THE HANDBOOK OF
MUNICIPAL BONDS
AND
PUBLIC FINANCE

Robert Lamb • James Leigland
Stephen Rappaport

NEW YORK INSTITUTE OF FINANCE

New York London Toronto Sydney Tokyo Singapore

Library of Congress Cataloging-in-Publication Data

The Handbook of municipal bonds and public finance / [compiled and
    edited by] Robert Lamb, James Leigland, Stephen Rappaport.
        p. cm.
    Includes index.
    ISBN 0–13–373960–0
    1. Municipal bonds—United States—Handbooks, manuals, etc.
    2. Finance, Public—United States—Handbooks, manuals, etc.
    I. Lamb, Robert. II. Leigland, James. III. Rappaport,
Stephen P.
    HG4952.H33   1992
    332.63'233'0973—dc20   92–26109
                                                                 CIP

© 1993 by NYIF Corp.
Simon & Schuster
A Paramount Communications Company

ISBN 0-13-373960-0

Printed in the United States of America
10 9 8 7 6 5 4 3 2 1

This book is dedicated to our wives
for all their love and support.
For Nancy Lamb,
Bonnie Leigland and
Arlene Markowitz Rappaport, M.D.

Contents

PART TWO   CREDIT QUALITY ANALYSIS, 115

Chapter **8**   ## Credit Fundamentals—The Rating Agency Perspective, 117

Freda S. Johnson
(Government Finance Associates, Inc.)

Chapter **9**   ## Analyzing Government Credit, 127

Claire Gorham Cohen
(Fitch Investors Service, Inc.)

Introduction

Perhaps, never before in the history of the securities industry has a single segment been subject to such urgent pressures for profound change, from such a wide variety of forces as the municipal securities market has been since the late 1970s. Over the last 15 years, Congressional action has changed fundamentally the nature of tax exemption; a ground-breaking 1988 Supreme Court decision invited even more widespread Congressional action in the future; and federal aid to state and local governments began to diminish at a time when needs to promote economic development and replace failing infrastructure were already reaching crisis proportions.

Within the industry, changes in procedures and processes have been widespread, with even broader changes on the horizon. Types of debt instruments and debt issuing practices have proliferated, as have the numbers of individuals and organizations who must play well-informed roles as participants in the debt issuing process. Finally, the need for market participants to understand the growing and ever-changing complexities of the market has increased in geometrical fashion.

This book is designed to help professionals in a variety of fields understand the most important of the new developments in the municipal securities industry and evaluate the most innovative solutions to emerging public finance problems. Above all, the book is intended to help professionals in and around the municipal marketplace cope with the changes and challenges that lie ahead.

THE CHANGING FEDERAL ROLE IN MUNICIPAL FINANCE

For many years, the issuance of tax-exempt municipal bonds was carried out with regularity and widespread acceptance. During the early 1980s, however, the new issue volume of municipals soared at roughly the same time that some of those who had either supported or permitted the growth began to withhold their approval.

The tax-exempt status of municipal bonds, long widely accepted as a quasi-constitutional right, already was gradually being eroded by Congressional action. That right had been formalized by the Supreme Court in the 1895 decision of *Pollock v. Farmers' Loan & Trust Co.*, when interest earned on state bonds was found to be immune from federal taxation. A series of subsequent actions by the U.S. Congress to undermine this right culminated in the Tax Reform Act of 1986, which removed or limited the tax-exempt status of newly defined "private activity" bonds. These kinds of securities traditionally had been considered "public" purpose and rightfully tax exempt. The attacks by Congress on tax exemption during the 1980s were given extra force by federal determination to move toward a balanced federal budget. The partial elimination of tax exemption was seen as one additional way of increasing Treasury Department revenues.

At the same time, however, and for similar reasons, the federal government began making severe cuts in funding normally targeted state and local governments, thus subjecting these two tiers of government to tremendous financial strain and increasing their need to raise capital through the issuance of municipal bonds. Making matters worse has been the desperate need of states and localities for money to repair and replace rapidly deteriorating infrastructure—the capital facilities used in the provision of important public services such as transportation, water supply, wastewater treatment, and so on. By the late 1980s, the municipal market was caught in a whipsaw of conflicting pressures.

What some believed to be the death knell in the continuing struggle between municipal bond market participants and Congress over the tax-exemption issue came in 1988 with a Supreme Court decision in the case of *South Carolina v. Baker.* The Court ruled that, "Subsequent case law has overruled the holding in *Pollock* that state bond interest is immune from a non-discriminatory federal tax." The Court also determined that,

The owners of state bonds have no constitutional entitlement not to pay taxes on income they earn from state bonds, and states have no Constitutional entitlement to issue bonds paying lower interest rates than other issuers.

INDUSTRY CHANGES IN PROCESSES AND PROCEDURES

These pressures began to appear during a period of transition in which many of the practices and procedures used by participants in the municipal securities industry were undergoing considerable change. In the wake of the New York City fiscal crisis in 1975 and the default of the Washington Public Power Supply System (or WPPSS) in 1983, disclosure practices in municipal securities offerings were identified by the industry as requiring reform. Paramount concern was focused on the amount of disclosure and its method, both for revenue bond issues as well as the more traditional general obligation bonds brought to market by states and local governments of general jurisdiction. Although revenue bond issues had been subject to considerably greater and more structured disclosure practices, it was believed by industry participants that the same standards should be applied to general obligation issues, and that additional detail should be included in official statements for all kinds of municipal securities.

The need for more complete disclosure was coupled with the need for clearer and more regularized accounting practices on the part of states and localities. Associations of accountants, as well as similar types of organizations for public officials, pressed for all municipal issuers to make use of generally accepted accounting principles (GAAP) in the preparation of their financial statements. This would not only regularize accounting at the state and local levels, making it understandable to analysts and investors, but also and perhaps more importantly would encourage certain issuers to put their fiscal houses in what the municipal industry considers to be appropriate order.

With the skyrocketing interest rates of the early 1980s, the municipal industry grafted onto the issuance of its securities many new types of market-related debt vehicles adapted from the world of corporate securities. These devices forced issuers and underwriters alike to become more sophisticated in the practice of bringing securities to market and more attuned to the financial needs of the particular kinds of investors who ultimately would be purchasers of these securities.

By the late 1980s, the growing complexity of the market—with accelerating demands for disclosure and clear feasibility, proliferating kinds of debt instruments and issuing techniques, and the growing frequency of legal change—required the widespread adoption of a "project" or "team" approach in bringing securities to market. Each financing necessarily brought together a large number of different types of professionals who were forced to cooperate in developing the necessary financial, feasibility, contractual, credit, budget, and other supporting material that had become essential parts of the issuing process.

THE GROWING NEED FOR INFORMATION

The turmoil of the 1980s emphasized as never before that a pivotal requirement for the successful issuance and management of municipal debt is access to a variety of different kinds of information. In order to design debt financing programs, issuers, underwriters and bond counsel can benefit from examples of plans, procedures, problems, and possibilities of financings in other states and/or localities. The team approach to issuance requires that all of those involved in processing transactions have much more than a modest knowledge of the details of the financing process, as well as the specific roles and responsibilities of the various participants.

Growing market complexities have also focused concern on the need among state and local officials for more information about state-of-the-art financial management techniques. Crucial to the financial viability of state and local governments in the years ahead will be their success in cash and debt management, their ability to establish and maintain effective financial accounting systems, the quality of their short- and long-term plans for meeting future public service needs, and the linkages between such plans and government budgets. By the early 1990s, first-rate public financial management has become an essential foundation for cost-effective public borrowing.

FUTURE TRENDS IN THE MUNICIPAL MARKET

A number of issues and trends that began to affect the municipal markets in the 1980s are likely to continue to be of critical importance during the later 1990s. General efficiency in government operations will continue to be important, as will be strategy and target selection for the repair and revitalization of infrastructure. Innovations in financing techniques will continue to appear, particularly those tied to the self-financing character of particular projects. By the same token, general obligation financings are likely to be increasingly limited. Overall, tension is likely to increase between the need for public works programs and slow growth in public revenues, particularly if federal deficit problems continue to strain federal aid to states and localities.

Many crucial public financing decisions in the 1990s will certainly be umpired by voters, but it is also likely that financial solutions will be generated by those professionals who earn their livelihood working in and around the municipal bond industry, including those associated with it through their positions in state and local government, or on the public finance faculties and staff of universities and research organizations.

THE ROLE OF THIS BOOK

This book is a broadly focused treatise written by a variety of well-known professionals in the municipal bond and public finance industry. The book is designed to be forward-looking and to present a variety of views rather than the single perspective of one or two authors. As such, the book is written for a more professional audience than most texts covering a specific field or any part of one. Government officials, professionals in the investment banking and brokerage industry, institutional and individual purchasers of municipal bonds, and university faculty and students studying the market for state and local debt should find of interest at least some of the chapters of this volume.

As illustrated above, so much has taken place over the last 15 years in the municipal bond and public finance industry that even market participants have been unable to keep abreast of new developments and state-of-the-art techniques. And until now, authoritative information on a broad range of such issues has not appeared in a single volume. To be sure, books on the municipal bond industry have been published for more general readership, and trade publications have appeared focusing on the broad field of fixed income securities or more specific aspects of municipal bonds, such as credit analysis. But little or nothing has been published covering the latest developments in the municipal bond and public finance industry, relating to both how issues and problems have been solved at the state and local levels as well as the market making of the securities themselves. This volume is intended to fill that void.

Topics such as debt management, financial controls, bonding versus pay-as-you-go decisions, financing infrastructure improvements, and techniques for meeting the needs of today's state and local service-oriented economies occupy important chapters in this book. More market-oriented sections include those on mutual funds and unit trusts, portfolio management, swaps, futures, high yield securities, and refundings. The role of the financial advisor, privatization, bond insurance, letters of credit as additional security mechanisms, and even historically oriented sections written by notable industry journalists explain current issues and suggest future developments.

The editors of this volume are fortunate to have been able to assemble as contributors a group of notable industry professionals, all of whom possess the ability to clearly convey what they do and how they do it. Also included among the contributors are a wide variety of authors distinguished for their own publications on the municipal bond market and public finance issues. In all, the book includes pieces by a diverse group, including underwriters, investment bankers, economists, academics, government officials, attorneys, rating agency personnel, market makers, and journalists, to name a few. Each author was given wide latitude as to the nature and extent of coverage of his or her selected topic. Each author, writing as an expert in his or her field, has determined the critical information needed by a professional audience for a detailed overview of the topics under review.

As the municipal marketplace passes into the middle years of the 1990s, challenges abound. At no other time in its history has the market more urgently needed a reasonably comprehensive compilation of knowledge to assist market participants in charting the journey ahead.

Robert Boyden Lamb
James Leigland
Stephen P. Rappaport

Acknowledgments

The editors of THE HANDBOOK OF MUNICIPAL BONDS AND PUBLIC FINANCE owe a special debt of gratitude to our colleague Gregory K. Marks. The editors also wish to express their deep appreciation to the editors at Simon and Schuster and the New York Institute of Finance, and Rose Kernan who worked on the production process of this volume over many months.

The editors and authors of this volume also wish to acknowledge the support of a number of other individuals including: Edward T. O'Brien, President, Securities Industry Association; Hardwick Simmons, James Gahan, Leland Paton, Howard Whitman, Gerald Mc-Bride, and John Frary, all of Prudential Securities; Dean Richard West, Dean Richard Brief, Dean Daniel Diamond, Edward Altman, Ingo Walter, Roy Smith, Martin Gruber, Edwin Elton, Stephen Figlewski, Robert Kavesh, Robert Lindsay, Oscar Ornati, Rita Maldonado-Bear, David Rogers, Ernest Block, William Silber, Lawrence Ritter, Paul Samuelson, and William Cuth all of New York University's Stern School of Business; Arthur Centonze, Basheer Ahmed, Clarke Johnson, and John Dorey, all of the Lubin Graduate School of Business, Pace University; Jeffrey Liddle of Liddle, O'Connor, Finklestein, & Robinson, Esqs. at Staats Pellett of Bessemer Trust. We also owe a debt of gratitude to Franco Modigliani and Lester Thurow of The Sloan School of the

Massachusetts Institute of Technology, Donald Haider of the Kellogg Graduate School of Management, Northwestern University, Herman B. Leonard of the John F. Kennedy School of Government, Harvard University; Peter Lorange of the Wharton School, The University of Pennsylvania; Bruce Henderson of Vanderbilt University; Elizabeth Holtzman and Darcy Bradbury of the Comptrollers Office of the City of New York; Edward Martinez of the Dade County, Florida Finance Department; Austin Tobin of the Delphis Hanover Corporation; Kenneth Frankel of Drake Securities; David Juliana, CPA; Patricia Corbin of P.G. Corbin & Company; Sylvan G. Feldstein of Merrill Lynch; Heather Ruth and Carolyn Benn of the Public Securities Association; and Christopher Taylor of the Municipal Securities Rulemaking Board.

A special note of appreciation is given to Alfred M. Markowitz, M.D., College of Physicians and Surgeons of Columbia University and Columbia Presbyterian Medical Center for his encouragement, support, and help on this and other related projects.

About the Editors

Robert B. Lamb is a Clinical Full Professor of Management and Finance at New York University, Graduate School of Business Administration. He has also taught at Wharton School of Finance, University of Pennsylvania and Columbia University.

Professor Lamb has served as debt advisor to the U.S. Federal Reserve Board, U.S. Treasury Department and U.S. Justice Department. He is currently Debt Advisor to New York City and New York State and coordinates issues with the Port Authority of New York and New Jersey. He has been debt advisor to the City of Chicago on the funding of a new Chicago airport. He has advised the State of Illinois University System on bond redemptions. He has advised the Housing Development Corporation of New York, Nevada Housing Authority, as well as various municipalities and public authorities.

Professor Lamb has also advised U.S. and foreign commercial banks, investment banks, and corporations. Professor Lamb has worked with Morgan Guaranty Trust, Deutsche Bank, Creditanstalt, Sanwa Bank and various other firms to set up international municipal bond markets and project finance markets. For Creditanstalt, Professor Lamb is developing methods to integrate securities markets in order to finance the massive infrastructure development, transportation systems and environmental clean-up of Central Europe.

Professor Lamb has served as an Expert in legal cases for Paul Weiss Rifkind Wharton & Garrison, Cravath Swaine & Moore, Kirkland & Ellis, Chapman & Cutler, and others. He served as expert advisor to the U.S. Department of Justice and Treasury in the U.S. Supreme Court case *South Carolina v. James Baker*, Secretary of the Treasury of the United States.

Professor Lamb has been strategic management advisor and business ethics advisor to many U.S. and foreign companies and organizations including Citibank, Metropolitan Life Insurance, The Young President's Organization, and the Internal Revenue Service. He is founder and editor-in-chief of *The Journal of Business Strategy* and on the Board of Editors of *The Municipal Finance Journal*.

James Leigland is a member of the senior consulting staff of the Institute of Public Administration, New York, NY, where he has worked with a large variety of clients involved in state and local government finance. He is a former faculty member of the Martin School of Public Administration, Lexington, Kentucky, and continues to contribute to academic publications on public financial management issues. He is co-author, with Robert B. Lamb, of *WPPSS: Who is to Blame for the WPPSS Disaster*, published by Ballinger/Harper & Row.

Stephen P. Rappaport is Senior Vice President and Manager of the Municipal Research and Financial Services Department of Prudential Securities. Mr. Rappaport is co-author with Robert Lamb of *Municipal Bonds: The Comprehensive Review of Tax-Exempt Securities and Public Finance* published by the McGraw-Hill Book Company. He is also the author of *Management on Wall Street: Making Securities Firms Work* which was published by Dow Jones-Irwin, and *The Affluent Investor: Investment Strategies for All Markets*, published by the New York Institute of Finance, division of Simon & Schuster. Mr. Rappaport received a B.A. from Colby College, magna cum laude, Phi Beta Kappa; an M.A. and an M. Phil. from Columbia University as a President's Fellow; and anticipates a doctorate. He is also an adjunct professor of finance in the Lubin Graduate School of Business, Pace University.

About the Contributors

Aaron S. Gurwitz is Vice President, Fixed Income Research Division, Goldman, Sachs and Co. Mr. Gurwitz is a senior economist and his area of responsibility encompasses the monitoring and analysis of developments across all fixed income markets. He is responsible for municipal bond market analysis as well as relative value research. Aaron has published extensively on subjects related to fixed income markets, public finance, and regional economic development. Before joining Goldman Sachs, Mr. Gurwitz was Vice President in charge of municipal bond market research at Salomon Brothers Inc. He has also held positions as Senior Economist at the Federal Reserve Bank of New York and at the Rand Corporation. Mr. Gurwitz holds a Ph.D. in Economics from Stanford University.

Claire Gorham Cohen is Executive Vice President, Fitch Investors Service, Inc. Ms. Gorham Cohen came to Fitch in 1989 from Moody's Investors Service, where she was vice president and managing director for state ratings and a chairman of the public finance department rating committee. Her nearly 30-year career at Dun & Bradstreet and Moody's spanned virtually all aspects of the municipal market as well as international experience with sovereign issuers. Acknowledged to be the country's leading expert on state ratings, Claire was previously associate director of the municipal department at Moody's. Claire started her career at Dun & Bradstreet (subsequently acquired by Moody's) on receiving her BA degree from Radcliffe College. She has served as chairman of the Municipal Analysts Group of New York and on the Board of Governors of the National Federation of Municipal Analysts. Claire also is a member of the Municipal Forum.

Howard Mischel is a Vice President and Managing Director in the Public Finance Department of Moody's Investors Service. Previously he has worked as a public finance banker for Union Bank of Switzerland and as the Director of Municipal Research at Marine Midland Bank.

James H. Burr is a Vice President and Assistant Director of Legal Analysis in the Public Finance Department of Moody's Investors Service. Admitted to the New York Bar in 1980, Mr. Burr has also worked at the New York City Office of Management and Budget and the New York State Financial Control Board for the City of New York.

Katherine McManus is a Vice President and Manager of Legal Analysis in the Public Finance Department of Moody's Investors Service. Previously she was a Director of a low income housing group at the New York City Department of Housing Preservation and Development.

David R. Ambler is currently a Vice President-Assistant Director of Regional Ratings at Moody's Investors Service. In his eight year tenure, he has focused on credits primarily in California and the Pacific Northwest.

Diana L. Roswick is a Vice President and Assistant Director of Moody's Regional Ratings Group. Prior to her current position, she was Managing Editor of Moody's public finance publications and Manager of the Great Lakes Ratings Group. Diana holds a masters in urban affairs from the New School for Social Research and an undergraduate degree from Cornell University.

Hyman C. Grossman is Managing Director—Municipal Finance at Standard & Poor's Ratings Group and is a spokesman for S&P's debt rating policies. Mr. Grossman has been with S&P since 1963, when he joined the Municipal Bond Department as an analyst. Over the years, he has appeared before regional and national groups concerned with municipal finance, has received recognition awards, served on special task forces, and has also written extensively on the subject. He is a 1958 graduate of New York University.

Martin Ives, CPA, is Vice Chairman of the Governmental Accounting Standards Board, and was also its first Director of Research. He served as First Deputy Comptroller of New York City from 1976–1983, and as Deputy Comptroller of New York State from 1963–1976. He is also a member of the Federal Accounting Standards Advisory Board.

Robert Berne is Associate Dean and Professor of Public Administration at the Robert F. Wagner Graduate School of Public Service, New York University. Professor Berne is the co-author of *The Financial Analysis of Governments* and has recently completed a research study, "The Relationships between Financial Reporting and the Measurement of Financial Condition," for the Governmental Accounting Standards Board. He is also carrying out extensive research on educational policy issues including finance, performance measurement, and governance. He received his Ph.D. and M.B.A. from Cornell University.

Merl Hackbart is Special Assistant to the Chancellor of the University of Kentucky, Lexington Campus, and Professor of Finance and Public Administration. He has twice served as State Budget Director for the State of Kentucky. His research has focused on public financial management including portfolio management, debt financing and public budgeting issues.

Clement W. Mikowski is the Financial Manager of Florida's Turnpike. He is also a Certified Public Accountant; graduated from Aquinas College with a B.S. in Business Administration and Accounting; received a Masters of Public Administration from Western Michigan University and was recently designated a position on the Wall of Distinction at Western Michigan University for professional accomplishments. Mr. Mikowski has a diverse background in public service and was formerly the Director of Florida's Division of Bond Finance and, prior to that, the Administrator of Debt Management for the State of Michigan where he was also President of the Michigan Association of Accountants, Auditors and Business Administrators and concurrently represented the state treasurer on several boards and committees.

John Petersen, President, Government Finance Group, Inc. With 25 years experience, Mr. Petersen has built his professional career on serving governments in all phases of financial analysis and management. As Senior Director of the Government Finance Research Center for over 17 years, Petersen was responsible for more than 250 research and consulting projects and a service that since 1985 has advised on approximately 100 financings, amounting to over $1.5 billion. He has written or co-edited numerous books and technical publications including the *Disclosure Guidelines for State and Local Government Securities* and *Local Government Finance: Concepts and Practices.* Dr. Petersen has a B.A. from Northwestern University, an M.B.A. from the Wharton School and a Ph.D. from the University of Pennsylvania.

Arthur M. Miller is a Vice President of Goldman, Sachs and Co., in New York, New York. He is the co-head of the quantitative analytics group and new products development for the Municipal Finance Department.

Mr. Miller was previously an Associate Attorney in the Tax Department at Mudge Rose Guthrie Alexander & Ferdon in New York, New York. Mr. Miller heads the American Bar Association's Task Force on Advance Refundings of the Tax Section on Tax-Exempt Financing, and is also a Member of the Public Securities Association's Federal Legislation Committee. Mr. Miller is a graduate of Princeton University (AB); the University of North Carolina (MA History); Duke University (JD); and New York University (LLM Taxation).

Michelle D. Monticciolo, Associate, Fixed Income Research, Goldman, Sachs and Co. Michelle (Deligiannis) Monticciolo is a member of the Market Research Group of Fixed Income Research at Goldman, Sachs and Co. She is responsible for market analysis for the short-term sectors of the fixed income markets and provides research and analytical support for the municipal markets. Ms. Monticciolo holds a B.B.A. in Finance from The College of William and Mary in Virginia.

Alison M. Martier is a Managing Director at Equitable Capital Management Corporation in New York City. She is a Portfolio Manager of fixed income accounts with assets over $900 million. Mrs. Martier is a Chartered Financial Analyst, and a member of the Society of Financial Analysts and the New York Society of Security Analysts. She is a graduate of Northwestern University and holds an M.B.A. from New York University.

Julie C. Morrone is a Vice President in Lehman Brother's Municipal Research Department where she specializes in the analysis of a wide range of tax-exempt securities. Her career in municipal finance has involved work in both the commercial and investment banking sectors of the market. Ms. Morrone holds an M.B.A. in accounting and international business and a B.S. in finance from New York University.

Allen J. Proctor is currently Executive Director of the New York State Financial Control Board. He previously served as Deputy Director of the Office of Management and Budget for New York City and as Chief of the Bank Analysis and Monetary Analysis Divisions of the Federal Reserve Bank of New York. He holds a Ph.D. in economics from the University of Wisconsin—Madison.

Joan Perry and **Michael Satz** have taught "Public Debt Management" at the New York University Graduate School of Public Administration. Each draws on extensive experience in public finance. Dr. Perry has more than twenty years experience in municipal credit analysis, has worked for a municipal issuer and has been involved on both the "buy" and "sell" sides of Wall Street. Dr. Perry was employed at AMBAC as Executive Vice President, having served as the Chief Underwriting Officer. Mr. Satz has acted as bond counsel and underwriter's counsel while associated with the law firm of Willkie Farr & Gallagher in the area of public finance. Mr. Satz joined AMBAC as General Counsel, and thereafter served in the capacity of Senior Executive Vice President and Chief Operating Officer. Mr. Satz was the first President of the Association of Financial Guaranty Insurors; he is currently the Chairman and Chief Executive Officer of Capital Reinsurance Company.

Abraham Losice is a Vice President at Standard & Poor's Corporation. He is the manager of the Letter of Credit Group. Mr. Losice holds an MBA from New York University and a bachelors degree from Brooklyn College.

Annette L. De Lara is the Assistant Superintendent for Finance and Capital Budget for the School Board of Dade County, Florida.

William W. Cobbs and **Wesley C. Hough** are principals in Public Resources Advisory Group, a financial advisory firm.

Catherine Holstein, is the president of Export Technology, Inc., a major exporter of computer related products. Previously, Ms. Holstein was a member of the Government Finance Research Center's Financial Advisory Group. She holds a MBA in Finance and a BS in Management Information Systems from the State University of New York at Albany.

William B. James, C.F.A. is a Managing Director in the Public Finance Department of Prudential Securities Incorporated in New York. He is a member of the USEPA-sponsored Environmental Financial Advisory Board and the Advisory Committee to the Anthony Commission on Public Finance. He is also a member of the Board of Directors of the Council of Infrastructure Financing Authorities. Mr. James is a member of the New York Society of Securities Analysts, the Association for Investment Management and Research, the Municipal Bond Club of New York and the Municipal Forum of New York. He received his MBA from the Wharton Graduate School of University of Pennsylvania in 1975 where he was a recipient of a Wharton Graduate Fellowship.

Matthew Kreps, Steven Dickson, Joan Pryde, and **Joe Mysak** are contributors and editors for *The Bond Buyer.* Their work has appeared in the centennial edition of *The Bond Buyer.*

Stephen Peters, Stephanie Smith Lovette, and **K. Tina Choe** co-authored the article on Emerging Borrowing Priorities. Ms. Smith Lovette is with the Public Finance Department of Sutro & Co., Inc., while Mr. Peters and Ms. Choe are with Shearson Lehman Bros.

A. Michael Lipper, CFA is President of Lipper Analytical Services which produces the most widely followed analytical standards for the investment company industry. He has long been active in industry affairs with the New York Society of Security Analysts and the Securities Industry Association.

William Dawson is a senior vice president of Federated Research Corp. in charge of various fixed income portfolios. In the late 1970s and early 1980s, he was the portfolio manager of Federated Tax-Free Trust referenced in this chapter. As such, he pioneered many of the original tax-free variable rate demand notes used in this industry.

James R. Ramsey is the Vice President for Administration and Technology at Western Kentucky University. He also serves as a Professor in the Economics Department. Previously, Dr. Ramsey was the Chief State Economist for the Commonwealth of Kentucky.

Part One

THE MUNICIPAL MARKET

CHAPTER 1

The Characteristics of Outstanding Municipal Bonds*

Aaron Gurwitz
Goldman, Sachs and Co.

Analysts and investors in the municipal bond market have been handicapped by the limited amount of available knowledge regarding the characteristics of outstanding municipal bonds. Simple descriptive statistics, such as the weighted distribution of maturities, coupons, credit ratings, and interest payment dates, have been unobtainable— even though such information has long been available for the markets in U.S. government and corporate bonds and mortgage-backed securities. The problem in the municipal market has been the very large number of different municipal "issues"—including both serial and term bonds, the total exceeds two million—and the fact that the standard municipal issue data bases do not include the original dollar amount of each maturity or the dollar amount currently outstanding.

To fill this knowledge gap, Goldman Sachs is conducting an extended statistical study of outstanding municipal bonds. Specifically, we have selected a stratified random sample of 1,000 CUSIP numbers.[1] We drew indicative information on the coupon, maturity, issuer, rating,

---

[1] CUSIP stands for Committee on Uniform Security Identification Procedures. The CUSIP number uniquely identifies each publicly offered security. Each municipal bond— characterized by coupon, issue date, and maturity—is assigned a distinct CUSIP number.

use of proceeds, call and put features and credit rating from the Kinney Information Systems data base. We took information on original issue amount and amount currently outstanding from a variety of sources, including official statements and direct inquiries to issuers and bond trustees. We believe that this sample is large enough to provide statistically reliable estimates of key characteristics of the population of outstanding municipal bonds.[2] So far we have assembled complete information on more than 90% of the bonds in the sample (totaling slightly more than $4 billion in original issue amount). We do not expect the information we collect on the remaining issues to alter our conclusions appreciably. However, you should view the results reported here as preliminary, and we have labeled them accordingly.

SUMMARY FINDINGS

Table 1.1 summarizes the preliminary findings of our study. None of the conclusions are particularly surprising. In the aggregate or on average, outstanding municipal bonds are intermediate-term, high quality securities with high coupons relative to current interest rates. To some extent these "average" characteristics reflect the fact that approximately 21.2% of all outstanding municipal bonds are pre-refunded issues. Approximately 9% of the sample bonds incorporate put features. Nearly 35% of bonds in the sample mature in either January or July and, most likely, make semiannual interest payments on those dates.

These summary statistics conceal one of the most important findings of this study. Although the *average* effective maturity date of the bonds in the sample is in 2003, the distribution of maturities is distinctly bimodal. A large proportion of outstanding bonds matures or is scheduled for redemptions during the coming five years, and another large proportion is scheduled to mature 18 or more years in the future. Bonds that mature between six and 17 years in the future are relatively scarce.

Furthermore, an investor who owns a "market portfolio" of municipal bonds should assume that a substantial proportion of current holdings will be redeemed through current refunding over the next five years. *In fact, an owner of the market portfolio can expect that 50% of bonds held at present will be gone in five years through scheduled maturities,*

---

[2] We include additional information on the sampling methodology in the Appendix on page M9.

TABLE 1.1
Summary Results

• Weighted average coupon:	8.582%
• Weighted average maturity date:	November 16, 2003
• Weighted median maturity date:	November 6, 2001
• Percent pre-refundeds:	21.2%
• Percent putable:	9.15%
• Percent January and July maturities:	34.83%
• Percent Aaa or Aa:	55.1%

scheduled redemptions of pre-refunded issues, or likely currently refunding of high coupon nonpre-refunded issues.

Given the proportion of outstanding bonds scheduled to mature or be redeemed between now and 1995, unless gross new issue volume in the municipal market grows substantially faster than it has in recent years, the total volume of municipal bonds outstanding is unlikely to grow appreciably between 1993 and 1995. In fact, there may very well be quarters during that period when the volume of outstanding bonds actually contracts. Meanwhile, the demand for municipal bonds is likely to continue growing. A rising volume of household savings and the gradual return of property/casualty insurance companies to the municipal market as buyers should, in fact, combine to accelerate demand growth over the next several years.

This analysis, therefore, suggests that tax-exempt bonds will become very scarce commodities over the next five years. Investors should, therefore, do what they can now to "lock in" municipal holdings for the mid-decade period. Investment strategies directed at this goal include purchasing longer-term, call-protected municipal bonds and buying whatever municipal forwards may be offered. Investors who are concerned that interest rates might rise over the next few years should hedge the duration exposure of their municipal portfolios with short positions in taxable markets. A large, relatively permanent position long municipal and short Treasuries is not, of course, risk-free. Fiscal pressures on state and local governments along with more vigorous efforts to address the infrastructure problem could accelerate municipal issuance substantially. The demand for bonds might stagnate if the current recession is long and if insurance companies do not return to profitability. And as always, there is a risk that Congress may pass tax legislation that jeopardizes the value of municipal bonds. These very real risks notwithstanding, it appears likely that yields on municipal bonds will trend downward relative to Treasury yields over the next several years.

MATURITIES, EFFECTIVE MATURITY, AND EXPECTED MATURITIES

Figure 1.1 summarizes information on the effective maturities of the bonds in the sample. The pattern of maturities highlights the bimodal distribution of maturities. A large proportion of bonds, weighted by original issue amount, is scheduled to mature or be redeemed before 1995. There are relatively few bonds maturing between 2000 and 2007, and another large proportion matures in 2008 and thereafter. Bonds that have not been pre-refunded but carry coupons above 8% are treated separately; we do not include them among the longer-maturity issues, but present them separately on the assumption that they will be refunded on their first call date.

We present this same information in another way in Figure 1.2. To understand this chart, assume that a portfolio manager holds the municipal "market portfolio," that is, he owns small equal proportions of each outstanding bond (or each bond in the sample). Assume further that the manager never sells any of these bonds and never buys any new bonds. The bars in Figure 1.2 indicate what proportion of the dollar amount of bonds held in that portfolio at the end of 1990 would be "gone" by the end of each of the following years. As the

FIGURE 1.1
Preliminary Results: Annual Redemptions of Sample Bonds

(\$, millions)

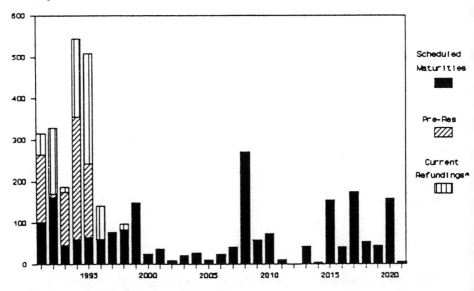

*Long-term bonds with coupons above 8%.

FIGURE 1.2
Preliminary Results: Cumulative Percentage of Currently Outstanding
Municipal Bonds Maturing or Redeemed, by Year

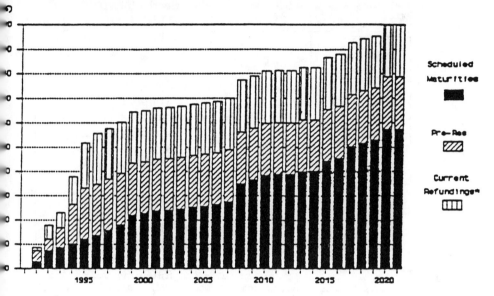

*Long-term bonds with coupons above 8%.

chart indicates, half of this hypothetical portfolio would be converted
into cash by the end of 1995.

The Projected Size of the Municipal Market: A Simulation

Figure 1.3 takes this analysis one step farther. The purpose of this exercise is to assess the effect of the large volume of pre-1995 maturities
on the total volume of municipal bonds outstanding. The simulations
assume the following:

(1) Municipal bonds valued at $800 billion were outstanding at the
    end of 1990.
(2) In each subsequent year, a proportion of those bonds matures or is
    redeemed as scheduled under an advance refunding. The propor-
    tion that matures or is redeemed is equal to the proportion of
    bonds in our sample that matures or is redeemed in that year.
(3) Gross new issue volume totals $100 in 1991 and grows thereafter at
    0%, 1.25%, 2.5%, 5%, or 10% per year.

8 The Characteristics of Outstanding Municipal Bonds

FIGURE 1.3
Simulation Results: Projected Municipals Outstanding by Growth Rate of
New Issue Volume

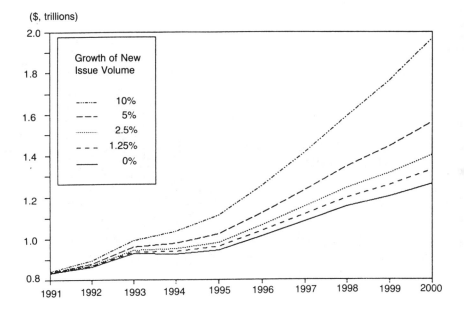

($, trillions)

(4) The maturity distribution of all newly issued bonds is the same as
the maturity structure of sample bonds that were issued in 1989.

As the simulation results depicted in Figure 1.3 suggest, the total volume of outstanding municipal bonds is likely to increase gradually in
1991 and 1992, even if new issue volume grows very slowly. Between
1993 and 1994, however, unless new issue volume grows by more than
5%, the total volume of bonds outstanding will stagnate. At lower
growth rates, total outstandings remain basically flat for this two-
year period. If so, given the seasonality of municipal issuance, it is
likely that the aggregate size of the market will actually decline over
some quarters between 1993 QI and 1995 QIV.

DISTRIBUTION BY COUPON

As with the maturity distribution, the weighted coupon distribution
of the outstanding stock of municipal bonds is bimodal. As Figure 1.4
indicates, a large proportion of municipal bonds outstanding,
weighted by original issue amount, has coupons in the 7%–7.99%

FIGURE 1.4
Preliminary Results: Weighted Distribution of Sample Bonds* by Coupon

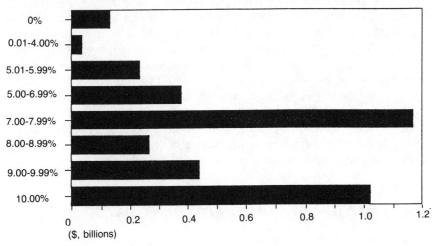

*Weighted by original amount outstanding.

FIGURE 1.5
Weighted Distribution of Sample Bonds* by Coupon and Maturity

($, millions

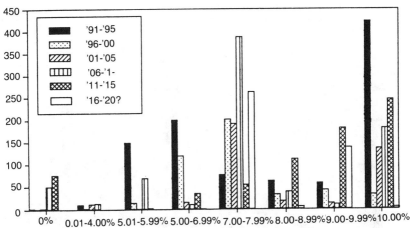

*Weighted by original amount outstanding.

range. Another large proportion of bonds carries coupons above 9%. Coupons below 7% and in the 8%–8.99% range are relatively scarce.

The shape of the distribution is likely to change substantially over the next few years. Figure 1.5 indicates that a large proportion of the highest and lowest coupon bonds is scheduled to mature or be redeemed before 1995. Thereafter, unless the market moves up or down substantially in the meantime, the weighted distribution of coupons will become much more highly concentrated in the 7–7.99% range. To the extent that high or low coupon bonds are attractive to certain categories of investors, bonds with coupons below 7% or above 8% that will remain outstanding after 1995 should become relatively more valuable over the next five years. Noncallable intermediate- and long-term premium bonds should perform particularly well.

DISTRIBUTION BY COUPON PAYMENT DATE

Observers of the municipal market have long suspected that a large proportion of bonds pays coupons in January and July. Our study confirms this conjecture. Although the data we have do not include coupon payment months, it is probably safe to assume that bonds mature on coupon payment dates; bonds that mature in October, say, probably make semiannual coupon payments in April and October.

FIGURE 1.6
Preliminary Results: Percentage of Sample Bond Principal Amounts by Month of Maturity

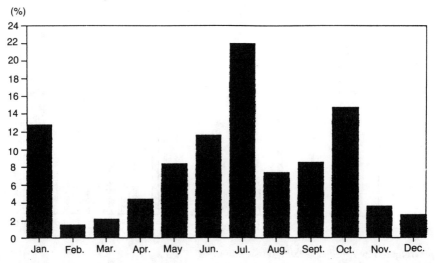

As Figure 1.6 indicates, July is the most common month for municipal bond maturities. January is also popular. Thus, January–July payment schedules are the most common. April–October payment schedules are the second most popular, followed closely by June–December.

It is interesting to note that on the assumption that monthly payment schedules are invariant with the level of the coupon, interest payments on municipal bonds total nearly $12 billion[3] in January and July.

APPENDIX: SAMPLE SELECTION METHODOLOGY

The total target sample size was 1,000 CUSIP numbers. Taking a random sample of all CUSIPs, however, would result in oversampling small issues. Data on new municipal bond issues brought to market since 1983 indicated that bond issues (serials plus term bonds) amounting to $50 million or more accounted for approximately 60% of the dollar amount of primary market volume. Therefore, we aimed to select 60% of our sample from issuers that, at some point between 1983 and 1990, had sold individual bond issues totaling $50 million or more. We identified the names and associated CUSIP numbers of all such issuers and selected 600 CUSIPs from this subpopulation. The remaining 400 CUSIPs were selected from all remaining CUSIPs after bonds sold by the large issuer group had been deleted.

[3] $800 billion in municipals outstanding times half of the 8.582% average coupon times 34.83% of coupon payments made on a January–July schedule.

CHAPTER 2

Household Demand for Tax-Exempt Investments*

Aaron Gurwitz
Goldman, Sachs and Co.

To begin, we will examine the investment behavior of the most important group of buyers of municipal bonds: households and their intermediaries. This chapter focuses in particular on what determines households' aggregate demand for tax-exempt investments. In ensuing chapters, we will deal with the considerations that influence decisions to buy bonds directly or through intermediaries and the types of bonds to buy.

Individuals and their surrogates—collectively termed "households"—have emerged as the most important group of buyers in the municipal market. As Figure 2.1 indicates, individuals, trusts, and open-end bond funds currently hold approximately 50% of the municipal bonds outstanding.[1] The role of the household sector as a net purchaser

---

[1] A review of the data sources on investor holdings of municipals may be useful. The main source of data on the volume of municipals outstanding and on the periodic flows of tax-exempt assets among market participants is the *Flow of Funds* report produced by the Federal Reserve Board. The Federal Reserve compiles data on the issuance and holdings of all types of financial assets and liabilities and releases quarterly statistical reports. For some types of investors, mostly federally regulated financial institutions, quarterly data on asset and liability holdings are readily available with only a brief lag. For other types of investors—insurance companies, for example—these data

FIGURE 2.1

Outstanding Tax-Exempt Obligations by Type of Holder

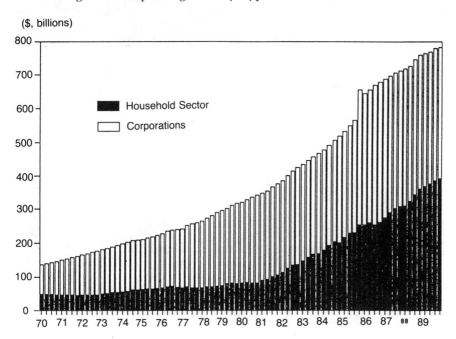

($, billions)

are available only on an annual basis after a substantial lag. In these cases analysts at the Federal Reserve estimate recent quarterly changes on the basis of historical behavior and current circumstantial evidence. No direct observations of "household" investments in various types of assets are available. Asset holdings of this sector—which includes direct individual investments and assets held by trusts and charitable institutions—are estimated by the Federal Reserve as a residual category. The Federal Reserve has a good fix on the total volume of various types of assets outstanding and on the holdings of all types of investors, in some cases with a lag, except the household sector. Any difference between the total volume of an asset category outstanding and the holdings that can be accounted for by direct observation is assumed to be held by the household sector. In the case of municipals, the Federal Reserve tracks the gross volume of new issues and estimates the volume of bonds that mature or are redeemed each quarter. Based on cumulative information on issuance, the Fed's analysts can estimate the total volume of tax-exempt bonds outstanding. Periodic regulatory reports filed by depository institutions contain information on the tax-exempt holdings of these investors, and other sources of data provide information on the size of municipal bond portfolios held by insurance companies and other institutional investors. These "hard" data on institutional holdings account for only about half of the estimated volume of municipals outstanding. Therefore, the Federal Reserve estimates that about half are held by the "unobserved" household sector.

FIGURE 2.2
Net Acquisition of Tax-Exempt Obligations by Type of Buyers

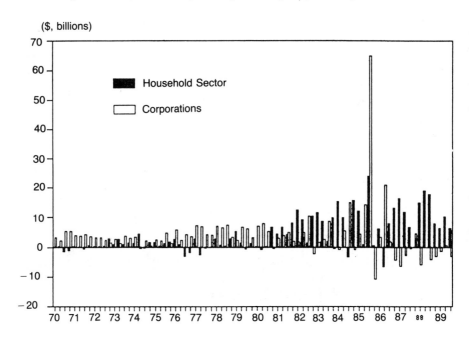

of newly issued municipals is even more dominant; in recent quarters, net acquisitions of tax-exempts by individuals, trusts, and open-end bond funds has been accounting for more than total net issuance (see Figure 2.2). In other words, according to the Federal Reserve's statistics, individual investors, trust departments, unit investment trusts, and managed bond funds have been bidding municipals away from other holders in the secondary market.

INDIVIDUALS' INVESTMENT CHOICES

To identify the forces that determine aggregate household demand for tax-exempt bonds, we need to analyze two simultaneous decisions. The first of these is the decision to save instead of spend current income. Once the aggregate savings decision is made, investors must decide on the distribution of assets among broad categories in their investment portfolios.

AGGREGATE SAVINGS

When individuals receive income, they have the choice of using the money for current consumption or of saving to finance future consumption. Households' allocation of current income to these two purposes responds to many determinants: the expected rate of return on investments, the anticipated variance of that return, cultural proclivities, existing net worth, consumer confidence regarding near- and long-term economic conditions, and so on. Among these determinants of the savings rate, the household's position in the life cycle is one of the most important. The life cycle theory of the savings rate is based on the observation that the allocation of current income to savings tends to be low during the early years after the household is formed, when major consumer durables are being purchased and, if the family owns a home, mortgage payments consist mostly of interest. Later in the life cycle, when earning power reaches its peak and retirement years begin to approach, the household's savings rate rises. Then, after retirement, the typical household enters a period of dissaving.

As each household's savings rate depends in part on the family's position in the life cycle, the aggregate savings rate in the economy depends on the distribution of households across the life cycle. As the

FIGURE 2.3
Aggregate Household Savings and the Savings Rate

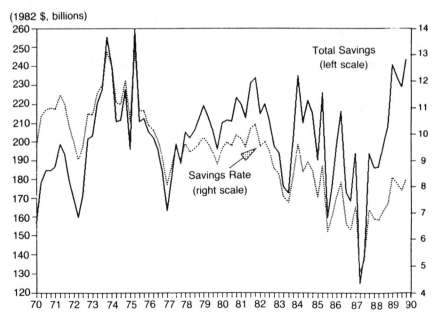

bulk of baby boom families move out of the household formation years into the peak savings phase of the life cycle, the aggregate savings rate in the economy should increase. As the historical data in Figure 2.3 indicate, the aggregate savings rate in the United States has been rising recently from extremely low levels, reflecting in part the underlying demographic trend.

HOUSEHOLD ASSET ALLOCATION DECISIONS

Once the aggregate level of savings is determined, households must decide how to allocate their aggregate net worth across asset categories: stocks, bank deposits, taxable fixed-income investments, tax-exempt fixed-income investments, real estate and so on. In part, this allocation decision will depend on the total size of the household's net worth; some investments are offered only in relatively large block sizes. This is one reason why the bulk of investment earnings received by low and moderate income households is taxable interest income (see Figure 2.4); small time deposits may be the only investment alternative available to families with minimal net worth.

Insights from Portfolio Theory

To analyze the investment choices of households that do have a broader array of potential choices, we make use of the insights provided by portfolio theory. The analysis begins with the observation that each asset category offers some combination of risk (i.e., variance of returns) and expected returns. Portfolios that consist of several asset categories also offer some combination of risk and expected returns. The riskiness of a portfolio will be higher to the extent that the performance patterns of the different assets in the portfolio are correlated. When the return patterns of portfolio assets are uncorrelated— that is, to the extent that the portfolio is "diversified"—the overall riskiness of the combined holdings will be lower.

Investors, faced with uncertainty about the likely performance of different investment vehicles, will chose a portfolio offering an optimal combination of expected returns and risk. The optimal combination of risk and expected returns is a subjective judgment. In general, investors will want to hold larger positions in an asset category to the extent that the category's expected returns are high, that the risk is low, and that the category's performance exhibits a low or negative correlation with the returns of other attractive asset categories.

From this perspective, the key characteristics of any investment alternative—including municipal bonds—are expected returns, the

FIGURE 2.4
Sources of Investment Income by Adjusted Gross Income

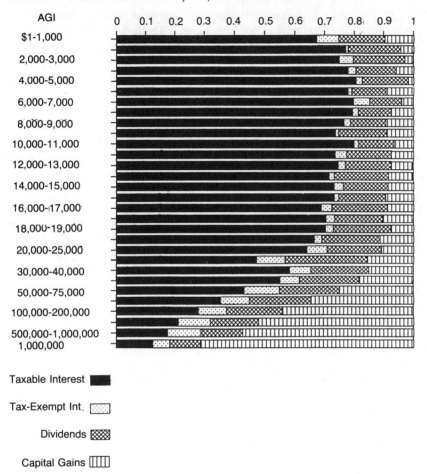

Taxable Interest ▮

Tax-Exempt Int. ▦

Dividends ▨

Capital Gains ‖‖‖

variance of expected returns, and the correlation of expected returns with those of other investments.

The Tax Treatment of Investment Alternatives

To apply general portfolio theory to households, we must take into account the fact that these investors are also taxpayers and will be aiming to optimize *after-tax* returns and *after-tax* risk. This would be straightforward except for the complexity of the tax treatment of investment returns. The periodic total return on an investment is the sum of coupon, dividend or rental income, and price appreciation. The tax treatment of each of these types of income varies by type of investment and changes substantially over time.

Current tax law with respect to investment income is relatively straightforward. Taxpayers are liable to pay their marginal tax rate times the amount of investment income, regardless of whether the earnings come in the form of coupon interest, stock dividends, rents, or capital gains. Capital gains are taxed only upon realization. Capital losses can be used to offset any capital gains realized in the same year and, to a limited degree, net losses can be used to offset ordinary taxable income. Individual investors pay one of three effective marginal tax rates: 15%, 28%, or 33%.[2] Coupon income on municipal bonds is exempt from federal taxes under the standard calculation, but capital gains realized upon the sale or redemption of a municipal bond are taxable.

The Alternative Minimum Tax

Before the passage of the Tax Reform Act of 1986 (TRA), the tax treatment of investment income was much more complicated. A proportion of realized capital gains was excluded from taxable income; taxpayers could defer tax payments on earnings on assets held in individual retirement accounts (IRAs); and the treatment of passive investment losses provided a wide variety of tax shelters. In this sense, the TRA simplified the tax treatment of investment income considerably. In another way, however, the TRA added to the complexity of the tax treatment of municipal bonds by expanding the alternative minimum tax (AMT).

Taxpayers who claim substantial itemized deductions are required to calculate their tax liability in two ways: once under the standard calculation described above and once under the rules governing the AMT.[3] The AMT calculation begins with the taxable income determined by the standard calculation and then adds back certain items that were excluded or deducted under the standard calculation. The sum of standard calculation taxable income and the deductions and exemptions added back is AMT taxable income. The AMT liability for individual taxpayers is 21% of AMT taxable income. The taxpayer is liable to pay the larger of the standard calculation or the AMT calculation.

---

[2] Officially, there are only two marginal rates: 15% and 28%. The 33% rate imposed on individual filers with taxable incomes between $43,150 and $89,560 and joint filers with incomes between $71,900 and $149,250 reflects the official 28% rate paid by these taxpayers and the gradual phase-out of the benefit of the 15% rate on the first $29,750 of income for joint filers and $17,850 for single filers.

[3] The discussion in this *Monthly Market Perspective* deals only with the AMT as it applies to households. The corporate AMT differs in several crucial aspects and will be discussed in a later installment of the *Back to Basics* series.

Among the items that are included in AMT income but not under standard calculation taxable income is interest paid on "private purpose" municipal bonds issued on or after August 7, 1986. This provision of the AMT creates an additional asset category, "AMT municipals," for investors to consider. The fact that the treatment of some categories of investment income is different under the two calculations adds an additional dimension of uncertainty into investment decision-making: uncertainty over which tax calculation will determine the final liability.

For taxpayers, the realized total return on investments depends on the tax treatment of those returns when they are received. Because the tax law as it applies to investment income changes frequently, investors must incorporate uncertainty about future tax treatment of different types of investment income into their decision-making. For example, investors at present must consider the possibility that the tax treatment of capital gains might change in the near future, increasing the relative attractiveness of investments that incorporate a relatively large proportion of price gains into their total returns. Also, the Bush Administration has proposed creating a new vehicle for tax-free investing, while some Congressional Democrats have proposed reinstituting IRAs.

THE PERFORMANCE CHARACTERISTICS OF ALTERNATIVE INVESTMENTS

Table 2.1 lists the mean annual returns on several asset categories over the 30-year period between 1959 and 1988, the standard deviation of annual returns, and the correlations among annual total returns. The calculations of after-tax returns are based on the treatment of investment income under the TRA of 1986. We also assume that all capital losses can be offset by capital gains or against ordinary income.

The results reported in the table offer several insights into the behavior of taxable investors. Note first that stocks have produced the highest average returns, both before- and after-tax. This high return comes at the cost of a higher variance of returns. Bonds have offered lower average returns with lower variance. Correlations between the returns on stocks and both categories of bonds are relatively low. Consequently, investors will benefit from holding both stocks and bonds in the portfolio. The proportions of the two asset categories any given household may hold will depend on the investor's attitude toward risk. Investors characterized by a high degree of risk aversion will hold proportionally more bonds; those less averse to risk will hold proportionally more stocks.

TABLE 2.1
Annual Total Return Statistics by Asset Type and Tax Treatment 1959–88

	After-Tax			Before-Tax		
Asset Category	Municipals	Stocks	L.T. Treasuries	Municipals	Stocks	L.T. Treasuries
Average	0.0506	0.0905	0.0426	0.0463	0.1257	0.0591
Std. Dev.	0.0692	0.1116	0.0735	0.0942	0.1550	0.1020
Correlation With:						
After-Tax						
Municipals	1.000	0.0925	0.5120	0.9952	0.0952	0.5120
Stocks		1.0000	0.1020	0.0805	1.000	0.1020
L.T. Treasuries			1.0000	0.4779	0.1020	1.0000
Before-Tax						
Municipals				1.0000	0.0805	0.4779
Stocks					1.0000	0.1020
L.T. Treasuries						1.0000

Somewhat surprisingly, the statistics also suggest that all investors, regardless of their tax liabilities, should hold both tax-exempt and taxable bonds. To be sure, the average after-tax returns on municipals are higher than those on Treasuries, while Treasuries offer higher before-tax returns. The correlations between the returns on the two bond categories, while positive and substantial, are far from perfect. This means that holding both municipals and Treasuries offers benefits in terms of portfolio diversification and risk reduction to *all* investors. This point having been made, however, investors who are taxpayers will want to concentrate a very large proportion of their fixed income portfolios in the tax-exempt sector because municipals offer both higher after-tax returns and lower variance of after-tax returns than Treasuries. Investors with no tax liabilities will want to hold only a very small proportion of their fixed income assets in municipals. In fact, in Table 2.1, the before-tax return on municipals averaged less than the after-tax return on these assets. Over this 30-year period, interest rates were generally rising, and bond holdings were generating capital losses. In the calculations underlying Table 2.1, after-tax losses were smaller than before-tax losses because we assumed that losses could be used to offset other taxable income.

The results in Table 2.1 offer one additional insight into taxpayers' investment behavior that is worth mentioning. To the extent that the investor receives some investment income that is subject to taxation and some that is not—through an IRA or Keogh plan, for example—the untaxed account should probably hold a larger proportion of equities than the taxed account. The ratio of the average after-tax return on stocks to the average after-tax return on municipals over this period was about 1.79 to 1. The ratio of the average before-tax return on stocks to the before-tax return on Treasuries was about 2.13 to 1. Therefore, fixed income investments are a better relative buy for taxpayers than for investors or accounts that are exempt from taxation.

SUMMARY: DETERMINANTS OF THE AGGREGATE DEMAND FOR MUNICIPALS

We can summarize this discussion in a list of the main determinants of the aggregate demand for municipals:

(1) *The higher aggregate household savings, the greater the demand.* Aggregate savings will increase to the extent that household disposable income grows rapidly or the savings rate increases. Both disposable income and the savings rate are likely to increase relatively quickly as the bulk of the U.S. population matures into the peak savings years of the life cycle.

(2) *The higher the expected after-tax returns on municipals relative to the after-tax yield on alternative investments, the greater the demand.* Credit-adjusted relative after-tax yields will rise when tax rates increase. Expected relative after-tax returns on municipals will tend to be lower to the extent that taxpayers anticipate the creation of new tax-advantaged investment vehicles.

(3) *The lower the variance in periodic after-tax returns on municipals relative to the variance of returns on alternative investments, the greater the demand.* Less uncertainty about future tax law and less volatility in the new issue calendar would tend to reduce the relative volatility of municipal returns.

(4) *The lower the correlation between the after-tax returns on municipals and those of alternative investments, the greater the demand.* Frequent changes in the yield relationship between municipal and taxable bonds tend to bring more investors into the market. At the same time, however, a lower correlation between municipal and U.S. Treasury bond returns might induce taxpayers to hold larger proportions of taxable bonds than they might otherwise.

CHAPTER 3

The Primary Market: Underwriting Municipal Bonds*

Robert Boyden Lamb
New York University

Municipal bonds are brought to market in two ways:

- Competitive public sale.
- Private sale (also known as negotiated sale).

Private (negotiated) underwritings have grown rapidly in recent years—from about $5 billion in 1972 to $53 billion a decade later. In that same period, competitive underwritings grew only about 20%. The dollar volume of negotiated underwritings is now about double that of competitive sales.

This chapter is reprinted from *Corporate and Municipal Securities: Volume III of the Library of Investment Banking* (Richard D. Irwin, Inc.: Homewood, IL) 1989, pp. 796–812.

*This chapter was derived from the following sources: Robert Boyden Lamb, "Municipal Debt," Chapter 4 in Securities Essential Program of Stanton C. Selbst's Financial Professional's Series; Robert Boyden Lamb and Henry P. Schott, Jr., "Price Efficiency of Competitive Bidding on New Issues in the Municipal Securities Market," *Municipal Finance Journal*, Volume 8:1, Winter 1987; and James Leigland and Robert Boyden Lamb, *Who Is to Blame for the WPP$$ Disaster?* Ballanger/Harper & Row 1987.

COMPETITIVE SALE

Competitive public sales are used by large issuers with strong credit and interest in their bonds among financial institutions. State and local laws may require that competitive public sales be used for offerings of general obligation (GO) bonds.

Official Announcement

A competitive public sale begins with an official announcement by the issuer in local newspapers and financial periodicals. This announcement sets forth the size, maturities, purpose, and structure of the proposed issue, along with instructions for submitting bids. An official statement may be prepared during this time. This document is both a disclosure and a selling document prepared by the issuer to inform the market of the issue's terms. It serves the same purpose as a prospectus in a corporate financing. (Municipal securities are not subject to the terms of the Securities Act of 1933 or the Securities and Exchange Act of 1934, including the SEC's registration and prospectus requirements. However, the *Anti-Fraud* provisions of The Securities Act *do* apply to Municipal Securities.) Often, ratings for a new issue are not established until after the official announcement is made.

Syndicate Letter

Securities underwriting firms then canvass each other to determine relative interest in bidding on the new issue and forming underwriting syndicates. This is accomplished by a syndicate letter sent by a firm organizing the group to each potential member of the group. The letter invites participation and explains terms under which the underwriting syndicate will operate. There is no requirement that a firm join a syndicate to participate in a municipal bond offering. Securities firms are free to submit single-handed bids to underwrite an entire issue themselves, and many do. Banks may participate in the primary offering of municipal bonds, but they are limited to participation in general obligation (GO) bonds, housing revenue bonds, student loan bonds, and other specified types.

Syndicate Meeting

On the day a bid is submitted, members of the syndicate gather at a syndicate meeting to discuss and agree on a bid. Any firm that disagrees with the consensus bid is free to drop out at this point. The remaining firms then agree on their individual underwriting liabilities—the portion of the syndicate's total responsibility for purchasing bonds allocated to each firm. These and other terms are set forth in the agreement among underwriters. The final bid is submitted in compliance with the issuer's instructions. The syndicate normally pays a good-faith deposit of 5% at this time.

Awarding Bids

At the designated hour, bids are opened and the bonds awarded to the bidding group that has submitted the lowest bid. Usually, this is defined in terms of the lowest interest cost to the issuer and is computed in one of two ways:

- Net interest cost (NIC)—This is a measure of the total interest to be paid in relation to the amount of principal outstanding over the life of the issue.
- True interest cost (TIC)—This is the interest rate of return that will be paid by the issuer to investors (i.e., the discount rate that will equal the sum of the present values of the issuer's cash payments).

The advantage of TIC to the issuer is that it takes into account the time value of money. This provides a more accurate indication of the cost to the issuer than NIC.

The winning syndicate members then begin to distribute the bonds to other firms, institutions, and the public. Often, the entire issue is spoken for in a matter of hours, or a few days at most.

NEGOTIATED SALE

In a negotiated (private) sale, the issuer works with a single underwriting syndicate to distribute the bonds, at an interest rate and price to be determined through negotiation. Revenue bonds, which are not often subject to public sale requirements (as are GO bonds) usually are sold through private negotiation.

Advantages to Issuers

Many issuers prefer negotiation because it gives more flexibility than a competitive sale. The issuer is free to modify key elements such as maturity dates and issue size right up until the date of sale. In a competitive sale, these terms must be locked in when the notice of sale is made, often two to three weeks prior to the sale date.

Choosing the Underwriting Syndicate

The issuer's choice of an underwriting syndicate is determined by past relationships and special expertise in selling the same type of securities. The underwriting firm selected by the issuer to manage the syndicate sends an invitation to other underwriters, setting forth terms and inviting them to participate.

The managers of the syndicate and officials of the issuer (typically a financial manager or treasurer of a city or county) work together on terms of the issue, including maturities, interest rates, call provisions, credit provisions, covenants, and so forth.

Red Herring and Indications of Interest

Once the issuer and lead underwriter are in agreement, a preliminary official statement (red herring) is printed and distributed to the offices of the syndicate members. A week or two before the sale, the issuer and syndicate managers agree on a preliminary price, which is actually a scale of interest rates and prices for the issue. This is communicated to the sales staff, which then solicits presale orders or indications of interest from clients.

If an insufficient level of interest is generated by the first preliminary price, the managers may increase the yield of the bonds (decrease the price) until sufficient demand surfaces.

Bond Purchase Contract

When the syndicate managers are reasonably confident they have set a yield that will enable the bonds to sell out, they make a final offer to purchase the bonds in the form of a bond purchase contact. If the issuer accepts the syndicate's offer, the contract is signed and the bonds are sold to the syndicate, which then distributes them.

DIVIDED AND UNDIVIDED ACCOUNTS

In both negotiated and competitive bond sales, the two basic types of underwriting accounts are:

- Divided, or Western, accounts.
- Undivided, or Eastern, accounts.

In a Western account, each syndicate member is responsible only for its own underwriting allocation. For example, if a member is allocated 10% of the issue, financial liability ends when its 10% share of the total has been distributed.

In an Eastern account, every underwriter is responsible for the entire underwriting in proportion to its original share of the total. An underwriter who is allocated 10% of the original allocation is liable for 10% of *any* bonds that are not sold by the syndicate as a whole. Large bond underwritings generally are undivided, and smaller underwritings are divided.

SALES AND SPREADS

The underwriting syndicate purchases the bonds from the issuer at a discount from the public offering price. The difference is called the gross spread. This is the total amount of money available to members of the syndicate for their efforts and the miscellaneous expenses of the offering such as legal fees and advertising.

The Takedown

The manager allocates bonds to syndicate members at the offering price less a part of the total discount. This part is called the takedown and is typically about 1 point ($10 per $1,000 principal amount). For example, if the takedown is 1 point and the bonds are offered to the public at par ($1,000), the syndicate members pays $990 to the manager per bond. The syndicate member will make $10 per bond. If the gross spread is $15 per bond, the syndicate manager keeps an additional $5 per bond for the syndicate.

If a nonmember of the syndicate has a client order to fill and buys bonds from the syndicate, the nonmember's compensation is called a selling concession. This usually is included in the takedown. For example, if the takedown is 1 point and the selling concession is $5/8$ of a point, the nonmember makes $6.25 for each $1,000 bond sold. The syndicate member who released the bond to the nonmember makes the additional $3.75 of the takedown. If the bonds did not come from a syndicate member (but from the syndicate itself) the remainder of the takedown is added to the underwriting profit of the syndicate.

Allocation Priorities and Procedures

Often, there are more orders for a municipal issue than bonds to go around. When this happens, in both competitive and negotiated offerings, the senior manager of the syndicate is responsible for establishing a set of priorities for determining which members receive bonds for sale. According to the rules of the Municipal Securities Rulemaking Board (MSRB), the Congressionally authorized body responsible for regulatory and disciplinary functions in municipal securities, the manager must formalize these priorities in advance of the sale and notify syndicate members. The following priorities are used for determining allocations:

(1) Presale orders. Orders received prior to the actual award of the bonds to the syndicate, and communicated to the manager during the presale period, receive first priority.

(2) Group account orders. Orders from major institutional investors, each of whom normally does business with members of the syndicate, are next in priority.

(3) Designated orders. Orders from major institutional buyers who wish to reward certain members of the syndicate by designating them as the members who receive credit for the sale are given next priority.

(4) Member's orders. Additional orders received by each member of the syndicate *after* the award of the bonds are last in priority.

Conditions of Sales

Sale of bonds by the underwriting syndicate generally are made on a "when, as and if issued" basis. That means the order is taken before the bonds are issued and subject to the timing (when issued) of the offering. Written confirmations of purchases usually must be sent within two days. Preliminary official statements (red herring) often are mailed to customers who request them with the confirmations, although there is no requirement that this be done. Municipal bond offerings often are completely allocated by the syndicate and sold to customers within a matter of days of the official announcement.

Bond Documents

Two to four weeks after the selling activity, the bond documents usually are ready for delivery to customers. Until recently, most of the delay has been a result of the printing of bond certificates. This delay is being eliminated through use of certificateless Book Entry Bonds or Citizen Bonds.

About a week before actual delivery of the bonds, the underwriters mail to their customers final confirmations that describe the amounts to be paid. The Municipal Securities Rulemaking Board (MSRB) rule G-32 requires that the confirmation include the underwriting spread earned by the syndicate, along with other information. The MSRB also requires that the underwriters send copies of the final official statement along with confirmations.

Dated Date

The date on which bondholders are entitled to begin earning interest is the dated date. This is determined by the issuer and the investment banker and is disclosed in the official statement. If bonds are delivered and paid for after the dated date, purchasers also must pay the interest that has accrued. This payment is made to the syndicate member who has held the bonds. In turn, purchasers collect and keep the full interest due on the first coupon date, which has the effect of repaying accrued interest.

COMMUNICATION AND MOTIVATION IN UNDERWRITING

When competitive bidding is used to sell debt, as we have seen, investment bankers join together in groups or syndicates that bid for the right to purchase the entire issue of securities and sell them again at a slightly higher price. Prior to officially bidding for the issue, members of each competing syndicate canvass potential buyers to get an idea of what they will offer for the bonds. In syndicate meetings the members discuss possible bids based on information from potential buyers, credit ratings, general market and economic conditions, and so on. They agree on specific interest rates considered attractive to investors and on a reoffering price for all of the bonds in the issue. Syndicate members are free to drop out at any time before the final bid is made. If enough drop out, the interest rate may be raised or the syndicate may decide not to bid.

The winning syndicate begins selling the securities immediately at the reoffering price, in the hopes of unloading them all within a few days. Occasionally, the interest of buyers is much lower than anticipated, and, after a designated period, members of the syndicate are allowed to offer the securities at whatever price the market will accept. Some members may choose to keep the securities until a later date when they can be sold at a more favorable price. Either way, because each member must still pay for its share of the issue at the agreed-upon price, the syndicate members usually experience financial losses.

Thus, there are a number of ways for underwriters and investors to communicate their opinions of a bond issue to the issuer. If an issue is unattractive, high interest rates may be established to attract investors, few bids may be received, and underwriters may have difficulty reselling the securities. These signals are not unambiguous. Many factors affect the establishment of interest rates in the underwriting process, and factors having nothing to do with the credit risk of bonds often influence investor enthusiasm.

Nor are underwriters, for example, particularly interested in credit quality. Their major focus is on buying the bonds and then selling them for a profit in as short a time as possible. Creditworthiness is considered only to the extent that it enhances or diminishes the attractiveness of the bonds in the eyes of customers to whom the underwriter tries to resell. And weak credit often can be offset by high interest offered to investors.

But a great deal of formal and informal communication takes place in the underwriting process, and underwriters and other investment firms seem quick to reach a general consensus about the investment quality of certain issues. When negative assessments of credit quality begin to appear, the news spreads rapidly through the investment community.

COMPETITIVE BIDDING VS. NEGOTIATED SALE

What are the relative benefits and drawbacks of competitive bidding versus negotiated sales? Since the number of issues sold through negotiation is constantly rising, this issue has great relevance in the present municipal market. Many issuers that can sell bonds through competitive bidding would prefer to have negotiated issues.

Pros and Cons of Competitive Bidding

The primary advantage of competitive bidding is that a syndicate's bid is final and cannot be changed, regardless of whether underwriters make or lose money on the issue. The advantages of competitive bids for investors are that reoffering yields cannot be changed by the syndicate, except to raise them if the issue is selling slowly, and investors can usually find out within hours whether they have received the bonds they ordered.

The main advantage of competitive bidding, on the other hand, can also be its primary detriment. Sometimes syndicate bids are too cheap, and the bonds can trade immediately at a premium from issue price. In other words, the bidding is inefficient, and the bonds rise in price to their true equilibrium level. This sometimes happens if the size of the issue is very large or if the issue is relatively unknown, causing a great deal of uncertainty among underwriters. This, in turn, leads to bids below the equilibrium prices of the bonds. A related drawback is the requirement in competitive bidding that bids received after a certain time may not be accepted. There are hundreds of cases in which the highest bid for an issue (i.e., the lowest interest cost) was late and not accepted because the person carrying the bid was delayed in traffic or caught in a slow elevator on his trip to the point of sale. Although such stories provide interesting copy for the press and give traders and syndicate members headaches, the more serious aspect of such cases is often overlooked, which is that rejecting a late bid can often cost a municipality millions of dollars over the life of the issue. If the late bid represents the lowest interest cost, rejecting it is an inefficiency of the market, for it means awarding bonds to a bid that is not the highest in the marketplace.

Pros and Cons of Negotiated Sales

Negotiated sales are able to adjust supply and demand much more easily than competitive sales. If there is a heavy demand for an issue at a certain price, yields can be reduced or the size of the issue can be increased or amounts reduced or the size of the issue can be increased to meet the demand. On the other hand, yields can be increased or amounts reduced if demand is sluggish for an issue. This cannot happen in a competitive sale, although some issuers selling bonds competitively are allowing underwriters more than one bidding option, or different maturity structures, in order to pay a lower net interest cost. The inefficiency of late bids is also avoided in a negotiated sale.

The major drawback of negotiated sales is that it often takes days for investors to find out whether they will receive the bonds they have ordered. Also, investors placing orders for negotiated issues are uncertain if the issue will be repriced and the yields lowered. (If yields are lowered, investors can refuse the bonds.)

What may be considered an attractive yield on Monday may not be that appealing on Thursday when syndicate allotments are made, since it can often take three days between first pricing and allocation. The length of the order period is one reason for the delay between pricing and final allocation. In negotiated sales, the order period is usually at least one full day, although the lead manager reserves the right to terminate it or extend it on the whole issue or on certain maturities. In competitive sales, order periods are usually for one hour after the time of sale, after which any unsold bonds are available on a first-come, first-served basis. Also, on very large negotiated issues, there are thousands of orders, and the allocation of bonds is a tedious and time-consuming process.

In the past, negotiated issues were often frowned upon by issuers, who felt that they would be treated unfairly by the negotiating syndicate. Fortunately, this attitude has changed in recent years, and many issuers prefer negotiated sales even though they could sell bonds competitively. The Municipal Assistance Corporation (MAC) of New York is such an issuer. MAC has sold only two competitive issues within its nine-year history, and its last seven issues have been via negotiation.

Although it may not appear so upon first glance, there is much competition between firms in negotiated issues. Senior managers for an issue are chosen for their ability to sell the issuer's bonds at the best prices, and if an issuer feels that it has been treated unfairly, it can and will change managers. Since managing negotiated issues is a highly lucrative business for securities firms, they are under extreme pressure to perform well for an issuer, or else they may lose their managership and the fees that go with it. This striving for managership of issues adds a strong degree of competition to negotiated sales. Indeed, the least competitive type of new issue is not a negotiated one but a competitive issue for which only one bid has been received. In such cases, the syndicate is under no pressure to perform for the issuer. Not surprisingly, the largest underwriting spreads are found in these issues.

MARKET EFFICIENCY IN PRICING NEW ISSUES

Despite the wealth of literature on new issue syndicates, there has been almost no work done on how close the syndicate bids are on competitive new issues. Such a study would give an indication of how efficiently information about the issuer is reflected in the marketplace. If the syndicate bids are very close, it would appear that all information about the issuer is accurately reflected in the prices of its bonds, and there would be little dispute by bidders over what a given issuer's bonds should yield in a certain year. On the other hand, if there is wide dispersion of syndicate bids, this means one of two things: either the market is inefficient in reflecting information about the issuer, or one syndicate has buyers that will pay higher prices for the issuer (and thereby accept lower yields) than the customers of the other bidding groups.

In order to measure how efficiently the market performs in pricing new issues, we examined a sample of 220 new issues that sold via competitive bid. These issues sold in November 1983, February 1984, and the entire six-month period from June to December 1984. Only issues that received at least three bids were selected, although this meant excluding several large issues that received only two bids. Also, no issues with final maturities of less than 10 years (1994) were included, since this would bias the sample. (Bidding would be much closer for issues with short maturities, since they carry much less risk of price volatility.) Furthermore, the issues were divided by size into three categories: $25 million and over, $5 million to $25 million, and under $5 million. Within these size divisions, the issues were subdivided by rating into AAA, AA, A, and BAA (or BBB) groups. When an issue carried different Moody's and Standard and Poor's ratings, the Moody's rating was used, since the marketplace gives more weight to that designation. The exception to this rule was insured issues, for which the Standard and Poor's AAA classification was used. (Moody's now rates MBIA and FGIC-insured issues AAA.) Finally, the sample was further divided into bank-eligible and nonbank-eligible issues (some revenue bonds are bank-eligible) to see whether any further insight could be gained into the question of whether banks should be allowed to underwrite revenue bonds.

The bidding results were categorized according to how many issues received two or three bids within 5 or 10 basis points, using the reported net interest cost or Canadian interest cost. If the market is truly efficient, the first three syndicate bids should be within at least 10 basis point of each other, since there should be very little difference of opinion among bidders as to what a given name should yield for a given year under any market conditions.

A preconception when this study was undertaken was that the bidding would be closest for the larger and more highly rated issues. Although the results are generally consistent with this presupposition, the dispersion of syndicate bids for smaller and lower-rated issues was much closer than initially expected. Exactly half of the 60 issues over $25 million received at least three bids within 10 basis points of each other; the two smaller categories exhibited this same closeness 40 percent of the time. These results suggest that the municipal market is fairly efficient in pricing new issues. Also, although the dispersion of bidding was a little closer for the AAA and AA groups in the $25 million and above category, in the two smaller categories the bidding was tighter for the A-rated issues. The overall total shows that 44 percent of all of the issues surveyed in the highest three rating categories received at least three bids within 10 basis points. Only the BAA category showed a wide dispersion of bids, with only 4 out of 18 issues receiving three close bids. Thus, although a definitive study on the subject is needed, we cannot claim to have found a great amount of inefficiency in the municipal market, at least in the dispersion of syndicate bids on new issues.

We also cannot claim that bank-eligible issues received tighter bids than ineligible ones, at least in the $25 million and above and $5 million to $25 million categories. Only in the smallest size category can we possibly assert that the presence of banks as bidders might have produced tighter bidding, and the sample of bank-ineligible issues is too small for us to make this claim with much conviction. The reason for the lack of discrepancy between eligible and ineligible issues is relatively easy to explain. Many of these issues are general market names, such as state general obligations, and they are purchased throughout the country. Also, many issues, even of regional names, are now insured by third parties, giving them a national appeal as well. This suggests that banks would not be able to find great numbers of buyers for the ineligible issues that nonbank dealers have not already located. On the other hand, our results hint that bank participation in smaller issues, which tend to be much more regional, would have a positive effect on reducing interest costs paid by the issuers.

Presently, however, the issue of bank participation in competitive revenue issues is largely moot. Roughly two-thirds of all public debt is revenue debt, with only one-third being general obligation debt. Moreover, the majority of revenue issues are negotiated. There are two main reasons for this. First, revenue issues are generally more complicated than general obligation issues, and a greater effort is required to sell them. A negotiated sale can be timed more easily to coincide with the selling effort. Second, even for large, bank-eligible competitive issues, there are usually no more than three syndicate bids, and often there are only two. The greatest number of bids is usually received on issues of between $10 million and $25 million, and it declines to two with most issues of over $100 million. Thus, for the larger issues, it appears that even with bank participation there are not enough buyers to support five or six syndicates. This is particularly true in regard to large institutions that are not covered by nonbank dealers. Also, since larger issues require a greater commitment of capital from securities firms, the number of members in syndicates for large issues is much higher than for issues of $10 million to $25 million. Therefore, even if banks were allowed to underwrite and trade revenue bonds, the number of bids for large issues probably would not increase. It is also probably not true that bank participation in revenue deals would cause many issuers to shift from negotiated sales to competitive bids. It is likely, however, that, if banks were allowed to underwrite and trade revenue bonds, the yield spread between revenue bonds and general obligations would narrow since there would be more firms making markets in revenue issues. This increased secondary market liquidity for revenue issues appears to be the primary benefit of allowing banks to underwrite revenue bonds. Hopefully, this increased competitiveness for revenue issues in the secondary market will cause greater competition in the bidding on new issues.

WHEN THE PROCESS FAILS: THE WPPSS DISASTER

While lawsuits and investigations proceed (such as with WPPSS), and until court decisions or legislation clarifies the legal responsibilities of the investment community, members of that community will continue to use what might be called their standard operating procedures. Most analysts, traders, underwriters, and so forth, admit that these procedures can be reduced to a single maxim: Whatever is profitable, and legal, will be done. This is the essence of street ethics, the code of behavior that governs Wall Street more as a fact of life than as a moral imperative.

Street Ethics

In other words, the individuals and organizations that make up the Wall Street community are not always motivated to fulfill the textbook role requirements. Street ethics considers it a mistake to assume that underwriters will question the need for a public debt financed project if the bonds can be sold at a profit and bond counsel declares the sale to be legal. Investment banking is a highly lucrative and highly competitive business.

Street ethics has also established that the traditional role of an analyst at an investment banking firm is to help market bonds. Most credit reports produced by these firms simply describe the issue, and reports seldom conflict with the marketing efforts of an investment firm's sell side. Street ethics also allows most major financial advisory firms to act at one time or another as underwriters for their advisees. This potential for underwriting clients' bonds contributes to limiting the financial advice given to marketing strategy.

How the Bonds Were Sold

In marketing bonds, especially when they are sold to individual purchasers, the rule that governs behavior is an even more freewheeling variation of the maxim mentioned above: whatever is profitable, and not illegal, will be used to retail bonds. In other words, no attorney stands by and approves the legality of marketing techniques in the way that bond counsel give opinions on the legality of bond issues. This maxim manifested itself in three ways as the WPPSS crisis took shape and billions of dollars' worth of bonds were sold.

On the Basis of Ratings. Above all, the bonds were sold on the basis of ratings that, by the 1980s, many salespeople knew to be unrealistically high. Until January 1983 both Standard & Poor's and Moody's gave bonds for WPPSS Projects 1, 2, and 3 a rating of AAA—the firms' highest. Roughly $6 billion in bonds were sold with the benefit of that rating. In June 1981 Standard and Poor's lowered its rating for Projects 4 and 5 bonds from A-plus to A, shortly after Moody's downgraded 4 and 5 to Baa 1. These actions resulted from the announcement that the total completion price for Projects 4 and 5 would be $12 billion, not the $8 billion estimate cited just months before. WPPSS 4 and 5 never came to market again. But $2.25 billion worth of Projects 4 and 5 bonds had been sold with the benefit of Moody's A-1 and S & P's A-plus ratings. The downgradings came too late to benefit the bond-buying public. By June 1983 Moody's had suspended ratings for Projects 1, 2, and 3. Project 4 and 5 bonds received Standard & Poor's highly speculative CC rating, the lowest possible rating for an issue that has not yet missed an interest payment.

Throughout this period the real significance of municipal ratings was obvious to anyone familiar with recent municipal defaults or near-defaults. Since the New York state crisis in 1975, all of the major municipal debt issues that eventually went into default were initially given investment-grade ratings. This includes the Urban Development Corporation and the bonds and notes of the Chicago Board of Education, which were rated investment grade in 1980 when the board was clearly in danger of default. When the Oklahoma Housing Finance Agency went into default in 1982, its construction bonds and notes were rated AAA and MIG-1 by Standard and Poor's and Moody's.

By 1975 Wall Street firms had already begun relying less on Moody's and Standard & Poor's credit ratings as indicators of credit quality. Even though in-house credit analyses still tended to support the activities of each firm's sell side, by the late 1970s these analyses were questioning the credit ratings assigned by the major rating agencies. For example, in February 1979, almost two and a half years before the major rating firms downgraded Projects 4 and 5 bonds, Susan Linden, an analyst at Merrill Lynch Fixed Income Research, published a report on WPPSS 4 and 5 that openly questioned the existing A+ ratings. Linden cited a management consulting report to emphasize the importance of construction cost overruns and construction delays and to show evidence of inadequate management capability. The Merrill Lynch report described Projects 4 and 5 as ". . . equivalent to a conditional low-range 'A.' The conditional nature of the rating will be removed and a higher credit level justifiable only upon successful operation of the project. Downward revision may be necessary unless timely financing and completion of the Projects occur."

But the growing lack of faith in the major rating agencies evidenced in Linden's reports and in those by analysts at other firms had little effect on the behavior of salespeople, especially when Moody's or

S & P's ratings could be used to sell bonds. In fact, Linden's approach to in-house analysis exemplifies well the already growing tension between analysts and salespeople.

Through UITs. Not only did ratings allow bond salesmen to retail billions of dollars of WPPSS bonds to individuals directly, but they also made possible indirect sales to sometimes unknown investors. This second method of retailing involves unit investment trusts (UITs). UITs represent one of the three ways in which individuals buy municipal bonds—direct purchases can be made of individual bonds (which are typically in $5,000 denominations) or of shares of managed municipal bond funds.

Participation in a UIT involves the purchase of a unit, or share, in a large portfolio of bonds maintained by an investment house. UITs are especially convenient for small investors who simply do not have enough money to put together a defensive portfolio of municipal bonds. Unit investment trusts, usually offered in $1,000 shares, consist of portfolios that generally limit single-issue concentration in a range of 7.5 to 10 percent.

The UITs bought WPPSS 4 and 5 early and often and stayed with the issues until 1981. When they stopped buying, the denial to WPPSS of market access was inevitable. Unlike bond funds, UITs do not involve actively managed portfolios; instead, UITs are supposed to contain reasonably safe collections of bonds that have the highest possible yield. The major UITs, such as the Nuveen Trust and the Municipal Investment Trust (sponsored by Merrill Lynch, Prudential-Bache, and Shearson Lehman Hutton, among others) have requirements specifying that only bonds with A ratings or better can be purchased for the trusts. It is possible that UITs purchased as much as 25% of all the WPPSS 4 and 5 bonds; they certainly combined to form the single largest category of institutional purchasing.

It is sometimes charged that the major brokerage firms, which were members of the WPPSS underwriting syndicates, simply used their UITs as a convenient place to dump a portion of their WPPSS underwritings. This may have been a consideration in some cases, but it pales beside the short-term competitive disadvantage that a UIT would have created for itself had it not used WPPSS bonds in its portfolio as other, competing UITs did. UITs are marketed to people who are assumed to know almost nothing about municipal bonds, and if all the bonds in all the competing UITs are rated A or better, the only apparent difference to the buyer is the portfolio yield. WPPSS provided tremendous extra yield. If a UIT decided to eliminate WPPSS from the portfolio, the yield became noncompetitive with the other trusts.

Not only did UITs buy a lot of WPPSS bonds, but they continued to buy and hold WPPSS bonds. In other words, they helped support the market for those bonds long after the denial of market access should have occurred. They also helped to withhold from individual investors the danger signal that an institutional dumping of WPPSS securities would have provided. If interest rates steadily rise during the purchase period, the current market value of the total holding will decline substantially below the original purchase price. A decision to sell holdings (for reasons of declining credit quality) results in a direct loss. An insurance company (a casualty company that buys municipal bonds) can write off the loss against taxes. A bank can do this also, but when a UIT sells a holding, the portfolio loss is directly passed on to the unit holder, whose individual tax status is unknown to the trust sponsor. UIT portfolio managers do not like to sell and pass through losses because, historically, most UITs have found it more in their interests to sit through a workout in default, or a near miss, than to sell bonds at sharply discounted prices. If a portfolio manager sells a major holding at a substantial loss and the issue later works out to par value, it will not reflect well on the manager's performance. Most institutions, especially UITs, held on to WPPSS bonds as long as possible.

Through Misinformation. A third technique for selling bonds to individual investors took advantage of the fact that most people—even those making direct purchases of bonds—know very little about municipal securities. This did not necessarily involve any misrepresentation of fact. It simply meant allowing potential investors to believe something that was not necessarily true. By the late 1970s the WPPSS staff was working closely with its financial advisers to tailor official statements to attract individual investors to its bonds. Whatever the actual intent of this tailoring, the effect was to make the careless reader or unsophisticated investor think the bonds were somehow backed by the federal government. Many investors in WPPSS bonds now consider this tailoring to be misrepresentation.

Widespread misuse of the term federal guarantee had a similar, if less profound, effect. So, too, did other inaccuracies in the press. A late 1981 *New York Times* article reported the high yields associated with bonds for WPPSS Projects 1, 2, and 3, which were then "trading to yield 14%—equivalent to 28% for a taxpayer in the 50% bracket." Moreover, the article reported that all three plants "steadily produce power."

Perhaps the best-known misstatement contributing to what may have been millions of dollars in sales of WPPSS bonds is the letter from Comptroller of the Currency James E. Smith to a vice president of a New York City bank. The August 27, 1975, letter was a response to a question about whether or not banks, prohibited from underwriting most revenue bond issues by the Glass-Steagall Banking Reform Act of 1933, could underwrite WPPSS Project 1, 2, and 3 bonds. After describing the net billing arrangements, Mr. Smith went on to conclude that

> Through these arrangements the United States acting through Bonneville has undertaken an obligation to make available to the system amounts sufficient to meet annual interest and principal payments on these bonds as well as all other costs of operating the Projects.
>
> It is our conclusion that the $175,000 Washington Public Power Supply System, Nuclear Project No. 1, 1975 Revenue Bonds are obligations of the United States under paragraph Seven of 12 U.S.C. 24 and are eligible for purchase, dealing in, underwriting and unlimited holding by national banks. (Smith 1975: 2)

In the process of upholding what has been a longstanding if informal policy of the comptroller's office to extend the area of national bank activity, Mr. Smith unwittingly helped brokers all over the country sell WPPSS bonds. Copies of the letter quickly circulated throughout Wall Street, and potential investors were soon being told that WPPSS Projects 1, 2, and 3 bonds were "obligations of the United States."

Let the Buyer Beware

One reality confirmed by the WPPSS disaster is that whether selling bonds to investors or advice to public borrowers, the investment community cannot be relied on to consider all of the issues of interest to its clients. But neither does the financial community actually claim to cover that full range. Issuers of tax-exempt securities, like purchasers of tax-exempt bonds, are responsible for recognizing what the investment community can and cannot do for them, given the standard operating procedures discussed above. The alliance of public entities, private financial institutions, and investors is a powerful one, but it works to benefit all only when the roles and responsibilities of each are clearly understood by all.

CHAPTER 4

The Secondary Market: Trading Municipal Bonds*

Robert Boyden Lamb
New York University

The secondary municipal market today is an over-the-counter market in which bond dealers trade and make markets in bonds using their own capital to maintain inventory. The actual buying and selling of previously issued municipals is conducted over the telephone in most cases, between dealers and customers or between two dealers.

HOW THE SYSTEM WORKS

If a telephone call does not result in a satisfactory execution, dealers with bonds to sell often employ the services of a broker's broker to locate another dealer with an interest in buying the bonds. These brokers are specialists in shopping the market for potential buyers and sellers. Some broker's brokers rely on the telephone to locate participants in a trade, while others use teletype wires connected to dealer offices around the country. These wires broadcast (print out) lists of bonds offered for sale. Broker's brokers usually charge a fee of at least

* This chapter is reprinted from *Corporate and Municipal Securities: Volume III of the Library of Investment Banking* (Richard D. Irwin, Inc.: Homewood, IL) 1989, pp. 813–831.

$^1/_8$% of the value of bonds sold as a commission. Since that works out to $1.25 per $1,000 traded, broker's brokers tend to focus on high-volume trading.

Blue List

If, after telephone calls and teletype surveys, a trade still has not been executed at an acceptable price, the next step is to consult the Blue List. This is a daily publication that lists bonds offered for sale by dealers. Listings are telephoned to the Blue List offices by 4 P.M. the day before publication. A problem in using this listing is that bonds may not be available at prices shown in the publication. They may already have been sold or withdrawn from the market. The Blue List does not contain credit ratings.

Computerized Trading

The secondary market for some Citizen bonds is the New York Stock Exchange. The NYSE computerized bond-trading system, known as the Automated Bond System (ABS), is used to execute all transactions involving small lots of bonds. Larger transactions are usually handled "upstairs" in the trading rooms of dealer firms. Computerized systems reduce the cost of executing bond trades to such low levels (approximately 50 to 75 cents per trade, once the transaction reaches the ABS system) that transactions involving Citizen bonds, even in amounts as small as $1,000, become quite cost effective.

The Daily Bond Buyer

The major periodical of record in the municipal bond industry is *The Daily Bond Buyer*. This publication features daily commentary on new issues entering the market. It also contains paid announcements from issuers of upcoming public bond sales and negotiated offerings, as well as lists of bonds that have been called.

The editorial staff of the *Bond Buyer* compiles a variety of indices relating to municipal obligations trading in the secondary market. Among them are the following:

- 20-Bond Index—This includes 20 medium-grade (Baa) to high-grade (Aaa) bonds with 20-year maturities and indicates a hypothetical composite bid by a dealer. The 20-Bond Index indicates the rate at which new issues should be priced to compete with outstanding issues.

- 11-Bond Index—This contains only high-grade (AAA, AA, and A) issues drawn from the 20-Bond Index. Its yield is lower than the 20-Bond Index because higher-quality bonds have lower yields.

The *Bond Buyer* staff also compiles statistics on the success of new municipal issues entering the market. The placement ratio is an estimate of new-issue bonds that have been sold to the public during the week, as a percentage of the total new bond inventory in the hands of dealers. A low placement ratio indicates reduced buying interest in new issues and a general feeling that current yields are not sufficient to facilitate the sale of new issues. *The Bond Buyer's* "30-Day Visible Supply Report" helps investors measure the amount of new issues that soon will come to market. Issuers use it to determine the optimal date to bring issues to market—periods when competition from other issues will be low.

GAUGING SECONDARY MARKET EFFICIENCY

In order to measure the overall efficiency of the secondary municipal bond market, we examined the bidding records of Chapdelaine and Co., one of the largest dealer-to-dealer brokers, from August 17 to September 4, 1984. If the secondary market is indeed efficient in pricing information, the bidding for secondary issues should be fairly close, since experienced bond traders are well versed in the relative yields, regardless of rating, on most major issues. Also, even for regional issues, local dealers in that region should be able to assess an issuer's value in the marketplace accurately.

Despite the fact that the difference between the highest and lowest bid for a bond could be as much as 10 points, our key to gauging efficiency is to look at the closeness of the top five bids. Often dealers deliberately bid low on an item, hoping to "steal" it. Essentially, dealers bidding low are hoping for the possibility of an arbitrage. If they are successful in buying the bonds on a low bid, they try to find a much higher bid for the item by using another dealer-to-dealer broker, waiting a couple of days before putting the bonds out for the bid again, or offering the bond to customers at a lower-than-expected price. Although arbitrage of this nature often occurs, the probability of dealers' buying bonds with a low bid from a broker such as Chapdelaine is very small.

Parameters of the Study

We divided over 500 secondary bid-wanted items into four size categories: $500,000 and above; $100,000 to $499,000; $25,000 to $99,000;

and $24,000 and below. Items that received as few as five bids were included; fortunately, most of the major bid-wanted items during our sample period received at least five bids (some received over 20). We were looking for three measures of price dispersion among the bidding: first, a spread of equal to or less than one-quarter of a point ($2.50 per $1,000) between the top bid and the second, or cover, bid; second; a spread of equal to or less than one-half of one point ($5,00 per $1,000) among the top three bids; and, third, a spread of equal to or less than one point ($10 per $1,000) among the top five bids. For the two smaller categories, we widened our dispersion measures to examine how many cover bids were within one-half of a point, how many times the top three bids were within one point of each, and how many instances occurred in which the top five bids ranged within less than two points ($20 per $1,000) of each other. The size categories were subdivided by rating.

Bidding Practices

Before turning to the results of our study, we must discuss two important aspects of bidding on municipal bonds: yield basis and spread, and how traders determine the bid.

Yield Basis and Spread. First, almost all bids on municipal bonds are composed of two parts: a yield basis and a spread, or concession. For example, if a trader bids an "eight basis less twelve-fifty" this means that he or she is bidding the dollar price corresponding to an 8% yield to maturity on the bonds, minus $12.50. If the trader is the high bid on a lot of bonds and buys them, he or she may reoffer the bonds to customers or to other dealers at a yield to maturity. If the trader is successful in selling the bonds at the offering price, the profit will be $12.50 per $1,000. (A trader is not prohibited from marking up the bonds to a lower yield, such as 7.75%. If the bonds can be sold at that yield, the profit margin is even greater. On the other hand, there is no assurance that any profit will be made.)

In bidding for municipal bonds, the lower the yield and the smaller the spread, the higher the bid will be. In our example, a bid of a 7.90% yield less $12.50 reflects a higher dollar price than does a bid of an eight basis less the same spread. An 8.00% yield less a $9 spread is also a higher bid. It is often possible, however, to bid a higher yield but smaller spread and still be the highest bid. Suppose that two bids on an item are received: an 8.00% yield less $15 and an 8.10% yield less $6. Although it would seem that the first bid is higher because of the lower yield, the second bid is actually the high one because the $9 difference in spread is more than the dollar value of the 10 basis points in yield. A dealer bids a smaller, or tighter, spread if he or she feels that the cost to find a buyer for the bonds is less than that of another dealer. Often, traders have orders for the bonds in hand before they make their bids.

How Traders Determine the Bid. Our second major point of discussion is how traders determine what to bid for any given bond. There are two main sources for that information: new issues and secondary trades that occur in the marketplace. Municipal bond yields are determined by the relationship of one issuer to another. For example, although there are great variations of yield within each rating class, it is nevertheless rare to see an issue rated A yield less than an AAA issue. If this occurs, it implies that the market considers the lower-rated bond less risky than the issue with the higher rating, an extremely rare occurrence. Therefore, no good trader will bid higher for an A-rated issue than he or she will for an AAA-rated one, except in unusual circumstances, such as when the A-rated bond has an active sinking fund.

Traders base their bids for bonds upon yield levels that have been established in the marketplace. Traders also base their bids for new items upon their bids for previous items. Dealer-to-dealer brokers always provide a comment to a trader about a bid for an item, such as "top five," "six to ten," or "way out." A trader in the top five who bids on one item may raise his or her bid a little in order to buy a similar item. On the other hand, a trader who has made the high bid on an item and who has a large cover, such as $15 per $1,000, may lower his or her bid for another similar lot of bonds.

Bid-ask spreads are determined in the same manner as are yields. Essentially, spreads are a function of the liquidity of a bond, which, in turn, is a function of several factors, such as rating, maturity, coupon, amount, and general market conditions. Generally, spreads narrow in rising markets since dealers feel that they will be able to sell their bonds faster and at a profit. Therefore, they are willing to work for a narrower spread. In other words, the costs they incur in searching for investors are less. The reverse is true in a falling market. If prices are falling, traders bid a larger spread; they are less certain of selling the bonds at a profit, and their search costs are greater. As in the case of relative yields, relative spreads also can be determined by traders through examining the spreads on new issues as well as on secondary market trades. Needless to say, the narrowest spreads occur on actively traded, or "dollar," bonds, since they have the most liquidity.

This practice of bidding bonds in terms of yield is the prime cause for the price dispersion in secondary market bids on municipal bonds. A difference of only 10 basis points between two bids can translate into almost a full point when the yield is converted to a dollar price, especially on bonds with long maturities; a difference of 10 basis points can equal almost two points. Therefore, our requirements for measuring efficiency are fairly stringent.

Results of the Study

It is not surprising that the greatest efficiency was recorded in the category of $500,000 and above. Almost 50% of the items sampled received at least five bids within one point of each other. (Items with less than a one-year maturity were excluded from the survey.) Within that category, each rating subdivision achieved virtually an equal percentage of tight bid dispersion. Within the $100,000 to $499,000 category, 35% of the items sampled received at least five bids within one point of each other and almost half of them had cover bids within one-quarter of a point. It is interesting that the highest percentage of items with five bids within one point in this category were in the BAA subdivision (12 out of 25). This is explained by the fact that almost all of the items in this category were either general obligation bonds from New York City or bonds from Puerto Rico; both locations have very active secondary markets. (Eighteen out of 25 items in this group received the two highest bids within one-quarter of a point of each other.) The results in the BAA subdivision suggest that a bond's seemingly low rating does not preclude it from receiving tight bids.

This tendency of lower-rated bonds to receive closer bids as the amount gets smaller is further emphasized in the results of the two smaller categories. In the $25,000 to $99,000 category, the highest percentages of close bids were in BAA- and A-rated bonds, in which 81% and 69%, respectively, received at least five bids within two point of each other. (The AAA subdivision, however, was a very close third, with a 68% total.) Finally, in the smallest category, the percentage of items receiving five bids within two points of each other was inversely proportional to the ratings of the bonds. Over 68% of the BAA-rated items received five close bids, followed by 59% of the A-rated bonds, 53% of the AA bonds, and a dismal 33% for the bonds with the highest rating.

This phenomenon is explained by two factors. First, the number of different names in the BAA rating group is small; this group is composed primarily of general obligation bonds from Puerto Rico, New York City, and Cleveland (which also has an active secondary market.) Second, the smaller lots of bonds are purchased mainly by individuals, who, more often than not, would probably prefer bonds with a higher yield as long as they carry an investment-grade rating. It takes a greater sales effort by dealers to find buyers for small lots of high-grade general obligation bonds than to find buyers for A-rated issues that yield considerably more. Thus, for larger blocks, most of which are purchased by institutions, the bidding is tighter for higher-rated items, whereas exactly the reverse occurs when the cost of the bonds goes below $100,000.

One other aspect of our survey is also worthy of mention. From our results, it cannot be concluded that bonds with shorter maturities receive closer bidding. In fact, the exact opposite often occurred—40-year bonds received as many as 10 bids within one point of each other. One reason for this is that many of the longer bonds with longer terms are large issues, which are followed by many dealers throughout the country because of their liquidity. Also, there is a large group of buyers for such issues—particularly tax-exempt unit trusts—and this translates into greater liquidity. It is surprising that the greatest price dispersion among bids occurred with regard to discount bonds with maturities of 10 to 12 years. The reason for this is that most bonds of this nature are serials with a small amount outstanding, thereby accounting for reduced liquidity and a relative scarcity of buyers.

From our study, we can conclude that the municipal secondary market is price-efficient to a great degree and that, despite the wide variations of yields among comparably rated issues, professional traders can determine what to bid for any given bond within a close range. This closeness of bidding shows that the prices of municipal bonds accurately reflect relevant information in the marketplace. Obviously, there can be wide dispersions of bids on some bonds, and there are also times when dealers are able to buy bonds with low bids and arbitrage them. However, instances of this sort do not prove that the whole municipal bond market is inefficient. Rather, they are examples of inefficiency that occur in an otherwise efficient market.

OPERATIONAL EFFICIENCY

The greatest inefficiencies of the municipal market occur in the time-consuming process of executing orders and in clearing trades. Since the municipal bond market is completely over-the-counter, and since it is a principal market, all trades are done either directly on a dealer-to-dealer basis or through a bond broker with another dealer. In any case, the process ensures a multiplicity of phone calls in order to consummate trades.

On inactively traded bonds, which constitute most of the municipal market, it can often take hours to get a bid. And there is no assurance that it will be the best bid in the marketplace. Unfortunately, there is no exchange where a quote can at least be registered even if no trading in that issue occurs. Obtaining offerings on inactively traded bonds can also be a cumbersome process. Although secondary market offerings are published daily in the Blue List and during the day over Munifacts, the municipal bond wire service, the only way for a dealer to determine whether the offering shown in either source still exists is to call the dealer that is showing the offering. Needless to say, it can be a tedious process to check offerings for customers, especially in active markets when offerings are changing constantly.

This discussion of the operation of the municipal market will focus first on the bid side, then on the offered side, and then on the process of clearing trades and reforms that are about to be implemented in municipal bond clearance.

How the Market Operates

We will use the system of order execution on the listed exchanges as our ideal example of an efficiently operating market. A customer of any member firm wishing to transact business in a listed stock (or one on NASDAQ) can obtain a quote on that security instantly from his broker. If the customer enters a market order on either the buy or sell side of the market, the customer learns, in a matter of minutes, that his trade has been executed and at what price. Also, the closing prices of all listed stocks are printed daily in major newspapers, so that investors can easily follow the prices of their securities. In other words, a customer spends virtually no time searching for the best bid or offering on a stock because the task is performed by the exchanges, which provide the highest bid and lowest offer on any listed stock at any given time.

In the municipal market, the most actively traded bonds are known as dollar bonds because they trade in a dollar value in units of $1/8$ of a point, or $1.25 per thousand, and not in terms of yield. Dollar bonds are issues with a large number of bonds in one maturity. They are often referred to as term bonds. In contrast, serial bonds are issued with a few bonds in many maturities. Because of the larger float, dollar bonds are traded by many firms. Thus, they are more liquid than serial bonds and trade on a narrower spread—often as little as $1/8$ of a point. Dollar bonds are displayed on screens provided by dealer-to-dealer brokers, and prices are constantly updated, so that it is possible for all dealers in the municipal bond market to know of price changes instantaneously in any actively traded bonds.

Unfortunately, there is currently no mechanism for transmitting municipal quotes from the dealer-to-dealer brokers to the general public. The only way for a customer to obtain a quote on his municipal bonds is to call his representative at a securities firm, who in turn must call his municipal trading desk.

Although obtaining a quote on a municipal dollar bond is the closest procedure to obtaining a quote on a listed stock in terms of time involved, there is a major difference. The quote a customer receives for a listed stock is from the exchange, and it represents the best bid and offer at that point in time. In the municipal bond market, the quote a customer receives is not the "inside" quote, but rather a mark-up or mark-down from that quote.

The reason for this markup or markdown is that a municipal trade is done on a principal basis, and the price that a customer receives or pays over the inside price represents the firm's commission. In stock transactions, commission is added to the price a customer pays or is deducted from the price he receives, since a securities firm is acting as agent in the transaction. A crucial difference between these two methods of charging a customer for the firm's services is that a firm's stock commission schedule can be easily obtained by the customer if he desires, while the markup or markdown from the execution price on a municipal trade does not have to be, and almost never is, disclosed. Moreover, most securities firms allow their sales representatives a considerable amount of discretion to determine how much they will charge their customers on municipal transactions. Some firms will set maximum guidelines, such as no more than $15 ($1^1/_2$ points) from the inside quote, while others will permit almost anything so long as it is not in excess of the National Association of Securities Dealers' (NASD) 5% guideline.

As one might imagine, there is a myriad of factors that will affect the markup or markdown: whether the client is considered a good customer, whether the client informs his broker that his securities firm is in competition with another firm, and what the broker considers fair, depending on how his business is at that time. Operationally, municipal dollar bonds are the closest examples in the municipal market to listed stocks, although there is a great deal of discretion and manipulation of quotes that do not exist with stocks listed on the exchanges.

The Bid Side

The operational efficiency for obtaining a bid on an inactively traded serial bond can range from fairly good to disastrous, depending on the amount of bonds the customer owns and how marketable the issue is. As one might expect, the larger the lot of bonds and the more recognizable the issuer, the easier it is to get a bid from a securities firm. Whether the customer obtains the best bid in the marketplace is another matter. Another firm could bid as much as $40 per thousand higher or lower, depending on market conditions, the rating of the bonds, their maturity, and the amount of the markdown charged by the sales representative.

Double-Brokering. The worst operational procedure results when a firm does not wish to bid on a particular lot of bonds owned by a customer, usually because the firm does not feel that its bid will be the best or because the firm does not feel that it can resell the bonds easily. In this case, the firm will give the customer's bonds to a dealer-to-dealer broker, also known as a bond broker. The largest broker is J. J. Kenny and Co., but there are at least 15 others throughout the country. Some have a national network with a wire service, such as Kenny and Chapdelaine and Co., while others specialize in bonds of a certain region, such as Helm, Nabori and Perry, which deals primarily in California bonds.

Unfortunately, bond brokers do not transact business with the individual or institutional investing public. Instead, they broker bonds only between bond dealers and dealer banks. The primary function of dealer-to-dealer brokers is to obtain the best bid on any given lot of bonds for a dealer, whether the bonds are from the dealer's inventory or are owned by a customer of the dealer. However, even with lots of $250,000, it is often difficult to get a quick bid (i.e., within a few minutes) because the bonds must be advertised on a wire or by phone by the broker. Then firms must decide whether they will bid the bonds and what they will bid, and brokers must round up all possible bids. Once the broker has obtained the best bid, it is submitted to the selling dealer, who may in turn have to pass it on to the customer, who must then decide whether or not to sell the bonds.

Customers often feel that a better bid will be obtained by instructing their securities firms to put their bonds out for a bid with a broker. (The alternative would be to ask one or more firms for their own bids.) This is not necessarily so because, in reality, their bonds are being double-brokered by the securities firm. Essentially, the customer will have to pay the broker's commission for obtaining a bid, as well as the dealer's commission for its service. Moreover, these commissions are not disclosed to the customer. The following example will better illustrate the process of double-brokering.

Example: A customer of a securities firm wishes a bid on Providence, Rhode Island, general obligation 6.00% due June 1, 1999. He calls his representative at the securities firm, who in turn calls his municipal trading desk for the bid. Since Providence is rated Baa, the securities firm would prefer not to bid the bonds for its own account. It asks a broker such as J. J. Kenny to obtain a bid. J. J. Kenny obtains the best bid on the bonds and then deducts a commission for its services. This commission is charged on a net basis (i.e., not as a separate charge, as stock commission is charged), and it varies with the amount of bonds in the lot. For a $5,000 lot, this commission could be as much as $10 per thousand. For $100,000 or more, it could be less than $1. (Obviously, the commission is greater per thousand for smaller lots of bonds, since the costs of processing a ticket are largely the same whether for $5,000 in bonds or $5 million.) If the highest bid to J. J. Kenny is 81.50, it will report a bid to the dealer of between 81.40 and 80.50, depending on the size of the lot of bonds.

After receiving the broker's bid, the securities firm then deducts a fee for putting the bonds out for the bid with a broker. Again, this is done on a net basis (e.g., the firm may show the customer a bid of between 81 and 79, and not disclose the amount of the charge). The amount of commission charged by the firm will depend on many factors.

As one can see from the example, the customer's bonds have been double-brokered from the firm with the highest bid (which is unknown to the selling firm and its customer) to the client, as both the client's firm and the broker have charged commissions for finding what they feel is the best bid on the customer's bonds. Ironically, by the time a customer has paid both his firm's and the broker's commissions, he might have received a higher bid if he had simply called two or three firms and asked for their bids. The best solution is to instruct one's firm to put out bonds for a bid with a broker, but to allow the firm to reserve the right to bid the bonds as well. Regardless of which method is used, however, the entire process is cumbersome. It can often take hours to get a bid on bonds, even large lots.

Lack of Disclosure. Even if the best bid from one broker has been received, there is no assurance that another broker could not have obtained a better bid. Moreover, it is somewhat difficult for a nonprofessional client to know whether the bid he receives is a good bid for his bonds. The best way to determine this is to look at the cover (second highest) bid and the number of bids received. The dealer-to-dealer broker will always disclose these facts to the securities firm, but they are not usually disclosed to the client. Needless to say, this lack of disclosure contributes to inefficiency because necessary market information is withheld from the customer, largely because clients are not aware that this information is readily available for the asking. Very often, customers' bonds are not sold to a bid that has a large cover, thereby implying that it is an excellent bid, simply because the client and his sales representative do not know that the high bid is "sticking out." This is an inefficiency, and although it rarely occurs with professional institutional accounts, it is commonplace among smaller individual investors.

The Variety of Bonds. Although this practice of obtaining bids through dealer-to-dealer brokers is cumbersome and inefficient, at least from an operational point of view, it will probably remain this way for three reasons. First, there are so many different municipal bonds issued with so many different coupons and maturities that the secondary market is fragmented.

Since issues and their sizes are so diverse and fragmented, trading is done in a multitude of auctions during any given day. In other words, a lot of bonds is put out for the bid, and firms bid the bonds. If the seller accepts the high bid, an equilibrium price has been established on that lot. This information will be relayed by brokers to the bidding firms, so that they can adjust their bids on other bonds accordingly. Thousands of these auctions occur daily.

Second, because of the myriad of different lots of bonds that are out for the bid on any given day, traders must spend a great deal of time determining what items they should bid on for their inventories for resale to their institutional and retail clients. Each time a firm makes a purchase, there is always a good deal of uncertainty that it can sell the bonds to its clients at a profit. Some names are simply more acceptable to clients than others. Much of a trader's day is spent canvassing a firm's institutional and retail sales force as to the salability of different issues to the firm's clientele.

Finally, as long as dealer-to-dealer brokers transact only with dealers and not the investing public, clients will be able to make use of their services only indirectly through their own securities firms. Despite the time-consuming process of using brokers to obtain bids on customers' bonds, it would be infinitely worse if dealer-to-dealer brokers did not exist and if traders had to call several firms directly each time a customer wanted a bid on an item that they did not care to bid. At a large wire house such as Merrill Lynch, which must bid hundreds of items each day for its customers, it would be virtual chaos if bond brokers did not exist. Using bond brokers to obtain bids is indubitably better than not having them at all.

Time Lag. One of the operational problems of secondary trading in the municipal market, as was mentioned above, is that it can take hours to get a bid on a lot of bonds, even round lots of $100,000 and above. Usually, it is possible to get an as-soon-as-possible (ASAP) bid only on a block of $1 million bonds or more. For a group of large lots, however, say 20 $1 million bond blocks, the market performs extremely slowly. It is virtually impossible for an institution, such as a casualty insurance company, to sell a large portion of its holdings at a moment's notice without severely depressing the market. What usually occurs is that the institution will contact several firms and notify them that it will take bids on a given list of items at a certain time a couple of days hence. (Sometimes the selling institution will use one securities firm as an agent to collect the bids and to advertise the list of items for sale in a special flier in the Blue List.)

Although it is usually necessary for large lists to be advertised two or three days in advance in order for the institution to get the best bids on its bonds, the seller is exposed to the market for two or three days until the bids are received. Needless to say, market conditions can change markedly in a couple of days, and there can be a great deal of uncertainty as to what the actual bids will be when the list is first announced.

There are several reasons why a one- or two-day lag between announcement and bidding is needed. First, securities firms must pare their inventories in order to prepare for the possibility of buying a large amount of the selling institution's bonds. Second, it gives securities firms time to develop buy orders for the bonds from other institutions. A securities firm will bid higher and work for less spread if it has an order on the other side for the bonds, since the transaction becomes riskless. Finally, advertising lists well in advance of the actual sale is an act of good faith on the part of the institutions to the dealer community.

Because all large institutions are covered by many securities firms, news of their activities travels rapidly through the marketplace. The quid pro quo for the institution, is return for advertising its list early, is that all firms are expected to perform in their bidding. Buy orders from institutions to securities firms are usually based on how well the firm has done in bidding the institution's bonds when the institution was a seller. This reciprocity ensures that institutions will get excellent bids on their bonds, but the time lag involved exposes them to the vicissitudes of the market.

Keeping Bids Firm. One prevalent practice in bidding municipals that impairs market efficiency is that of keeping bids firm for a period of time, in some cases two or three hours. By firm we mean that the bid cannot be lowered or withdrawn. In extreme circumstances, this means that a firm can bid on a block of bonds and be held to that bid for a period of time; in the meantime, a cheaper offering on the same bonds could appear in the marketplace. In other words, by being forced to keep his bid firm for a period of time, a bond dealer can be handed an instant loss.

The practice of keeping bids firm is detrimental to market efficiency, for it prevents bids as well as offerings from instantly adjusting in price to reflect new information that arrives in the marketplace. The justification of keeping bids firm is that it allows customers time to make up their minds whether to sell or not, or to evaluate the bids, or to calculate total proceeds if there is a long list being sold. This is a cogent argument, but it runs counter to the theory that the most competitive and efficient markets are those with the least amount of friction. No specialist on the New York Stock Exchange would be asked to bid a block of stock for his own account and keep the bid good for hours, yet such a practice exists in the municipal market with little danger of being eliminated in the near future.

The Offered Side

Unfortunately, the operational efficiency of the municipal market is not much better on the offered side of the market than it is on the bid side. We will examine the procedure for providing an offering on municipal bonds in three cases.

(1) on dollar bonds,
(2) on bonds that the firm owns, and
(3) on bonds that the firm does not own but can purchase from other dealers.

Dollar Bonds. In the case of dollar bonds, the operational procedure is very simple. A customer asks his representative at a securities firm for a quote on an actively traded bond. The representative calls his trading desk, where he is given the firm's inside (or wholesale) offered side. From this quote, the sales representative must add or subtract his commission.

Needless to say, there can be a great discrepancy between offering prices that a customer may receive on the same bond from different firms, and even from different salespeople at the same firm. The reasons for this are several. Some firms allow their salespeople to mark offerings to their customers from the bid side of the market if the firm owns bonds of that issue. Other firms use the offered side of the inside market, and less reputable firms use a price even above the offered side of the inside market. Obviously, there are many opportunities for abuse in their procedure by dealers, and firms are often penalized by the NASD for what are considered excessive markups on bonds. It is difficult, however, for retail customers to determine whether they are paying fair prices on bonds, since price information on municipals is hard to come by.

Bonds Owned by the Firm. Operationally, it is a relatively quick and easy process to obtain an offering on nondollar bonds that the firm has in position (i.e., in its inventory). Price efficiency, though, is another question. Some firms will allow their salespeople to take an additional markup from the firm's offering price; other firms prohibit the practice. It is a well-known fact that customers can "shop" one firm's offering price on bonds at another firm in order to try to get a better price. Customers can also purchase bonds at less than the stated offering prices from firms by giving them a bid surreptitiously for their bonds. In bad markets, customers are often successful in this practice.

Unfortunately, customers who feel that they are getting a bargain in these situations are often mistaken, because even if they are able to buy bonds at their bid, or reservation, prices, invariably it is because the market bid for the bonds is lower. It is virtually impossible for customers, as well as for salespeople at the securities firm, to determine the market bid for bonds, since they do not have access to the dealer-to-dealer brokers.

Institutional clients and institutional salespeople are the exception to this rule. Institutions are covered by so many firms that they have easy access to the best offerings in the marketplace. Managing an institutional portfolio, however, is a full-time occupation. Individual investors do not have the time and resources to devote to managing their portfolios. Therefore, the chances are good that individual investors are not receiving the best offering prices available in the marketplace when they purchase municipal bonds. This situation is usually not encountered in trading listed stock. The exchanges perform the market search function of finding the best bid and offer on any stock at any given time, and investors in stock can spend their time analyzing which stocks to buy or sell rather than calling different dealers to check prices.

Bonds Held by Another Firm. Operationally, the most cumbersome procedure is obtaining an offering on bonds held by another firm. As noted above, the only means of determining whether an offering shown in the Blue List or on Munifacts is correct, or if it still exists, is to call the firm showing the offering. Although this is an easy process when only one or two offerings must be checked, it can be quite tedious if a customer wants the best offering on a wide category of bonds, such as New York State general obligations between 1999 and 2010. As a consequence, salespeople at many securities firms are discouraged from soliciting orders from the Blue List or Munifacts. Some firms will not allow any additional markup from an offering price shown in the Blue List. In such cases, the salesperson earns the dealer discount, or concession, as his commission, but this amount is almost always less than the salesperson would earn on bonds held in his firm's inventory; thus, the desire for the markup. Although such a prohibition on markups is often justified by firms as a means of giving the best price to the customer, a more disingenuous motive for this policy is to limit business to the firm's inventory, so that a greater profit might be made.

Whether markups from the Blue List are allowed or not, it is virtually impossible for a retail customer to determine whether he is really obtaining the actual yield shown on the offering or it has been reduced (i.e., whether the price has been marked up). Very few retail customers have a subscription to the Blue List, a very expensive publication. Also, customers are not usually informed if an offering from the Blue List or Munifacts has been purchased at a cheaper price than the one shown.

Example: Suppose that a customer gives his firm an order for $25,000 Connecticut general obligations 5.00% due September 1, 2000, at a 9.10% yield, which are offered by another firm in the Blue List. The customer's firm may bid the other firm a 9.25% yield for the bonds, less a concession, such as half a point or $5 per bond. The other firm may deem the bid a fair one and "hit" the bid, or it may counter the bid with a cheaper offering, such as a 9.20% yield. (A 9.20% yield is about $6 per bond cheaper than a 9.10% yield.) If the customer's firm buys the bonds at a cheaper price, it may not pass the saving along to the customer, but increase the commission by that amount.

Bidding and Offering Inefficiencies

From the discussion above, we can conclude that there is a great deal of inefficiency in the process of bidding and offering municipal bonds, at least to retail customers. Perhaps the greatest inefficiency is that the offering process is so cumbersome that the set of investment possibilities in municipals for customers is usually very limited, particularly if firms discourage their salespeople from using the Blue List or Munifacts.

Moreover, even if offerings from other dealers via those sources are shown to customers, they may not be at the lowest offering prices. This occurs for two reasons. First, as we mentioned above, the customer's firm may mark the price of the bonds up or buy the bonds at a cheaper price and not pass the savings along to the customer. Second, firms often show cheaper prices on their bonds to their own sales forces than they show to other dealers. It is virtually impossible, however, for customers, or even other firms, to know that the cheaper offerings exist.

It must be admitted, though, that the reverse practice often occurs: sometimes traders at one firm will show a cheaper offering on their bonds to other dealers instead of to their own sales force. Practices of this kind, when discovered, cause a great deal of animosity and mistrust between a firm's traders and sales force. Also, because of the leeway given to sales representatives of firms in determining offering prices to their customers, it is quite possible for two customers to pay different prices for the same bond at the same time. This can occur because there is so little public information about municipal prices.

In fact, the transmission process of offerings in the municipal market is so cumbersome and outdated that dealers themselves are often the victims of the inefficiency. Dealers alone are responsible for updating their offerings in the Blue List, and some firms are much better than others at removing the offerings that no longer exist. It is common for traders to base bids and offerings of their bonds upon offerings of similar bonds that are shown in the Blue List, when in fact many of those offerings no longer exist. Moreover, a firm can show one price for its bonds in the Blue List and a higher or lower one on Munifacts for the same bonds. This is because the Blue List is published daily, whereas Munifacts runs throughout the day.

The greatest and most laughable example of the inefficiency of this transmission process occurs on days of extraordinary price changes on the upside. In times such as these, traders find that they can put bonds from their inventory out for the bid with dealer-to-dealer brokers and *receive higher bids than their published offering prices.* This occurs because prices are changing so rapidly that traders assume that all offerings in the Blue List have traded, so they pay attention only to bonds out for the bid with brokers. Thus, traders will bid higher through brokers on bonds that they could buy at a cheaper price out of the Blue List. Bidding through the offering is the greatest case of inefficiency in the municipal market. On certain days it can happen quite often because it is impossible for traders to check every offering in the Blue List or on Munifacts.

Clearing Trades

Until recently, one of the most inefficient areas of the municipal market was the clearance of trades and the resolution of trade problems. Before discussing the major reforms that have been implemented in the clearance of trades, let us first examine the most common types of trade problems and the cost to resolve them.

Trade Errors. In trading stock, errors generally fall into two types:

(1) a customer mistakenly sells stock that he does not own, thereby creating a short, or
(2) a customer is given a verbal execution price that is different from the price on the confirmation slip.

In the first case, it is a simple matter to cover the short, and the loss is usually minimal if it is discovered right away. In cases of a price discrepancy between the verbal and the written report, the firm will usually honor the best price for the customer and assume the loss if there is any. Losses will be major only in extremely volatile markets or in stocks with wide fluctuations.

Municipal errors, on the other hand, often can be quite difficult to resolve. The most common problems are very similar to those in stock trading, and they are of three general types:

(1) a customer sell bonds through a firm, without having the bonds at the firm, and delivers bonds with a different description, thereby causing a short position in the bond sold;

(2) a customer sells bonds at a firm without having them at the firm and never delivers them, thus causing the firm to be short the bonds; or

(3) errors are made when computing bids or offers from a yield basis to a dollar price.

The first two types of trade problems are the most difficult and costly to resolve because they create short positions that cannot be covered because there are so few similar bonds in existence. The problem is further complicated because the firm on the other side of the trade may not be willing to cancel the transaction. If the firm in error must provide an acceptable substitute to the other side, it can be quite costly—especially for smaller lots, where the bid-ask spread is often $30 to $40 per thousand. (Essentially, the firm in error would have to buy bonds on the offered side of the market and deliver them on the bid side of the market in order to satisfy the other party.)

The easiest solution to the above problem is for firms to require that bonds be in-house before a customer sells them, but this policy is not easy to enforce. Many customers sell bonds at one firm but hold them at another, or in their safe deposit boxes. If firms were to refuse to do business with customers unless they kept their bonds at the firm, they would lose a sizable amount of business.

The third type of error, miscalculation of dollar prices, can sometimes be easily resolved. If it occurs on a bond from the firm's inventory, either the incorrect price is honored, if it is in the customer's favor, or the trade is broken. This type of error can be very costly, however, when it happens on incorrectly computed bids or on bonds purchased from other firms. In the former case, the firm may put up a bid to the customer, receive the customer's approval to sell the bonds, and sell them to another firm. Once the error is discovered, the customer may change his mind and refuse to sell his bonds. In this case, the firm has a short position unless it can break the trade on the other side. If the firm has miscalculated the price on bonds it has purchased from another firm, the customer may refuse to purchase them once the error is discovered. In this situation, the firm will either make good on the error to the customer or keep the bonds. If the bonds are inactively traded or carry a large bid-ask spread, either solution to the problem could be costly.

Reforms. Fortunately, a few years ago, the municipal industry made several major reforms that have substantially reduced the inefficiency of clearing municipal trades. First, a CUSIP number or dated date of the bond must be provided by the selling party when all trades are consummated. In conjunction with this rule, a data base of all municipal issues has been established by the Municipal Securities Evaluation Service, a subsidiary of J. J. Kenny and Co. With the aid of the data base, all descriptions of municipals can be checked and verified as to call features, rating, and dated date. This service has had a revolutionary effect on reducing errors in municipal trades.

The greatest reform in the clearance of municipal trades occurred on February 1, 1985, when the Municipal Securities Rulemaking Board mandated that broker/dealer and institutional customer transactions must be *settled* in book-entry form at Depository Trust Company (DTC) without the use of certificates. This rule applies to any bonds of all issuers that are eligible for DTC settlement—that is, almost all major municipal issuers. Not only will firms be able to easily process many more trades in municipals, but also the cost of processing these trades will be a fraction of the former cost.

The magnitude and benefits of this new clearing process cannot be overemphasized, and this new procedure should drastically improve efficiency in the municipal market. Not only will the number of trade problems be greatly reduced, but spreads should also narrow, since the cost of processing trades will be less.

CHAPTER 5

Tax-Exempt Mutual and Closed-End Funds

A. Michael Lipper, C.F.A.
President, Lipper Analytical Services, Inc.

The tax-exempt segments of the mutual fund and closed-end fund industries are extensively described in 4 statistical services published by our firm. All statistical data presented in this chapter have been derived from these services:

(1) *LIPPER—Fixed Income Performance Analysis*—a monthly service providing investment performance data on all fixed income mutual funds (taxable and tax-exempt) over various time periods ranging from the most recent month back over the past 10 years. Our definition of investment performance means cumulated total investment returns, assuming reinvestment of all dividends, over the respective time periods. Additional supplements to this service also provide principal only returns, reflecting changes in market values, exclusive of dividend payments.

(2) *LIPPER—Portfolio Analysis Report on Fixed Income Funds*—a quarterly service providing portfolio structure analysis of all fixed income mutual funds (taxable and tax-exempt), broken down by types of investment, by quality ratings, and by maturity schedules.

(3) *LIPPER—Closed-End Fund Performance Analysis Service*—a monthly service covering investment performance of all closed-end funds

(both bond funds and equity funds) over various time periods ranging back 15 years.

(4) *LIPPER—Closed-End Bond Funds Analysis* and *LIPPER—Closed-End Equity Funds Analysis*—this is a 2-volume looseleaf quarterly service providing broad descriptive information on all of the domestic closed-end funds. The data includes financial and management fee information, expense ratios, investment performance, and portfolio structure comparisons.

While this chapter will cover both the mutual and closed-end tax-exempt funds, readers may also wish to explore still another closely similar medium of investment which falls beyond the scope of our coverage—the tax-exempt unit investment trust. These are fixed portfolios of municipal bonds assembled by underwriters and sold to the investing public, typically in minimum units ranging from $1,000 to $5,000.

While unit trusts offer the advantages of diversity and initial professional selection, unlike both mutual and closed-end funds, they do not carry the advantage of continued management supervision. Once assembled, the initial package of bonds is almost always held in its entirety until maturity. As various issues mature these trusts are gradually liquidated.

Unit trusts are typically sold upon initial offering with front-end sales fees ranging between 3% and 5%. Alternatively, they may be bought in the secondary market. However, that market may at times be non-existent or very inactive, with differences of 2% to 3% between bid and asked prices. The life span of unit trusts may range from three to thirty years, depending upon maturity policy. Since these trusts are not managed, annual operating costs are low and current yields tend to be slightly larger than for mutual or closed-end funds of similar quality and maturity.

TAX-EXEMPT MUTUAL FUNDS

At the close of 1990 total net assets of the entire mutual fund industry were approximately $1.0 trillion, of which about 80% consisted of 1912 fixed income funds with a total net asset value of $792.5 billion. This included 768 tax-exempt funds having total net assets of $205 billion. These in turn accounted for 40.17% of the total number of all fixed income funds, and 25.87% of the total net asset value—or about 20% of the entire $1.0 trillion mutual fund industry.

Table 5.1 (illustrated in Figure 5.1, 5.2, and 5.3) shows the remarkable 1980–1990 growth record of the tax-exempt segment of the mutual

TABLE 5.1
Fixed-Income Mutual Funds

Total Number and Market Values of Funds as of December 31, 1980–1990

Tax-Exempt Fund Totals vs. Totals for All Fixed Income Mutual Funds
(Values Are Total Net Assets, in Millions of Dollars)

| | *Tax-Exempt* | | *All Fixed Income* | | *Percent Tax-Exempt* | |
Dec. 31	*T.N.A.* *($ millions)*	*No. of* *Funds*	*T.N.A.* *($ millions)*	*No. of* *Funds*	*T.N.A.* *($ millions)*	*No. of* *Funds*
1990	$205,008	768	$792,518	1912	25.87%	40.17%
1989	179,544	685	717,616	1731	25.02	39.57
1988	155,459	645	608,536	1567	25.55	41.16
1987	141,909	570	583,949	1380	24.30	41.30
1986	143,248	409	550,718	1083	26.01	37.77
1985	78,641	299	376,371	881	20.89	33.94
1984	45,990	234	286,181	728	16.07	32.14
1983	32,790	145	212,720	595	15.41	24.37
1982	21,888	93	258,421	497	8.47	18.71
1981	8,493	77	200,260	380	4.24	20.26
1980	5,230	58	90,733	305	5.76	19.02

Source: LIPPER Fixed Income Performance Analysis, 1980–1990.

FIGURE 5.1
Growth in the Number of Taxable and Tax-Exempt Fixed Income Funds

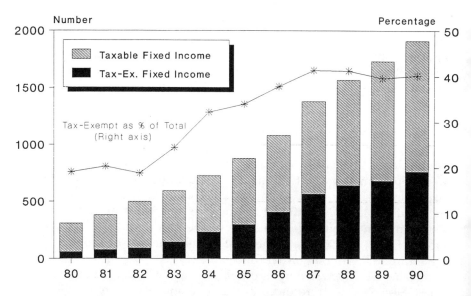

Source: LIPPER Fixed Income Fund Performance Analysis.

FIGURE 5.2
Tax-Exempt Funds as a Percentage of All Fixed Income Funds

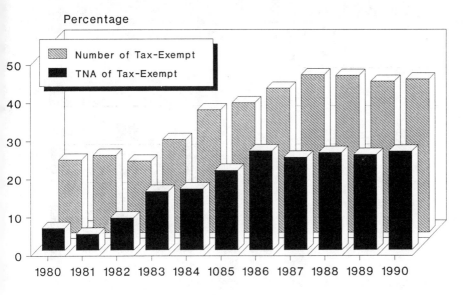

Source: LIPPER Fixed Income Fund Performance Analysis.

fund industry, compared with all fixed income mutual funds. Tax-exempt funds grew from a nominal 58 funds valued at $5.2 billion at the close of 1980 to 768 funds valued at $205 billion, while their percentage of total net assets grew from only 5.76% to 25.87% at the close of 1990. However, this strong relative growth occurred entirely during the years 1980–1986.

In absolute terms, very strong growth in both the number and value of tax-exempt funds continued over the next four years through 1990 but this was matched by corresponding growth in taxable fixed income funds so that the tax-exempt percentages stabilized at about 25% of total net assets and 40% of the total number of funds during this period.

The wide range of diversity offered by tax-exempt mutual bond funds is evident from Table 5.2. This describes our Lipper criteria for the classification of tax-exempt fixed income funds, with descriptions of the types of funds assigned to various categories. Note especially that there are now a large number of single state municipal bond funds, altogether accounting for about one-third of the total value of all tax-exempt mutual funds.

FIGURE 5.3
Tax-Exempt Mutual Fund Growth

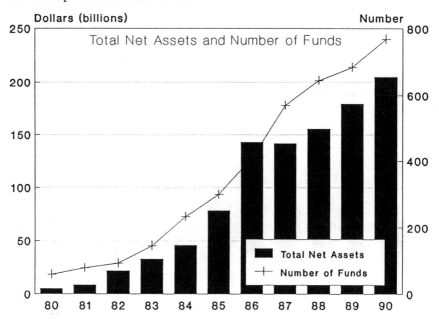

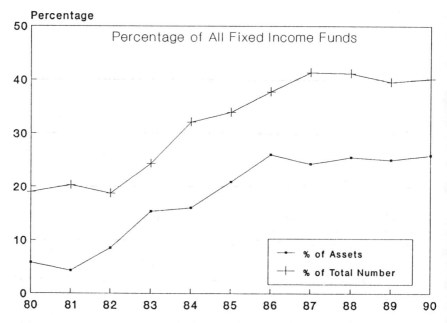

Source: LIPPER Fixed Income Fund Performance Analysis.

TABLE 5.2
Lipper Criteria for Classification of Tax-Exempt Fixed Income Funds

Short-Term Fixed Income Funds

GST   *General S-T Tax-Exempt Funds*—Invest assets in municipal obligations with dollar-weighted average maturities of less than 120 days. Intend to keep constant net asset value.

IST   *Institutional S-T Tax-Exempt Bond Funds*—Invest assets in municipal obligations with dollar-weighted average maturities of less than 120 days. Fund requires high minimum investments and has lower total expense ratios relative to other short-term funds. Intend to keep constant net asset value.

     California (CAS), New York (NYS) and Other States (OST) S-T Tax-Exempt Bond Funds—Invest assets in municipal obligations of a particular state (double tax-exempt) or city (triple tax-exempt) with dollar-weighted average maturities of less than 120 days. Intend to keep constant net asset value.

Municipal Bond Funds

SIB   *Short (1–5 Yr) Municipal Bond Funds*—Invest in municipal debt issues with maturities averaging less than 5 years.

IM   *Intermediate (5–10 Yr) Municipal Bond Funds*—Invest in municipal debt issues with maturities averaging five to ten years.

GM   *General Municipal Bond Funds*—Invest 65% or more of assets in municipal debt issues in the top four credit ratings.

MBI   *Insured Municipal Bond Funds*—Invest at least 65% of assets in municipal debt issues insured as to timely payment.

HM   *High Yield Municipal Bond Funds*—May invest 50% or more of assets in lower rated municipal debt issues.

     Single State Municipal Bond Funds—Limit assets to those securities which are exempt from taxation of a specified state (double tax-exempt) or city (triple tax-exempt).

Arizona	(AZ)	California	(CA)
Colorado	(CO)	Connecticut	(CT)
Florida	(FL)	Georgia	(GA)
Louisiana	(LA)	Maryland	(MD)
Massachusetts	(MA)	Michigan	(MI)
Minnesota	(MN)	New Jersey	(NJ)
New York	(NY)	North Carolina	(NC)
Ohio	(OH)	Oregon	(OR)
Pennsylvania	(PA)	Virginia	(VA)
Other States	(OTH)		

TABLE 5.2   *(continued)*

Criteria for Classification of Fixed Income Funds

Our assignment of funds to a specific investment classification is a matter of judgment. The statement of policy which is set forth in the prospectus is initially used in assigning the fund to one of the various classifications. As the fund matures and develops, clearly discernible investment policies and practices assume paramount importance in assigning the fund to a specific classification. Once assigned, funds are not reclassified without clear evidence of further change in portfolio management policy. A change in policy may be voted on by the shareholders or by the Board of Directors, or it may become more subtly evident from close observation and analysis of portfolio changes. Our *Lipper-Portfolio Analysis Report on Fixed Income Funds* is one of the most useful tools for this purpose.

Table 5.3 (illustrated in Figures 5.4 and 5.5) provides a statistical break-down of the principal types of tax-exempt mutual bond funds over the 1980–1990 decade. This should be studied in conjunction with Table 5.4, which summarizes the total net asset values and shows the percentage distribution. While there has been very substantial growth in the number of funds and the total net asset values in all categories over the decade, the net asset distribution as between the four principal maturity groups changed very little, as indicated below:

	Short-Term (Under 1 Yr.)	*Short (1–5 Yrs.)*	*Intermediate (5–10 Yrs.)*	*Long-Term (Over 10 Yrs.)*
12/31/90	40.3%	1.4%	2.4%	55.9%
12/31/80	41.3	—	1.5	57.2

However, within the Long-Term category there were sizable changes in the percentage distributions among the four different categories, as follows:

	12/31/80	*12/31/90*
General Tax-Exempt Municipals	49.3%	19.7%
Single State Tax-Exempt Municipals	—	24.2
Insured Tax-Exempt Municipals	—	4.5
High Yield Tax-Exempt Municipals	7.9	7.5
Total Long-Term Issues	57.2%	55.9%

The outstanding feature of the decade has been the development of single state (double or triple tax-exempt) municipal bond funds. At the close of 1990 these totaled $73.6 billion in value, accounting for 35.89%

TABLE 5.3
Tax-Exempt Mutual Bond Funds

Number of Funds, Value and Types of Funds as of December 31, 1980–1990
(Values Are Total Net Assets, in Millions of Dollars)

| | Short-Term Municipal Bond Funds (under 1-Year Maturity) | | | | | | | | | |
| | General | | Single State | | Total | | Short (1–5 Year Maturity) | | Intermediate (5–10 Year Maturity) | |
Dec. 31	T.N.A. ($ millions)	No. of Funds	T.N.A. ($ millions)	No. of Funds	T.N.A. ($ millions)	No. of Funds	T.N.A. ($ millions)	No. of Funds	T.N.A. ($ millions)	No. of Funds
1990	$58,581	152	$24,064	90	$82,645	242	$ 2819	17	$ 4988	35
1989	53,234	139	17,599	76	70,833	215	2646	19	4346	31
1988					65,580	186	2531	11	4175	32
1987					59,614	150	—	—	6710	40
1986					61,891	126	—	—	7725	29
1985					36,319	108	—	—	3780	24
1984					23,639	90	—	—	2049	20
1983					16,619	65	—	—	1633	16
1982					13,842	36	—	—	295	6
1981					5,223	27	—	—	85	5
1980					2,161	12	—	—	78	2

TABLE 5.3 (continued)

	General Municipal Bond Funds		Single State Municipal Bond Funds		Long-Term Municipal Bond Funds (over 10 Years) Insured Municipal Bond Funds		High Yield Municipal Bond Funds		Grand Totals—All Bond Funds	
Dec. 31	T.N.A. ($ millions)	No. of Funds	T.N.A. ($ millions)	No. of Funds	T.N.A. ($ millions)	No. of Funds	T.N.A. ($ millions)	No. of Funds	T.N.A. ($ millions)	No. of Funds
1990	$40,462	114	$49,518	310	$9202	24	$15,375	26	$205,008	768
1989	35,862	106	41,780	263	8213	24	15,865	27	179,544	685
1988	29,946	104	32,872	259	6416	24	13,939	29	155,459	645
1987	34,499	114	28,672	240			12,414	26	141,909	570
1986	32,315	94	26,792	137			14,525	23	143,248	409
1985	18,876	74	11,744	79			7924	14	78,641	299
1984	10,871	60	4,955	53			4476	11	45,990	234
1983	11,618	57					2920	7	32,790	145
1982	6,268	45					1483	6	21,888	93
1091	2,638	42					547	5	8,493	79
1980	2,580	39					411	5	5,230	59

Source: "LIPPER Fixed Income Fund Performance Analysis," 1980–1990.

FIGURE 5.4
Short- and Long-Term Tax-Exempt Fixed-Income Fund Assets

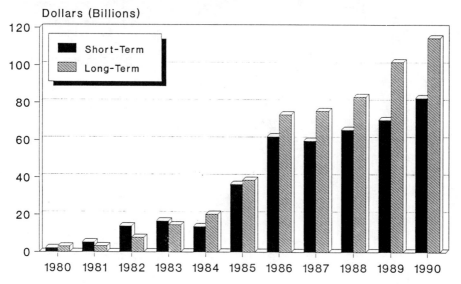

Source: LIPPER Fixed Income Fund Performance Analysis.

FIGURE 5.5
Share of Total Net Assets in Tax-Exempt Fixed Income Funds

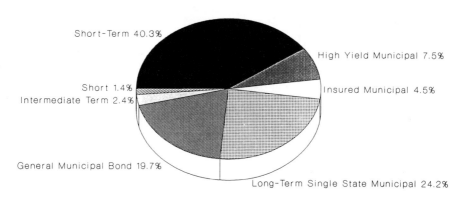

Source: LIPPER Fixed Income Fund Performance Analysis.

TABLE 5.4
Tax-Exempt Mutual Bond Funds

Total Net Asset Values of Major Types of Funds, December 31, 1980–1990 (Total Net Asset Values and Percentage Distribution)

Dec. 31	Short Term (under 1 Year)	Short (1–5 Years)	Intermediate 5–10 Years	Long-Term (over 10 Years)					Grand Totals
				General	Single State	Insured	High Yield	Total Long-Term	
				Total Net Asset Values (Millions of Dollars)					
1990	$82,645	$2819	$4988	$40,462	$49,518	$9202	$15,375	$114,557	$205,008
1989	70,833	2646	4346	35,862	41,780	8213	15,865	101,720	179,544
1988	65,580	2531	4175	29,946	32,872	6416	13,939	83,173	155,459
1987	59,614		6710	34,499	28,672		12,414	75,585	141,909
1986	61,891		7725	32,315	26,792		14,525	73,632	143,248
1985	36,319		3780	18,876	11,744		7,924	38,544	78,641
1984	23,639		2049	10,871	4,955		4,476	20,302	45,990
1983	16,619		1633	11,618			2,920	14,538	32,790
1982	13,842		295	6268			1,483	7,751	21,888
1981	5,223		85	2,638			547	3,185	8,493
1980	2,161		78	2,580			411	2,991	5,230
				Percentage Distribution					
1990	40.3%	1.4%	2.4%	19.7%	24.2%	4.5%	7.5%	55.9%	
1989	39.5	1.5	2.4	20.0	23.3	4.6	8.8	56.7	
1988	42.2	1.6	2.7	19.3	21.1	4.1	9.0	53.5	
1987	42.0		4.7	24.3	20.2		8.7	53.3	
1986	43.2		5.4	22.6	18.7		10.1	51.4	100.0%
1985	46.2		4.8	24.0	14.9		10.1	49.0	
1984	51.4		4.5	23.6	10.8		9.7	44.1	
1983	50.7		5.0	35.4			8.9	44.3	
1982	63.2		1.3	28.6			6.8	35.4	
1981	61.4		1.0	31.0			6.4	37.5	
1980	41.3		1.5	49.3			7.9	57.2	

Source: "LIPPER Fixed Income Performance Analysis," 1980–1990.

TABLE 5.5
Single State Municipal Bond Funds as of December 31, 1990

Maturity	California	New York State	All Other States	Totals
		Number of Funds		
Short-Term	34	30	26	90
Long-Term	60	51	199	310
Total	94	81	225	400
		Total Net Assets ($ Millions)		
Short-Term	$10,938	$ 6207	$ 6919	$24,064
Long-Term	22,914	11,271	15,333	49,518
Total	$33,852	$17,478	$22,252	$73,582
		Percentages of All Tax-Exempt Mutual Funds ($205 Billion)		
	16.51%	8.53%	10.85%	35.89%

Source: "LIPPER Tax Exempt Fixed Income Performance Analysis," Feb. 28, 1991

of the total net asset value of all tax-exempt municipal bond funds, as detailed in Table 5.5. California and New York are much the largest issuers, as summarized below:

	Number of Funds	Total Net Assets ($ Millions)	Percent of All Funds ($205 Million)
California	94	$33,852	16.51%
New York	81	17,478	8.53
All Other States	225	22,252	10.85
Total	400	$73,582	35.89%

Table 5.6 (illustrated in Figure 5.6) compares the total investment returns of various categories of taxable versus tax-exempt mutual funds of comparable maturity length over various time periods ranging from one year to ten years through December 31, 1990.

The column of returns for the 8-year period, December 31, 1982 to December 31, 1990 has been included because December 31, 1982 was the date after which for former Federal Reserve Board Regulation Q, which restricted interest rates on bank money market deposit accounts, was eliminated. Thereafter, banks were able to compete more effectively with their rapidly growing new competition from mutual fund money market accounts.

TABLE 5.6
Investment Performance Comparisons, 1980–1990

Taxable *vs.* Tax-Exempt Mutual Funds of Comparable Maturity Lengths
(Cumulated Total Reinvested Returns)

12/31/90 No. of Funds		1-Year 12/31/89 12/31/90	5-Years 12/31/85 12/31/90	8-Years 12/31/82* 12/31/90	10-Years 12/31/80 12/31/90	Average 12-Month Yield
	(A) Short-Term Funds (under 1 Year)					
277	Money Market Instrument Funds	7.77%	41.69%	82.68%	141.31%	7.5%
143	Short-Term U.S. Govt. Funds	7.65	39.96	78.47	131.11	7.4
152	General S-T Tax-Exempt Bond Funds	5.51	27.46	48.09	69.25	5.4
						Ratios
	Ratio Tax-Exempt to S-T U.S. Govt. Funds	72.0	68.7	61.3	52.8	73.0
	Ratio Tax-Exempt to Money Market Funds	70.9	65.9	58.2	49.0	72.0
	(B) Short (1–5 Year Maturity)					
34	Investment Grade Debt Funds	8.09%	47.55%	110.50%	N.A.	7.7%
27	U.S. Government Funds	8.99	47.82	99.92	N.A.	8.0
16	Tax-Exempt Bond Funds	6.39	35.76	65.33	99.25	6.1
						Ratios
	Ratio Tax-Exempt to U.S. Govt. Funds	71.1	74.8	65.4	N.A.	76.2
	Ratio Tax-Exempt to Inv. Grade Debt Funds	79.0	75.2	59.1	N.A.	79.2
	(C) Intermediate (5–10 Year Maturity)					
39	Investment Grade Debt Funds	7.20%	49.09%	116.09	198.14	8.4%
26	U.S. Government Funds	8.51	48.82	105.49	159.75	7.7
35	Tax-Exempt Bond Funds	6.48	41.70	87.91	153.11	6.2

					Ratios
Ratio Tax-Exempt to U.S. Govt. Funds	76.1	85.4	83.3	95.8	80.5
Ratio Tax-Exempt to Inv. Grade Debt Funds	90.0	84.9	75.7	77.3	73.8
(D) Long-Term (over 10-Year Maturity)					
46 Corporate Bond Funds (A-Rated)	6.79%	48.76%	122.47%	210.21%	8.2%
135 U.S. Government Funds	7.39	49.61	111.34	190.87	8.2
114 General Tax-Exempt Bond Funds	6.02	52.39	123.68	189.12	6.7
24 Insured Tax-Exempt Bond Funds	6.49	50.43	121.81	179.28	6.5
					Ratios
Ratio General Tax-Exempt to U.S. Govt. Funds	81.5	105.6	111.1	99.1	81.7
Ratio General Tax-Exempt to Corporate (A-Rated)	88.7	107.4	101.0	90.0	81.7
Ratio Insured Tax-Exempt to General Tax-Exempt	107.8	96.3	98.5	94.8	97.0
(E) High Current Yield Funds					
84 High Current Yield Taxable Funds	−11.08%	11.13%	69.15%	131.40%	16.3%
26 High Current Yield Tax-Exempt Funds	+5.05	51.82	127.21	196.76	7.5
					Ratios
Ratio Tax-Exempt to Taxable Funds	—	4.65×	1.84×	1.50×	46.0%
Ratio High Current Yield Tax-Exempt to Long-Term General Tax-Exempt Returns	85.2%	98.9%	102.8%	104.0%	111.9%

Note: December 1982 was the date after which Regulation Q restrictions upon bank Money Market Deposit Accounts were eliminated.

Source: "LIPPER Fixed Income Performance Analysis," 12/31/90.

FIGURE 5.6

Taxable vs. Tax-Exempt Reinvested Returns (Periods ending Dec. 31, 1990)

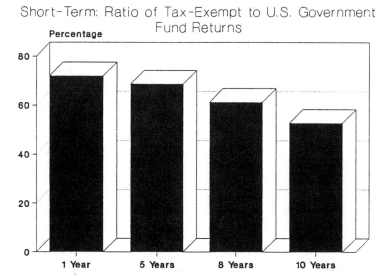

Short-Term: Ratio of Tax-Exempt to U.S. Government Fund Returns

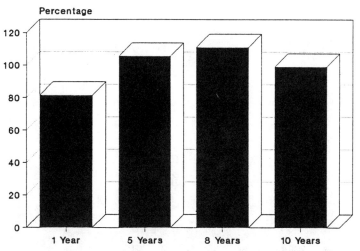

Long-Term: Ratio of General Municipal to U.S Government Bond Fund Returns

Source: LIPPER Fixed Income Fund Performance Analysis.

FIGURE 5.6 *(continued)*

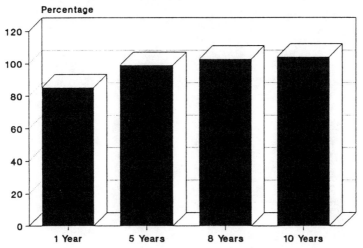

Long-Term: Ratio of High Current Yield Tax-Exempt to
General Municipal Bond Fund Returns

There is significant evidence that the abolishment of Regulation Q not only changed banking and financial conditions in the United States and possibly overseas, but it also fundamentally affected the interest rate spread in the fixed income market. The compound growth rate of money market returns for eight years was 7.83% in contrast with the 9.21% for 10 years, 138 basis points higher. However, the compound annual 8-year return was very close to the calendar year 1990 return of 7.77%, a difference of only 6 basis points.

Comparison (A) covers the respective *short-term* funds, having maturity lengths under one year. The two ratios of tax-exempt to taxable returns of U.S. government funds and money market funds over the 10-year period, 52.8% and 49.0%, respectively, were very low compared with more recent years, reflecting the relatively much higher personal income tax rates prevalent in the earlier years of this period. In contrast, the tax-exempt yield ratios for the most recent year 1990 had risen to 72.0% and 70.9%, respectively. This was closely reflective of the much lower marginal Federal tax rates for upper bracket individual taxpayers in that year.

Comparisons (B) and (C) show similar data for the Short (1–5 year maturity) and Intermediate (5–10 year maturity) groups of funds. As indicated previously, these two groups in total are of very small size and little consequence. In most of these comparisons, as would be expected, the intermediate maturity returns slightly exceed the corresponding Short maturity returns.

TABLE 5.7
Investment Performance Comparisons, 1980–1990

Taxable vs. Tax-Exempt Funds of Comparable Maturity Lengths
(Cumulated Total Reinvested Returns and Principal Only Returns Compared with C.P.I. Inflation Rate)

12/31/90 No. of Funds		Data Description*	1-Year 12/31/89 12/31/90	5-Years 12/31/85 12/31/90	10-Years 12/31/80 12/31/90
	Consumer Price Index (C.P.I.)		+6.11%	+22.42%	+55.11%
	(A) Short (1–5 Year Maturity)				
34	Investment Grade Debt Funds	TRR	+8.09%	+47.55%	N.A.%
27	U.S. Government Funds		8.99	47.82	N.A.
16	Tax-Exempt Bond Funds		6.39	35.76	99.25
34	Investment Grade Debt Funds	POR	0.13	9.78	N.A.
27	U.S. Government Funds		0.85	4.58	N.A.
16	Tax-Exempt Bond Funds		0.06	1.20	6.03
	(B) Intermediate (5–10 Year Maturity)				
39	Investment Grade Debt Funds	TRR	+7.20%	+49.09%	+198.14%
26	U.S. Government Funds		8.51	48.82	159.75
35	Tax-Exempt Bond Funds		6.48	41.70	153.11
39	Investment Grade Debt Funds	POR	–1.13	1.57	8.64
26	U.S. Government Funds		0.68	5.12	6.27
35	Tax-Exempt Bond Funds		0.10	3.30	19.13

(C) Long-Term (over 10-Year Maturity)

46	Corporate Bond Funds (A-Rated)		+6.79%	+48.76%	+210.21%
135	U.S. Government Funds		7.39	49.61	190.87
114	General Tax-Exempt Bond Funds	TRR	6.02	52.39	189.12
24	Insured Tax-Exempt Bond Funds		6.49	50.43	179.28
46	Corporate Bond Funds (A-Rated)		−1.68%	−2.93%	8.04
135	U.S. Government Funds	POR	−0.81	0.56	4.55
114	General Tax-Exempt Funds		−0.36	6.88	28.47
24	Insured Tax-Exempt Funds		−0.25	6.96	21.51

(D) High Current Yield Funds

84	High Current Yield Taxable Funds	TRR	−11.08%	+11.13%	+131.40%
26	High Current Yield Tax-Exempt Funds		5.05	51.82	196.76
84	High Current Yield Taxable Funds	POR	−22.69	−40.44	−36.30
26	High Current Yield Tax-Exempt Funds		−2.49	3.27	23.88

Note: TRR—Total Reinvested Returns, including reinvested dividends
POR—Principal only Returns, excludng dividends

Source: "LIPPER Fixed Income Performance Analysis," 12/31/90 Principal only issue.

However, one anomaly for which we find no rational explanation is that the two ratios of tax-exempt to taxable yields have been much higher in all time periods for the Intermediate than for the corresponding Short maturity groups. In retrospect, therefore, tax-exempt Intermediate maturity securities would have provided superior net returns for taxpayers in nearly all brackets over the past ten years.

Comparison D covers a large number of long-term funds (over 10-year maturity). Here again, several anomalies, perhaps reflecting market inefficiencies, become strikingly apparent, to wit:

- In both the one and 5-year periods ended 12/31/90 the returns of U.S. government bond funds exceeded the returns of A-rated corporate bond funds.

- Over both the five and 8-year periods the returns of both general and insured tax-exempt bond funds exceeded the returns on U.S. government bond funds.

- In 1990, the returns on insured tax-exempt exceeded the returns on general (uninsured) tax-exempt funds—and in the longer time periods the yield differential was small enough to make the insurance cost possibly well worthwhile.

Comparison E matches the returns of high current yield taxable funds (i.e., junk bond funds) against high current yield tax-exempt funds. It is strikingly apparent that the latter are of far higher calibre than the former, having provided vastly superior returns in all time periods. However, this record also provides no sound basis for argument in favor of high current yield funds of any kind, taxable or tax-exempt.

Despite relatively high risk the returns on high current yield tax-exempt funds have not matched those of the much higher quality general tax-exempt funds over the past five years, and were only nominally better over the 8 and 10-year periods.

Hopefully, this review of market anomalies and inefficiencies which have developed over the past ten years, and often persisted for long time periods, may alert investors to similar market opportunities which are bound to occur in the future.

Table 5.7 compares total reinvested returns (TRR) with principal only returns (POR)—the latter excluding reinvested dividends—for the same groups of funds shown previously in Table 5.6. With the notable exception of high current yield taxable funds (Comparison D—third line) there have been at least moderate positive returns on the principal only basis for most groups in most time periods, and the few negative returns have been nominal in amount.

For example, the long-term general tax-exempt funds (Comparison C) on the principal only basis show a return of 28.47% over the past 10 years, 6.88% over the past 5 years, and a loss of only 0.36% for 1990. However, these nominal principal returns should realistically be viewed in the light of corresponding inflation rates, measured by changes in the consumer price index, as follows:

10 Years Ended 12/31/90	5 Years Ended 12/31/90	1 Year Ended 12/31/90
+55.11%	+22.42%	+6.11%

With exception of the relatively low returns on all of the high current yield funds (Comparison D), all of the *total reinvested returns* (TRR) exceed the corresponding inflation rates by appreciable margins, with only one narrow exception (i.e., general tax-exempt bond funds in 1990 returned only 6.02%, slightly below the 6.11% inflation rate).

However, without exception all of the *principal only* returns shown in Table 5.7 are appreciably less than the corresponding inflation rates, resulting in real net loss of principal for all fund groups in all time periods, as illustrated below for the long-term general tax-exempt funds (Comparison C):

	10 Years Ended 12/31/90	5 Years Ended 12/31/90	1 Year Ended 12/31/90
Principal Only Return	28.47%	6.88%	−0.36%
C.P.I. Inflation Rate	55.11	22.42	6.11
Real Net Loss	−26.64	−15.54	−6.47

The bitter lesson from these observations is that bondholders especially, who are primary victims of inflation, would be well advised to compute real rates of return and to spend each year only that portion of portfolio earnings which exceeds the prevailing inflation rate. Only in that manner can the real purchasing power of capital be maintained.

The particularly poor returns achieved by all of the *high current yield funds* (Comparison D) are especially worth comment:

	10 Years Ended 12/31/90	5 Years Ended 12/31/90	1 Year Ended 12/31/90
Taxable Funds			
Principal Only Return	−36.30%	−40.44%	−22.69%
C.P.I. Inflation Rate	55.11	22.42	6.11
Real Net Loss	−91.41	−62.86	−28.80
Tax-Exempt Funds			
Principal Only Return	+23.88%	+3.27%	−2.49%
C.P.I. Inflation Rate	55.11	22.42	6.11
Real Net Loss	−31.23	−19.15	−8.60

While the high current yield tax-exempt funds have the better record, it still does not compare well with returns of the much higher quality *general tax-exempt funds,* as we have previously observed. In short, their higher degree of risk has not been adequately rewarded by the market.

TAX-EXEMPT CLOSED-END FUNDS

In contrast with the relatively large size and broad diversification available from tax-exempt mutual funds, the tax-exempt closed-end fund industry is very small, with a limited array of choice available. At the close of 1990, our services tracked only 50 tax-exempt closed-end funds, having total net assets of $13.6 billion—altogether less than 7% as large as the tax-exempt mutual fund industry. Further, this is a quite recent addition to the tax-exempt fund industry, with a short track record since none of these funds existed five years ago.

Our Lipper criteria for the classification of tax-exempt closed-end funds are described below:

> *General & Insured Municipal Bond Funds:*
>> *General Municipal Bond Funds*—Invest at least 65% of assets in municipal debt issues rated in the top four grades.
>> *Insured Municipal Bond Funds*—Invest at least 65% of assets in municipal debt issues insured as to timely payment.
>
> *High Yield Municipal Bond Funds:*
>> May invest 50% or more of assets in lower rated municipal debt issues.
>
> *Specific State Municipal Bond Funds:*
>> Limit assets to those securities which are exempt from taxation by the respective States of issue.

At the close of 1990 we tracked 50 closed-end municipal bond funds, having total net assets of $13.6 billion, as follows:

	12/31/90 Total Net Assets ($ Millions)	12/31/90 Number of Funds
General & Insured Municipal Bond Funds	$ 9,675	23
High Yield Municipal Bond Funds	2,446	11
Specific State Municpal Bond Funds	1,492	16
Totals	$13,613	50

Among the 23 general and insured funds, 1990 year-end yields averaged 7.2%, falling within a range of 6.2% to 8.4%, and market prices averaged only a fraction below par, with an average discount of only −0.1%.

The 11 high yield funds had an average yield of 8.5%, and average market discount of −3.9%.

All 16 of the specific state funds held bonds issued either by New York State or California. Their average yield was 6.4%, and average market premium +2.7%. Prospective investors should carefully compare these issues, on a comparable quality and maturity basis, with the large number of available New York State and California tax-exempt mutual funds reviewed earlier in this chapter.

Despite the small size and limited marketability of the tax-exempt closed-end fund universe, a careful search of this market may occasionally uncover worth-while investments. However, at mid-year 1991 nearly all of the closed-end municipal bond funds were selling at premiums above their net asset values. This may be disadvantageous compared with mutual funds of comparable quality and maturity, available by subscription at their net asset values.

CHAPTER 6

Techniques of Municipal Bond Portfolio Management*

Stephen P. Rappaport
Prudential Securities, Incorporated

Much of fixed income portfolio management today, especially that wholly relating to particular market sectors such as municipal bonds, stands astride an abyss-like body of knowledge. Indeed, on one side of the spectrum are some highly sophisticated computerized programs touted as the endall and be-all of the bond selection and portfolio design process. On the other side of the aisle, are many portfolio managers who, making only a modest use of such techniques as linear programming and the like, self-style their portfolios on a daily basis, sometimes with great success. Herein lies the difficulty of applying portfolio theory embodied in intricate programs to the day-to-day securities trading, buying, and selling activities, while taking into account the critically important individualized decision making processes made by portfolio managers and traders.

To be sure, strict adherence to a programmed portfolio model can work well in situations which have pre-determined purchasing constraints and specified targets for investment returns. Usually, however, constraints are employed only as guidelines and allow deviations from those specified parameters. As a result, applied portfolio models only work well in very specific cases which are difficult, if not, impossible, to

---

* Reprinted with permission from "Fixed-Income Portfolio Management: Capitalizing on Municipal Market Trends," by Stephen P. Rappaport, Prudential Securities, 1987.

replicate. In other instances, there is such great leeway allowed in re-structuring a given portfolio that much of the decision making is left to the portfolio manager. There is nothing wrong with this; it is probably as it should be. But this assumption implies that portfolio decisions which are not subject to specific, stringent, and quantifiable constraints are made based on available information which only the portfolio manager or trader individually digests and evaluates, with their own view towards what the future might be. Nevertheless, absent both a method to assess the character of a particular market and the relative trading patterns of particular securities, such as a thorough and quasi-quantified way to rationally make sense out of the available data, and a means to prescribe what might come in the market, too much is left to chance. This paper, therefore, is directed to developing useful and understandable decision making techniques for municipal portfolio management.

INTRODUCTION

This chapter deals with municipal portfolio management and analysis. This chapter will introduce a structural framework which takes into account both traditional portfolio management concepts and techniques and the specific peculiarities of the municipal market. It will also focus on such contemporary topics as hedging and futures, among others. Much of this material has not yet been systemized so as to better maximize the use of available data in an effort to achieve better portfolio returns.

For the purposes of this chapter, the general parameters for our hypothetical portfolio will be basic ones. The portfolio will be fully invested in tax-exempt securities and measured on a total return basis. Maximum yield will be sought, and there will also be an emphasis on achieving some balance among credit quality groups and generic bond sectors, across the whole range of maturities, depending upon the anticipated direction of interest rates. Of course, there can be innumerable combinations of constraints that may be created within this universe, and various ones will result in different securities being purchased and sold with wide ranging effects on the total portfolio. When applicable for illustrative purposes, some of these portfolio parameters will be specified throughout this report.

A SNAPSHOT LOOK AT THE PORTFOLIO IMPROVEMENT PROCESS

Any portfolio can be improved once it is structured because the securities markets are in a perennial state of flux. This situation gives rise to five principal occurrences which result in portfolio restructuring opportunities. The first and perhaps most fundamental one is a change in the shape of the yield curve. The second and third are alterations in relative yield differentials of credit quality categories or sector groups (i.e., different types of the same security). The fourth is changes in the trading relationships of particular securities. The fifth is an opportunity afforded by newly originated securities issues coming to market. These give rise to critically important, but often unrecognized, portfolio theory concepts which must be both understood and employed to successfully manage any given portfolio.

The Individualized Dimension

More than anything else, the assessment of market data at the time of decision making is an individualized task which often yields strikingly divergent evaluations and resultant actions from one portfolio manager or trader to another. For one thing, with literally hundreds of different relationships, such as yield differentials of different sectors, maturities, and credit quality categories for perhaps thousands of securities, there can be an almost limitless number of opinions upon which portfolio decisions can be made. Most of these decisions can be accomplished within the constraints in which many portfolio managers operate.

For instance, depending upon the slope of the yield curve, different yield relationships can occur among securities of different maturities, sectors, and credit quality categories. In the municipal bond arena, specifically, as yields fluctuate and as the supply of bonds varies in particular sectors, such as housing and general obligations, different yield relationships emerge. But the analysis of these relationships with a view towards buying and selling opportunities, begins and ends with those who engage in this activity. And not every portfolio professional will arrive at the same conclusion, if for the only reason that not all of them are presented with the same alternatives for buying and selling securities. As a result, much of the analysis of market-related data as well as the portfolio decision making which subsequently takes place is highly personalized and varies among portfolio managers.

Assessing Market Data: An Historical and Descriptive Analysis

Making portfolio decisions based purely on how a particular security is trading compared to how it traded three to nine months ago is a two-edged sword. On the one hand, taking advantage of anomalies in the market can certainly allow one to capture short-term gains. But as the market changes over time, so do relationships among securities so that it is possible that the gain received from bonds trading out of "sync" with their usual trading pattern relative to other securities could be reversed in a relatively short time. On the other hand, taking advantage of historical yield spreads when bonds are not trading like they usually do may provide positive results because it often takes a couple of months for the securities to resume their normal trading patterns.

This discussion, then, really weds the concepts of historical trading patterns with those which are descriptive of what is presently occurring. As a result, any portfolio restructuring could capitalize on one of four possible combinations of market-related events. These are as follows:

(1) securities which are trading differently than they historically have, and in a pattern which is likely to continue;

(2) securities which are trading like they have been historically, but in a pattern which is unlikely to continue;

(3) securities which are trading unlike their historic patterns, and in a way which is unlikely to continue; and

(4) securities which are trading like they historically have, and are likely to continue to do so.

These alternatives could be represented by Table 6.1:

TABLE 6.1
Evaluating Trading Patterns

Cases	Past (Historical)	Present (Descriptive)	Future (Prescriptive)
(1)	A	B	B
(2)	A	A	B
(3)	A	B	A
(4)	A	A	A

A Prescriptive Market Analysis

The analysis of what the market will look like in the future is also a critical element of portfolio management. It greatly affects what portfolio managers do each day to optimize the future gains of their portfolio based on the present positioning of securities with a view towards what they expect to occur within a foreseeable time frame. This activity has three basic elements to it. They include yield analysis, the evaluation of sector relationships, and the analysis of comparable trading relationships of particular securities. Predictions of future yield levels, which include the expected change in the slope of the yield curve and speed with which interest rates move, is, to a large extent, fueled by an individual's experience and predictive abilities. Interest rate changes affect sector relationships of generic securities areas, such as corporate or municipal bonds by impacting different maturities, and securities of different credit quality categories. This is critical to the portfolio improvement process.

Credit Quality Determinations

One of the more unquantifiable aspects of portfolio management is the determination which must be made about the credit quality of particular issuers. This must be done from two perspectives. The first is the relative credit quality at the point in time which a decision must be made about how that particular security usually trades relative to how it is trading at that moment. The second is an evaluation of the future direction of the issuer's credit quality—namely, a trend analysis. In this instance, the portfolio manager must make some determination as to whether a credit is likely to be upgraded or downgraded in the future.

In the municipal bond area, trading ranges of particular securities can vary greatly, even if they have the same credit ratings. This is often the case when securities are in the same sector, such as within public power, housing, or general obligation bond groups. Determinations must be made by portfolio managers and traders as to the relative under or over valuation of particular sectors. Similar analysis must also be made among specific securities relative to their credit ratings. Furthermore, an evaluation must be made as to how a particular bond usually trades relative to how it is trading at the given point in time that a decision must be made. For instance, a bond may be trading cheap to other bonds in a given sector such as public power and the sector may be cheap to the market. Both of these circumstances may usually be the case, even when ratings are taken into account. As a result, the issue of whether to purchase the cheaper selling bond depends not on whether it is trading cheap to other similar types of securities with, perhaps, a similar rating and the same maturity, but rather the extent to which it is trading cheaper than it usually does.

The direction or trend in credit quality of a security is also a critical determinant in whether a portfolio manager will purchase a particular security, especially if the manager intends to hold the issue for any length of time. Whether or not a security will be upgraded is not as much a concern to a portfolio manager as is the potential for a credit to be downgraded. In this case, the portfolio manager runs the risk of losing interest income, and perhaps, even the principal amount that was invested. Consequently, negative credit-related information on the issuer is reviewed carefully by portfolio managers. But the ultimate decision as to whether or not to invest in a security which runs a higher risk of being downgraded than others, which are investment alternatives at the moment, must be made by the portfolio manager and, therefore, is first and last an individual one.

More will be said about these concepts later, but it is sufficient to state that credit quality determinations as they relate to both relative yield differentials among sectors and particular issuers as well as the direction or trend in the quality of specific credits are fundamentally individual evaluations. As such, they will vary among portfolio professionals as will the actions taken by them as a result of such analyses.

THE FLEXIBILITY OF CONSTRAINTS

Forming the basis of many portfolio management decisions are the constraints under which portfolio managers operate. These include such identifiable targets such as duration, average maturity, yield to maturity, and percentage distributions of credit quality, types of bonds, and sector of bond types, among other items. However, there are two critical points which must be recognized regarding the seemingly tightly structured parameters which many believe are the framework in which portfolio decisions are made.

(1) Portfolio constraints are not as rigid as many perceive them to be. As a matter of fact, there are often wide allowable limits of many portfolio parameters. For instance, a credit quality constraint for a portfolio may specify that an allowable limit of 10% to 20% of the total dollar value of the portfolio be invested in securities rated "double-A" or better. In other cases, portfolio parameters may include only broad limits on the types of bonds which can be purchased. For example, a constraint might require that at most 10% of the portfolio may be invested in hospital bonds, or up to 50% be invested in state or local general obligation bonds rated above the "single-A" credit quality category.

(2) Even more important to note is that portfolio constraints change over time. And, much more often than not, the time frame over which they change is relatively short.

What must be emphasized here is that the allowable limits and the changing nature of most portfolio parameters results in decision making which is rather individualized. And these decisions are fueled by a portfolio manager's beliefs about what has and is happening in the market at a given point in time and the relative price relationships of securities at that moment coupled with the manager's perception of what is likely to occur at some foreseeable point in the future. Once again, even within the often broad portfolio constraints, historical, descriptive, and prescriptive analyses of market-related facts and relationships must be made by the portfolio manager or trader.

THE CONCEPT OF THE "MOVING TARGET"

The most appropriate security selection made at a given time results in the successful achievement of a target objective. By their very nature, these decisions are proactive portfolio management ones accomplished on a moment-to-moment basis. They are based on at least some analysis of the market and all the investment alternatives available at a given point in time with a view towards what may happen in the future. Yet, any particular decision will vary from individual to individual based on each one's perception of all the available data. As a result, the optimum solution or the best decision is always, for lack of a better description, "a moving target." It is therefore rather difficult to design any given model or formula to take into account all the variables existing at a given moment in an effort to make the best selection. This is so because the security which is the "best fit" at a given moment may not be later, because of changes in circumstances which are then interpreted by the portfolio manager and trader who must make the ultimate decision.

INCREMENTAL DECISION MAKING IN PORTFOLIO MANAGEMENT

The active portfolio decision making process is actually one where a decision occurs at different moments along a time horizon towards a "moving target" or best fit based on available data. The portfolio management process, therefore, is also an incremental one.

Incremental decision making, be definition, implies that decisions are made over time based on information that is accrued and restructured because of the constant influx of new data. The evaluation of this new information takes on historical, descriptive, and prescriptive forms. It is historical and descriptive in the sense that it accounts for what has been and is available in the marketplace. It is also prescriptive because it interprets information indicating what might happen in the market at some later date. Finally, decisions are also made based on some combination of an analysis of all three of these dimensions. Thus, the portfolio restructuring process is incrementally accomplished to take advantage of what has and does exist in the marketplace so as to optimize the chances of capturing value at some future date.

WITHER "THE SEAT OF THE PANTS" SYNDROME!

All of the foregoing is not to say that portfolio management based solely on mathematical techniques is undoable or that the portfolio management process involves so many qualitative decision-oriented factors that a quantitatively constructed model is impossible to implement. But it does suggest that applied quantitative methods, in such an arena as the municipal bond one, is difficult because so many factors which do not lend themselves to such evaluations must be individually assessed and weighted. Each portfolio decision becomes a personalized one, even in situations with identical portfolio parameters.

As a consequence, the approach which is suggested here and which will be outlined in subsequent reports is a "decision-tree" one. It will take into account the unusual aspects of the municipal market, then isolate what data is and is not important. Ultimately, a set of rules will be developed as to how the data should be viewed, what questions should be asked, and how they might be answered so that better portfolio management decisions may be made.

THE AVAILABLE DATA IN THE MUNICIPAL MARKET

There is actually a tremendous amount of data on the municipal market available from a number of sources, such as "The Bond Buyer" and Municipal Market Data, Inc., in the form of "Municipal Market Data-Line" information.

Yet, it also must be emphasized that the municipal market does not serve up definitive information about the trading characteristics, and bid and asked prices for all securities which would be available through a "black-box" type of system. The market for municipal bonds is anything but "pure." Nevertheless, it is absolutely critical that certain selected information which is available be understood as to how it may be best employed to make more appropriate investment decisions.

The Municipal and Treasury Markets: Just for the Record

The municipal market is obviously greatly affected by the market for treasury securities, and there exists substantial data on the relative spread differentials between taxable government bonds and selected tax-exempt securities. From such information can be garnered the appropriate times that it would generally be advantageous to invest in tax-exempt securities as opposed to taxable ones and vice-versa.

Also useful is data on the volatility and/or direction of government bond interest rates, on a historical and projected basis. To be sure, the use of this data can be very effective when employed for purposes of managing a municipal bond position. But it is also important to portfolio managers by helping them assess both the present disparities in the prices of particular securities and sectors as well as the future direction of interest rates. An analysis of the government bond market should also focus on whether or not the movement of interest rates is a medium to long-term trend or is more transitory.

Some portfolio managers argue that they are only dealing with activity in the municipal market, but, as a result, they are attempting to assess all the impacts that would normally be reflected in changes in municipal bond prices. As such, the treasury market is one single indicator, albeit an important one. In this regard, it is generally considered that interest rates in the municipal market typically lag those in the government bond market, but this is not always so. Additionally, there has been no discernible set lag time. The municipal market can be affected almost immediately to a very large extent, over a few days to a lesser extent, or even in a moderate way over a relatively long period of time. But for municipal portfolio managers who have to make active decisions on a moment-to-moment basis, the critical assessment which must be made is the extent and depth of the impact that the treasury market is making on the municipal one.

The Municipal Yield Curve

The general shape of the yield curve of particular municipal bonds, such as a "triple-A" rated securities, is useful for historical type of analyses, especially when compared to treasury securities and when assessing the direction of interest rates. This data is even more useful if the sector and quality of a *particular* bond are specified and prescriptive information as to what is likely to come for the yield spread relationships of specific securities are able to be discerned from this information. As will be discussed later, this data, when taken together with certain other indices, can be particularly useful in predicting market trends and helping to make better portfolio selections.

The Actively Traded Dollar Bonds Deviation Index

This index produced by Municipal Market Data, Inc., is an indicator of price momentum and oversold and overbought conditions in the municipal market today. The Deviation Index "plots the rate of price change of the actively traded dollar bonds index, providing a measurement of price momentum. The current level of the Actively Traded Dollar Bonds Index is recorded as a percentage above or below its 30-day moving average, the zero line on the graph." The Actively Traded Dollar Bonds Index "measures the daily percentage price change of term bonds most recently sold in the municipal marketplace." The Index is "comprised of a variable group of current coupon active dollar bonds continually altered to include newly issued bonds and delete older, less actively traded securities."

For those interested in charting overbought and oversold conditions in the municipal marketplace, the Deviation Index is valuable. According to Municipal Market Data, Inc., overbought conditions "exist when prices rise substantially above the moving average." These are conditions "when prices have experienced significant advances over a short time period, signaling possible near-term downward corrections." Oversold conditions, conversely, "develop as prices fall substantially below the moving average." These are conditions "when prices have experienced significant declines over a short time period, signaling possible near term upward corrections." The Deviation Index "tends to fluctuate between +5% and −5%, rates of change which historically have not been sustainable."

In and of itself, the Deviation Index may be useful in a prescriptive sense for trading a position, and it is certainly worth employing in the portfolio management process. However, it may also be used effectively in isolating other significant characteristics and relationships within the municipal market that are expected to either be sustained into the future or occur at a later date.

The Visible Supply

One of the more significant predictors of relative yield levels in the municipal marketplace is the 30-day visible supply. This provides information about the expected level of volume in the municipal market over the forthcoming month. To derive the greatest leverage from this data for portfolio management purposes, it is best used in conjunction with a number of other indicators not the least important of which is the 30-day visible supply when broken down by sector and credit quality.

Although total figures and relative ones can be valuable for portfolio management purposes, it is their deviation from historical norms that is especially important. Indeed, it is critical to find the extent to which the numerical data on the visible supply provided is unrepresentative of the total issuance in the municipal market, whether it is less than the expected average issuance over a given year or more than that, and the extent to which this is so. In other words, the data is most useful when aspects of it are significantly out-of-line with the recent past or anticipated future.

Municipal Sector and Securities' Spreads

Sector spread relationships in the municipal bond arena are regulated largely by the relative supply of bonds. But this must be tempered by estimates as to the future percentage of a particular sector's supply on a *relative* basis. In other words, an evaluation must be made of the future supply of bonds of a given sector as a percentage more or less than its *usual* relative supply based on historical sector volume and resultant spread of different sectors. The point here is to capitalize on spread relationships among various sectors at a given point in time based on what is expected to occur.

To be sure, it is important to estimate how volume relationships will change based on the future availability or unavailability of bonds in a given sector, *but only when* the relative supply will be out-of-line compared to what it usually has been. It is critical to note here that this calls for a judgement by the portfolio manager about what the future will hold for sector relationships based on an evaluation of past, present and projected data.

These kinds of decisions, if they are to be made with a high degree of accuracy, must have as their basis a great deal of information about how securities have been and are trading for general generic sectors in the municipal market and credit quality categories under different interest rate scenarios, and different issuance volumes. However, much of the data which is available in the municipal market really does not come close to providing this kind of information which portfolio managers must have at their disposal in order to make the best or most optimum decision at a given point in time. For instance, much of what is presently available in the area of sector related. Information only covers how specific sectors relatively trade which are rated in a particular credit category, such as "single-A" rated housing and "triple-A" rated general obligation bonds.

Nevertheless, carrying this line of reasoning further, perhaps the most critical elements in a portfolio manager's decision to buy or sell a particular security are the yield spreads among different sectors and bonds within a particular sector with a view towards expected supply. Decisions are made about the extent to which a particular sector of municipal bonds, such as housing, hospitals, or public power bonds are trading relative to others in the given market, and then, the extent to which a single bond in a particular sector, is trading relative to other securities within that sector, all compared against historical trading relationships and future supply. In other words, if it is generally perceived that public power issues are trading at levels which are now much cheaper than they have been relative to general obligation bonds, and if a particular public power issue is trading at a level which is cheaper than it would usually trade at, the purchase of that particular public power bond and perhaps the sale of the general obligation bond would be a likely portfolio decision, if supply considerations support that action. Of course, the maturity of the bond must be taken into account as much as the credit quality of that particular security.

SOME TECHNICAL ISSUES

Total Return

In the real world, somehow or other the relative success of portfolios is likely to be ultimately judged by the "total return" concept. This takes into account not only investment or coupon income, but also the change in the portfolio's value, which of necessity, includes capital gains and losses. These result when the prices of bonds fluctuate through the *horizon* period for measuring the portfolio's return. (The extent of a bond's price change depends on its initial yield, its coupon, its maturity, and interest rate changes.)

Discount and Premium Bonds

Premium bonds tend to drop in price slower than discounts, while discounts, which are more volatile, go up in price more quickly. As a result, premium bonds are generally purchased when interest rates are moving up, and discount bonds are purchased as interest rates head downward. Similarly, a current coupon bond is less volatile than a discount one.

THE "PURE CASE"

As alluded to earlier, the most productive portfolio management techniques can be operationalized when there is a given universe of securities, such as municipal bonds, which have been tracked over a long period of time as to their trading relationships under different market conditions. The situation would also be one where there would only be a secondary market, thus eliminating the impact that newly issued securities have on the market for those which are outstanding. In this theoretical marketplace, a database could be developed and updated showing various trading relationships of securities across different sectors, maturities, and credit quality categories, all during different market conditions. And as municipal professionals became more accustomed to using the database, it would be likely that more profitable operations would be the result.

This type of situation would still leave ample room for individuals to make judgements about the market and the relative attractiveness of particular municipal securities. Certainly, different portfolios would have different parameters and objectives, all of which would change in both the short and the long run. But the transactions which would ultimately result as a consequence of using this broad-based database would approach the more optimum "moving target" at any decision making point rather than when portfolio decisions would have been made without this data. However, like most hypothetical illustrations, this optimum situation is not a realistic one. It is, in a few words, a "pure case."

At the present time, there is a tremendous gulf between what information could optimally be available and what actually is. And this gulf is not likely to be filled soon. Consequently, it is the purpose of analysts and advisors to try to fill this void with guidelines which help portfolio managers to limit their downside by making decisions which are less structured, less regulated, and more intuitive. Intuition about any market plays a major role in the portfolio management process. Yet, where there is much at stake and where there is a tremendous amount of market-related material available, but where there is much more which is not, there needs to be a set of strictures upon which professionals can make decisions which will result in the greatest gains with the smallest amount of risk. The following set of decision making tools is designed to meet this need.

QUANTITATIVE ANALYTICAL TOOLS: MUNICIPAL MARKET DATA, INC.

Great strides have been made in the development of a useful database on the trading patterns of municipal securities, and this information may be used to help make better portfolio management decisions. The development of this system, which entails tracking the trading patterns of municipal securities over significant time periods and along a number of quantitatively defined characteristics, results in information which resembles the so-called "pure case" previously discussed. The only difference is that, in this situation, a limited number of municipal securities have been tracked and only a few, albeit significant, quantitative techniques have been applied to that securities database. Indeed, most of the municipal securities which have been studied are in the general category of actively traded dollar bonds or general market names. Nevertheless, it is generally considered that anywhere from 80 to 175 or so municipal issuers comprise the universe of securities which are consistently traded by most tax-exempt market participants. Many consider this to be representative of approximately 50% of the municipal bonds which are actively traded market names. The remaining 50% are comprised of general market names which are largely traded on a regional basis. But these are just approximations.

A database has been developed by Municipal Market Data, Inc. and is presently employed by some major municipal market participants nationwide so as to better their portfolio management techniques and trading decisions. These include quantitative measures of trading patterns of municipal securities which are general market names and are bought, sold, and traded in the municipal market on a regular basis. These measures are designed to be decision making tools, and each municipal professional is likely to employ them in somewhat varying ways. Nevertheless, definitions of them and a discussion of how they might be used is a mandatory precursor to the portfolio decision-making process. *The definitions of the terms below are derived from Municipal Market Data, Inc. and will be quoted when applicable.*

Beta

Beta analysis is a "measure of the price relationship between two variables." Beta quantifies the percentage of price movement of a dependent variable compared to the independent variable. The beta value, therefore, is the number of units the dependent variable is likely to move for each unit change of the independent variable.

The Correlation Value: r^2

The correlation value "expresses the percentage of movement in one variable that is 'explained' by the movement of the other variable." The value "measures the degree of similarity of movement between the two variables being compared. A value close to 0% suggests very little correlation" between the price movements of two variables, "while a value close to 100% indicates very similar price movements."

Standard Deviation

The standard deviation is generally used as a "measure of the spread or distribution of data points in a set of observations." It is generally employed with a normal distribution curve around a definable average. Measures of standard deviation are used in this particular genre to "accurately define 'overbought' and 'oversold' conditions of the market for shorter periods of time. 'Oversold' conditions develop when current values fall more than 1.0 standard deviation below the average. Conversely, 'overbought' conditions occur when the values exceed plus 1.0 standard deviation."

Duration

Duration was generally defined years ago by Frederick Macauley. The modified use of the term duration was, and is still considered to be, the estimate of volatility or sensitivity of the market value of a portfolio or a security to a change in the direction of interest rates.

Much can be made of these quantitative tools in the trading, buying, and selling of municipal bonds for portfolio purposes. They can be used, as will be noted below, for comparing specific securities against some indices generally employed in the municipal market, or even against each other. They can be used when taken together or as separate and distinct measures of the trading relationships of securities in the marketplace. Not every portfolio manager or trader will employ quantitative measures in the same way all of the time, and not every municipal market participant will arrive at the same conclusions about the data and will take exactly the same resultant actions.

HOW TO USE SOME TECHNICAL CONCEPTS

The Benchmark Idea

Comparing yield levels of specific securities to certain benchmark yields, which are generally considered to be baseline upon which yields on other securities are measured, is not a new idea. Typically, the richness or cheapness of many securities in the municipal market were compared against long-term "triple-A" rated general obligation (G.O.) bonds. However, because there are many "triple-A" G.O. issues, which trade much differently from one another, it is often a difficult comparison to employ, and one which is likely to yield widely varying results. Some market participants like to compare the yields on municipal securities to a specific "triple-A" rated credit, but this too has its potential uncertainties. Perhaps the most important one is the fact that the shape of the yield curve of a particular "triple-A" rated security can fluctuate widely when compared against the "triple-A" yield curve of a group of securities. This is so because the yield curve of a single security is much more subject to the supply and demand pressures of the marketplace and the activity of particular buyers, among other changing variables.

Very often the yield of a particular security or its beta value is also compared to various Bond Buyer indices. This too can be useful, but it also carries with it some inherent problems. For instance, the indices may have less actively traded names, and thus may lag general market movements by significant amounts of time. As a result, such comparisons may be an after-the-fact phenomenon.

The index which many consider to be the most accurate reflection of activity in the municipal marketplace is the Actively Traded Dollar Bonds Index. This Index is useful not only because it reacts more quickly than other indices as the market moves, but also because it includes more actively traded securities. Consequently, portfolio improvements could be made just by dealing with some of the securities which comprise it.

Yield Spreads

Yield spreads of particular securities as they compare to others can be especially helpful in making purchasing decisions. But to take the best advantage of this type of information, a trend must be present in the spread relationships of two securities over a significant period of time. This is so because, in many instances, yield spread relationships between two securities have vacillated in the past. This presents the observer with a "double helix" type of relationship where, in the most recent historical period, the yield to maturity or yield to call of a particular security is significantly above that of the other, while in the more distant past, the relationship was totally the reverse. And depending on market conditions, this relationship could switch back to its original one. As a result, one of the key concepts in studying yield spread relationships of particular securities, especially with only a recent historical database, is to make sure that there is a continuing and chartable trend. The relationship should also be discernible when the spreads are charted against a particular benchmark, such as the Actively Traded Dollar Bonds Index.

If the yield spread relationship between two securities is such that it is worth taking advantage of, it should not always remain the same when the Index changes. If it does remain the same, it is likely that other factors are at work on the spread relationship and further analyses should be undertaken.

The Use and Abuse of Quantitative Measurements

The beta of a particular security provides an indication of the extent to which it moves in price when compared to an index or simply another variable. Put differently, the analyst can tell the extent to which a bond's price movement was more or less volatile than a particular index. This may be supported by high correlation values. For instance, a security, whose beta value is 1.00 and whose correlation value is 98%, is one which is likely to closely track the particular index at an approximate level which the beta value indicates. In making a decision about a purchase or sale of a security relative to another one based on beta, one could, and perhaps even should, look to a high correlation value in support of that decision. Similarly, in certain types of markets, it may be wiser to purchase a particular security with beta close to 1.0 which is supported by a high correlation value, but a low duration factor indicating less potential volatility, so that the downside risk is limited. In up markets, the duration factor may not be as important, because weathering a downside risk as a result of greater volatility is a less significant factor.

Many portfolio decisions, however, are initially based on a cheap/ rich indicator. A standard deviation measurement could be appropriately employed as such as indicator when it is used with an index which is reflective of market trends. When a bond with a high beta and duration supported by a high correlation value is trading cheap to the market or an index (as indicated by a relatively high negative standard deviation), it may be a bond to purchase if the market is on an anticipated upswing.

Conversely, all these factors can be employed on the sell side in a down market. A highly volatile bond, as seen by its duration, could be sold, especially if it is rich to the market or an index as indicated by its standard deviation. This decision would carry even more weight if it was supported by a high beta and a high correlation value.

Rich and Cheap Relationships

As in the analysis of yield relationships across sector lines, there are certain similar factors which must be considered in evaluating rich and cheap spread relationships of actively traded dollar bonds. In these cases, a comparison between two particular dollar bonds is usually made by relating the securities' maximum and minimum spread relationship with the average and current one. However, there are now a number of factors which must be considered together with how the current spread relationship relates to the average one before a portfolio move is made.

First of all, the spread relationship between the two securities should be supported by a similar sector spread relationship, if the bonds which are being compared are from two different sectors, such as housing and hospital groups. Also, if, for instance, a hospital bond is trading cheap to a housing bond, it would be even better if the visible supply of hospital bonds for the foreseeable future is significantly below what it is usually expected to be. If two bonds of the same sector are being compared, such as two public power issues, it would be a positive indication if public power bonds were already cheap to the market as seen through their sector spreads and are expected to continue to be so, for any number of reasons, not the least of which would be expected visible supply. Similarly, if the sale of a particular security is contemplated, it should be one where the expected visible supply of that particular bond is likely to be significantly greater than it historically has been because it may be able to purchase even cheaper securities of that particular sector in the future.

In all of this, it is critical to note that, if a purchase or a sale of a particular security as against another one is to be made, the current spread between the two is significantly above or below its average so that the spread relationship is likely to continue. This relationship should be supported by the future supply estimates. Put differently, the closer to the average spread that the current spread between two securities is, the more likely that market movements can bring the current spread closer to the average one, so that the purchase or sale of a particular security would have a minimum impact on the yield of a particular portfolio. There are no set limits above or below the average spreads which can be deemed minimally adequate enough to make a purchase or sale of a security, but 20% above or below the average spread is likely to justify a market making decision.

RULES OF THE ROAD: A MODIFIED
DECISION-TREE METHOD OF BOND SELECTION

The key underlying rationale for portfolio decisions, certainly in the municipal and corporate area, is to make purchases and sales in order to take advantage of disparities in the marketplace. Indeed, portfolio managers have, as their goal, the uncovering of unusual spread differentials among sectors of a particular securities market at a given point in time and which are likely to continue and then to find similar value in bonds within a given sector or among sectors. In other words, by taking advantage of spread differentials in the marketplace, portfolio decisions are made based on a relative value concept. Even if interest rates move either upward or downward, the purchase or sale decision would have been made on a generally relative basis and is likely to hold for the short term, such as three months or so (except in the unlikely event of an unusual reshaping of the yield curve and a distortion of the sector relationships which results in a degree of permanence).

For practical purposes, a time horizon of three months may be used. While sector relationships and the trading patterns of securities can go back much further, portfolio decisions are, for our purposes, expected to be made based on trading patterns of particular securities at a given point in time and which show a *trend* perhaps over the previous three months, but which can generally be supported by their historical trading patterns over a longer period of time.

Decision 1: Determine the Direction of Interest Rates for the Short Term

It is obviously important to make some determination of what is likely to be the direction of interest rates, at least for the foreseeable future, and the speed with which a change, if any, of the yield curve is likely to take place. There are numerous ways to make these evaluations. In any event, a historical analysis of the treasury bond yield curve compared to the municipal bond "triple-A" rated yield curve is important as are all factors which are perceived to impact interest rates. Yet, in determining the future direction of municipal bond interest rates, the Actively Traded Dollar Bonds Index should be reviewed carefully as should other indices.

(1) What has been the recent historical relationship between the treasury bond yield curve and the municipal bond "triple-A" yield curve and/or the Actively Traded Dollar Bond Index?

(2) Is there a lag phenomenon present?

(3) Is the municipal bond market oversold or overbought as seen through the Actively Traded Dollar Bonds Deviation Index?

(4) To what extent are interest rates expected to remain stable, move upward, or move downward based upon the above information?

(5) Is the direction of interest rates supported overall by a higher or lower than average 30-day visible supply of municipals?

Decision 2: Determine the Best Value Generally in the Market Based on Maturity and Credit Quality

A determination of where the greatest value in the yield curve lies across all major rating categories for specific maturities must be made. A cursory evaluation provides information on which particular maturities will produce proportionately greater returns. A similar analysis can then be done for credit rating categories as a function of the risk factor. This information can show generally how much additional yield may be picked-up for each maturity year and for each rating category. For instance, a conclusion might be that the greatest value versus the risk lies in purchasing "double-A" rated securities in the 10- to 15-year maturity range and that there is really no additional proportionate reward available by purchasing securities which carry lower ratings and/or longer maturities. What this data may indicate, however, is where it is likely for a portfolio manager to pick up the greatest yield so that a proportionately greater share of a portfolio may be invested advantageously in those particular maturity ranges and credit quality categories.

Obviously, the lower the credit is rated and the longer the maturity, the more likely it is that there will be greater yield. But for portfolio management purposes, this information must be evaluated on a value-added basis. Oftentimes, longer maturities and lower credits do not justify the risks involved; the pick-up in yield, for instance, might be minimal beyond say, the 20-year maturity range and for credits which are rated below "single-A." Nevertheless, the information distilled here must really be supported on a sector basis.

(1) In what maturity does it appear that a significantly greater yield becomes apparent?

(2) In what credit rating category does a significantly greater yield occur?

(3) For what maturity ranges and credit rating categories are their significant yield advantages?

When the maturity ranges and credit categories of most significant yield are isolated, there are maturities and credit categories *both* above and below it which do not afford purchasers significant yield advantages. This may indicate selling opportunities.

Decision 3: Determine the Ranking of Sectors Which Provide the Greatest Relative Yield Levels

Critical to the portfolio decision making process is a determination of the relative ranking of generic municipal bond sectors as to how cheap and rich they are trading in general terms relative to one another. This is not to say that actions should be taken simply based on the fact that a particular sector is trading cheap to another one. Nor does it necessarily mean that another sector should be totally avoided; diversity in and of itself may be useful. But rather this may suggest that it is wise to invest in a particular sector versus another one even though that sector is trading significantly higher than it would usually trade relative to the other one, perhaps at a level which is 20% higher.

In addition, a relative ranking of how sectors are trading against one another, especially over maturity ranges and specific credit rating categories, is critical. It is conceivable that the portfolio manager can get an idea of the relative cheapness or richness of sectors across specific spot maturities such as every 5 years. Similarly, it is also likely that only information about a specific credit category of a sector is available, as noted earlier. For instance, comparisons in the data may only be made among "single-A" rated housing and hospital bonds. Yet, this information may still be useful because the preponderance of the dollar volume of both these types of bonds may be rated in this category and, if not, are rated very close to it.

Once again, however, there are no hard and fast rules as to what should or should not be purchased based on a sector analysis of spreads. Rather, this data provides a general idea of how a portfolio might be proportionately structured so as to capture the greatest potential yield advantage for a particular sector at a given maturity level. This data would be especially useful if the decision is supported by the expected visible supply.

(1) On a relative basis, which sector is trading significantly cheaper to any other sector when compared against the way it has historically traded?

(2) What maturity ranges in each sector are trading significantly cheaper than they normally trade?

(3) How do the sectors rank according to how they are trading from cheapest to richest?

(4) Where can the greatest yield be gained across all maturities and all sectors?

(5) Is this supported by the expected future visible supply in the sectors? If not, what variations should take place as sectors continually get cheaper or richer? What should the purchasing patterns be as a function of this information?

Decision 4: Determine Which Bonds on an Intra- and Inter-Sector Basis are Worthy of Purchase or Sale

With the above available data, especially that which relates to the relative richness and cheapness of securities it is possible, at this point, to begin making decisions as to which bonds should be purchased and which should be sold. Initially, this information should come from an analysis of intra-sector spreads (i.e., the differences in spreads of bonds within the same sector, such as public power or housing bonds). As discussed earlier, a yield spread with a differential of more than 20% of what a particular bond has historically traded lends support to these buying and selling decisions. If this is supported by appropriate information about the trading pattern of a particular sector as it relates to other sectors as well as the foreseeable visible supply, it may be an indication that a portfolio decision or restructuring is in order.

Keep in mind, that in this instance, we are dealing only with bonds within a particular sector. Not only are such comparisons more ideal because bonds of a given sector generally trade relative to one another more closely than bonds trade on an inter-sector basis, but also because these comparisons are more quantitatively definable and often more meaningful to portfolio managers, traders, and analysts who truly understand the trading and credit dynamics of bonds within a given sector and the sector as a whole.

A similar determination should be made of specific bonds on an inter-sector basis which have been isolated as appropriate purchases and/or sales based on inter-sector trading relationships which are supported by such factors as sector spreads as a function of expected visible supply.

Decision 5: Determine if the Selection of Securities for Purchase or Sale Is Supported

As alluded to earlier, purchases of securities are held through changing markets, and there is no more important a change effecting a bond market than that which relates to the direction of interest rates. As a result, the selected security's volatility and the extent to which it does and does not move with certain indices are particularly important in the ultimate purchase or sale decision. Furthermore, these characteristics should be evaluated in relation to the Actively Traded Dollar Bonds Deviation Index, indicating the extent to which the market is overbought or oversold. Additionally, whether or not the environment suggests the purchase of discount or premium securities is also critical to the portfolio management process. Much of this material and the way these variables interact with and support each other was discussed earlier in this paper. But as a general decision making tool, it is important that an analysis of these characteristics as they affect portfolio decisions be made at this point.

*Decision 6: Determine Whether or Not any of the
Securities Selected are Expected to Have Their Ratings
Upgraded or Downgraded*

It is no "state secret" that every portfolio manager, and indeed perhaps even every municipal market participant, has some fairly strong opinions about certain credits, and many simply steer away from those issuers which they believe may have credit problems in the foreseeable future. More significantly, portfolio managers must make these decisions when they have received a significant amount of credit related information from any number of sources. It is in these situations that a portfolio manager may decide that certain credits could conceivably have difficulties and, therefore, are ones which should be avoided even if quantitative data indicates that they may be a candidate for purchase. As a matter of fact, many believe that the reason these kinds of credits may be trading cheap to the market is that there are other market participants who share similar perceptions about them.

Likewise, there are certain credits which quantitative data would indicate should be purchased and may even be upgraded by the rating agencies. This kind of information simply adds value to the quantitative and qualitative analysis done by portfolio managers which isolate these securities as purchasing targets.

Other general credit-related concepts include the fact that lower rated credits are more volatile than higher rated ones. In down or volatile markets, it is best to steer away from the more volatile credits because of the potentially greater downside risk. This concept also applies to those credits perceived to be either overrated or are expected to have credit quality problems.

In any case, credit determinations are made in the final analysis of the portfolio decision making process. Although they are, in a way, "the icing on the cake," many believe they are some of the most important decisions any portfolio manager or trader is likely to make.

BIBLIOGRAPHY

Darst, David M. *The Handbook of the Bond and Money Markets.* New York: McGraw-Hill Book Company, 1981.

Fabozzi, Frank J. and Pollack, Irving M. *The Handbook of Fixed Income Securities.* Illinois: Dow Jones-Irwin, 1987.

Homer, Sidney and Liebowitz, Martin L. *Inside the Yield Book.* New Jersey: Prentice-Hall, Inc. and New York: New York Institute of Finance, 1972.

Municipal Market Data, Inc. *Municipal/Futures Data-Line.* Massachusetts, 1985.

Municipal Market Data, Inc. *Municipal Market Data-Line.* Massachusetts, 1985.

CHAPTER 7

Ups and Downs of Municipal Bonds' Volume and Yields in the Past Century*

Matthew Kreps

On November 14, 1985, the New Jersey Turnpike Authority put the capstone on the municipal bond market's record year by pricing $2 billion of bonds in a single offering. It remains the largest municipal bond sale ever. In the final six weeks of 1985, $75.6 billion of new issues flooded the market, pushing the year's total above $200 billion, a record twice the size of the largest year before it.

The turnpike issue stands, in its sheer bulk and complexity, as a particularly apt symbol of the modern municipal market and the wrenching changes the market endured during the 100 years since William F. G. Shanks founded *The Daily Bond Buyer*. If the founder had been told the story of the Turnpike bonds in 1891, he would have contemptuously dismissed it as a Jules Verne fantasy.

A $2 billion issue, in a market that had never sold more than $200 million in an entire year? An issuer who didn't collect taxes and would have to repay the debt solely from revenues from *automobile tolls?* Securities that could be sold back to the issuer from six weeks to five years later? Coupon rates that could be changed *every week,* or at *whatever period the issuer wanted?* And all of them sold through negotiation *8 days*

---

* Reprinted with permission from *The Bond Buyer*, One State Street Plaza, New York, NY 10004-1549.

after it was announced to the public? With interest rates ranging up to 7%? *Seven percent,* in a market that had, at its worst in 1873, never paid more than *5.50%?* What sort of fool would issue bonds like that? What sort of fool would *buy* them?

The editors who followed him for the next 60 years would have asked much the same questions. Public authorities that issued bonds did not exist until 1921, when the Port of New York Authority was chartered. The bond market did not reach the $2 billion total sales mark for an entire year until 1947. Interest rates did not crack the 7% barrier until 1970. Negotiated bonds did not become prominent until the mid-1970s. Revenue bonds were not permitted until 1905 and did not dominate the market until the late 1970s. And variable-rate put bonds were unheard of before the early 1980s, when they were created for issuers desperately trying to avoid paying 13% on long-term bonds.

It is not likely, however, that Mr. Shanks and his successors would have spent much time thinking about such fantasies. They may have dealt with bond structures and procedures that were simple, almost unchanging, in their day, but they had their hands full tracking a market that already was selling more than 2,000 issues in 1897—without benefit of telephones, computers, or electronic typesetting.

By 1904, more than 3,500 issues were marketed, and the 1920s saw more than 7,000 issues a year. Those figures are surprisingly not that far below modern times; in 1989, the busiest year ever in the market, 11,766 issues were sold.

The bond market's most astonishing growth over the past century lies in the sums involved. The 3,500 issues sold in 1904 raised just $422 million. Forty-three years later, in 1947, the market sold 4,300 issues that raised $3.31 billion—nearly 8 times as much. Forty-three years after that, in 1990, issuers sold 11,500 issues and raised $162.3 billion—49 times as much.

The Bond Buyer's first 100 years also paid witness to 5 great interest rate swings—3 bull markets (1874 to 1900, 1921 to 1946, and 1982 on) and 2 bear markets (1901 to 1920 and 1947 to 1982). The greatest of the bull markets, 1921 through mid-1946, concluded with the lowest interest rates in U.S. history. Less than 40 years later, the worst bear market of all time ended with the highest interest rates.

Municipal bonds were sold from the beginning of the Republic, but became popular only in the 1820s, as America's cities grew. The market expanded rapidly until the Panic of 1873, which caused a depression that stunted all financial markets for a time.

All of these bonds were general obligations of the cities that issued them. Revenue bonds, mostly for water supply systems, were sold, but they were of the "double-barreled" type that also had a city's full faith and credit behind them.

These 19th-century bonds were sold at rates not so far below today's. Homer Sidney, in his *A History of Interest Rates* (1977), shows New England municipal bond yields fluctuating from 6.30% to 5.02% from 1798 through 1819, and from 5.51% to 4.37% from 1820 until the Panic of 1873. The first of the great bull markets began after the Panic, as yields dropped from the 1873 high of 5.58% to 4.22% in 1879 and 3.45% in 1889. The bull market that began in 1874 lasted until the end of the decade. New England bond yields fell from 3.42% in 1890 to 3.10% in 1899, the lowest yield reported for the 19th century.

In 1896, the first year for which *The Daily Bond Buyer* has complete new-issue figures, municipal governments sold 1,283 bond and note issues (known then as "permanent loans" and "temporary loans") totaling $130 million. In the final three years of the 1890s, issuers reported more than 2,000 sales a year, but the dollar amounts ranged only from $129 million to $163 million. *The Bond Buyer's* lists did not limit themselves to U.S. cities and counties, but included street railway companies, ferry companies, gas and electric utilities, and even Canadian governments.

THE 1900s

The first decade of the 20th century clearly shows a historical trend that persists today—municipal bond sales and rates rising and falling in tandem. This relationship exists mainly because of supply and demand—an increase in new-issue supply tends to drive prices down and yields up.

Municipal volume climbed from 2,600 issues and $168 million in 1901 to 4,700 issues and $478 million in 1909. Bond yields, as represented by the 20-Bond Index of general obligation yields, began the first bear market of the century with a steady rise from 3.10% in 1901 to 3.76% in 1909.

The decade's high for both volume and rates came in 1908, when $530 million of bonds and notes were issued and the 20-Bond Index hit 3.87%. (The 20-Bond Index was not created until 1917, but editors of *The Daily Bond Buyer* were able to use historical data on bond prices to calculate it retroactively to 1900.) Short-term notes made their first appearance in *Bond Buyer* tables in 1905, when it reported $150 million of sales. This market sector remained under $200 million a year until 1914.

THE TEENS

The municipal market was rattled by two pivotal events—the enactment of the federal income tax in 1913, which separated municipal bonds from their U.S. government and corporate cousins, and World War I, which shut the financial markets during the second half of 1914 and frequently monopolized the industry's attention with Victory and Liberty bond drives.

Long-term volume rose from $324 million in 1910 to $770 million in 1919. Short-term sales jumped quickly from $197 million in 1910 to $483 million in 1913, dropped below $400 million from 1914 through 1917, and finally moved above $450 million in 1918 and 1919.

The bear market that began in 1901 continued apace, pushing the 20-Bond Index up from 3.91% in 1910 to 4.51% in December 1919. The index broke through the 4% barrier for the first time in 1912 and got as high as 4.45% in 1913. It then dropped back to the low 4s in 1917, but this respite was short-lived, as it shot up to the decade's high of 4.74% in June 1918 and remained close to 4.50% for the next 18 months.

THE TWENTIES

The municipal market roared right along with all the other markets, embarking on a 26-year rally that ended with the lowest interest rates of all time. The recovery began after September 1920, when the 20-Bond Index reached the decade's high of 5.27%. Less than two years later, it was down in the low 4s and it remained there, with occasional dips into the high 3s, for the rest of the decade. Its low for the 1920s was 3.87%, in January, February, and March of 1928.

The market achieved its first billion-dollar year of long-term sales in 1921, with 6,720 issues totaling $1.38 billion. But that was the last major growth spurt for 26 years; the long-term sector would not rise above $1.5 billion until 1947. Short-term notes, on the other hand, doubled during the decade, topping the $500 million mark for the first time in 1920 and finishing 1929 at $921 million. Revenue bonds firmly planted their roots during the 1920s. Kentucky sold the first state revenue bond in 1920, an issue secured by a first lien on State Fair property and repaid out of State Board of Agriculture income.

The grandfather of all bond authorities, the Port of New York Authority, was created in 1921 and sold its first issue for $24 million in 1926. *The Bond Buyer* also devoted considerable coverage to state bond sales for soldiers' bonuses, foreign government bonds, and a burgeoning number of road and highway bonds.

THE THIRTIES

The Great Depression severely damaged municipal finance. *The Bond Buyer's* 11-Bond Index of high-grade municipal bonds shows just how bad the damage was: In 1928, Moody's Investors Service rated all 11 bonds Aaa, but by 1934, all 11 were down to Aa or A. By 1939, when ratings were listed for all 20 bonds in the 20-Bond Index, six were Baa, nine were A, four were Aa, and only one, the City of Baltimore, was Aaa.

Long-term bond volume collapsed early, from $1.38 billion in 1930 to $937 million in 1933. It remained in the $1.1 billion range for the rest of the decade. The short-term note market pierced the $1 billion level in 1931 and 1932, but it dropped below that in 1933 and did not get back over $1 billion until 1938.

Not even the very first $100 million bond sale, a New York City offering of corporate stock and various serial bonds, on March 4, 1931, offered much solace to an unhappy market. A second $100 million issue by New York City, in January 1932, was the last of that size until the end of World War II.

Bond prices also collapsed in the early 1930s. The 20-Bond Index moved above 5% in 1932 and jumped more than 100 basis points in early 1933 to a then-record high of 5.69% by May. But the bulls reasserted themselves, and yields began to drop again, falling below 4% by November 1934 and below 3% in July 1936. The index remained in the low 3s and high 2s for the rest of the decade, reaching as low as 2.62% in January 1937.

When World War II broke out on September 1, 1939, *The Daily Bond Buyer* considered it important enough not to wait the usual 30 days, until October 1, to calculate the 20-Bond Index. A special calculation on September 15 revealed a whopping 79-basis-point jump, from 3.21% to 4.00%. But the market recovered nearly completely in the next two weeks and dropped the index back to 3.30% on October 1.

THE FORTIES

When the world went to war, most investment capital went with it, and the municipal market sank to its lowest ebb since the late 1910s. After flirting with the $1.5 billion mark in 1940, long-term bond sales dropped to just $576 million in 1942 and $507 million in 1943—the smallest totals since 1918. Short-term note issuance also fell sharply, from $1.63 billion in 1940 to $711 million in 1943, $568 million in 1944, and $665 million in 1945.

Revenue bonds accounted for 39% of the volume in 1942, the first year in which *The Daily Bond Buyer* began tracking them, but their share of the market dropped to 17% by 1946 and remained at that level through the end of the decade.

Refunding issues were heavy during the war years of 1943 through 1945, but they declined to almost nothing in 1946 and 1947.

The Treasury's estimates of municipal debt outstanding show a 21% decline for 1940 through 1946, from $19.9 billion to $15.6 billion.

With municipal bonds so scarce, and federal income tax brackets raised to new highs—the top bracket leaped during the war years from 79% in 1940 to 94% in 1944 and 1945—the bull market for tax-exempt bonds forged ahead.

After the 20-Bond Index hit 3% in June 1940, it never touched that level again for 13 years. It dropped below 2% for the first time ever in November 1941, and remained there from June 1943 until November 1947.

This greatest of bull markets reached its peak for 8 weeks in February, March, and April 1946 when the Index sat at its all-time low of 1.29%. The higher-grade 11-Bond Index even flirted with the 1% barrier, sitting at 1.04% for the same eight weeks in early 1946.

That was the high-water mark for municipal bond prices. The war was over, the nation embarked on a great economic expansion, and municipal bond sales and yields began to rise. Long-term bond sales finally topped $2 billion in 1947 and approached $3 billion in 1948 and 1949.

At the same time, the 20-Bond Index more than doubled, from 1.29% in April 1946 to 2.48% in February 1948 before easing slightly to the low 2s through the end of the decade. Mr. Sidney blamed the decline in prices on the burgeoning supply: "Large new municipal issues overtaxed the limited resources of high-bracket investors and forced the market to seek a wider clientele."

Bond issues definitely were getting larger. Michigan sold the first $200 million municipal issue on March 4, 1947, and Illinois followed with the first $300 million issue on April 29. Both were soldiers' bonus bonds.

Turnpike authorities, which would dominate the "Hundred-Million Club" in the next decade, celebrated their first big sale in 1948, when the Pennsylvania Turnpike Commission sold $134 million of bonds on August 10. Two months later, the New Jersey Turnpike Authority was born.

THE FIFTIES

America's great economic boom carried the municipal bond market to new heights during the 1950s. Long-term sales broke records regularly throughout the years, exceeding $3 billion in 1950, $4 billion in 1952, $5 billion in 1953, $6 billion in 1954, and $7 billion in 1958.

Short-term notes followed suit, breaking above $2 billion in 1952, $3 billion in 1954, and $4 billion in 1959. More than 50 issues of $100 million or more were sold during the 1950s, compared with only 10 in all the years before. Municipal debt outstanding nearly tripled, from

$23.3 billion in 1950 to $67.1 billion in 1959. Many of the big sales were revenue bonds for turnpikes and electric power, which increased revenue bonds' share of the market to 30% most years during the next two decades.

The New Jersey Turnpike Authority set a record with its very first issue, when it sold $220 million of revenue bonds on February 17, 1950. All of the bonds were privately placed with insurance companies and New Jersey state funds, making the sale the biggest municipal private placement of the times.

Another turnpike authority, the Illinois Toll Road Commission, brought the market its first $400-million-plus issue, with a $415 million sale on October 25, 1955.

The 1950s also saw the first sales of public housing authority bonds and notes which were authorized by a 1949 amendment to the U.S. Housing Act of 1937. The bonds made their debut on July 17, 1951, with a $171 million issue, and 17 more $100-million-plus sales followed in the 1950s. These bonds, which were the highest-priced municipals of all because they were G.O. bonds guaranteed by the U.S. government, were sold until 1974; the note sales continued through mid-1984.

The rising sales carried bond yields up with them. The 20-Bond Index rose 141%, from the 1950s low of 1.58% on February 8, 1951, to the high of 3.81% on September 1959. It hovered in the high 1s and low 2s from January 1950 to mid-1952, rose to the 3% level by mid-1953, dropped back to the mid-2s halfway through the decade, and rose steadily thereafter. The steady increase in rates kept refunding sales at a minimal level—never more than 2.3% of the overall volume from 1953 on.

THE SIXTIES

The municipal bond market thrived in the early 1960s, as the economy entered what Mr. Sidney called "the most unusual period of stability in the postwar period." Long-term bonds exceeded $8 billion in 1961, $10 billion in 1963, and $11 billion in 1965, while short-term notes broke through the $5 billion level in 1963 and the $6 billion mark in 1965. Outstanding debt jumped from $72.9 billion in 1960 to $106.6 billion in 1966.

All the while, the 20-Bond Index meandered below the 3.50% level, hitting the decade's low of 2.98% on October 18, 1962. That was the last time the 20-Bond Index has been below 3%.

Municipal bond prices had managed to survive two world wars and the Korean conflict, but they could not withstand the price inflation created by America's two wars of the late 1960s—the Vietnam

War and the War Against Poverty. The 20-Bond Index rose above 4% in 1967, 4.50% in 1968, and shot to historic highs by 1969. It broke through the 6% barrier—a level not seen in U.S. municipal bonds since the 18th century—on August 21, 1969, and reached its all-time high of 6.90% on December 18, 1969.

Long-term bond sales continued unabated, topping $14 billion in 1967 and $16 billion in 1968, before plunging nearly $5 billion, to $11 billion, in 1969. Note sales rose to $8 billion in 1967 and $11.8 billion in 1969. By the end of the decade, $133.5 billion of municipal bonds and notes were outstanding.

The Bond Buyer began tracking the purposes of municipal financing at the beginning of the 1960s, and found in 1960 that schools were the leading purpose, with $2.43 billion of new issues, followed by transportation with $1.07 billion and utilities with $1.01 billion. In addition, $383 million of bonds were sold for public housing authorities and $200 million for veterans loans in California, which left $2.13 billion for general-purpose issues.

Industrial development bonds become popular early in the decade, rising from $46 million in 1960 to $1.59 billion in 1968. The wide use of these bonds to benefit private-sector companies did what a number of influential congressmen, federal officials, and even President Franklin D. Roosevelt could not do from the 1910s through the 1950s—persuade Congress to restrict municipal bonds.

The Revenue and Expenditure Control Act of 1968, the first law to put any restrictions on municipal financing, nearly wiped out the industrial development bond market, cutting the IDB total to just $24 million in 1969.

THE SEVENTIES

The 20-Bond Index began the decade by crashing through 7% on May 21, 1970, marking the first time in American history that municipal bonds yielded so much. The market then gained a brief respite, as the index dropped to the 5% range through 1973, reaching the decade's low of 4.96% on December 7, 1972. But the index began to rise again in early 1974 and spiked sharply higher in late 1975 to the decade's high of 7.67% on October 2. It eased again in 1977 and 1978, but rose again in the final three months of 1979 to the low 7s.

State and local governments, desperately trying to keep their debt costs down, turned to the short-term note market, where yields were substantially lower. As a result, short-term notes caught fire in the first half of the 1970s, skyrocketing from $17.9 billion in 1970 to $29 billion in 1974 and $28 billion in 1975. Long-term bond sales grew more slowly but still respectably, topping $24 billion in 1971 and $30 billion in 1976.

New York City's financial crisis in 1975, which led to a moratorium on its note payments, slammed the brakes on the short-term market, and volume fell to the $20 billion range for the rest of the decade. Long-term bonds picked up the slack in 1977 and jumped to $45 billion, and remained above $40 billion in 1978 and 1979. Refunding bond sales jumped sharply in 1976, 1977, and 1978, when rates came down from the then-historic highs of 1975.

The Municipal Assistance Corporation for the City of New York, created in the turmoil of New York City's fiscal crisis, made a name for itself on July 2, 1975, when it sold the market's first $1 billion issue. The sale shattered the previous record of $476 million, sold by New York City in October 1974, by more than $500 million. It would be another decade before the New Jersey Turnpike Authority smashed the MAC record with its $2 billion colossus.

This was the decade for revenue bonds, which grew from one-third of the market to about two-thirds by end of decade. Their biggest leap forward came in 1977, when revenue bond sales soared from $17 billion to $27 billion and they definitively outstripped G.O. volume for the first time ever.

Taxpayer revolts against property tax rates curbed the general obligation sector, and the uses for revenue bonds expanded dramatically, to include single-family and multifamily housing, hospitals, industrial pollution control, public power projects, stadiums and convention centers, airports, and universities and colleges. By decade's end, revenue bonds were prominent enough to encourage *The Bond Buyer* to create its 30-year Revenue Bond Index in September 1979.

Issuers also turned away decisively from competitive bids and toward negotiated sales during the 1970s. In 1973, the first year in which *The Bond Buyer* tracks negotiated volume, $5.92 billion of bonds, or 26% of the total, were negotiated. Two years later, negotiated bonds accounted for 40% of the market, and by 1977 they had 56% of the total. They would reach their peak in 1985 with 82% of the record $204 billion market and remain at three-quarters of the volume thereafter.

THE EIGHTIES

The last decade of *The Bond Buyer's* first century was easily the most tumultuous. The market endured the highest interest rates in recorded history, annual changes in tax law that spurred one issuing frenzy after another and a vast wave of innovations, and a crashing second-half bust that pushed yields down to more bearable levels but also put major bond firms and thousands of employees out of work.

Issuers suffered the highest municipal bond yields ever early in the decade, as the 20-Bond Index blew through one record high after another in rapid succession, sailing above 8% on February 21, 1980, 9% on March 13, 1980, 10% on December 11, 1980, 11% on July 16, 1981, 12% on August 20, 1981, and 13% on September 3, 1981.

Four months later, on January 14, 1982, the 20-Bond Index reached its all-time high of 13.44%. Eight days later, the Washington Public Power Supply System set the stage for the biggest ($2.25 billion) municipal bond default of all time when it canceled construction of two power projects.

The record high yields were accompanied by swings so volatile that many issuers and underwriters scrambled for protection against rate shock. Variable-rate bonds, which took advantage of sharply lower short-term yields, went from nil to $4.8 billion, or 6% of the market, in 1983. Even *The Bond Buyer* and the Chicago Board of Trade offered a solution to market risk: a daily Municipal Bond Index to be used for trading municipal bond futures as a hedge against price movements.

January 1982 marked the lowest depth of this great bear bond market. Prices then began a long ascent, dropping the 20-Bond Index in fits and starts from 1983 through 1986. It fell below 10% during 1983, bounced back over 10% in 1984, dropped again to the low 8s during 1985 and the low 7s in 1986, and hit a cyclical low of 6.54% in March 1987.

Two sharp spikes pushed the index back up over the next six months, until it topped 9% on October 15, 1987. Four days later, the stock market's Black Monday, when the Dow Jones industrial average plunged 509 points in a single horrifying session, sent investors fleeing to fixed-income havens. The index fell back to around 8% by the end of 1987, spent 1988 in the mid- to high 7s and eased to the low to mid-7s in 1989, 1990, and the first quarter of 1991, with occasional brushes with the high 6s.

Municipal bond sales mushroomed quickly in the early 1980s, leaping from the $40 billion level in the late 1970s to $77 billion in 1982, $102 billion in 1984, and the all-time high of $204 billion in 1985.

The note market hit its peak in 1982 with $43.4 billion, spurred by record high long-term rates and accelerating sales of housing project and urban renewal notes. Note sales shrank dramatically in 1985, as the housing and urban renewal note programs were terminated, long-term rates declined, and variable-rate bonds became more popular.

The record $204 billion volume in 1985 was driven, in part, by the federal government's desire to eliminate tax-exempt bonds. The Treasury Department proposals first came to light in May 1985 and eventually metamorphosed into a House bill, H.R. 3838, that sought the most severe restrictions ever on municipal bonds.

The threat was strong enough to drive issuers into the greatest bond-selling frenzy in history. They jammed $108.8 billion of new bonds through the market in the final three months of the year. December's volume of $55 billion exceeded the market's entire 55-year output for 1896 through 1951.

More than half of 1985's vast volume was for the "private-activity" purposes, such as housing, health care, public power, industrial development, and industrial pollution control, that the Treasury so vigorously detested. This sector exploded in 1985 because bonds were rushed to market ahead of the proposed restrictions, and once the restrictions were enacted, it shrank just as dramatically. By 1990, only housing and health care retained the prominent positions they held five years earlier. The three purposes that had dominated the market for decades—education, transportation, and utilities—were back among the leaders.

New-issue sales declined dramatically for the next two years, to $151 billion in 1986 and $105 billion in 1987, as issuers adjusted to the new tax laws and worked through the massive amounts of bond funds stockpiled in 1985. Sales rebounded thereafter, to $117 billion in 1988, $125 billion in 1989, and $128 billion for 1990.

Short-term notes began to revive toward the close of the decade, rising from the low $20-billion level of 1985 to 1988 to $29 billion in 1989 and $34 billion in 1990, as more state and local governments used cash-flow financings to tide them through budget crises.

The municipal bond market begins its second century closer in spirit to the 1890s than the 1980s. The 20-bond index, hovering around 7%, is closer to its low levels of 100 years ago than to its worst peaks of 10 years ago. Bond sales are expected to grow slowly and traditional purposes such as schools, highways, and utilities are expected to lead the market through the rest of 1990s.

That would echo the steady but unspectacular growth of the 1950s more closely than the violent swings of recent years. The market certainly will never return full-circle to the old days—the federal government's rules, regulations, and restrictions have seen to that—but it also expects and hopes that it will not see the likes of the 1980s again, either.

Part Two

CREDIT QUALITY ANALYSIS

CHAPTER 8

Credit Fundamentals—The Rating Agency Perspective

Freda S. Johnson
Formerly of Moody's Investors Service—1979–1990
Director of Public Finance Department
Currently: Special Consultant, Government Finance Associates, Inc.,
Independent Public Finance Consultant

Historically, the financing of the vast capital needs of local government—ranging from sidewalk repair to the construction of roads, schools, bridges and water and sewer systems—has been met generally from 3 basic sources:

(1) Internally generated revenues;

(2) grants and other forms of inter-governmental contributions; and

(3) the municipal bond market.

The strength and resiliency of the municipal market to provide a significant portion of local capital financing requirements can be attributed to the integrity and ingenuity of units of government to withstand frequent economic, political, and financial pressures and yet achieve an unrivaled record of repayment. The security of investments historically offered by municipal obligations together with their usual tax-exempt status have made municipal issues particularly attractive to the investor. However, tax status is not a credit factor. The same analytical approach to the rating of municipal obligations is used whether they are issued as tax-exempt or taxable.

An issuer which decides to raise capital through the municipal bond market must answer a multitude of questions including:

- What is the purpose of the borrowing?
- Is it essential or non-essential?
- Is there the legal ability to borrow?
- What legal restraints need to be addressed?
- How will the debt be secured?
- What is the best way to structure the debt?
- Should the debt be long- or short-term?
- What are the tradeoffs between a broad or narrow revenue pledge?
- What expertise is needed to structure and market the issue?
- What is involved in getting the issue rated?

THE RATING AGENCY

Given all these complexities, a rating agency facilitates bringing an issue to market in a number of ways. Most importantly, it provides an independent, objective assessment of the relative creditworthiness of debt obligations for the municipal market. The rating system is an easy-to-understand ranking which both key parties in a municipal transaction, issuers and investors, use as an aid in the capital formation process. For units of government, ratings expedite the process of obtaining needed capital funds by providing issuers with information that they can use to explain to investors (the buyers of municipal obligations) about the level of risk contained in the repayment of the debt. Investors use the rating in making their purchase decisions as a substitute for or enhancement of their own research about a particular municipal issue. This, even within this generally safe market, ratings act to differentiate among issues and, in a sense, provide some discipline in an otherwise largely unregulated market.

THE RATING PROCESS

The rating process begins with an application for a rating by the issuer, its advisor or underwriter. The request should be made several weeks in advance of the expected sale date to permit ample time for both the analysis and timely release and publication of the rating.

In order to assign a rating, a credit analyst will look both to historical trends and current conditions and will review a number of documents including a preliminary official statement, annual financial reports, the most recent operating and capital budgets and all legal documents relating to debt security. Extensive demographic and labor market data is also examined. When necessary, the review of submitted information is augmented by a meeting with the rating agency, either in New York or on-site. Such visits are particularly important for complex financings or where there has been a significant change in credit quality.

After thoroughly examining the financial, demographic, debt, legal and other information, the analyst will discuss the rating recommendation with the area manager and then present it to the Municipal Department Rating Committee, which consists of the senior members of the department who serve on a rotational basis. The ultimate rating decision rests with Rating Committee, which evaluates the information presented, reaches a consensus, and then officially assigns the rating.

CREDIT ANALYSIS

Credit analysis is the assessment of the relative strengths and weaknesses of those factors which have a bearing on the likely repayment of debt obligations. Ultimately, the repayment of a debt depends on both the borrower's ability and willingness to make repayment. To judge ability to pay, what is really measured is the degree of control that the obligor can exert to call forth and manage its resources so that its obligations can be met in full and on time. Determination of relative degrees of control or measurement of ability to pay is a major focus of the rating process.

The other component of credit analysis, the one that is less easily measured, is willingness to pay. Tax and expenditure limitation initiatives, voter rejection of millage budgets and bond issues, or the unwillingness of officials to make the often difficult decisions to assure budget balance are looked upon as symptoms of a possible unwillingness to pay. A consistent trend of positive performance, particularly when achieved in an environment of economic stress or under restrictive bond covenants, can provide the analyst with strong evidence of willingness to pay. An analyst's determination of credit quality, expressed in a credit rating, is based on an assessment of those factors affecting ability and willingness to pay.

These fundamental concepts of bond analysis, ability and willingness to pay, apply equally to general obligation, special tax bond analysis, and to the analysis of enterprise revenue bonds. The analysis of more limited liability revenue bonds also encompasses additional considerations relating to the future sound operation of the enterprise over the life of the bond issue. Both sets of analytical approaches are summarized in this chapter. It is important to note, however, that no one single factor in the process can be considered as most important.

ECONOMIC FACTORS

The economy is probably the least controllable and often the most difficult factor to predict in municipal credit analysis. Local performance during recent recessionary and inflationary periods has emphasized how little any one community can do to offset the effects of national economic trends. Even with these limitations, measures of local economic control are nevertheless very important to credit analysis.

Decennial U.S. census statistics of population and housing characteristics and various measures of employment, unemployment, and economic production provide a profile of the community's economy and the well being of its residents. These basic statistics are necessarily augmented by locally derived information. Especially in smaller communities, this information is needed to determine a community's dependence on a single industry or the dominance of a single employer.

Analysts are also interested in what the management of a municipality can do to encourage economic activity. In the case of a revenue bond, information on competitive factors relating to the service being provided by the enterprise is vital to the analyst. The size of the primary and secondary service areas and what duplication of services by other competitive units existing within those service areas are key issues which are reviewed.

Economic control can also be measured in terms of how sensitive a municipality's or enterprise's financial condition is to the performance of the local economy. Cyclical sensitivity of revenues, such as personal and business income taxes and sales taxes or fees and charges to industrial or commercial users, can be an indicator of financial vulnerability. Economic downturns are also reflected in higher property tax delinquencies and increasing accounts receivable.

Many municipalities have also shown particular sensitivity to interest rate movements either because of reduced investment earnings when rates fall or because of reduced private investment when rates rise.

ADMINISTRATION OF SERVICES

To be able to evaluate the ability of a community or enterprise to control financial conditions, it is particularly important to understand the scope and powers of the municipality's administration. How is the government organized? Are powers, particularly financial and budgetary responsibilities, clearly delineated? Are powers vested in a chief executive or are they spread among several offices? Is there a professional manager who can supply continuity between elected administrations? Are municipal enterprise operations supervised directly by the general government or are they managed by a professional administrator? What services is the government responsible for? U.S. municipal governmental arrangements vary widely and this is a key reason why it is difficult to quantify standards of municipal performance.

Intergovernmental relationships become important considerations when provision for services to a common group of taxpayers is shared. At one extreme are relatively independent units that provide all local government services that in other places are traditionally provided by multiple layers of government. At the other extreme are governmental arrangements where even such basic services as police and fire are the responsibility of independent special service districts or where regional financing authorities, such as those for transit and sewer purposes, legally separate the financing of a service from the responsibility of service provision. Intergovernmental relationships are particularly important to understand in joint action agency financings where the benefits of using the financing approach can be outweighed by the risks; that can be true primarily when there is lack of centralized responsibility or when a large variety of units participate, many of which have different objectives to be achieved by the financing. Experience indicates that membership in a joint action agency should be undertaken cautiously by the governmental participant, and such membership is carefully examined by the municipal analyst.

In addition to understanding the scope of municipal services, it is also important to understand the degree of flexibility in providing these services. Some proportion of any budget's expenditures is likely to be fixed, including the servicing of debt and other contractual obligations and contributions to employee pensions. Certain costs, particularly pension expenses or maintenance of municipal facilities, can be deferred without immediate consequences; however, the prudent funding of these accrued expenses is critical to building a solid base for future operations.

THE REVENUE COMPONENT

Just as it is important for the analyst to examine the degree of spending flexibility, revenue-raising powers must also be considered in the assessment of financial performance. Some governments have broad powers to raise tax rates and other fees independently, providing a strong means of controlling future financial condition. The analyst is particularly interested in the way revenue-raising authority is used. Some communities undertake a revenue review as part of the annual budget process and implement marginal tax rate adjustments as needed, while in other communities tax rate increases tend to be traumatic events, usually implemented only when crisis conditions are at hand.

Different types of enterprises (i.e., hospitals versus water systems) operate under widely different regulatory climates. Some must comply with separate rate review agencies while others are able to set rates at their own discretion, with covenants made to bondholders and competitive forces the main constraints.

When restrictions on revenue-raising authority exist, they take on greater significance in credit analysis because of the already inherent limitations to revenue structure of all government units.

DEBT MANAGEMENT

Control of debt position is particularly critical to any kind of credit analysis. Honoring the promise to repay and the fulfillment of all legal covenants with bondholders are the ultimate tests of a borrower's ability and willingness to pay. The starting point for debt analysis is the pledged legal security and other bondholder protections, and it is the task of the bond analyst to determine whether the borrower will meet these commitments. Although legal security for the debt provides the foundation and remains a central component of debt analysis, other analytical considerations are equally important. The economic feasibility and necessity of the project being financed must be determined. The relationship between the magnitude of debt to be repaid and the perceived benefit to be derived from the uses of that debt has become very critical.

Empirical evidence strongly suggests that when public indebtedness becomes too burdensome, an inability or unwillingness to pay may follow. Analysts employ certain measures of relative indebtedness to measure the burden of debt. Also considered is the impact of all debt obligations and the ability of taxpayers to meet them. Capital planning for future debt can be a very meaningful way of demonstrating control. For tax-supported debt analysis, total debt includes not only the debt obligations issued by the borrowing government, which is called the direct debt, but also the proportionate share of the debt obligations of overlapping governmental units. The analysis here must cover all debt supported by the same group of taxpayers, regardless of who issues the debt. This overall debt is then related to population and to the broadest and most generally available measure of the wealth of the community—the assessed valuation of all taxable property adjusted to reflect market value as nearly as possible.

For revenue debt analysis, coverage of annual debt service by net revenues[1] affords the analyst the ability to trace the trend of coverage over time, an indicator of both debt protection and sound management practices. Coverage calculations can also act as a supplemental indicator of the margins of protection available to bondholders, with the primary indicator of protection being the debt service safety margin ratio.[2] The ability of a municipal enterprise to repay its debt is always evaluated on a net revenue basis. We take this "harshest" text view in order to assure ourselves that sufficient revenues are available to operate and maintain the enterprise over the life of the debt. We also need affirmation that all covenants to bondholders have been met as a basic indicator of willingness to pay.

Another indicator is the rate of debt retirement relative both to tax base growth projections and the purposes for which the mix between the debt was issued. A key indicator is the mix between long-term and short-term debt. Reduced control of financial position is usually associated with an overreliance on short-term debt. The need for future market access always introduces some degree of vulnerability. Heavy reliance on bond anticipation notes that require subsequent refinancing and on annual operating loans or heavy use of variable rate debt with demand options reduce the level of financial control by increasing vulnerability to market uncertainties.

FINANCIAL PERFORMANCE

Annual operating performance and resultant year-end position are the ultimate measures of management's control. Regardless of economic, spending, and taxing realities, a municipal government is expected to balance its budget. Financial results are deemed satisfactory when annual revenues meet or exceed annual expenditures and sufficient

---

[1] Revenue bond debt service coverage is one of the most commonly used statistics within the municipal market. It is the ratio of net revenues to debt service requirements. For example, 1.50 times coverage refers to net revenue equaling $1^1/_2$ times debt service. In most resolutions authorizing the issuance of revenue bonds, it is standard for the issuer to offer bondholders added protection by a covenant to maintain rates and charges to yield net revenues sufficient to achieve at least a minimum coverage level. The requirement that certain coverage levels be met before additional debt may be issued is also standard.

[2] Defined as net revenues less debt service for the year divided by gross revenue and income.

financial resources have been accumulated to meet unforeseen contingencies and normal liquidity requirements.

Important to the analysis of any enterprise is clear evidence of the sound maintenance of plant investment. Operations are judged by the quality of annual balance as measured by a multi-year trend of results and through detailed analysis to determine that ongoing expenditures are financed by recurring revenues. Normal costs should be covered from basic charges for service, without reliance on one-time connection or other such timely rate adjustments. Regular rate review prevents the occurrence of periodic large rate increases and potential customer resistance.

The level of fund balance is related to the likelihood of drawing upon these accumulations. Generally, a fund balance of 5% of the budget is deemed prudent. A smaller balance may be justified by a long-term trend of annual budget surplus, while a larger balance may be warranted, particularly if budget revenues and expenses are economically sensitive or otherwise not easily forecasted. While positive operating results and a large fund balance provide financial strength, a planned drawdown of balances and actual performance consistently close to original budget estimates are evidence of strong management control. Prudent management will also insure that the investment of cash balances is done carefully and conservatively.

Accumulated balances should provide for the maintenance of debt service and other reserves at covenanted levels and also for the availability of monies for unforeseen contingencies, extraordinary maintenance needs and certain capital improvements. The outflow of surplus from the enterprise's funds flow, to finance other governmental purposes, is viewed cautiously to assure that all of the needs of the enterprise are fully met prior to any transfer.

LEGAL FACTORS

Critical to any analysis, particularly for revenue bonds, are the legal provisions contained within the resolution, indenture, state statute, or local law authorizing the debt issuance. The analyst evaluates the specific revenue that has been pledged for debt repayment. Also reviewed are provisions concerning the flow of funds, additional bonds' test governing further debt issuance, the required level of any reserve, and the "rate covenant." The latter three are essential components of any analyst's review of a revenue bond as they can have a direct bearing on overall security.

A liberal additional bonds' test offers weak protection in the future against significant further borrowing. A weak rate covenant (i.e., a low coverage requirement) offers little security in terms of added financial operating cushions. Finally, a weak reserve requirement also provides little comfort, particularly in the event an issuer enters an unexpected period of financial stress.

At the same time, analysts clearly recognize that legal provisions should not be structured to overly restrict an issuer's ability to operate efficiently. Rather, legal provisions should represent a fair balance between the legitimate security concerns of a bondholder and the issuer.

SHORT-TERM OBLIGATIONS

It should be noted that there is no direct correlation between bond and note ratings. Although many of the same credit factors are considered in assessing long-term and short-term credit positions, their level of importance differs with each situation. There are criteria used exclusively to analyze notes.

Notes sold in anticipation of taxes, specified revenues, or grants (TANs, RANs, GANs) are subjected to cash flow analysis. Such analysis is a judgment of the relative ability to obtain on a timely basis the revenues pledged to repay notes. It also evaluates the amounts and timing of all other receipts and disbursements, as well as the means by which sufficient monies to pay note principal and interest will be accumulated, all within the context of the issuer's normal operations. Actual cash flows from recent years are studied to identify trends. These historic results are compared with a cash flow projection for the year(s) in which a note will be outstanding and retired. One can then gauge whether the forecast is realistic and the degree of reliability of the pledged revenue.

Repayment of bond anticipation notes (BANs) is, in fact as well as in theory, dependent upon ultimate refinancing. Accordingly, analysis of market access is a prime consideration in assigning a rating to a bond anticipation note. This requires forecasting market reception for a sale of either bonds or renewal notes. Market access is not seen as being either available or unavailable but rather in terms of relative ease of market entry. The number of bids received for a prior bond issue and its net interest cost in comparison to like-rated issues are valuable measures of future market access. Also, such factors as statutory interest rate limits may bear on marketability.

SUMMARY

Ideally, the analyst looks for a municipality or an enterprise to be in a position to exert maximum control over its ability to repay its debts and to demonstrate a clear willingness to honor its commitments. The local economy should be strong and prospering. There should be no constraints on revenue raising abilities; in fact there should be a great deal of discretion in determining service levels. A proven track record of careful management should exist which has provided for the build-up of financial reserves to address unforeseen contingencies. What the analyst looks for is a clear trend of sound performance, both financially and operational, that is reinforced by a record of management's responsiveness to bondholder needs.

Over the last several years, the municipal market has grown at a phenomenal pace. At the same time, debt instruments have become more varied and complex. Yet despite these changes in the market, the fundamentals of credit analysis—evaluating the borrower's ability and willingness to pay—remain constant.

CHAPTER 9

Analyzing Governmental Credit

Claire Gorham Cohen
Fitch Investors Service, Inc.

All debt must be repaid from the existing and potential sources of income available to the borrower. For governments, by definition this means the taxes, fees and charges which may be levied on the citizens, individual or corporate. Even government enterprises which charge for use of their products and facilities are included, as governments may, by direct action or franchising, limit competition or create monopolies. While it might appear that all government borrowing should have the highest credit standing because of the innate ability to expropriate whatever amounts may be needed through taxation or control of resources, history, practical experience and the fear of citizen revolt (best expressed in the United States at the polls) dictate a careful analysis of both the ability and the willingness of a government to meet the terms of a debt contract.

Credit analysis can be directed toward tests of two conditions: the harshest imaginable or that expected in the foreseeable future. Probably the best approach is a mix so that vulnerabilities under stress can be recognized and yet reasonable expectation prevails.

For state and municipal governments, only one period in this century, the Great Depression, is a reliable guide to behavior under extreme stress. Although conditions have changed since the 1930s with the introduction of protective social safety nets, more aggressive government action, and a different socio-economic profile of the nation's population, some things remain the same. Governments continue to receive their income through taxation and revenues remain vulnerable to volatility in the economy. Borrowing policies may still be unwise or suited only to extended prosperity.

GENERAL FACTORS OF GOVERNMENTAL CREDIT ANALYSIS

Government credit analysis has long sought to identify the resources available to be taxed, which measure the ability to pay. It has also looked toward the record of actions taken, especially under adverse circumstances, which measures the willingness to live up to obligations that have been undertaken. For governments, analysts have reached agreement on the sensitivity of several factors: the extent and nature of debt obligations contracted; financial operations (including sources of revenues, spending requirements, and unencumbered money on hand); the structure of the government; and the economic and social characteristics of the populace which constitute the body politic.

STATE DEBT AND THE CONCEPT OF SOVEREIGNTY

The analysis of state bonds requires the same basic methods used in assessing the creditworthiness of any debt obligation of a government; however, state bonds differ from municipal bonds, although both have shared the benefit of tax exemption, primarily because of the aspects of sovereignty enjoyed by states. The analyst examining a state bond must first consider what sovereignty is and what it means. Sovereignty is defined as "supreme power especially over a body politic, an autonomous state." Each of the 50 states is sovereign within its own borders and has retained those powers which were not given to the federal government under the provisions of the United States Constitution.

The powers accorded to a state within the concept of sovereignty are of major interest to the bond analyst. The state can define its own ability to create debt and can levy taxes in any area not preempted by the federal government. Most importantly, it can repudiate debt without retribution as no state can be sued without its consent. Further, when sovereign immunity to suit has been waived, as is often the case, there is still no way for the bondholder to enforce the judgement; all disbursements must be by legislative appropriation. In addition to this legal distinction, state bond analysis varies from municipal bond analysis because of the broader base of the state. Any state has actual or potential debt incurring powers which transcend those of its creations, the municipal corporations. Its revenue base is broader and its economy larger and more diverse. While state resources and powers tend to lead to a higher level of creditworthiness, they can also lead to more rapid improvement or deterioration.

HISTORY OF STATE BORROWING

The first governmental borrowing on the North American continent occurred over 300 years ago. While this seems remote today, state and colonial debt history shows that the purposes for which states have borrowed remain amazingly constant over time. It can also identify the situations which have led either to default on payment or to sacrifice to live up to contractual responsibility. While history never quite repeats itself, similarities over time do emerge. Another reason for studying the debt history of states is that the legal provisions governing various aspects of debt, whether followed or by-passed, often exist to avert future repetition of past mistakes. To understand why and how one state borrows and another does not, the past is an excellent guide to the future.

State borrowing dates from 1690 when the Commonwealth of Massachusetts issued bills of credit. An expeditionary force had been sent to Quebec and was expected to receive its pay from the capture of booty. Unfortunately, the booty did not materialize. Upon the return of an army expecting recompense for its efforts, the Commonwealth issued the bills to the soldiers, for, it was said, the want of money in the treasury. Over the years, this reason has been a recurring cause of state borrowing. Massachusetts enlarged on the experiment and other colonies joined her. Reportedly, the bills were not legal tender but were valid for payment of property taxes (so they have been considered to be the forerunner of tax anticipation notes). As might be expected, the levy of taxes for repayment was delayed, the bills depreciated while they circulated, and eventually became interest bearing. During this period, refunding also occurred and borrowing to create loan funds was originated. Borrowing for money supply and to finance the Revolutionary War continued until 1789. In 1790, the newly created federal government assumed the debt of the states, in exchange for which they were forbidden to create money. This effectively curtailed state borrowing.

In the next period of state borrowing, beginning around 1820, debt was issued to finance internal improvements, largely for transportation. When the projects failed to produce adequate revenue, nine states defaulted in the mid-1840s and others narrowly avoided ignominy. While federal assumption was proposed, especially by bondholders, it was not again adopted and most states resumed payments in later years, although Mississippi repudiated certain of its debt. States borrowed heavily to finance the Civil War, and there were several repudiations by the states of the Confederacy. Reconstruction was also a period of state debt issuance with many of the bonds ending either in repudiation or in the scaling down of amounts owed.

In the later part of the nineteenth century, state debt increased, especially for highway financing, and this trend continued, supplemented by borrowing for rural credit. By the 1930s, borrowing expanded for purposes of relief and for aid to local governments which were then unable to meet their financial commitments. Some deficits were funded as well. During the Great Depression, only Arkansas defaulted, but other states, such as Tennessee, were forced to reorganize their debt to avoid nonpayment. World War II halted state borrowing expansion, as by that time the federal government was responsible for financing the conflict and national resources were directed to the war effort.

In the postwar period, state debt grew dramatically, propelled in part by the 1956 passage of the National System of Interstate and Defense Highway Act. The interstate system legislation provided for vast expenditure for highway construction, with the federal government contributing 90% and the states 10%, with actual construction done by the states. This both enlarged the scope of state financial operations and promoted borrowing. Education has also been a major force as states have become more responsible for financing their school systems. More recently, state borrowing has been directed toward economic development whether in the form of transportation, state building complexes (often for urban renewal purposes within declining inner-city areas in the state capital) and housing.

In 1990, long-term state debt was estimated by the U.S. Bureau of the Census at $315.5 billion of which $303.1 billion was classified to as having been issued for general government functions; of that amount, about half was allocated as public debt for private purposes. The current reporting method obscures the actual purposes for state borrowing but earlier series indicated around 11 to 12% for higher education, 7 to 8% for highways and 9% for hospitals.

The themes and variations of state borrowing continue to be repeated. States have shown a tendency to be more willing to borrow than to tax and economic development, in its many guises, has always been tantalizing. Over 300 years of history, the purposes of state debt have remained primarily the funding of deficits, transportation, and loan funding. New purposes are often in response to functional shifts under our federal system. Only once has the federal government assumed the debts of the states, but states have in various periods assumed the debts or the functions of the local units. Shifting responsibility among the various levels of government has expanded the role of states in recent years as the federal government has contracted domestically and local governments have lacked adequate funding resources to carry out their traditional functions. Default experience has tended to result from a change in expectations, from unwillingness to tax when projects fail, and from assumption of debts unable to be maintained under adverse economic conditions.

CONSTITUTIONAL LIMITS

Because of their sovereignty, states are limited in their borrowing capacity only by the provisions of the federal and their own constitutions. The constitution of the State of Vermont, adopted in 1790, does not even address debt, leaving all arrangements to statute. Most other New England constitutions are almost as liberal, allowing issuance solely by legislative approval. For other states, however, the power to incur debt is strictly limited. The common restrictions are:

(1) an outright prohibition of debt, except for defense or, minimally, to cover casual deficits:

(2) voter approval;

(3) a limitation related either to debt as a percent of property value or debt service as a percent of revenues.

These restrictions generally reflect a reaction to some adverse event in the past. The limit, while designed to address past failure, will likely become obsolete, representing an obstacle to be surmounted by creative interpretation.

A major development in state debt accumulation has come from the application and variation of the special fund doctrine. The special fund doctrine holds that debt secured by a dedicated revenue does not constitute legal debt. By application of the doctrine, for instance, bonds payable from a sales tax do not constitute "debt" within a legal meaning. Variations on the doctrine include the granting of indirect state credit through a pledge to make rental payments or replenishing deficiencies in a reserve fund promised to be maintained at a level equal to debt service on bonds issued by an agency or some similar device.

In many states, particularly Wisconsin and Georgia, the movement to circumvent unreasonable limitations led to the creation of authorities empowered to borrow to finance facilities to be leased back to the state, thus creating debt through a lease rental device. Other states such as Florida achieved the same purpose by dedication of taxes. The inefficiency and higher cost of such practices led to widespread constitutional reform in the 1960s and 1970s, when Wisconsin, Georgia, Florida, Minnesota, Montana, Washington, Illinois, Louisiana, Pennsylvania, and Virginia all adopted changes which liberalized borrowing requirements. At the same time, a counter-trend has been in motion. States such as New York, which requires voter approval, began to encourage borrowing by state agencies, with only a relatively infrequent use of the full credit of the state itself. Virginia has increasingly turned to non-general obligation borrowing despite its constitutional change.

Most state debt structures today include general obligation bonds, lease rental obligations, and their close kin, the appropriation bond, and perhaps debts issued by agencies with either a dedicated tax pledge or a statement of intent to replenish any deficiencies in a debt service reserve. The last, sometimes called a "moral obligation," can be interpreted to infer that the state is ultimately responsible for debt service, but there can be no legal enforcement. The types of debt are many and varied, generally reflecting either debt limits (constitutional or statutory) or the use of limited, rather than general, credit to back narrow-purpose projects.

DEBT FACTORS

Identification of Debt

The analyst must first identify all of the debt attributable to a state, regardless of the name of the issuer. Ideally, all contingent liabilities should be evident, and debt that does not currently require state support can be deducted. The resulting figure, classified as net tax supported debt, represents the debt now constituting a burden on financial resources. The amounts deducted and the contingencies represent what can conceivably in the future represent the full burden.

To assess the pledge of full faith and credit, the analysis must take into account the resources and prospects for the state. For general obligation debt supported by project revenues, the overall assessment should include both fundamental credit and an assessment of the viability of the project; failure of the project's earnings can only reduce general credit. For special tax debt, the yield of the tax in question must be a factor, as it is the legal source of payment, but, in turn, its strength depends on general credit factors. It is unlikely that special tax debt will have a standing superior to that of general credit unless the state in question has pledged away its major sources of revenue, or is in such financial disarray that the creditor will accept only an obligation backed by a major revenue source. In either of such cases, there is little left to support a general obligation.

Modern Debt Structures

State debt structures tend to be a result, or circumvention, of self-imposed restrictions on debt incurrence, largely originated from prior bad judgements. Historically, broad public purpose debt obligations have a better record than those issued for narrow special purposes. In the postwar period, when limited obligations have flourished, defaults have occurred in only a few instances. Moral obligation debts have been honored in several cases, including payments of an agency's debt service by the State of New York and the call of bonds by the State of Rhode Island. While limited or contingent commitments can easily be honored in prosperous periods, they may be susceptible when there is extreme stress. There has been little testing of this type of commitment. The adoption of generally accepted principles of accounting (GAAP) has helped to identify these instruments as obligations and should be a factor in enforcing responsibility.

Debt Measurements

After an examination of debt history, debt limitation and debt structuring, the next step is a measurement, both absolute and relative, of the debt burden of both the state and its constituent local governments. In several states, lack of accurate data precludes this practice, but a knowledge of state-by-state financing practices can be a rough guide.

Using state data alone, net and gross tax-supported debt can be related to a few standard measurements. One is per capita debt, which relates the burden of debt to the number of people benefited, although it does not reflect ability to pay. Relating state debt to the market value of property is generally imprecise but does provide a wealth measure. Perhaps the best measure is that of debt to personal income which is not only a wealth measure but is also related to the base on which state taxes are levied. Average debt ratios have changed little over the past three decades, excluding per capita figures which are distorted by inflation. Debt related to personal income on average has been in the 2 to 4% range while the relation to full value has been around 1%. In most states, ratios to personal income have declined since the mid 1970s, as borrowing increased less than inflation.

Debt service as a percent of revenues is an excellent measure of the burden of debt. It is most easily employed where there is an inclusive general fund and a highway fund. The measures are far less precise where there are several funds and several types of debt supported by earmarked taxes. Most states devote only a small portion of general revenues to debt service. An accepted upper limit is 8 to 10% with the average being closer to 2 to 5%. This measure should be used carefully, as a state with few functions and limited revenues may show a larger proportion of revenues devoted to debt service than a state which acts as general collector of revenues for its local units (which collections are in essence fixed costs). If figures were available, the best measure would be debt service as a percentage of revenues that can be freely appropriated.

Debt analysis should take note of the allocation of functions between state and local governments in each state to understand fully the meanings of high and low debt ratios. For example, the State of Hawaii has a relatively heavy debt burden with its local units having low burdens, due to state centralization, while in Indiana borrowing is done almost exclusively at the local levels.

FINANCIAL ANALYSIS

A major part of credit analysis depends on the assessment of both existing and available financial resources. Those available, but not used, belong more properly to the assessment of the underlying economy. While surplus, or unappropriated balance, is a handy guide, it only measures the amount of money in hand at any given time, before it is appropriated for operations or for special purposes. Surplus is most meaningful in states which have consistently employed it as a working balance to be used in recession and rebuilt in prosperity. So-called "rainy day" funds (very popular in the 1980s) have yet to meet this test. The massive revenue failures of 1989 through 1991 generally depleted this type of reserve, indicating that unless the situation is truly temporary the real rainy day fund role may be to delay needed financial decisions. Whether the reserves will be rebuilt remains to be seen. However, a good target level of surplus or reserve should be around 5% of general recurring revenue as casual non-realization of budget estimates rarely exceeds this amount.

State revenue systems will dictate the source of the government's working funds and should provide a measure of susceptibility to economic downturns. While diversity is a positive factor, both the recessions of the early 1980s and 1990s highlighted the reliance of the major taxes on the same employment and income base. In 1990, state revenue systems as a whole received 33% of total intake from sales taxes, 32% from individual income taxes, 7% from corporate taxes, and 10% from gas taxes and motor vehicle fees. In earlier years, distribution was quite different. In 1960, sales taxes provided 23%, individual income taxes only 12%, and highway revenues 25%. By 1970, the trend toward greater use of the broad based taxes was evident, with sales taxes accounting for 30% and individual income taxes rising to 19%; highway revenues had declined to 18%. Corporate taxes have contributed a stable 7 to 9% over the three decades. Federal aid has declined as a revenue contributor from around 22% in 1960 and 1970 to 19% now. Property taxes, perhaps the most stable and predictable source of government revenue, are not a factor overall in state revenue systems.

As revenue systems have shifted to reliance on sales and income taxes, they have become more susceptible to general economic conditions and more difficult to predict. Forecasting, which has become very precise, must rely on accurate economic information if it is to be valid and there is always a risk that the models will not properly reflect changes in taxpayer behavior. Financial vulnerability has also been increased by the practice of appropriating little or no surplus to cushion the effects for mis-estimation. The attraction of broad based taxes, which have large revenue-raising capacity and do not offend any one specific group, has also diminished the role of specific excise taxes, such as the gas tax. This has been detrimental to highway systems which typically rely on dedicated highway user taxes for their financing. Interim reporting on tax collections is of great value although not all states make such data available. Where possible, the analyst should measure them both against budget and against the previous year. The vulnerability of systems dependent on variable sources such as mineral or land income is obvious. A state's ability to achieve its revenue forecasts is essential to orderly budgeting. A sudden or unexpected revenue failure can lead to competition for available dollars among the government's functions, which include general debt service and a potential appropriation for a contingent liability.

Based on 1990 composite data furnished by the Bureau of the Census, total state expenditures were about $517 billion, excluding insurance trust accounts. Of the total, education accounted for 36%, social service for 20%, transportation 9%, health and hospitals 8%, and interest on general debt 4%. For individual states, there is considerable variation, but the percentages show the overall expenditure distribution of the states. Some 33% of the total was for intergovernmental purposes, more than half accounted for by education. The expenditure profile can indicate the burdens being placed on the state. Some states, such as Wisconsin and Minnesota act as tax collectors for their local units and have perhaps functioned as circuit breakers for rising property taxes by providing state-shared taxes for replacement purposes. Other states, such as New Hampshire, provide relatively little aid for their local units.

An assessment of public needs can be applied against the functions for which an individual state has declared responsibility. One guide is the relative local tax burden and the rate at which property values are accelerating. As tax rates rise and property values grow more rapidly than incomes, the property tax limitation movement has led to state assumption of costs or to heightened roles for fiscal intermediaries. In California and Massachusetts, voter-imposed limits on property taxation have led the former to more or less assume educational financing and the latter to increase vastly its share of local funding. Nevada has granted property tax relief through an increase in state-shared taxes. In the 1960s, when Minnesota first imposed a sales tax, it was identified as property tax relief and replaced a mill levy.

A careful analysis of expenditure patterns reveals the role of the state in public finance and indicates pressure points. Evidence of local strain has been apt to result in a future expansion of the state's responsibility. More recently, pressure at the state level is now leading to a devolution to the local level, either of functions supported by new taxing options or by an outright reduction of state aid.

ECONOMIC AND SOCIAL FACTORS

A state's economic activity provides the foundation for its debt and fiscal patterns. A strong state will have diverse employment, high wealth levels, forward-looking industries, educational and social characteristics which can support change, and sustained economic growth. In fact, few if any states can claim all these characteristics over time. Whether credit is best enhanced by consistent stability or by vibrant, if erratic growth remains problematic. States provide better statistical data for performance measurement than do local units. While Census statistics, including population, are generally available, employment data for states is more current and more detailed. Personal income is reported annually in great detail and on a more limited basis quarterly. On the other hand, specific economic events, such as the closing of a major industrial facility, are more easily analyzed on the local level.

Personal income per capita, its growth and its relation to regional and national averages remain excellent indicators of economic position. Long-term trend data highlights relative expansion or decline. Such data is particularly useful because of the relationship between personal income growth and the state revenue yield. Employment growth and the changing distribution within overall employment are equally valuable. Other statistics, such as weekly and hourly earnings by type of worker, aid in understanding the direction the economy is taking.

As the United States moves from an industrial to a service economy, a state's educational levels reflect the ability of its population to adapt successfully to this change. This awareness is underscored by today's emphasis on improving education in nearly every state.

Economic development is a major priority now. While it has many phases, including better education, vocational education, subsidies, and transportation, state policies should be investigated. The economy and its health dictate available revenues and often indicate the needs for borrowing. While expansion can rightly lead to greater spending and borrowing, an increase in debt and expenditure fit poorly with a stagnant or deteriorating economy.

INTERGOVERNMENTAL RELATIONS

The states occupy a vulnerable position in our federal system. Once supreme, they delegated many important powers to the federal government. The inability in the 1930s to collect locally levied revenue and the rise in social need led to a shift in power to the federal government, which was in a position to create money. As programs developed which involved federal-state cost sharing, the states began to increase the yield from their revenue systems. Today, with the federal government reducing its commitments to domestic areas, the states are developing approaches to social and economic problems, with or without adequate resources. To some extent, it can be said that state policies and activities are in response to federal policies.

The responsibilities of the states vis-á-vis their local units are unclear. Municipalities are the creations of states which provide for specific powers and duties. Yet, when municipalities are under stress, does the state have ultimate responsibility? When New York City faced crisis in 1975, the scope of the problem was too large for New York State to consider. In Ohio, when several school districts as well as Cleveland had severe difficulties, Constitutional interpretation turned to local responsibility. But, excluding the exceptions, generally states have relieved municipalities of burdensome taxation and expenditures in recent years.

The states are highly vulnerable to shifts in attitude or capacity from both the higher and lower levels of government. Their relative role has increased as their revenue systems have expanded. At the present time, they are being asked both to grant relief to their local governments and to assume functions formerly provided by the federal government.

Recent trends in state debt would indicate that the states have the capacity to carry a larger debt burden. Overall, debt has grown more slowly then resources. Not only is the average for debt as a percent of personal income about the same today as it was in 1960 but it is below the bulge of the 1970s. In addition, those states with a relatively high ratio have moved closer to the average. The most notable correlation is the constant and conservative relation between debt and resources.

ASSESSING STATE CREDIT

State general obligation bonds have traditionally been favorable credits, mostly classified in the high grade group, the top two rating categories. The primary reasons for the superior credit standing of state bonds include the already discussed powers of sovereignty as well as the long-established record of conservatism in both debt and financial operations.

Overall state credit quality has been declining, with a noticeable perception that few states should be accorded the top credit standing. Several general factors may be cited as contributory, especially the greater responsibilities taken on by the states which become non-discretionary expenditures. When coupled with revenue failure, the result has been a series of state financial crises, damaging creditworthiness. Improved financial reporting has made potential deficits known both more generally and more quickly, and press coverage of state financial operations has increased.

Whether state financial problems of recent years are of temporary or permanent nature is difficult to discern. There are some large areas involved in public discussion relating to federal-state-local financing responsibilities, and to the appropriate size and role of government at each level. The outcome as well as the course of the economy will provide the background for state credit considerations.

In summary, state bond analysis must be based on fundamental credit factors and their interrelationships. The approach should be modified by an understanding of the sovereign powers of states, particularly in the areas of debt policy and revenue raising. The strengths and weaknesses emanating from the reactive role of states in the federal system are major factors in understanding their actions and pressures. But the thoughtful analyst will also study the historical framework and the actual record of each individual state as well as the unique characteristics of states as a class of borrower.

LOCAL DEBT

The analysis of local debt obligations relies on an examination of the same basic factors crucial to all government credit—debt, financial operations, administrative or governmental factors, and the economy and social characteristics of the populace. Local governments lack sovereign characteristics as they are the creatures of their parents, the states, and have what powers have been allocated to them.

Local debt in 1989 was set by the U.S. Bureau of the Census at $502 billion, or about two-thirds of state and local debt combined. Local debt is diffuse as there are many types of governments and borrowers. Municipalities accounted for 40% of the total, followed in importance by special districts 28%, counties 22%, school districts 9% and townships 2%. (The school district proportion must be seen in context, as in many states, municipalities or counties are responsible for school financing.)

The primary functions of local government are education, public safety, streets, and provision of water and sewer services. Their service delivery is more direct than that of states and in general their constituencies are closer to and more involved in their governments. The primary funding base, other than intergovernmental aid, remains the property tax, at once both a more stable and predictable source and one that is under constant attack by constituents for relief.

Some aspects of local debt analysis are more tangible than that of state debt analysis, due to the smaller base and the specificity of the economy within the government's borders. This is offset by the dearth of current economic statistics as well as shortcomings in timeliness, and sometimes the content, of official economic information.

DEBT FACTORS

To assess local debt properly, all borrowing supported by the same tax base must be included. While at the state level, the comprehensive figure is called net tax supported debt, at the local level, it is called net direct and overlapping debt. This would include the debt for which the government itself is responsible (direct debt) and its share (based on estimated full value of property) of the debt of other jurisdictions having the same tax base, less any debt which is self-supporting from enterprise operations.

Most local debt is general obligation, although there are some states such as Indiana and Kentucky where the form is primarily lease rental, and others, such as New Mexico and Colorado where sales tax bonds are prevalent. Generally localities do not have the authority to enter into contingent commitments but the trend where possible has been to create enterprise operations which can issue bonds backed only by generated revenues (revenue bonds), with no claim on general credit.

Local general obligation bonds are attached to the local tax base and are either backed by an unlimited or limited property tax. The repayment promise is to levy on that tax base and the creditor may sue to enforce the promise, unlike the state general obligations where the promise to pay is usually unsecured. The traditional measurements of the weight of local debt are the per capita figure and the relationship of debt to estimated full value of property. (Personal income measurements are limited to the county level.) Permissible levels are somewhat hard to define as the functions vary among different types of governments, but in relation to full value, the figure of 10%

should serve as a top level beyond which serious questions should be raised, unless the unit is capitally intensive such as a park district where its levy is essentially for debt service.

Per capita figures again measure the burden per citizen but not the ability of the tax base to support debt. Probably not more than 8 to 10% of revenues should be devoted to debt service. On average, local debt burdens (debt as a percentage of full value) are probably in the range of 2 to 5%, again indicating that government borrowing has remained moderate. While local debt measurements are more precise than state burdens due to the direct relationship between the tax base (wealth) and the revenue system, there are problems. First, the accuracy of assessments has always been questionable. Secondly, developments of recent years may have created serious distortion.

In many areas of the country, real estate values have escalated far apace of the money income of their owners. In other words, many owners of expensive real estate are neither rich nor are they really able to afford the carrying costs of their asset. This has tended to show the burden of local debt as much lower than it probably is and the analyst should depreciate the full value figure by perhaps 20 to 30% to get an accurate reading of the true tax base. This development has also been a factor in the shifting of financial responsibility upward to the states in the wake of widespread resistance to local tax increases.

FINANCIAL CONSIDERATIONS

Local finances are very different from state finances but own source revenues account for over 60% of local revenues in aggregate, with the state aid about 33%. The property tax continues to be the major own source revenue provider, 74%, in 1989. The trend has been away from property taxes, which in 1969 were 85% of the total. The major other sources of local revenue have been particularly the sales tax, which rose from 7% in 1969 to 15% in 1989, with income taxes rising from 4% to 6%. Possibly the states were developing the income tax for themselves, letting local units add to the sales tax level which has been more acceptable because an element of choice has been seen as involved.

Local expenditures remain concentrated in education, 42% of the total, with none of the other items such as public safety, health and hospitals, sewerage and solid waste, accounting for as much as 10%. With notable exceptions such as New York, most local governments are not responsible for the burgeoning costs of welfare and Medicaid. However, education and public safety are notably labor intensive and place pressure not only on current operations but also on such areas as pension funding.

Local budgeting differs from state budgeting. It is more rational as likely expenditures can be identified and the tax level with provision for uncollectibles can be set. While more predictable, the practical limits are what the citizens will bear.

The property tax has been an area of great pressure on local governments for over a decade. Statewide movements such as Proposition 13 in California and $2^1/2$ in Massachusetts are well known, but there have also been many local referenda accomplishing the same purpose. In 1990, Oregon adopted a tax limitation which directly accomplished what the others had done indirectly. It shifted funding of school costs largely to the state. While this is a direct and specified mandate, the result of other initiatives relating to the property tax, whether enacted or threatened, lead to the same result.

In the 1950s and 1960s, local governments looked to Washington for help with financial problems, and it is meaningful that today the largest item of federal aid is housing and community development, a holdover from the urban fears of yesterday. Today the local governments have been looking to the states for help which they have received, largely for property tax relief. The trend now is reversing. States are looking downward, as they seem to have reached their political limits on the ability to raise revenue and their financial resources must increasingly be devoted to the social purposes formerly the preserve of the federal government, which is now deeply involved in containment of domestic expenditure.

ECONOMIC CONSIDERATIONS

The economy of a community is generally definable. Diversity and stability can be identified through the top tax payers and employers which are usually available and in addition plant closings or openings are announced. As the country has shifted from manufacturing toward services, the suburban community has become stronger credit while the urban area has become weaker.

The best profile for a good municipal credit is wealth, a stable and educated populace, and an economy based on the future. This is seen rarely and in fact, the analyst looks for prudent debt which can be supported by the tax base, for stable financial operations, untroubled by tax revolt.

SUMMARY

In summary, local credit is much more diffuse than state credit. There are many more local governments, either with a general or a special purpose. Local governments have always been dependent upon the property tax to finance their operations, which primarily concern education and other basics of community life. States have taken over increasing burdens from local governments, to some extent politically, when federal government support receded.

But today states are in no financial condition to continue this path and in fact are now beginning to divest of previously assumed burdens. Local governments have no lower levels on which to devolve responsibilities, except for the citizenry, through termination of service provision. As financial pressure continues at all governmental levels, this may increasingly be an option that is exercised. The best municipal credits are those which have learned to relate to their citizenry, contain expenditures within resources and look to themselves rather than to other levels of government.

CHAPTER 10

Revenue Bond Credit Analysis

David Ambler

James Burr

Katherine McManus

Howard Mischel

Diana Roswick
Moody's Investors Service—Public Finance Department

In his book, *The Power Broker,* Robert Caro describes how Robert Moses assembled an empire of potent public agencies in part by attending to the minutiae of the authorizing legislation and the indentures for various revenue bonds, issued to fund the construction of bridges, highways and other public projects throughout New York. Because these revenue bond indentures allowed excess toll revenues to flow annually back to the issuing agency, Moses was able to amass substantial financial muscle that could be applied to numerous other capital projects. Moses' empire building aside, the anecdote graphically illustrates a fundamental aspect of the revenue bond that sets it apart from a general obligation bond, and which is key to understanding creditworthiness. This aspect is that the essential legal nature and structure of a revenue bond—its pledged revenues, flow of funds, events of default, and all

Moody's would like to acknowledge the contribution of Alfred Medioli to this publication.

other characteristics—are not at all generic. They are, instead, very particular to the individual revenue bond indenture, which creates a distinct legal universe specific for that bond. Revenue bonds tend to be unique, created and defined to fit particular financing situations.

Revenue bond credit analysis, therefore, must be equally attuned to those particular situations and the specific set of legal rules created in each indenture. Most important, because revenue bonds by definition are dependent on a particular revenue, the source, context, and variability of that revenue are paramount.

While revenue bonds have been in use since the 1930s, it is only in the past several decades that they have become relatively common. Indeed, once they were considered to be fairly radical financing instruments. Instead of the all-encompassing general obligation pledge, here was a bond pledging repayment from a single source of revenues only, often derived from a single facility, whose construction and subsequent use may well have posed risks. It was this narrowness of pledge and its association with project finance and limited purpose authorities that caused revenue bonds to require various legal protections such as reserve funds, rate covenants and additional bonds tests. This association with riskiness was not unfounded. Among the largest of the very infrequent municipal bond defaults in the United States have been project revenue bonds, such as those of the Washington Public Power Supply System and large toll road undertakings such as the Chesapeake Bay Bridge and Tunnel or the Calumet Skyway.

But much has changed since the 1930s as well. Revenue bonds became more common, particularly with the advent of national environmental legislation beginning in the late 1960s, where the condition for the receipt of federal pollution abatement grants encouraged the use of revenue bond financing. Since then, environmental issues—whether relating to air quality, water pollution, sewage, storm drainage, or solid waste—have continued to drive much of the public finance revenue bond market. And over this period, the municipal enterprises set up to operate water, electric, or sewer operations have grown and matured, and otherwise demonstrated their long term reliability.

REVENUE BOND CREDIT RATINGS

As with the credit assessment of any debt obligation, a credit evaluation of a revenue bond involves a judgment about the issuer's willingness and ability to pay. In general, because of the narrower pledge, revenue bonds tend to have lower credit ratings than general obligation bonds. Indeed, only 0.6% of the revenue bonds rated by Moody's Investors

Services have ratings that are in the two highest rating categories, *Aaa* and *Aa1*, as compared with almost 3.0% for general obligation bonds. Conversely, a greater portion of revenue bonds bear "below investment grade" ratings (that is, ratings below *Baa*)—2.2% compared with 0.8% for general obligation bonds.

On the other hand, many revenue bonds are strong enough to achieve a high quality rating of *Aa*. Some 9.4% of revenue bonds are rated *Aa* by Moody's, a figure which compares favorably with the proportion of general obligation bonds that are rated *Aa* (9.1%).[1] In some instances, a revenue bond, particularly one issued for a purpose that is integral to municipal operations, can be equal in credit quality to a general obligation from the same issuer. After all, the same citizens, whether they are paying through property taxes or user charges, are supporting the debt. Occasionally, the revenue bond is the stronger of the two securities. One advantage that many enterprise systems enjoy is a relative insulation from the political process, including the ramifications of voter resistance to property tax increases. Related to this is the typical ability of revenue systems to enforce payment for services; a water or electric system will turn off your service in a month or two after a non-payment notice, whereas a repossession and tax sale of property can be highly politicized and take years. Even for non-essential enterprise systems, payment enforcement is strong—you can't get into a stadium or onto a toll bridge without paying up front. For all these reasons, it is not uncommon to see a revenue enterprise system with more stable financial operations than the General Fund of the same municipality. In fact, as some general government credits weaken, because of limited revenue raising powers and rising, often legally mandated social service costs, the enterprise systems serving that same area can well remain secure because of their financial strengths.

ESSENTIALITY VS. DISCRETIONARY USE: THE VITAL QUESTION OF DEMAND

Because the revenue bond by definition is secured by a narrow stream of revenues, as opposed to the all-encompassing general obligation pledge, the scope of the enterprise system producing that single stream of revenues becomes paramount to credit analysis. Specifically, the linkage of a revenue bond to the local economic base depends on the extent, importance, and simple need for the enterprise

---

[1] All figures cited exclude ratings based on credit enhancements.

itself. This may effectively place a ceiling on the creditworthiness of the bond that other factors—such as debt level and structure, or financial performance—may not be able to raise. Thus, a bond secured by the net revenues of an essential, citywide enterprise such as water supply can be as strong as the citywide economy itself, because the absolute need for water ensures that system usage—and the flow of water system net revenues—will mirror the performance of the citywide economy. If the economy is thriving, the creditworthiness of the revenue bond may be very high indeed, subject to other factors such as the system's physical condition, capital needs, debt load, financial operations, and management.

The citywide water system may be contrasted with several other examples. A bond secured by the net revenues of a convention center, for instance, is only tenuously linked to the city economy. While everyone within the city may use the convention center, this use is entirely discretionary, and depends on such variables as the attractiveness of the center's shows and exhibitions, and the cost of admission. Thus, the demand for a convention center is likely to be very difficult to predict with any degree of accuracy, and will exhibit much greater elasticity than will demand for the water system's essential service.

A parking revenue bond is similarly subject to much discretionary and price-sensitive usage, but unlike the convention center, a parking system composed of only a few garages will not even be available to the larger city economy. The economic base of the parking system may be only those few square blocks within walking distance of the garages, and may have very little to do with the city's

TABLE 10.1
Relative Demand for Revenue Bond-Financed Services and Facilities

Essential	Important but Demand-sensitive	Discretionary, Non-essential
public power	toll bridge, highway	convention center
water	mass transit	
sanitary sewer	university	parking facility
storm drainage	commercial airport	stadium
solid waste disposal	major hospital	marina
	non-potable water supply	general aviation airport
	seaport	golf, tennis, skating facilities, etc.

larger economy. The credit analysis in this case becomes as specific as that for a real estate transaction. In addition to price elasticity and the vagaries of the several-square-block economy, the parking revenue flow is also subject to a third variable that of competition from street and lot parking as well as other garages. Airports, ports, universities and colleges, toll bridges and highways, and health care facilities are similarly subject to competitive pressures of varying geographic extent. The several large toll facility revenue bond defaults mentioned earlier all resulted from significantly weaker-than-forecast demand that resulted in part from competition from non-toll highways.

FEASIBILITY STUDIES

Because the issue of demand is such an important variable for the creditworthiness of any revenue bond, a new revenue financing (as opposed to a refunding) is typically accompanied by a feasibility analysis that addresses the reasonableness of demand forecasts and the projected revenue flows. For a long-established and essential infrastructure system with a demonstrated service area demand, demand forecasting may be relatively simple unless the financing involves a major new extension of service. However, for more discretionary and non-essential enterprises, much greater depth of forecast analysis is typically required, including elasticity and sensitivity studies. In the case of facilities such as ports and hub airfields, the demand largely depends on private transportation operators—air carriers and shipping lines—and the analysis must commensurately extend to these industrial sectors.

Feasibility studies typically include information that ranges from data on the physical and engineering aspects of a project, to economic and operational concerns and, of critical importance, the estimation of operating revenue and expenses. Whether the feasibility study speaks to technical feasibility, financial feasibility, or both, credit analysts must carefully consider the comprehensiveness of the data and the assumptions behind it, because there is an enormously wide range in the scope and quality of these studies. Because there is as much art as science in the preparation of a feasibility study, the fact that the study concludes that a project is feasible offers no assurance of the ultimate financial success and long-term credit quality of the bonds issued to finance the capital project under consideration.

A well-structured feasibility study ought to go beyond simply identifying the likely users of the enterprise service, projecting levels of consumption and concluding with a projection of the issuer's ability to pay and debt service coverage. Key components to look for in a feasibility study include:

(1) A project overview, including a description of the purpose and scope of the project proposed, including cost estimates and contingencies, future financing requirements, and sources of funding.

(2) A description of existing facilities or system, if any, in both physical and operational terms.

(3) A project construction schedule, including any future financing and construction required.

(4) A definition of major financial and operating policies, including key conditions, assumptions, laws, policies, or other factors that will affect operations or the conduct of business.

(5) An analysis of project demand or needs survey, including a discussion of competitive issues, where appropriate. This may include comparison with other similar systems currently in operation.

(6) An analysis of both historical and anticipated operating trends.

(7) An analysis of historical and anticipated revenue and expenditure trends.

(8) An evaluation of customer base and user trends.

(9) Debt service requirements.

(10) Estimates of future rates and charges that will be necessary to provide sufficient revenues and their feasibility, including socioeconomic/demographic considerations.

(11) A discussion of revenue and expenditure performance under the indenture which may differ from GAAP.

(12) Revenue and expenditure reconciliation between GAAP and indenture accounting.

(13) A discussion of the derivation of rates and charges under the ordinance or other agreements.

(14) A comparison to costs at competing facilities.

(15) A description of the methodology and assumptions employed in the preparation of the study.

(16) Conclusions and recommendations.

There have been numerous cases presented over the years of unrealistic performance expectations and flawed projections. In some cases, this can be directly attributed to the quality of work by the party which prepared the study: either erroneous, overly optimistic assumptions are made or insufficient attention is paid to key variables.

Sources of information may be questionable, or inadequate effort put into analyzing the historical experience of the particular industry or enterprise. Since it is rare to see a study that does not endorse the feasibility of a project, careful scrutiny and healthy skepticism are critical to an effective evaluation of a study's results.

NET VS. GROSS REVENUE: OPERATIONS AND THE MATTER OF LEGAL PLEDGE

If an enterprise system is a legally closed or self-contained one, as defined by its own indenture, it is typically also a closed system in terms of financial operations. It carries out its services, pays its employees and its suppliers, maintains its plant and vehicles, and funds its capital needs out of the charges imposed for the services it provides. It typically has no taxing power and no revenue-raising ability not directly linked to its basic role of service provider. Unlike many other municipal operations that issue debt, it closely approximates the workings of a business; like a business, it may also make in-lieu-of-tax payments to the related local general government. And thus, long term credit quality depends on the continued, business-like operation of the enterprise to provide services and generate revenues.

For these critical reasons, the use of a gross revenue pledge—wherein debt service payments are made before payment of operating and maintenance (O&M) costs—does not provide any meaningful improvement in credit quality over a net revenue pledge, wherein debt service is paid after O&M costs. In either case, a net revenue analysis is necessary because of the direct linkage between credit quality and the long term viability of the enterprise itself. It should be noted that this concern extends well beyond the matters of annual O&M and debt service. "Long-term viability" also includes the condition of plant and related capital needs, the retention and protection of rate-making flexibility, managerial quality and stability, and other attributes of a truly businesslike enterprise operation.

COVERAGE AND OTHER MEASURES OF RESILIENCE

Traditional revenue bond credit analysis has often focused on debt service coverage as a primary indicator of credit quality—the higher the coverage of annual debt service by annual system net revenues, the better the credit quality. In certain of the generic, non-essential or demand sensitive enterprise systems described above, relatively high levels of coverage are in fact desirable because they can offset various exogenous events affecting demand that are simply too difficult to predict with any accuracy. These kinds of events would include the creation of a successful competing convention center, international labor or trade agreements that alter the economics of steamship companies, or the ability of a private developer to build a competitive parking garage.

On the other hand, in certain enterprise systems, the revenue and legal structure can render debt coverage virtually meaningless as a credit factor. For most airport revenue bonds, for example, basic funds flow is governed primarily by the set of airport/air carrier operating agreements that exist outside the bond indenture itself. In many cases, these agreements stipulate that air carriers cover all airport operating expenses and debt service up to the covenanted amount, and no higher. The resulting 125% annual debt service coverage thus demonstrated by most large airports reveals very little of these airports' relative ability to repay debt.

While essential service public enterprise systems tend not to have the coverage-limiting, external funds flow dependence typical of airports, too much can be made of debt service coverage at the expense of other, very relevant issues. Such issues include service area economy, price or cost of service, condition of plant, and the overall efficiency and quality of system management. The legislative or legal ability of most enterprise systems to raise rates quickly is also critical, and is an important difference between many municipal enterprises and private utilities, which are more often subject to regulatory rate review. In this sense, long-term credit quality can be seen as a measure of resilience, or the ability of the enterprise system to respond to reasonably foreseeable events while continuing to operate the system and pay debt service.

While many of these factors are not directly quantifiable, there are useful analytic ratios that are not related to debt service, including operating ratio and net take down. The operating ratio expresses operating expenditures as a percentage of operating revenues, and essentially measures the comfort margin between annually recurring costs and revenues. An enterprise system that must rely on non-recurring, non-operating revenues (such as investment income or water/sewer connection fees linked to building permit activity) is thus a potentially weak credit. The net take-down measures the overall net annual profitability of the system, or net revenue as a percentage of gross system earnings. Each of these ratios can be compared across types of systems to test for aberrations or unusual patterns from year to year which could reveal either stability or vulnerability.

EVALUATING DEBT LEVELS AND STRUCTURES

For most enterprise systems, debt levels are likely to look high relative to those for tax-supported debt of the same issuer. This is because the scope of an enterprise system's assets cannot compare to the wealth encompassed in a tax base. A commonly used measure for evaluating the relative debt load of an enterprise system is the "debt ratio," a figure calculated by dividing a system's debt (net of debt reserves and other debt service funds) by its fixed assets and working capital. The debt ratio reflects the system's reliance on debt financing relative to its assets and also assesses its capacity to support additional debt. Because the capital needs of different types of enterprises vary widely, different types of revenue systems have to be judged by separate standards. For example, airports tend to have more complex and extensive capital needs, relative to their assets, than water or sewer systems. Not surprisingly, a typical debt ratio for an airport is more than twice that for a water and sewer system (57% versus 27%).[2] Some revenue systems have debt ratios approaching 100%. This is not necessarily a negative credit factor if the system is well managed and its capital plans are reasonable. (See Table 10.2.)

Debt structure can be as important as debt levels. In general, long-term fixed-rate debt instruments that have lives no longer than the projects being financed are appropriate. These instruments allow annual debt service costs to be predictable and to occur over a time period when users are getting maximum benefit from the respective project. Debt structures that involve heavy reliance on short-term instruments, such as bond anticipation notes and variable rate obligations, subject the issuer to market conditions, which can fluctuate. Moreover, they can make planning, forecasting and rate-setting more difficult. The ability to handle short-term and variable rate debt depends on the extent of the system's cash reserves, the sophistication of management, and the ease with which user charges can be raised when needed.

EVALUATING MANAGEMENT

Since each enterprise faces challenges that can vary greatly, it is difficult to devise a standard by which to evaluate management.

[2] Moody's Investors Service Public Finance Department, 1992 *Medians, Selected Indicators of Municipal Performance.*

TABLE 10.2
Moody's Financial and Debt Medians for Selected Enterprise Systems

	Water	Sewer	Electric Distribution	Electric Generation and Transmission	Airport
Operating Ratio (%)[1]	64.6	62.4	88.2	76.3	54.00
Net Take-Down (%)[2]	41.7	44.4	14.5	29.1	49.8
Debt Service Coverage (x)[3]	2.2	2.0	2.9	2.3	1.7
Debt Service Safety Margin (%)[4]	19.1	24.6	11.0	15.6	21.4
Debt Ratio (%)[5]	32.1	29.9	32.9	50.4	56.9

Source: Moody's Investors Service, Public Finance Department, *1992 Medians, selected Indicators of Municipal Performance.*

[1] Operating and maintenance expenses divided by total operating revenues.

[2] Net revenues divided by gross revenue and income.

[3] Net revenues divided by principal and interest requirements for year.

[4] Net revenues less principal and interest requirements for year divided by gross revenue and income.

[5] Net funded debt divided by the sum of net fixed assets plus net working capital.

However, an analyst must determine to what extent management dictates the direction of the enterprise, as this is an important facet of credit assessment. Management's ability to interact with political, natural, and regulatory forces without severely compromising its agenda is the key to this portion of municipal credit analysis.

The key in assessing the proficiency of system management is to look beyond any group of individuals and determine to what degree strong managerial practices and philosophies are institutionalized within the enterprise's organization. Analyzing practices, such as budgeting techniques, methodologies for capital planning, construction management programs, and responsiveness to regulatory pressures are good indicators of management's effectiveness. More often than not, an organization that has institutionalized strong managerial programs also displays a historically stable and cohesive relationship between the board and administrative staff. At times, however, relationships between these parties can become politically charged, especially if an election is pending, often to the detriment of effective management of the system. Determining the nature of these relationships requires a good degree of analytical judgment. Review of the board's voting records, campaign issues of a recent election, attendance levels at public hearings, and coverage by local print media can often add insight into the assessment of managerial cohesiveness.

PROTECTION PROVIDED BY BOND COVENANTS

Since the legally pledged security for revenue bonds is a limited one, the market has historically demanded that additional legal protections be built into the legal documents as a condition of purchasing these bonds. Strong legal covenants in and of themselves cannot guarantee strong debt security. The underlying fundamentals—a satisfactory customer base, good finances, manageable debt levels, and the like—must be present for debt to be well-secured. Bond covenants can require certain debt service coverage levels, but if there is lower-than-expected demand for the project's services and the system cannot raise adequate revenues, the system will be unable to meet the coverage requirement.

Because of the inherent limitations of legal covenants in preventing a default and the generally successful track record that revenue bonds have demonstrated, bond covenants have tended to become less stringent over time. Nevertheless, they continue to play an important role for three reasons. First, revenue bond covenants can provide bondholders with some protection in helping to avert a bankruptcy or default. Second, they can provide bondholders with remedies in the event that a bankruptcy or default does occur. Finally, bond covenants tend to promote more prudent management by creating certain ground rules for financial operations. The weaker and riskier the enterprise, the greater the need for strong legal protections to promote financial discipline and diffuse the potential for default.

In addition to the pledge of revenues (net versus gross) discussed earlier, among the legal protections typically found in bond documents are provisions for the debt service reserve fund, rate covenant, flow of funds requirements, additional bonds test, investment limitations and, with some financings, a mortgage of the underlying asset.

Debt Service Reserve Fund

Historically, the debt service reserve fund, financed from bond proceeds at a level equal to maximum annual debt service, served two functions:

(1) it bought time for a workout to prevent a default in the event of a catastrophe or some occurrence that could lead to a shortfall in pledged revenues to pay the debt; and

(2) it served notice that, in the event the reserve fund had to be tapped to pay bondholders, serious and timely actions would be taken (a "tripwire" use).

While these functions are still valuable, the debt service reserve fund has been reduced in importance by the provisions of the 1986 Tax Reform Act, which reduced the maximum funding of a debt service reserve fund to 10% of the issue size; and by a growing recognition that for strong issuers, the likelihood of the debt service reserve fund being needed was minimal. However, for project financings, where adverse developments cannot be shared over an entire system, or even for weak systems, the reserve fund is still important as a security feature.

Rate Covenant

The rate covenant is a legal pledge whereby the obligor agrees to set rates and charges sufficiently high so as to generate adequate funds to cover operating costs and debt service. The purpose of the covenant is to ensure that rates and fees are set high enough to ensure payment of debt service, even in the event of a major shortfall in revenues or unplanned increase in expenditures. Initially, rate covenants provided for substantial coverage (net revenue would be required to cover debt service by a minimum of 1.5–2.0 times). More recently, however they have become much less stringent, sometimes only calling for 1.0 times coverage. Even though the typical rate covenant has weakened, for most enterprise systems actual coverage is usually higher—often by a significant amount—than the legally required minimum.

Flow of Funds

The *flow of funds* requirements reflect the process by which monies are allocated to the various funds held under the trust indenture. Typically, revenues are deposited as received into a general revenue fund, from which funds flow out, in the following order: to pay operations and maintenance costs; debt service; replenish the debt service reserve fund if depleted for any reason; fund a depreciation or maintenance fund; and fund contingencies or a rate stabilization fund.

One key analytic issue is whether funds may flow totally out of the system, for example, to a parent government to pay overhead expenses or general obligation debt supported by a subordinate claim on revenues, or must be retained within the system (*open* and *closed* loops, respectively). There are obvious benefits to bondholders of retaining funds within the system, either as working capital or to finance *pay-as-you-go* capital projects, rather than issuing additional debt. At the same time, the need to generate sufficient funds to pay general obligation bonds may be beneficial to holders of revenue debt that has a senior claim on net revenues of the system.

A related point is that, because funds flow first to pay senior lien debt, senior lien obligations will often be of higher credit quality than the same system's junior lien revenue debt. It should be noted, however, that the credit distinction between senior and junior lien bonds is unlikely to be large, since an enterprise system must generate enough revenues to remain an ongoing concern and to cover all its obligations.

The deposit of all system revenues to a *lock-box*, held by the revenue bond trustee, can be beneficial in ensuring that all monies pledged to bondholders flow through the trustee. Similarly, the inclusion of a rate stabilization fund, whether in an open- or closed-loop system, may provide additional security to bondholders by reducing the need for required rate increases under adverse economic conditions or other undesirable circumstances.

Additional Bonds Test

The additional bonds test requires the issuer to demonstrate that the revenue stream is sufficient to pay both the old and the new debt as a condition to new issuances. This test is intended to ensure that future debt issuance does not reduce bondholder security by placing too high a burden on the revenue stream. Early tests required that financial results reflect actual coverage of both old and new debt service costs by actual historical net revenues of the system or project by several multiples of the maximum annual debt service on both old and new bonds. Gradually, as the market became more comfortable with revenue bonds and began to recognize the detrimental effects of unnecessarily high debt service coverage as a legal requirement, required coverage levels began to decrease and various special adjustments could be made to demonstrate sufficient coverage. In addition, a variety of other debt instruments—variable rate demand obligations, commercial paper, subordinate lien bonds, and so on—were often not readily susceptible to treatment under a conventional test and, as a result, were not made subject to the test. These various factors, in turn, served to undermine the importance of the classical test, rendering it very weak, if not meaningless in some cases. The additional bonds test, if it is a "true" and reasonable test, can help promote appropriate debt management and can be a favorable credit factor, particularly for weaker systems or those that are growing very rapidly.

Investment Limitations

Limitations on the investment of monies held under the revenue bond trust indenture are particularly critical for stand-alone project financings. In the absence of a refunding or the issuance of additional completion bonds, the inability to complete the project will preclude the generation of revenues to pay bondholders. In the case of a system with existing revenue-generating capacity, these concerns are somewhat mitigated, since debt service costs can be spread over the system through rate increases until additional funds can be found. Nonetheless, prudent investment is always desirable. In order to allay any concerns about default risk related to investments, investments should be limited to government securities or federal agencies, highly rated corporate or municipal debt, highly rated asset-backed investments and repurchase/ reverse repurchase agreements with rated counterparties and structural protections to meet counterparty bankruptcy concerns. Avoiding obvious market rate risks by matching investment maturities with expected needs should not be overlooked, even for a revenue bonds supported by system, rather than project, revenues.

Mortgages

Historically, revenue bond legal documents incorporated a grant to the trustee for the benefit of the bondholders of a mortgage on the property or facility being financed. This was instituted ostensibly to increase bondholder security in the event of a default. Currently, many municipal market participants place little analytic weight on this provision. This reflects the belief that enforcement of this legal remedy (i.e., foreclosure on the public facility) would probably be precluded as a matter of public policy, if the property or facility were to any degree to be deemed essential to the public safety or welfare. In the case of a 501(c)(3) borrower, such enforcement might not be precluded as a post-default remedy. However, the nature of the financed facility might limit its ready disposal without a significant loss to bondholders. More important, however, is that any such remedy would only be exercisable after the occurrence of a default.

Recent Changes in U.S. Bankruptcy Code

Revenue bondholders should benefit from recent changes in Chapter 9 of the U.S. Bankruptcy Code in the event that the issuer of their bonds files a petition for bankruptcy. First, the risk to bondholders that debt service payments could be disgorged as voidable preferences has been eliminated by the abolition of the concept of preference for municipal bonds and notes. Second, possible delays in payments to bondholders under the "automatic stay" provision (section 362(a)) to trustee-held debt service payments has been eliminated for holders of bonds supported by "special revenues," which would include most, if not all, revenue bondholders. Finally, the lien on system revenues possessed by the bondholders is not extinguished post-bankruptcy, as would be the case in a corporate or other bankruptcy filing. These changes are beneficial to bondholders, but are applicable only post-bankruptcy, whether or not there has been a default on the actual bonds.

TYPES OF ENTERPRISE SYSTEMS

In evaluating a revenue bond, the credit analyst must first decide whether the debt is issued for a "simple" or "complex" system. While most revenue bonds reflect the pledge and operations of a "simple" single enterprise, the financing of very large facilities—power plants, central sewage treatment complexes, or water systems—is often done as a joint effort by several individual enterprise systems. Many smaller cities, for example, might pool their resources to build an otherwise unaffordable plant. This is typically achieved through the workings of a *joint action* or *joint powers agency* (JPA), which adds a level of legal and administrative issues to the credit analysis. These issues include such elements as the strength of the administering authority's oversight powers; the nature of the individual participant's payment as a form of parity net revenue pledge or simple operating payment; and the specific commitment of the various participants to make up any shortfalls in the payments of others, such as through a step-up provision. Another variation of the complex system is a single issuer pledging the revenues of a combined or multiple utility system, wherein an analysis of the component systems is appropriate.

Whether simple or complex in nature, each enterprise system must be evaluated in light of the technical, regulatory, and operational issues that are particular to its industry. Following is a brief discussion of some of the unique analytical concerns for different types of enterprises.

Enterprise Systems that Provide Essential Services

Water and Sewer. Many of the key issues for water and sewer systems involve compliance with environmental mandates, most notably the Clean Water Act. Meeting federal and state standards for such things as secondary and tertiary treatment of sewage is often costly and complicated. Moreover, in the process of meeting these mandates, many older, urban sewer enterprises need to address problems stemming from the fact that they have combined systems for storm and sanitary sewers. Because separating the two functions is expensive, municipalities tend to look for alternatives, such as building retention facilities or developing methods to keep potential overflows within sewer lines for longer periods. Arranging for sludge disposal is also a growing problem. It should be pointed out that while most systems are grappling with making improvements to meet environmental mandates, the paramount issue for other systems, such as those in California, is the procurement of an adequate water supply. In these cases, an assessment of the quality and sufficiency of the potential water source will be a key credit concern.

Credit assessment of water and sewer debt has taken on new dimensions with changing financing trends. Major water and sewer problems initially involved bigger urban systems, most of which issued their own debt. In recent years, however, there has been a proliferation of debt issues for smaller systems. This has resulted in an increased use of pooled financings for water and sewer purposes. The replacement of federal grant programs with *state revolving funds* (SRFs), backed in part by the revenues of water and sewer systems, has introduced additional credit issues. For pooled financings and SRFs, credit analysis must focus on the operations of the individual water and sewer system participants as well as on the structural characteristics of the pool.

Public Power. Many of the key analytic concerns for public power involve the type of system (generation, transmission and/or distribution), the nature and source of the power supply, and the ability of the system to meet baseload and peak demand in the most cost-effective way. Generating systems typically have greater capital needs than distribution systems. However, they also have more control over their power supply as well as the ability to enhance revenues by selling excess power. The credit quality of debt sold by generating systems reflects the value of their power relative to that of other providers, including investor-owned utilities. In contrast, the credit quality of distribution systems reflects the nature and structure of their power purchase contracts. In either case, electric systems operate in a more competitive environment than enterprises such as water and sewer systems and need to deal with this in the rate-setting process.

A key determinant of rates for electric enterprises is the cost of their fuel sources relative to alternatives. Complicating the analysis of the relative strengths of various fuel sources is the fact that changes in the economy and regulatory climate can make an enormous difference. Oil and gas were considered cheap until the Arab oil embargo, and are now again relatively inexpensive. Nuclear power was originally seen by many as a cost-effective way to provide massive amounts of new energy but has obvious safety and environmental concerns, highlighted by the incident at Three Mile Island. Currently, reliance on coal, particularly low sulfur coal, is an advantage, since such power plants can more easily comply with Clean Air Act standards.

A final key analytic concern for many larger power systems is the nature of the contracts between the JPA and its participants. *Take-or-pay* contracts (in which each participant must pay whether or not it receives service) are stronger than *take-and-pay* contracts (in which each participant only pays if it receives service). It should be noted, however, that while take-or-pay contracts have been upheld in some states, such as Massachusetts, they remain untested in most states. Of course, if the power project is not economically viable, there will be more incentive on the part of the participants to find legal means to negate their obligations.

Solid Waste/Resource Recovery. The creation of resource recovery facilities is a step in the evolution of solid waste disposal from a concern to a full-blown enterprise. Only a few systems have so matured. Major credit issues for resource recovery facilities include the choice of technology, political difficulties in siting facilities, and the role of the vendor in project design, construction and operation. Issues of technology and politics have rendered most single-facility approaches obsolete in favor of a more flexible "system approach" including the use of landfills and other alternatives to mass burn and other resource recovery facilities. The flow of funds is usually a key credit issue and typically, the general government must be willing to be a "deep pocket" to cover operating deficits until the facility is self-supporting.

Storm Water/Flood Control. This type of enterprise debt reflects the recognition and growth of an essentially new utility. While storm drainage had generally been addressed as part of street and road operations, it has become a more critical and broader concern with the extensive suburbanization of development in 1980s, and the consequent problems with increased storm water runoff. Storm water utilities mix land-use controls and planning with *hard* construction (channels, catch basins, and the like), *soft* measures (such as the preservation and maintenance of swales, ravines, and other natural drainage features).

An interesting credit aspect of a storm water/flood control system is the adaptation of the traditional revenue bond to a system providing a service that, although essential, reflects non-metered "consumption." The problem of how to charge users fairly for the storm water system has typically been solved through the generation of a "runoff coefficient," similar to a user fee, for each parcel of property, which assesses that property's contribution to the storm water problem based on parcel type, size, and amount of paving. This type of assessment depends on a systemwide master plan, but has been effectively used for some systems.

Systems That Provide Important but Demand-Sensitive Services

Airports. A key market issue in the analysis of *general airport revenue bonds* (GARBs) is the mix of *origin-and-destination* (O&D) traffic versus that derived from hubbing activities. The facility's economic base is generally a more significant credit consideration for airports that have a high proportion of O&D traffic, while the health of the dominant air carrier(s) will carry more weight in an airport devoted primarily to hubbing. Also key to evaluating an airport's credit position is an assessment of the extent to which various airline operating agreements afford the airport flexibility. An airport generates substantial revenue from a variety of sources including concessions, parking, ground transportation, and building and ground rentals. However, these revenues may or may not accrue to the direct benefit of the airport, depending on the way they are handled in the airport's rate-making methodology.

The degree to which an airport exercises control over its gates and other facilities has become an extremely important credit factor. It is gate control more than any other element that determines whether or not an airport can access its passenger market and take advantage of any resilience within its rates and charges should the failure of a dominant carrier threaten a disruption in operations. If the airport does not have control over its gates, that is to say, if gates are exclusively leased by carriers with preferential or usage-based clauses, in a worst-case scenario, it could be a bankruptcy court and not the airport administration, that determines utilization. Because of consolidation among airlines and reduced competitiveness, which has led to the more frequent domination of individual airports by single carriers, debt ratings may be closely linked to the fortunes of a dominant carrier. This relationship will depend on a variety of factors, including the role that the airport and its market play in the air carrier's overall operations, and the degree of the air carrier's commitment to that facility.

Seaports. Seaports are similar to airports in that operating revenues depend on external private entities, which in this case are steamship companies, as well as a host of specialized firms related to shipping, such as freight forwarders, brokers and insurers. As with air transportation, shipping is an industry heavily influenced by competition from other modes, shifts in international trade patterns and tariffs, and changes in the costs of labor and fuel. Any of these factors could determine whether the cheapest sea freight route to the United States from Singapore is via an Atlantic or Pacific port, which heavily affects utilization at these particular facilities. One important trend is the shift by container freight operators to larger vessels that make fewer stops, in the interest of reducing costly stays in ports. Given that container freight is the high-value activity for a port (as opposed to bulk or break-bulk freight), competition to attract shipping companies is becoming intense. One final, salient issue from the perspective of credit quality is that many port operations enjoy heavy state subsidies and, therefore, are not comparable to pure port revenue systems.

Toll Roads and Bridges. For toll roads and bridges, the issue of competitive demand—often within a localized geographic area—is paramount. Some of the municipal market's major revenue bond defaults—West Virginia Turnpike, the Calumet Skyway, and the Chesapeake Bay Bridge and Tunnel—all resulted from underestimations of traffic growth related to the competition from other roads. As a result of the inability to control competing modes and facilities, new toll systems are generally considered to be very risky. Most recent toll bond issues therefore involve the funding of relatively minor extensions or improvements to large and well-established systems, wherein debt service coverage from existing operations is ample.

Mass Transit. Given the often substantial capital needs of transit systems, as well as the cost of operations, farebox revenues alone rarely if ever provide adequate funds to allow the transit system to be self-supporting. However, because mass transit is critical to the smooth functioning of the local economy, particularly in larger cities, transit systems often receive sizable federal and/or state grants. In many cases, mass transit systems that issue debt derive subsidies from local sales tax revenues. While the credit analysis of these systems must examine overall operations and system-wide net revenues, the debt is essentially special tax-supported, as opposed to revenue, debt.

Higher Education. Analytic distinctions for university and college bonds are twofold—first, whether the bonds have a broad revenue pledge such as tuition and fees, or a narrow one such as dormitory rents; and second, whether the institution is public or private. For a public university, trends in state aid, the place of higher education on the state's list of competing priorities, and the state's own financial position are important credit considerations. For a private university, more weight would be given to other factors such as the size of the endowment, debt-to-asset ratios, and the competitiveness of tuition levels.

Competition for applicants is a top concern for both public and private institutions, as demographics shift and baby boomers no longer provide a swelling body of potential students. Consequently, colleges across the country are becoming more sophisticated in marketing themselves, and in offering scholarships and other financial incentives to prospective students. Credit analysis of university bonds must address how effective these strategies are and their impact on the university's finances, particularly given cutbacks in federal research grants and fluctuations in private and corporate contributions. For many private universities and colleges, effective management of endowments is also a key financial concern. Tightening finances are worsened in some instances by the university's connection with a hospital, which itself may be strapped due to the competitive forces and reimbursement challenges in the health care industry. Generally, the larger and more prominent universities have continued to do well, despite some financial tightening. The most vulnerable institutions are the smaller, private ones that have limited resources and lack a national or even statewide prominence.

Health Care. Because of concern over rapidly rising health care costs, the various payers of hospital bills (government programs such as Medicare and Medicaid, and private health insuers) have been aggressively attempting to limit payment increases to hospitals. In addition, a number of states have established rate setting commissions or budget review procedures which tend to further limit hospital revenues. As a result of these factors, revenues are not keeping pace with costs at many hospitals, and consequently some institutions are experiencing serious financial problems.

The health care industry is extremely competitive. Hospitals must compete for patients, for doctors and other skilled personnel, and for new medical technologies. This competition is of particular concern in many areas of the country where there remains an overcapacity of hospital facilities. Nevertheless, overall utilization of hospitals is likely to stay relatively strong due to the important nature of health services and the aging of the American population.

Tax-exempt hospital revenue bonds are issued on behalf of a wide variety of hospitals, from large teaching institutions affiliated with prestigious medical schools, to small rural hospitals that serve sparsely populated, often poor, areas. The manner in which the reimbursement climate and demand for health care services affects any individual institution will depend on its specific mix of services, its particular niche in the market, and how effectively it deals with changes in its revenue and cost structures. Ultimately, some hospitals will gain at the expense of others. Greater operating efficiencies, more consolidations, and additional hospital closures and bankruptcies are likely to be characteristics of this industry, for some time to come.

Systems Providing Discretionary Services

Convention Centers. Convention centers are typically built to promote economic development. Indeed, activity stemming from large conferences held at such facilities can be a boom to the local economy. However, as costly, non-essential service providers, convention centers and similar facilities are rarely if ever self-supporting. Consequently, bonds are usually serviced by a variety of hotel/motel and other sales taxes that supplement income from the operation of the facility itself.

Key to the success of a convention center is a strategic decision about the facility's "mission" (for example, whether it will accommodate large trade shows and compete nationally, or host smaller conferences and compete regionally). Location is also key—a convention center is most likely to thrive in a community that is seen by conventioneers as a desirable place to visit. Proximity to an adequate number of hotels and motels, as well as to retail and recreational facilities, is equally critical. In addition, the facility must be competitive in terms of cost, accessibility and convenience.

Because of the frequent need for accompanying commercial development, competition from similar facilities in the region and/or nation, and the vulnerability of demand to overall economic conditions, convention centers and related facilities are very risky ventures. Since the enterprise is unlikely to be self-supporting, the credit analyst will need to analyze trends in the related hotel, motel, and amusement tax revenues in order to determine whether projected revenues from these sources will be adequate to pay debt service and operations and management.

Parking. The location of the parking facility and the level of existing competition are critical factors in evaluating parking revenue bonds. Because a parking garage serves a relatively restricted service area, it is imperative that the analysis include a thorough evaluation of that area and the activities likely to generate a flow of traffic. Business closings, fuel shortages, or other unanticipated economic events can have sharp or sudden effects on parking demand. A relatively positive credit scenario is presented by parking garages that are part of a diverse, municipally owned system, pre-lease a significant portion of their available spaces, encounter limited competition from private competitors, and possess a reasonable degree of elasticity in their rate structure. Garages that are stand-alone facilities, positioned in a highly competitive environment, or that suffer from an inability to raise rates should be viewed with caution. A record of timely rate review and revision, an adequate record of maintenance provision, and appropriate hazard-insurance levels speak to quality of management and are positive credit factors.

Golf Courses, Ice Rinks, and Other Recreation Facilities. Bonds sold for golf courses, ice rinks, and other recreational facilities are among the riskiest municipal securities because they are stand-alone, non-essential facilities with very narrow revenue streams. Demand can fluctuate greatly for such facilities, depending on weather conditions, economic circumstances, and consumer preferences. Such facilities should have adequate hazard insurance and the bonds sold on their behalf should have strong legal protections.

CREDIT OUTLOOK FOR ENTERPRISE SYSTEMS

The credit outlook for any individual revenue bond depends on the strength and interplay of the various credit factors—the economy, financial performance, debt, management, and legal structure. As a broad group, however, revenue bonds—particularly those issued for essential services—have been improving in credit quality. Usually segregated from municipal general funds, essential service enterprise systems are largely shielded from diversions to help pay for municipal programs that have suffered large decreases in federal and state aid. Additionally, although the revenue streams of these systems are narrowly defined, the process by which rates can be raised is usually far easier than bolstering general purpose revenues for a municipality in these tax defiant times. The more narrowly defined agenda of an enterprise system tends to provide an advantage in the political arena.

The single-purpose focus of such enterprise systems also tends to facilitate management. Although these systems are often vulnerable to the forces of nature and regulatory change, on the whole, they have demonstrated remarkable long-term reliability. For example, California's major water utilities' credit ratings remain as strong as they were in pre-drought days. The track record of these utilities proves that they can endure periods of hardship.

The future challenge for these systems will be their ability to adapt to ever-increasing levels of regulatory pressure. Until recently, consumer rates for enterprise system services like sewage treatment have been kept relatively low because of expanding customer bases as well as generous federal grant programs for pollution control. Now, with generally slowed customer base expansion and the disappearance of such federal grant programs, these enterprise systems will have to confront their customers with the real costs of meeting increased regulatory demands.

Despite such challenges, the credit quality of the debt of many of these systems, is likely to remain stable or to improve. Mature enterprise systems that provide essential services and have a long track record of successful operations are increasingly likely to have debt that is equivalent in credit quality to bonds secured by the general obligation pledge of the same municipality.

CHAPTER 11

Civil War, Railroads, and Road Bonds: Bond Repudiations in the Days of Yore*

Steven Dickson

As the Civil War was coming to an end in the mid-1860s, the United States began an effort to unite by rail a nation that had been so recently divided by war. The eventual result was one of the most extensive and impressive railroad systems for its time in the world. In the interim, it generated one of the first major default stories covered in depth by *The Daily Bond Buyer*—railroad aid bonds and Southern repudiation of Reconstruction-era debt.

Throughout the 1860s, Congress offered companies and municipalities massive subsidies and land grants to link the Mississippi River to the Pacific Ocean by rail, hoping the effort would help develop territories acquired in the Louisiana Purchase. Construction began in Council Bluffs, Iowa, and Sacramento, Calif. As the two railroads—the Union Pacific and the Central Pacific—snaked their way to an eventual rendezvous in Promontory Point, Utah, in 1869, state and local governments along the way seized the opportunity to issue millions of dollars of bonds to pay for access routes and branch roads, many of them unnecessary and overly lavish.

* Reprinted with permission from *The Bond Buyer*, One State Street Plaza, New York, NY 10004-1549.

Other railroads, including ties from New Orleans to Los Angeles and St. Paul to Portland, also carried the baggage of large-scale state and local bond issuance. "An immense volume of railroad aid bonds was placed upon the market, in some cases recklessly, in others corruptly, and in almost all cases extravagantly," as *The Daily Bond Buyer* put it in 1901.

Eventually, many Southern states trying to recover from the ravages of war and from the recession of 1873 simply passed laws declaring invalid the outstanding railroad debt and numerous other bond obligations, most notably bonds issued to capitalize new banks. Millions of dollars of bonds issued by corrupt "carpet bag" governments that took over state legislatures throughout the South following the Civil War added to the mess. When citizens eventually were permitted to vote the officials out of office, new lawmakers added their predecessors' bond issuance to the long list of repudiated debt.

Relying on Section 4 of the U.S. Constitution's 14th Amendment, which prohibited any state from paying debt incurred to fund rebellion against the federal government, states greatly reduced the amount they were willing to pay. In all, a total of 10 Southern states repudiated almost $300 million, including accumulated interest, by the turn of the century, with Virginia leading the pack at $72 million, according to a count by *The Daily Bond Buyer* in 1904.

CREATIVE COLLECTION ATTEMPTS

Not to be deterred, investors stuck with the worthless bonds found creative ways to try to make recalcitrant states pay up. One such effort, chronicled in *The Daily Bond Buyer* in 1901, featured a partnership between North American Trust Co. of New York and two English blokes, identified only as "Messrs. Fairbairn and Wingfield of London."

The team put out a circular, reprinted in the newspaper, calling on all holders of repudiated Southern debt to turn their bonds over to the company. Partners in the group said they saw a "reasonable chance to make valuable what is now absolutely worthless." And all they wanted in exchange was 50% of whatever was recovered.

Although one bondholder wired North American Trust that he had found "a trunk full of the [repudiated] bonds" and was preparing to send them to New York, no further mention was ever made on the fate of the effort. In all likelihood, North American Trust's problem was the same one that tripped up most bondholders seeking to force states to make good on their old promises: a constitutional prohibition against individuals suing a state.

But at least one industrious victim of the repudiation era found a way over that hurdle in 1904. Simon Schafer, a member of the firm Schafer & Brothers at 35 Wall Street, realized that while he might be prevented from suing North Carolina to recover his lost $10,000 investment, the law did not prevent another state from acting as his proxy.

In a strategy eventually upheld by the United States Supreme Court, Mr. Schafer convinced the South Dakota Legislature to accept his "gift" of $10,000 of repudiated bonds issued by North Carolina, a state that had reneged on a total of about $48 million. In accepting the bonds, the state in turn promised it would sue North Carolina to recover the lost principal, plus interest and costs. South Dakota would get to keep $10,000 of the judgment for state charities, and would have to pay Mr. Schafer whatever was left.

As it turned out, $17,400 was left. And not only did the judge in the case rule that North Carolina had to pay South Dakota the full $27,400, but he also directed that if North Carolina seemed to be dawdling, the U.S. Marshal could seize any assets of the state and "sell them from the east front steps of the Capitol at Washington." Suddenly bondholders around the country were tearing apart attics and old trunks, dusting off their bonds, and recalculating back interest.

UNDUE FEARS AND HOPES

Not so fast, *The Daily Bond Buyer* advised. "There is no need to get unduly excited at the South by fears or at the North by hopes," the paper wrote after the Supreme Court upheld the judgment against North Carolina. States like South Dakota that would be willing to take on such lawsuits would be rare, and many of the defaulting states would be unable to make the payments even if the Supreme Court ruled that they must, the paper predicted.

"At any rate it is not worthwhile just yet for Southern papers to suggest another secession movement rather than pay up, or for any Northern paper to suggest that the United States assume these defaulted millions and issue national bonds to take up the repudiated state bonds." Nevertheless, an ambitious ex-Senator from Sioux Falls, South Dakota, R.F. Pettigrew, said a few months later that he was ready to take up where Mr. Schafer left off. After obtaining contracts from bondholders of six Southern states, Mr. Pettigrew announced he would make a go at collecting between $20 million and $30 million of repudiated debt. Again *The Daily Bond Buyer* advised caution, seeing a potential for far-reaching consequences if a new standoff between the North and South developed over bad debt.

"To encumber the South, just entering upon a new career of prosperity, with the task of paying by taxation repudiated bonds which have been accumulating interest in many instances for fifty years would be manifestly, not unjust, but clearly destructive of development of this great natural section of our common country," the paper wrote in October 1904. The editor urged President Theodore Roosevelt to present the matter to Congress, to find a way to allow the South "to avoid the destructive consequences of the mistakes of the preceding generations." Still more time passed without a resolution, and more practical problems emerged. Georgia, for example, faced interest and principal payments on its repudiated debt of as much as $14 million by late 1904. But officials there said they could no longer find documentation of when or how the bonds had been repudiated. Pretty soon, they warned, there would no longer by any "living witnesses" to the repudiation, and therefore no way to undo it either.

In some Southern circles, however, the idea was catching on that if the states were to regain credibility among out-of-state investors, some of the old debts would have to be repaid. The Abbeville, S.C., *Press and Banner*, for example, called several of the state's repudiations "shameful." "Ought not the chivalric old Palmetto State be made to pay her honest debts?" the *Press and Banner* asked.

That was not the prevailing view. In July 1905, Gov. Robert Brodnex Glenn of North Carolina traveled north, after learning that New York State had acquired a chunk of his state's repudiated debt with an eye toward a Simon Schafer-style lawsuit. After discussing the matter with New York Gov. Frank W. Higgins, Gov. Glenn issued a statement warning that any attempt to sue for payment of the bonds would mean costly and futile litigation. The Supreme Court judgment against his state applied strictly to the Schafer bonds, which were secured by stock in a railroad company, the governor argued. The bonds held by New York, on the other hand, were issued by a "carpet bag government." "My state would not pay them, and there [is] no court in the land which would decide that they ought to be paid when the conditions under which they were issued were taken into consideration," Gov. Higgins said.

If New York did decide to sue, *The Daily Bond Buyer* must have decided it unworthy of coverage. In any event, by 1911, the same amount of repudiated North Carolina debt was still being mentioned on the pages of the newspaper, as occasional speculators picked up chunks here and there at a rate of about $5 per $1,000 face value.

REOPENING OLD WOUNDS

But as time went on, old repudiation wounds continued to reopen. After World War I, when the United States was trying to get Great Britain to pay war debts, the issue was raised by London bankers holding tight to their old Southern bond coupons. Why should they pay debt to a nation which refused to honor its own, the bankers argued. Even 62 years after the end of the Civil War, the issue continued to trigger fierce debate.

The governor of North Carolina, called upon again in July 1927 to defend his position on the state's repudiation, said in the pages of *The Daily Bond Buyer* that the unpaid bonds were not the responsibility of his state, since they were issued by the carpet baggers and "negroes" that usurped power in North Carolina and across the South at the close of the war. Later attempts to secure payment met the same resistance. In 1928, the state of Connecticut filed suit against North Carolina, hoping to win payment of $300,000 for a pile of 1869 bonds.

Eventually, and in fulfillment of *The Daily Bond Buyer's* prediction of 1904 that sister states would not have the stomach for lawsuits against each other, Connecticut dropped its suit, albeit after an unfavorable U.S. Supreme Court ruling involving a technicality.

Other creative methods reminiscent of Mr. Schafer's original strategy appeared and disappeared from the pages of the newspaper, including one chronicling Cuba's mysteriously abandoned attempt to sue North Carolina. And in 1933, the Principality of Monaco served notice on the state of Mississippi that it would sue over $7 million of bonds issued 90 years earlier to capitalize two banks. But the U.S. Supreme Court promptly ended that effort, ruling that a foreign power could not sue a state without that state's permission.

No other mention was ever made of a successful attempt to force payment of repudiated Southern debt, and eventually, apparently through the passage of time, the issue for the most part stopped being a credit concern. As efforts to force Southern states to acknowledge their repudiated bonds languished, *The Daily Bond Buyer* shifted its attention to other risky credits.

THE ANCESTORS OF "DIRT DISTRICTS"

One such case centered on the Arkansas Legislature's 1920 "good roads" acts, which authorized local roads commissioners to issue bonds virtually at will. The result was about 350 special road districts selling bonds with virtually little regard for the ability of the local economy to support it.

The Daily Bond Buyer reprinted at length investigative articles on the matter which ran in March 1921 in *The New York Times*, though the paper noted that some investment bankers involved in selling the Arkansas road bonds found the articles "vicious" and "apparently maliciously inspired."

Nevertheless, the articles explained in detail how taxes were rising to such absurd levels to back the bonds that the security of the issues seemed in doubt. One Arkansas "widow," for example, was reported to have a total annual income of $4,000 and a road tax bill of $2,800. Gov. Thomas C. McRae called the situation the "greatest disaster that has ever befallen the people of Arkansas." And in one district, taxpayers so overburdened by the assessments levied to back the bonds marched into a meeting and secured the resignation of the road commissioners at gunpoint.

Still, Gov. McRae recognized that default would only cause the state more harm. He said the obligations would be met "honestly and manfully." A week later, the paper ran an article from the *St. Louis Post Dispatch*, which argued that many of the *Times's* points were exaggerated. The *Post-Dispatch* reporter found that people in Arkansas were having a tough time paying their taxes because the market for their crops had disintegrated, not because the taxes had become exorbitant. The "widow" cited by the *Times* who owed $2,800 was actually a wealthy resident of Washington, D.C., whose land was worth $150,000, the paper reported.

While Arkansas's situation in 1920 may not have been as bad as the *Times* first reported, it was a precursor to an era of special district defaults. As the decade of the 1920s roared its way toward eventual collapse, real estate values rose dramatically and special districts sprang up around the nation in response. And as was the case in Arkansas, many of the districts were empowered to sell bonds and levy taxes with very little public input.

By 1926, a group of about 100 Texans had had enough with their local district. When their votes against a new bond issue were overruled by wealthy landowners elsewhere in their Archer County community, the group filed suit to stop the $300,000 bond sale. The U.S. Supreme Court eventually supported them, finding that the proposed road would provide them with no benefit whatsoever and that the special district's ability to tax them without their full input was "repugnant to the due process clause of the fourteenth amendment."

The fallout was immediate. Now that the highest court in the nation had found Texas' special district laws unconstitutional, what would that mean for the nearly $100 million of outstanding bonds already issued under the law's provisions, not to mention the hundreds of millions of dollars of bonds issued around the country under laws virtually identical to the one in Texas?

Texas officials immediately scrambled to find a way to validate the state's outstanding issues and calm the market for its bonds. Speculation was raised that taxes to back the bonds might not legally be collectible, or that some county treasurers might decide not to apply the taxes that were collected against debt service obligations. A special legislative session was called to deal with the issue, and every road district in the state took action to have their bonds validated.

Eventually the state Supreme Court upheld the 555 validating laws—one for each special district—needed to bring Texas back into good standing with the credit markets. Courts and legislatures around the nation took similar action to protect their own credit from the implications of the Supreme Court ruling.

The actions averted widespread defaults, which historically have been a rarity in the municipal bond markets. But troubled credits have always generated situations involving time-consuming and complicated workout scenarios, and The Bond Buyer's interest in such matters in the first half of the century continued into the second.

One of the most notorious defaults in recent times was the Calumet Skyway in Chicago, which stopped paying debt service on $100 million of bonds in 1963 when lower-than-expected traffic levels strangled the highway's finances.

New York City's default in 1975 is another of the industry's low points. After years of spending beyond its means and trying to pay off old note issues with new note issues, the credit markets finally shut their doors to New York. The resulting default by decree of the state legislature forced reforms and the institution of oversight boards that gradually restored the city to the status of a sound credit risk.

Although the reforms have not been enough to save New York from a new round of severe fiscal distress in recent years, they have so far prevented the problem from spiraling into catastrophe, which happened in 1983 in the most famous municipal bond default of all time—the Washington Public Power Supply System, or WPPSS. The power system won the distinction of the largest municipal bond default ever when $2.25 billion of revenue bonds tanked in 1983. The Bond Buyer has covered that default and the years of costly litigation and cleanup ever since.

Despite the massive publicity that accompanies such major default and risky credit stories, the municipal bond industry is generally credited with one of the lowest default rates of any market, with most estimates pegging the figure at historically less than 1% of the market. About $6 billion in defaults have been recorded, and one recent analysis put the odds of default at about four in 10,000. Even Southern states that repudiated 19th century debt have now, for the most part, rebuilt their credit reputations.

Nevertheless, reports continue to pop up in the financial press that point to distressed cities like Philadelphia and Bridgeport, Conn., as proof the industry is heading for trouble. Despite such speculation, finance officials nationwide maintain default is still all but unthinkable. Even climbing the steps of bankruptcy court in June 1991, Bridgeport Mayor Mary Moran said the collapse of the city would not mean bonds would go unpaid.

And Philadelphia officials have been just as adamant. No large American city has endured a major bond default in at least half a century, Mayor W. Wilson Goode told Pennsylvania legislators in a plea for aid in May 1991. "Such an event would haunt the city's reputation and damage its economy for years to come."

Just ask Mississippi. When state officials traveled to London in 1987 to try to sell a taxable Eurobond issue, investors there told them the state's credit was no good. Mississippi, the bankers explained, still owed London bankers principal and interest on $7 million of defaulted state debt—sold 156 years earlier and repudiated in 1857.

CHAPTER 12

Credit Trends

Hyman C. Grossman
Managing Director
Standard & Poor's Ratings Group

From time to time, certain clear cut credit trends emerge and are worth noting. Spotting deteriorating or positive events would seem to be a priority of those engaged in credit evaluation. The purpose of this chapter is not necessarily to make any predictions but to share some ideas and clues about credit trends in an attempt to suggest what to look for and when to do so.

In a recent column, George Will pointed out that "the future has a way of arriving unannounced. Its arrival is jolting when people have not prepared for it. One way to prepare is by governing with a two-word truism: Nothing lasts." Indeed, this chapter suggests what the data bases will likely be telling us by the end of the decade.

ECONOMIC TRENDS

The stock market shock and the following economic recession can be viewed as the flashpoint of what was happening at that time in several aspects of the economy. However, it must be quickly stated that other forces affecting economic regions and hence credit potential were noticeable months before the debacle of October 16-19, 1988. And as has often been said in the past, management responses to these challenges can also make a difference in the analyst's credit assessment.

For example, the reversal of the decline in the midwest manufacturing center was becoming apparent in late 1986. It was affected by our dollar devaluation versus overseas currencies, modernization, and restructuring. This steady trend has enhanced a streamlined manufacturing base in Ohio, Michigan, Indiana, and, to some extent, Pennsylvania. A number of regional and state economies will benefit from enhanced exports, including the middle American states, but also New York (upstate and downstate tourism), California (manufacturing and tourism), Hawaii (tourism), and Florida (tourism).

But even this is only part of the picture in these states and regions. What else is happening in these economies? Diversification is a key to rolling with the next economic adjustment. In examining total employment trends and prospects, a key factor in those sections that experienced the greatest growth was growth in financial services, services in general, government, and construction employment. That is the general trend. But when you get to specifics, you find that personal income growth in terms of sectors did not show parallel trends. Thus, the largest component in personal income growth in New York City in recent years has come in financial services—the commercial and investment banks which are experiencing significant job and income losses. New Jersey and, to a lesser extent, Pennsylvania, while showing strong growth trends had far less income growth out of financial services and, therefore, probably should have a lesser negative trend out of this sector in the 1988–1989 economy. However, New Jersey and New York had important income dependency on construction and financial services that has slowed down and will stay fairly depressed for a while longer.

From data of the Bureau of Economic Analysis we learned that, during the 1975–1985 period, earnings in New York from services were up 21% while the finance, insurance, and real estate group (FIRE) grew by 33%. New Jersey saw services grow by 33% and FIRE by only 18%. In Pennsylvania, service-related earnings soared by 44% as FIRE rose a significant 26%. It is important then for analysts to probe where income and earnings are coming from, how vulnerable they might be, and then tie this into state and local government revenue capacity and trends.

To some extent, enhanced export activity will help offset job and income losses in regions that had experienced the largest growth of the 1980s. Looking beyond the mid-Atlantic region, overconcentration or lack of diversification in recent years was most apparent in the oil rich states such as Louisiana, Oklahoma, and Texas. But Texas is more diversified and has reluctantly realized that a modern revenue and fiscal system is a prerequisite for meeting the challenges of the approaching twenty-first century. The jury is still out on Louisiana and Oklahoma. Alaska is a special case in that revenues are virtually entirely dependent upon the price of oil and gas but the Permanent Fund has prudently been developed as a major offsetting asset.

During the economic restructuring of the past 15 years—manufacturing to services—as recent studies have pointed out, not all manufacturing jobs are high pay and not all service jobs are low pay. Biotechnology and pharmaceuticals can be listed in manufacturing and be highly paid. But textiles and related jobs are lower paid. An equally important factor in anticipating economic trends is an examination of demographics. These trends not only include population and in-migration patterns but the labor supply being generated out of the 18–25 year-old group. Recently, and for the next several years, this age group is a direct outgrowth of declining high school enrollment of recent years and will be a factor for another 8–10 years following the noticeable increase in the birth rate of the last 3–4 years. Household formations also follow these trends and have an impact on housing patterns and demands.

But the labor market will get tighter and a premium will be paid for talented people. To attract talented people and the ultimate support of the demands of a more sophisticated economic engine requires housing, school, energy, transportation and related amenities that are available at reasonable costs. Otherwise regions can cost themselves out of economic growth. Where in-migration is taking place such as in Arizona and Florida, the labor pool is growing but the challenge is the necessary training to meet demands of an expanding economic base.

So, examine labor supply, its quality, labor force and employment trends and opportunities, real estate values, office space vacancies, and likely demand in these sectors. Examine the budget assumptions more closely and watch for sale of assets or other non-recurring types of "resource enhancements."

Spending pressures in education, infrastructure, health services, solid waste, and housing will continue to be areas of concern to governments as well as credit analysts. On a national basis, issues of concern include growing dependency on overseas energy sources as well as the controversy about power plant sitings for facilities that most assuredly will be needed before too long. Regions with oil dependency are likely to get hurt at some point in the next five years.

CONCLUSION: THE MANAGEMENT CHALLENGE

The key to meeting all of these challenges, in my view, will be management's response to problems and trends. In recent years, there has developed an enhanced degree of professionalism and competence in many more states and cities. It has become apparent that one could not leave government completely to the vagaries of elected politicians. A core of competent and dedicated people is needed at the helm day-to-day—using better information systems. It has even been politically attractive to cite that one's government is "on GAAP" even if one is not quite sure of what it means. The fact that New York City, for example, is anticipating the challenge is a positive step. Fifteen years ago, the response by city officials would have been "What challenge?"

In summary then, clues to emerging credit trends will be found in examining the present credit profile in all of its aspects (primarily the economy and management), the factors that brought it to this point, and the changing nature of trends that will most likely impact the future.

Part Three

BUDGETING, ACCOUNTING, AND DEBT MANAGEMENT

CHAPTER 13

Municipal Financing and the Budget Process

Dall W. Forsythe
Former Director—New York State Division of the Budget

In the Tax Reform Act of 1986, Congress eliminated tax-exempt financing for some purposes and sharply restricted its use in other areas by creating state caps on the allowable financing for most nongovernmental purposes. As a result, the pursuit of arbitrage earnings has ceased to be the driving force behind the issuance of many special types of municipal bonds. Instead, tax-exempt financing under the new tax code will be used predominantly for general governmental purposes—financing of roads, bridges, sewers, school buildings, and other capital needs subsumed under the clumsy rubric of "infrastructure."

Most financings by states and cities for such purposes and facilities have their roots in the budgetary process. While the politics and processes of governmental budgets may not always be easily comprehensible to issuers, bankers and credit analysts, successful completion of those municipal bond financings will depend in part on an understanding of the budgetary origins of bond or note sales, and the legal and accounting rules underlying them. Some sense of the dynamics of choice in the budget process and the perspectives and expectations of the politicians and bureaucrats who make budgets also will allow interested parties to comment on those transactions at earlier stages in their development, and to avoid steps during marketing that fly in the face of the original intentions of executive branch and legislative decision makers. Finally, an enhanced understanding of those processes will also help rating analysts and municipal bond buyers better gauge the willingness of government decision makers to stand behind the commitments embodied in the bonds they sell in the municipal marketplace.

Tax-exempt financing is tightly constrained not only by federal tax rules, but also by state and local law. The regiments of lawyers that are associated with the marketing of municipal notes and bonds make visible the legislative origins of tax exempt (and now taxable) municipal financing.

For other players in the municipal bond markets, it is also vital to understand that prior to and concurrent with the legislative process, a budget process operates. Complex and detailed budgeting decisions are made allocating the financial resources of the government in question, based on technical, programmatic, and political concerns.

Financing for general governmental purposes is typically shaped by three broad sets of financial imperatives. First, and most obvious, is the capital planning process, where decisions are made about which specific capital projects should proceed and when. Second, the fundamental requirement to balance the operating budget means that fiscal sufficiency is a constraint even after capital needs are approved. Government officials must decide how to pay for capital facilities and still fund the other competing demands made by their constituencies, all within a balanced operating budget. Third, and finally, state and local governments must also deal with shorter-range and highly sensitive questions of cash flow management, typically but not always within a single fiscal year. Informed by these three imperatives, choices are made, first by the executive and then by the legislative branches, culminating in allocations of scarce resources, in decisions about financing programs, and eventually in sales of bonds and notes.

This brief chapter discusses those imperatives and some of the choices they create. Most of the examples are drawn from New York's experience, reflecting the author's own background and sources of data. Because it has suffered through several straight years of fiscal stress, New York State also provides a particularly rich menu of budget-driven financing decisions. However, similar dynamics and decisions can be found in many other states and local governments, especially during times of fiscal stringency.

ASSESSING CAPITAL NEEDS

Most state and many local governments attempt to analyze, more or less comprehensively, the capital needs of their agency sub-units.

This process, which culminates in the capital budgets proposed by mayors and governors, involves both line agencies and staff agencies (especially budget offices, planning agencies, and construction management offices).

Central to the capital planning process are the proposals and priorities of the operating line units of government. Functions requiring significant capital resources fall into a number of categories, as outlined below.

Transportation

Capital requirements for roads and bridges continue to grow. Even in regions where the basic transportation infrastructure exists, major maintenance and reconstruction needs remain. Where populations continue to grow, pressures to expand the capacity of existing roads can be strong. Mass transit is also heavily capital intensive, with the costs of buses and garages paling in comparison to the price tags for new rail programs or major modernizations of subways and light rail systems. In New York, the capital needs of transportation, whether financed by cities, by the State or by independent authorities like the Metropolitan Transportation Authority (MTA), outweigh the capital requirements of all other functions combined.

Institutional Populations

Government agencies which house sizable populations in institutional settings have costly capital needs. These include corrections departments (serving both adult and juvenile populations) and agencies serving the mentally ill and mentally retarded. In New York and all across the nation, rapidly growing prison populations have created heavy capital requirements during the last decade. In the State's mental hygiene agencies, capital spending has been driven by attempts to shrink mental institutions and create smaller facilities in community settings, as well as more aggressive monitoring and tougher standards set by oversight agencies responsible for accreditation and certification. (Capital planning for mental health in New York is discussed in more detail below.)

Education

In rapidly growing areas, new buildings for elementary and secondary schools are a high priority for capital spending, and the building programs of public universities never seem to stop. In inner cities, programs to reduce class size also create pressures on building capacity. Even in communities with stable populations, buildings need modernization and major rehabilitation, and new trends in sports and science curricula often create pressures for new facilities.

Other Governmental Buildings

In much the same fashion, other government functions require office buildings, garages, and other storage and work buildings. New capital needs reflect either staff growth, new technical requirements for laboratories or computer facilities, or simply the modernization of antiquated or unsafe buildings or facilities.

Environmental Facilities

More and more money is required to complete waste water treatment facilities, cope with solid waste, or clean up hazardous waste sites. Estimating the need for capital in these areas is often complicated by government's difficulty in deciding what programmatic and technological approaches it will take in response to these issues.

Other Needs

Other areas of need, while important in and of themselves, are much less costly in absolute terms than the functions outlined above. Nonetheless, state and local governments spend capital dollars for parks and other recreational facilities; for court facilities; and for equipment. New York State has also lent its credit to non-profit hospitals in poor communities and, like several other states, has committed funds for subsidies for affordable housing.

Capital Priorities

In most governments, the initial list of capital needs will far outstrip the resources available to fund those needs. In those circumstances, central planning and budgeting offices typically rank needs according to several criteria. Health and safety requirements are generally at the top of the list of priorities. Additional criteria include the management capacity of a project to generate revenue or save operating dollars, and conformity of a project to programmatic concerns. Finally, the management capacity of an agency to actually carry through to successful completion the planning, design and oversight of capital projects constitutes an additional factor in the capital needs equation.

In 1986, the New York State Division of the Budget (DOB) reassessed the capital needs of its two largest mental hygiene agencies. At that time, the Office of Mental Health (OMH) operated 31 psychiatric centers, housing approximately 19,000 mental patients. Its operating budget of more than $2.2 billion supported more than 35,000 employees. The Office of Mental Retardation and Developmental Disabilities (OMRDD) housed 9,200 clients in State operated institutions, provided residential care in community settings for another 18,000 clients and employed about 27,000 staff with its $1.5 billion budget. For years, State policy had been to reduce the residential census in these State-operated institutions by limiting admissions and providing residential and out-patient care in community settings. Maintenance in those facilities had been deferred, more stringent accreditation standards had led to complaints about patient's needs, and, in some cases, had caused lessened federal funding. Indeed, even the policy of shrinking State-operated facilities created capital needs, since demolition or conversion of unused facilities to other uses was sometimes necessary to reduce operating and maintenance costs.

In fiscal year 1986–1987,[1] the State Budget Division (DOB) estimated capital needs for those mental hygiene agencies at $101.5 million a year. After the reassessment of capital needs in 1986, Budget Division staff projected that capital requirements would grow to nearly $186.6 million for fiscal year 1987–1988, and would total $1.49 billion during the time horizon of their five-year capital plan. Postponing those capital outlays could further jeopardize federal funding if State institutions lost their accreditation because of deficiencies in those facilities. Program staff in the Governor's office and the mental hygiene agencies were also anxious to proceed with necessary improvements for client health and safety requirements. As outlined below, the stage was set for a debt financing program to help meet the State's massive needs for capital for its mental hygiene system.

After agency-level priorities are established, a similar ranking is made across agency lines, emphasizing once again criteria such as health and safety, savings and revenue yield, and programmatic emphasis. The resulting totals are then winnowed down to a level that can be funded within a government's projected resources. New York State's five year projection of spending for capital needs was $21.2 billion beginning in fiscal year 1991–1992. Because the total of $21.2 billion includes only outlays expected to be appropriated by the State Legislature during the budget process, it significantly understates the total volume of disbursements for all State purposes during this period. For example, the New York State Thruway Authority anticipates spending over $1 billion during this five-year period. In much the

---

[1] In New York, the fiscal year begins April 1. Because the legislature stays in session until July, budgets are usually passed long after the beginning of the fiscal year. Since 1990, changing the date of the fiscal year has been a topic of discussion between the legislature and the governor.

same fashion, Dormitory Authority disbursements for the State and City Universities are projected to total over a billion dollars beyond the spending for education. The Budget Division estimates that total disbursements over the five years will grow from $21.2 billion to more than $50 billion when capital spending from all State authorities is included.

BALANCING THE BUDGET

After priorities are established for a governmental unit's capital requirements, those needs must compete for funding with all other demands for government dollars. Decisions about how to fund those needs are typically made in an environment where the question of balancing the budget is often primary. If the operating budget of a state or local government has current revenues sufficient to fund all of its base needs, together with its new programs and capital requirements, a government may decide to fund all of its capital needs on a "pay-as-you-go" basis. More likely in recent years, spending pressures will outrun current revenues, and bond financing will often be used to help close the gap between planned expenditures and projected revenues.

Financing capital needs with bonds can alleviate fiscal pressures in several ways. Initially, of course, annual debt service costs are less than the full one-time costs of purchasing capital goods, although total outlays for principal, interest, and costs of issuance over the life of a facility will be much larger than pay-as-you-go expenditures. Second, bond financings can be used to justify the creation of or increases in user fees to pay for capital facilities. Finally, interest rate shifts or other more unusual circumstances can create opportunities to reduce budget outlays through refinancings.

Pay-as-You-Go versus Debt Financing

Some governments, such as the State of Iowa, usually fund all of their capital needs out of current revenues. This approach leaves the State's balance sheet strong, but may mean that some capital needs are postponed to help avoid increases in taxes or fees. In other governments, bond proceeds are used to pay for virtually all capital outlays. Using the issuing authority of Municipal Assistance Corporation (MAC) and the New York City Water Authority to supplement its own general obligation bonds, New York City has issued more than $32.1 billion in long-term debt to fund its capital needs since City fiscal year 1981. By contrast, during that period, the City made pay-as-you-go contributions of only $147 million in support of those capital outlays.

Until its most recent round of tight budgets, New York State steered a middle course. A significant share of its capital needs—generally about a third—were funded with tax dollars transferred from the tax-supported General Fund to the Capital Projects Fund. Those transfers, called "hard dollars" by State officials, represent a pay-as-you-go contribution to capital that, while smaller than some, was still substantial. The rest of its capital requirements were funded by a combination of federal funds and debt financing instruments, including *general obligation* (GO) bonds and debt subject to annual appropriation, such as lease purchase and service contract bonds and *certificates of participation* (COPs). During the five years preceding fiscal year 1987–1988, "hard dollars" provided pay-as-you-go funding for an average of 38% of all capital disbursements.

In public finance theory, decisions about the balance between pay-as-you-go and debt financing are cast as choices about which generation will bear the burden of paying for public facilities. When a facility is financed out of general revenues, the current generation of taxpayers foots the entire bill. However, by definition, capital facilities have long useful lives, and it is often argued that it is unfair to require today's taxpayers to pay the full costs associated with a facility which will benefit another generation of taxpayers. On those grounds, the theory holds, decisions are made to finance capital projects with bonds or other debt instruments with terms tailored to the useful life of the facilities.

In fact, fiscal realities and tight budgetary conditions are more likely to result in decisions to shift the proportion of pay-as-you-go financing. In New York State's Executive Budget for fiscal year 1987–1988, Governor Cuomo proposed a spending cap which would hold the growth in the State's General Fund at or below the growth rate in the State's personal income as a whole. His purpose in making such a proposal was to prevent tax-supported State spending from consuming a larger share of New York's economic output, and to allow further cuts in tax rates. Although the legislature did not enact a multi-year cap until 1990, it did enact a budget at the level proposed by Cuomo in 1987, accepting his spending cap on a *de facto* basis.

As intended, the spending cap constrained total outlays. At the same time, however, legitimate capital requirements were increasing, most markedly in the area of mental hygiene, as outlined above. One result of those conflicting pressures was adoption of a major debt financing program for mental hygiene, leading to a reduction in the overall proportion of capital needs financed on a pay-as-you-go basis.

The new financing program for mental hygiene initiated in 1987 used key elements of an earlier structure for mental hygiene bonds. These bonds, issued between 1963 and 1977, were secured by revenues flowing into what the mental hygiene department called its "Patient

Income Account," which included payments from Medicare, third-party reimbursements from private insurers, and Medicaid. Although patient care income revenues were very large, the original financing structure buttressed this revenue pledge with debt service reserves covering two years of debt service requirements together with a moral obligation pledge. (Details of New York State's moral obligation credit structure can be found below.) Legislation passed in 1987 authorized a new mental hygiene financing program, eliminated the moral obligation pledge, authorized refunding of the $465 million in existing mental hygiene bonds, and reduced the debt service reserve fund to six months' requirements. To defease the outstanding bonds, the New York State Medical Care Facilities Financing Agency issued $395 million in refunding bonds, and $317 million in special obligation bonds. Costs of issuance for the refunding bonds were offset by reinvestment of a portion of the debt service reserves from the old bonds at an unrestricted yield, and additional proceeds from the elimination of excess reserves were sufficient to provide approximately $80 million in budget relief for the 1988–1989 General Fund.

As suggested above, one consequence of these expanded bonding programs was a reduction in pay-as-you-go support for New York State's capital program. From the average level of 38% during the previous five years, "hard dollar" funding in fiscal year 1987–1988 fell to about 22% of total capital funding of $1.8 billion. In addition to increased levels of bond financing, surplus funds from the State Insurance Fund were appropriated in 1987 directly to the Capital Projects Fund, contributing to the marked reduction in pay-as-you-go support from the General Fund.

In the years from 1989–1990 to 1991–1992, the percentage of pay-as-you-go funding further dropped from 22% to 12% as budget shortfalls made "hard dollars" scarcer and bond financing much more attractive to elected officials. Major programs to replace pay-as-you-go financing with debt included new transportation bonding programs carried out by the Thruway Authority, and the issuance of taxable and tax-exempt debt to maintain subsidies for low and moderate income housing.

Debt financing can be used to postpone some of the costs of capital facilities, and refinancings can reduce the cost of debt service, shift debt service payment dates, or otherwise reduce pressure on the operating budget. Although most governmental outlays under *generally accepted accounting principles* (GAAP) are recognized as expenditures on a modified accrual basis, debt service is typically accounted for on a cash basis, so changes of this nature can improve a government's GAAP operating statements as well as its cash position.

In 1989, as New York's budget problems worsened, the governor proposed and the legislature agreed to refinance all of the $2.1 billion of outstanding bonds of the State University of New York (SUNY). Like the mental hygiene bonds discussed above, the existing SUNY bonds had debt service reserves larger than required by current standards. These excess reserves in part offset the present value losses on the refinancing of SUNY bonds, leaving a net present value loss of about $6 million. Restructuring of SUNY debt service provided nearly $400 million in budget relief during fiscal years 1989–1990 and 1990–1991. While the rating agencies expressed concern about this refinancing and a similar but smaller refinancing of a portion of the debt associated with the South Mall in Albany, they did not reduce the State's ratings until FY 1990–1991, when the State finished its third straight year with an operating deficit. As revenue estimates plummeted in the first four months of FY 1990–1991, the governor and the legislature agreed to a gap-closing package of nearly $1.9 billion in non-recurring actions. While no additional refinancings were included, new Thruway Authority and housing bond programs were created, and steps were taken to restructure debt service reserves to provide budget relief. Before the FY 1990–1991 budget was completed, Standard and Poor's reduced its rating from AA- to A. Moody's downgraded the State from A1 to A upon enactment of that budget.

Bonds can be used to reduce the immediate costs of capital requirements or to provide budget relief through refinancings or restructuring. Revenue bonds can also be used to justify new or additional user fees, thereby actually adding to the revenue stream available to fund capital needs. An instructive example is the case of New York City's Municipal Water Authority, created in 1984 by an act of the State Legislature to help finance an $8 billion capital improvement program proposed for the City's water supply and sewerage system between 1986 and 1996. Sewer and water rates in New York City were low, compared to other localities, and the City began a program to increase those rates even while the legislature was contemplating the Municipal Water Authority and its financing package. Water and sewer rates were unchanged from 1971 to 1980. Between 1980 and 1987, unmetered (or "flat") rates for single-family homes increased by 62%, and sewer rates shot up by more than 350% during that same period. Debt service on bonds issued by the Water Authority will serve as the basis for significant new increases in water and sewer charges for New York City landowners, and as the impetus for a program of universal water metering. Between 1985, when the Water Authority issued its first bonds, and 1991, water rates increased by more than 150%, and sewer rates increased by 345%.

In addition to providing a justification for fee increases for City residents, the Water Authority revenue bond structure also short-circuited political obstacles to rate hikes. The legislation shifted the locus for decision making on sewer and water fees from the City Council, an elected body, to a Water Board, a newly created entity appointed by, and submissive to, the Mayor. Through these mechanisms, the creation of a new revenue bond program was used to facilitate a significant increase in revenues available for support of New York City's water and waste water capital infrastructure.

Choices Among Debt Instruments

New York State and other governments use a variety of mechanisms for the issuance of tax-supported debt. In New York, general obligation bonds can be issued after a vote of the Legislature and a referendum. General obligation debt carries the highest credit rating because of the pledge of the State's full faith and credit, and because debt service can be paid even in the absence of a legislative appropriation. Because of the length of time required for this complex approval process, and because voters have rejected bond issues for prison construction and for environmental purposes, the State has also used debt structures other than general obligation bonds.

When a general obligation prison bond issue was defeated in 1983, prison debt was authorized by the legislature and issued by the Urban Development Corporation (UDC) under a lease-purchase arrangement subject to annual appropriation by the State. This program was initiated over the vigorous objections of the State Comptroller, who argued that the voters' choice should be honored. In 1982, the Metropolitan Transportation Authority was also authorized to issue bonds backed by a service contract with the State. Moreover, the State itself has issued Certificates of Participation for capital equipment and school and office buildings, under legislation enacted in 1986. All of the bonds issued under these programs are subject to annual appropriation, like the mental hygiene and SUNY debt discussed above.

New York also has sizable amounts of older bonds outstanding backed by the State's *moral obligation* (MO) pledge, whereby the legislature pledges to make up any draws on debt service reserves. The annual appropriation programs outlined above are sometimes confused with New York's moral obligation debt. The MO credit structure was created to hedge the crucial question of appropriation risk, and was discredited after the State's default on UDC securities in the 1970s, even though the State met all of its moral obligation requirements. As outlined above in the discussion of mental hygiene financing, State officials are reducing the level of moral obligation debt as quickly as possible. Moreover, several new programs have been created using the State's credit without either a moral obligation or a general obligation pledge, including the distressed hospital financing on behalf of voluntary hospital lacking the financial strength to issue their own debt. State officials have gone to some pains to emphasize the differences between the State's moral obligation bonds, and debt issued subject to annual appropriation under service contract, lease purchase, COPs and similar credit structures.

CASH FLOW

As suggested above, pressures to balance a government's operating budget can provide the impetus for new debt financing programs or for the refinancing of existing debt. Note financings most frequently reflect cash flow requirements, typically but not always within a single fiscal year, and have only a secondary relationship to operating budget requirements. However, because note transactions are often the largest financings a government undertakes, and because those note sales provide a regular opportunity for rating agencies to review a state or city's short-term credit rating, cash flow borrowings are often among the most sensitive of a government's fiscal activities.

Cash flow imbalances in governments reflect variations in the schedule of receipts and disbursements. Some receipts, such as sales tax collections, are relatively evenly distributed throughout a fiscal year. Others, such as corporate or personal income tax receipts, varied widely from month to month and season to season. In much the same fashion, some disbursements—payroll costs, for example—are spread out fairly evenly from month to month, while others may be more concentrated.

Before the passage of tax reform legislation in 1986, governments were permitted to borrow more than the amount required simply to fund their cash flow deficit. The tax code allowed the sale of notes sufficient to fund the cash imbalances which resulted from these factors, less the opening balance of its general fund. Governments were also authorized to borrow at tax exempt rates an amount equal to an additional month's disbursements. Because these additional funds were never drawn down, a government could invest them at taxable rates and earn arbitrage. Most states and cities took advantage of these arbitrage opportunities, and some went to some lengths to maximize their arbitrage borrowing. In 1985, for example, the State of California moved its Reserve for Economic Uncertainty out of its general fund so the cash in that fund would not be counted in the arbitrage calculation for note borrowing. As a result, California's note borrowing increased from $1.2 billion in 1984 to $1.9 billion in 1985. State officials estimated that they earned an additional $15 million from this maneuver. Other states and cities reduced interfund borrowing and increased the issuance of tax exempt notes, a step which also increased arbitrage earnings. Changes to the tax code since 1986 have eliminated most of the arbitrage opportunities associated with cash flow borrowing.

Over the years, New York State has represented an extreme case of cash imbalance, most visibly reflected in its "spring borrowing," which has usually been the largest financing by a non-federal governmental unit in America. At its peak in 1984 and 1985, New York State issued $4.3 billion in tax and revenue anticipation notes (TRANS) to meet its massive cash flow needs. New York State's fiscal year, which begins April 1st, overlaps the fiscal years of its local governmental units, including its school boards, which usually begin July 1. New York used this anomaly of the fiscal calendar to increase aid to schools and local government, but postpone payment of that aid until the next fiscal year. The State accomplished this goal by making payments for those aid increases in April, May, and June, the first quarter of the State's fiscal year, and the last quarter for the schools and most local governments. Through the use of this device, which came to be called "the magic window," New York State eventually compressed into its first quarter almost 46% of its disbursements for local assistance, a budget category which itself represented more than two-thirds percent of total spending. Other budget balancing steps—primarily delays in tax refunds and pension payments—increased cash needs in the State's first quarter.

At the same time, corporate income tax payments and sales tax collections were accelerated across fiscal year boundaries, facilitating budget balance in years when the State was particularly hard pressed, but moving a crucial source of receipts from the State's first quarter to its last. The resulting funds were available to help repay the massive note borrowing at the end of the fiscal year in March, but were no longer available to directly fund the first quarter's outlays. Because New York's cash needs were severe and its borrowing so large, the State did not borrow for arbitrage purposes, but restricted the size of its note offerings to its actual cash flow requirements.

In recent years, New York State has taken steps to reduce its cash flow borrowing, initially by using budget surpluses to fund reserves, and later by an agreement with its largest pension system to restructure its pension payments, which had been made in June, the month of maximum cash needs for the State. Because pension payments totalling more than $750 million a year had been made fifteen months late, the State Comptroller—who heads the pension system—initially refused to agree to an additional delay to move the payment out of the State's overburdened first quarter. In 1986, Governor Cuomo proposed to begin a program to fully amortize the 15-month lag, and to move the pension payment, which would not be current, to the final month of the fiscal year. The Comptroller and the Legislature agreed, and New York began making an annual payment of $140 million, sufficient to pay off its $1.4 billion pension lag over a period of 17 years at the pension system's actuarial interest rate. The initial cost of the payment was offset by reductions in overall pension funding needs and reduced debt service costs on the spring borrowing, which dropped from $4.3 billion to $3.5 billion. Further steps, including the use of cash generated by a significant budget surplus in fiscal year 1987–1988, reduced the borrowing in 1987 to $2.6 billion.

By 1988, operating surpluses were succeeded by deficits, and the spring borrowing began to increase again. In 1990, the State borrowed $4.1 billion and the Legislature agreed to a proposal by the Governor to bond out the spring borrowing. A new issuing agency was created called the New York Local Government Assistance Corporation (LGAC). It was authorized to issue bonds to provide up to $4.7 billion in proceeds to restructure the State's cash flow and eliminate the spring borrowing. Debt service on those bonds, while subject to annual appropriation by the Legislature, was also backed by the segregation of 1% of the State's sales tax into a special fund. In February 1991, LGAC issued $910 million in bonds to begin to reduce the spring borrowing. As the spring borrowing falls, the State's accumulated general fund deficit—totalling approximately $6 billion in 1991—will be reduced by a like amount.

SUMMARY AND CONCLUSIONS

As segments of the tax-exempt market are curtailed by tax reform, a greater proportion of new municipal securities will be issued to finance traditional governmental functions—transportation, public protection, education, environmental protection, and others. Decisions about those financing programs will be made, at least in part, through state and local budget processes. As a result, participants in the municipal markets will be well-advised to learn more about the players and incentives operating in the budgetary process. Although political factors can be powerful influences in the making of budgets, this brief chapter focuses on several important fiscal imperatives. First, decision makers sort out competing capital needs and establish priorities for funding. Second, those capital needs compete with other spending requirements, and financing programs using a variety of credit structures can be used to spread the costs of capital needs. Finally, short-term notes remain a key tool in managing the sensitive question of cash flow needs within a government's fiscal year, although the value of notes as arbitrage instruments has sharply diminished.

In times of fiscal scarcity—the early 1990s, for example—all of these fiscal pressures are magnified. So, of course, are the pressures on politicians to maintain popular spending programs and avoid tax increases. The result is likely to be increased use of non-recurring and non-traditional budget balancing actions, often achieved by the issuance of municipal bonds. The challenge for state and local governments will be to reverse those trends in more comfortable fiscal circumstances, rebuilding reserves and pay-as-you-go capital commitments before the next downturn in the business cycle is upon them.

CHAPTER 14

Public Funds Management: Current Practices and Future Trends

James R. Ramsey
Western Kentucky University

Merl M. Hackbart
University of Kentucky

The management of the operating or day-to-day portfolio of a city or state involves investing tax receipts, user fees, and other funds which are continually being collected and held until needed for expenditures. These investments are generally made in short-term money market instruments with maturities ranging from one day to perhaps one or two years. The management of these short-term public sector portfolios began to receive greater attention in the 1970s as the opportunity cost of holding idle funds grew significantly with increased interest rates.[1] In fact, in the high interest rate environment of the late 1970s and early 1980s, it became easy for public funds managers to earn significant interest income on their idle cash balances and as a result, interest income became a relied upon source of non-tax revenue for budget and expenditure plans.

The relative lower interest rate environment of recent years has forced public funds managers to re-evaluate their portfolio management

---

[1] See: Advisory Commission on Intergovernmental Relations, *Understanding State and Local Cash Management* (Washington, D.C.: Advisory Commission on Intergovernmental Relations, 1977), p. ll, and Jack Kiley, "A Perspective on Public Cash Management in the 1980s," *Government Finance* (December, 1989).

programs. For example, many public funds managers have developed comprehensive cash management programs to allow funds to be invested for longer periods of time and, hence, increase investment earnings. Some public funds managers have sought legislative authorization to broaden the array of permissible assets in which public funds can be invested in the expectation that higher returns can be earned with only modest increases in credit risk. In other instances, new investment techniques such as tri-party repurchase agreements, reverse repurchase agreements and securities lending programs have gained acceptance as techniques to provide "value added" to public sector portfolios. More recently, the use of options has evolved as part of an overall portfolio management strategy, particularly for private sector portfolio managers.

The purpose of this chapter is to discuss the investment management challenge facing public funds managers today. This challenge is: "How to maximize investment income in an environment of both lower and uncertain interest rates." We begin with a description of a comprehensive cash management program for public funds. Four components of a cash management program are identified. It is shown that through the development and implementation of a comprehensive cash management program, the public funds manager can maximize the time funds are available for investment and hence earn greater income regardless of the interest rate environment.

Finally, a comparison is provided of the portfolio characteristics of the "typical" state government portfolio with that of a "typical" private sector portfolio. It is shown that state portfolios are more concentrated in assets issued by the federal government and its agencies, or assets "backed by" and collateralized by federal or agency securities. On the other hand, private sector portfolios are concentrated in a broader array of money market assets. Credit risk and the implications of broadening asset holdings as a portfolio enhancer are discussed.

The chapter then presents a discussion of investment management strategies with special focus on techniques being used by public funds managers to achieve "value added" on a core portfolio of treasury securities.

CASH MANAGEMENT: THE BASIC ELEMENTS

The goal of a cash management program is to "reduce the amount of cash that is being used within the firm so as to increase organizational profitability, but without lessening business activity or exposing the firm to undue risk in meeting its financial obligations."[2] While

---

[2] Smith, K.V., *Guide to Working Capital Management*, (New York, N.Y.: McGraw-Hill, Inc., 1979), p. 72.

this definition was developed for the private sector, it is equally applicable to the public sector. The concept of cash management suggests that an organization should maintain an objective of minimizing cash holdings in order to maximize investment return, or "profitability."

A cash management program consists of four distinct components. These are:

(1) cash mobilization;

(2) cash forecasting;

(3) banking relationships; and

(4) investment management.

Each of these components will be specifically discussed in greater detail below. The "bottom line" for a comprehensive cash management program is the common sense tenet that one cannot invest funds that they do not have. Therefore, a cash management program's goal is to ensure that funds are deposited as quickly as possible and that bills are paid on time so that funds may be invested consistent with the defined investment objectives.

Cash Mobilization

The cash mobilization component of a cash management program involves the maximization of cash available for investment. This includes two fundamental processes:

(1) accelerating the receipt of revenues; and

(2) controlling the disbursement of funds.

The processes and activities involved in carrying out these functions will depend on the fund being managed (including its source and use) and the organizational and geographical characteristics of the state and local governments. Alternative cash mobilization procedures used by the state and local government cash manager to mobilize cash are briefly described below.

Revenue Acceleration. As noted earlier, state and local government receipts come from four principal sources. The receipt date for tax collections may be specified in enabling statutes or ordinances and, therefore, may be beyond the policy or operational influence of the cash manager. In other cases, state and local governments may find that by requiring taxpayers to remit payments more rapidly (e.g., income withholding taxes, sales taxes, corporate taxes, etc.) and perhaps, more often, allows funds to be invested for longer periods, thus increasing investment income. The date for the closing of a bond sale is typically included in the official statement for the bond sale and is normally subject to the discretion of the financial manager given the condition of the financial markets, processing times, and the need for funds.

Intergovernmental transfer receipt dates have historically tended to be flexible and subject to negotiation when federal and state laws were silent as to the transfer date and when ownership of funds transferred between levels of government. Ownership patterns among federal agencies were typically guided by the generic type of transfer which might be involved including cost reimbursement (followed for years by the U.S. Department of Transportation) to the "delayed drawdown" procedures (followed by the U.S. Department of Health and Human Resources). However, the recently enacted Cash Management Improvement Act of 1990[3] defines uniform and consistent procedures for the receipt and disbursement of funds between the federal government and state and local governments. States have until 1992 to comply with this new legislation and its impact on state and local governments will be significant.

Agency fund collections include both "earmarked" tax revenues and agency receipts including enterprise funds (e.g., user fees at parks departments). Enterprise funds mirror cash acceleration options available to the private sector while other earmarked taxes and agency receipts such as tuition payments tend to follow statutory requirements or policies promulgated by special authorities. Therefore, acceleration options available to the cash manager tend to be limited. By contrast, government enterprise activities have the option of following normal private sector speed-up processes including:

(1) modifying the paying behavior of the enterprise's customers; or

(2) improving the delivery system for such payments.[4]

Since state and local government cash managers often have little control over time receipt technicalities of tax and other revenues, cash

---

[3] Due to the use of a variety of cash management procedures by different federal agencies, the State/Federal Cash Management Reform Task Force was formed with representation from the Office for Management and Budget, the Department of Treasury, the National Association of State Auditors, Comptrollers, and Treasurers (NASACT), and the National Association of State Budget Officers (NASBO) to develop one comprehensive set of cash management procedures to be used by federal, state and local governments. This joint cooperative effort resulted in the passage of the Cash Management Improvement Act of 1990.

[4] Smith, *op cit.*

mobilization emphasis is typically directed toward expediting the collection and deposit of tax and other revenues within their depository institutions. Such activities are referred to as the "minimization of the negative float" associated with the receipt of funds. *Negative float* is the time delay between the disbursement of tax receipts by an individual or corporation and the availability of "good" funds by the state treasurer or appropriate finance official.

Negative float can be divided into three subcategories.[5] These are:

- *Mail float* is the lag between the time the taxpayer or other revenue source mails his payment and the moment at which the state or local government unit receives the payment.
- *Processing float* is the time lapse between the receipt of the tax payment or revenue source and the deposit of such funds in the appropriate banking institution. This float category, essentially, represents the time required to appropriately record and process the payment by the Treasurer, Comptroller, or appropriate finance official.
- *Clearing float* is the time lapse which may occur between the deposit of the check in the bank and the time at which the bank recognizes the check as a legitimate source of funds. This float arises due to the processing time required to clear funds through the various banking institutions and Federal Reserve System.

The various categories of float are further depicted in Figure 14.1. Mail float is represented by the time lapse between taxpayer disbursement, Point A, and collection Point B. Processing float occurs between Point B and Point C and involves tax processing activities. Check clearing float is represented by the time lapse between the time of deposit by the Treasurer and the recognition of "good funds" by the bank at Point D.

Efforts to minimize negative float include the use of

(1) lock box systems;

(2) cash concentration accounts; and

(3) electronic funds transfers.

Lock box systems are designed to reduce mail float while concentration accounts are utilized to mitigate processing float.[6]

---

[5] *Ibid*, p. 71.

[6] Bretschneider, S., Hackbart, M., and Ward, B., *State Cash Flow Management: The Kentucky System* (Lexington, Kentucky: Martin Center for Public Administration, University of Kentucky, 1982), p. 35.

FIGURE 14.1
Float Representation

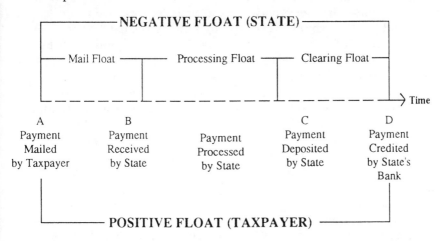

The use of lock box systems has had mixed reactions by state governments. For example, in some states, lock box systems have been used in combination with check encoding and sorting machines to transmit revenue receipts to regional banks for clearance. Both mail and processing float have been reduced as a result of this innovation. In other states, concerns have been raised by various state officials regarding the taxpayer's right to privacy of tax receipt information. If returns are handled with the same degree of concern for confidentiality and security as those processed by state agencies, no adverse taxpayers' right to privacy problems should occur.[7] Moreover, when used in combination with wire transfers, lock box systems can significantly reduce negative float from tax and other revenue receipts.

Like lock box systems, the use of concentration accounts is often more applicable to state governments than to local governments and municipalities. The concentration account is a regional account which is utilized by multiple funds for initial deposits. Subsequently, funds are disbursed to the centralized depository account for investment or disbursement to payees. In addition, funds are typically wire transferred to the central depository bank/account to reduce mail float. Processing float may also be reduced by turning processing activities over to commercial banks which might have more efficient, cost-effective processing techniques than do state agencies.

Disbursement Management. As noted by one cash management expert, "cash mobilization is as dependent on a government's disburse-

---

[7] *Ibid.*

ment policies as it is on practices designed to accelerate the deposit of revenue."[8] Characterized as positive float, there is value associated with the time difference between the time a check is written to pay bills and the time the check is actually paid by the bank. Management of that time difference along with the timing of the initial disbursement authorization to take into account discounts while not paying debts prior to a due date if a discount is not available constitute the key features of an effective disbursement management system.

The importance of a properly managed disbursement system has been shown to be significant. For example, if a payment that is due in 30 days carries a 1% discount if paid in full in 10 days (20 days in advance), the savings were shown to be equivalent to an annual rate of return of 18%.[9] Such rates must be compared to the "opportunity interest foregone" to determine the optimal disbursement pattern.

In addition to timing of disbursements, the means of disbursement is also an important consideration. Disbursement float can be eliminated via a zero-balance account. With such an account, a single general account is maintained along with single clearing accounts for different agencies or funds.[10] the special clearing accounts are maintained with zero balances until checks are presented for payment. At that time, funds are transferred from the general account to cover the payment or payments scheduled for that time period. The funds in the general account are, of course, invested in relatively liquid securities which can be converted to cash as the need arises to cover the clearing demands of the separate clearing accounts.

Cash Forecasting

The objective of cash forecasting is to provide the investment or portfolio manager with reliable information regarding patterns of revenue receipts and expenditures by investment fund. Such information permits the funds to be invested in longer term, higher yielding assets. As shown in Figure 14.2, different funds tend to realize different receipt and expenditure patterns. At the same time, different assets have different yield curve patterns as displayed in Figure 14.3. The matching of investable funds, given receipt and expenditure patterns, becomes the challenge of the cash forecasting process. Obviously, in making cash

---

[8] Kiley, J., "A Perspective on Public Cash Management in the 1980s," *Government Finance* (December, 1981), p. 5.

[9] Legislative Research Commission, *Program Evaluation: Commonwealth Cash Management*, No. 124 (Frankfort, Kentucky: Legislative Research Commission, 1982), p. 18.

[10] ACIR, *op. cit.*, p. 14.

FIGURE 14.2
Revenue and Expenditure Patterns by Fund

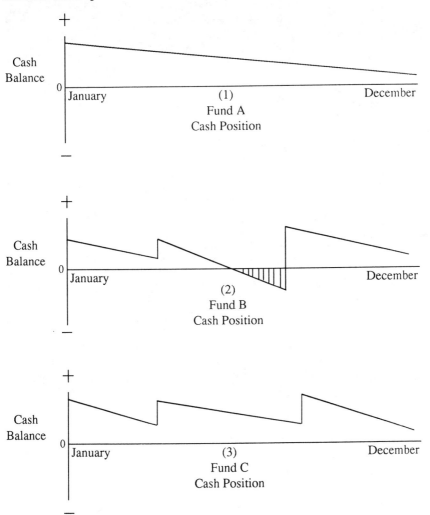

Source: Advisory Commission on Intergovernmental Relations, *Understanding State and Local Cash Management*, (Washington, D.C.: Advisory Commission on Intergovernmental Relations, 1977), p. 11.

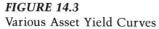

FIGURE 14.3
Various Asset Yield Curves

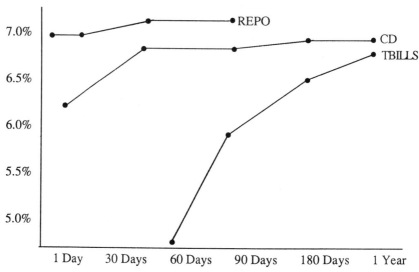

Source: J. R. Ramsey and M. M. Hackbart, *Introduction to Cash Management,* (Concord, New Hampshire Governor's Finance Officers Association, State of New Hampshire, 1987).

forecasts, accuracy is of utmost importance. If an asset is prematurely liquidated due to unanticipated cash flow needs, income from that investment may be severely reduced. Therefore, forecasting precision is critical to effective cash management.

Forecasts may be made by:

(1) subjective judgment or evaluations based upon past patterns of receipts and expenditures;

(2) by time series analysis which utilizes statistical equations to predict the future flows based upon the supposition that past patterns best predict the future; and

(3) by economic analysis which explains past cash flow relationships including tax and other revenues and expenditures and economic performance to predict future cash flows through mathematical and statistical equations.[11]

Such cash forecasts can be short term involving daily, weekly, or monthly assessments of cash flow patterns. Short-term forecasts are vital for the

[11] Bretschneider, S., *et al.,* p. 62.

management of the portfolio within the fiscal year period as the investment manager may want to realize all investment income within the fiscal year if the government unit is operating on a cash or a quasi-cash accounting system. Longer term forecasts (beyond the fiscal year) provide the cash manager with early indications of potential cash flow problems in the out years. Long-run forecasts can also assist the investment manager in selecting higher yielding long-term assets when appropriate. An example would be a capital construction fund or agency revolving fund which does not have to be managed so as to realize investment income within a single fiscal year period.[12]

Bank Relationships

Banking relationships are another element of a complete cash management system. As suppliers of services to state and local governments (including operating and maintaining depository accounts, lockbox systems, processing checks and providing other financial services) banking institutions provide an integral component of the cash management process. In addition to providing transaction services, banks facilitate investment activities and may provide an investment option for public funds managers as a provider of certificates of deposit or repurchase agreements.

Banking policy issues for state and local governments include such issues as:

(1) whether single or multiple depository accounts should be maintained;

(2) whether banking services will be paid for with fees for services provided or whether a "compensating" balance will be maintained with the selected depository bank or banks; and

(3) whether banking services will be bid or negotiated.

Issues surrounding single or multiple depository accounts have both efficiency and structural implications. A single depository bank provides an opportunity to locate all fund balances or investable funds in a single banking institution. In such a situation, zero-balance accounts and/or concentration accounts may be facilitated. The state's banking structure also impacts the decision process regarding a single or multiple depository banking choice. With cross-state or branch banking, one major banking institution may be able to provide a complete set of cash management services including

---

[12] *Ibid.*

lockboxes, concentration accounts, zero-balance accounts, and other routine banking services. In such a situation, a single statewide bank as a depository may be an efficient model. In other states with more limiting banking laws, different combinations of depository and banking service arrangements may be more desirable.

As noted, the method of paying for banking services involves a choice between paying fees for individual banking services such as check clearing and the like or maintaining a compensating balance. With a fee for service approach, bidding or negotiation determines the fee structure for each service performed while a compensating balance approach involves an "estimate" of the aggregate services or an actual account of services performed and the concomitant determination of the appropriate balance of funds which, if invested by the bank at the current market rate, will yield a comparable total compensation package. Some states and localities statutorily forbid direct payment for banking services. In such cases, the compensating balance approach becomes the preferred method due to statutory limitations. In less restrictive settings, the state or local government may select the preferred bank compensation method.

Investment Management

The final component of a comprehensive cash management program is the actual investment of the available funds. The investment of public funds is usually carried out pursuant to the achievement of three goals:

(1) safety;
(2) liquidity; and
(3) maximization of the return on the investment of funds.[13]

The relative weighting of the three objectives varies depending upon the fund and its cash flow characteristics, the willingness of the governmental unit to trade off risk for return, and staff expertise and capability to manage the portfolio.

Goals

Safety. Like the trade-off between maturity and rate of return, trade-offs also exist between rate of return and risk. In other words, certain investment assets contain a credit risk premium to reflect the

---

[13] See Girard Miller, *Investing Public Funds* (Government Finance Officers Association, Chicago, Illinois: 1986), pp. 99–107 for a full discussion of public funds goals.

FIGURE 14.4
Predictability of Portfolio Assets

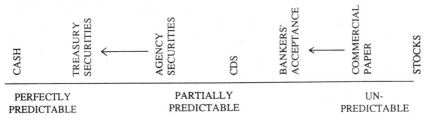

| PERFECTLY | PARTIALLY | UN- |
| PREDICTABLE | PREDICTABLE | PREDICTABLE |

probability that the original cash value may not be realized at the maturity of the investment asset.[14] Safety may also refer to the degree to which an asset's cash value may be determined at any point in time or its predictability. Figure 14.4 indicates, in relative terms, the predictability associated with several categories of investable assets. Cash, of course, is perfectly predictable with its nominal value known at any point in time. The market value of the other assets may change with changes in interest rates prior to maturity. At maturity, the value of the asset is then known with certainty. A more detailed discussion of the different types of risks is included later.

Two issues arise for the investment manager as a result of concern over safety. First, the manager must determine the degree to which the government unit will accept risk in return for potentially higher investment returns. As discussed later, risk acceptance may be specified by statute or ordinance in the form of a listing of permissible assets—assets in which the governmental unit can legally invest. The second issue facing the investment manager involves the identification of means of predicting cash flow requirements so as to reduce the need to convert assets to cash. To the degree this can be accomplished, higher yielding but less predictable assets might be selected for need to convert investment assets into cash for expenditure purposes. This reinforces the need for a good cash forecasting model.

Liquidity. Liquidity refers to speed and ease of conversion of an investment asset to cash. Liquidity is measured in the credit markets by the strength of the secondary market for the asset (the bid/ask spread). There is a very active secondary market for Treasury securities, so they are considered to be very liquid. Real estate, on the other hand, often has a less active secondary market and is therefore

---

[14] For a full discussion of credit risk and other categories of risk see: Fong, H. Gifford, and Fabozzi, Frank J., *Fixed Income Portfolio Management* (Homewood, Illinois: Dow-Jones-Irwin, 1985).

considered less liquid. Liquidity is an important investment consideration for the previously discussed reasons.

Yield. The yield, or total return, on a public funds portfolio, is comprised of three components:

(1) direct coupon or interest income;
(2) capital gains income; and
(3) income derived from special "value added" programs.

Direct coupon or interest income is the actual interest income earned while an asset is held in the portfolio. For example, if a portfolio manager has made a $1 million investment at a 6% interest rate, the coupon or interest income for one year would be $60,000 (interest income could be compounded daily, quarterly, semi-annually). For certain assets such as Treasury Bills, the portfolio manager purchases the asset at a price less than the par or maturity amount of the asset (i.e., at a discount) and the coupon or interest income is the difference between the purchase price and the maturity amount.

The second component of yield or total return is any capital gains income that may be realized. The best analogy for understanding this concept is the stock market. An individual investor may buy shares of IBM at $100 per share and have the opportunity to later sell those shares at $110 per share, or a $10 capital gain per share. In like manner, assets held by public funds portfolio managers may appreciate or depreciate in value while held in the portfolio.

As earlier noted in the discussion on safety and predictability, many assets held by public funds managers have a known value only at their maturity date. For example, a two-year Treasury note purchased today will have a fixed value upon maturity two years later. However, the value of the Treasury note will fluctuate during the life of the asset with changes in interest rates. As the general level of interest rates increase, the value of the asset will decrease, and as the general level of interest rates decreases, the value of the asset will increase. As will be discussed later, for those portfolio managers who pursue active portfolio management strategies, as the general level of interest rates declines, and assets such as Treasury Securities appreciate in value, the funds manager may sell these assets in the secondary market to realize a capital gain.

The third component of yield or total return on a portfolio is any additional income earned from special "value added" programs as will be discussed later. Such programs include securities lending, options, and the like.

Permissible Assets. Given cash flow characteristics, the cash manager attempts to select a set of assets which will maximize returns of the portfolio. The public investment manager is, however, typically constrained regarding the specific assets which can be used in the portfolio. As noted, such constraints emerge from an overriding concern for portfolio security and may involve statutory or regulatory restrictions. Results of a recent survey are presented later on in the chapter where we summarize these legal restrictions.

INVESTMENT STRATEGIES FOR PUBLIC FUNDS MANAGERS

As noted, the goals of public sector portfolio management are most often safety, liquidity, and yield. Further, it has been found that state portfolio managers specify safety and liquidity as their most important investment goals. In pursuing these goals, public funds managers may sacrifice potential yield to ensure the safety and liquidity of the portfolio. Also as previously discussed, public funds managers attempt to achieve the safety goal by carefully selecting the assets they purchase. Given this safety constraint, selected portfolio management strategies are pursued by the public funds manager to maximize yield. In general, one of three investment strategies are pursued by public funds managers:

(1) passive investment strategies;

(2) active investment strategies; or

(3) hybrid investment strategies.

Passive Management Strategies

The manager utilizing passive strategies assumes that the credit markets are efficient.[15] That is, a passive portfolio manager assumes that perfect information is transmitted instantaneously to an infinite number of buyers and sellers in the credit markets so that the opportunity to realize price appreciation from the existence of temporary price disequilibriums in the markets will not exist. In addition, the passive portfolio manager does not formulate a market expectation that either interest rates will go up or down in an effort to achieve price appreciation. Thus, the passive manager seeks to maximize only

---

[15] For a discussion of market efficiency, see Walton, Edwin J. and Gruber, Martin J., *Modern Portfolio Theory and Investment Analysis* (John Wiley and Sons, New York, New York: 1981), pp. 358–388.

coupon income and does this with a buy and hold approach whereby securities are bought and held to maturity.[16]

Active Management Strategies

The active portfolio manager, on the other hand, assumes that the credit markets are not efficient. The active manager assumes that temporary price disequilibriums do occur in the markets and that by taking advantage of these trading opportunities, the public funds manager can increase portfolio yield through asset price appreciation. The active manager is willing to make a market call or forecast of future interest rates, in an effort to structure the portfolio to take advantage of price movements.[17] While the passive manager is risk averse and attempts to ignore interest rate risk, the active manager is willing to take a predetermined amount of risk in order to achieve a greater portfolio return.[18] An active manager for example may have cash to invest for ninety days. The active management may expect interest rates to fall and security prices to rise. Therefore, this manager may buy a two-year Treasury note with the expectation that in 90 days the security can be sold for a capital gain.

Hybrid Management Strategies

The final portfolio strategy is the category of hybrid approaches which contain elements of both the passive and active strategies. The portfolio manager following a hybrid strategy attempts to create a portfolio with an assured return for a specific time horizon regardless of interest rate movements. Unlike the active manager, the hybrid approach does not attempt to maximize overall portfolio return but rather seeks a target portfolio return. Unlike the passive manager, the hybrid approach does not accept interest rate volatility and the price movements which accompany it but rather, through continual restructuring of the portfolio, attempts to smooth out the impacts of interest rate movements. As with an active approach, this requires the recognition of the total yield or return of the portfolio.

A common hybrid approach is the Treasury roll.[19] For example, the portfolio manager may buy a two-year Treasury note. The next month, the portfolio manager sells this security and the "new" two-year Treasury being sold by the U.S. Treasury is purchased. The process

---

[16] Fong and Fabozzi, pp. 93–114.

[17] *Ibid.*, pp. 162–228.

[18] *Ibid.* The risks discussed here are generally not default risks as the active and passive portfolio managers may be restricted to the same array of asset choices.

[19] *Ibid.*, pp. 115–161.

continues every month. If interest rates go up while the security is held in the portfolio, the value of the security goes down and the portfolio realizes a capital loss when the security is sold. However, if the new interest rate is higher, more interest income will be earned to offset the capital loss. Conversely, if interest rates fall while the security is held in the portfolio, a capital gain is realized by the funds will be reinvested at a lower interest rate. This "rolling" strategy allows for the achievement of a target rate of return.

The actual set of strategies used by a portfolio manager will be a function of the specific goals adopted for the portfolio. In addition, since active and hybrid strategies require greater management time and expertise, very practical considerations often are important in the selection of an investment strategy. Also, within a portfolio, one strategy may be appropriate for one governmental fund or set of accounts and another strategy may be more appropriate for other funds or sets of accounts. The same portfolio may use a combination of strategies.

The Concept of Value Added

As we will discuss later on, the public funds manager concentrates most heavily in the purchase of treasury and agency securities and securities collateralized by treasuries and agencies. Given the relative risk free nature of these holdings, it would be expected that public funds will yield less return than a portfolio that is subject to even a marginal amount of additional risk. As a result, public funds managers often pursue active or hybrid investment strategies in an attempt to realize capital gains as a source of investment return. Further, in recent years as the general level of interest rates has fallen from the peak interest rate periods of the early 1980s portfolio managers have sought to implement "value added" programs that will provide additional income on their core holding of treasury and agency securities.

For example, a common "value added" program utilized by many states today is a securities lending or reverse repurchase agreement program. As noted earlier most states are legally able to invest in repurchase agreements. A securities lending or reverse repurchase agreement program can be described as follows:

(1) the public funds manager loans all or a portion of its treasury securities held in the portfolio to a bank or an investment bank;

(2) the bank or investment bank borrowing the treasury and agency securities agrees to collateralize the loan with another set of assets (generally other types of agency securities or mortgage-backed securities);

(3) the bank or investment bank borrowing the treasuries and agency securities from the public funds agrees to pay the public funds portfolio manager a fee for the use of these treasury securities for a specified period of time; and

(4) at a designated date in the future the transaction is reversed with the treasury securities returned to the public funds portfolio and the collateral returned to the bank or investment bank.

If properly structured, a securities lending program can generate additional investment income to the public funds manager with no additional risk. To insure the safety of the public funds being loaned it is necessary to

(1) carefully specify the type of collateral that will be accepted from the bank or investment bank;

(2) establish margin requirements in excess of the given value of securities being loaned; and

(3) continually reprice the securities pledged as collateral for the loan and the posting of additional collateral if the market value of the collateral has declined.

Other programs have also evolved as public funds managers have sought to earn additional income given the statutory restrictions on their investment opportunities and the general concern for safety. While the options market is generally thought of as a speculative trading vehicle, the use of a disciplined option program can in fact reduce public sector portfolio management risk and provide for value added. The next section discusses the use of the over-the-counter treasury options market as a public sector portfolio management technique that can be used by public funds managers to achieve value added to their portfolio return.

Options as a Portfolio Management Strategy

The emergence of the options markets over the last two decades can be attributed to two significant factors:

(1) research leading to the development of option pricing models;[20] and

(2) the October 1979 shift in Federal Reserve policy to the use of open market operations to target the money supply rather than interest

---

[20] See: Blitz, Steven, and Hardee, Sidney, *Monthly Review of Futures and Options— December, 1988* (Salomon Brothers, New York, New York: 1988) for a discussion of the development of options pricing models.

rates and the unprecedented interest rate volatility which resulted from this policy shift.[21]

Today, options contracts have become an integral component of the financial markets.

Since the purpose of this presentation is to discuss the applications of options to a public portfolio, a brief set of definitions will be presented to assist this effort. An option is the right, but not the obligation, to buy or sell an underlying security (e.g., a treasury security) at a specified price—called the strike (or exercise) price—on or before a specified expiration date. An option to buy a security is a call option and an option to sell a security is a put option. An option exercisable only on the expiration date is a European option, while an option exercisable on or before the expiration date is an American option. The price the buyer of a call option or put option pays is called the option premium.[22] For example, if a portfolio manager sells to someone else the right to buy a Treasury note at the price of 100.00 (par) at a specific date in the future, the manager has sold an European call (the security can be called away only at that specific date) at a strike price of 100.00. The seller of a call will be paid a premium to give up the right to have the security called away. It should also be noted that Treasury securities and hence option premiums are quoted in terms of thirty-seconds.

The Application of Options to a Public Sector Portfolio. The strategy of selling a call on a Treasury security is called covered call writing. In a covered call writing strategy, the strike price is generally set at a price greater than the original purchase price of the security so that the portfolio manager will not only collect premium income but will also realize a capital gain if the option is exercised and the security is called. It must be realized that an "opportunity loss" may be incurred if the call is exercised since the security without an option could have been held and sold for a higher price in the cash market.[23] While the covered call writer either believes that the market will remain at present levels or that yields will rise, the call writer must choose a strike price at which he would be comfortable selling the security should interest rates decline and the option be exercised yielding a given capital gain.[24]

---

[21] Johnson, Cal, *An Introduction to Options* (Salomon Brothers, New York, New York: 1987), p. 1.

[22] See Johnson and *Option Reference Guide* published by Central Bank of the South.

[23] The cash market refers to the normal market whereby securities are bought and sold for cash settlement as opposed to the options market.

[24] See Johnson and Central Bank of the South.

A covered call writing strategy allows the price of the underlying security to decline by an amount equal to the option premium without the portfolio position showing an accounting or book loss (i.e., the premium income can be used to cover accounting losses on the portfolio in a declining price market). Once the cushion provided by the premium is depleted, the portfolio position shows an accounting or book loss point-for-point with the price declines of the underlying security.

Puts may also be sold by public funds managers to generate premium income and protect against interest rate movements. Whereas the call writer must choose strike prices at which he would be willing to sell a security, the put writer must choose a strike price at which he would be willing to buy the security. For example, suppose that a Treasury note is trading at par and that a portfolio manager would be willing to buy the security at par in 30 days since the portfolio manager has a known source of investable funds in 30 days. This manager might consider selling a put at 100.00. If the market price increases to 101.00 in 30 days, the security will not be put to the portfolio manager since the holder of the option can sell the security in the cash market at this higher price. However, the premium income earned when the put was sold can be used to offset the current cash market price at which the security must be purchased. If on the other hand, the price of the security in 30 days fell to 99.00, the security will be "put to" or sold to the portfolio manager at par, a higher price than he would have paid in the cash market. However, again the portfolio manager has earned premium income and has purchased a security at a yield that satisfies the original portfolio objectives.[25]

Options Management: A Case Study. In late 1986, the Commonwealth of Kentucky initiated a case study over-the-counter (OTC) Options Treasury Management Program to determine whether the state could utilize puts and calls on treasury securities to enhance return without affecting the portfolio's safety or liquidity. The pilot program was implemented with specific policy parameters established by the state's governing investment board to limit the "speculative" myth concerning options.

At the conclusion of the pilot program an independent evaluation of the program was performed. Table 14.1 presents a summary of the option activity during the test period. As seen in Table 14.1, a total of 17 options were written, seven calls and 10 put options. Two calls and four puts were exercised during the test period with an exercise rate of 35%. It should be noted an abnormally high exercise

---

[25] *Ibid.*

TABLE 14.1
Commonwealth of Kentucky OTC Treasury Options Case Study
Performance Evaluaton

Number of Options Sold		
Call Options	=	7
Put Options	=	10
Total	=	17
Number of Options Exercised		
Calls	=	2
Puts	=	4
Total	=	6
Exercise Rate	=	35%

Option Premium Income

Total Gross Income	=	$386,718.75
Less: Repurchase of call options of cover positions	=	(6,250.00)
Less: Foregone capital gains as a result of exercise of put and call options	=	(28,875.50)
NET PREMIUM INCOME	=	$351,593.25

Source: Hackbart, Merl M. and Officer, Dennis T., "An Evaluation of Kentucky OTC Options Treasury Management Program" (Lexington, Kentucky: unpublished, 1987).

rate suggests that the market expectations of the portfolio manager have been incorrect and option premium income could be distorted by the potential "opportunity loss" or the cost of buying back the option to avoid the option being exercised. However, the relatively small number of options written in the pilot program did not permit any statistically significant conclusions concerning the state's exercise rate.[26]

During the case study period, the OTC Options Treasury Management Program generated a total of $386,718.75 in gross option premium income. The independent evaluation of the case study suggested that two factors mitigated gross premium income:

(1) the repurchase of call options; and

(2) the opportunity losses incurred.

[26] Hackbart, Merl M., and Officer, Dennis T., "An Evaluation of Kentucky OTC Options Treasury Management Program" (unpublished, Lexington, Kentucky: 1987).

In two instances, outstanding call options were repurchased at a profit to prevent the option on the underlying security from being exercised. The cost of repurchasing the option must be deducted from gross premium income. Also, as a result of the exercise of six options, the state sold (in the case of calls) or purchased (in the case of puts) securities at exercise prices which were lower or higher than the existing market prices at the time the options were exercised.

This opportunity loss was calculated by collecting market prices of the six securities at the expiration of the option and comparing their values to the strike prices on the options. The value of the foregone prices during the test period was $28,875.50. This represented the dollar value opportunity loss as a result of selling securities below their market value due to a call option exercise or purchasing securities above their market value as a result of a put option exercise. After consideration of call option repurchases and foregone prices as a result of exercise, the OTC Options Treasury Management Program generated a net premium income of $351,593.25 for the test period.[27, 28]

To put the revenue enhancement of options in perspective, an estimate was derived of what the investment income would have been on the $25 million portfolio during the case study period if only a buy-and-hold strategy had been employed. The $25 million portfolio would have yielded, in the absence of the deployment of any active portfolio management strategy, a rate of return during the seven-month period of approximately 6.5% and, investment income of $947,916.66. The 6.5% return was estimated based on the average Treasury note rate during the period of the case study. The options revenue of $351,593.25 represents a 37% enhancement of investment income for the "options portfolio" for the case study period.[29] Based upon these results the Commonwealth of Kentucky developed a detailed program guideline to be followed in the implementation of a full scale options program.[30] Such a

---

[27] *Ibid.*

[28] It has been suggested that since interest rates during the latter 1980s were lower than in the earlier part of the 1980s that Treasury securities in general would have appreciated in value and thus any active management strategy would result in capital gains. This analysis shows that an options strategy enhanced the portfolio's value added beyond that of capital gains income by the amount of the premium income generated. That is, an OTC Treasury options program provided during this time period both capital gains and premium income. Also the total enhanced portfolio income is "net" of the "opportunity costs" represented by market prices higher than the options strike price.

[29] *Ibid.*

[30] Strong internal controls and procedures are a critical component of a successful options trading strategy. As a result of the case study, the following guidelines were adopted:

full scale program has been operational since the case study and has become an integral part of the state's portfolio management strategy.[31]

STATE AND CORPORATE CASH MANAGEMENT: A COMPARISON

The following information on state portfolio management practices resulted from a survey conducted by the authors and sponsored by the Council of State Governments and the National Association of State Treasurers (NAST), hereinafter referred to as the NAST study.[32] The investment management practices for corporate cash managers were derived from an earlier study by Kamath and others.[33] The NAST and

---

(1) A plan must be defined for each option trade.

(2) The interest rate trend on a long-, intermediate- and short-term basis is to be identified through the use of tools such as moving averages.

(3) Trades only with the intermediate-term trend (i.e., writing of covered calls in a sideways or rising interest rate environment) will be executed. This minimizes the probability that securities will be called away and reduces reinvestment risk.

(4) Optionable securities will be selected and only those securities the state is willing to let go at a specified price will be chosen.

(5) Duration will be limited to no more than 90 days. Liquidity needs and forecast can change quickly in volatile markets.

(6) A minimum of three competitive bids from approved dealers will be obtained.

(7) The initial plan will be adhered to; short-term alterations will not affect carefully laid plans.

[31] A recent analysis performed for the state indicates that the state's expanded options program has represented a 63.4% increase over and above the interest income otherwise generated on the state's Treasury portfolio for this period of time. See: Ray, Russ; Brandi, Jay; and Ramsey, James R. "Options and Public Monies: A Case Study," unpublished, 1990.

[32] The survey document was distributed by the Council of State Governments (CSG) and the National Association of State Treasurers (NAST) to all state treasurers' offices in June of 1987. Telephone follow-up was used to encourage participation and to clarify responses to the questionnaire. Respondents were asked to complete the survey based on May 1987 data and practices. The survey was completed in September 1987 and 34 states responded. The response rate of 70% compares favorably with a survey by Ravindra R. Kamath, Shahriar Khaksari, Heidi Hylton Meier, and John Winklepleck regarding corporate cash management practices, which was distributed to Fortune's second 500 firms, as reported in "Management of Excess Cash: Practices and Developments," *Financial Management*, 14 (Autumn 1985), which has a response rate of 41.5 to 50%. It is noted that the questionnaire used in this study was modeled after the Kamath *et al.* survey.

[33] Kamath, R., Khaksari, S., Meier, H., and Winklepleck, J., "Management of Excess Cash: Practices and Developments." *Financial Management*, 14 (Autumn 1985). The study by Kamath *et al.* involved three surveys of *Fortune's* second 500 firms over the

the Kamath study groups possess environmental and institutional characteristics which are unique and different. Such different characteristics include:

(1) size of portfolio;

(2) constraints to management; and

(3) investment goals and practices.

Such differences might, logically, lead to different cash and investment management practices.

At the same time, the fundamental cash management functions carried out by both groups suggest similarities of cash management goals and practices. Such similarities include

(1) maximizing currently available cash;

(2) investing excess cash; and

(3) meeting challenges of maximizing return subject to acceptable levels of risk.

These similarities and differences are discussed below.

Respondent Portfolio Sizes

The Kamath study focused on *Fortune's* second 500 industrial companies.[34] The mean portfolio size for the 199 firms responding to the 1984 study was $18,340,000 with approximately 8% having portfolios over $50 million. By comparison, the mean portfolio for the 34 states reporting to the NAST survey was $2.1 billion.

Legal Investment for States

As noted, the composition of state portfolios typically is constrained by state statutes while corporate portfolios are not similarly constrained. Such state statutes vary from state-to-state and change in response to the investment experience of other states, the availability of new investable assets, changing investment environments, and other state policy factors.

1979–1984 period. The questionnaires were sent to the highest ranking financial officer of each firm during the first quarter of 1979, 1982, and 1984 and the data reported in the study were drawn from the respective previous years. The comparisons in this study were principally drawn on the 1983 data reported in the Kamath *et al.* study.

[34] *Ibid.*

To determine the array of investment options available to the states, states were asked to indicate which securities were statutorily permissible for short-term cash reserve investments.

Table 14.2 indicates the number of states which identified each security as a legal investment instrument along with abbreviations used to represent these assets in this chapter. Thirty-three states were permitted to acquire Treasury bills and repurchase agreements while 31 could legally purchase and hold agency securities. Such statutory restraints are not existent for corporations.

Number of Assets Held

Kamath and others reported in their study of corporate portfolios that the mean number of different types of instruments used by corporations rose from 3.72 in 1978 to 3.79 in 1981. By 1983, corpora-

TABLE 14.2

Securities Most Frequently Held by States and Corporations and Number of States Indicating Legal Securities by Type[a]

Securities[b]	Number of States Permitted to Hold
U.S. Treasury Bills (TB)	33
U.S. Agency Issues (AG)	31
Repurchase Agreements (RP)	33
Certificates of Deposit (CD)	30
Negotiable Certificates of Deposit (NCD)	0
Yankee Certificates of Deposit (YCD)	8
Eurodollar Certificates of Deposit (ECD)	0
Bankers' Acceptances (BA)	23
Commercial Paper (CP)	22
Off Shore Deposits (Eurodollar Deposits) (OSD)	9
Municipal Securities (Tax Exempt Notes or Bonds) (MUNI)	16
OTHER[c]	12

Source: NAST Survey, 1987.

[a] Match of security categories between the Kamath et al. and NAST studies was constrained, somewhat, by portfolio managers' term usage. For example, the Kamath et al. study used the term tax exempt notes or bonds while the NAST study used municipal securities, to refer to, essentially, the same group of securities.

[b] The frequently used assets shown are displayed in an order relatively consistent with common default risk rankings.

[c] Includes securities that three or fewer states identified as permissible such as money market funds, special savings accounts, and the like.

tions held, on the average, 4.18 different classes of assets.[35] By comparison, the states responding to the NAST survey indicated that the mean number of assets held in short-term portfolio was 5.26. It was also indicated that the mean number of "permissible" assets which could be held by the states was 6.35. In other words, the states held, on the average, more types of assets in their portfolios than did the corporations while not holding, on the average, all of the assets they could hold given the states' statutory environment regarding permissible assets.

The growth in the number of assets held by the corporations participating in the Kamath[36] study is consistent with growth in the number of assets available to portfolio managers, increasing sophistication of managers, and the need for increased flexibility in the selection of assets to match excess funds' investment with cash needs. While exactly comparable data are not readily available for the states, a 1975 study[37] of state portfolio management practices indicated that only 29% of the states used commercial paper in their portfolio compared to 47% in 1987 (see Table 14.3). Meanwhile, only 3% of the states used Banker's Acceptances in 1975 compared to 38% in 1987 (Table 14.3). Therefore, it appears that state portfolio managers have been influenced by availability of new assets and investment options even though they operate in a more restrictive environment.

The use by the responding states of money market securities can be compared to the corporate sector data regarding asset usage by also considering Table 14.4.[38] Repurchase agreements and treasury bills were the most frequently used instruments by states followed closely by certificates of deposit and agency issues. By comparison, repurchase agreements were the most preferred marketable securities held by the corporation respondents followed by negotiable certificates of deposit, commercial paper, and off shore deposits or Eurodollar securities. It is noted that the Kamath et al. study also indicated that Eurodeposits experienced the fastest growth among the money market securities for short-term corporate portfolios between 1979 and 1983.[39]

[35] *Ibid.*

[36] *Ibid.*

[37] Hackbart, H., and Johnson, R., *State Cash Balance Management Policy* (The Council of State Governments, Lexington, Kentucky: 1975).

[38] Kamath.

[39] *Ibid.*

TABLE 14.3
Corporate and State Usage of Money Market Instruments in
Percentage Terms[a]

| Security | Corporations[b] | | States | |
	Percent Using	Rank	Percent Using	Rank
TB	42.9	5	88.2	2
AG	—	—	76.5	4
RP	76.5	1	94.1	1
CD	—	—	82.4	3
NCD	68.7	2	—	—
YCD	—	—	26.5	7
ECD	39.9	6	—	—
BA	34.4	8	38.2	6
CP	68.3	3	47.1	5
OSD	52.5	4	5.8	9
MUNI	18.7	9	11.8	8
Other	35.2	7	26.5	7

Sources: NAST Survey, June 1987, and Ravindra R. Kamath, Shahriar Khaksari, Heidi Hylton Meier, and John Winklepleck, "Management of Excess Cash: Practices and Developments," *Financial Management,* 14 (Autumn 1985), Exhibit 5, 73.

[a] Indicates percent of state and corporations responding to the respective studies which used the respective investment instruments. It should be noted, again, that not all states can hold these assets.

[b] For the corporations, this group includes money market funds, Merrill Lynch Ready Asset Accounts, Canadian CDs and variable preferred among others. For the states, the other category indicates that 73.33% of the states held at least one security note listed. However, less than 10% of all 34 states responding held one of the assets not listed on this table.

TABLE 14.4
Ranking and Relative Importance of Criteria Considered by
States in Selecting Money Market Instruments
(1 = Most Important and 6 = Least Important)

Factors	Weight	Rank	Relative Importance Score
State Statute	185	1	100.00
Preserve Capital	157	2	84.86
Liquidity	115	3	62.16
Rate of Return	112	4	60.54
Convenience	67	5	36.22
Other	6	6	3.24

Source: NAST Survey, 1987.

Investment Criteria

In order to examine the relative importance of money market investment criteria, the states in the NAST study were asked to rank six specific criteria, ranging from state statute to rate of return in terms of their relative importance in selecting investment assets. The criteria options for the state respondents were the same as those used by the Kamath study with the exception that the Kamath study considered corporate policy as an option while the NAST study considered state statute as a criterion option. The responses were separated into two exhibits. Table 14.5 lists the relative importance of the various criteria as reported by the states. The criteria weighting system used to rank the criteria specified by the states follows the presentation by Kamath and others.[40] The findings indicate that state statutes are the dominant factor among the states for choosing money market securities followed by preservation of capital and liquidity. By comparison, Kamath and others determined that company policy ranked third behind preservation of capital and rate of return as the major reasons for selecting corporate portfolio assets.

Table 14.5 extends the analysis of factors influencing asset choice by adding the dimension of investment size to the investment asset decision. Preservation of capital ranked as the single most important factor for selecting state investment for portfolios both below and above $1,000,000 in size and portfolio assets after statute limitations. In the Kamath[41] study, size of investment also had little impact on the ranking of the six criteria in terms of their relative importance in influencing asset selection. The priority ranking of

(1) preservation of capital;

(2) rate of return;

(3) company policy;

(4) liquidity;

(5) convenience; and

---

[40] Since there are six criteria, each criterion, or factor, would have a certain frequency for it under the classification of "most important," and so on, as assigned by the respondents in each survey. The frequency of responses under the "most important" were assigned a weight of six, the next five, and so on all the way down to a weight of one to responses listed last. By multiplying the response frequencies by the appropriate weights and editing, a total score was obtained for each criterion which, in turn, was utilized to rank the relative importance of the various criteria. Specifically, the total score or weight of each criterion was divided by the highest total score (that of state statute in this case) and multiplied by 100 to arrive at the relative importance scores.

[41] Kamath.

TABLE 14.5
Ranking and Relative Importance of Criteria Considered by States in
Selecting Money Market Instruments by Investment Size
(1 = Most Important and 7 = Least Important)

Factors	$100,000 to $999,000			Over $1,000,000		
	Weight	Rank	Percent	Weight	Rank	Percent
State Statute	175	1	100.00	209	1	100.00
Preserve Capital	142	2	81.14	181	2	86.00
Rate of Return	102	3	58.29	135	3	64.59
Liquidity	98	4	56.00	133	4	63.64
Available Instrument*	83	5	47.43	103	5	49.28
Convenience	69	6	39.43	70	6	33.49
Other	5	7	2.86	5	7	2.39

(6) other factors remained constant for the corporate group as investment portfolio size varied.

Because short-term cash management in both the public and private sectors often involves investment of funds already committed for future expenditures, the importance of capital preservation appears to be a
logical high priority for both groups. Finally, it is noted that "availability
of instrument" defined as whether the required minimum denomination
of an asset purchase limited the availability of an asset as an investment
alternative was added to the list of asset selection criteria. This was done
in order to determine whether investment size restrictions might affect
asset choice. The study results indicated that investment size did not appear to restrict asset choice for the state portfolio managers.

Investment Holding Period and Portfolio Composition

Another issue considered in the state portfolio study was the potential
impact that investment holding period might have on asset preference.
To determine such an impact, state portfolio managers were asked to
specify the three money market securities they preferred when they
wanted to invest for less than 30 days and for 30 days or more. Repurchase agreements were the preferred asset for investment periods less
than 30 days (Table 14.6), followed by commercial paper. For longer
periods, treasury bills, followed by certificates of deposit, were the
preferred securities. By comparison, Kamath and others reported that,
for corporations, repurchase agreements were the highest ranked securities for maturities of less than 30 days while negotiable CDs

TABLE 14.6
State Portfolio Managers' Security Preferences
Investment Holding Period

	Less Than 30 Days (Percent) First Choice	More Than 30 Days (Percent) First Choice
TB	6.90	31.03
AG	0.00	6.90
RP	51.72	10.34
CD	10.34	27.59
BA	0.00	3.45
CP	27.59	20.69
Other	3.45	0.00

Source: NAST Survey, 1987.

ranked highest for longer maturities.[42] Commercial paper was the second most preferred instrument for both maturity categories while Eurodollar deposits ranked third for both durations. Corporate managers displayed considerable variation in their selection choice for their fourth through eighth rankings.

Denominations of Investments

Table 14.7 indicates state preferences regarding investment increment size for various investment instruments. As can be seen, 62% of the CD placements were in denominations of less than $1,000,000 while 97% of the TB placements were in denominations of over $1,000,000 and 100% of AGs, RPs, YCDs, BAs, OSDs, and CP investments were over $1,000,000 in size. (It should be noted that YCD and OSD denomination data involved only one response and MUNIs involved only two responses.) Municipal investment denominations were split between less than and greater than $1,000,000.

The corporations had a similar pattern of denomination investments with 64% of the BAs, 70% of the NCDs, 76% of the CPs, 81% of the ECDs, 64% of the RPs, 70% of the MUNI notes (Municipals), 74% of the TBs, and 88% of the other investments being made in denominations of over $1,000,000.[43]

By investing denominations of less than $1,000,000 (i.e., CDs and MUNIs), states may be pursuing economic development and other

[42] Ibid.

[43] Ibid.

TABLE 14.7

Typical Dollar Denominations of Investments for Various Money Market
Instruments by States

	Number of Responses	$0–99,999	Denomination Amounts $100,000–999,999	$1,000,000 and over
TB	32	3.13	0.00	96.88
AG	27	0.00	0.00	100.00
RP	33	0.00	0.00	100.00
CD	29	3.45	58.62	37.93
YCD	1	0.00	0.00	100.00
BA	17	0.00	0.00	100.00
CP	18	0.00	0.00	100.00
OSD	1	0.00	0.00	100.00
MUNI	2	0.00	50.00	50.00
Other	9	0.00	44.44	55.56

Source: NAST Survey, 1987.

Note: Tabular values are percentages of respondents using each instrument.

goals within their state. Such pursuits may be counter to economies of
scale and higher rates of return achieved by larger investments. This is
particularly evident relative to the use of MUNIs in the state portfolios as MUNIs have lower yields due to the tax exempt nature of these
assets and relatively higher transaction costs. It is noted, however, that
states often purchase MUNIs to

(1) provide a market for their own securities; and
(2) to avoid arbitrage rebate calculation and filings with the Internal
    Revenue Service.

These data regarding denomination size support the work of Kamath and others[44] in finding that the most common denomination for
the various investments was in increments of $1,000,000 or more. Fur-
thermore, the concentration of investments in larger increments reduces
the number of securities which need to be managed and monitored.
Since state portfolios turn over very frequently (securities mature and
the proceeds reinvested), transaction costs can be reduced by increasing
the typical size of investment. Similar results are expected for corporate
investors.

[44] Ibid.

A comparison of public sector portfolios with their private sector counterparts suggest that while there are similarities in investment practices, the different operating environments in which the public funds and private sector portfolio managers operate dictates that there are real differences in actual assets held and in the time period of investments. In particular, public funds managers operate in an environment constrained by statutory and policy guidelines as to asset types that may be purchased and as a result, public funds are more frequently invested in treasury and agency securities and assets backed or collateralized by treasuries and agencies. Some states have moved to broader asset diversification in an attempt to enhance market return. Still, as a group, public funds managers concentrate their portfolios in a more restricted basket of securities than their private sector counterparts.

CONCLUSIONS

The management of state and local government cash reserves has emerged as a major financial management issue in the 1980s. State and local governments have begun to more fully realize that effective cash management can be a significant source of additional non-tax revenue. Therefore, a growing need exists to identify the most efficient and effective techniques and processes to improve the cash management process.

As noted, there are four major components of the cash management process including cash mobilization, cash forecasting, banking relationships and investment management. Each of these cash management system components involves a series of steps or activities which can enhance investment earnings. Cash mobilization activities as well as cash investment management processes of state and local governments can be significantly improved by drawing on private sector practices and procedures. Activities such as lockboxes, concentration accounts, zero-balance accounts, and cash forecasting practices described in this chapter are among the adoptable practices.

As state and local governments continue to increase their cash management capability, portfolio management, cash forecasting and mobilization procedures will be enhanced. The financial sector is changing rapidly as a result of changing regulations, technology and approaches to financial management. The challenge to the public sector funds management is to continue to identify and adopt new practices so that financial resources are optimized. To do less would be to breach the public trust.

CHAPTER 15

Governmental Accounting and Financial Reporting

Martin Ives
Governmental Accounting Standards Board

Accounting and financial reporting by state and local governments is based on the standards set by the Governmental Accounting Standards Board (GASB), created in 1984, and its predecessor, the National Council on Governmental Accounting (NCGA). In addition to these standards, the standards established for business enterprise accounting by the Financial Accounting Standards Board (FASB), previous accounting standard-setting bodies, such as the Accounting Principles Board of the American Institute of Certified Public Accountants (AICPA), and the body of accounting and financial reporting theory developed over the years also have an effect on governmental accounting. These standards, conventions, and procedures are known collectively as *generally accepted accounting principles* (GAAP).

The standards developed by the GASB become GAAP after extensive due process. The GASB's due process includes the use of task forces composed of knowledgeable individuals, exposing proposed standards to a broad group of financial report preparers, attestors and users, public hearings (as appropriate), and careful consideration of the comments received during that exposure. Once established, the standards have the force of the CPA profession's Code of Professional Ethics. AICPA Ethics Rule 203 provides that a member of the AICPA, when giving an opinion on financial statements, must follow GASB and FASB standards unless the attestor can demonstrate that, due to unusual circumstances, following the standards would cause the financial statements to be misleading.

The statutes of many states require that financial statements prepared by the state and its local governments be prepared in accordance with GAAP. Furthermore, financial reports prepared by state and local governments as a result of the Federal Single Audit Act must say whether the statements were prepared in accordance with GAAP. Some state statutes specifically define GAAP as the principles established by the GASB, and bond rating agencies encourage reporting in accordance with those principles.

The GASB was established as the successor to the NCGA, which together with its predecessor organizations, had developed accounting and financial reporting standards for state and local governments since the mid-1930s. Shortly after it came into existence, the GASB affirmed the then effective NCGA standards as GAAP, until modified or superseded by subsequent GASB standards. Several NCGA standards have already been modified or superseded by GASB standards. Because the GASB is in the process of examining the basic accounting and financial reporting structure for governments, many other changes can be expected. All standards specifically applicable to governmental entities are included in the GASB's *Codification of Governmental Accounting and Financial Reporting Standards*, which is updated periodically. (References made in this chapter to specific parts of the GASB Codification will use the term GASB Cod. Section XX.)

Governmental accounting and financial reporting differs in several significant respects from business enterprise accounting and financial reporting, particularly for "governmental-type" services financed by taxation (like police and fire protection, sanitation, health, education, and welfare). For governmental business-type activities operated through separate funds or separate corporations (like public utilities and public authorities), governmental accounting is similar to business enterprise accounting, although there are some differences. GASB accounting and financial reporting standards apply both to governmental activities accomplished through a legally constituted general government and to activities operated by separately constituted special-purpose governmental organizations.

This chapter first discusses the factors influencing governmental accounting, fund accounting, and the principles for recognizing and measuring revenues, expenditures, assets and liabilities. It then discusses the principles of financial reporting, including the objectives of reporting, the reporting entity, the structure of financial statements, the content of those statements, and other elements of financial reporting such as statistical data. Also included is a more detailed review of some specific aspects of financial reporting that are important to an analysis of governmental financial statements. Finally, there is a discussion of some major accounting and financial reporting issues currently on the GASB's agenda that are likely to affect some of the matters discussed in this chapter.

GOVERNMENTAL ACCOUNTING PRINCIPLES

Factors Influencing Governmental Accounting and Financial Reporting

As noted, governmental accounting and financial reporting differs from the private sector in several significant respects. Knowledge of the factors affecting governmental accounting and financial reporting will make those differences easier to understand. The most significant factors are:

(a) the role of the governmental budget;

(b) the use of fund accounting as a means of control; and

(c) the nature of the relationship between governmental resources (and resource providers) and expenditures.

The budget is perhaps the single most significant financial document in government. The budget is a statement of financial intent, setting forth the proposed expenditures for the year and the means of financing them. In most governmental jurisdictions, the executive branch prepares a budget and submits appropriation bills to the legislative branch. Once they become law by action of the legislature, these bills serve not only as *authorizations of* amounts that may be spent for particular purposes, but also as *limitations on* (that is, as controls over) those amounts. The executive branch of government is accountable to the legislative branch within the context of the appropriation laws; generally, budgetary authorizations may not be exceeded without due process.

The idea of a "balanced budget" is basic to governmental finance in most jurisdictions. The budget shows how revenues will be raised and purports to demonstrate (although it doesn't always do so) fiscal responsibility by living within those revenues. The result of the budgetary process is fund balance—the amount left over at period-end for future governmental expenditures. (The laws of some jurisdictions require that the fund balance be retained in a "rainy day" fund or be used to reduce future years' taxes.) Because of its central role in the governmental financial process, the budget has had a major influence on governmental accounting and financial reporting.

Another means of controlling governmental expenditures is the use of fund accounting. A *fund* is a fiscal mechanism that creates an accounting entity—a self-balancing set of accounts for recording (and segregating) the financial transactions related to a specific activity or activities. Funds are intended to provide assurance that moneys raised for a particular purpose are used for that purpose and none other. For example, if a special tax is placed on gasoline sales to finance a highway repair program, a special highway fund may be established to provide accountability for the related revenues and expenditures. Similarly, property taxes raised to make debt service payments on general obligation debt may be placed into a debt service fund to demonstrate accountability for those taxes.

Governmental accounting and financial reporting has also been influenced by the nature of the relationship between the basic providers of governmental resources (the taxpayers) and the services they use. Business enterprise transactions are typically characterized by an exchange relationship—a simultaneous benefit and sacrifice to both the enterprise and the consumer. From the viewpoint of the enterprise, this exchange results in the ability to match costs and revenues, providing a measure of performance: net profit. In government, there is generally no exchange relationship. Instead, resources are marshalled from taxpayers, who provide those resources in a manner (for example, personal income and property taxes) and to an extent that does not necessarily match the benefits received by those individual taxpayers. Whatever matching exists is on a community-wide basis, relating to a specific period of time. Except where user charges are made for specific governmental services, there is no need to measure "profits" or to balance revenues with costs on a transaction basis; instead, financial resources are balanced with financial expenditures.

The lack of an overall performance measure (like profit or loss) and the fact that individual taxpayers may not receive benefits in relation to resources provided, makes government look to other ways to demonstrate accountability; the executive branch must be accountable to the legislature, and both must be accountable to the citizen/taxpayer. The need for demonstrating accountability results in reporting by fund and fund type and in making comparisons between budgeted and actual revenues and expenditures. Future governmental financial reporting will likely expand on the notion of accountability; for example, by expanding reporting to include measures of service efforts and accomplishments.

Fund Accounting

Governmental accounting is characterized by fund accounting. A fund is defined in GASB Cod. Section 1300 as "a fiscal and accounting entity with a self-balancing set of accounts recording cash and other financial resources, together with all related liabilities and residual equities or balances, and changes therein, which are segregated for the purpose of carrying on specific activities or attaining certain objectives in accordance with special regulations, restrictions, or limitations." From an accounting and financial management perspective, general purpose governmental entities like states, cities and counties are a combination of several (sometimes many) funds. Special purpose governmental entities, like public authorities, often accomplish their accounting through a single, integrated set of accounts, but some use more than one fund. Generally, separate funds are created because of legal (constitutional, statutory, or contractual) requirements to do so; however, they may also be established for administrative reasons. Using funds makes it easier to demonstrate accountability. It provides a control mechanism that helps to show that funds raised for specific purposes are used for those purposes and none other. Aside from legal requirements, however, there is no absolute need to account by means of separate funds; accountability can also be achieved by using separate accounts within a particular fund. Governmental accounting standards suggest establishing only the minimum number of funds to meet legal and operating requirements, because unnecessary funds result in lack of flexibility and undue complexity. Further, fund accounting does not necessarily mean that assets have been physically segregated; for example, even with fund accounting, cash applicable to several funds may be kept in a single bank account unless there is a legal requirement for separate bank accounts.

The funds used by governments fall into three general categories: governmental fund types, proprietary fund types, and fiduciary fund types. There are four governmental fund types: the general fund, special revenue funds, debt service funds, and capital projects funds. (A fifth governmental fund type, special assessment funds, was eliminated as a result of GASB Statement No. 6, *Accounting and Financial Reporting for Special Assessments,* effective for financial statements issued for periods beginning after June 15, 1987.) There are two proprietary fund types: enterprise funds and internal service funds. Trust and agency funds are generally considered together as constituting the fiduciary fund types.

Not every governmental entity uses every type of fund. Neither does every governmental entity account for similar transactions in the same fund type; nor does every governmental entity maintain the same number of funds to account for the same type of transactions. For example, some governmental entities have numerous special revenue funds; some have only a few. Some report transactions in the general fund that others report in a special revenue fund. Some report debt service transactions in debt service funds, while others use the general fund. Some even account for activities in a special revenue fund what others account for by using an enterprise fund. The financial statement user can generally determine the fund structure of a particular governmental entity by reading the "statement of significant accounting policies" note to the financial statements.

Governmental Fund Types. Most governmental functions are accounted for in governmental fund types. These funds are, in essence, segregations of *financial* resources. (The term financial resources is used to distinguish these resources from an entity's capital resources. The significance of this distinction will become apparent in the discussion of measurement focus/basis of accounting, which follows below.)

The General Fund. The general fund is sometimes described as the fund that accounts for all financial resources other than those required to be accounted for in another fund. This description tends to understate the significance of the general fund, because the general fund usually accounts for most of the day-to-day operating activities of government, that is, those that are financed by general tax revenues and miscellaneous revenues. In a city, for example, the general fund ordinarily accounts for the financial resources (such as property, sales and other taxes and miscellaneous revenues) used to finance the police, fire, and sanitation departments, the street maintenance department, and other day-to-day operating activities—a large portion of the services a government provides.

Special Revenue Funds. These funds are used to account for revenues that are legally restricted to expenditure by the government for specified purposes. Most special revenue fund activities are of a current operating nature, similar to activities financed by general fund resources. For example, a special revenue fund may be used to account for park user fees intended solely for park maintenance, even though other park activities are financed by general fund revenues. Some governmental entities account for federal grants through special revenue funds, while others account for them through appropriate accounting segregations in the general fund. Year-end balances in the special revenue funds are restricted to expenditure for similar purposes in future years; whether the restrictions are numerous or limited depends on the laws that establish the individual funds.

Debt Service Funds. Debt service funds are used to account for the accumulation of resources for, and the payment of, general long-term debt principal and interest. Debt service funds may be financed by specific taxes (such as a specified portion of the property tax) credited directly to the debt service fund, or by transfers of financial resources from other funds. Debt service funds may be used to accumulate resources intended to pay debt service due in the immediate future on serial bonds or to pay debt service due in the longer term (as a sinking fund, for example). They may also be used to accumulate resources for debt service reserves. Not all government debt service, however, is accounted for in debt service funds.

Debt service expenditures are sometimes made directly from the general fund. Debt related to and paid from user charges of an enterprise fund is accounted for in the enterprise fund, even if the debt carries the full faith and credit of the governmental entity.

Capital Projects Funds. Capital projects funds are used to account for financial resources to be used for the acquisition or construction of major capital facilities. Not all capital outlays, however, are accounted for in a capital projects fund; those related to proprietary and trust funds are accounted for in those funds. And minor capital outlays are frequently financed directly through the general or other operating-type funds. Resources to finance capital projects may come from bond proceeds, grants from other governments, transfers from other funds, or from other sources such as dedicated tax revenues. The financial resources remain in the capital projects fund until they are expended for capital purposes. Capital projects funds are not used to account for capital assets once constructed or acquired; if at all, those assets are accounted for in the general fixed assets account group, discussed below. Capital projects financed with special assessment debt are accounted for like any other capital project.

Account Groups. Because governmental funds are used to account only for *financial* resources—and as described later, only for *current* financial resources and liabilities—accounting within the governmental fund types is incomplete. To complete the accounting process, account groups are used to record the government's general fixed assets and general long-term debt. The general fixed assets account group (GFAAG) is not a fund because the assets it records are not resources available for expenditure. The general long-term debt account group (GLTDAG) is not part of a fund because the liabilities it records did not require use of financial resources during the current accounting period. Both account groups are self-balancing in the sense that the offset to the general fixed assets is reported simply as "investment in general fixed assets" and the offset to the liabilities is reported as "amount to be provided."

General Fixed Assets Account Group. As discussed in GASB Cod. Section 1400, the GFAAG is used to account for a governmental entity's fixed assets other than those accounted for in proprietary funds or trust funds. Under current accounting standards, recording infrastructure fixed assets (roads, bridges, curbs and gutters, streets and sidewalks, street lighting systems and similar assets that are immovable and of value only to the governmental unit) is optional; as a result, GFAAG assets usually include only land, buildings, machinery and equipment, and capitalized leases. Recording accumulated depreciation against the GFAAG fixed assets is optional; even when recorded, however, depreciation is not treated as a charge in the governmental funds themselves. The fixed assets are accounted for at cost, which may be estimated if original cost is not practicably determinable.

General Long-Term Debt Account Group. As discussed in GASB Cod. Section 1500, the GLTDAG includes two types of long-term obligations: (a) those resulting from the issuance of debt instruments, such as general obligation debt, and (b) those resulting from certain operating events, transactions, or circumstances that occurred in the past, but that are not current liabilities recorded in governmental funds. The first category is the unmatured principal of bonds, warrants, notes, or other forms of long-term general obligation indebtedness that is not a specific liability of a proprietary or trust fund. The latter includes the noncurrent portion of the general government liability for pensions, claims, judgments, compensated absences and certain other liabilities.

Proprietary Fund Types. Proprietary funds are used to account for activities similar to those often found in business enterprise. Because these funds measure net income, they account for all resources used by the activity (including capital resources) rather than only financial resources. There are two types of proprietary funds.

Enterprise Funds. Enterprise funds are used to account for the transactions of entities that engage in business-type activities for the benefit of the citizenry. Enterprise funds are established when the intent of the governing body is that the costs (including depreciation) of providing goods or services be recovered primarily through user charges or when the governing body decides that periodic determination of revenues, expenses and net income is appropriate for public policy, capital maintenance or other purposes. (Some business-type activities are accounted for as special revenue funds because the governing body believes it is more appropriate to measure financial resource flows than net income.) Some enterprise funds are activities of the legally constituted governmental entity; for example, a department of government may operate a water supply activity, an electric utility or a municipal hospital. Others are organized as separate legally constituted entities, such as public authorities. The fact that an activity is accounted for in an enterprise fund does not necessarily mean that all of its operating costs are financed from charges against the users of the specific services provided by the activity. Many enterprise funds, whether organized as departments of general government or as separately constituted public authorities, are subsidized by general governmental revenues, specifically dedicated tax revenues, and intergovernmental grants. Other enterprises may generate sufficient cash flows to provide revenues to the general government itself.

Internal Service Funds. Internal service funds are used to account for the financing of goods and services provided by one governmental department or agency to another, on a cost-reimbursement basis. Internal service funds accumulate the costs of specific activities (including depreciation of capital assets) and charge those costs to other governmental departments or funds. Activities sometimes financed through internal service funds include motor pools, computer services, and self-insurance.

Fiduciary Fund Types. The fiduciary funds, commonly referred to as trust and agency funds, account for resources held by the governmental entity in a trust or agency capacity. Often, the resources held in a trust or agency capacity are for the benefit of individuals, private organizations, or other governmental entities, but sometimes the beneficiary of the fund is the governmental entity itself. The most common form of trust fund is the pension trust fund, where resources are held for ultimate payment to the employees of the governmental entity or other governmental entities. Another common form of trust fund is the endowment fund, in which the beneficiary may be the government itself or certain groups of individuals. Agency funds are used typically to account for income taxes withheld from employee salaries, deferred compensation under Section 457 of the Internal Revenue Code, and property or other taxes collected by one governmental entity for subsequent transmittal to another. The distinction between trust funds and agency funds is often a very fine one, even though accounting for the two fund types differs somewhat.

Measurement Focus and Basis of Accounting

Understanding the measurement focus and basis of accounting in governmental accounting is essential to financial statement analysis. Measurement focus refers to *what* is being measured. For example, one may want to determine the year's net income for a particular activity; or one may want to measure the inflows and outflows of financial resources during the year; or to determine whether there was sufficient cash flow to meet debt service requirements. Basis of accounting refers to *when* revenues and expenditures are recognized in the financial statements. The accounts might, for example, report on a full accrual basis (revenues are recognized when earned and expenses when incurred regardless of when cash is received or paid); a modified accrual basis (revenues are recognized when measurable and available to finance current period expenditures and expenditures are recognized if they would normally be liquidated with expendable available financial resources); or a cash basis (revenues are recognized when cash is received and expenditures when cash is paid). The basis of accounting helps to accomplish a particular measurement focus; for example, accrual accounting is better than cash accounting if the focus is to measure net income.

Proprietary Funds. To show the contrast with governmental fund accounting, it is useful to start with a discussion of the measurement focus and basis of accounting used by proprietary funds. Most governmental business-type activities (including those organized as public authorities) use proprietary fund accounting, which is similar to business enterprise accounting. Business enterprise transactions generally take the form of exchanges, in which both the provider of goods or services and the consumer make simultaneous sacrifices to obtain benefits. To measure business enterprise profits, there is a need to match the revenues from a transaction (the benefit) with the costs of the transaction (the sacrifice). Business enterprises use accrual accounting, in which transactions, events, and circumstances are recognized when they occur, rather than when cash changes hands. Revenues are recognized in the period they are earned and expenses are matched against those revenues.

Accrual accounting (as applied to expenses) is comprised of two elements: (a) accruals, in which a charge is made to a particular accounting period based on the occurrence of a transaction, event, or circumstance, even though cash is paid at a later date, and (b) deferrals and amortizations, in which a charge is made to the period benefited even though cash may have been paid in a previous period. Depreciation of capital assets is a significant form of deferral and amortization; the using up of a capital asset is recognized as an expense in a systematic and rational method over the life of that asset. In proprietary fund accounting, all economic resources, both financial and capital, are included in a single fund. There is no need for a series of funds and account groups to separate financial and capital transactions, assets, and liabilities, as there is in governmental fund accounting.

Governmental Funds. General governments (states, cities, counties, towns) and other governmental entities that are accounted for in governmental funds are not concerned with measuring net income, but rather with measuring the flows of financial resources. The primary purpose of governmental fund accounting is to account for the sources and uses of financial resources, so that the net financial resources available for subsequent appropriation and expenditure are known. Governmental fund accounting considers the budgetary process. As indicated earlier, most governmental revenues come not from exchanges, but from the marshalling of resources from taxpayers to pay for the general expenditures of running the government. There is no direct relationship between a particular revenue source, such as property tax, and a particular type of expenditure, such as police protection.

There is no need to match revenues with costs from exchanges, to determine net income. Once financial resources have been expended to acquire capital assets, those resources are no longer available for future appropriation. If a capital asset is acquired from the proceeds of debt, the focus is on accumulating financial resources to pay off the debt, not on deferring the original cost of the fixed asset and spreading that cost over future periods. Note the relationship between the focus on measuring financial resource flows and the definition of governmental funds as segregations of *financial* resources.

Under current governmental accounting standards, governmental funds focus only on *current* inflows and outflows of *financial* resources; revenues and expenditures not received or paid either during the year or shortly thereafter are not recognized as part of that year's revenues and expenditures. To measure the inflows and outflows of current financial resources, governmental funds recognize revenues and expenditures on what is known as the *modified accrual* basis of accounting. (See discussion at end of this section concerning forthcoming changes based on changes in GASB standards.) The modified accrual basis of accounting is described in GASB Cod. Section 1600; its effect on recognizing and measuring specific items of revenue and expenditure is described below.

Revenue Recognition. Revenues and other governmental fund financial resource increments are recognized in the accounting period that they become both *measurable* and *available* to finance the expenditures of the period. The term "available" means collectible within the current period or soon enough thereafter to be used to pay the liabilities of the current period. For the most common source of local governmental revenues—property taxes—this means that revenues are recognized in the fiscal period for which the taxes are levied, provided they are due to be received within that period and are actually received either before the period, during the period, or soon enough thereafter to be able to pay the bills of the period. The term "soon enough thereafter" is intended normally to be a period not greater than 60 days; if received more than 60 days after the end of the period, the revenues would ordinarily not be recognized until the next period. If property taxes are actually received before the period they are intended to finance, those revenues are deferred and recognized in the period they are intended to finance. (See GASB Cod. Section P70.)

Sales taxes and taxpayer-assessed income taxes (personal and corporate) are generally recognized when the cash is received, although accruals are made by some state and local governments. Current standards say that it is neither necessary nor practical to attempt to accrue those taxes unless taxpayer liability and collectibility have been clearly established, as when tax returns have been filed, but collection is delayed beyond the normal time of receipt. Therefore, sales taxes collected by merchants are generally recognized as revenues when received from the merchant. However, sales taxes collected and held by one governmental entity for another at year-end are generally accrued if they are received in time to pay obligations incurred. (See GASB Cod. Section S10.) For personal income and corporation taxes, most governmental jurisdictions have adopted systems of withholding and estimated tax payments and recognize revenue as cash is received. If personal income taxes have been overwithheld by a governmental entity, the amount overwithheld should be estimated and treated as a reduction of revenues. Fees, inspection charges, parking meter receipts, parking violation fines, and miscellaneous revenues are generally recognized when cash is received.

Expenditure Recognition. Expenditures from governmental funds are generally recognized when the related liability is incurred, but there are a number of significant exceptions to the general rule as well as some options. (Note that an "expenditure" is a decrease in financial resources; the term "expenses" is not used because that term includes allocations of the cost of assets acquired with previously expended financial resources, such as depreciation.) The major governmental expenditure—salaries—is recognized in the period that an employee provides services, regardless of when paid. Items purchased for inventory may be treated as expenditures either when purchased or when used. Financial resources are usually appropriated for maturing principal and interest on general long-term debt when those payments are due, and debt service expenditures are ordinarily recognized when due. However, if resources have been provided during the current year for payment of principal and interest due early in the following year, the expenditure may be recognized in the current year.

Certain types of expenditures resulting from transactions, events or circumstances that occur in a particular accounting period may not result in current cash outflows, that is, outflows either during the period or shortly thereafter. They include such items as claims (which may not be settled in some jurisdictions for five or more years), compensated absences (vacation and sick leave, which employees may be allowed to accumulate, at least in part, until retirement) and pensions (which some governments may choose to fund only partially or not at all). These expenditures may not require the use of available expendable resources. Current governmental fund expenditure recognition standards require that they be recognized as expenditures only to the extent reasonably expected to be paid from existing fund assets; that is, to the extent settled (in the case of claims), appropriated (in the case of pensions), and due because of retirement (in the case of compensated absences). The difference between the amount recognized as an expenditure in the current period and the amount applicable to the period (in the case of pensions, for example, an amount calculated in accordance with an acceptable actuarial method) is reported in the GLTDAG, offset by an "amount to be provided." That amount does not flow through the governmental fund's operating statement until paid or expected to be paid from available expendable resources. Therefore, a complete understanding of the long-term financial effect of current-period governmental fund transactions, events and circumstances requires analysis not only of the fund accounts, but also of the GLTDAG. (See GASB Cod. Sections C50, C60, T25, and P 20.110-113.)

Capital Acquisitions Financed with Debt. As previously indicated, the capital projects fund is a governmental fund and reports only the financial resources available to meet capital expenditures. Also, most governments segregate the financial resources available to meet debt service expenditures from other financial resources by accounting for them in debt service funds. As a result, accounting for most capital assets acquired by incurring debt is accomplished through two fund types (generally, capital projects and debt service funds) and two account groups (GFAAG and GLTDAG). The debt issued is reported in the GLTDAG. The financial resources obtained as a result of issuing the debt are reported as an "other financing source" in the capital projects fund, and the expenditures for purchasing or constructing capital assets are also reported in that fund. The asset acquired or constructed is reported in the GFAAG, unless it is an infrastructure fixed asset, for which GFAAG reporting is optional. The expenditure of financial resources for debt service is reported in the debt service fund, if a debt service fund is required; if not, those expenditures may be reported in the general fund. In some governments, resources being accumulated to pay debt service may be reported initially in the general fund and then transferred to the debt service fund as an operating transfer.

Change in Measurement Focus and Basis of Accounting—Governmental Funds. As a result of GASB Statement No. 11, issued in May 1990, there will be significant changes in the measurement focus and basis of accounting for governmental funds, effective for financial statements for periods beginning after June 15, 1994. The measurement focus will change from *current* financial resources to *total* financial resources (referred to simply as financial resources) and the basis of accounting and will change from *modified accrual* to *accrual*. This means that governmental fund operating statements will recognize the effects of transactions or events on financial resources when they take place, regardless of when cash is received or paid. Except for capital transactions and depreciation, financial statement recognition and measurement procedures for governmental and proprietary funds will be essentially the same.

Under the new standards, tax revenues will be recognized in the financial statements when an "underlying" transaction or event has occurred and the government has demanded the taxes, regardless of when cash is received. For example, property taxes will be recognized in the budgetary period for which the taxes are levied, provided the government has demanded the taxes on or before the end of the period, regardless of when the cash is received by the government. Operating expenditures will be recognized when transactions that result in claims against financial resources take place, regardless of when cash is paid. Hence, expenditures like claims, compensated absences and pensions will be recognized in the financial statements when the events occur or the employees earn the benefits. These significant changes will result in greater consistency and comparability of reporting within and among governments.

FINANCIAL REPORTING PRINCIPLES

Introduction

Governmental financial reporting standards recommend the publication of a comprehensive annual financial report (CAFR) containing:

(1) the general purpose financial statements (GPFS) prepared by *fund type* and account group; and

(2) more detailed data on *individual funds*, as well as statistical data and supplementary information.

The GPFS are the primary or basic financial statements issued by governmental entities; those statements together with the related notes and required supplementary information are required for a fair presentation in accordance with GAAP. Certified public accountants generally express their opinion only on the GPFS. The GPFS are ordinarily included in official statements issued by the governmental entity for bond offering purposes. Because they are prepared by fund type, the GPFS provide an overview of the governmental entity's financial position and results of operations; the remainder of the CAFR provides details by fund, details within a fund (such as schedules of revenues that may have been summarized in the GPFS), and important statistical information.

Governmental financial reporting considers the needs of those who use the reports and the environment in which governments operate. The major users of governmental financial reports have been identified generally as those to whom the government is primarily accountable (the citizen/taxpayer), those who represent the citizenry (legislative and oversight bodies), and those who lend or who participate in the lending process (investors and creditors). The needs of other financial report users, such as higher level grantor agencies, are generally considered to be included within the needs of the major users. Internal management is also considered to be an important user of financial reports, although management has the ability to satisfy its needs through internal reports.

In assessing the kind of information that may be available through financial reporting, the financial analyst needs to understand the limitations of financial reporting. These limitations include: the fact that users have both similar and different needs, so that general purpose financial reporting is designed to meet the common needs of all users; the fact that financial information is often based on estimates and judgments; and the fact that information has a cost to prepare and attest, so that reporting standards are established on the basis of the standard-setters' judgments of whether the cost to produce a particular element of information is worth the benefits expected to be derived from that information.

Financial Reporting Objectives

As previously indicated, governmental financial reporting is in a state of evolution. One of the GASB's first projects was Statement of Governmental Accounting Concepts No. 1, *Objectives of Financial Reporting* (May, 1987). The Statement says that governmental financial reporting should provide information to assist users in assessing accountability and making economic, social, and political decisions. Traditional emphasis on accountability in governmental financial reporting has already resulted in differences from business enterprise financial reporting (for example, governmental financial reporting requires a comparison of budgeted revenues and expenditures with actual) and is likely to result in more. The financial reporting objectives listed below are from the Statement. Specific standards will need to be developed by the GASB before some of them [particularly items a.(3) and c.(2)] can be met.

a. Financial reporting should assist in fulfilling government's duty to be publicly accountable and should enable users to assess that accountability by:

(1) Providing information to determine whether current-year revenues were sufficient to pay for current-year services

(2) Demonstrating whether resources were obtained and used in accordance with the entity's legally adopted budget, and demonstrating compliance with other finance-related legal or contractual requirements

(3) Providing information to assist users in assessing the service efforts, costs, and accomplishments of the governmental entity

b. Financial reporting should assist users in evaluating the operating results of the governmental entity for the year by:

(1) Providing information about sources and uses of financial resources

(2) Providing information about how it financed its activities and met its cash requirements

(3) Providing information necessary to determine whether its financial position improved or deteriorated as a result of the year's operations

c. Financial reporting should assist users in assessing the level of services that can be provided by the governmental entity and its ability to meet its obligations as they become due by:

(1) Providing information about its financial position and condition

(2) Providing information about its physical and other nonfinancial resources having useful lives that extend beyond the current year, including information that can be used to assess the service potential of those resources

(3) Disclosing legal or contractual restrictions on resources and the risk of potential loss of resources.

Financial Reporting Entity

The fact that governmental entities have similar designations, like "states" or "cities," does not necessarily mean that all similarly designated entities are organized and perform their activities in the same way. Some entities create separately constituted legal units like public authorities and special districts to perform certain functions. For greater comparability and more comprehensive financial reporting, the governmental financial reporting entity has been defined to include separately constituted organizations that meet certain criteria. The governmental financial reporting entity is comprised of (1) "component units," which are the separate governmental units, agencies or corporations that meet the criteria for combining with other component units to form the financial reporting entity and (2) the "oversight unit," which is the "core" government, the component unit that has the ability to exercise oversight responsibility over all other component units.

As discussed in GASB Cod. Section 2100, the basic, but not the only, criterion for including a governmental department, agency, public authority, or other governmental organization in a reporting entity for financial reporting purposes is the ability of the oversight unit's elected officials to exercise *oversight responsibility* over that agency. The most significant manifestation of oversight responsibility is *financial interdependency*. An oversight unit and a potential component unit are financially interdependent if the potential component unit imposes a financial burden on or provides a financial benefit to the oversight unit; for example, financial interdependency exists if the oversight unit is responsible for financing a potential component unit's deficits, receiving its surpluses, or guaranteeing (or being "morally responsible" for) its debt. A specific example of this relationship is a public authority created to build office buildings for the oversight unit, with debt service on the authority's "moral obligation" bonds financed by "rental payments" from the oversight unit.

Other manifestations of the ability of an oversight unit to exercise oversight responsibility are: selecting the potential component unit's governing authority, appointing its management, significantly influencing its operations (for example, by approving budgets, signing contracts, and hiring key personnel), and retaining accountability for fiscal matters. Other factors may be considered in borderline situations, such as where there is a special financing relationship and the failure to include a potential component unit may be misleading; the Municipal Assistance Corporation (MAC) for the City of New York is an example of this situation because MAC has issued debt on behalf of the City backed by what had previously been the City's sales tax revenues. The preparer of financial statements must exercise professional judgment in deciding which potential component units to include or exclude from the financial reporting entity, and the municipal analyst will be helped by reading the notes to financial statements that describe the reporting entity.

The financial statements of the component units comprising the financial reporting entity are incorporated with the statements of the oversight unit by fund type and account group in the general purpose financial statements. Most public authorities are classified as enterprise funds, so the accounts of those authorities are generally combined with the accounts of the other enterprise funds of the oversight unit. However, some public authorities, such as building authorities, may be classified as debt service funds and some as special revenue funds, depending on the nature of the authority's activity. Colleges and universities are frequently reported in a separate column because they use a basis of accounting different from that of the governmental funds and the proprietary funds. Details of the individual component unit financial statements are included in the CAFR's combining statements. More significant details about enterprise funds can be found in the notes to financial statements as "segment" information.

GASB Statement No. 14, issued in June 1991, makes certain changes in the reporting entity standards, effective for financial statements for periods beginning after December 15, 1992. The most significant change will be in the way the entity is reported in the financial statements.

The new definition of the reporting entity, which is not significantly different from the current definition, is based on the notion of financial accountability. A primary government is financially accountable for organizations that make up its legal entity and for legally separate organizations if (a) its officials appoint a voting majority of the organization's governing body *and* either it is able to impose its will on that organization or there is a potential for the organization to provide specific financial benefits to, or to impose specific financial burdens on, the primary government or (b) the organization is fiscally dependent on the primary government.

The change in financial reporting resulted primarily from concern of analysts over the high degree of aggregation in the current reporting standards. Under the new standards, report users will be able to distinguish more readily between the primary government and its component units. As a general rule, component unit financial data will be reported in a column or columns separate from that of the primary government. Details concerning individual component units will be presented in separate statements or in the notes.

Financial Reporting Structure

As described in GASB Cod. Section 1900, governmental financial reporting is organized in the form of a pyramid, with increasing levels of detail provided farther down the pyramid. It is expected that the preparer will go as far down the pyramid as necessary to report the financial position and operating results of the *individual* funds and account groups, to demonstrate compliance with finance-related legal and contractual requirements, and to provide adequate disclosure at the individual fund level. The levels of the pyramid (in descending order) are:

(1) General purpose financial statements (combined statements). These statements provide a summary overview of the financial position of

all funds and account groups and of the operating results of all funds. (As previously indicated, under the new financial reporting standards, financial data of component units will be in a separate column or columns.) At this level of the pyramid, the individual funds within a particular fund type are combined, so that, for example, the operating results of all the special revenue funds are reported combined into a single figure. The combined statements are prepared in a multi-columnar format, with separate columns used for each fund type and account group.

(2) Combining statements, by fund type. These statements provide the link between the combined information included in the GPFS and the individual fund statements, showing how the balances in the individual fund statements aggregate to the totals appearing in the GPFS. They, too, are prepared in a multi-columnar format.

(3) Individual fund and account group statements. Generally, these statements are prepared to provide additional details on the individual funds and account groups. They may, for example, show comparisons of budgeted and actual revenues and expenditures by individual fund, and comparisons of current-year and prior-year data by individual fund.

(4) Schedules. Schedules provide additional details considered useful. For example, schedules may provide information on debt (by bond issue), revenues (by department), and tax delinquencies (by year). Schedules may also be provided to show compliance with bond agreement provisions. Comparisons of amounts appropriated by individual unit of appropriation with actual expenditures may also be shown.

General Purpose Financial Statements

The basic financial statements, the GPFS, are designed to be "liftable" from the CAFR, for widespread distribution to those who may not need the details included in the CAFR and for inclusion in bond offering statements. They are the statements that, together with the notes to financial statements, constitute "fair presentation in accordance with GAAP." Because these financial statements are presented by fund type and account group, each statement contains as many columns as there are fund types and account groups. For example, a municipality that has all the fund types and account groups will present nine columns of information in its balance sheet, for the four governmental fund types, the two proprietary fund types, the fiduciary fund types, and the two account groups.

The statements may also have total columns, labeled "memorandum only" because the totals are not comparable to a consolidation and because those totals do not purport to show data in conformity with GAAP as do the separate fund type columns. Although the multi-columnar fund type/account group format is designed to constitute "fair presentation" and omitting a particular column is likely to cause an audit exception, including a particular column does not necessarily mean that the "core" government has unlimited access to all of the assets presented for that fund type. For example, the assets of many trust and agency funds are the legal property of others, the assets of enterprise funds may be accessible only by the individual organizations whose accounts are included in those funds, and the assets of some funds may be restricted to use for particular purposes, such as for paying debt service.

Ordinarily, the GPFS is comprised of these five statements.

(1) Combined balance sheet—all fund types and account groups.

(2) Combined statement of revenues, expenditures, and changes in fund balances—all governmental fund types and expendable trust funds. This statement does not present the operations of the proprietary fund types because they have a different measurement focus/basis of accounting and, therefore, are presented separately.

(3) Combined statements of revenues, expenditures, and changes in fund balances—budget and actual—general and special revenue fund types and similar governmental fund types for which annual budgets have been legally adopted. This statement is prepared primarily for accountability purposes, but is also useful for analytical purposes. To assure that the information presented in this statement is internally consistent, the *actual* revenues and expenditures reported in this statement are reported on the same basis of accounting as the budget. As a result, the "actuals" shown in this statement will often not agree with that shown in the preceding statement, which is prepared on a GAAP basis. A reconciliation of the differences between the two sets of "actuals" is required to be presented either on the face of the financial statements or in the accompanying notes. Many of the differences result from accruals made for reporting in accordance with GAAP, and by including encumbrances for materials and services ordered but not received as of the balance sheet date as expenditures for budgetary purposes. Other differences may be caused by factors such as differences in the fund, organization, and appropriation structures as between the budget and the GAAP presentations.

(4) Combined statement of revenues, expenses, and changes in retained earnings (or equity)—all proprietary fund types (and similar trust funds). This is the proprietary fund operating statement counterpart to the statement shown in (2) above for governmental funds. "Segment" information on individual proprietary funds must be

disclosed in the notes if financial data for two or more of those funds have been combined or additional disclosures are needed to make the GPFS not misleading.

(5) Combined statement of cash flows—all proprietary fund types (and similar trust funds). This Statement, required by GASB Statement No. 9, effective for financial statements for fiscal years beginning after December 15, 1989, replaces the statement of changes in financial position. It classifies cash receipts and payments according to whether they result from operating, noncapital financing, capital and related financing, or investing activities.

Notes to Financial Statements and Required Supplementary Information

The notes to the financial statements are an integral part of the statements and must be read with them. The notes are intended to provide information essential for a fair presentation of the GPFS that is not readily apparent from, or cannot be included in, the GPFS. It is expected that the financial statement preparer will exercise judgment in preparing the notes, and some statements contain more detailed notes than others. GASB Cod. Section 2300 contains a listing of notes considered essential for fair presentation as well as additional disclosures that should be made, if applicable. GASB Statement No. 5 on pension disclosures also requires presentation of certain supplementary information outside the notes to financial statements that is necessary to meet the objectives of the GASB's pension disclosure requirements; this information is particularly helpful to analysts.

Among the notes considered essential to a fair presentation of the GPFS is a summary of significant accounting policies. This summary usually describes the principles used in determining the scope of the reporting entity for financial reporting purposes, the fund types used in presenting the statements, the revenue and expenditure/expense recognition policies of the funds, and the accounting policies for various assets and liabilities. General budget policies, including the budgetary basis of accounting, may also be found in this section of the notes. Some preparers also include significant operating information when describing the accounting policies (such as tax due dates and insurance information), so this note should be read carefully.

Other notes considered essential for fair presentation include: significant contingent liabilities (such as those resulting from lawsuits and claims); significant effects of events subsequent to the balance sheet date (such as new debt and refundings of old debt); pension plan obligations; material violations of finance-related legal and contractual provisions; debt service requirements to maturity (often shown annually for the first five years after the balance sheet date and in five-year totals thereafter); commitments under noncapitalized leases, construction, and other significant commitments; changes in general long-term debt; deficits in fund balances or retained earnings of significant funds; inter-fund receivables and payables; cash deposits with financial institutions; and investments. GASB Statement No. 12, effective for financial statements for periods beginning after June 15, 1990, requires certain disclosures about postemployment benefits other than pension benefits.

Other information of concern to the municipal analyst that may be in the notes includes: key operating and balance sheet accounts for certain enterprise funds (known as segment information); the effect on debt service requirements and the economic gain or loss resulting from advance refundings; outstanding short-term debt instruments; interfund eliminations in combined financial statements that may not be readily apparent from column headings; significant accounting policies and other information concerning public authorities; and the budget basis-GAAP basis operating statement reconciliation.

Statistical Tables

Information of particular use to municipal analysts can also be found outside of the GPFS, in statistical tables included in the CAFR. Statistical tables provide comparative financial data, often for ten years or more, as well as nonaccounting data, such as demographic and economic information. Among the statistical tables that may be found in the CAFR, as discussed in GASB Cod. Section 2800, are:

(1) Trend information of general governmental expenditures by function and general governmental revenues by source.
(2) Trend information about property taxes, such as tax levies and collections, assessed and estimated actual value of taxable property, and property tax rates of overlapping governments.
(3) Trend information about debt and debt service, such as the ratio of net general bonded debt to assessed value of property, per capita debt, the ratio of debt service to total general expenditures, and revenue bond coverage. Also, other debt information, such as the legal debt margin and overlapping debt.
(4) Economic indicators, such as property value, construction, and bank deposit trends.

Auditor's Opinion

The primary purpose of an independent audit is to express an opinion on whether the financial statements present fairly the entity's financial position and results of operations, in conformity with generally accepted accounting principles. A so-called "clean" opinion does not mean that the financial statements are absolutely correct, but rather that they are free from material misstatement. Neither does a "clean" opinion mean that the entity is free from any and all financial problems. The auditor is, however, expected to call attention to situations where a question arises about the ability of the governmental unit to meet its debts as they come due.

If engaged to audit an entity's combined general purpose financial statements, the auditor will express an opinion on the financial position of the governmental entity, the results of its operations, and the cash flows of its proprietary fund types. An auditor may also be engaged to express an opinion on the entity's combining individual fund and account group financial statements and supporting schedules, in which case the auditor will also express an opinion on whether those statements are fairly presented in all material respects in relation to the general purpose financial statements taken as a whole. Omission of one or more financial statements, fund types, funds, account groups, or component units that should have been included in the combined statements (such as the "budget versus actual" statement, the general fixed assets account group or an enterprise fund) may result in a qualified opinion because of a departure from GAAP.

COMMENTARY ON SPECIFIC ACCOUNTS, NOTES, AND STATEMENTS

This part of the chapter covers some specific financial statement elements, accounts, and notes, as well as some of the interrelationships among the financial statements. It is based partly on questions frequently asked of the author and is intended to help analyze governmental financial statements.

Pensions

Until recently, analysis of governmental pension obligations had been hindered by the diversity of actuarial funding methods, differing pension funding objectives, and the lack of financial reporting standards. As a result, pension obligation analysis focused on the size of the unfunded pension obligation at a point in time or on ratios of pension system revenues (typically, from employer contributions, employee contributions, and earnings from assets) versus expenditures (for employee benefits, employee withdrawals, and administrative expenses) for the current year. GASB Statement No. 5, *Disclosure of Pension Information by Public*

Employee Retirement Systems and State and Local Governmental Employers, attempts to provide more useful information for analytical purposes by standardizing the measure of the pension obligation; requiring disclosure of trends in certain pension funding ratios; and also requiring disclosure of the actuarial assumptions used in calculating the pension obligation. This GASB Statement was effective for financial reports issued for fiscal years beginning after December 15, 1986.

The standardized pension obligation measure (referred to in financial statements as the *pension benefit obligation*) will help in making comparisons among governmental employers and pension systems. The pension benefit obligation is the present value of benefits estimated to be payable in the future as a result of employee service to the date of the actuarial valuation or actuarial update, computed by attributing an equal benefit amount to each year of credited and expected future employee service. In calculating benefits, the effects of both projected salary increases and any step-rate benefits are included. This standardized measure must be disclosed regardless of the actuarial method used for pension funding purposes and even if pensions are not actuarially funded.

Pension reporting requirements for governmental employers necessarily differ depending on the type (single-employer, "agent" multiple-employer, or "cost-sharing" multiple employer) of public employee retirement system (PERS) to which an employer contributes. All PERS and certain employers must show the pension benefit obligation segregated among four major components (amounts applicable to retirees and beneficiaries currently receiving benefits and terminated employees entitled to benefits but not yet receiving them, accumulated employee contributions and related investment income, employer-financed share for vested current employees, and employer-financed share for nonvested current employees). Net assets available for benefits must also be disclosed; comparison of that amount with the components of the pension benefit obligation provides an indication (in the financial sense, rather than legal sense) of the extent to which those components are covered by the assets.

Employers contributing to single-employer PERS and "agent" multiple-employer PERS are required to disclose these ratios for a three-year period:

• Net assets available for benefits, expressed as percentages of the pension benefit obligation. (This calculation is often called the funded ratio. Generally, the greater the percentage, the stronger the pension system, so that a gradually increasing percentage implies that the system's funded status is improving over time. A system is said to be "fully funded" if the percentage is 100.)

- Unfunded pension benefit obligation (difference between the pension benefit obligation and net assets available for benefits), expressed as percentages of the annual covered payroll. (Generally, decreasing percentages over time imply improving pension system funding.)
- Employer contributions, expressed as percentages of annual covered payroll. Also, a statement as to whether contributions were made in accordance with actuarially determined requirements. (These percentages provide a measure of the relative burden on the employer of the annual pension contribution.)

PERS are required to disclose the details of the first two ratios for a 10-year period, together with information about changes in benefits, actuarial assumptions, and other matters that affect trends over that period. In addition, PERS are required to show the details of revenues by source and expenses by type for a 10-year period, which provides information for the more traditional pay-in versus pay-out pension analysis.

GLTDAG

As previously stated, the general long-term debt account group (GLTDAG) includes long-term obligations resulting from two types of transactions: (1) capital transactions and (2) current operating transactions not paid with expendable available financial resources. Note disclosure of changes in general long-term debt is considered essential to fair presentation of the GPFS, and governmental entities should reconcile bonds payable at the beginning and end of the fiscal year, showing new debt issued and old debt redeemed. Equally important to the municipal analyst is a reconciliation of the beginning and ending balances of the long-term obligations arising out of current operating transactions. Because certain current period transactions, events, and circumstances are reported in the governmental operating funds only to the extent financed from expendable available financial resources, a complete picture of the current year's operations cannot be obtained without analyzing the changes in the beginning and ending balances of the individual GLTDAG accounts.

Sometimes an analysis of the year's GLTDAG activity will be shown parenthetically in the captions on the face of the financial statements, sometimes it will appear in the notes, or sometimes not at all. Based on current accounting standards, the operating transactions that may be reported partially in the GLTDAG include pensions, claims and judgments, compensated absences, and special termination benefits. It is possible, however, that other operating expenditures, attributable to the past but to be paid in the future, will also be reported partially in the GLTDAG.

Interfund Transfers

Interfund transfers are a frequent cause of concern and confusion when analyzing governmental financial statements. Part of the concern results from the fact that amounts reported as transfers may be material relative to the amounts immediately preceding them (excess of revenues over or under expenditures). Part of the confusion results from the fact that transfers are not explained in the notes as often as they should.

It is appropriate to first describe what interfund transfers are *not*. Interfund transactions that would be treated as revenues, expenditures or expenses if they had involved organizations *external* to the governmental entity are not reported as transfers; these are known as quasi-external transactions. For example, routine contributions from the general fund to the pension trust fund, most internal service fund billings, and payments in lieu of taxes from an enterprise fund to the general fund are reported as revenues, expenditures, or expenses of the affected funds and not as transfers. (Payments to internal service funds for self-insurance may be reported currently as transfers, but GASB Statement No. 10 requires those payments to be reported as expenditures in periods beginning after June 15, 1994.)

Also, an expenditure or expense may be paid initially by one fund and subsequently reimbursed by the affected fund. These interfund transactions, which are called *reimbursements,* are also reported as expenditures or expenses of the affected fund and reductions of the expenditures or expenses of the fund that originally made the payment, and not as transfers. Interfund loans or advances are also not transfers; outstanding interfund loans (normally expected to be repaid in the next year) are reported in the balance sheet "due to/due from" accounts, and outstanding interfund advances (loans that are intended to be repaid over a period longer than one year) should be reported as advances in the balance sheet.

Two kinds of interfund transactions are reported as transfers: residual equity transfers and operating transfers.

(1) *Residual equity* transfers are nonrecurring or nonroutine transfers of *equity* between funds; for example, if a general fund contributes the initial capital to start an enterprise fund or an internal service fund or if a particular fund is discontinued and its residual equity balance is transferred to the general fund. Because these are equity transfers, they are reported as additions to or deductions

from the beginning fund balance of governmental funds; residual equity transfers to proprietary funds are reported as additions to contributed capital.

(2) *Operating* transfers are sometimes routine and sometimes not. Even routine operating transfers may be growing or declining in amount. That is why knowledge of the nature, cause, amount, and trend of the detail of the operating transfers is important in assessing the financial condition of particular funds and the reporting entity itself. Operating transfers include such items as: transfers from the general fund or a special revenue fund to an enterprise fund that are made to subsidize the operations of the enterprise fund; transfers from an enterprise fund to the general fund (other than payments in lieu of taxes) that help to finance general fund expenditures; budgeted transfers from the general fund to the capital projects fund, which have the effect of using operating resources rather than bonds to finance capital projects; and routine annual transfers of tax revenues from the general fund to the debt service fund. Some operating transfers (such as transfers to an enterprise fund or a component unit public authority) may represent a continuing and growing drain on the health of the entity, some (such as transfers to the capital projects fund) may indicate an improvement in the entity's health, and some may have no particular significance.

Operating transfers, like residual equity transfers, are distinguished from revenues, expenditures and expenses in the financial statements. Operating transfers are reported in the "other financing sources (uses)" section of the governmental fund operating statement and in the "operating transfers" section of the proprietary fund operating statement. Transfers of resources from a fund legally authorized to receive them to a fund legally authorized to expend them may, as an alternative, be reported as deductions from gross revenues in the former and additions to revenues in the latter.

The municipal analyst should also have an understanding of the causes of the "due to/due from" accounts in the balance sheet, because they may result from any of the transactions discussed. Often, they are merely the result of timing differences between the recognition of a quasi-external, reimbursement, or transfer transaction, and the outflow of cash. Sometimes, however, these balances are caused by interfund loans; for example, general fund cash may be used to finance capital projects pending the issuance of bonds or to cover temporary cash shortages in other funds. The analyst may want to inquire about the cause of the "due to/due from" accounts and the source and timing of their repayment.

Intragovernmental and Intergovernmental Relationships

Interfund transfers, described previously, provide some evidence of the financial relationships between the oversight unit and its components. Additional information can be obtained from the notes to the financial statements about the debt of the component units and the obligations, if any, assumed by the oversight unit for the payment of those debts. In addition to these *intra*governmental relationships, financial statement analysis also provides information about a governmental entity's *inter*governmental relationships, such as those of a city with the state and the federal government.

(1) The extent to which an oversight unit is responsible for the debts of its components varies considerably from government to government and among component units within a particular governmental entity. The debts of some component units may be formally guaranteed by the oversight unit's constitution or statutes; the debts of some may be a contractual obligation of the oversight unit (as often occurs in a public authority responsible for office building construction); the debts of some may be subject to the so-called "moral make-up clause," wherein the oversight unit's budget director is authorized to seek appropriations to restore the component's debt service funds to a particular level; the debts of some may carry no "makeup" provision at all, but the financial health of the component is so vital to the economy of the oversight unit that the oversight unit is likely to provide financial assistance, if needed; and assumption of the debts of others may be clearly forbidden by the oversight unit's constitution. Knowledge of these nuances, some of which may be obtained from the notes to financial statements, is necessary to understanding the financial condition of both the oversight unit and its component units.

(2) It is also useful to know the extent to which a governmental entity obtains revenues from external sources, since excessive dependency on external sources could result in financial difficulties if those sources were to cut back their support. Details of revenues from external sources may not always appear in the GPFS, and it may be necessary to analyze the individual fund statements or the detailed schedules. A helpful analytical tool is a statement showing a matrix of expenditures by type and revenues by source.

Budget versus Actual Comparisons

Typically, the budgetary amounts appearing in the combined statement of revenues, expenditures, and changes in fund balances—budget and actual—are based not on the original legally adopted budget, but rather on the budget as modified by amendments throughout the year (and sometimes even after the end of the year). Comparison of actual revenues and expenditures with the modified budget is useful for demonstrating accountability, but may not be as valuable to the municipal analyst as a comparison with the original budget. Comparison with the original budget helps to show how the governmental entity responded to changes to economic events such as revenue shortfalls. It also shows which particular programs experienced cutbacks or overruns during the year, providing evidence of program problems and management priorities. Analysis of the reconciliation between actual expenditures on a budgetary basis and actual expenditures on a GAAP basis might indicate a future drain on a government's financial resources.

Deferred Revenues

The deferred revenues account on the balance sheet sometimes causes confusion because deferred revenues result from several kinds of transactions. Revenue that is "deferred" will not be recognized as revenue until a subsequent year. However, a corresponding asset (cash or accounts receivable) is recognized when the revenue is deferred. Deferred revenues might represent:

(1) taxes normally billed and possibly even collected before the period they are intended to finance, such as property taxes received in November for a budget period starting the following January;

(2) taxes or miscellaneous revenues deliberately billed and collected before the period they would normally finance, because a municipality has been experiencing cash flow difficulties; and

(3) revenues like property taxes that were billed for the period just ended, but not expected to be collected until more than 60 days after the start of the new fiscal year and, therefore, not "available" to meet expenditures of the period just ended.

In the first two cases, the cash might have been received before the end of the year; in the third, the cash would not have been received and the deferred revenue would be offset by a like amount of accounts receivable. The municipal analyst may wish to inquire into the causes of growing amounts of deferred revenues or the sudden appearance of deferred revenues, if the causes are not readily apparent.

Factors Affecting Liquidity

Liquidity as shown by period-end cash balances may not be representative of the liquidity of the governmental entity throughout the fiscal year. Some governmental entities collect most of their taxes before the fiscal year begins, some ratably throughout the year, some essentially at year-end, and some not until the following year. Yet, cash outflows from governmental operating activities tend to occur ratably during the year. Cash inflows from intergovernmental revenues may also not match related cash outflows. Analysis of balance sheet account trends, notes to the financial statements, and statistical data included in the CAFR will aid the municipal analyst in assessing liquidity. For example, tax calendars may be included in the notes to the financial statements or elsewhere in the CAFR. Some governmental entities provide monthly cash flow statements in the CAFR.

Analysis of trends in taxes receivable and accounts receivable (measured as a percentage of revenues) may indicate either poor billing and collection practices or declining economic health of the governmental jurisdiction. Trend analysis of taxes receivable, assessed values of real property, and tax collections in the year of the levy is particularly helpful. A declining percentage of collections in the year of the levy may indicate developing problems in assessment practices, economic climate, or both. (In the period preceding New York City's mid-1970s fiscal crisis, for example, collections in the year of the tax levy declined, indicating the continued appearance on the tax rolls of properties that were not producing taxes.)

CURRENT ACCOUNTING AND FINANCIAL REPORTING ISSUES

Many fundamental issues affecting governmental accounting and financial reporting are on the GASB's current agenda. In addition to the newly issued standards referred to previously (some of which are not yet effective), it is likely that the GASB will issue standards affecting many other matters discussed above within the next few years. Some of the more significant issues currently on the GASB agenda are discussed here.

Financial Reporting Model

The most significant project currently on the GASB agenda is the financial reporting model. These are some of the issues being considered in the reexamination of the financial reporting model:

- Where should the assets and liabilities resulting from the change in measurement focus and basis of accounting for governmental funds be reported, in the funds or in the GLTDAG? (The GASB has tentatively decided to retain the traditional notion of "fund balance;" hence, the problem concerns the most informative way to report it.) What other changes are needed to improve the reporting of financial position?

- Should there be a clear "bottom line" (results of operations) on the operating statement, or should the operating statement be presented in an "all-inclusive" format where the final line is "fund balance?"

- What degree of aggregation should be reported in the general purpose financial statements? Should there be an additional financial statement, aggregating the fund type information in some manner? Should the general purpose financial statements also include less aggregated financial data; for example, should fund type information be supported with individual fund data?

- What is the most informative method of reporting fiduciary funds? (Some believe that reporting all fiduciary funds as part of the basic financial statements may be misleading to some users of those statements.)

Enterprise Funds

The GASB is reexamining the definition and measurement focus of enterprise funds. As noted elsewhere in this chapter, business-type activities are sometimes reported in special revenue funds rather than enterprise funds. The major issue is whether it is more useful to report debt principal payments rather than depreciation on the operating statement, particularly in those instances where the pricing of services is geared to the recovery of debt service and other cash outflows.

Pensions and Other Post-Employment Benefits

The GASB is currently examining recognition and measurement of pension expenditure/expense, assets, and liabilities, for both employers and public employee retirement systems. Perhaps the most significant issue concerns how the employer pension expenditure/expense is measured. Should pension measurement in government be similar to the way pension expense is measured in the private sector or should governmental pension accounting measurement be based on whatever method is used for pension funding purposes so long as the funding contribution requirement is based on a "systematic and rational" method? The GASB has also started research on recognition and measurement of post-employment benefits other than pensions, such as post-employment health care benefits.

Fixed Assets/Infrastructure

The GASB is also considering how to improve reporting of information regarding governmental capital plant. Among the questions being considered are:

- Should infrastructure fixed assets be reported? Should information on capital asset serviceability (condition, age, deferred maintenance) and capacity be disclosed?
- Should information on capital plans and planned versus actual expenditures be disclosed?
- Should the using up of fixed assets be reported?
- Should fixed assets be valued at some measure of current cost?

Users of governmental financial reports will need to be aware of developments in governmental accounting and financial reporting over the next few years, because of the likelihood of major changes.

Governmental Accounting and Financial Reporting and the Measurement of Financial Condition

Robert Berne
Associate Dean and Professor of Public Administration,
Robert F. Wagner Graduate School of Public Service,
New York University

One of the objectives of governmental financial reporting, as stated by the Governmental Accounting Standards Board (GASB), is to "provide information about the financial position and condition of a governmental entity. Financial reporting should provide information about resources and obligations, both actual and contingent, current and noncurrent."[1] For many participants in the municipal borrowing process, the measurement of a an issuer's financial condition is a critical concern. Many chapters in this handbook address financial condition analysis and, regardless of the approach, virtually all of these rely heavily on the information presented in governmental financial reports. But, as novice and experienced readers of governmental financial reports know, the identification and interpretation of the necessary information for analysis is not always simple and straightforward.

The previous chapter described the important features and principles of governmental accounting and financial reporting. The objective of this chapter is to illustrate how the information included in governmental financial reports is used in financial condition analysis. In the

---

[1] Governmental Accounting Standards Board, *Objectives of Financial Reporting,* Stamford, Conn.: Governmental Accounting Standards Board, May 1987, p. 28.

next section of this chapter, a definition of financial condition is presented which provides the basic framework for the examination of the government's financial reports. Each succeeding section of the chapter examines a different part of the governmental financial report and relates the financial report to the measurement of financial condition.

Two other introductory comments are appropriate. First, virtually no analysis of financial condition can rely exclusively on the information presented in governmental financial reports. Information from statutes, budgets, forecasts, economic and demographic reports, and specific industry analyses are often essential for a thorough financial analysis. However, since the information in governmental financial reports is so essential and is often presented in such a way that its interpretation requires specific knowledge that is typically not included with the information, this chapter focuses on the understanding of governmental financial reports. Second, the illustrations and examples in this chapter are not substitutes for the details included in one of the several excellent texts on governmental and not-for-profit accounting.[2]

A DEFINITION OF GOVERNMENTAL FINANCIAL CONDITION

While understanding a government's financial condition is a critical part of the issuance of and investment in municipal securities, the diversity among issuers and investors means that the specific context influences the definition of financial condition. Instead of devoting a large part of this chapter to a series of alternatives, a generic definition of financial condition is used to capture the key components of every assessment of governmental financial condition.[3]

In this chapter, the term "financial condition" is used synonymously with financial health, solvency, strength, and stress. A general definition of financial condition is the probability that a government will meet its financial obligations to all relevant parties including creditors, consumers, employees, taxpayers, suppliers, constituents, and others as

---

[2] See Robert J. Freeman, Craig D. Shoulders, and Edward S. Lynn, *Governmental and Nonprofit Accounting: Theory and Practice,* Third Edition, Englewood Cliffs, N.J.: Prentice-Hall, 1988; Leon E. Hay, *Accounting for Governmental and Nonprofit Entities,* Seventh Edition, Homewood, Illinois: Richard D. Irwin, 1985; Emerson O. Henke, *Introduction to Nonprofit Organization Accounting,* Second Edition, Boston, Massachusetts, 1985; and Joseph R. Razek and Gordon A. Hosch, *Introduction to Governmental and Not-for-Profit Accounting,* Englewood Cliffs, N.J.: Prentice-Hall, 1985.

[3] For more details on the measurement of financial condition using this framework, see Robert Berne and Richard Schramm, *The Financial Analysis of Governments,* Englewood Cliffs, N.J.: Prentice-Hall, 1986.

they come due. These financial obligations can be viewed as pressures on the government for expenditures, and its ability to meet these pressures with available resources is an elaboration of this definition of financial condition. Thus the measurement of financial condition involves the assessment of the sources of available resources and pressures for expenditures. Before discussing how financial condition is measured, several additional features of this definition should be noted.

First, financial condition has a time dimension. Available resources and expenditure pressures can vary in the short- as opposed to the long-run. It is possible for a government to have severe problems in the long-run, but not face a serious threat in the short-run, and vice versa. Of course in many cases short- and long-term financial condition move in the same direction.

Second, financial condition has an important economic dimension. The underlying economies affecting a government are major determinants of the government's available resources and needs for expenditures. Moreover, not just the economy of the area of the government in question, but neighboring economies as well as the economies of larger units of government are often important in measuring financial condition. Thus, while the focus of this chapter is on the financial information needed for financial analysis, economic relationships are often key determinants of the financial results.

Third, financial condition is viewed here as a multi-dimensional concept. For example, financial inflows come from taxpayers, other governments, users of services, and creditors; financial outflows go to consumer groups, suppliers, employees, bondholders, banks, and pensioners. As a result, financial condition cannot be measured solely with respect to a government's financial obligations to a single group, such as creditors, but has to be viewed as the net result of obligations to all governmental clientele receiving or providing resources. It requires analysis of all major sources and uses of resources and not just one aspect.

Fourth, financial condition often involves implicit as well as explicit financial obligations, where implicit obligations are changes in resource and service flows or requirements that do not reveal themselves explicitly in financial transactions. For example, a government with little outstanding debt but with a severely deteriorating physical infrastructure has implicit obligations that differ from explicit financial ones. Or a government with large cash reserves and untapped resources in a community that has substantial unmet needs for government services is, in an overall sense, less financially healthy than it appears from a strict analysis of the government's finances.

Finally, financial condition is a composite variable, encompassing financial strengths and weaknesses, not a simple one dimensional measure of well-being. Financial condition can vary over a continuum from excellent financial condition on many dimensions to financial insolvency.

Due to the different perspectives taken by the various participants in municipal securities transactions, and due to the differences among the securities themselves, the generic approach taken in this chapter is necessary to generalize about the relationships between the measurement of financial condition and governmental financial reporting. Before turning to the actual financial reports themselves, additional details on the actual measurement of financial condition are presented.

Financial condition, defined as the probability that a government will meet its financial obligations, depends upon the level of expenditure demands on the government (expenditure pressures) relative to the total resources available to meet those demands (available resources). In this context, the slack or gap between expenditure pressures and available resources becomes a measure of financial condition. A government that faces little pressure for additional expenditures and has substantial capacity to raise additional revenues is in good financial condition; a government with considerable pressures to increase its spending, but very little unused revenue capacity, is in poor financial condition.

Figure 16.1 displays this representation of financial condition and the internal and external factors related to a government's well-being. Expenditure pressures result both from demands for greater quantity (or better quality) of services, and from increases in costs just to provide the existing levels of outputs. Thus, the factors increasing the quantity, quality, and/or per unit cost of outputs will adversely affect financial condition. Both current and capital expenditures may be part

FIGURE 16.1
Components of Financial Condition Analysis

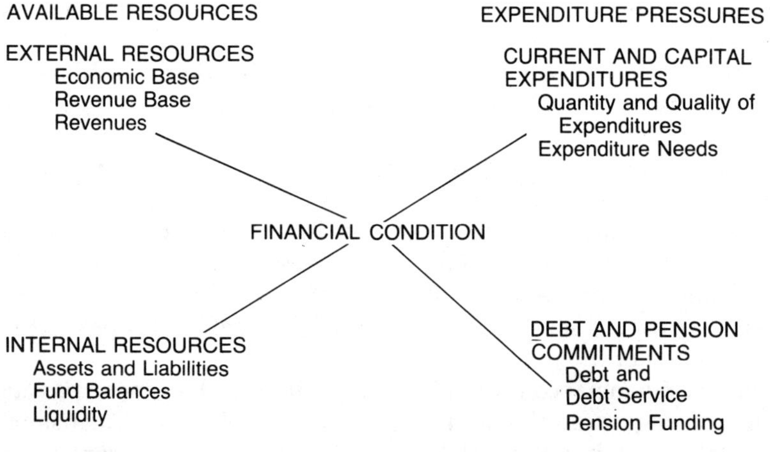

AVAILABLE RESOURCES

EXPENDITURE PRESSURES

EXTERNAL RESOURCES
Economic Base
Revenue Base
Revenues

CURRENT AND CAPITAL
EXPENDITURES
Quantity and Quality of
Expenditures
Expenditure Needs

FINANCIAL CONDITION

INTERNAL RESOURCES
Assets and Liabilities
Fund Balances
Liquidity

DEBT AND PENSION
COMMITMENTS
Debt and
Debt Service
Pension Funding

of this pressure. Expenditure pressures also come from past decisions to meet needs that resulted in liabilities faced currently by government, primarily from debt and pension commitments.

Available resources can be either external or internal. A government will have, at any point in time, an external resource base, both local and nonlocal, that it can draw upon. The availability of this external base depends on, for example, the level of unused tax capacity and other revenue capacity and intergovernmental revenue sources. Internal resources depend on the levels of different assets, relative to liabilities, and the ease with which these resources can be converted to cash.

Thus the framework for the assessment of financial condition, displayed in Figure 16.1, includes components that address the analysis of revenues, expenditures, debt, pensions, and internal resources. To complete this discussion of financial condition, the specific measures that are employed to quantify these components are examined.

Figure 16.2 presents a list of selected measures that are employed to assess the components of governmental financial condition.

FIGURE 16.2
Selected Measures for the Analysis of Financial Condition

Economic Base

Population (total, age distribution, education levels)

Income (per capita, per family; averages, medians)

Labor force and employment (total employment, participation rates, unemployment rates, employment by industry and occupation, largest employers)

Industrial structure (export employment and earnings)

Revenue Base

Property base (equalized value, assessed value, by categories, building permits)

Sales tax base

Income tax base

Other tax bases

Revenue base elasticities

Revenues

Revenues (total and per capita, nominal and real, by source)

Legal limits and percentages of limits currently used

Tax and revenue capacity

Tax and revenue reserves

Tax burdens and efforts

FIGURE 16.2   (continued)

Percentages of capacity utilized

Tax rates

Intergovernmental revenues and distribution systems

Current and Capital Expenditures

Expenditures (total and per capita, nominal and real, by function and object)

Government employees (total and per 1,000 population)

Price indexes

Measures of expenditure needs (poverty levels, crime measures, age of housing, health data)

Debt

Outstanding debt by security (to determine debt of the government, separate from enterprises)

Overlapping debt

Legal limits on debt and percentages of debt currently used

Maturity structure of debt

Short term debt (amounts and uses)

Debt service

Debt compared to income

Debt compared to population

Debt compared to full value of property

Debt service compared to total and own source revenues

Pensions

Pension structure and funding methods

Unfunded liabilities (total and compared to population, full value of property, and annual payroll)

Funded ratio

Pension assets compared to benefits

Pension receipts compared to pension disbursements

Pension contributions compared to salaries

Pension earnings compared to benefits

Percentage of calculated contribution actually made

Internal Resources

Fund balances (total, compared to revenues, compared to population)

Surpluses and deficits (total, compared to revenues)

Current assets compared to current liabilities

Tax delinquencies and other collection and payment rates

Receipts and disbursements and short term borrowing

Transfers to and from other funds and enterprises

The measures included in this figure are discussed in the credit analysis and bond insurance chapters in this handbook. The first three categories of measures, economic base, revenue base, and revenue, are aimed at the external revenues available to the government. These measures examine the basic economic strength of the government, the resources that can be tapped, the capacity of the government to generate revenues, and the actual revenues raised. Taxes, user charges, and intergovernmental revenues are assessed as part of this analysis.

The expenditure category includes measures that assess the need for current and capital expenditures, and the pressure on the government for additional expenditures. Different measures of expenditure needs are used for current versus capital expenditures. Comparisons of expenditure needs and actual expenditures help determine the pressure on the government for additional expenditures.

Borrowing by governments leads to commitments to bondholders, and these commitments are the focus of debt analysis. Leases and other debt-like instruments should be incorporated into debt analysis. Debt analysis examines the existing levels of outstanding debt, repayment schedules, and the debt burden imposed by current and planned borrowing.

Pensions are also structured so that promises in the past and present lead to commitments in the future. But since pension funding can vary considerably, this part of financial condition analysis is concerned about the future burdens that pensions will place on the government. Actuarially computed unfunded liabilities and cash flow measures are commonly used to assess pensions.

The final component examines the internal resources available to the government. Surpluses and deficits and fund balances are examined along with liquidity measures. In addition, as part of this analysis government enterprises are examined to determine whether they affect the overall financial condition of the government.

The measures presented in this chapter do not all apply to the same parts of the government. The discussion of government accounting in the previous chapter noted that governments are divided into funds for accounting and financial reporting purposes. For an analysis of financial condition, it is useful to be able to divide the government's accounting transactions into four parts, corresponding to the operating, capital, enterprise, and trust activities of the government. The trust activities are examined separately since these assets are being held separately, usually with specific requirements such as in a pension fund. The enterprise activities are those that are operated on a break even basis by the government, and these are usually funded primarily by user charges. If a government runs enterprises that fail to break even, then these activities can be placed in the operating part. The capital activities are those that lead to the acquisition of assets that have a useful life that extends beyond the operating cycle, normally a fiscal year. Thus expenditures for buildings, equipment, land, and infrastructure fall into the capital part. The operating part includes the activities associated with the normal, on-going service delivery and funding aspects of the government.

There is often a rough correspondence between these four divisions of the government and the government's fund structure. Trust funds are generally independent from the other funds, however resource flows among the trust and other funds need to be understood. The enterprise part is usually represented by internal service and enterprise funds, although there are occasions when enterprises are not accounted for in separate funds. When internal service functions or enterprises are not operating on a break even basis, it is appropriate to include them as part of the operating analysis. The capital part typically includes the capital projects funds, and may include resources in the general or special revenue funds if they support significant capital activities. For most governments, the general, debt service and appropriate parts of the special revenue funds comprise the operating part. Thus, the existing fund structure of a government determines the potential groupings of funds that can be used in financial analysis, yet some modifications or adjustments may be necessary. The feasibility of these adjustments depends upon the level of detail that is disclosed.

When using most measures of financial condition, *absolute* benchmarks are usually not available to interpret the measures. Instead, a good deal of financial analysis employs various forms of comparative analysis. Critical comparisons are the trends in the measures over time, or, in other words, how the does the government compare with itself in the past. Time series analyses assess whether a government's financial condition is improving or getting worse. But often the absolute levels of the measures are difficult to interpret without comparing them to those for other governments. While this is a necessary part of financial condition analysis, the differences among government structure, functions, financing, and accounting systems require that care be exercised when cross-jurisdictional comparisons are used. Because so many of the differences across governments vary systematically by state, comparisons within states are often sounder that comparisons across states. In either case, data must be extracted from financial reports with care when cross-jurisdictional and time series comparisons are used.

Financial condition analysis uses measures such as the ones listed in Figure 16.2, however due to its complexity financial condition analysis still includes a substantial amount of subjective analysis as noted throughout this handbook. A key objective of any analysis of financial condition is to understand the past trends to be able to predict the current and future financial condition of the government.

THE COMPREHENSIVE ANNUAL
FINANCIAL REPORT

According to generally accepted accounting principles (GAAP), every governmental unit is required to prepare a comprehensive annual financial report and the information contained in this report is an essential ingredient in financial condition analysis.[4] The principal features of this annual financial report were described in the preceding chapter. Yet, despite the requirement to publish an annual financial report and the objective, stated above, that financial reporting should provide information on the government's financial condition, the financial report does not typically contain a section designed to define, measure, and assess the government's financial condition. Instead, the assessment of a government's financial condition usually requires that a reasonably knowledgeable analyst gather information, define financial condition, and apply the appropriate techniques. Therefore, knowing how to identify and interpret the relevant information in governmental annual financial reports is a necessary part of financial analysis. This is addressed in the remainder of this chapter.

The examination of the financial report is guided by the approach to financial condition measurement described previously. Each of the next sections focuses on a different part of the annual financial report. Not exclusively, though, because the linkages among the information in different parts of the financial report is often critical. Quickly skimming the annual financial report is a useful first step before examining each part in depth. This first reading provides the analyst with a basic understanding of the array of information that is available and, equally importantly, its organization. One way to obtain an initial overview is to begin with the introductory material, then turn to the auditor's opinion and the combined financial statements including the notes to the financial statements, after which the statistical section can be reviewed, followed by a quick examination of the individual fund statements and other material.

The review of each of these parts of the financial report in this chapter follows this sequence. Throughout this chapter, examples from actual financial statements are presented. These are presented to illustrate how to relate information in financial reports to financial condition analysis and are not presented to endorse a particular presentation format. In order to examine a variety of issues, the examples

---

[4] For a description of generally accepted accounting principles, see Governmental Accounting Standards Board, *Codification of Governmental Accounting and Reporting Standards as of June 15, 1987,* Second Edition, Stamford, Conn.: Governmental Accounting Standards Board, 1987.

have been chosen from several different financial reports. A final point worth emphasizing is that a particular aspect of a financial report can be puzzling, even to the most experienced reader. Therefore, asking questions of the officials from the preparing government should always be part of an analytical routine.

The Introductory Section

A table of contents and one or more transmittal letters are typically included in the introductory section. In addition, a summary of the key financial events or a brief assessment of the financial condition of the government may be included in this introductory section.

A transmittal letter is usually written by the chief financial officer, but a letter or report from another official in the introductory section is not unusual. As noted by Freeman, Shoulders, and Lynn, "the transmittal letter from the chief financial officer is an extremely important part of the CAFR [Comprehensive Annual Financial Report]. Indeed, like the president's letter in private corporation reports, most readers direct their attention here initially for an overview of the financial position of the city at year end and the results of operations for the year. Readers also expect that the major significant events that occurred during the year, whether good or bad, will be highlighted here."[5]

The degree to which readers expectations are fulfilled on this latter point varies considerably from one financial report to another. In many cases, these letters are simply statements indicating that the government is fulfilling its requirement to produce an annual report, with one or two additional paragraphs that highlight several important financial events or findings. Even these relatively short letters may be revealing to the financial analyst. In other cases, the transmittal letters are considerably more detailed, summarizing significant accounting policies, government structure, and financial results for the government, often with tables and graphics. In these cases, the transmittal letters contribute a great deal to the analysis of financial condition.

Figure 16.3 presents excerpts from the transmittal letter from the Comptroller of the City of Chicago to the Mayor and Members of the City Council in the annual financial report for year-end December 31, 1986. The first page of Figure 16.3 contains the beginning of the transmittal letter and it indicates that Chicago is striving for, but has not yet received, the Government Finance Officers Association's (GFOA)

---

[5] Robert J. Freeman, Craig D. Shoulders, and Edward S. Lynn, *Governmental and Nonprofit Accounting: Theory and Practice,* Third Edition, Englewood Cliffs, N.J., 1988, p. 626.

FIGURE 16.3
Excerpts from Transmittal Letter

CITY OF CHICAGO
DEPARTMENT OF FINANCE

RONALD D. PICUR
COMPTROLLER

HAROLD WASHINGTON
MAYOR

October 31, 1987

The Honorable Mayor Harold Washington
and the Members of the City Council
of the City of Chicago

Ladies and Gentlemen:

I am pleased to submit the Comprehensive Annual Financial Report (CAFR) of the City of Chicago for the Year Ended December 31, 1986, prepared in accordance with generally accepted accounting principles. The CAFR is designed to present fairly the financial position and results of financial operations of the City in all material respects, and to demonstrate compliance with applicable finance-related legal and contractual provisions. The principle of full disclosure has been followed so that the reader may gain the maximum understanding of the City's financial affairs. Steps are being taken to achieve the goal of attaining the Certificate of Achievement for Excellence in Financial Reporting, awarded by the Government Finance Officers Association (GFOA).

REPORTING AUTHORITY AND STANDARDS

This report is published in accordance with Section 7-21 of the Municipal Code of Chicago, which requires the City Comptroller to prepare an annual report, giving a full and detailed statement of all receipts and expenditures, the resources and liabilities of the City, and all other data necessary to exhibit its true financial condition.

The City Comptroller's Office has prepared this report and is responsible for its completeness and fairness of presentation. The financial statements in this report have been prepared to conform with the most current standards of governmental accounting and reporting, as promulgated by the Governmental Accounting Standards Board (GASB). The GASB has succeeded the National Council on Governmental Accounting (NCGA) in setting generally accepted accounting principles (GAAP) applicable to state and local governmental units. In complying with GAAP, this year the report includes additional disclosures regarding investments, as required by GASB Statement No. 3, and early application of the new standard of accounting for special assessments, as called for in GASB Statement No. 6.

Source: City of Chicago, *Comprehensive Annual Financial Report,* for Fiscal Year Ended December 31, 1986, pp. 7–14.

FIGURE 16.3 (continued)

GOVERNMENT STRUCTURE AND FINANCIAL MANAGEMENT

Incorporated in 1837, the City of Chicago is a municipal corporation and home rule unit of local government under the Illinois Constitution. As such, the City may exercise the power to tax, license and incur debt. It can perform a broad range of municipal functions for the protection of public safety, health and welfare.

The City has a mayor-council form of government. The Mayor is the Chief Executive Officer of the City and is elected to a four-year term. The City Council is the legislative body of Chicago and consists of 50 aldermen who are elected by ward for four-year terms.

Responsibility for governing the City's finances is vested in the Mayor, the City Comptroller and the Budget Director (both being appointed by the Mayor with the advice and consent of the City Council), as well as the independently-elected City Treasurer, and the City Council.

The Mayor, assisted by the Budget Director, is responsible for preparing and recommending the City's annual budget to the City Council. The Mayor, assisted by the City Comptroller, is responsible for initiating and executing debt issuances. The Mayor has broad appointment powers with respect to all executive departments and certain boards and commissions.

The City Comptroller, as head of the Department of Finance, serves as the City's Chief Financial Officer and is responsible for the management and control of the City's financial operations. The Comptroller is responsible for maintaining the financial records of the City, publishing an annual report for each fiscal year, and performing investigative and audit functions.

The City Treasurer receives and is custodian of all the City's monies and maintains the cash accounts of each fund. The Treasurer is the custodian of securities held by the City and maintains the cash accounts for the City's four pension funds and the Chicago Board of Education.

The City Council passes all financial ordinances of the City. Its Committee on the Budget and Government Operations is responsible for reviewing and acting on the Mayor's executive budget. This Committee recommends the budget to the City Council as the basis for the adoption of the annual appropriation ordinance. The Committee on Finance is responsible for reviewing the revenues in the Mayor's executive budget, including recommending the property tax levy to the City Council. The Committee on Finance also reviews all ordinances for the issuance of debt.

REPORTING ENTITY AND ITS SERVICES

This report, prepared in accordance with generally accepted accounting principles, encompasses all funds, account groups, boards, commissions and agencies under the control of, or financially dependent upon, the City's executive and legislative branches. The City services include police, fire, streets and sanitation, public works, water, sewer, health, aviation and inspectional services.

Within the City, additional services are provided by the following coterminous or overlapping units of government: the Chicago Board of Education, the Chicago School Finance Authority, the Chicago City Colleges (Community College District No. 508), the Chicago Park District, Cook County, the Forest Preserve District of Cook County and the Metropolitan Sanitary District of Greater Chicago. Each of these units of government derives its power and authority under laws of the State of Illinois, has an independent governing board and its own tax levy, and maintains its own financial records and accounts. These governments have not been included in this report because they are substantially self-governing and are not financially dependent on the City.

FIGURE 16.3 *(continued)*

General Fund – Fund Balance Increase

Fund balances reflect the accumulated excess (shortfall) of revenues and other financing sources over (under) expenditures and other uses. For the General Fund, the City ended 1986 with a fund balance of $19.8 million. This positive result is the first since 1983, the year in which the City began reporting on a GAAP basis.

During 1986, the City eliminated the Working Cash Fund which resulted in a residual equity transfer of $32 million to the General Fund. Historically, the Working Cash Fund issued debt to provide working capital for current operating uses. Currently, the City obtains working capital through the issuance of General Obligation Tender Notes, which are financed through the Debt Service Fund.

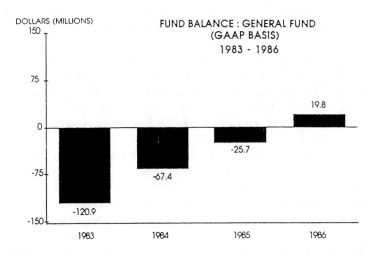

Debt Administration

The successful use of General Obligation Tender Notes for short-term financing was continued in 1986 with a total of $335.8 million issued in four series. Proceeds are used primarily to meet the cash flow requirements of the City, including the effect of the one-year lag in collection of Illinois property tax levies. A total of $235.8 million was outstanding at year-end, $155.3 million of which was classified as long-term debt as a result of refinancing arrangements. The average interest rate for this indebtedness was less than 5%.

The City also undertook to reduce future interest expenditures by refunding the majority of a 1985 General Obligation Bond issue, which carried interest rates up to 9-7/8%, with a $204 million 1986 refunding issue having a maximum rate of 7.4%.

Overall, the City's outstanding long-term debt totalled $897.1 million in 1986. Direct debt burden represents 1.75% of estimated fair market value of taxable properties.

In 1987, both of the nation's major credit rating agencies upgraded the City's bond rating. The City's 1986 results were a primary factor in these upgrades, combined with the City's improving financial position and economic base revitalization. Standard and Poor's Corporation raised the City's rating from BBB+ to A-, while Moody's Investors Service, Inc. upgraded the City from Baa1 to A. The Standard and Poor's increase is the first in 24 years, Moody's the first in 13 years.

Certificate of Achievement for Excellence in Financial Reporting. This is a peer reviewed program that identifies financial reports that meet high standards.[6] The last paragraph on this page indicates that several of the newer standards promulgated by the GASB are incorporated in this report.[7]

The second page of Figure 16.3 displays two additional sections of the City of Chicago transmittal letter that explains the government structure and budget process and also summarizes the reporting entity definition used in the report. Since the government structure and budget process vary substantially across governments, an explanation such as the one presented in this letter is useful for the financial analyst, especially if questions arise concerning current and future policies. The selection of the reporting entity is particularly important since it affects virtually every component of financial condition discussed in the previous section. In this case, the exclusion of other coterminous jurisdictions such as the Chicago Board of Education signals to the financial analyst that there are other local governments, besides the county, whose tax base, revenue capacity, and ability to borrow interact with the City of Chicago. The entity is often more fully described in the notes to the financial statements, but this is an example of a critical issue that is highlighted in the transmittal letter.

The third page of Figure 16.3 includes sections of the City of Chicago transmittal letter that address specific components of the financial condition framework. The graph clearly presents the increasing fund balance in the general fund from 1983 through 1986, and the text discloses that part of the increase from 1985 to 1986 was due to a "residual equity transfer" because of the elimination of a fund. Both the trend in the general fund balance and the use of this transfer are important inputs for the analysis of financial condition. The section on debt financing describes a few features of the complex debt position of the City of Chicago and discloses the bond rating increases that took place during 1987. Clearly the financial information presented in the transmittal letter is not at the level of detail necessary for financial condition analysis. Nonetheless, the information disclosed is a useful introduction and it highlights particular concerns for further analysis.

---

[6] Close to 1,000 governmental jurisdictions received the GFOA's Certificate of Achievement for Excellence in Financial Reporting for fiscal year 1986, compared to around 600 for fiscal year 1983. When a government receives this certificate, a copy of the certificate is often included in the introductory section of the annual financial report.

[7] The letter from the independent auditor which will be reviewed shortly presents a more detailed review of compliance with GAAP.

The incidence of more detailed and analytical transmittal letters is consistent with the improvements in financial reporting for governments. Since there are currently no specific standards on the information to be included in such transmittal letters and because these letters are not subject to the scrutiny of the external auditors, substantial diversity is likely to continue to exist. There may be an implicit bias to be more forthcoming with "good" news as opposed to "bad" news, but this is an untested hypothesis at this point in time.

All other information presented in the introductory section should be closely scrutinized in financial condition analysis. Governments often present an organizational chart. This information is useful in knowing who to contact to assess lines of responsibility and for follow-up questions.

The Independent Auditor's Statement

Many annual financial reports of governments are reviewed by external auditors who present an opinion on the report. Auditors are guided by professional standards and are required to assess the report in question against those standards.[8] The auditor's statement should disclose which parts of the financial report have been reviewed by the auditor, where the report contains information that was reviewed by other auditors, whether the report presents information in accordance with generally accepted accounting principles (GAAP), and whether there have been any significant changes in accounting principles compared to previous reports.

A careful reading of the auditor's letter is essential for financial condition analysis. First, it is important to know which information is unaudited because the analyst should not have the same confidence in this compared to the audited part. Second, the analyst must be alert to the parts of the report that do not conform to GAAP, since this may require special treatment or interpretation. For example, there are still elements of cash accounting used by some governments, and this should be noted in the auditor's opinion if it is not in conformance with GAAP. Third, since financial condition analysis requires the construction of financial trends, it is important to know when financial reporting varies with previous presentations.

Figure 16.4 presents several paragraphs from different letters from external auditors. The first paragraph on the figure is the beginning of the letter from the external auditors from the 1986 City of Chicago

---

[8] Of course, just as with any profession, an auditor's statement is not a *guarantee*. It is a professional opinion in a field where the opinion, itself, is one of the critical services offered by the auditor.

FIGURE 16.4
Excerpts from Letters from External Auditors

From City of Chicago's Annual Financial Report

To the City Council of the
City of Chicago, Illinois

We have examined the combined financial statements of the City of Chicago, Illinois, as of and for the year ended December 31, 1986, as listed in the table of contents. Our examination was made in accordance with generally accepted auditing standards and, accordingly, included such tests of the accounting records and such other auditing procedures as we considered necessary in the circumstances. We did not examine the financial statements of the City's Pension and Deferred Compensation Plans which, in the aggregate, represent substantially all of the assets of the Fiduciary Fund Type. Those statements were examined by other auditors whose reports thereon have been furnished to us and our opinion expressed herein, insofar as it relates to the amounts included for such Plans, is based solely upon the reports of the other auditors. The financial statements of the General Fixed Assets Account Group have not been audited (See Note 1).

From City of Buffalo's Annual Financial Report

As described in Note 5 to the financial statements, the City has been involved in litigation for property tax refunds. As a result the City has proposed a settlement plan the costs of which have been accrued for in the financial statements. However, this proposed settlement plan has not been accepted by the taxpayers who are parties to the litigation nor has it been imposed by the courts. As such, the terms of any final settlement to this litigation cannot be determined.

As described in Note 4 to the financial statements, BURA is involved in litigation for various claims. The ultimate outcome of these claims and lawsuits cannot presently be determined.

In the course of administering its grant activities, BURA has acquired numerous parcels of land located throughout the City of Buffalo. The value of such land, which is held for resale, is not included in the financial statements described above as BURA has not maintained the records necessary to accumulate the cost of these assets.

As discussed in Note 1j to the financial statements, the Board and BURA do not account for the General Fixed Assets Account Group in accordance with generally accepted accounting principles. It was not practicable to audit the cumulative balances as presented for the Board of $176,400,000 or to determine the difference between the presented amounts and the amounts that would have resulted from the application of generally accepted accounting principles.

FIGURE 16.4 (*continued*)

From City of New York's Annual Financial Report

In our opinion, based on our examination and the reports of the other auditors referred to above, the general purpose financial statements referred to above present fairly the financial position of The City of New York at June 30, 1986, and the results of its operations and the changes in financial position of its enterprise and pension trust funds for the year then ended, in conformity with generally accepted accounting principles applied on a basis consistent with that of the preceding year, except for the transfer of the operations and fixed asset accounts of the New York City Water Board previously included in the general fund and general fixed assets account group, respectively, to the enterprise fund, with which we concur, as described in Notes A and N to the financial statements. Also, in our opinion, the combining, individual, and account group financial statements referred to above present fairly the financial position of the individual funds and account groups of The City of New York, at June 30, 1986, and the results of operations of such funds and the changes in financial position of the individual enterprise and pension trust funds for the year then ended, in conformity with generally accepted accounting principles applied on a basis consistent with that of the preceding year, except for the previously mentioned change with which we concur.

Source: City of Chicago, *Comprehensive Annual Financial Report,* for Fiscal Year Ended December 31, 1986, p. 14; City of Buffalo, New York, *Comprehensive Annual Financial Report,* for the Fiscal Year Ended June 30, 1987, p. 2; and City of New York, *Comprehensive Annual Financial Report of the Comptroller,* for the Year Ended June 30, 1986, p. 3.

financial report, and this indicates that the fixed asset account group is not audited. This finding, and the note to the financial statement that states that the city is upgrading its capital asset accounting systems, could be viewed as an invitation to the analyst to go beyond the financial report for information on fixed assets.

The four paragraphs on Figure 16.4 from the City of Buffalo's financial report for year ending June 30, 1987 show how the external auditor can highlight aspects of the financial statement that require additional explanation. The first paragraph should alert the analyst to the possibility of property tax refunds and the analyst would have to determine the significance of such litigation for the city's revenue structure. The second and third paragraphs signal other uncertainties that may affect the government's financial condition. The final paragraph is an example of an accounting practice that does not conform to GAAP.

The final example shown on Figure 16.4 is a paragraph from the external auditor's statement from the City of New York's annual financial report for year ending June 30, 1986 noting a change from the previous presentation regarding accounting for water and sewer activities. Since certain activities that were accounted for in the general fund are now included in an enterprise fund, trends in revenues and expenditures will be affected and the analyst will have to investigate to determine how to take this change into account.

The Combined Financial Statements

As noted in the previous chapter, according to GAAP, governments are required to present five combined financial statements. Each *fund type* is represented in these combined statements and, in many cases, this level of aggregation is appropriate for financial analysis. These combined financial statements are the source for many of the financial variables needed to calculate the measures presented in Figure 16.2. In some cases, the financial variables are computed for several years in other places in the report, particularly the statistical section. Even when trends in the variables are presented, the analyst needs to compare the calculated trends with the data in the combined statements to insure that the variables in the trends are defined appropriately for financial condition analysis. Although the combined statements are illustrated separately from the notes to the financial statements, in practice the notes and the statements should be examined together.

The first combined statement is the balance sheet, and an example from the State of New York for the year ending March 31, 1987 is presented in Table 16.1. New York State uses a fairly typical fund structure, however the enterprises are called "public benefit corporations." Several measures of financial condition in Figure 16.2 in the internal resource component, such as fund balances and liquidity ratios, use information from the balance sheet. The significant negative undesignated fund balance in the general fund is a critical input to financial condition analysis, but it has a different interpretation compared to the negative undesignated fund balance in the capital projects fund. In the case of the general fund it reflects the excess of expenditures over revenues in the prior years, while in the capital projects fund there are encumbrances which will require additional revenues, probably in the form of new borrowing. The assets, liabilities, and fund equities may require further analysis, and the details presented in the combined balance sheet is a logical starting point. Again, for New York State, the general fund's assets, liabilities, and fund balances deserve further scrutiny in a financial condition analysis.

The second combined statement is the statement of revenues, expenditures, and changes in fund balances for all governmental funds. An example from New York State is shown in Table 16.2. This statement typically provides the input needed to calculate the many of the revenue and expenditure variables that are a critical part of financial condition analysis. In the case of New York State, the financial analyst may choose to examine the general fund separately, or combine it with the special revenue and debt service funds, or both. Regardless, the capital projects fund should be examined separately. Note that the general fund is primarily supported by taxes; federal funds and lottery proceeds support the special revenue fund; while tuition and fees and patient fees are the primary revenues of the debt service fund. The expenditures of the general and special revenue fund cover many of the same activities, while debt service is the only expenditure of the debt service fund.

This statement also alerts the analyst to the use of interfund transfers by the government. The use of these transfers needs to be understood, however this is often not possible from this statement alone. The notes to the financial statement or information obtained directly from the government may be required to fully comprehend the use and meaning of the interfund transfers. Table 16.2 signifies to the analyst that interfund transfers play a role in the financing of the governmental funds in New York State.

The combined statement of revenues, expenditures, and changes in fund balances with comparisons of budget and actual for general and special revenue fund types and similar governmental fund types with legally adopted budgets is the third combined statement in the annual financial report. The basis of accounting used in the budget is used in this statement, therefore the basis of accounting in this and the previous two combined statements may differ, sometimes significantly. The comparisons of budget and actual are often examined by analysts as indicators of the predictability of the financial environment and may also serve as an indirect reading of the financial capability of the government. Because there can be significant variation in the version of the budget that is used in this statement, for example the adopted or amended budget, clarification may be needed before the statement can be interpreted fully. The key differences should be explained either in the statement or in a note to the financial statement.

Table 16.3 presents such a statement for New York State, however since a cash basis of accounting is used as the budgetary basis in New York State, this statement is labelled a "statement of cash receipts and disbursements." The "financial plan" is New York State's equivalent of the budget, and a note to the statement explains that the plan is amended three months before the end of the fiscal year. This helps explain why the variances between the financial plan and the actuals shown in Table 16.3 are relatively small.[9]

---

[9] The note to New York State's financial statements that explains the two bases of accounting is reproduced later in this chapter.

TABLE 16.1
Illustration of Combined Balance Sheet

STATE OF NEW YORK

Combined Balance Sheet

ALL FUND TYPES AND ACCOUNT GROUPS
March 31, 1987
(Amounts in thousands)

Governmental Fund Types

	General	Special Revenue	Debt Service	Capital Projects
ASSETS:				
Cash and marketable securities	$ 1,084,206	$ 674,323	$ 1,092,885	$ 386,171
Retirement systems investments	—	—	—	—
Receivables, net of allowances for uncollectibles:				
Taxes	3,927,112	49,239	—	—
Due from Federal government	—	1,402,944	—	100,131
Loans and leases	—	—	—	—
Other	293,070	33,251	297,944	39,088
Due from other funds	149,309	42,232	18,874	507
Marketable securities held in lieu of retainage	—	—	—	46,265
Fixed assets	—	—	—	—
Other assets	79,568	4,108	—	—
Assets available for future debt service	—	—	—	—
Resources to be provided for retirement of general long-term obligations	—	—	—	—
Total assets	$ 5,533,265	$ 2,206,097	$ 1,409,703	$ 572,162
LIABILITIES:				
Tax refunds payable	$ 3,040,512	$ 8,459	$ —	$ —
Payable to local governments	3,517,546	418,815	—	—
Pension contributions payable	518,003	—	—	—
Accounts payable	235,602	53,206	1,168	292,075
Accrued liabilities	1,289,451	892,295	—	1,853
Due to other funds	92,215	102,313	10,844	40,244
Deferred revenues	119,156	1,268	100,381	8,884
Notes payable	—	—	—	130,010
Bonds payable	—	—	—	—
Obligations under lease/purchase and other financing agreements	—	—	—	—
Other long-term liabilities	—	—	—	—
Total liabilities	8,812,485	1,476,356	112,393	473,066
EQUITY (DEFICIT):				
Fund balances (deficits):				
Reserved for:				
Encumbrances	394,824	75,208	—	2,101,594
Unemployment benefits	—	—	—	—
Debt service	—	—	818,318	—
Tax stabilization	201,373	—	—	—
Education accumulation	431,400	—	—	—
Other specified purposes	66,861	—	—	37,373
Unreserved				
Designated	—	654,533	478,992	—
Undesignated	(4,373,678)	—	—	(2,039,871)
Investment in general fixed assets	—	—	—	—
Net retirement systems assets available for benefits	—	—	—	—
Equity of public benefit corporations	—	—	—	—
Total equity (deficit)	(3,279,220)	729,741	1,297,310	99,096
Commitments and contingencies				
Total liabilities and equity	$ 5,533,265	$ 2,206,097	$ 1,409,703	$ 572,162

Source: State of New York, *Comprehensive Annual Financial Report of the Comptroller,* for the Fiscal Year Ending March 31, 1987, pp. 20–21.

TABLE 16.1   *(continued)*

EXHIBIT A

	Account Groups		Fiduciary Fund Types		Proprietary Fund Type
	General Fixed Assets	General Long-term Obligations	Trust and Agency	State Administered Retirement Systems	Public Benefit Corporations
$ —	$ —	$ 5,331,553	$ —	$ 13,699,695
—	—	—	35,621,792	—
—	—	727,146	—	—
—	—	47,909	—	62
—	—	—	—	9,966,018
—	—	237,697	3,162,072	1,103,192
—	—	73,153	—	—
—	—	—	—	—
4,698,920	—	—	—	10,912,979
—	—	92	7,223	775,993
—	1,297,310	—	—	—
—	11,913,900	—	—	—
$ 4,698,920	$ 13,211,210	$ 6,417,550	$ 38,791,087	$ 36,457,939
$ —	$ —	$ —	$ —	$ —
—	—	1,198,793	—	—
—	720,323	—	—	1,495,636
—	—	77,708	—	209,528
—	—	1,816,270	551,162	4,251,720
—	—	38,459	—	—
—	—	34,328	—	539,505
—	—	—	—	323,415
—	3,754,662	—	—	20,955,815
—	6,934,594	—	—	—
—	1,801,631	—	—	1,178,697
—	13,211,210	3,165,558	551,162	28,954,316
—	—	2,749,879	—	—
—	—	—	—	—
—	—	—	—	—
—	—	502,113	—	—
—	—	—	—	—
4,690,920	—	—	—	—
—	—	—	38,239,925	—
—	—	—	—	7,503,623
4,698,920	—	3,251,992	38,239,925	7,503,623
$ 4,698,920	$ 13,211,210	$ 6,417,550	$ 38,791,087	$ 36,457,939

TABLE 16.2

Illustration of Combined Statement of Revenues, Expenditures, and Changes in Fund Balances for all Governmental Funds

STATE OF NEW YORK

Combined Statement of Revenues, Expenditures and Changes in Fund Balances

ALL GOVERNMENTAL FUND TYPES AND EXPENDABLE TRUST FUNDS
Year Ended March 31, 1987
(Amounts in thousands)

Governmental

	General	Special Revenue	Debt Service
REVENUES:			
Taxes:			
Personal income	$ 13,074,740	$ —	$ —
General business	3,283,365	485,253	
Consumption and use	6,438,691	199,484	30,418
Unemployment	—	—	—
Other	1,518,308	—	—
Federal grants	62,167	8,717,716	13,766
Lottery	—	1,383,196	—
Tuition and fees	—	—	676,296
Patient fees	—	—	580,885
Miscellaneous	1,375,875	125,228	125,673
Total revenues	25,753,146	10,910,877	1,427,038
EXPENDITURES:			
Grants to local governments:			
Education	7,122,925	1,353,685	—
Social services	4,914,349	5,905,585	—
Non-categorical aid	1,195,653	—	—
Health and environmental	181,520	163,100	—
Transportation	407,697	547,845	—
Mental hygiene	542,485	34,416	—
Criminal justice	153,985	7,065	—
Other programs	387,428	295,171	—
Operation of state departments and agencies:			
Personal service costs	6,324,231	362,713	—
Non-personal service costs	2,404,828	1,048,209	—
Pension contribution	540,971	42,708	—
Other fringe benefits	1,161,075	65,955	—
Debt service, including payments on financing agreements	151,710	—	1,183,453
Capital construction	—	—	—
Unemployment benefits	—	—	—
Total expenditures	25,488,857	9,826,452	1,183,453
Excess (deficiency) of revenues over expenditures	264,289	1,084,425	243,585
OTHER FINANCING SOURCES (USES):			
Operating transfers from other funds	2,175,946	4,322	1,581,426
Operating transfers to other funds	(1,438,754)	(832,190)	(1,754,283)
Proceeds of general obligation bonds	—	—	—
Proceeds from financing agreements	—	—	404,690
Net other financing sources (uses)	737,192	(827,868)	231,833
Excess of revenues and other financing sources over expenditures and other financing uses	1,001,481	256,557	475,418
Fund balances (deficits) at April 1, 1986	(4,280,701)	473,184	821,892
Fund balances (deficits) at March 31, 1987	$ (3,279,220)	$ 729,741	$ 1,297,310

Source: State of New York, *Comprehensive Annual Financial Report of the Comptroller,* for the Fiscal Year Ending March 31, 1987, pp. 22–23.

TABLE 16.2 *(continued)*

STATE OF NEW YORK

EXHIBIT B

	Fund Types		Fiduciary Fund Type
	Capital Projects	Total (Memorandum Only)	Expendable Trust
$ —	$ 13,074,740	$ —
—	3,768,618	—
—	6,668,593	—
—	—	1,463,849
—	1,518,308	—
642,076	9,435,725	19,935
—	1,383,196	—
—	676,296	—
—	580,885	—
35,635	1,662,411	250,729
677,711	38,768,772	1,734,513
4,662	8,481,272	—
—	10,819,934	—
—	1,195,653	—
78,238	422,858	—
56,420	1,011,962	—
23,042	599,943	—
..	161,050	—
15,170	697,769	3,557
—	6,686,944	2,188
—	3,453,037	77,559
—	583,679	—
—	1,227,030	583
—	1,335,163	—
1,748,869	1,748,869	—
—	—	1,210,896
1,926,401	38,425,163	1,294,783
(1,248,690)	343,609	439,730
711,480	4,473,174	—
(122,947)	(4,148,174)	—
436,000	436,000	—
461,759	866,449	—
1,486,292	1,627,449	—
237,602	1,971,058	439,730
(138,506)	(3,124,131)	2,511,893
$ 99,096	$ (1,153,073)	$ 2,951,623

TABLE 16.3
Illustration of Combined Statement of Revenues, Expenditures, and
Changes in Fund Balances, Budget and Actual, for Governmental Funds
with Approved Budgets

STATE OF NEW YORK

Combined Statement of
Cash Receipts and Disbursements

BUDGETARY BASIS—FINANCIAL PLAN AND ACTUAL
GOVERNMENTAL FUND TYPES
Year Ended March 31, 1987
(Amounts in thousands)

	General			Special Revenue		
	Financial Plan	Actual	Favorable (Unfavorable) Variance	Financial Plan	Actual	Favorable (Unfavorable) Variance
RECEIPTS:						
Taxes	$ 23,301,000	$ 23,415,400	$ 114,400	$ 660,000	$ 672,900	$ 12,900
Miscellaneous	1,197,000	1,213,700	16,700	1,691,000	1,636,100	(54,900)
Federal grants	79,000	58,800	(20,200)	8,462,000	8,641,700	179,700
Total receipts	24,577,000	24,687,900	110,900	10,813,000	10,950,700	137,700
DISBURSEMENTS:						
Grants to local governments	15,348,000	15,338,600	9,400	8,224,000	8,447,700	(223,700)
Departmental operations	6,178,000	6,229,100	(51,100)	2,690,000	2,589,900	100,100
General state charges	1,723,000	1,733,300	(10,300)	188,000	167,900	20,100
Debt service	153,000	151,700	1,300	—	—	—
Capital projects	—	—	—	21,000	4,700	16,300
Total disbursements	23,402,000	23,452,700	(50,700)	11,123,000	11,210,200	(87,200)
Receipts over (under) disbursements	1,175,000	1,235,200	60,200	(310,000)	(259,500)	50,500
OTHER FINANCING SOURCES (USES):						
Bond proceeds, net	—	—	—	—	—	—
Transfers from other funds	159,200	161,100	1,900	1,646,000	1,641,900	(4,100)
Transfers to other funds	(1,318,000)	(1,379,900)	(61,900)	(896,000)	(924,000)	(28,000)
Net other financing sources (uses)	(1,158,800)	(1,218,800)	(60,000)	750,000	717,900	(32,100)
Receipts and other financing sources over (under) disbursements and other financing uses	16,200	16,400	200	440,000	458,400	18,400
Fund balances at April 1, 1986	152,600	152,600	—	617,400	617,400	—
Fund balances at March 31, 1987	$ 168,800	$ 169,000	$ 200	$ 1,057,400	$ 1,075,800	$ 18,400

Source: State of New York, *Comprehensive Annual Financial Report of the Comptroller,* for
the Fiscal Year Ending March 31, 1987, pp. 24–25.

TABLE 16.3   (*continued*)

EXHIBIT C

	Debt Service			Capital Projects		
	Financial Plan	Actual	Favorable (Unfavorable) Variance	Financial Plan	Actual	Favorable (Unfavorable) Variance
$	30,000 $	30,400 $	400 $	— $	— $	—
	1,139,000	1,180,400	41,400	205,000	158,100	(46,900)
	12,000	13,800	1,800	621,000	619,800	(1,200)
	1,181,000	1,224,600	43,600	826,000	777,900	(48,100)
	—	—	—	5,000	3,700	1,300
	—	—	—	—	500	(500)
	947,000	944,000	3,000	—	—	—
	—	—	—	1,860,000	1,816,600	43,400
	947,000	944,000	3,000	1,865,000	1,820,800	44,200
	234,000	280,600	46,600	(1,039,000)	(1,042,900)	(3,900)
	—	—	—	455,000	410,800	(44,200)
	1,378,000	1,346,200	(31,800)	651,000	734,500	83,500
	(1,648,000)	(1,594,400)	53,600	—	(6,900)	(6,900)
	(270,000)	(248,200)	21,800	1,106,000	1,138,400	32,400
	(36,000)	32,400	68,400	67,000	95,500	28,500
	170,900	170,900	—	130,200	130,200	—
$	134,900 $	203,300 $	68,400 $	197,200 $	225,700 $	28,500

There are differences between the comparable observations in Tables 16.2 and 16.3 in the case of New York State. For example, general fund revenues shown in Table 16.2 on a GAAP basis are $25.753 billion while the general fund "receipts" on a budget basis are $24.688 billion. And the special revenue fund expenditures on a GAAP basis are $9.826 billion and the special revenue fund disbursements on a budgetary basis are $11.210 billion. Because financial condition is concerned with the future, and budgetary data are often substantially more current, the differences between the actual inflows and outflows reported on a GAAP basis and the budgeted inflows and outflows, which may be reported on a different basis of accounting, need to be incorporated in trend analyses that utilize actual and budgeted data. Not only the inflows and outflows, but the fund balances reported in this statement use the budgetary basis of accounting. In the case of the fund balance of the general fund in New York State on March 31, 1987, the GAAP basis reports a deficit of $3.279 billion (Tables 16.1 and 16.2) while the budgetary basis reports a fund balance of $169 million (Table 16.3); this latter amount is simply a cash balance. Clearly comparisons between this and the previous two GAAP statements must be made with care.

The fourth statement in the annual financial report is the combined statement of revenues, expenses, and changes in retained earnings/fund balances for all proprietary fund types and similar trust funds. Recall from the discussion in the previous chapter that proprietary funds use a full accrual basis of accounting similar to that used by for-profit organizations. A key concern for the financial analyst is the degree to which the non-enterprise funds support the various enterprises and this statement is a starting point for that issue.

Table 16.4 is an example of a statement of revenues and expenses for New York City's enterprise and trust funds for the year ending June 30, 1987. This statement presents the revenues and expenses for each enterprise separately, however many governments present a single column for all enterprise funds, combined, which would be equivalent to the total column in Table 16.4. This statement is an excellent example of why the analyst must examine the entire financial statement, including the notes before reaching a conclusion. If the question of the role of the government's general revenues is raised in connection with the Health and Hospital Corporation (HHC) in Table 16.4, what would be the conclusion? Judging just by the data in the figure alone, a $100 million transfer from the general fund to the HHC is the only apparent connection. However, the notes to the financial statements indicate that virtually all of the "operating revenue" shown in Table 16.4 is city general revenue used to pay for indigent health care costs. Thus the comment to "see accompanying notes to financial statements" included on these and most other

TABLE 16.4

Illustration of Combined Statement of Revenues, Expenses and Changes in Retained Earnings/Fund Balances for Proprietary Fund Types and Similar Trust Funds

THE CITY OF NEW YORK
COMBINED STATEMENT OF REVENUES. EXPENSES AND CHANGES IN
FUND EQUITY—PROPRIETARY FUND TYPE
AND SIMILAR TRUST FUND
FOR THE YEAR ENDED JUNE 30, 1987
(in thousands)

	Proprietary Fund Type					Fiduciary Fund Type
	Health and Hospitals Corporation	Off-Track Betting Corporation	Housing and Economic Development Funds	Water and Sewer System	Total	Pension Trust
REVENUES:						
Patient service revenues, net	$1,655,196	$ —	$ —	$ —	$1,655,196	$ —
Operating revenue	567,663	230,004	28,872	451,273	1,277,812	—
Interest income	4,244	828	238,089	—	243,161	—
Other revenues	32,362	—	60,573	—	92,935	—
Employer, employee contributions	—	—	—	—	—	2,240,690
Investment income, net	—	—	—	13,550	13,550	4,266,799
Total revenues	2,259,465	230,832	327,534	464,823	3,282,654	6,507,489
EXPENSES:						
Personal services	1,390,377	—	18,023	—	1,408,400	—
Affiliation	302,047	—	—	—	302,047	—
Racing industry compensation	—	59,174	—	—	59,174	—
Interest expense	57,465	—	173,979	37,563	269,007	—
Administrative and selling	—	12,866	—	—	12,866	—
Depreciation and amortization	84,470	1,528	464	70,307	156,769	—
Benefit payments and withdrawals	—	—	—	—	—	2,166,782
Other operating	396,667	88,367	34,769	427,847	947,650	—
Total expenses	2,231,026	161,935	227,235	535,717	3,155,913	2,166,782
Allocation to the State and other local governments	—	28,263	—	—	28,263	—
	2,231,026	190,198	227,235	535,717	3,184,176	2,166,782
EXCESS (DEFICIT) OF REVENUES OVER EXPENSES BEFORE OTHER ITEMS	28,439	40,634	100,299	(70,894)	98,478	4,340,707
NON-OPERATING REVENUES AND PAYMENTS						
Special subsidy from New York City	100,000	—	—	—	100,000	—
Amounts from other OTB communities	—	6,933	—	—	6,933	—
Payments to other funds	—	—	—	—	—	(339,367)
Other	—	—	(3,343)	2,360	(983)	—
EXCESS (DEFICIT) OF REVENUES OVER EXPENSES BEFORE EXTRAORDINARY ITEM	128,439	47,567	96,956	(68,534)	204,428	4,001,340
EXTRAORDINARY ITEM:						
Loss on defeasance of bonds	—	—	—	(30,016)	(30,016)	—
EXCESS (DEFICIT) OF REVENUES OVER EXPENSES AFTER EXTRAORDINARY ITEM AND BEFORE ALLOCATION TO THE GENERAL FUND	128,439	47,567	96,956	(98,550)	174,412	4,001,340
Allocation of net revenues to General Fund	—	(47,567)	—	—	(47,567)	—
EXCESS (DEFICIT) OF REVENUES OVER EXPENSES	128,439	—	96,956	(98,550)	126,845	4,001,340
FUND EQUITY AT BEGINNING OF YEAR	1,000,397	—	247,567	5,017,727	6,265,691	27,964,749
Contributed fixed assets	65,527	—	—	46,660	112,187	—
Allocation of net income to contributed capital	—	—	—	67,356	67,356	—
Net increase in donor restricted funds	1,178	—	—	—	1,178	—
FUND EQUITY AT END OF YEAR						
Reserved	949,313	—	272,907	4,981,433	6,203,653	—
Reserved for pension benefits	—	—	—	—	—	31,966,089
Unreserved	246,228	—	71,616	51,760	369,604	—
FUND EQUITY AT END OF YEAR	$1,195,541	$ —	$344,523	$5,033,193	$6,573,257	$31,966,089

See accompanying notes to financial statements.

Source: City of New York, *Comprehensive Annual Financial Report of the Comptroller,* for the Fiscal Year Ended June 30, 1987, p. 10.

governmental financial statements is absolutely essential for the financial analyst.

The fifth and final combined statement in the government's annual financial report has undergone changes due to the Financial Accounting Standards Board's Statement No. 95, which mandates that a statement of cash flows must now be presented instead of the more traditional statement of changes in financial position. The new statement will be clearer than the former statement, but analysts will need to be able to interpret the changes in financial position statement when several years of statements are examined together. Table 16.5 presents a combined statement of changes in financial position for New York City's proprietary and trust funds for the year ending June 30, 1987. Notice that the cash is provided by operations and non-operating sources including changes in current assets and liabilities. Principal payments which are not shown on the revenue and expense statements are often disclosed on the financial position (or cash flow) statement.

These five combined statements, also known as the general purpose financial statements, present the financial information of the government in the most aggregate format. Most of the time in financial analysis, these combined statements are as detailed as necessary, but there are instances where the analyst must go further. In some cases, more detailed information is often disclosed in combined statements by fund type where the single column on the general purpose statement is subdivided to show the individual funds. Table 16.6 is an example of a more detailed statement for the City of Chicago's special revenue funds and this would enable the analyst to separate the transactions of the several special revenue funds. The total column on the right is identical to the special revenue column on the combined balance sheet.

There are also cases where additional detail is presented for a particular fund in the financial statement. Individual revenue items or expenditures are sometimes presented for the general fund.

The Notes to the Financial Statements

The notes to the financial statements are as essential to the financial analyst as the statements themselves. In fact, in many annual financial reports, the notes are lengthier than the statements. The notes accompany the general purpose financial statements discussed above, and are designed to insure that the statements and the notes, together, fairly present the financial position of the government. Also the notes may disclose more detailed information at the fund level. This may duplicate information contained in separate fund statements but is necessary since the general purpose financial statements and the notes are sometimes presented separately, for example as an appendix in an official statement for a bond.

TABLE 16.5

Illustration of Combined Statement Changes in Financial Position
Statement for Proprietary Fund Types and Similar Trust Funds

THE CITY OF NEW YORK
COMBINED STATEMENT OF CHANGES IN FINANCIAL POSITION
PROPRIETARY FUND TYPE AND SIMILAR TRUST FUND
FOR THE YEAR ENDED JUNE 30, 1987
(in thousands)

	Proprietary Fund Type					Fiduciary Fund Type
	Health and Hospitals Corporation	Off-Track Betting Corporation	Housing and Economic Development Funds	Water and Sewer System	Total	Pension Trust
CASH PROVIDED BY:						
Excess (Deficit) of revenues over expenses before extraordinary item	$128,439	$47,567	$ 96,956	$ (68,534)	$ 204,428	$4,001,340
Depreciation and amortization	84,470	1,528	464	70,307	156,769	—
Net adjustment for other noncash items	—	—	9,645	—	9,645	(749,978)
Cash provided by operations before extraordinary item	212,909	49,095	107,065	1,773	370,842	3,251,362
Extraordinary Item:						
Loss on defeasance of bonds	—	—	—	(30,016)	(30,016)	—
Cash provided by (used in) operations	212,909	49,095	107,065	(28,243)	340,826	3,251,362
Payments from the City not included above	56,156	—	1,366	—	57,522	—
Decrease in assets whose use is limited	16,481	—	—	—	16,481	—
Changes in patient receivables:						
Increase in patients' accounts receivable	(71,773)	—	—	—	(71,773)	—
Retroactive rate adjustment receivable	50,435	—	—	—	50,435	—
Retroactive rate adjustment accrued	7,604	—	—	—	7,604	—
Increase (decrease) in accounts payable and other liabilities	(23,367)	10,630	8,790	37,698	33,751	104,942
Increase in deferred revenues	—	—	4,681	10,172	14,853	—
Increase in payables to the State and other local governments	—	177	—	—	177	—
Increase in accrued benefits payable	—	—	—	—	—	26,010
Other, net	(45,554)	4,522	(309,037)	(65,838)	(415,907)	3,572
Increase in accrued salaries and wages	4,427	—	—	—	4,427	—
Proceeds from bonds and notes issuances	—	—	365,085	587,877	952,962	—
Mortgage principal repayment	—	—	241,394	—	241,394	—
Increase in contributed capital	—	—	—	114,014	114,014	—
Total cash provided	207,318	64,424	419,344	655,680	1,346,766	3,385,886
CASH USED FOR:						
Payments to the General Fund	—	51,439	—	—	51,439	—
Decrease in accrued interest and dividends	—	—	—	—	—	(42,307)
Decrease in payables to other retirement systems	—	—	—	—	—	182,038
Decrease in accrued pension costs	666	—	—	—	666	—
Increase in gross investments	—	—	—	—	—	3,147,095
Fixed assets	96,814	10,462	1,264	483,812	592,352	—
Increase in mortgages, loans, distributions and advances to mortgagors	—	—	212,364	—	212,364	—
Principal repayments on bonds and notes	—	—	196,093	166,140	362,233	—
Bond and note issuance cost	—	—	3,998	3,734	7,732	—
Decrease in bonds payable	6,185	—	—	—	6,185	—
Total cash used	103,665	61,901	413,719	653,686	1,232,971	3,286,826
NET CASH PROVIDED	103,653	2,523	5,625	1,994	113,795	99,060
CASH AND CASH EQUIVALENTS AT BEGINNING OF YEAR	84,448	1,553	26,583	4,443	117,027	17,371
CASH AND CASH EQUIVALENTS AT END OF YEAR	$188,101	$ 4,076	$ 32,208	$ 6,437	$ 230,822	$ 116,431

See accompanying notes to financial statements.

Source: City of New York, *Comprehensive Annual Financial Report of the Comptroller*, for the Fiscal Year Ended June 20, 1987, p. 11.

TABLE 16.6

Illustration of Combined Balance Sheet for a Particular Fund Type

Schedule B-1
CITY OF CHICAGO, ILLINOIS
SPECIAL REVENUE FUNDS
COMBINING BALANCE SHEET
December 31, 1986
With Comparative Totals for December 31, 1985
(Amounts are in Thousands of Dollars)

	Vehicle Tax	Motor Fuel Tax	Judgment Tax	Pension
ASSETS				
Cash and Investments	$ 9,402	$ 54,606	$ 1,948	$ 6,234
Cash with Escrow Agent	–	–	–	–
Receivables (Net of Allowance):				
Property Taxes	–	–	20,608	158,954
Accounts	149	154	7	–
Due from Other Funds	11,175	1	119	–
Due from Other Governments	–	3,579	–	3,633
Total Assets	$ 20,726	$ 58,340	$ 22,682	$168,821
LIABILITIES AND FUND BALANCE				
Liabilities:				
Voucher Warrants Payable	$ 1,547	$ 6,964	$ 1,934	$ –
Tax Anticipation Notes	–	–	18,170	–
Due to Other Funds	12,335	21,521	(351)	15,719
Accrued and Other Liabilities	1,207	–	–	–
Judgments, Including Accrued Interest	–	–	12,709	–
Deferred Revenue	–	–	19,836	153,102
Total Liabilities	$ 15,089	$ 28,485	$ 52,298	$168,821
Fund Balance (Deficit):				
Reserve for Encumbrances	$ 1,293	$ 6,968	$ –	$ –
Reserve for Debt Service	–	–	–	–
Unreserved	4,344	22,887	(29,616)	–
Total Fund Balance (Deficit)	$ 5,637	$ 29,855	$(29,616)	$ –
Total Liabilities and Fund Balance (Deficit)	$ 20,726	$ 58,340	$ 22,682	$168,821

Source: City of Chicago, *Comprehensive Annual Financial Report,* for Fiscal Year Ended December 31, 1986, pp. 76–77.

TABLE 16.6 (continued)

Public Building Commission	Traction and Transit	Chicago Public Library	Municipal Hotel Operators' Tax	City Relief	Spec. Serv. Area No. 1, No. 2 & No. 7 Maintenance	Totals 1986	1985
$ 4,082	$ (1,688)	$ 17,339	$ (292)	$ 1,019	$ 4,938	$ 97,588	$ 61,687
49	–	–	–	–	–	49	49
13,554	–	33,187	–	14,442	493	241,238	238,682
–	–	84	–	1	5	400	326
–	69	1,874	9	–	271	13,518	8,446
11,756	1	19	733	–	–	19,721	20,594
$ 29,441	$ (1,618)	$ 52,503	$ 450	$ 15,462	$ 5,707	$ 372,514	$ 329,784
$ –	$ –	$ 2,472	$ 135	$ 938	$ 18	$ 14,008	$ 18,925
–	–	29,200	–	12,730	–	60,100	61,000
–	1	4,956	246	82	297	54,806	13,607
49	–	722	22	–	–	2,000	1,643
–	–	–	–	–	–	12,709	13,855
13,043	–	31,944	–	13,879	462	232,266	221,962
$ 13,092	$ 1	$ 69,294	$ 403	$ 27,629	$ 777	$ 375,889	$ 330,992
$ –	$ –	$ 3,383	$ –	$ –	$ –	$ 11,644	$ 8,902
16,349	–	–	–	–	–	16,349	17,214
–	(1,619)	(20,174)	47	(12,167)	4,930	(31,368)	(27,324)
$ 16,349	$ (1,619)	$ (16,791)	$ 47	$ (12,167)	$ 4,930	$ (3,375)	$ (1,208)
$ 29,441	$ (1,618)	$ 52,503	$ 450	$ 15,462	$ 5,707	$ 372,514	$ 329,784

Many of the measures included in Figure 16.2 require information contained in the notes to the financial statements, either in conjunction with the financial statement or by itself. Figure 16.5 lists the notes that are designated as "essential for fair presentation" by the GASB, and the additional notes that may be necessary for full disclosure. These need to be read in the initial examination of the financial statements, and then more fully digested as part of the financial analysis. Although every note may relate to the measurement of financial condition, only a sample of the relevant notes are discussed in this chapter.

The first note is usually an explanation of the significant accounting policies. Two parts of this note that help the analyst decide the most appropriate structure for the assessment of financial condition are the explanation of the entity and the funds used by the government. Questions such as whether the school district is included with the city, whether the economic development agency is treated separately, and whether the government uses a debt service fund can be answered by this note. Also included in this note is the description of the basis of accounting, which is needed for the proper interpretation of the government's financial information. Many of the assets, liabilities, and fund equities on the combined balance sheet are also explained in this note.

FIGURE 16.5
Notes to Annual Governmental Financial Statements

Notes Essential for Fair Presentation

    Summary of significant accounting policies
        Description of reporting entity
        Revenue recognition policies
        Encumbrance accounting
        Infrastructure asset reporting
        Interest cost capitalization
    Cash deposits with financial institutions
    Investments
    Significant contingent liabilities
    Encumbrances outstanding
    Encumbrances outstanding
    Significant effects of subsequent events
    Pension plan obligations
    Material violations of finance-related legal and contractual provisions
    Debt service requirements to maturity
    Commitments under noncapitalized (operating) leases
    Construction and other significant commitments

FIGURE 16.5 *(continued)*

Changes in general fixed assets
Changes in general long-term debt
Any excess of expenditures over appropriations in individual funds
Deficit fund balance or retained earnings of individual funds
Interfund receivables and payables

Additional Notes that May Be Necessary

Claims and judgments
Property taxes
Segment information for enterprise funds
Budget basis of accounting and differences with GAAP
Short-term debt instruments and liquidity
Related party transactions
Capital leases
Contingencies
Joint ventures
Special termination benefits
Extinguishment of debt
Grants entitlements and shared revenues
Nature of total column use in combined statements
Method of estimation of fixed asset costs
Fund balance designation
Interfund eliminations in combined financial statements not apparent
  from headings
Pension plans in both separately issued plan financial statements and
  employer statements
Bond, tax, or revenue anticipation notes excluded from fund or current
  liabilities
Nature and amount of inconsistencies in financial statements caused by
  transactions between component units with different fiscal year ends
Separate summary of significant accounting policies for discrete
  presentations
Relationship of component unit to oversight unit in separately issued
  component statements and reports
Deferred compensation plans
Reverse repurchase and dollar repurchase agreements
Special assessment debt and related activities
Demand bonds

Source: Governmental Accounting Standards Board, *Codification of Governmental Accounting and Reporting Standards and of June 15, 1987,* Second Edition, Stamford, Connecticut: Governmental Accounting Standards Board, 1987, pp. 173–75.

While the note on significant accounting policies is critical information for the overall analysis, other notes may be the only available source of information for the calculation of several of the important financial condition measures. For example, financial analysts often have to make judgments concerning the outstanding debt of the government, particularly whether the debt is being repaid by the general revenues of the government or by the revenues of a self-supporting enterprise. Moreover, now that governments take advantage of the variety of debt instruments available, the task of identifying, understanding, and classifying the outstanding debt of a government is no longer a simple matter. Thus the notes that disclose the debt and debt-like liabilities of the government form a critical part of debt analysis. But even with the information provided by the notes on outstanding debt, the analyst may have to carry out additional research to fully understand the government's debt structure.

Table 16.7 includes notes 6, 7, 8, and 12 from New York State's annual financial report for year ending March 31, 1987 as an example of a series of notes that describe a government's outstanding debt. These notes are needed to distinguish between short- and long-term financing, and to determine which debt will be repaid from the state's general revenues. New York State issues several billion dollars of short-term financing every year, and this debt is usually outstanding for most of the fiscal year. But since the short-term debt is fully repaid by the last day of the fiscal year, it does not appear on the balance sheet. Instead, it is disclosed in note 6.

The debt structure of New York State is probably more complex than most. In addition to general obligation debt, the state uses lease/purchase agreements and moral obligation bonds rather extensively, and the analyst must determine how these forms of debt are used in the debt analysis. For example, under the moral obligation category, the $8.370 billion in Municipal Assistance Corporation debt that is usually treated as debt of the City of New York because it is repaid from city revenues. In the case of New York State, the State Comptroller issued a separate report defining "tax-supported debt" but not all analysts would agree with this particular interpretation.

When the combined financial statement that compares budget and actual for the governmental funds uses a budgetary basis of accounting that differs from the accounting basis, a note that explains this difference is important to the financial analyst when linking budgets with financial statements to assess financial trends with the most up-to-date information. For example, Table 16.3 presented the comparisons of budget to actual for the governmental funds in New York State. The "financial plan" column in Table 16.3 is the modified budget, and the actual column uses the budgetary basis of accounting.

The note displayed in Table 16.8 from the New York State annual report shows the changes that were made to the original budget to obtain the financial plan and presents a reconciliation between the GAAP and budgetary bases of accounting. The note also explains the budget modifications and shows how the entity, fund structure and basis of accounting contribute to the differences between budget reporting and GAAP. There is about a $1 billion difference between the surplus on a GAAP and budgetary basis that the financial analyst must recognize.

TABLE 16.7
Excerpts from Notes to Financial Statements on Governmental Debt

Note 6
SHORT-TERM FINANCING

Notes, including commercial paper and bond anticipation notes, are issued by the State in anticipation of the proceeds of voter-authorized bond issues. Notes may be issued for a term not exceeding two years. The notes may legally be redeemed only from the proceeds of permanent bonds or reissued notes. Notes outstanding at March 31, 1987 were issued at rates of 3.4% to 4.5% and included $129.9 million of commercial paper.

Changes in notes during the year (not including renewals) were as follows (amounts in thousands):

Purpose	Outstanding April 1, 1986	Issued	Redeemed	Outstanding March 31, 1987
Environmental quality protection—water	$ 37,925	$ —	$ 37,925	$ —
Housing-urban renewal	340	140	340	140
Parks and recreation land acquisition	500	—	500	—
Pure waters	20,060	—	20,060	—
Transportation capital facilities:				
Mass transportation	1,500	—	1,500	—
Aviation	5,910	—	5,910	—
Rebuild New York transportation renewal	89,005	129,870	89,005	129,870
Total	$ 155,240	$130,010	$ 155,240	$ 130,010

The State issues tax and revenue anticipation notes in bearer form annually, at the inception of each fiscal year. These notes are issued primarily because the State makes almost one-half of its payments of grants to local governments and a substantial portion of the personal income tax refunds during the first quarter of the fiscal year while tax and other revenues are received more ratably over the fiscal year.

In April 1987 the State issued such notes in the aggregate amount of $2.6 billion. The notes were issued at an interest rate of 5.35% and are payable on March 31, 1988. The notes are general obligations of the State and have the full faith and credit of the State. The principal and interest will be paid from taxes and miscellaneous revenues of the General Fund. The State Comptroller is required by statute to impound sufficient funds in a separate bank account to pay principal and interest on the notes at maturity. Similarly, tax and revenue anticipation notes of $3.5 billion were issued in April 1986 and repaid by March 31, 1987.

Source: State of New York, *Comprehensive Annual Financial Report of the Comptroller,* for the Fiscal Year Ending March 31, 1987, pp. 34–44.

TABLE 16.7   *(continued)*

Note 7

BONDS PAYABLE

General obligation bonds are backed by the full faith and credit of the State and must be repaid in equal annual installments beginning not more than one year after issuance of such bonds. Changes for the year were as follows (amounts in thousands):

Purpose	Outstanding April 1, 1986	Issued	Redeemed	Outstanding March 31, 1987
Grade crossing elimination (2.5%-4.0%)	$ 1,900	$ —	$ 1,100	$ 800
Environmental quality protection:				
Air (5.25%-12.5%)	52,100	—	5,020	47,080
Land (5.1%-12.5%)	114,255	93,165	8,220	199,200
Wetlands (5.25%-6.0%)	1,627	—	231	1,396
Water (3.75%-12.5%)	255,628	72,450	14,044	314,034
Higher education (2.0%-6.5%)	96,880	—	5,800	91,080
Highway construction (3.4%-4.2%)	26,300	—	13,150	13,150
Housing:				
Low cost (1.0%-7.0%)	446,764	—	19,054	427,710
Middle income (3.25%-10.0%)	119,274	—	2,022	117,252
Urban renewal (6.0%-10.0%)	8,770	400	475	8,695
Mental health construction (4.75%-6.0%)	7,400	—	4,000	3,400
Outdoor recreation (3.0%-12.5%)	77,315	—	8,840	68,475
Parks and recreation land acquisition (5.0%-12.5%)	8,860	500	930	8,430
Pure waters (2.0%-12.5%)	513,735	38,100	27,600	524,235
Rail preservation (4.5%-12.5%)	177,030	26,285	8,630	194,685
Transportation capital facilities:				
Highways (2.0%-7.0%)	375,250	—	60,250	315,000
Mass transportation (2.0%-12.5%)	655,800	3,000	35,525	623,275
Aviation (3.0%-12.5%)	116,245	27,600	6,375	137,470
Energy conservation through improved transportation (6.0%-12.5%)	391,545	21,000	26,860	385,685
Rebuild New York-transportation renewal:				
Highways, parkways, bridges (5.1%-10.6%)	115,630	87,300	11,920	191,010
Ports, waterways (6.0%-10.6%)	14,600	20,700	1,000	34,300
Rapid transit, rail, aviation (6.0%-10.6%)	2,900	45,500	100	48,300
Total	**$ 3,579,808**	**$436,000**	**$ 261,146**	**$ 3,754,662**

Debt service expenditures related to general obligation bonds during the year were $504 million.

Debt service requirements for general obligation bonds in future years, which are financed by transfers from the General Fund, are as follows (amounts in thousands)

Year	Principal	Interest	Total
1988	$ 282,765	$ 242,648	$ 525,413
1989	267,314	223,539	490,853
1990	260,009	205,402	465,411
1991	252,485	188,036	440,521
1992	236,271	171,768	408,039
Thereafter	2,455,818	1,398,671	3,854,489
Total	**$ 3,754,662**	**$ 2,430,064**	**$ 6,184,726**

The total amount of general obligation bonds authorized but not issued at March 31, 1987 was $2.930 billion.

On August 7, 1986 the State issued $405 million of general obligation refunding bonds with an interest range of 5.90-12.00%. The bonds were issued to effect a crossover refunding through the redemption of an equal amount of certain maturities of existing general obligation bonds with an interest range of 8.00-12.00%. The proceeds of the refunding bonds have been placed in an escrow account to provide for the redemptions which will take place on six specific dates between 1990 and 1992. The State expects to reduce its debt service expenditures by approximately $73 million, having a present value discounted semiannually at a rate of interest equal to the yield of the bonds, of approximately $32 million. Debt service expenditures related to general obligation refunding bonds during the year were $9 million.

Interest on the refunding bonds will be paid from the escrow account until the refunded bonds are redeemed. The proceeds of the issue are reported in the Debt Service Funds as proceeds from financing agreements and a reservation of fund balance. The debt is reported in the General Long-term Obligations Account Group as other long-term liabilities.

TABLE 16.7 *(continued)*

Note 8

OBLIGATIONS UNDER LEASE/ PURCHASE AND OTHER FINANCING AGREEMENTS

The State has entered into lease purchase agreements with certain public benefit corporations, municipalities and other entities for various capital facilities. Under these agreements construction costs are initially paid by the State from appropriations (reported as capital construction expenditures in the Capital Projects Funds). These appropriations are then repaid to the State from the proceeds of bonds issued by the public benefit corporations or other entities (reported as proceeds from financing agreements in the Capital Projects Funds). The State becomes the tenant of the facility under a lease purchase agreement which provides for the payment of rentals sufficient to cover the related bond debt service and for the passage of title to the State after the bonds have been repaid.

The State has also entered into contractual obligation financing arrangements (also referred to as "service contract bonds") with the Metropolitan Transportation Authority ($933 million) and the Urban Development Corporation ($44 million). The terms of these arrangements require the State to fund the debt service requirements of the specific debt issued by these entities. The public benefit corporations retain title to the assets acquired with the bond proceeds.

During the year the State entered into various arrangements for the refinancing and purchase of equipment and real property through the issuance of certificates of participation. These certificates are issued through a trustee and the State is responsible for payments to the trustee that approximate the interest and principal payments made by the trustee to the certificate holders. The State maintains custody and use of the equipment and real property. However, title is held by the trustees as security for the certificate holders, until such time as the certificates are fully paid. Proceeds from the issuance of these certificates and the related capital expenditures are accounted for in the same manner as lease/purchase agreements.

Changes for the year were as follows (amounts in thousands):

	Outstanding April 1, 1986	Additions	Payments	Outstanding March 31, 1987
Public Benefit Corporations (see Note 15):				
Housing Finance Agency	$ 2,600,855	$ 127,265	$ 92,845	$ 2,635,275
Dormitory Authority	1,126,045	211,235	31,935	1,305,345
Thruway Authority	161,310	—	6,275	155,035
Triborough Bridge and Tunnel Authority	437,460	—	5,720	431,740
Metropolitan Transportation Authority	882,590	57,310	6,785	933,115
Urban Development Corporation	350,335	230,682	12,450	568,567
Total PBCs	5,558,595	626,492	156,010	6,029,077
Other Entities:				
County of Albany	473,010	—	46,130	426,880
Other municipalities	27,900	—	2,915	24,985
Retirement systems	1,045	—	703	342
Total PBCs and other entities	6,060,550	626,492	205,758	6,481,284
Certificates of Participation	117,984	354,060	18,734	453,310
Total	$ 6,178,534	$ 980,552	$ 224,492	$ 6,934,594

Debt service expenditures for the aforementioned obligations during the year were $670 million. These expenditures are financed primarily by the revenues reported in the Debt Service Funds along with transfers of medicaid monies from the Special Revenue Funds (see Note 9).

Certain of the underlying bond indentures require the maintenance of a rental reserve, usually amounting to one year of debt service. Such amounts ($323 million) are reported as cash of the appropriate Debt Service Fund with a corresponding reservation of fund balance.

Following is a summary of the future minimum rental payments for lease/purchase and contractual obligations financing agreements including interest at 3.25% to 13.75% (amounts in thousands):

Fiscal Year	Principal	Interest	Total
1988	$ 201,435	$ 400,999	$ 602,434
1989	211,917	398,468	610,385
1990	221,741	395,830	617,571
1991	225,412	392,574	617,986
1992	228,875	390,440	619,315
Thereafter	5,391,904	5,704,205	11,096,109
Total	$ 6,481,284	$ 7,682,516	$ 14,163,800

Certain certificate of participation issues require the maintenance of a reserve. These amounts ($60 million) are reported as cash of the appropriate Debt Service Fund with a corresponding reservation of fund balance.

Debt service requirements for certificates of participation, which are financed by transfers from the General Fund, including interest at 3.50% to 8.00%, are as follows (amounts in thousands):

Fiscal Year	Principal	Interest	Total
1988	$ 28,602	$ 28,898	$ 57,500
1989	36,212	27,234	63,446
1990	33,981	25,250	59,231
1991	41,266	23,267	64,533
1992	32,243	20,739	52,982
Thereafter	281,006	173,980	454,986
Total	$ 453,310	$ 299,368	$ 752,678

The State is also committed under numerous operating leases covering real property and equipment. Rental expenditures reported for the year ended March 31, 1987 under such operating leases totaled $208 million and were financed

TABLE 16.7 *(continued)*

primarily from the General Fund. Following is a summary of the future minimum rental commitments under noncancellable real property and equipment leases with terms exceeding one year (amounts in thousands):

Fiscal Year

1988	$ 95,235
1989	81,797
1990	73,578
1991	66,858
1992	50,446

Note 12

GUARANTEED AND MORAL OBLIGATION DEBT

The New York State Constitution provides that the State may guarantee repayment of certain borrowings of the New York State Thruway Authority, the Job Development Authority and the Port Authority of New York and New Jersey to carry out designated projects. The State has never been called upon to make any direct payments pursuant to such guarantees. Except as now authorized, no further State guaranteed debt may be incurred without voter approval. As of March 31, 1987 such State-guaranteed bonds and State-guaranteed bond anticipation notes outstanding (with an additional $314 million authorized but not issued) were as follows (amounts in thousands):

Issuer	Bonds	Notes	Total
Port Authority	$ 96,690	$ —	$ 96,690
Thruway Authority	199,750	—	199,750
Job Development Authority	267,130	22,500	289,630
Total	**$563,570**	**$ 22,500**	**$586,070**

In order to provide additional inducement to investors to purchase the obligations of certain public benefit corporations, the legislation creating these corporations authorizes the State to make up any deficiencies in their debt service reserve funds, subject to legislative appropriation (effectively, a "moral obligation" to back the corporations' credit). Since such "moral obligations" do not constitute full faith and credit obligations of the State, voter approval of such obligations was not obtained.

The State has enacted "capping legislation" which restricts the amount of moral obligation bonds each corporation (other than the Municipal Assistance Corporation) may issue. The cap is set at the amounts of bonds and notes outstanding as of April 1, 1976 plus, within specific dollar limitations, additional bonds and notes required to finance projects then in progress. As moral obligation bonds within the cap are repaid (other than by refunding) the maximum cap is reduced accordingly. Public benefit corporations with no bonds or notes outstanding when this legislation became effective are prohibited from issuing moral obligation debt. This legislation also imposed maximum limitations on lease/purchase financing for certain authorities.

As of March 31, 1987 approximately $12.8 billion in moral obligation bonds were outstanding as follows (amounts in thousands):

Issuer	
Battery Park City Authority	$ 184,900
Dormitory Authority of the State of New York	370,035
New York State Energy Research and Development Authority	5,620
New York State Environmental Facilities Corporation	1,618
New York State Housing Finance Agency	2,458,913
New York State Job Development Authority	1,450
New York State Medical Care Facilities Finance Agency	212,830
New York State Project Finance Agency	212,170
State of New York Mortgage Agency	152,565
United Nations Development Corporation	32,745
Urban Development Corporation	827,735
Municipal Assistance Corporation for the City of New York	8,369,533
Total	**$ 12,830,114**

While the State Legislature is not required to restore any deficiency in a debt service reserve fund, as of March 31, 1987, it had made appropriations pursuant to its "moral obligation" to make up such deficiencies under obligations issued by certain public benefit corporations, notably the Housing Finance Agency (HFA), Urban Development Corporation and Battery Park City Authority. Generally, these amounts are included as appropriated loans receivable. Pursuant to this "moral obligation", the State appropriated and paid $6.5 million during the current year to replenish HFA's debt service reserve funds.

TABLE 16.8

Excerpts from Notes to Financial Statements on Comparison of GAAP and Budgetary Bases of Reporting

Note 10

BUDGETARY BASIS REPORTING

The State Constitution requires the Governor to submit annually an Executive Budget which contains a complete plan for all funds of expenditures for the ensuing fiscal year and all monies and revenues estimated to be available therefore accompanied by bills containing all recommended appropriations or reappropriations and any proposed legislation necessary to provide monies and revenues sufficient to meet such proposed expenditures. Included in the proposed appropriation bills is a provision for spending authority for unanticipated revenues or unforeseen emergencies in accordance with statutory requirements. The Executive Budget includes a cash basis financial plan which must be in balance, i.e., disbursements must not exceed receipts. It also contains a five year financial projection for governmental funds and a five year capital plan. A GAAP basis financial plan for the ensuing fiscal year is presented for informational purposes.

The Legislature enacts appropriation bills and revenue measures embodying those parts of the Executive Budget it has approved or modified. The Legislature may also enact a supplemental appropriation bill and numerous special appropriation bills. When the Legislature convenes in January it generally enacts a deficiency appropriation bill which authorizes additional unforeseen expenditures for the then current fiscal year.

An appropriation is a statutory authorization against which expenditures may be made during a specific fiscal year. An appropriation represents the maximum spending authority and is not a mandate to spend. There are expenditure controls within the State's central accounting system that ensure the maximum spending authority is not exceeded. Generally an appropriation lapses at the end of the fiscal year except for appropriations for which obligations have been incurred, in which case the appropriation lapses the following September 15. The funds to be appropriated

are determined in accordance with constitutional and statutory requirements.

Once the appropriation and revenue bills become law, the cash basis and the GAAP basis financial plans are revised by the Governor to reflect legislative actions. The cash basis financial plan serves as the basis for the administration of the State's finances during the fiscal year. Furthermore, the State Comptroller and Director of the Budget must certify that it is in balance to permit the annual issuance of the tax and revenue anticipation notes (see Note 6). Accordingly, the cash basis financial plan is generally considered to be the State's budget and the appropriate plan to present in Exhibit C. The financial plans are updated quarterly by the Governor or more frequently if necessary. The Governor is required to provide a report to the Legislature showing a comparison of the actual year-to-date results with the latest revised plans providing an explanation of any major deviations and any significant changes to the financial plans.

The annual budget cycle normally begins during the summer prior to the commencement of the fiscal year with the State departments developing their budget requests for submission to the Division of the Budget in September. During the Fall, the departmental requests are analyzed by the Division of the Budget, formal budget hearings are held and major policy decisions are made by the Governor. The Executive Branch phase of the process culminates in the submission of the Executive Budget to the Legislature in late January. The Legislative fiscal committees review the Executive Budget, the Legislature holds public hearings and generally the appropriation bills are enacted by April 1.

The following represents a comparison of the State's cash basis financial plan as originally published by the Governor in April 1986 with subsequent modifications by the Governor to reflect changes during the fiscal year (amounts in millions):

	April 1986	Modifications	January 1987
GENERAL			
Receipts:			
Taxes	$ 23,200	$ 101	$ 23,301
Miscellaneous	1,340	(143)	1,197
Federal grants	90	(11)	79
Total receipts	24,630	(53)	24,577
Disbursements:			
Grants to local governments	15,356	(8)	15,348
Departmental operations	6,156	22	6,178
General state charges	1,731	(8)	1,723
Debt service	157	(4)	153
Total disbursements	23,400	2	23,402
Other financing sources (uses):			
Transfers from other funds	159	—	159
Transfers to other funds	(1,373)	(55)	(1,318)
Net other financing sources (uses)	(1,214)	(55)	(1,159)
Receipts and other financing sources over disbursements and other financing uses	$ 16	$ —	$ 16

Source: State of New York, *Comprehensive Annual Financial Report of the Comptroller,* for the Fiscal Year Ending March 31, 1987, pp. 39–42.

TABLE 16.8 *(continued)*

	April 1986	Modifications	January 1987
SPECIAL REVENUE			
Receipts:			
Taxes	$ 425	$ 235	$ 660
Miscellaneous	1,547	144	1,691
Federal grants	8,579	(117)	8,462
Total receipts	10,551	262	10,813
Disbursements:			
Grants to local governments	8,342	(118)	8,224
Departmental operations	2,773	(83)	2,690
General state charges	191	(3)	188
Capital projects	19	2	21
Total disbursements	11,325	(202)	11,123
Other financing sources (uses):			
Transfers from other funds	1,719	(73)	1,646
Transfers to other funds	(882)	(14)	(896)
Net other financing sources (uses)	837	(87)	750
Receipts and other financing sources over disbursements and other financing uses	$ 63	$ 377	$ 440
DEBT SERVICE			
Receipts:			
Taxes	$ 30	$ —	$ 30
Miscellaneous	1,185	(46)	1,139
Federal grants	12	—	12
Total receipts	1,227	(46)	1,181
Disbursements:			
Debt service	954	(7)	947
Other financing sources (uses):			
Transfers from other funds	1,384	(6)	1,378
Transfers to other funds	(1,694)	46	(1,648)
Net other financing sources (uses)	(310)	40	(270)
Receipts and other financing sources over (under) disbursements and other financing uses	$ (37)	$ 1	$ (36)
CAPITAL PROJECTS			
Receipts:			
Miscellaneous	$ 213	$ (8)	$ 205
Federal grants	508	113	621
Total receipts	721	105	826
Disbursements:			
Departmental operations	5	—	5
Capital projects	1,894	(34)	1,860
Total disbursements	1,899	(34)	1,865
Other financing sources (uses):			
Bond proceeds, net	475	(20)	455
Transfers from other funds	692	(41)	651
Transfers to other funds	—	—	—
Net other financing sources (uses)	1,167	(61)	1,106
Receipts and other financing sources over (under) disbursements and other financing uses	$ (11)	$ 78	$ 67

The modifications indicated above generally reflect revisions to projections based on actual receipts and disbursements for interim periods. The primary revisions are described below:

—General Fund receipts decreased due to lower than anticipated collections of miscellaneous receipts. The reduction in miscellaneous receipts was partially offset by increases in collections of other taxes and business and user taxes. The increase in other taxes reflect the extraordinary year-end real estate market and the impact of the strong stock market on estate tax collections.

TABLE 16.8   *(continued)*

STATE OF NEW YORK

—Special Revenue Funds receipts increased due primarily to tax collections received in the Mass Transportation Operating Assistance Fund as a result of the extension of business tax surcharges. Increased miscellaneous receipts due to a transfer of investment earnings from the Higher Education Services Corporation and receipt of certain petroleum overcharge funds was offset by a reduction in federal grants as a result of a revised projection of Federally supported spending. Transfers from other funds decreased primarily as a result of lower receipts of the State University of New York.

—Special Revenue Funds disbursements for both grants to local governments and departmental operations decreased due to lower than originally anticipated spending for certain Federally supported programs.

—Capital Project Funds receipts were revised upward due to an increase in the drawdown of Federal grants based on actual Federally financed disbursements. This increase was partially offset by lower than anticipated proceeds from the issuance of bonds and a decrease in transfers from other funds due to a decline in capital spending for certain housing and transportation programs.

Exhibit C provides a comparison of the estimated data in the revised Financial Plan with the actual results on the cash basis of accounting for appropriated Governmental Fund Types, whereas Exhibit B presents operating results for the Governmental Fund Types in conformity with generally accepted accounting principles. The following presents a reconciliation of the budgetary cash basis operating results per Exhibit C with the GAAP based operating results per Exhibit B (amounts in thousands):

	General	Special Revenue	Debt Service	Capital Projects
Receipts and other financing sources over disbursements and other financing uses per Exhibit C	$ 16,400	$ 458,400	$ 32,400	$ 95,500
Entity differences:				
Receipts and other financing sources over disbursements and other financing uses for funds and accounts not included in the cash basis financial plan	254,074	383	418,340	101,773
Perspective difference:				
Receipts and other financing sources over disbursements and other financing uses of the Earmarked Revenue Account which is treated as a Special Revenue Fund in the financial plan and part of the General Fund for GAAP reporting......................................	170,991	(170,991)	—	—
Basis of accounting differences:				
Net increase in taxes receivable...........................	902,947	8,886	—	—
Net increase in due from Federal government	—	80,973	—	30,221
Net increase (decrease) in other revenue and asset accruals ...	389,901	(27,080)	34,766	12,991
Net (increase) in tax refunds payable	(281,706)	(3,263)	—	—
Net (increase) in payable to local governments	(404,666)	(8,328)	—	—
Net (increase) in other payables and accrued liabilities	(46,460)	(82,423)	(10,088)	(2,883)
Excess of revenues and other financing sources over expenditures and other financing uses per Exhibit B	$ 1,001,481	$ 256,557	$ 475,418	$ 237,602

The entity differences relate to the presentation of CUNY and its related entities, the inclusion of certain funds considered to be proprietary funds in the budget process, the inclusion of certain sole custody bank accounts, and the inclusion of the proceeds of the crossover refunding (see Note 7). Additionally, the cash basis financial plan presents the State's subsidy of CUNY as grants to local governments ($504 million) whereas this amount in addition to the remainder of CUNY operations are presented as operations of State departments and agencies on Exhibit B.

The perspective difference relates to the Earmarked Revenue Account which is presented on a cash basis (amounts in thousands):

RECEIPTS:	
General business taxes	$ 11,000
Federal grants	5,093
Miscellaneous	804,592
	820,685
DISBURSEMENTS:	
Grants to local governments	200,134
Departmental operations	1,866,703
General state charges	62,499
	2,129,336
OTHER FINANCING SOURCES (USES):	
Transfers from other funds	1,607,301
Transfers to other funds	(127,659)
	1,479,642
Receipts and other financing sources over disbursements and other financing uses	$ 170,991

The assessment of the funding of a government's pensions are a component of financial analysis that usually relies upon the information presented in the notes to the financial statements. In addition, GASB Statement No. 5 requires that governments report certain actuarial calculations for ten years as supplementary information in the financial report. A new requirement of Statement No. 5 is the reporting of pension liabilities calculated using a standard methodology which will improve the analysts' ability to compare and assess the status of the government's pensions.

Table 16.9 presents part of the note from New York City's annual financial statement, year ending June 30, 1987, that presents information on the city's pension systems. New York City actually uses five pension systems and information on all the systems are disclosed in the same note. The note describes the systems, reports on the assets held by the systems, summarizes the actuarial assumptions used to calculate contributions, presents the city's pension contributions, and displays the calculation of the unfunded liabilities for five pension systems. The evaluation of the government's pension systems by the financial analyst relies heavily on this type of information.

Additional information on New York City's pension systems are included in the statistical section of the report. Table 16.10 presents five tables, each containing ten years of information for all five pension systems in New York City. Not shown here are the detailed tables for each of the five systems. Similar information will be reported by all pension systems once GASB Statement No. 5 is implemented. The first part of Table 16.10 computes net assets available for benefits as a percentage of total actuarial present value of credited projected benefits which is a measure of the funding status of the pension system. The second part compares the unfunded actuarial present value of credited benefits to the active annual payroll. The third part shows the percentages of various components of the actuarial present value of credited projected benefits that are covered by the assets available for benefits. The measures of the funding status of New York City's pension systems shown in the three tables exhibit improvement in the combined pension systems over the decade. The fourth and fifth parts of Table 16.10 present the sources of revenues and the components of expenses of the pension system over the decade. This type of supplementary information, which will soon be presented for all governmental pension systems, will substantially improve the analysts's ability to assess the funding status of governmental pension systems. A larger number of the most useful measures of a pension system will be available, and the standard methodology and assumptions used to calculate them will significantly enhance their interpretability.

Many of the other notes listed on Figure 16.5 are essential to the measurement of financial condition, but the importance of individual

TABLE 16.9

Excerpts from Notes to Financial Statements on Pension Systems

G. PENSION PLANS

The City sponsors or participates in pension plans covering substantially all full-time employees. Most plans require employee contributions. The plans provide pension benefits to retired employees based on salary and length of service and also provide cost-of-living and other supplemental pensions to certain retirees and beneficiaries. In the event of disability during employment, participants may receive retirement allowances based on satisfaction of certain service requirements and other plan provisions.

The majority of City employees are members of one of the following five major actuarial systems:

1. New York City Employees' Retirement System (NYCERS), a multiple-employer system, for full time employees of the City not covered by one of the other systems and employees of certain component units of the City and certain other government units.

2. Teachers' Retirement System of The City of New York-Qualified Pension Plan (TRS), a multiple-employer system for teachers in the public schools of the City and certain other specified school and college members.

3. New York City Board of Education Retirement System-Qualified Pension Plan (BERS), a single employer system, for non-pedagogical, permanent, full-time employees of the Board of Education.

4. New York Police Department Pension Fund—Article 2 (Police), a single employer system, for full-time uniformed employees of the Police Department.

5. New York Fire Department Pension Fund—Article 1-B (Fire), a single employer system, for full-time uniformed employees of the Fire Department.

Investments by Pension Trust Funds in debt securities and mortgages are stated at cost, increased or decreased by amortization of purchase discounts or premiums. Investments in equity securities are stated at the last reported sales price on a national securities exchange on the last business day of the fiscal year. Securities purchased pursuant to agreements to resell are carried at the contract price, exclusive of interest, at which the securities will be resold.

Realized gains or losses on sales of securities are based on the average cost of securities. Dividend income is recorded on the ex-dividend date. Interest income is recorded as earned on an accrual basis.

The net assets of the five major actuarial trust funds at June 30, 1987 and 1986 are summarized as follows:

	1987		1986	
	Book Value	Market Value(1)	Book Value	Market Value
		(in millions)		
Securities purchased under agreements to resell	$ 353	$ 353	$ 402	$ 402
Other short-term investments	1,760	1,760	4,064	4,064
Debt securities:				
City of New York and other related public benefit corporations	365	358	471	463
U.S. Government	14,506	14,837	10,135	10,057
Corporate debt	3,030	3,020	3,048	3,406
Other	533	571	449	487
Equity securities at market value (cost was $7,224 million and $6,115 million respectively)	10,922	10,922	9,063	9,063
Mortgages	101	(2)	156	(2)
Guaranteed investment contracts	606	606	491	491
Total investments	32,176		28,279	
Other, net	(210)		(314)	
Net assets available for pension benefits	$31,966		$27,965	

(1) The market value of securities as of October 27, 1987 reflects a decline in value from June 30, 1987 of approximately $2.3 billion. Management does not believe that such decline will have a significant effect on future pension cost.
(2) Market values for these investments are not readily determinable.

Net assets available for pension benefits by plan were as follows:

	1987	1986
	(in millions)	
NYCERS	$13,918	$12,046
TRS	11,092	9,902
BERS	460	419
POLICE	4,749	4,108
FIRE	1,747	1,490
	$31,966	$27,965

Source: City of New York, *Comprehensive Annual Financial Report of the Comptroller,* for the Fiscal Year Ended June 30, 1987, pp. 24–27.

TABLE 16.9 *(continued)*

Upon termination of employment before retirement, certain members are entitled to refunds of their own contributions including accumulated interest less any loans outstanding. The net total of those categories included in fund balances on the Statement of Assets, Liabilities and Net Assets Available for Pension Benefits were approximately:

	1987	1986
	(in millions)	
NYCERS	$ 1,042	$ 973
TRS	1,051	985
BERS	58	53
POLICE	245	227
FIRE	66	59
	$ 2,462	$2,297

The more significant assumptions used in the actuarial calculations for employers' contributions are as follows:

Assumed rate of return on investments	8% (4% for benefits payable under the variable annuity programs)
Mortality basis	Tables based on prior experience
Turnover	Moderate scales
Retirement	Varies from earliest age a member is eligible to retire until age at end of published tables.
Asset valuation	For NYCERS, Police and Fire, a five-year moving average of market value for equities and amortized cost for other investments. For TRS and BERS, market value for equities and amortized cost for other investments. Realized gains and losses related to bond sales are deferred and amortized.
Salary	In general, merit and promotion component averaging 1% per year plus assumed general increase of 5.5% per year. (For the Teachers' Retirement System, the general wage assumption has been decreased .5% since the 1985 valuation; for the Board of Education Retirement Systems the merit and promotion component averaging 1% per year plus assumed general increase of 6.0% per year).
Unfunded actuarial accrued liabilities	A portion of the frozen initial actuarial accrued liability as of June 30, 1975 remaining unfunded as of June 30, 1980 is being amortized principally over a 35-year period beginning July 1, 1980. Other components of the unfunded actuarial accrued liability are being amortized over 10 to 40 years.

The City's expenditures for pension costs, exclusive of employee contributions, for the years ended June 30, 1987 and 1986 were approximately $1.8 billion and $1.7 billion, respectively for each year and were equal to the amounts recommended by the Systems' actuary. The expenditures recommended by the actuary for the current year are as follows:

		Expenditures for		Expenditures as a percentage of covered employee payroll
	Normal cost	Amortization of actuarial accrued liability	Total	
		(in millions)		
New York City Employees' Retirement System (net)	$291.7	$194.7	$ 486.4	21.1%
Teachers' Retirement System (net)	226.4	222.9	449.3	20.3%
Board of Education Retirement System	16.5	9.4	25.9	16.6%
Police Pension Fund—Article 2	332.2	148.5	480.7	49.0%
Fire Department Pension Fund—Article 1-B	130.4	94.4	224.8	45.1%
Other systems and programs	N/A	N/A	112.4	—
Total			$1,779.5	

Included in the above total is approximately $50.1 million of payments (net of revenue received from the State as reimbursement) for State employees in the City's pension systems and payments made on behalf of certain employees in the New York City Transit Authority and the New York City Housing Authority. These payments and the related reimbursements are recorded as either expenditures or revenues in individual program categories rather than as pension expenditures in the Combined Statement of Revenues, Expenditures and Changes in Fund Balance.

TABLE 16.9 *(continued)*

Also included in the total is approximately $112 million contributed to three other actuarial retirement systems and seven non-actuarial retirement systems for certain employees, retirees and beneficiaries not covered by any of the five major actuarial systems. The City also contributes per diem amounts into certain union-administered annuity funds.

An actuarial valuation, including a review of the continued reasonableness of the actuarial assumptions, is performed annually for each of the five major actuarial systems. The following is a comparison of the actuarial present value of credited projected benefits and net assets available for benefits for the five major actuarial systems as of June 30, 1987:

	Actuarial present value of					
	Projected benefits for retirees, beneficiaries and terminated vested participants	Credited projected benefits for		Total actuarial present value of credited projected benefits**	Net assets available for benefits***	Unfunded actuarial present value of credited projected benefits
		Vested active participants*	Non-vested active participants*			
			(in millions)			
New York City Employees' Retirement System	$ 4,233.6	$ 3,177.0	$1,556.7	$ 8,967.3	$ 7,153.2	$1,814.1
Teachers' Retirement System	4,221.2	6,307.1	749.3	11,277.6	9,544.5	1,733.1
Board of Education Retirement System	220.1	250.9	61.6	532.6	405.3	127.3
Police Pension Fund Article 2	3,844.6	1,842.2	1,860.2	7,547.0	3,827.8	3,719.2
Fire Pension Fund Article 1-B	1,391.4	1,205.9	745.9	3,343.2	1,446.6	1,896.6
Total	$13,910.9	$12,783.1	$4,973.7	$31,667.7	$22,377.4	$9,290.3

* Excludes amounts attributable to employee contributions subject to refund upon termination of employment before retirement.

** Includes $1,265.7 million and $6,185.5 million attributable to City component unit employers and non City employers, respectively, of NYCERS and TRS.

*** Based on actuarial assumptions asset valuations (see page 26).

The actuarial present values of credited projected benefits for active participants are based on current salaries with projected increases to retirement. As of June 30, 1987, the actuarial present value of future benefits for the three non-actuarial pension funds of the City is approximately $486 million.

The net assets available for benefits shown in these financial statements exclude the accrued pension contribution of $2,797 million for amortization of the two-year payment lag reported in the Long-term Obligations Account Group, $122 million reported in the Enterprise funds and $416 million from other government units. Prior to fiscal year 1981 pension contributions had been made on a statutory basis which reflected pension costs incurred two years earlier and a phase-in of certain actuarial assumptions. The City's liability resulting from the two-year lag is being amortized over 40 years.

The Comptroller of the City is custodian for the Systems' assets and was designated investment manager for most funds. Securities are held by certain banks under custodial agreements. The Trustees of the various systems utilize investment advisors to help manage the investment portfolios. Actuarial services are provided to the Systems by an actuary employed by the Systems. The City's Corporation Counsel provides legal services to the Systems and other administrative services are provided by the City.

TABLE 16.10

Additional Information on Pension Systems

Major Actuarial Pension Systems—Schedule 1

COMPARATIVE SUMMARY OF NET ASSETS AVAILABLE FOR BENEFITS AND TOTAL ACTUARIAL
PRESENT VALUE OF CREDITED PROJECTED BENEFITS*

Fiscal Year	Net Assets Available for Benefits** (in thousands)		Total Actuarial Present Value of Credited Projected Benefits	Percentage
	(A)	(B)	(D)	(B) ÷ (D)
1978	$10,568,657	$10,644,299	$20,971,655	50.8%
1979	11,735,118	11,658,326	22,442,931	51.9
1980	13,241,708	12,978,862	24,158,246	53.7
1981	14,839,212	14,317,987	25,586,481	56.0
1982	15,499,762	15,315,155	26,677,721	57.4
1983	19,064,033	17,910,070	29,407,749	60.9
1984	19,944,756	19,443,707	31,482,399	61.8
1985	23,820,879	22,523,583	33,940,651	66.4
1986	28,385,442	26,268,971	38,843,692	67.6
1987	32,343,377	30,143,409	41,871,852	72.0

Combined—All Five Pension Systems (Memorandum Only)

(A) Market value for equities and amortized cost for bonds.
(B) For TRS and Bd. of Ed.: Market value for equities and amortized cost for bonds.
For NYCERS, Police and Fire: Five-year moving average of market value for equities and amortized cost for bonds.

Major Actuarial Pension Systems—Schedule 2

COMPARATIVE SUMMARY OF UNFUNDED ACTUARIAL PRESENT VALUE OF CREDITED
PROJECTED BENEFITS AND ANNUAL ACTIVE MEMBER PAYROLL

Fiscal Year	Unfunded Actuarial Present Value of Credited Projected Benefits (in thousands)	Annual Active Member Payroll	Percentage
	(A)	(B)	(A) ÷ (B)
1978	$10,327,356	$4,529,450	228.0%
1979	10,784,605	4,585,520	235.2
1980	11,179,384	4,913,254	227.5
1981	11,268,494	5,435,731	207.3
1982	11,362,566	6,002,017	189.3
1983	11,497,679	6,594,603	174.3
1984	12,038,693	7,186,547	167.5
1985	11,417,069	7,677,546	148.7
1986	12,574,721	8,398,194	149.7
1987	11,728,443	8,981,718	130.6

Combined—All Five Pension Systems (Memorandum Only)

Source: City of New York, *Comprehensive Annual Financial Report of the Comptroller,* for the Fiscal Year Ended June 30, 1987, pp. 276–85.

TABLE 16.10 (continued)

Major Actuarial Pension Systems—Schedule 3

COMPARATIVE SUMMARY OF ACTUARIAL VALUES AND PERCENTAGES COVERED BY NET ASSETS
AVAILABLE FOR BENEFITS
Actuarial Present Value of Credited Projected Benefits

Fiscal Year	Member Contributions	Current Retirants and Beneficiaries	Terminated Vested Participants*	Active Members Employer Financed Portion	Net Assets Available for Benefits	Percentage of Actuarial Values Covered by Net Assets Available for Benefits			
				(In thousands)					
				Combined—All Five Pension Systems (Memorandum Only)					
	(A)	(B)	(C)	(D)		(A)	(B)	(C)	(D)
1978	$1,428,248	$ 8,452,618	$381,325	$10,709,465	$10,644,299	100%	100%	100%	3.6%
1979	1,521,250	9,146,643	261,673	11,513,365	11,658,326	100	100	100	6.3
1980	1,608,189	9,857,501	271,377	12,421,179	12,978,862	100	100	100	10.0
1981	1,736,942	9,566,727	313,968	13,968,843	14,317,987	100	100	100	19.3
1982	1,797,641	10,048,010	396,878	14,435,192	15,315,155	100	100	100	21.3
1983	1,920,653	11,311,655	237,890	15,937,551	17,910,070	100	100	100	27.9
1984	1,994,413	12,166,416	357,883	17,071,086	19,443,707	100	100	100	28.8
1985	2,177,504	13,101,204	536,956	18,124,986	22,523,583	100	100	100	37.0
1986	2,486,560	15,497,665	572,164	20,287,303	26,268,971	100	100	100	38.0
1987	2,752,906	17,076,564	416,912	21,625,470	30,143,409	100	100	100	45.8

Major Actuarial Pension Systems—Schedule 4

COMPARATIVE SUMMARY OF REVENUES BY SOURCE

Fiscal Year	Member Contributions	Employer Contributions	Investment Income	Other	Total
		(in thousands)			
		Combined—All Five Pension Systems (Memorandum Only)			
1978*	$212,145	$1,233,272	$ 610,347	$38,769	$2,094,533
1979	115,071	1,373,950	816,937	—	2,305,958
1980	86,699	1,466,305	1,192,170	—	2,745,174
1981	98,153	2,295,942	1,129,628	—	3,523,723
1982	4,647	1,672,763	266,108	7,696	1,951,214
1983	70,199	1,762,126	3,335,029	8,163	5,175,517
1984	127,791	1,814,243	518,835	137	2,461,006
1985	120,797	1,897,608	3,590,360	6,366	5,615,131
1986	151,904	2,021,422	4,760,978	346	6,934,650
1987	171,572	2,049,654	4,266,799	490	6,488,515

Major Actuarial Pension Systems—Schedule 5

COMPARATIVE SUMMARY OF EXPENSES BY TYPE

Fiscal Year	Benefits	Refunds	Administrative Expenses	Other	Total
		(In thousands)			
		Combined—All Five Pension Systems (Memorandum Only)			
1978*	$ 908,460	$30,354	$1,488	$427,898	$1,368,200
1979	963,027	35,883	91	18,673	1,017,674
1980	1,068,227	54,274	116	11,418	1,134,035
1981	1,116,040	68,684	107	5,679	1,190,510
1982	1,268,378	42,205	196	44,198	1,354,977
1983	1,410,078	34,423	413	39,563	1,484,477
1984	1,584,843	39,238	301	25,016	1,649,398
1985	1,704,756	45,921	292	27,121	1,778,090
1986	1,900,506	47,124	368	540,473	2,488,471
1987	2,084,013	82,153	323	340,150	2,506,639

notes for specific governments will vary from case to case. Notes on interfund transfers and obligations are often needed by the financial analyst to understand the relationships among the funds. Other notes may disclose critical information for financial condition analysis, and may be very important in selected instances. For example, many governments will have no pending lawsuits that individually or in the aggregate will materially affect financial condition. But when such litigation exists, it should be disclosed in the notes to the financial statements. Table 16.11 is a note from the City of Buffalo financial statements, year ending June 30, 1987, explaining both the pending litigation that could result in significant liabilities, and the inclusion of part of that liability in the long-term debt group of accounts and the debt service fund.

The Statistical Section

The final component of the annual financial report discussed in this chapter, the statistical section, is of great use in the analysis of financial condition. The statistical section includes both accounting and non-accounting data which in many cases includes various measures listed in Figure 16.2. According to a publication that includes extensive illustrations of tables and figures from statistical sections, "the statistical section is intended to provide CAFR [comprehensive annual financial report] users with a broader and deeper perspective on the financial affairs of the reporting government than is provided in the letter of transmittal contained in the CAFR's introductory section

TABLE 16.11
Excerpts from Notes to Financial Statements on Pending Litigation

---

5. General Property Tax Litigation

Since a 1974 decision in the Hurd case, in which the State Court of Appeals struck down statutes intended to provide a means to enable the City to tax above its constitutional limits, the City has been a party to numerous claims and lawsuits in which taxpayers sought refunds for taxes collected in excess of the constitutional limit.

With respect to City tax levies prior to the use of the State Special Equalization Ratios, the City of Buffalo was found liable in the case of Central Buffalo Project Corporation v. City of Buffalo for tax refunds for the fiscal years 1974–75 through 1977–78, aggregating approximately $876,000, a determination which was upheld by the State Court of Appeals.

After several years of litigation the City was faced with the prospect of a multitude of separate actions for tax refunds as a result of one large successful claimant and, accordingly commenced a class action in March 1981, entitled *City of Buffalo v. Wysocki, et al.* to determine the extent of its liability and a plan for repayment, as required, in an orderly manner.

TABLE 16.11 (continued)

Motions for summary judgment in *City of Buffalo v. Wysocki, et al.* were heard on January 6, 1982. The Court ruled in favor of taxpayers who paid under protest (written protest at time of payment). Judgments have been entered for members of the Fourth Sub-class which, total $7.4 million in principal plus interest which through June 30, 1987, totals approximately $5.6 million.

The City estimates that the maximum amount of refunds, excluding interest, that could be paid as a result of litigation stemming from the Hurd decision is $58,100,000 as follows:

Total amount levied in excess of the 2% limitation for fiscal years 1974–75 through 1977–78	$88,500,000
Less:	
Amount of 1974–75 excess levy estimated to be excluded on the basis of the six-year statute of limitations	21,100,000
Amount cancelled through foreclosure proceedings	3,300,000
Amount of excess taxes never paid	5,100,000
Refunds paid through June 30, 1987	900,000
	$58,100,000

The Wysocki proceedings are now in Supreme Court, Erie County where a proposed plan to attempt to resolve all claims was submitted. To date, this proposed plan has not been accepted by the Fourth Sub-class claimants nor imposed by the Court.

The City of Buffalo's proposed plan has been modeled, to some extent, after Rochester New York's settlement plan for similar litigation and includes the following key provisions:

- Payment of outstanding judgments to the Fourth Sub-class an amount equal to 61% of principal is full settlement of these claims except that if other classes in the Wysocki litigation were to receive a higher percentage then such Fourth Sub-class claimants would be paid pari passu.

- Engagement of an independent CPA firm to identify, verify and process payment of valid claims for other classes in the Wysocki case.

- Petitions to New York State elected officials for assistance in funding future claims.

- Set aside of any undesignated, unreserved general fund balances as a City funded downpayment for refunds to the other sub-classes.

In connection with these matters the City has accrued $31,250,000 in the general long-term debt group of accounts (which represents 61% of the original principle amount of over taxation in all other sub-classes) and $6,325,000 in the Debt Service Fund (which represents 61% of the original principle amount of over taxation for the Fourth Sub-class and estimated administrative costs of claims processing.

Source: City of Buffalo, New York, *Comprehensive Annual Financial Report,* June 30, 1987, pp. 16 and 17.

FIGURE 16.6
Statistical Tables Required by GASB for Inclusion in Comprehensive
Annual Financial Reports

Statistical Tables Covering the Last Ten Fiscal Years

General Government Expenditures by Function

General Revenues by Source

Property Tax Levies and Collections

Assessed and Estimated Actual Value of Taxable Property

Property Tax Rates, All Overlapping Governments

Special Assessment Billings and Collections

Ratio of Net General Bonded Debt to Assessed Value and Net Bonded
Debt Per Capita

Ratio of Annual Debt Service for General Bonded Debt to Total General
Expenditures

Revenue Bond Coverage

Property Value, Constructions, and Bank Deposits

Other Statistical Tables

Computation of Legal Debt Margin if Not Presented in the General
Purpose Financial Statements (GPFS)

Computation of Overlapping Debt, if not presented in the GPFS

Demographic Statistics

Principal Taxpayers

Miscellaneous Statistics

Source: Governmental Accounting Standards Board, *Codification of Governmental Accounting and Reporting Standards as of June 15, 1987,* Second Edition, Stamford, Connecticut: Governmental Accounting Standards Board, 1987, p. 211.

and in the financial statements and supporting schedules presented in the CAFR's financial section."[10]

Unlike the financial statements and notes, the statistical section is usually not audited by the external auditor. In most cases, the financial analyst must rely on the sources of the information cited in the report to assess the quality of the information.

Figure 16.6 lists the statistical tables required by the GASB for inclusion in the comprehensive annual financial report. In cases where the item is not relevant, such as when a government has no

[10] Paul E. Glick, *Illustrations of Statistical Sections of Comprehensive Annual Financial Reports of State and Local Governments,* Chicago, Illinois: Government Finance Officers Association, 1984, p. 1.

debt, the table is not required. For the financial analyst, it is tremendously valuable to have key financial variables computed for ten years using consistent definitions. When an accounting definition changes over the period, a note is often included in the table indicating that the entire time series is not completely comparable. In most of the cases, the variables presented in the statistical tables are listed in Figure 16.2 as measures of one of the components of financial condition, so that the a complete statistical section is a real asset to the financial analyst. And while the presentation of complete statistical sections is improving over time, an analyst cannot assume that all of the tables required by the GASB will be included in all reports.[11] Although examples of all of the required statistical tables are not included in this chapter, several are presented to document their usefulness to the financial analyst.

Because time series analyses of revenues and expenditures are an important part of financial analysis, the ten-year tables of revenues and expenditures are very useful. The particular fund structure used in these ten-year time series is often explained on the table because these trends often encompass the revenues and expenditures in more than one fund. A table of revenues and expenditures from New York State's statistical section is presented in Table 16.12. Note that the totals for 1986–87 correspond to the "Total" column in the combined statement shown in Table 16.2. In this case, the ten-year trend table includes the revenues and expenditures from the four governmental funds in New York State. Since this includes the capital projects fund, this time series may not be optimally designed for certain aspects of revenue and expenditure analysis. Since it is indicated that the state used a cash basis of accounting during the early part of the time series, the data are not comparable over the entire ten-year period.

The list of required tables in Figure 16.6 includes several that examine the property tax because it is the major tax source for local governments. Table 16.13, from the statistical section in New York City's comprehensive annual financial report, is an example of the property tax information that is included in this section. Information on collections, assessed and full value, and components of the property tax base are important variables in financial condition analysis. Additional information is often required to interpret a particular government's property tax performance due to the variations in property tax classification systems, collection policies, and methods used to obtain full values from assessed values.

---

[11] See, for example, Robert W. Ingram and Walter A. Robbins, *Financial Reporting Practices of Local Governments*, Stamford, Conn.: Governmental Accounting Standards Board, 1987.

TABLE 16.12
Illustration of Statistical Section Information on Revenues and
Expenditures
STATE OF NEW YORK

Schedule of Revenues, Expenditures and Other Financing Sources (Uses)

ALL GOVERNMENTAL FUNDS

For the Ten Past Fiscal Years

(Amounts in millions) (Unaudited)

	1977-78	1978-79
REVENUES:		
Taxes	$ 10,491	$ 11,005
Miscellaneous revenues	1,355	1,502
Federal grants	4,772	5,473
Receivables from other government units	1,025	1,011
Repayment of advances by public authorities	42	24
Total revenues	17,685	19,015
EXPENDITURES:		
Grants to local governments	ʰ 10,569	11,303
Operations of state departments and agencies	4,839	5,347
Debt service	779	840
Capital projects	774	1,015
Advances and miscellaneous	886	900
Total expenditures	17,847	19,405
Revenues over (under) expenditures	(162)	(390)
OTHER FINANCING SOURCES (USES):		
Bond proceeds	279	99
Tax and revenue anticipation note proceeds	—	—
Transfers from other funds	—	—
Transfers to other funds	—	—
Net other financing sources	279	99
Operating revenues and other financing sources over		
(under) expenditures and other financing uses	$ 117	$ (291)

Footnote: Amounts prior to 1980-81 fiscal year are cash basis amounts

Source: Office of the State Comptroller

Source: State of New York, *Comprehensive Annual Financial Report of the Comptroller,* for
the Fiscal Year Ending March 31, 1987, pp. 120–21.

TABLE 16.12 (*continued*)

STATE OF NEW YORK

1979-80	1980-81	1981-82	1982-83	1983-84	1984-85	1985-86	1986-87
$ 12,320	$ 13,597	$ 15,060	$ 16,252	$ 18,498	$ 20,803	$ 22,255	$ 25,030
1,768	2,140	2,782	3,191	2,943	3,555	3,798	4,303
6,113	5,936	6,955	7,047	7,432	8,195	8,999	9,436
135	—	—	—	—	—	—	—
32	—	—	—	—	—	—	—
20,368	21,673	24,797	26,490	28,873	32,553	35,052	38,769
12,168	13,136	15,705	17,005	17,737	19,591	21,405	23,390
6,033	7,144	8,097	9,018	9,543	10,625	11,165	11,951
896	858	701	1,143	1,229	1,309	1,315	1,335
1,194	1,016	996	1,294	1,109	1,328	1,521	1,749
122	—	—	—	—	—	—	—
20,413	22,154	25,499	28,460	29,618	32,853	35,406	38,425
(45)	(481)	(702)	(1,970)	(745)	(300)	(354)	344
283	240	123	529	295	274	655	1,302
—	—	—	218	—	—	—	—
—	23	3,348	3,908	3,396	3,770	3,794	4,473
—	—	(3,093)	(3,512)	(3,396)	(3,770)	(3,794)	(4,148)
283	263	378	1,143	295	274	655	1,627
$ 238	$ (218)	$ (324)	$ (827)	$ (450)	$ (26)	$ 301	$ 1,971

The government's outstanding debt is obviously a critical part of financial condition analysis, and several of the tables in the statistical section typically address this issue. From an analytical perspective, these tables often have the advantages of time series data and consistent definitions. The analyst must always assess whether the definitions are consistent with the analytical objectives. Table 16.14 and Figure 16.7 present debt information from the statistical section in the City of Chicago's annual report. The first table is an example of how the

TABLE 16.13

Illustration of Statistical Information on the Property Tax

Real Estate Tax

Real Estate Tax Collections

Fiscal Year	Tax Levy	Year of Levy	1st Year After Year of Levy	2nd Year After Year of Levy	3rd Year After Year of Levy	Remaining Uncollected June 30, 1987
			Percent of Tax Levy Collected Within			
1978 and prior	$ —	—	—	—	—	$ 3,798,936
1979	3,318,582,535	94.10	1.14	0.33	0.13	1,551,540
1980	3,329,997,998	94.14	1.13	0.30	0.05	3,176,800
1981	3,499,080,204	93.43	0.94	0.16	0.07	6,666,459
1982	3,798,603,761	92.92	0.47	(0.26)	(0.02)	6,200,649
1983	3,996,382,508	93.91	0.47	0.01	0.11	4,710,522
1984	4,200,566,636	93.73	0.46	0.16	0.09	1,958,950
1985	4,476,957,607	93.25	0.67	0.20	—	28,889,596
1986	4,867,969,237	92.78	0.71	—	—	38,422,663
1987	5,108,944,117	94.82	—	—	—	97,222,651

Real Estate Assessments

Fiscal Year	Taxable Assessed Value(1)	Full Value(2)	Tax Levy	Tax Rate Per $100 of Assessed Value	Tax Rate Per $100 of Full Value
1978	$38,611,805,862	$ 86,246,235,249	$3,378,611,468	8.75	3.92
1979	37,926,135,100	86,646,897,955	3,318,582,535	8.75	3.83
1980	38,055,969,696	84,385,108,529	3,329,997,998	8.75	3.95
1981	39,428,721,277	87,108,314,857	3,499,080,204	8.85[3]	4.02
1982	42,545,394,486	107,442,669,992	3,798,603,761	8.95	3.54
1983	43,824,841,468	129,950,789,485	3,996,382,508	9.12[4]	3.08
1984	45,644,829,501	158,875,146,192	4,200,566,636	9.21[4]	2.65
1985	48,384,099,158	177,882,717,493	4,476,957,607	9.26[4]	2.52
1986	52,643,593,088	199,105,874,009	4,867,969,237	9.26[4]	2.45
1987	55,287,807,367	220,357,940,881	5,108,944,117	9.32[4]	2.34

(1) Excludes value of certain property eligible for the veteran's real property exemption.
(2) Full valuation for each fiscal year shown is based on the special equalization rates as reported to the City Council for purposes of fixing the tax rate for such year.
(3) Tax rate was increased from 8.75 to 8.95 effective January 1, 1981 resulting in an average rate of 8.85 for the fiscal year.
(4) Beginning with the City's 1983 fiscal year, taxable real property in the City is divided into four classes with an individual real estate tax rate for each class. The rate per full dollar of valuation is based on the weighted average of these individual rates.

Source: City of New York, *Comprehensive Annual Financial Report of the Comptroller*, for the Fiscal Year Ended June 30, 1987, pp. 24–45.

TABLE 16.13 (continued)

Real Estate Tax

COLLECTIONS, CANCELLATIONS, ABATEMENTS AND OTHER CREDITS AS A
PERCENT OF TAX LEVY

Fiscal Year	Tax Levy (in millions)	Collections	Cancellations	Abatements	Percent of Tax Levy through June 30, 1987 Prepayment Discounts	Section 626 Deduction(1)	Uncollected Balance June 30, 1987	Uncollected Balance End of Levy Year
1978	$3,378.6	93.9%	5.1%	0.7%	0.1%	0.2%	0.0%	4.7%
1979	3,318.6	95.1	3.7	0.8	0.2	0.2	0.0	3.6
1980	3,330.0	95.4	3.4	0.9	0.1	0.2	0.0	3.6
1981	3,499.1	94.6	3.9	1.0	0.1	0.2	0.2	3.7
1982	3,798.6	93.2	5.3	1.1	0.1	0.2	0.1	3.2
1983	3,996.4	94.6	4.2	1.0	0.0	0.1	0.1	2.9
1984	4,200.6	94.5	4.2	1.1	0.0	0.2	0.0	3.0
1985	4,477.0	94.1	4.0	1.1	0.0	0.2	0.6	3.0
1986	4,868.0	93.5	4.6	0.9	0.0	0.2	0.8	2.0
1987	5,108.9	94.8	2.4	0.9	0.0	0.0	1.9	1.9

Total uncollected balance at June 30, 1987 less allowance for uncollectible amounts equals net realizable amount (real estate taxes receivable).

1) Deduction allowed against taxes levied on a special franchise for certain other payments made by special franchise owners to The City of New York.

ASSESSED VALUATION OF TOTAL REAL ESTATE BY COMPONENTS

Type of Property	Fiscal Year 1987 Assessed Value (in millions)	Percentage Of Taxable Real Estate	Fiscal Year 1986 Assessed Value (in millions)	Percentage Of Taxable Real Estate	Fiscal Year 1985 Assessed Value (in millions)	Percentage Of Taxable Real Estate
One Family Dwellings	$ 3,385.6	6.1%	$ 3,358.9	6.4%	$ 3,234.6	6.7%
Two Family Dwellings	2,660.8	4.8	2,684.4	5.1	2,585.0	5.3
Walk-Up Apartments	3,962.2	7.2	3,833.3	7.3	3,749.8	7.8
Elevator Apartments	10,214.7	18.5	9,782.7	18.6	9,049.9	18.7
Warehouses	577.1	1.0	554.7	1.1	541.0	1.1
Factories	1,110.9	2.0	1,090.4	2.1	1,068.0	2.2
Garages	653.4	1.2	623.3	1.2	612.1	1.3
Hotels	1,030.0	1.9	975.1	1.9	920.6	1.9
Theatres	134.6	0.2	129.7	0.2	122.7	0.3
Store Buildings	2,765.7	5.0	2,550.9	4.8	2,348.5	4.9
Lofts	1,815.9	3.3	1,615.5	3.1	1,482.7	3.1
Office Buildings	14,899.2	26.9	13,046.3	24.8	11,547.0	23.9
Miscellaneous Buildings	1,997.3	3.6	1,838.1	3.5	1,661.5	3.4
Vacant Land	509.2	0.9	503.7	1.0	522.5	1.1
Real Estate of Public Utilities and Special Franchises	9,571.2	17.3	10.056.6	19.1	8,938.2	18.5
Total	$55,287.8	100.0%	$52,643.6	100.0%	$48,384.1	100.0%

NOTE: Details may not add up due to rounding. Totals do not include the value of certain property eligible for the veterans' real property tax exemption.

TABLE 16.14

Illustration of Statistical Information on Outstanding Debt

Table 8
CITY OF CHICAGO, ILLINOIS
COMPUTATION OF OVERLAPPING DEBT (1)
December 31, 1986
(Amounts are In Thousands of Dollars)

	Outstanding Debt	Percentage of Overlapping Debt	Debt Applicable
City of Chicago Bonds, Notes and Capitalized Lease Obligations	$ 897,098 (2)	100.00%	$ 897,098 (2)
Board of Education	229,141	100.00	229,141
Chicago School Finance Authority	648,855	100.00	648,855
Chicago Park District	277,679	100.00	277,679
City Colleges of Chicago	225,541	100.00	225,541
Cook County	149,646	41.35	61,879
Forest Preserve District	12,550	41.35	5,189
Sanitary District	273,911	42.31	115,892
Total Direct and Overlapping Debt	$ 2,714,421		$ 2,461,274

NOTES:

(1) Source: The Civic Federation.

(2) The Civic Federation computation for the City of Chicago's Outstanding Debt differs from the City Comptroller's Office as follows:

Outstanding Debt (Table 11)		$ 897,098
Add: Public Building Commission Debt		67,774
		964,872
Less:		
Federal Housing Administration Bonds	$ 670	
North Loop and Special Service Area Bonds	61,615	
Capitalized Lease Obligations	71,873	
General Obligation Daily Tender Notes Series–1986D	125,340	(259,498)
Outstanding Debt (Civic Federation)		$ 705,374

Table 9
CITY OF CHICAGO, ILLINOIS
RATIO OF ANNUAL DEBT SERVICE FUNDS EXPENDITURES
TO TOTAL GENERAL FUND EXPENDITURES
Last Ten Years Ended December 31, 1986
(Amounts are In Thousands of Dollars)

Year	Principal	Interest	Debt Service Funds Expenditures	General Fund Expenditures	Ratio of Debt Service to General Fund Expenditures
1977	$ 26,700	$ 15,299	$ 41,999	$ 687,031	6.1%
1978	26,915	15,699	42,614	723,608	5.9
1979	27,205	14,474	41,679	817,290	5.1
1980	27,445	13,102	40,547	828,716	4.9
1981	46,795	32,114	78,909	974,478	8.1
1982	44,090	40,916	85,006	1,083,790	7.8
1983	44,480	46,744	91,224	1,150,395	7.9
1984	55,424	43,064	98,488	1,139,597	8.6
1985	56,625	41,522	98,147	1,170,560	8.4
1986	42,925	46,718	89,643	1,263,496	7.1

Source: City of Chicago, *Comprehensive Annual Financial Report,* for Fiscal Year Ended December 31, 1986, pp. 142–43.

TABLE 16.14   *(continued)*

Table 10
CITY OF CHICAGO, ILLINOIS
DEBT STATISTICS
Last Five Years
(Amounts are In Thousands of Dollars)

	1982	1983	1984	1985	1986
Direct Debt..........................	$ 543,022	$ 556,316	$ 541,507	$ 698,200	$ 897,098
Overlapping Debt	1,720,137	1,739,989	1,800,003	1,773,893	1,564,176
Total Debt	$ 2,263,159	$ 2,296,305	$ 2,341,510	$ 2,472,093	$ 2,461,274
Full Valuation (Estimated Fair Market Value) (1)	$46,643,915	$47,469,194	$49,461,048	$51,193,280	$ 58,036,788
Direct Debt Burden (2)	1.15%	1.19%	1.14%	1.41%	1.75%
Total Debt Burden (2)......	4.80%	4.92%	4.93%	5.00%	4.81%

NOTES:

(1)   Source: The Civic Federation.

(2)   Due to the one-year lag in the State Equalized Assessed Valuation, the direct debt burden and total (direct and overlapping) debt burden are computed utilizing the prior year's full valuation estimate. The full value estimated for 1981 is $47,102,061 thousand.

definition of a government's outstanding debt can vary. The importance of overlapping debt is also clear from these tables.

Finally, the statistical section often includes several tables that present non-accounting demographic and economic data. It is clear from Figure 16.2 that these variables are necessary for financial condition analysis and, in fact, the analyst will almost always need to go further than the information provided in the statistical section. Thus, the demographic and economic information in the statistical

FIGURE 16.7
Direct and Overlapping Debt (1982–1986)

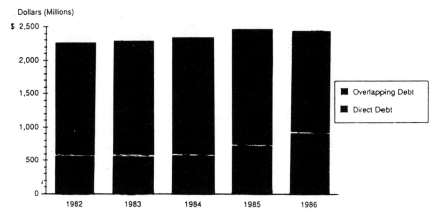

TABLE 16.15

Illustration of Statistical Information on Demographic and Economic Variables

Table 17
CITY OF CHICAGO, ILLINOIS
POPULATION AND INCOME STATISTICS
Last Ten Years Ended December 31, 1986

Year	Population (1)	Median Age (2)	Number of Households (2)	Per Capita Income (2)
1977	3,062,881	30.8	1,162,200	$ 6,720
1978	3,042,000	31.1	1,160,900	6,950
1979	3,020,898	31.2	1,143,700	7,607
1980	3,004,192	31.1	1,138,300	8,099
1981	3,000,674	30.4	1,089,700	8,254
1982	2,997,155	30.7	1,089,300	8,611
1983	2,994,814	31.0	1,102,600	9,043
1984	2,992,472	31.3	1,102,400	10,131
1985	2,989,513	31.5	1,122,200	11,072
1986	3,007,603	31.9	1,131,200	11,669

NOTES:

(1) Source: City of Chicago Department of Planning.

(2) Source: Sales and Marketing Management magazine. Reprinted by permission of Sales & Marketing Management. Copyright: July 27, 1987, Survey of Buying Power.

Table 18
CITY OF CHICAGO, ILLINOIS
LABOR FORCE, EMPLOYMENT AND UNEMPLOYMENT
Last Ten Years, Annual Averages
(Amounts are In Thousands)

Year	Civilian Labor Force Number	Percent of Population	Employment Number	Percent of Population	Unemployment Rate
1977	1,241	58.0%	1,129	52.8%	9.1%
1978	1,275	60.4	1,159	54.9	9.1
1979	1,261	60.1	1,168	55.7	7.4
1980	1,394	61.0	1,237	54.2	11.3
1981	1,351	61.1	1,189	53.8	12.0
1982	1,347	61.2	1,115	50.6	17.2
1983	1,298	60.2	1,080	50.1	16.8
1984	1,338	58.8	1,144	50.3	14.5
1985	1,384	60.6	1,181	51.8	14.7
1986	1,376	60.6	1,196	52.7	13.1

NOTE:

Source: City of Chicago, *Comprehensive Annual Financial Report,* for Fiscal Year Ended December 31, 1986, p. 150.

section can be viewed as a starting point. Table 16.15 displays two tables from the City of Chicago's statistical section that presents information on population, income, and employment, three important variables in financial condition analysis. When comparing data from statistical sections with data from other sources and other cities, attention must be paid to the definitions used since terms such as income and employment can be defined differently in various sources.

CONCLUSIONS

The evaluation of a government's financial condition is a critical part of the municipal securities transaction. The annual financial report of the government is one of the most essential sources of information for financial condition analysis, and this chapter described the linkages between these financial reports and the measurement of financial condition. All parts of the comprehensive annual financial report, including the transmittal letter, auditor's opinion, general purpose financial statements, notes to the financial statements, and statistical section, provide valuable information for the analyst.

Although there is no doubt that governmental financial reporting has improved over the last 15 years, there is still a considerable burden on the analyst who must correctly interpret the information in the financial reports as part of a relatively complex assessment of a government's financial condition. Despite the fact that the reporting of a government's financial condition is a stated objective of financial reporting, most reports do not present a free-standing, comprehensive assessment of the government's financial condition.

The question can be asked whether the objectives of financial reporting, presented in this and the previous chapters, are fulfilled with the current state of affairs. Do governments who present their reports according to GAAP disclose information on their financial condition in a satisfactory manner? Or should the issuer be required to synthesize the information on its financial condition in a form that is understandable to a broader segment of the users of financial reporting? In response to questions such as these, the GASB currently has a study underway to assess how financial condition is reported and to determine whether there are alternatives so that the user of financial reports can be more fully informed on the government's financial condition without confronting an array of complexities, some of which are discussed in this chapter.

CHAPTER 17

Debt Management and Debt Capacity

Merl Hackbart
Professor of Finance and Public Administration
University of Kentucky

James R. Ramsey
Vice-President for Administration and
Professor of Economics
Western Kentucky University

Debt capacity and debt management have emerged as priority state and local government financial management issues during the past decade. Concern over debt affordability and debt capacity levels has resulted from major growth in state and local government debt financing in the 1980s.[1] The emergence of that concern has led researchers, policymakers and policy analysts to focus attention on overall debt levels and measures and indicators of debt affordability. Attention has also been directed to the quantity of debt outstanding by the bond rating agencies (Fitch's, Moody's, and Standard and Poor's)[2] as they consider the impact of growing debt levels on the credit worthiness or rating of new bond issues coming to market.

While debt level and debt affordability concerns have dominated the capital acquisition issue agenda of state and local governments, attention has also been given to gaining a better understanding of the options and opportunities available to more effectively manage overall

---

[1] Hackbart, M. and Leigland, J., "State Debt Policy: A National Survey," *Public Budgeting and Finance*, Vol. 10, No. 2, Spring 1990.

[2] Standard and Poor's Corporation, *S&P's Municipal Finance Criteria*, (New York, NY, 1989).

debt policy and issuance practices and processes. Such attention has emerged as state and local governments search for more efficient means of procuring debt financed capital and more effective ways of managing diverse and independent debt issuing agencies and authorities. Operational debt management concerns, therefore, emanate from the desire to reduce the administrative costs of debt issuance processing, the desire to find new, less costly sources of capital and the need to develop more effective oversight mechanisms for new and existing debt issuing authorities.

Unfortunately, research regarding these topics has only recently emerged. As a result, state and local governments as well as rating agencies often have to rely on rules of thumb and/or industry standards to estimate affordable debt levels. Likewise, they have little information to rely on to manage debt issuance, manage debt policy and oversee debt authority establishment and operation.

While these issues have tended to dominate the state and local government agenda regarding debt management in the past decade, effective consideration of these issues requires an understanding of:

(1) the role and use of debt financing in the overall financial management of state and local government; and

(2) the exploration of the relationship between capital budgeting and the use of bonds to procure the capital to finance state and local government capital projects.

While the field of public finance has considered the "appropriate role" of debt financing for capital acquisition issue from a variety of standpoints, there appears to be a growing perception that debt financing of capital needs is a relatively painless method of acquiring additional financial capital. This is particularly true when governments face fiscal stress and financial pressure due to deteriorating economic conditions or unanticipated growth in the demand for capital. In recent years, such capital demand growth has been the result of at least three factors:

(1) an expansion of the array of capital investments which state and local governments are expected to provide for the operation of government programs;

(2) growing expectations that state and local governments should support private sector economic development (oftentimes via infrastructure investment); and

(3) a replacement of infrastructure development financial support which has been provided by the federal government.

The latter factor has been particularly pronounced during the last decade as the federal government has chosen to reduce infrastructure development support as a result of federal fiscal and budgetary problems.

While the set of debt financing issues facing state and local governments are highly interrelated, it is useful to categorize them in order to focus on their policy and operational implications. Toward that end, the following topics are considered in this chapter:

(1) theoretical and operational issues involved in debt financing and capital budgeting;

(2) debt capacity and debt affordability;

(3) debt management issues and debt authorities; and

(4) new state and local government capital sources including foreign capital markets.

Each of the sections consider debt financing issues from a conceptual and operational viewpoint and include references to recent research regarding these topics.

CAPITAL BUDGETING AND DEBT FINANCING

The separation of state and local government budgets into capital and operating components is becoming more commonplace. The separation, while somewhat arbitrary, is based upon the fundamental reality that certain public expenditures yield benefits over an extended period of time (more than one fiscal year) while other program expenditures provide a benefit stream over a more near-term horizon, typically within a specific fiscal year. The separation into "capital" and "noncapital" components also provides for a more appropriate alignment of funding sources.

A recent study indicated that at least 40 states have some form of capital budget.[3] Such an indication of the extensive use of capital budgeting suggests that states perceive policy and management benefits from the development of a capital budget. John Mikesell has identified several reasons for the use of a capital budget including:

(1) improved efficiency and equity of the provision and finance of nonrecurrent projects with long-term service flows (i.e., spreading the

---

[3] Thomassen, H., "Capital Budgeting for a State," *Public Budgeting and Finance*, Vol. 10, No. 4, Winter, 1990, p. 72.

cost of long-term projects among beneficiaries of such projects—
such matching is often accommodated by debt financing of multi-
year projects so as to match costs and benefits of such projects);

(2) improved stability of tax rates when large multi-year projects are
paid for over several fiscal or budgetary periods;

(3) improved project review procedures which are unique for multi-
year capital investment projects which have long-term operational
and program limiting characteristics; and

(4) enhanced ability to "regularize" construction activities and smooth
out peaks and valleys of spending requirements, tax resources and
debt limits.[4]

As noted, increased capital demands along with severe fiscal stress
led to increased use of debt financing of state and local government capital projects in the past decade. A further indication of the importance of
debt financing in the overall state capital investment picture emanates
from the earlier referenced study which indicated that 20 of the 40 states
reporting the use of capital budgets also indicated that their budgeting
processes *required* that debt service payments, associated with their debt
financing of capital projects, be identified and charged to either their
"capital" or "operating budgets."[5] By budgetarily focusing on the cost of
debt financed capital in this way, states highlight the fact that debt service cost and affordability are critical budgeting factors. In fact, the
analysis of debt service requirements is an integral component of the
budgeting process in many states and local governments. Such information, therefore, becomes important data in the determination of whether
proposed capital projects are affordable given overall budgetary and financial constraints.

The use of debt financing to support all or a portion of a state or
local government capital budget increases the complexity of the budget
allocation decision process. Rather than relying on estimates of current
revenues (generated by taxes, usage fees, federal funds and other special
sources) to establish the expenditure base for a state or local government, debt financing provides an additional source of funds for the overall operating and capital budget and expenditure plan. However, with
such supplemental funds, policy makers are forced to consider the
implications of financing capital acquisitions from borrowed funds
which will require a future stream of debt service payments to retire the
acquired debt. While the use of such financing is normally justified for

[4] Mikesell, J.L., *Fiscal Administration: Analysis and Applications for the Public Sector,*
(The Dorsey Press: Chicago, IL, 1986), pp. 184–86.

[5] Thomassen, H., *op. cit.*

capital projects based upon the benefits received principle, the implications of such decisions include the possible "crowding out" of future operating program expenditures and/or the need to increase taxes or other revenue sources to support, simultaneously, operating programs and debt service payments.

Moreover, debt service becomes a *nondiscretionary* expenditure in a state or local government's budget. Consequently, a state or local government's assessment of its ability to sustain debt service payments along with its on-going operating programs focuses attention on debt affordability or "debt capacity." Such affordability issues are particularly acute during periods of economic recession and associated revenue shortfalls. If budgets are cut, the impact of such costs fall, necessarily, disproportionately, on operating programs as debt service payments are nondiscretionary. On the other hand, if such cuts are substantial, policy makers might have to choose between "high priority" operating programs and meeting bond debt service. Thus, a state or local government's assessment of debt capacity must focus upon both its current and future ability to pay. As discussed in more detail later, the municipal bond rating agencies (Moody's, Standard and Poor's, and Fitch's) attempt to assess an issuer's ability to meet future debt service obligations when assigning credit ratings.[6]

Thus, an effective capital budgeting process for state and local governments must include an estimate of the amount of *new debt* that the government can incur without overextending its commitment of future revenues to meet debt service. If such an estimate can be developed, policy makers will have information regarding the amount of new debt that the debt issuer can incur without significantly displacing other state and local government expenditures and, thus, maintain its current and future financial integrity.

Theory of Debt Finance: Further Considerations

As noted, the conventional wisdom of municipal finance is that state and local governments finance current operating expenses (personnel, utilities, rent, travel, and the like) with current revenue sources (taxes, user fees and recurring governmental transfers) and that capital projects (those expenditures with an asset life of more than one fiscal year) may be financed with the same revenue or with long-term bonds.[7]

---

[6] Lamb, R., and Rappaport, S.P., *Municipal Bonds, The Comprehensive Review of Tax Exempt Securities and Public Finance*, (New York: McGraw-Hill Company, 1987), pp. 61–81.

[7] Oates, W., *Fiscal Federalism*, (New York: Harcourt Brace Jouanovich, Inc., 1972), pp. 153–61.

The rationale for this conventional wisdom is the benefit principle of taxation. The benefit principle of taxation suggests that those consumers who benefit from the consumption of a public good are the taxpayers who should pay for the good. If an individual does not consume a particular good, the benefit principle of taxation would suggest that the individual should not be expected to pay taxes for the good. Since capital projects have a multi-year life, the benefit principle suggests that future users of capital projects should pay their share of the cost of projects. Bond financing of capital projects provides for such a linkage. Therefore, the conventional wisdom of public finance suggests that financing capital projects with bonds allows some of the project cost to be shifted to future beneficiaries and, therefore, represents an appropriate financial management strategy.

It should be noted that this conventional wisdom of public finance has been challenged by those who assume the existence of perfect capital markets and the existence of a "Tiebout world." This challenge to the conventional wisdom suggests that it is impossible to shift costs of government services financed by bonds to future taxpayers.[8] The existence of perfect capital markets implies that all participants in the debt markets have the opportunity to borrow at the same costs. Therefore, an individual would be able to access funds at the same interest rate as would state government. The "Tiebout world" concept is the notion that taxpayers vote with their feet. That is, an individual taxpayer selects the state in which to reside based on the total package of public services offered and the tax payments used to support those services. If a particular state changed its mix of services or taxes, an individual in a "Tiebout world" would move to another state which offered the basket of services and taxes more compatible with his or her tastes and preferences.

Therefore, the challenge of the conventional wisdom of public finance argues that if an individual lives in State A and State A elects to finance a public project through the issuance of bonds, and the individual prefers that the project be paid out of current revenues instead of borrowing, the individual can go to the capital market and purchase a security which will yield a stream of payments equal to their future tax liability. Alternatively, in a "Tiebout world," the individual can move to another state that does not use debt finance. In this manner, an individual can avoid paying for debt financed capital projects in the future.

While a full discussion of the challenge to the conventional wisdom is not presented here, it is worthwhile to briefly consider the market for state bonds since an understanding of this market supports the conventional wisdom and refutes the assumptions upon which the

[8] *Ibid.*

challenges to it rely. Governmental bonds, as defined by the Tax Reform Act of 1986, retain their total tax exemption for individual purchasers of the bonds.[9] This tax exemption is the most important and distinctive characteristic of municipal bonds since municipal issuers are able to borrow funds at interest rates which are below the rates at which individuals or businesses can borrow. Therefore, credit markets are not perfect. The interest rate differentials in the taxable and tax-exempt markets impact a governmental issuer's decision to pay for capital projects from available revenues or the issuance of long-term debt. Conceptionally, a municipal issuer that has funds available to pay for a long-term capital asset can invest those funds in the taxable securities market and the investment earnings will exceed the debt service cost on long-term bonds issued to finance the project in the tax-exempt securities market. Again, this supports the conventional wisdom that the use of debt financing by municipal issuers is often appropriate.

By example, if a state government decides to build a park that has an asset life of many years and the state park seeks to have those individuals who will benefit from the park to pay for the park, the governmental unit may issue long-term bonds to finance the facility. In such a case, consumers of the park, both now and in the future, would share in the cost of the park over the life of the bonds. Therefore, bond financing of long-term capital projects allows for the cost of projects to be shifted to the beneficiaries of the project.

It can also be argued that borrowing by state governments is appropriate for several practical reasons. First, many public projects (buildings, road projects, prisons) are extremely expensive and debt financing is the only practical means of paying for needed projects. Second, debt financing avoids tax friction, or the constant changing of tax rates up and down to provide the revenue needed to finance expensive capital projects on a pay as you go basis.

It can then be concluded that debt financing by state and local governments is an appropriate means of financing capital projects. This is not to say, however, that all capital projects should be financed through borrowing or that there is not a limit on the amount of debt financing which a state can afford given its revenue sources. However, while a number of capital projects may be economically viable

---

[9] The Tax Reform Act of 1986 defined two general types of municipal bonds: governmental and private activity bonds (PAB). The latter are bonds which are issued for the benefit of an individual (such as a student loan bond) or business (such as industrial revenue bonds). PAB are subject to the Alternative Minimum Tax for individuals. Thus, for the first time, municipal bonds are not totally tax exempt. Government bonds are used for public purpose projects (government office buildings, roads, parks and the like) and retain their tax exemptions.

and justified, the revenue constraints of a state, along with other factors, define a debt affordability level for that state. This issue is explored in a later section of this chapter.

Capital Budgeting: Further Considerations

As indicated earlier, capital budgeting has emerged as an integral component of state and local government budgeting procedures. While the principal driving force behind this emergence has, probably, been the need to develop the capability to more fully consider the overall financial implications of increased public capital investments, there is also a desire to utilize more consistent, rational procedures for making capital investment decisions. Such a desire recognizes the fact that:

(1) there is a need for a framework for determining which projects are justified in terms of benefits and costs to taxpayers;

(2) total financial resources (current revenue available for capital projects and affordable debt financed capital combined) are insufficient to support all "justified" projects; and

(3) there is a need to have a basis for making trade-off decisions among competing projects for scarce capital resources.

Direct applications or adaptations of benefit-cost analysis has emerged as the "accepted" basic operating framework for project assessment. While the basic benefit-cost model is well established and discussed elsewhere,[10] there are several operational capital budgeting application policy dilemmas which require resolution and are worthy of review here. Among these are:

(1) the determination of the appropriate discount rate for the application of benefit-cost analysis;

(2) the selection of the appropriate decision criteria or specific discounted net benefit-cost model to utilize in setting capital project priorities; and

(3) decision problems associated with allocating limited capital to a set of projects which have been "justified" in that they have met basic selection criteria for acceptable capital investment projects for a state or local government.

The Discount Rate Issue. Until recently, government decision-makers believed that the appropriate rate of discount to apply to public

---

[10] Mikesell, J.L., *op, cit.*, pp. 192–210.

expenditures was the cost of borrowing money; which for the government has been low relative to other interest rates due to the perceived credit quality of treasury securities (resulting in a lower discount rate and a higher present value of a project). It can be argued that government should recognize that its investments withdraw resources from the private sector of the economy and that the correct discount rate for government expenditures is the opportunity cost of capital (i.e., the rate of return in the private sector). That is to say, if the rate of return on private investment projects is 10 to 15% (say this is what GM or IBM earns on their capital investments) then any use of resources by the government which yields less than 10 to 15% is inefficient. Therefore, if we have efficient capital markets, the appropriate discount rate is the rate of return on private investment projects.

It can still be argued that government often uses resources that would not otherwise have been made available for private investment, therefore, the private opportunity cost is irrelevant. Accordingly, the source of government's investable funds determines the appropriate discount rate. In general, the sources of funds rule yields a *lower* discount rate for public investments than the private opportunity cost rule (again, this is due to the existence of market imperfections).

A final argument regarding the appropriate rate of discount to be used is based upon the notion that public investments are qualitatively different from private investments and that the private motivations leading to a determination of the market interest rate should not be allowed to influence government investments. In other words, there are many expenditures or investments that will not be undertaken in the private market. Therefore, individual consumers and producers cannot be relied upon to express society's preferences for future capital goods because the time horizon of individuals is much shorter than that of society. Thus, government should make the decision as to the rate of time preference of society and this rate of social time preference is then the appropriate rate of discount for government expenditures.[11]

Another argument to support the use of the rate of social time preference as the discount rate is that since we cannot quantify all of the benefits of public expenditures, they tend to be undervalued. Therefore, we can compensate for this undervaluation by discounting future output at a lower discount rate. This approach is not entirely satisfactory, however, because such rates understate the costs of government investment projects. Therefore, there continues to be some question regarding the appropriate discount rate to use in the

---

[11] Baumol, W.J., "On the Discount Rate for Public Projects," in *Public Expenditure and Policy Analysis*, ed. Haveman, R.H. and Margolis, J., (Chicago: Markham Publishing, 1970) p. 274.

calculation of the present value of benefits arising from government expenditures.

Decision Criteria. The two most common criterion used in making priority rankings of capital projects are:

(1) the benefit-cost ratio; and

(2) the net present value.

If the benefit-cost ratio is determined to exceed 1 or if the net present value is determined to be positive, analysis indicates that a project meets the test of economic efficiency. Meeting that test implies that the completion of the project will enhance economic efficiency or that the economic well-being of the community proposing the project will be improved. The use of either of these criterion, however, does not consider other policy-relevant information such as distributional impacts and other special state or local government concerns.

As implied, the use of either of these criteria or an alternative (the internal rate of return) will provide similar results regarding the fundamental issue of improved economic efficiency. A more difficult problem arises when decision makers must rank competing capital projects (assuming scarce financial capital supplies due to limited current revenues or limited debt affordability). In such an application, the benefit-cost ratio and discounted present value criterions can produce conflicting rankings of projects. This is particularly true if project scope for the competing projects differ and or if sufficient data are not available to compare different project scope and investment stream options (i.e., net present value implies that the alternative investment streams are determined or fixed while the ratio approach may imply that the project scope or investment stream may be enhanced or reduced without affecting the relative benefit-cost ratio).[12] When such conflicting interpretations of results arise, capital budgeting decisions must be based upon analysis of feasible combinations of project sizes given available capital investment resources.

Capital Allocation Decision Making. Capital allocation decision making is the final dilemma often encountered in the application of capital budgeting decision criteria. This dilemma may be best examined by a simplified example. As part of the budget preparation phase of the budget cycle, assume that the capital projects listed in Table 17.1 are all candidates for debt financing, since each project has

---

[12] Mikesell, J.L., *op. cit.*, pp. 192–210.

TABLE 17.1
Capital Budgeting Process

Project	Ratio of Present Value of Benefits to Present Value of Costs	Debt Service Associated with 20-Year Bond Issue to Finance Project
1	2.5	$ 200,00
2	2.0	1,000,000
3	1.6	50,000
4	1.6	250,000
5	1.3	400,000
6	1.1	100,000
		$2,000,000

a discounted benefit to cost ratio which is greater than one. In other words, each project listed in Table 17.1 is economically viable because the residents of the region contemplating the projects would clearly benefit from their completion. Table 17.1 also lists the estimated annual debt service for each project, assuming the projects are financed by fixed-rate long-term bonds.

While, as noted, all six projects listed in Table 17.1 are economically viable, a key budgetary decision which must be considered is whether all six projects are affordable? If sufficient state revenues are available, the budget office could recommend all of the projects for funding; if resources are limited, the budget office could establish a target benefit to cost ratio, net present value, or internal rate of return and elect to fund only those projects that exceed the target rate. However, from a more practical budgetary perspective, the question is how many of these projects can be afforded for debt financing with current and future revenues given competing uses for such funds? Or, more fundamentally, a state must decide, as part of the budgetary process, the level of available resources it can or should commit to debt service on capital projects given other competing needs (operating programs) for available state resources.

As shown on Table 17.1, if bonds are sold to finance the projects, the total annual debt service is estimated to be $2,000,000. Now, let us assume that the issuer has defined its *affordable* level of debt so that debt service should not exceed five percent of its available revenues so as to limit the displacement of operating programs which higher debt service to total budget ratios would require. In this instance, the projected growth in new revenue in the year being budgeted for must be $40,000 for all six economically viable projects to be affordable.[13] If

[13] ($2,000,000 ÷ .05 = $40,000)

the upcoming budget year revenue estimate indicates revenue growth of only $30,000,000, the new affordable level of debt or the debt capacity, given this approach, is those projects which will not cost more than $1,500,000 in annual debt service. Therefore, on a purely financial basis, only the first four projects would be financed if the ratio of present value benefits to present value costs were used as the capital allocating criterion.[14]

DEBT CAPACITY AND DEBT AFFORDABILITY

The issuance of bonds represents a long-term commitment of resources and, consequently, has direct implications regarding a state or local government's ability to provide other critical services. Although the exact impact of debt issuance on a state or local government's ability to meet other expenditure obligations is unclear, some "crowding out" of other programs is inevitable. Moreover, the ultimate crowding-out impact of public bond issuance is difficult to estimate at any point in time, due to the growing use of moral obligation bonds (potential resource liabilities) and the use of lease-back financing (such as certificates of participation), which may be used to avoid constitutionally specified debt limitations that constrain new debt issuance. With such arrangements, future appropriations are, potentially, being committed to debt service, although such commitments may be indirect.

Consequently, the possibility of crowding-out effects resulting from excessive debt service obligations (whether general obligation revenue, or moral obligation) is increasingly a concern of state and local government policy makers and the rating agencies as they attempt to assess the relative credit worthiness of new debt issues. Such concern is typically raised by the credit rating agencies through the rating process. At the same time, policy makers often focus debt policy management guidelines on ratings, because a general rating downgrade is often perceived by the public as an indication of excessive increases in debt holdings, ineffective financial management, or a combination of these factors. Any of these perceptions can have serious financial and political implications. Moreover, a credit rating downgrade increases the cost of debt-financed capital, which can induce further crowding out and the displacement of other operating programs. Therefore, state and local governments, often, formally or informally, impose stable-credit-rating requirements as a precondition to the issuance of new bonds.

---

[14] Total debt service for projects 1, 2, 3, and 4 would be $1,500,000.

Debt Capacity: A Theoretical Perspective

From a theoretical point of view, the concept of the appropriate level of debt service expenditure which indirectly reflects the appropriate or affordable level of debt outstanding may be represented as the level of state resources committed to debt service that maximizes the utility of the residents of the state. The commitment of resources to debt-financed capital (i.e., debt service) then simply represents one of a set of public goods expenditures available to the residents of the state.[15]

The equilibrium allocation of public resources to debt-financed capital is defined in Equation 17.1 as those values of G_1, G_2, and R that maximize the state's utility function, subject to its budget or fiscal constrain as specified in Equation 17.2.[16]

$$\text{Maximize: } U = F(G_1, G_2, R) \qquad\qquad 17.1$$

$$\text{Subject to: } FC = P_2(G_2) + [P_1(G_1) + P_3(R)] \qquad 17.2$$

Where:

U = Utility function of goods and services consumed by the residents of a state

G_1 = Quantity of operating goods provided by the state for the public

G_2 = Quantity of capital goods provided by the state and financed with bonds

R = Quantity of private goods consumed by the public

FC = Aggregate fiscal constraint (budget of the state including all publicized or private resources available to utilize in the acquisition of G_1, G_2, or R by individuals or by public decision makers)

P_1 = Price of operating goods provided by the state

P_2 = Debt-financed capital costs

P_3 = Price of private goods

Given this budget constraint and utility function, you could assume that:

(1) the historical equilibrating behavior of the political process regarding the selection of debt-financed capital goods vis-á-vis other

---

[15] Hackbart, M. and Ramsey, J., "State Debt Level Management: A Stable Credit Rating Model," *Municipal Finance Journal*, Vol. 11, No. 1, Spring 1990.

[16] *Ibid.*

public and private goods, given state preference patterns, is observable; and

(2) the financial market's perception of that behavior, given the risk
and uncertainty regarding future economic and demographic conditions of the state, are reflected in the current credit rating of
each state.

As discussed below, if an "overallocation" of state-appropriated
funds is made to debt service, a lower bond credit rating might result,
increasing P_2 in Equation 17.2. As shown in Figure 17.1, a higher price
of debt-financed capital projects (P_2') would cause the budget constraint (FC) to rotate counterclockwise to FC_1, resulting in a new point
of utility maximum (E'): a point that is lower than the original level of
maximum utility (E) that existed prior to the overallocation of resources to debt finance. Therefore, in this framework, there is a level
of debt that exceeds a defined appropriate level for the state and
thereby reduces a state's point of maximum utility.

It follows, then, that a state would pursue a policy of maintaining
an acceptable credit rating on its bonds and that this credit rating defines, indirectly, the state's target appropriate level of debt. By maintaining a constant rating, the cost of debt would be maintained in
approximate equilibrium with alternative uses of the state's resources
(assuming constant consumer preferences).

FIGURE 17.1
Equilibrium Model for Public and Private Goods
Given Increased Cost of Debt-Financed Capital

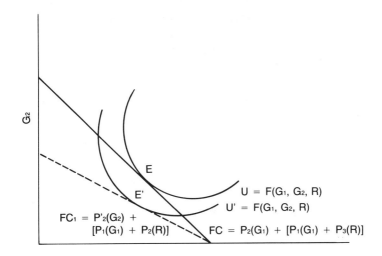

Thus, a key component of an effective debt affordability management program for a state or local government must include an estimate of the amount of *new debt* that it can incur without overextending its commitment of future revenues to meet debt service. If such an estimate can be developed, policy makers will have better information regarding the amount of new debt that can be issued without significantly displacing other expenditures and, thus, maintain its current and future financial integrity. Oftentimes, policy makers assume that credit ratings indirectly reflect (at least as perceived by the rating agency) a state or local government's ability to meet future debt service and attempt to avoid rating downgrades which might suggest that it is financially overextending itself thus limiting its ability to meet other priority needs.

It is well-documented that rating differentials can often result in significantly different borrowing costs to issuers. The spread between bonds with the highest and lowest investment grade credit ratings has averaged between 80 and 100 basis points in recent years.[17] Therefore, credit rating assignments influence borrowing rates for issuers, future debt service payments, and thus, indirectly, future debt capacity. At the same time, the level of debt of a governmental unit is one of the key financial variables reviewed by the rating agencies when assigning a rating. Thus, Figure 17.2 depicts the relationship between the rating process and an issuers' debt capacity. As shown, current debt levels influence ratings which, in turn, influence capital costs, debt service payments and debt capacity and/or debt levels. Since the rating assigned to state and local debt is a key variable influencing the issuer's borrowing cost and level of debt holdings, it is useful to briefly discuss the rating process.

A difficulty with the rating process is that neither issuers of bonds nor the users of ratings assigned by the major rating agencies are fully informed about either the variables used to determine rating assignments or the weight assignment to these variables.[18] Although Standard & Poors Corporation publishes a useful manual that discusses the key factors influencing a rating, a detailed checklist of factors and weights for each different rating assignment is not provided.[19] Several studies

[17] Willson, S., "Credit Ratings and General Obligation Bonds: A Statistical Alternative," *Government Finance Review*, Vol. 2, No. 3, June 1986.

[18] For example, see Carleton and Lerner, "Statistical Credit Scoring of Municipal Bonds," *Journal of Money, Credit and Banking* (Nov. 1969) pp. 750–64; Horton, "A Statistical Rating Index for Municipal Bonds," *Financial Analysts Journal* (March/April 1969) pp. 72–75; and Rubinfield, "Credit Ratings and the Market for General Obligation Municipal Bonds," *National Tax Journal* (March 1978) pp. 17–21.

[19] Standard and Poor's Corporation, *S&P's Municipal Finance Criteria*, (New York, NY, 1989).

FIGURE 17.2
Relationship Between Rating and Debt Capacity

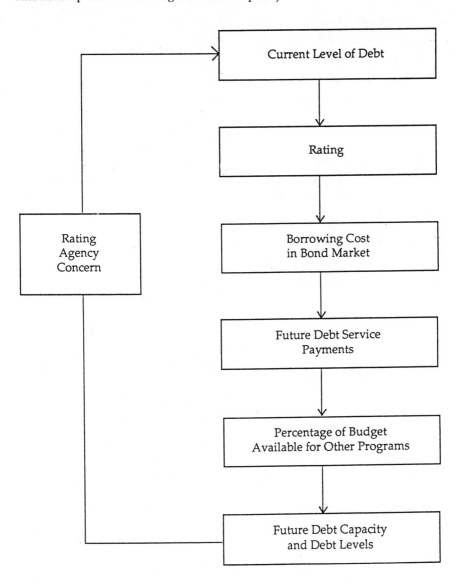

have been designed to determine a surrogate set of credit rating variables that statistically relate to rating assignments. One such study identified the following surrogate variables for state issuers:

(1) debt;

(2) revenues;

(3) personal income of residents;

(4) population;

(5) expenditures;

(6) agricultural activity;

(7) mineral extraction activities;

(8) manufacturing; and

(9) general demographic information.[20]

Another study concluded that for local governments, only economic variables show any real discriminating ability in their determination of rating assignments.[21] One authoritative text on municipal bonds identifies "red flags" or trends which would pose potential problems in the fiscal stability of state and municipalities. The categories of "red flags" include:

(1) revenue based indicators;

(2) expenditure based indicators;

(3) cash management indicators; and

(4) debt indicators.[22]

To determine various approaches to calculating debt capacity, a survey of state issuers was carried out to identify "guideposts" for calculating optimal or maximum debt levels.[23] To focus upon debt capacity "guideposts" used by state issuers, discussions were held with representatives of the National Association of State Treasurers, the Government Finance Officer's Association, various investment banking firms, and the two major rating agencies to determine those states which have developed procedures for identifying debt capacity levels. Twelve states were identified and studied. Table 17.2 summarizes the variable(s) as identified by these twelve states as most important in calculating their debt capacities. As can be seen, the most frequently cited factor is revenue (6 of the 12 states). The other factors identified as determinants of debt capacity were: personal income (3 states), population/population

---

[20] Osteryoung, J.S. and Blevins, D.R., "State General Obligation Bond Credit Ratings," *Growth and Change*, (July 1978) pp. 29–35.

[21] Willson, *op. cit.* 7, p. 21.

[22] Lamb and Rappaport, *op. cit.*

[23] Ramsey, J.R., Gritz, T. and Hackbart, M.M., "State Approaches to Debt Capacity Assessment: A Further Evaluation," *International Journal of Public Administration*, Vol. 11, No. 2, 1988.

TABLE 17.2
Independent Variables as Used by States in Calculating Debt Capacity

Revenue	Personal Income	Population/ Population Growth	Assessed Property Value	Historical Debt
Alaska	Maryland	California	Oregon	Vermont
Maryland	California	Wisconsin	Wisconsin	California
South Carolina	New York	New York		
Tennessee				
New York				
Connecticut				

growth (3 states), assessed value of real property (2 states), and historical debt levels within the state (2 states).[24]

Debt Capacity Assessment

In addition to the rule-of-thumb and overall guideline approaches utilized by a number of state and local governments to manage debt levels, efforts have been undertaken to more precisely estimate debt or debt service capacities based upon statistical models which focus on economic, demographic and financial variables which have been identified by the rating agencies and others as affecting or being closely associated with the estimation of state debt capacity.

Such efforts by Ramsey and Hackbart[25] utilized multiple regression estimating techniques (ordinary least squares) to estimate a stable credit rating debt expenditure model for various states. In their model, it is assumed that a state's ability to present evidence of ability to sustain a given level of debt represents a proxy for the state's debt capacity for that debt or credit rating level.

While recognizing that many factors, both qualitative and quantitative, affect a state's ability to support a given level of debt and/or retain its credit rating, the authors identified:

(1) per capita income;

(2) state revenues;

(3) population; and

[24] *Ibid.*

[25] Ramsey, J. and Hackbart, M., "State and Local Debt Capacity: An Index Measure," *Municipal Finance Journal*, Vol. 9, No. 1, 1988.

(4) assessed value of real property as the variables which have been identified as ones for which data are available for the states to utilize in empirically estimating levels of debt which are sustainable thus warranting stable credit ratings.

Also, these variables represent measures of the income or wealth of an issuer and thus represent proxies of a state's fiscal constraint or ability to meet its debt service obligations. This modeling approach also assumes that states typically attempt to maintain a stable credit rating. Therefore, by predicting a level of debt which will maintain a stable debt rating, a sustainable level of debt (or debt capacity for the state) can be estimated.

Their model is structured as follows:

$$Y = a + b_1x_1 + b_2x_2 + b_3x_3 + b_4x_4$$

Where:

Y = a state's debt outstanding

x_1 = a state's per capita income

x_2 = a state's revenue

x_3 = a state's population

x_4 = a state's full value of assessed real property

Theoretically, they assume a positive relationship should exist between debt outstanding and each of the independent variables. That is, the greater the per capita income in a state, the greater the state's fiscal capacity and the more debt and other expenditures the state can afford. It should be noted, that in this context, that a state's revenues include taxes, agency or user fees, and recurring intergovernmental grants. State population is a proxy for the demographic characteristics of a state, and it is expected that the larger a state's population, the more taxpayers there are and the greater the state's ability to pay for debt service and other purchases. The full value of assessed real property is a proxy for a state's wealth base, which would have similar implications.

In their research, data were collected for the 50 states for the time period 1972 to 1984 and a multiple regression estimating technique (ordinary least squares) was used to estimate their stable credit rating debt level equation. The results of this estimation were:

$$Y = -4450.00 + .5317X_1 + 240.599X_2 + .0528X_3 - .0352X_4$$

$$(58416.512) \quad (.0466) \quad (23.997) \quad (.008856) \quad (.002215)$$

$$\text{ADJ } R^2 = .8454$$

The values in parenthesis below the coefficients represent the standard errors. The independent variables taken as a whole were statistically significant (F test) and each of the independent variables tested alone proved to be statistically significant (t test).[26] Therefore, their equation appeared to represent a good model or statistical approach for explaining past debt levels and predicting future debt capacity.

For statistical estimating reasons (the possible existence of multi-collinearity), several further statistical analysis of the results were undertaken.[27] While a detailed discussion of this analysis is not presented here, their analysis suggested that the use of the above equation to estimate debt capacity levels may:

(1) result in biased estimates due to specification problems; and

(2) a simpler statistical model could be developed that would produce statistically significant estimates of debt capacity.

Therefore, a stepwise regression was performed for each individual state to determine if, for a given state, any of the independent variables could be dropped from this equation without reducing the statistical significance of the equation. That is, the authors suggest that some of the dependent variables in the equation may not help define a state's sustainable credit rating debt level.

Performing a stepwise regression[28] approach to the equation for each of the fifty states, they found that the revenue variable alone best explains past debt levels and can be used to predict future debt for 12 states, the personal income variable best explains past debt levels in four states, the assessed value of real property variable best explains past debt levels in six states, the population variable best explains past debt for 10 states, while none of the independent variables in Equation 17.1 were statistically significant in explaining past levels of debt of 18 states. (See Table 17.3.)

To estimate future debt capacity levels for an individual state using the conceptual approach,[29] it is necessary to determine which variable best explains past debt levels for a particular state and to estimate future values for that variable. For example, revenue was found to be statistically significant in explaining past debt levels for the state of Kentucky. To use this approach to estimating future sustainable debt levels or debt

[26] Tested for alpha equal 5%.

[27] Ramsey, J. and Hackbart, M., *op. cit.*

[28] *Ibid.*

[29] *Ibid.*

TABLE 17.3
Variable Which Best Explains Post-Debt Levels by
Number of States

Variable	Number of States
State Revenue	12
Personal Income	4
Assessed Value of Real Property	6
Population	10
None of the Analyzed Variables	18

capacity, future revenues for Kentucky must be estimated (this would normally be done as part of a state's budget preparation process) and used in the appropriate statistical equation for Kentucky. Using the official revenue estimates for Kentucky for 1988 to 1989 and 1989 to 1990 (1988 to 1990 biennium), the state's debt capacity for the next two-year budget period was estimated. Kentucky's debt capacity was estimated to be approximately $390 million in new debt financed projects in the next biennium (1988 to 1990 biennium).

Table 17.4 displays the historical ratios of state debt to revenues ratios for the state as well as the ratios for 1989 and 1990 which would

TABLE 17.4
Debt Service to Revenue Ratios for Kentucky 1980–1990

Year	Total Revenue (000)	Debt Service (000)	Debt Service as a Percent of Revenue
1980	2,895,178	156,751	5.4
1981	3,099,448	165,539	5.3
1982	3,242,716	170,667	5.3
1983	3,452,400	184,887	5.4
1984	3,738,248	201,024	5.4
1985	3,959,214	209,671	5.3
1986	4,248,081	247,384	5.8
1987	4,934,001	247,419	5.0
1988	5,464,858*	275,711	5.1
1989	5,783,459*	335,441*	5.8
1990	6,037,309*	350,164*	5.8

*Estimated.

Source: Kentucky Financial Report, various issues, and calculations by authors.

exist if the new debt levels estimated as being acceptable by this model were, in fact, authorized by Kentucky's General Assembly.

The projected amount of new sustainable debt estimated with this statistical technique[30] is, obviously, a function of projected growth in the variable identified as the most important factor for explaining debt in an individual state. For Kentucky, if revenue growth is more or less than the amount estimated, the amount of new debt that can be supported will vary accordingly. In addition, the projected amount of new debt service assumes that the proportion of revenues spent for debt service that has existed for approximately the last 20 years should continue in the future. This, of course, is a policy decision which could be changed in the future. Finally, as previously noted, rating agencies analyze many more factors than those identified in this statistical analysis in the determination of a rating. Consequently, an issuer's debt capacity may be impacted, positively or negatively, by nonquantitative factors that cannot be estimated statistically.

DEBT AUTHORITIES AND DEBT MANAGEMENT ISSUES

By any measure (debt outstanding, issuing activity, or number of issuing entities or authorities), debt issuing activity by state and local governments has increased significantly in the past decade.[31] Moreover, the complexity of the debt issuing and management process has grown as a result of the increase in the number of debt issuing entities as well as a rapid expansion of debt structuring innovations and variations. Complexity has also been added due to such factors as expanded use of moral obligation bonds, lease back arrangements and changing federal tax laws. As a result, state and local governments have had to take a more pro-active management stance regarding the policies and practices associated with the issuance of debt.

Other policy issues of concern to state governments include the impact of constitutional constraints on debt issuing practice, the changing environment of debt issuing authority, and emerging trends in the formulation, and implementation of overall state debt management policy. A recent survey by the National Association of State Treasurers (NAST) and others considered these issues among others in a survey study of the states designed to provide background and a

[30] *Ibid.*

[31] Hackbart, M. and Leigland, J., *op. cit.*

TABLE 17.5
State-Level Special Purpose Governments* with Debt
Outstanding 1977, 1987

	1977	1987
Authority	131	213
Commission	36	43
Corporation	18	40
Board	16	20
Other**	23	38
Totals	224	354

*Exclusive of educational institutions.

**Other names include administration, association, bank, center, company, cooperative, council, district, fund, hospital, port, system, turnpike.

Source: Moody's Investors Service, *Moody's Municipal and Government Manual* (New York: Moody's Investors Service, 1977); *Moody's Municipal and Government Mnaual* (New York: Moody's Investors Service, 1987).

frame of reference for states to use in managing the evolution of their overall debt management policies and procedures.[32]

Among other results, the 50 state survey indicated that there has been a 50% increase in the number of state-level entities or authorities issuing revenue-backed debt, which is not directly guaranteed by state government (Table 17.5) from 1977 to 1987. During the approximate same period, state long-term nonguaranteed debt outstanding increased from $44.3 billion to $197.3 billion. This quadrupling of the amount of non-guaranteed debt outstanding compares to an approximate 50 percent increase in the level of full faith and credit outstanding of state issues ($42.9 billion in 1976 compared to $66.8 billion in 1986).[33] While the increase in the number of separate debt issuing entities influenced the structural shift to nonguaranteed issues, specific state restrictions on the issuance of full faith and credit debt, including special approval procedures, as well as other factors such as convenience probably encouraged the shift toward the nonguaranteed debt by the states.

[32] Hackbart, M., Leigland, J., Riherd, R. and Reid, M., "Debt and Duty: Accountability and Efficiency in State Debt Management," (The Council of State Governments, Lexington, Kentucky, 1990).

[33] *Ibid.*

The study[34] also indicated that some forty states operate with constitutionally imposed limitations on state debt issuance and approval procedures. Among such limitations are specific dollar limits on outstanding debt, approval of issues including referenda and/or extraordinary legislative majorities, and flexible debt limits tied to revenue collection, property values and the like. Such requirements have strongly influenced the debt issuance and management practices of the states. For example, eight of the 11 states which currently do not issue full faith and credit bonds have some kind of dollar limit on debt, suggesting that this type of debt limit may severely constrain state borrowing behavior. States may, however, circumvent constitutional limits by foregoing full faith and credit debt completely and, instead, issuing nonguaranteed or revenue-backed debt, as in Arizona or Colorado. They may also create semi-autonomous government corporations to issue such nonguaranteed debt, as in the case of Indiana and Kentucky.

The sale of state debt involves a series of processes, including decisions regarding the use of bond proceeds (e.g., as part of the capital budgeting process), the authorization of specific proposals to issue debt, the assembly of a team of expert advisors (e.g., bond counsel, financial advisor, other legal advisors, accountants, auditors, and other experts), the design and structuring of the bond issue (decisions regarding size, timing, nature of the debt instrument used and the like), selection of underwriter or underwriting syndicate (via negotiation or formal competition), arrangements for credit ratings and the like. The study found significant variation among the states regarding the degree of centralization and decentralization and degree of autonomy of issuing entities in carrying out these functions. Centralization and control were more pronounced among the states in the structuring and selling issuance of full faith and credit bonds (27 of 39 states issuing such debt do so through a "central" finance office) and state revenue debt (17 of 34 states issuing such debt) than in the issuance of special purpose or special authority debt. (See Table 17.6.) Only 3 states indicated that they maintain Central Executive Branch control over the structuring and sale of debt for special purpose governments or special authorities. This strong decentralization bias apparently exists even though, as indicated, such entities constitute the major growth area for new state bond issues in the decade of the 1980s. A similar pattern of "decentralization" of special authority debt issuance is shown in Table 17.7 which classifies states according to the entities with principal roles in authorizing state

[34] *Ibid.*

TABLE 17.6

States Classified According to Types of Entities with Principal Roles in Structuring and Selling State Debt

Type of Authorizing Entity	Type of Debt Issued		
	State General Obligation Debt (39 states)	State Revenue Debt (34 states)	Special Authority Revenue Debt (49 states)
Central Executive Branch Finance Office	AL, AR, CA, CT, DE, HI, IL, ME, MD, MA, MI, MN, MS, MT, NV, NH, NJ, NY, NC, OK, OR, PA, RI, SC, UT, VT, WI	AR, CA, HI, IL, KY, MS, MT, NV, NH, NJ, NC, OR, RI, SC, UT, WI, WY	KY, NC, OR
Executive Branch Commission, Authority or Board	AK, FL, MO, NM, OH, TX, VA, WA, WV	AK, FL, KS, MO, NE, NM, TX, VA, WV	KS
Joint Leg/Exec Commission or Board	GA, LA, TN		GA, TN
Individual Departments, Agencies, or Authorities		AZ, CO, CT, IA, MA, MI, ND, OH	AL, AK, AZ, AR, CA, CO, CT, DE, FL, HI, ID, IL, IN, IA, LA, ME, MD, MA, MI, MN, MS, MO, MT, NE, NH, NJ, NY, NM, ND, OH, OK, PA, RI, SC, SD, TX, UT, VT, VA, WA, WV, WI, WY

Source: NAST/Council of State Governments National Survey, 1988.

TABLE 17.7

States Classified According to Types of Entities with Principal Roles in Authorizing Specific State Bond Issues

Type of Authorizing Entity	Type of Debt Issued		
	State General Obligation Debt (39 states)	State Revenue Debt (34 states)	Special Authority Revenue Debt (49 states)
Central Executive Branch Finance Office		AR, CO, NH, NJ, NC, OR, RI, WY	KY, NC, OR
Executive Branch Commission, Authority or Board	MS	AZ, FL, MA, MI, MS, NM, TX, VA	DE, MS, NM
Joint Leg/Exec Commission or Board	CT, SC	SC	LA, SC, TN
Legislative Majority	DE, GA, HI, IL, LA, MD, MA, MN, MO, MT, NH, NC, RI, UT, VT, TN, WI	AK, CA, CT, HI, IL, IA, KS, KY, MO, MT, NE, NV, ND, UT, WV, WI	AL, CA, GA, HI, ID, KS, ND, WV
Electorate (referendum)	AL, AK, AR, CA, FL, ME, MI, NV, NJ, NM, NY, OH, OK, OR, PA, TX, VA, WA, WV		
Individual Departments, Agencies, or Authorities		OH	AK, AZ, AR, CO, CT, FL, IL, IN, IA, ME, MD, MA, MI, MN, MO, MT, NE, NH, NJ, NY, OH, OK, PA, RI, SD, TX, UT, VT, VA, WA, WI, WY

Source: NAST/Council of State Governments National Survey, 1988.

bond issues. For example, as shown, some 32 states indicated that special authority revenue debt is authorized by the individual Department, Agency or Authority in contrast to requirements for legislative or electorate authorization approval which predominates for state general obligation or revenue debt.

With the emergence of increased state government concern with debt ratings, debt levels and related issues, debt oversight has emerged as a critical state management issue.

Included here are periodic calculations of outstanding debt levels, on-going and direct review and approval of capital construction plans and debt issuance supervision and control. The issuance of state GO and revenue debt is typically subjected to oversight by a variety of elected and appointed officials of state government. Most debt-issuing state special authorities appear to be relatively free from oversight, other than that exercised by their boards of directors. According to this study, the principal means of overseeing the activities of these entities is through appointments to the boards of trustees (bodies that also authorize specific bond issues in 32 states, as noted above). Typically, such appointments are made by the governor.

In California, Maine, Massachusetts, Pennsylvania and Vermont, for example, the State Treasurer sits on the boards of all special purpose governments issuing debt. In Maine, Missouri, New York and many other states, the governor appoints the trustees of each state's authority. A second means of oversight for special authorities involves formal requirements for regular reporting by these entities. For example, Arizona's Salt River Power District sets its own debt limits and structures its own bond issues, but is required to report amounts of its outstanding debt to the Department of Revenue.

A third means of oversight involves direct controls over special authority actions in the form of specific review and approval powers exercised by officials of regular state governments. For example, the State Treasurers in Delaware, Oregon, and North Carolina must approve capital plans of issuing authorities in those states. The Kentucky Office of Investment and Debt Management reviews and approves all authority capital projects, and manages debt service payments. The governors of New York and New Jersey may veto the board minutes (and thus any and all board actions) of certain authorities in those states, thus affording them a powerful, but rarely used, form of oversight.

As indicated, however, most state authorities, commissions, districts, and the like, appear to be relatively free from oversight. For example, the Arkansas Development Finance Authority maintains its own information on debt issues, and is not required to report information to state officials. Similarly, Colorado's authorities are not subject to formal reporting requirements, and are not supervised by any state office. The same is true of special purpose governments in Idaho, Connecticut, Delaware, Montana, Nebraska, Ohio, and a number of other states as evidenced by the NAST study.[35]

As indicated by the results of the NAST study,[36] there is significant diversity among the states in their approach to the management of debt issuing entities and overall debt levels. Concomitantly, the states approach oversight of special authorities in different ways depending on their organizational and statutory environment. Undoubtedly, state and local governments will be devoting increased attention to policy and management issues associated with special debt authorities as well as their own revenue and general obligation debt in the future. Such attention will result from the realization of the potential and real interrelationships between special authorities and the overall financial integrity and credit rating position of state and local governments.

NEW CAPITAL SOURCES: FOREIGN CAPITAL MARKETS

Since the mid-1980s, there has been increased state and local government interest in the taxable bond market as a source of capital. This interest has resulted from, among other factors, restrictions imposed on the use of nontaxable revenue bonds as a capital source for economic and industrial development loan programs. Such restrictions were part of the Tax Reform Act of 1986.[37] That Act resulted, partially, from the capital subsidies that state governments were using extensively to attract firms to their state and to promote economic development. Such subsidies supported by nontaxable municipal issues, in turn, represented tax expenditures for the federal government and a growing source of foregone federal revenue.

Several states have begun to utilize the taxable bond markets as a source of economic development capital and as a means of reacting to the tax-exempt bond restrictions. As a result, they have initiated searches for the most efficient source of such taxable bond capital. Among the options considered was acquisition of capital in foreign capital markets. Private sector corporations have frequently accessed foreign capital markets to take advantage of lower interest rates and reduced finance costs. By contrast, state and local governments have

---

[35] *Ibid.*

[36] *Ibid.*

[37] Ramsey, J. and Hackbart, M., "Municipal Debt Issues in Foreign Markets: Managing Currency and Interest Rate Risk," *Public Budgeting and Finance*, Vol. 11, No. 4, Winter, 1991.

only recently turned their attention to such markets. This section considers some of the policy issues associated with the implementation of such a capital acquisition policy option.

While the potential capital cost advantages associated with foreign capital markets may be attractive to municipal issuers, such transactions expose the borrower to currency exchange risk. Such risk arises since bond principal and interest payments are paid in the currency in which the debt is originally denominated. For instance, a United States borrower in the Japanese market will be required to make principal and interest repayment in yen instead of dollars if the bond issue was denominated in yen. Obviously, movements in the dollar/yen exchange rate over the life time of the issue will impact, either positively or negatively, the final total borrowing cost of the issuer.[38]

Given the fact that state and local governments tend to be risk averse, municipal issuers tend to consider currency risk hedging options when considering a foreign currency denominated issue to mitigate such risk. Such hedges may, of course, reduce the initial cost advantage of acquiring capital in foreign markets. However, given the risk aversion of municipal issuers, it is appropriate to consider the foreign capital acquisition option from a "hedged cost" framework. Hedging options are considered here and Appendix A of this Chapter reviews an example of a hedging strategy utilized by the Kentucky Development Finance Authority of Kentucky when it issued bonds in the Japanese Samurai Bond market. That example provides a more detailed perspective on the issues involved in foreign currency denominated municipal bond issue.

Currency Hedging Strategy Alternatives

Three general categories of hedging strategies are available for borrowers in foreign capital markets. These are:

(1) the forward exchange market;

(2) the futures exchange market; and

(3) the swap market.[39]

Each strategy has unique characteristics which provide advantages for conducting current exchange rate hedges. The selection of the "optimal" strategy typically depends on the nature of the transaction and the

---

[38] *Ibid.*

[39] For a more complete discussion, see Jones, E.T. and Jones, D.L., *Hedging Foreign Exchange*, (New York: John Wiley and Sons, 1987).

institutional characteristics and requirements of the borrower. Each of those strategies is explained here.

The Forward Exchange Hedge. A forward exchange transaction is a contractual commitment to buy or sell a specified quantity of foreign currency on a designated future date (maturity date of contract) for a designated price (forward exchange rate). These transactions are arranged through a market-maker, such as a bank, who receives a fee for arranging the transaction. Forward rates may be quoted at a price higher than the prevailing exchange rate (i.e., at a "premium" or at a lower rate such as a "discount").

Pricing of the forward rate is linked to the theory of interest rate parity which states that a difference in national interest rates for securities of a similar risk and maturity should be equal but opposite in sign of a foreign exchange rate discount or premium.[40] For example, if the interest on a 10-year security in Country A is 5% and the interest rate on a similar security in Country B is 10%, the market "expects" Country B's exchange rate to decline over the life of the issue. Specifically, since the interest rate differential is 500 basis points (1% equals 100 basis points), Country B's exchange rate should decline 50% over the life of the security. However, there are often opportunities to negotiate the forward exchange rate since the pricing mechanism described above is based on the assumption that markets operate efficiently. For long-term contracts, this assumption may not be as appropriate.[41]

Transactionally, forward contacts are flexible and simple. As long as a counterparty can be found, any amount and any maturity can be exchanged. In particular, the forward contract has been a very popular instrument for hedging long-term currency exposure for generally one to five years. The market liquidity is considered less beyond the five-year time horizon. Because of the forward market's flexibility and the size of potential profits to market-makers, investors with larger transactions have dominated that market.

Futures Exchange Markets. Currency futures markets are distinct from the currency forward market both mechanically and structurally since currency futures contracts are traded, as are other futures commodities, on organized futures exchanges. All futures contracts are of a standard size and their maturity dates are standardized, falling on the third Wednesday of March, June, September, and December. Generally,

---

[40] See Levi, M., *International Finance: Financial Management and International Economy*, (New York: McGraw-Hill Book Company, 1983), Chapters 5 and 6.

[41] Jones and Jones, *op. cit.*

FIGURE 17.3

Cash Flows Associated with a Basic Currency Swap

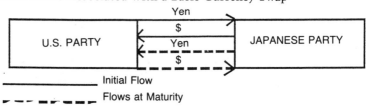

Note: This example assumes that the U.S. party has borrowed in yen.

smaller investors with transactions less than $1 million dominate the currency futures market since larger investors have the ability to tailor their risk management strategies to their specific program needs. Few public entities utilize this market to manage currency risk due to high transaction costs and the constant management of risk that is required.[42]

Swap Markets. A third currency hedging alternative is the swap market.[43] A currency swap is an agreement to make an initial exchange of currency between counterparties and a re-exchange of those currencies at maturity at a predetermined exchange rate. This rate is often the same as the initial rate but may be at premium or discount to the initial exchange rate. An example of these flows is provided in Figure 17.3.[44]

An extension of this type of currency swap can be transacted which also includes a coupon, or interest rate swap, whereby two parties essentially exchange debt service obligations in addition to the principal amounts. For example, an American counterparty may borrow yen in the Japanese capital markets and a Japanese counterparty may borrow

[42] *Ibid.*

[43] Ramsey, J., Smith, B. and Hilliard, B., *Public Finance and the International Markets: A Primer,* (Frankfort, Kentucky: Office of Revenue Estimating and Economic Analysis Working Paper Series, No. 2, 1989).

[44] The steps involved in such a transaction are:

(1) Counterparties borrow funds in the foreign market.

(2) Borrowed funds are swapped at the existing spot rate.

(3) Throughout the life of the loans, the American counterparty pays dollar interest payments to the Japanese counterparty who pay its creditors and the Japanese counterparty pays yen interest payments to the American counterparty who pays its creditors.

(4) At maturity, the American counterparty pays the dollar principal amount to the Japanese counterparty and the Japanese counterparty pays the yen principal amount to the American counterparty. Both then repay their creditors.

FIGURE 17.4
Sample Currency Interest Rate Swap

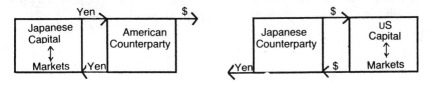

dollars in the U.S. capital markets. The parties may desire to access funds in their own domestic markets but are limited in their ability to do so or, each may seek to limit their exchange rate risk in making interest and principal payments. As a result, these two parties may enter into a currency/interest rate swap agreement where the Japanese counterparty pays the American counterparty the yen interest payments due on its loan and the American counterparty pays the Japanese counterparty the dollar interest payments due on its loan. At maturity, the principal payment is also assumed by the counterparties. Each party is still obligated to its initial creditors but the funds flow as shown in Figure 17.4.[45] In this manner, both counterparties have essentially accessed their domestic markets and have eliminated any uncertainty in their cash flows which may have resulted from movements in exchange rates.

An interest rate swap does not necessarily have to be combined with a currency swap. Without exchanging principal payments, two counterparties may effectively alter their interest payments/income streams. If a borrower is unable to access the fixed capital markets but for portfolio management reasons desires to do so, it may swap a floating-rate liability for a fixed-rate liability with a counterparty desiring to take the opposite position. In addition, many transactions involve several swaps, both interest rate and currency, which allow for the most desirable position for a given portfolio.

Regardless of the hedging strategy selected, state or local governments would normally reduce currency risk exposure by adopting one

---

[45] An interest rate risk management strategy may be important when foreign bond proceeds are used for economic development loans because declining interest rates increase the probability of loan non-origination. For example, non-origination is often a problem with single family mortgage revenue bonds sold by public entities. If bonds are sold that result in a mortgage interest rate of 10 percent, and prior to the origination and closing on the loans, the general level of interest rate declines, then alternate sources of mortgage money may become more attractive. In the domestic tax-exempt markets, such non-origination is often handled by bond indenture provisions which allow extraordinary calls. Such calls are not permitted in some foreign capital markets such as the Samurai market in Japan.

or more of the hedging strategies considered here. In designing a foreign capital market transaction, state and local governments may also design complimentary interest rate hedges. As indicated, an example of a hedging strategy is included in Appendix A.

SUMMARY

The emergence of debt affordability and debt management as major state and local government fiscal management issues has occurred as a result of several factors including a changing intergovernmental fiscal environment, changing attitudes regarding the role of the public sector in economic development and an emerging financial capital investment needs environment which has forced state and local governments to identify new, innovative approaches to capital acquisition and management. Such enhanced state and local government interest in debt management issues has fostered new research and renewed focus on these issues during the past decade. Issues such as debt capacity, debt affordability, and other broad debt management issues are complex concepts and even more difficult to deal with from either a policy or administrative perspective.

This chapter was intended to provide both a conceptual and an operational perspective for state and local government financial managers to utilize in relating to and managing these emerging policy issues. The concepts considered, however, represent a status report on these issues rather than a final answer. To that extent, the content is exemplary of the evolution of information and knowledge regarding the overall financial management of public policy and institutions.

APPENDIX *17.1**

Currency and Interest Rate Hedging: The KDFA Example

THE AUTHORITY AND THE ISSUE

The Kentucky Development Finance Authority was established in 1958 by the Kentucky legislature and has been a primary economic development assistance tool for the Commonwealth of Kentucky since that time. KDFA historically received appropriations from the State's General Fund as its source of loanable funds. In 1982, however, in an effort to expand the activities of KDFA, the Kentucky General Assembly authorized the issuance of $50 million of bonds to provide an equity contribution to KDFA. The significance of this bond transaction was that the bonds were fully supported by General Fund appropriations of the Commonwealth. That is, while the $50 million proceeds from the bond issue were made available to KDFA for loan purposes, loan repayments were not security for the repayment of the bonds. The sole source of repayment to the bondholder was General Fund appropriations.

---

* This Appendix draws heavily on an article by Ramsey, J. and Hackbart, M., *Municipal Debt Issues in Foreign Markets: Managing Currency and Interest Rate Risk, Public Budgeting and Finance*, Vol. 11, No. 4, Winter, 1991.

In 1988, in a further effort to expand its economic development programs and activities, KDFA requested additional General Fund appropriations to support its loan activities. However, due to State budgetary constraints, the General Assembly failed to authorize additional state-supported bonds for KDFA. Therefore, KDFA began to analyze alternatives for raising capital in the most economical taxable market possible to expand its economic development efforts including issuing bonds in the Japanese markets.

After considerable analysis, it was determined that KDFA could borrow for ten years in the Japanese Samurai market at approximately 5.00 to 5.50% and in the domestic taxable market at 10.50 to 11.00%; a 500 basis point differential. Because of these savings, KDFA issued bonds in the Japanese Samurai Bond market in March of 1989. Samurai bonds are publicly issued bonds by foreigners in Japanese markets.[46] KDFA chose to borrow funds in this market:

(1) due to the interest rate savings that could be achieved vis-á-vis the domestic taxable market; and

(2) to further enhance the Commonwealth's economic development programs and attractiveness to Japanese investors.[47]

Issuing bonds in the Samurai market, would, of course, leave KDFA initially exposed to currency exchange rate risk since the interest payments due over the life of the issue and the repayment of principal would be made in yen. As a matter of public policy,[48] it was determined that any exposure to such risk was unacceptable. To protect against this risk, KDFA elected to manage its risk in the swap market. The main considerations in structuring KDFA's swaps were:

---

[46] The Japanese capital markets are accessible through several financial instruments. These include:

(1) Samurai bonds, which are yen-denominated bonds and are publicly issued by foreigners in Japanese markets;

(2) Shogun bonds, which are foreign-currency denominated bonds;

(3) Shibosai bonds, which are yen-denominated private placements by foreign borrowers; and

(4) the Euroyen bond, which is yen-denominated but issued publicly outside of the Japanese market, typically in Europe.

[47] Ramsey, J.R. and Smith, J.B., "Kentucky Development Finance Authority's Samurai Bond Finance," presentation to National Conference of State Legislatures, September 11, 1989.

[48] *Ibid.*

(1) minimizing KDFA's currency exchange rate risk; and

(2) eliminating interest rate risk due to uncertain loan origination dates.[49]

THE KDFA SWAPS HEDGING STRUCTURE

A series of swaps was constructed by KDFA which involved the following steps:

(1) KDFA issued Yen 10 billion of Samurai bonds at Yen fixed rate of 5.4%. (See Figure 17.5.)

(2) KDFA then entered into a 10-year liability currency/interest rate swap agreement with the Industrial Bank of Japan (IBJ), a AAA-rated bank, whereby KDFA initially swapped the bond proceeds for $77,674,418.60.[50] At maturity, IBJ will provide KDFA with Yen 10,020,000,000—the principal amount needed to pay the bondholders and the 0.2% principal repayment fee, and KDFA will provide IBJ with $77,674,418.60. In addition, an interest rate swap was transacted in which KDFA exchanged its 5.4% yen semi-annual interest payments on the bonds and its 0.3% interest payment fee (Yen 270,810,000 each payment period) with IBJ for a semi-annual 6-month US$ LIBOR[51] + 18.5 basis point interest rate on $77,674,418.60. IBJ effectively pays KDFA's yen semi-annual payments and KDFA provides IBJ semi-annual interest payments as described above. Therefore, KDFA effectively has a floating dollar liability of 6 months US$ LIBOR + 18.5 basis point. (See Figure 17.6.)

(3) To assure KDFA's assets earn an income stream matching KDFA's liability stream, a set of asset swaps was transacted. The dollar proceeds KDFA received from the bond issue were used to purchase AAA and AA-rated securities paying dollar denominated interest flows.[52] (See Figure 17.7.)

---

[49] See Note 44 above.

[50] IBJ has since been downgraded to AA by Standard & Poor's and is rated AA+ by Fitch.

[51] LIBOR is the acronym for *London Interbank Offering Rate*. This interest rate is more frequently cited as a benchmark interest rate by banks and financial institutions in the international markets than the prime lending rate, fed fund rates, U.S. treasury bill rate or other rates frequently cited in the United States. LIBOR is a short-term rate set by large money center banks and is quoted daily and listed in *The Wall Street Journal* and other financial publications.

[52] The specific securities purchased are listed in Table 1.

FIGURE 17.5
Samurai Bond Cash Flows

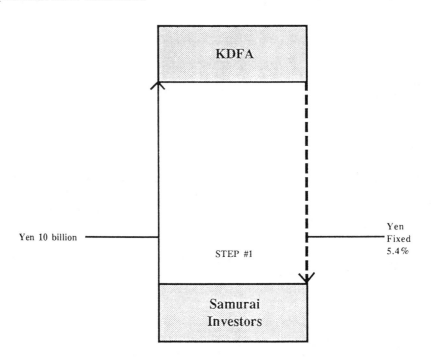

————————— Initial Flows

— — — — — — —Interim Flows

(4) KDFA then swapped these dollar interest flows with the asset swap
    counterparty, Bankers Trust, for a 6-month US$ LIBOR − 10 basis
    points interest income stream. Essentially, KDFA's net asset stream
    is now 6-month US$ LIBOR − 10 basis points. (See Figure 17.8.)
    KDFA's assets and liabilities were then matched in terms of interest
    rate with the exception of the negative arbitrage equaling 28.5 bp.
    This negative arbitrage would have been present regardless of
    whether the money was raised domestically or in a foreign market.
    Further, a comparison of the all-in-borrowing costs from this struc-
    ture and that available in the domestic taxable markets indicated
    that KDFA was able to borrow funds at a savings of approximately 30
    basis points over the cost of funds in the domestic market.

FIGURE 17.6
Currency Interest Rate Swap Transaction

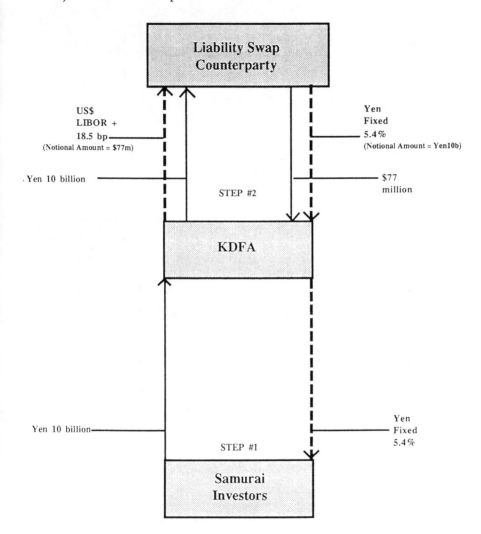

Initial Flows

Interim Flows

FIGURE 17.7
Investment of Swap Proceeds ($)

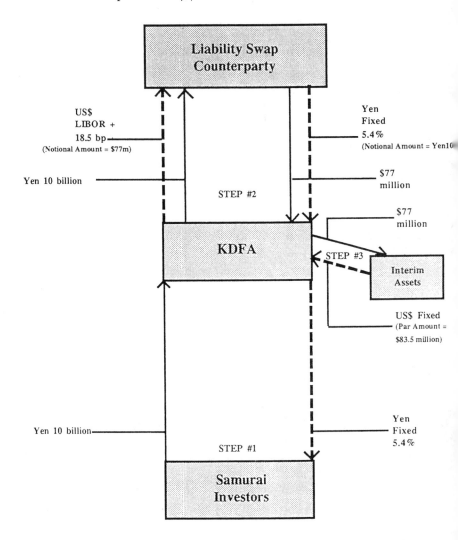

Initial Flows

Interim Flows

FIGURE 17.8
Asset Swap Cash Flow

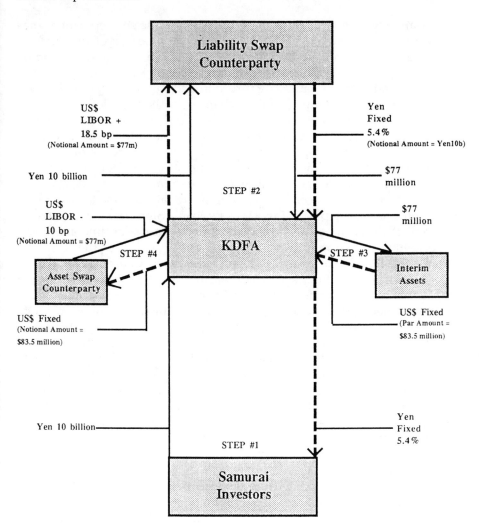

LOAN ORIGINATION AND SECOND GENERATION HEDGING

As already noted, KDFA is the primary economic development agency of the Commonwealth of Kentucky and the proceeds of the Samurai bond transaction were designed to be an additional source of capital to compliment KDFA's existing loan programs. KDFA, using the currency and interest rate structure outlined above, was initially perfectly hedged to protect against changes in the yen/dollar exchange rate and changes in interest rates. In addition, this structure provides KDFA the ability to make yen or dollar denominated loans and fixed or variable rate loans. However, the use of bond proceeds to originate fixed rate loans require that second generation hedges be constructed to maintain KDFA's risk management program.

As fixed rate economic development loans are made, securities, as outlined in Step 3, are replaced by loans. Since the income stream from the securities was swapped in Step 4 of the outline above, the original asset swap must be unwound and a portion of the securities must be liquidated to fund the loan to be made. Conceptually, the existence of efficient markets would ensure that the value of a swap and the value of the underlying security move in opposite directions, at approximately the same magnitude. For example, if interest rates go down following the initial swap transaction, the counterparty receiving the fixed interest rate has value in the swap. Therefore, the fixed rate payer would have to pay the fixed rate receiver a premium to "unwind" the initial transaction. However, the fixed rate payer (i.e., the holder of the underlying security yielding a fixed coupon) has seen the value of that security appreciate. Conceptually, the increased security value should offset the "unwind cost" on the swap. As already noted, markets are not efficient and the unwind cost may exceed the gain on the security.

March, 1990, was the second interest payment date with respect to the KDFA Samurai bonds. KDFA was prepared to make $8.5 million in loans; a $6 million fixed interest rate loan and a $2.5 million floating rate loan.[53] Therefore, KDFA was faced with a dual decision:

(1) which asset to sell; and

(2) how to eliminate the corresponding asset swap liability.

---

[53] In September, 1989, the first loan was originated with the proceeds of the Yen issue. In this case, the asset swap counterparty bought a portion of the securities held to provide funding for the loan and unwound the swap on the cash flow from the security. Since the loan originated was a variable-rate loan pegged to LIBOR, no new interest rate swap was required to match the liability swap detailed in Step 2.

TABLE 17.8
Bids on Swap Unwind/Reassignment

Firm A

Security	Initial Price* at Purchase	Par Value**	Accrued Interest	Best Bid*** Purchase Price	Current Market Price	Net Gain on Sale	Firm A Reassign Cost	Net Cost to KDFA	Cost Per Notional $
Dresdner	$36,500,000	$36,500,000	$120,652.77	99.93	$36,474,450	$ 95,103	($ 376,000)	($280,897)	($0.0077)
Footworks	$10,406,614	$12,000,000	$209,625.00	89.92	$10,790,400	$ 593,411	($ 740,000)	($146,589)	($0.0141)
Furukawa	$15,236,517	$18,000,000	$422,812.50	89.83	$16,169,400	$1,355,696	($1,555,000)	($199,305)	($0.0131)
Nakanagumi	$ 8,531,288	$10,000,000	$215,000.00	90.15	$ 9,015,000	$ 698,712	($ 790,000)	($ 91,288)	($0.0107)

Firm B

Security	Initial Price* at Purchase	Par Value**	Accrued Interest	Best*** Purchase Price	Current Market Price	Net Gain on Sale	Unwinding Cost	Net Cost to KDFA	Cost Per Notional $
Dresdner	$36,500,000	$36,500,000	$120,652.77	99.93	$36,474,450	$ 95,103	($ 393,801)	($298,698)	($0.0082)
Footworks	$10,406,614	$12,000,000	$209,625.00	89.92	$10,790,400	$ 593,411	($ 741,020)	($147,609)	($0.0142)
Furukawa	$15,236,517	$18,000,000	$422,812.50	89.83	$16,169,400	$1,355,696	($1,568,939)	($213,244)	($0.0140)
Nakanagumi	$ 8,531,288	$10,000,000	$215,000.00	90.15	$ 9,015,000	$ 698,712	($ 837,207)	($138,494)	($0.0162)

Firm C

Security	Initial Price* at Purchase	Par Value**	Accrued Interest	Best*** Purchase Price	Current Market Price	Net Gain on Sale	Firm C Reassign Cost	Net Cost to KDFA	Cost Per Notional $
Dresdner	$36,500,000	$36,500,000	$120,652.77	99.93	$36,474,450	$ 95,103	NO BID	NO BID	NO BID
Footworks	$10,406,614	$12,000,000	$209,625.00	89.92	$10,790,400	$ 593,411	($ 715,000)	($121,589)	($0.0177)
Furukawa	$15,236,517	$18,000,000	$422,812.50	89.83	$16,169,400	$1,355,696	($1,530,000)	($174,305)	($0.0114)
Nakanagumi	$ 8,531,288	$10,000,000	$215,000.00	90.15	$ 9,015,000	$ 698,712	($ 800,000)	($101,288)	($0.0119)

*This is the notional amount used to calculate original asset swap conterparty's interest payments to KDFA.
**This is the notional amount used to calculate KDFA's interest payments to Asset swap counterparty.
***Bids were independently taken to determine the best sell price for the securities and then the best bid was used to determine the most effective unwind/reassignment alternative.

FIGURE 17.9
Making a KDFA Fixed-Rate Loan

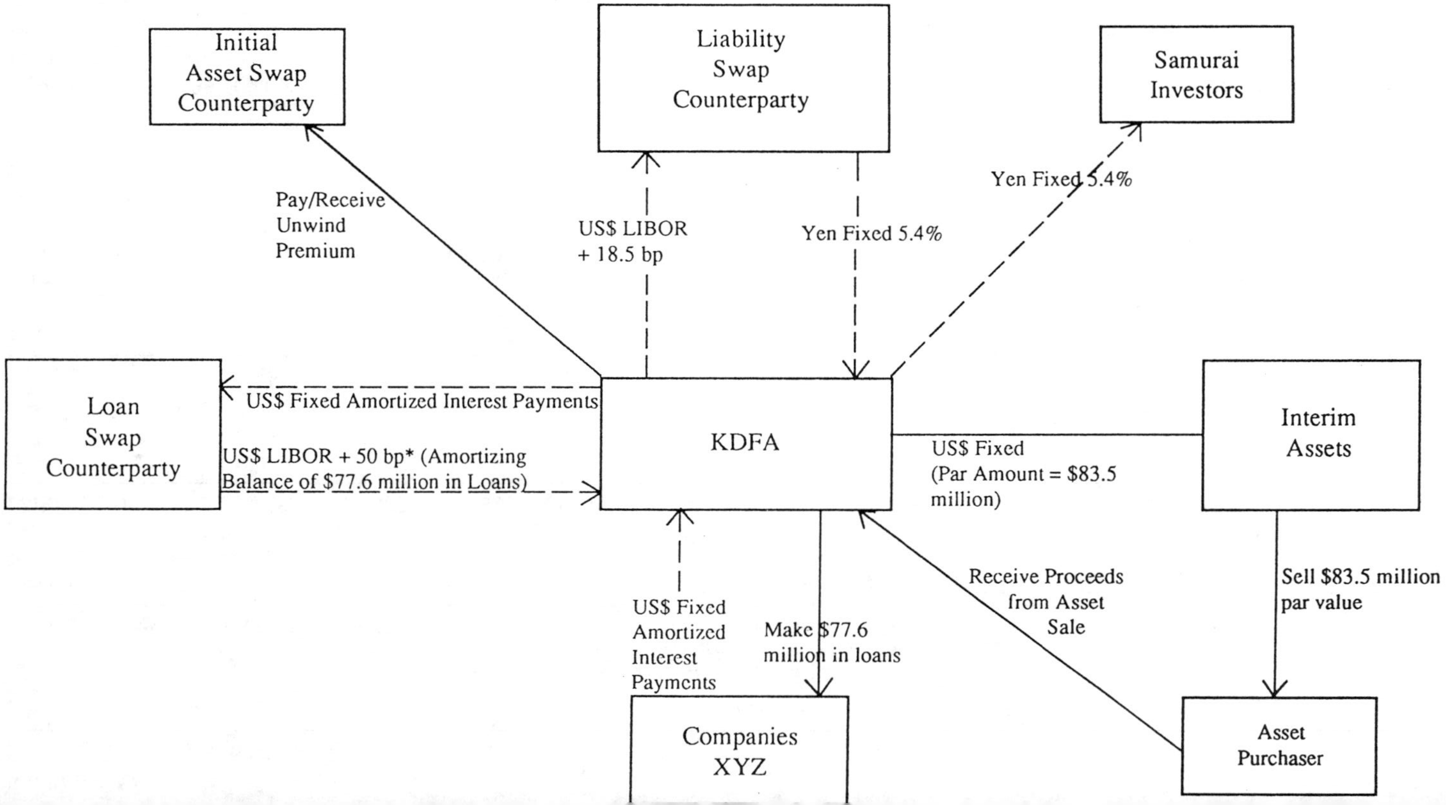

Two options were available for purposes of eliminating the asset swap liability constructed in Step 4. KDFA could "unwind" (i.e., directly eliminate its contractual agreement with its asset swap counterparty, or KDFA could "reassign" the asset swap to another institution desiring to assume KDFA's position). KDFA had to then liquidate a security, or portion thereof, to provide the loan funds. Table 17.8 outlines the "bid" information KDFA used to analyze this dual decision. Three institutions bid on the purchase of the securities. Based on these bids, the best price for each security was selected (Column #5) and subsequently any gain or loss on the sale of the securities was calculated (Column #7).

Two institutions bid "reassign" prices which were compared with the actual "unwind" cost bid by the institution with whom the swaps were originally constructed. The difference between the "reassign/unwind" costs and the gain on the security sale was subsequently calculated and put on a per notional[54] swap dollar basis to make comparisons as shown in Table 17.8. The "reassign" cost bid by Firm A on the Dresdner securities was the most competitive, and in fact, Firm A had also provided the best bids on the purchase of these bonds. Therefore, KDFA:

(1) Sold $8.5 million of its Dresdner bonds; and

(2) Reassigned its corresponding portion of the asset swap to Firm A.

The net cost to KDFA to eliminate this swap liability was $65,450 ($8,500,000 @ .0077/notional $).

Since the $2.5 million loan was at a variable rate, KDFA's assets and liabilities were effectively matched. The $6 million fixed-rate loan required an additional transaction for it to become a LIBOR-bearing asset matched to the original liability swap. Therefore, as in Step 4 of the previous outline, KDFA swapped this fixed interest cash flow for a LIBOR based cash flow, thus rehedging the portfolio. Figure 17.9 portrays graphically all the transactions required when making a fixed rate loan. Through this series of currency and interest rate swaps, KDFA was able to effectively hedge the currency and interest rate risks associated with a foreign bond issue and still raise capital at an all-in-cost less than had the funds been raised in the domestic taxable market.

---

[54] Notional refers to the agreed fixed principal amount upon which swap payments are calculated. As the value of securities change with changes in interest rates, the notional amount upon which the swap is based remains the same for swap calculation purposes.

CHAPTER 18

Organizational Dynamics of State Debt Issuance

Clement Mikowski
Former Director, Division of Bond Finance, State of Florida

This chapter will address the organizational dynamics and characteristics of typical state tax-exempt debt issuers. The first section will compare government organization and style between Michigan and Florida during recent years of economic change with the evolution of federal regulations and accountability for state budgeting and reporting. Current topics of interest and concern to the state debt administrator will be reviewed in the second section of this chapter. As perceived by the issuer of debt, this author will not attempt to delve into technical marketing aspects and current investment banking industry disciplines but will provide an adequate perspective of the issuers' needs based on their characteristics. Organization of government and legal construction of different types of debt issuance are the key elements in determining authority, responsibility, and structuring options for capital financing needs of state issuers. That is the key concept we are about to explore for the benefit of issuers, buyers, and all other participants in the state or municipal debt market.

As with municipalities, states vary in size, population, geography, location, climate, resources, major industries, and politics. All have a bearing on and influence how the 50 diverse sovereign entities are organized and governed. Historical development is another important element in this analysis. The major differences between states and municipalities are size, form of government and program needs. Typically, states have legislative, executive, and judicial arms of government that all insist on participating in the development and administration of debt financed programs. Our first objective is to develop a working knowledge of the issuer's government and other characteristics pertinent to debt administration.

Two states that provide interesting contrasts for comparison are Michigan and Florida which, by chance, are states where I have served as debt administrator. Historically, both states first borrowed in the early 1800s for territorial development based on the capital strength of the state banks. Thereafter, borrowing was initiated to finance major wars, development and extension of railroads, and the early stages of the industrial revolution based upon revenues of the system and whatever limited taxing powers were in place. Defaults were not uncommon and the buyers were mostly commercial banks both domestic and foreign where the banking systems were first developed.

During the 1900s, the highway systems and the development of municipalities generated growing demand for state borrowing with major restructuring of programs subsequent to the great depression of the 1930s. The greatest frequency of default was experienced during that depression. Since the 1930s water and sewer facilities, educational facilities, power facilities, and airport development have probably been the major sources of debt in addition to the continuing need for highways. During the 1970s, special purpose authorities for housing, hospitals, and industrial development became very active issuers as separate and distinct legal entities within state governments.

Also, during the 1900s, tax structures became more sophisticated with greater reliance upon general obligation *or* full faith and credit debt for general public purpose projects. About the time special purpose authorities were expanding, there was a tax revolt that generated several tax limitation referendums on states' ballots throughout the country. This constitutionally restricted the use of unlimited ad valorem taxes for certain states such as Michigan and California.

From the late 1970s to the present, an unprecedented onslaught of federal regulations, standard accounting and reporting principles and procedures, and industry generated rules and regulations have transformed a rather simple and adequate tax-exempt debt industry to one of the most complicated, restrictive, and burdensome disciplines of current time. For some reason, whenever the federal government gets involved in regulating an industry it seems to follow that trend.

The most recent complication is the severe reduction in the use of tax-exempt debt for industrial development, pollution control, housing, and other areas previously granted access to the tax-exempt market, but not restricted by federal tax law. In addition, state and municipal issuers are limited by severe federal arbitrage regulations as to the investment of debt finance capital for partial financing or reduction of total project or program costs. *Most state constitutions, statutes, and administrative procedures are not flexible or diversified sufficiently to absorb such major evolution in regulations and industry changes without great organizational and political stress being placed upon the state government and the debt service structure.*

GOVERNMENT ORGANIZATIONS AND STYLE

Michigan

Michigan is the twenty-third largest state with an area of 56,954 square miles located in the East North Central Region of the United States and bordering on four of the five Great Lakes. According to the 1980 census, Michigan ranked eighth among the 50 states with a population of 9.3 million. Michigan has 83 counties, 271 incorporated cities, and 263 incorporated villages.

The economy of the State is highly industrialized and dependent to a great degree on manufacturing of durable goods with heavy concentration in motor vehicles and equipment, non-electrical machinery, fabricated metal products and primary metal products. Other major manufacturing includes chemicals, pharmaceuticals, paper products, cereal products, and furniture. Economic activity tends to be more cyclical on average than the nation as a whole.

The legislative branch of government consists of 38 Senators and 110 Representatives of the House. Legislative sessions commence in January of each year for a session of indeterminate length or a full-time legislature in a practical sense.

The executive power of the State is vested with the Governor who is elected. Other elected officials are the Lieutenant Governor, Secretary of State, and Attorney General. The State Treasurer is appointed by and serves at the convenience of the Governor.

Michigan's judicial branch of government consists of the Supreme Court, the Court of Appeals, the Circuit Courts, the Probate Courts, and other courts of more limited jurisdiction.

The state operates on an annual budget submitted by the Governor to the Legislature for approval. Michigan has a strong Governor with a concentration of power and authority over 19 principal executive departments created under provisions of the State Constitution. The Governor also has the legal authority to veto legislation passed by the Legislature, including budget line items. The Legislature may override the Governor's veto, but it takes a two-thirds vote of the members of each house.

Michigan first adopted a Constitution in 1835, two years before becoming a State. Subsequently, Constitutions were adopted in 1850, 1908, and, most recently, in 1963 to take effect in 1964.

Michigan Debt

Michigan has issued three types of debt in recent times. They are general obligation, special obligation, and other state-related revenue debt. The 1963 State Constitution limits general obligation debt to:

(1) short-term debt for State operating purposes;

(2) short- and long-term debt for the purpose of making loans to school districts; and

(3) long-term debt for voter-approved purposes.

Currently, the only active general obligation debt program in Michigan is the School Bond Loan Program which incidentally is one of the premier pool bond programs in the country.

Originated in the late 1950s, the School Bond Loan Program assists local school districts with partial loans for capital construction bond issues and/or payment of local school districts principal and interest on their debt if necessary. Some bonds are outstanding for Water Pollution Control, Public Recreation, and Vietnam Veteran Bonus programs. General obligation debt is structured and sold by the State Treasurer with authorization to issue from the State Administrative Board which is composed of the Governor, Lieutenant Governor, Secretary of State, Attorney General, Superintendent of Public Instruction, and State Treasurer. The Board is authorized to provide for the issuance of bonds and notes of the State and for their repayment. Only about $200 million worth of bonds are outstanding for general obligation debt.

Special obligation debt is authorized by Constitution or by legislation to finance the cost of State revenue supported or appropriation supported capital projects usually approved by the Legislature. The State Transportation Commission issues bonds for comprehensive transportation purposes and highway purposes which are supported by motor fuel taxes, vehicle registration fees, and certain designated sales taxes. Approximately $450 million worth of these bonds are outstanding. A State Building Authority, created by the Legislature, issues bonds to acquire, construct, improve and maintain buildings for use of the State or any of its agencies. Leases are executed to be paid by State appropriations based upon true rental values. Projects are approved by the Legislature. Approximately $550 million worth of these bonds are outstanding.

Other State-related revenue debt is a catchall for special purpose agencies and authorities created by the Legislature, by statute, to issue revenue bonds payable from designated revenues or fees. Such bonds are not obligations of the State and the State has no obligation to appropriate moneys to meet debt service payments. Most notable in this category are the Michigan State Housing Development Authority with in excess of $2 billion worth of bonds and notes outstanding and the Michigan State Hospital Finance Authority with in excess of $1.5 billion worth of bonds outstanding. To date, the Legislature has created as many as 15 special purpose agencies and authorities with separate boards and commissions and staffs to provide services including, but not limited to, bridge construction and management, farm loans, island property development, student loans, park development, private college loans, industrial development, loans to municipalities, and the like. Each agency is authorized to sell its own debt without any State centralization of debt issuance or policy administration except for limited review by the State Treasurer. Total other State-related debt issuance is approximately $5 billion of which approximately $450 million is debt of State universities and colleges. Not all special purpose agencies and authorities are active and some have been superseded by second generation agencies or authorities created by new administrations. The Michigan Strategic Fund and Michigan Municipal Bond Authority are the most recently created agencies.

In brief, of the total debt outstanding for the State of Michigan and its agencies or authorities, approximately 3% is general obligation, 16% is special obligation and 81% is other state-related revenue debt.

The preceding paragraphs give a brief perspective of Michigan government and debt, which only touch upon major aspects of organization and structure. With this framework established, it is necessary to review several other matters of importance to complete this overview of Michigan debt.

Michigan has *recently* survived one of the most dire economic times in the history of the states. From the late 1960s through the mid 1980s, the State maintained its access to the market given the following:

(1) Detroit riots in 1967.

(2) Oil supply limitations and crisis in the 1970s that reduced demand for automobiles and increased efficiency standards while engine effluence standards were also increased.

(3) Major growth in competition from foreign auto suppliers that continues today.

(4) Retooling of outdated auto, and related industry, facilities and associated employment reductions to generate cost savings.

(5) Serious taxpayer revolt with constitutional amendments limiting the State's ability to raise taxes and effectuate new programs.

(6) Major reductions in Federal revenue sharing for state and local governments.

(7) In 1981 and 1982, the worst national economic recession since the 1930s.

At its worst, in the fall of 1982, the recession had generated a $1.5 billion state deficit and unemployment rates as high as 17% on a monthly seasonally adjusted basis and a declining State population in 1981 through 1983. The State's credit ratings were reduced to A+ by Standard and Poors and Baa-1 by Moody's. Starting in 1983, the Governor took full control of State government and finances. The State's personal income tax was increased, programs were reduced, State employment was reduced and with the help of a healing national economy the State's economy became more productive.

During the crisis period, the State used its Constitutional ability to issue general obligation notes for short-term cash flow needs. Such borrowing was initiated from 1978 through September of 1986. With the combination of executive order budget cuts, delayed payments, interfund borrowing and short-term note issuance, the State survived its crisis. To its credit the State never exceeded borrowing $500 million short-term while certain other states greatly exceeded that amount with one borrowing as much as $4.3 billion short-term.

During this same period, the State had to enhance its borrowings as its note rating had been reduced from a Moody's MIG-1 to MIG-2 and further reductions were anticipated without enhancement. The State retained a financial advisor, bond counsel, and major investment and commercial banking firms. Together they structured the first major foreign letter of credit for a State issuer; amended most debt-related statutes to provide for negotiated sale and all other dynamics of a negotiated or credit enhanced debt issue; developed sophisticated rating agency presentations with charts and diagrams; conducted buyer information meetings; developed elaborate pricing books that provided a valuable factual and historical reference document for all; and perfected mandatory set-aside trust funds with independent trust agents for repayment of debt.

Two other items that protected the State's access to debt markets were a statutory work-out remedy for late payment of principal and interest on debt and the famous "Rainy-Day" fund. A 1982 statute assigns the State Treasurer the duty to pay principal and interest on any full faith and credit obligation of the State, not paid when due, from the first State money or revenue which then or thereafter come under his control or custody other than retirement funds, trust and agency funds, bond proceeds funds, debt service funds, restricted gifts and grants, or revenue restricted by the State Constitution of 1963 for other purposes. In 1977, the State created by legislation the Budget Stabilization (Rainy Day) Fund which is a counter-cyclical stabilization fund. This fund is designed to accumulate balances during years of significant economic growth to be used in years when the State's economy experiences cyclical downturns. The fund was depleted at different times from 1981 through 1983, but in 1984 in excess of $300 million was transferred to the fund. More recently, the Fund has had additional sizeable transfers.

Today Michigan's G.O. ratings are restored to AA− by Standard and Poor's and A1 by Moody's and the State is flush with cash, but there will be future recessions and auto industry problems. Given past experiences, the State will survive and continue to prosper and diversify. Government power will continue to be centralized and other State-related revenue debt will continue to grow because it is not subject to voter approval or other constitutional restrictions that apply to general obligation debt.

Florida

Florida is the twenty-second largest state with an area of 58,560 square miles located in the extreme South Eastern Region of the United States bordering the Atlantic Ocean on the East and the Gulf of Mexico on the West. According to the 1980 census, Florida ranked seventh among the 50 states with a population of 9.75 million. Florida has 67 counties and 390 incorporated cities.

Florida's economy is nicely diversified with an employment spread as follows: 27.0% in trade, 25.6% in services, 15.2% in government, 11.8% in manufacturing and mining, 7.6% in construction, 7.3% in finance, insurance, and real estate, and 5.5% in transportation, communication, and public utilities. Of the total jobs, 19.4% are goods producing and 80.6% are non-goods producing. This is important to credit analysts for two reasons. During the last two major recessions, goods producing jobs declined significantly while non-goods producing jobs remained constant or actually rose in the service employment areas. Secondly, the Federal Tax Reform Act of 1986 leans more heavily upon capital-intensive heavy industries which lose investment tax credits and generous depreciation allowances while service industries are affected to a much lesser degree from lower maximum corporate tax rates.

The legislative branch of government consists of 40 Senators and 120 Representatives of the House. Legislative sessions commence in April of each year for a term of sixty days, with provisions for special sessions if necessary. A part-time legislature in a practical sense, which allows the State to conduct its business for approximately nine months without legislative action or statutory changes as in Michigan.

The executive branch of government is decentralized and consists of a Governor, Lieutenant Governor and six Cabinet members as follows: Attorney General, Commissioner of Agriculture, Commissioner of Education, Comptroller, Treasurer, and Secretary of State. All are elected officials who serve terms of four years. The State Constitution provides that all functions of the executive branch shall be allotted among not more than 25 departments. Each department must be under the direct supervision of the Governor, Lt. Governor, Governor and Cabinet, or a Cabinet Member. This is a much weaker form of Governor than is present in Michigan which reduces the amount and degree of transition between elections depending on the results of Cabinet office elections.

Florida's Constitution, as amended in 1972, provides for one of the most modern court systems in the nation with the power of the judicial branch vested in a Supreme Court, District Courts of Appeal, Circuit Courts and County Courts. Important to State debt issuance is the fact that new bonding programs and new series of bonds within programs generally have to be validated, that is, a determination of legal validity to issue in a State Circuit Court. In Michigan, and most other states, validation is contained in the constitutional and statutory authority to issue and does not require separate and independent findings by the Circuit Court prior to issuance. Unfortunately, a disgruntled citizen can intervene during the validation procedure and actually stop the progress of sizeable, timely and needed bond issues as in major transportation programs.

The state operates on a biennial budget, which is formulated in the even numbered years and is presented by the Governor to the Legislature in the odd numbered years. In even numbered years, a supplemental budget request is used to refine and modify the major submission. This greatly reduces the number of man hours required to prepare a full-course annual State budget and enhances consistency in long-term capital planning. With less time spent on development, more emphasis is placed on planning, evaluation and control of the budget. The Governor of Florida has line item veto power or can veto an entire bill as in Michigan. Also, the Legislature may override the Governor's veto with a two-thirds vote of the members of each house.

Florida became a State in 1845 and has had six constitutional conventions in all. Current debt authorization is contained in the fifth Constitution as adopted in 1885 and the sixth Constitution as adopted in 1968.

Florida Debt

Florida has six basic bonding programs for which bonds are structured and sold by the Division of Bond Finance of the Department of General Services. The Division of Bond Finance is a centralized debt management staff authorized to sell debt of the State agencies and local governments. The six bonding categories are education, environmental and coastal preservation, fixed capital outlay, housing, pollution control, and transportation. Florida has never authorized a statewide ad valorem tax and, unlike Michigan, Florida has no personal income tax. Further, the state sales tax, which is the largest single source of revenue, is constitutionally restricted from pledging to secure bonds.

Prior to 1968, Florida had extremely limited bonding authority, except for the purposes of repelling invasion or suppressing insurrection and limited tax bonds for education, transportation, state buildings, and outdoor recreation bonds. Such constraint was imposed on the State due to several unsuccessful prior bond issues which resulted in default and in some cases actual repudiation of previously incurred debt. Strangely enough, most of the defaults were at the local level, but such restrictions were not locally applied. During the depression of the 1930s, Florida's local units led the nation with 621 defaults. It wasn't until the 1968 Constitution that State Bonds were authorized to be issued pledging the full faith and credit of the State.

Florida's full faith and credit pledge is not an absolute general obligation pledge with automatic appropriation of debt service monies from the general fund. By Constitution, such bonds are issued with a primary pledge of special taxes levied for the discharge of such bonds and, in addition, the full faith and credit is pledged but not to create a general lien or charge upon unspecified revenues, moneys, or income. The State acknowledges indebtedness for the bonds and that such indebtedness is enforceable should the special taxes or revenues pledged for the bonds be insufficient. In addition, the State will act in good faith to use its resources as authorized or required by law for the prompt payment of principal and interest. This is very similar to the statutory work-out remedy available to Michigan's bondholders if payment is past due on principal and interest; in addition to the fact that Michigan does have automatic appropriation of funds for its general obligation pledge.

Florida has in excess of $5.1 billion outstanding in 1985 of which, unlike Michigan, $3.1 billion (61%) are full faith and credit special tax bonds. Of the remaining balance, $439 million (8.6%) are limited tax bonds, $257 million (5.0%) are revenue bonds, and $1.3 billion (25.4%) are housing bonds. Subsequently, the State has issued in excess of $1 billion education refunding and new project bonds that are full faith and credit special tax bonds. In addition, the State has issued $564 million of appropriation supported new program fixed capital outlay debt for state buildings purchase or construction and financing of a pool of funds for equipment leasing.

Special taxes pledged for full faith and credit bonds include tolls, if any, and a designated second gas tax for road projects; motor vehicle tax for county education projects; and, gross receipts tax for higher education bonds; and revenues from pollution control projects. All these bonds are limited by specific coverage requirements. The limited tax bonds, mentioned above, were issued prior to the 1968 Constitution and do not include a full faith and credit pledge. *Revenue bonds by definition* are supported by revenues of the system.

Florida Division of Bond Finance

The Division of Bond Finance was created and exists under the provisions of the "State Bond Act," being sections 215.57 through 215.83 of the Florida Statutes. The "State Bond Act" authorizes the Division to issue any bonds of the State or on behalf of any State agency, and to exercise all of the powers relating to the issuance of bonds of State agencies. The Governing Board of the Division is composed of the Governor and Cabinet consisting of the Comptroller, Treasurer, Attorney General, Commissioner of Agriculture, Commissioner of Education and Secretary of State. The Division of Bond Finance is considered one of the nations best organized debt administration agencies. Given serious constitutional and statutory limitations on the construction of debt and forms of security, the Division has consistently delivered bond proceeds for badly needed capital finance programs in one of the fastest growing economies in the country. Recently, the Division sought and obtained legislation to negotiate the sale of refunding bonds. In Florida, it is still required that practically all bonds at the State level be sold by competitive bid except for the more recent housing and fixed capital outlay programs.

The Division is in the process of refunding out and restructuring outstanding State debt with anticipated gross cost savings of approximately $200 million. With a staff of 16, consisting of legal and financial professionals and clerical staff, the Division works closely with the Governor and Cabinet to administer state debt; develop new program and regulatory legislation; protect the State's credit; and accommodate federal regulations by administering allocation formulas, arbitrage requirements and other legal restrictions. The Division also collects information on local issuance of debt for the Governor, Cabinet, and Legislature. To its credit, the Division has had its Glossary of Municipal Bond Terms adapted by the Municipal Securities Rulemaking Board in its Glossary of Municipal Securities Terms.

Another agency pertinent to the issuance of debt in Florida is the State Board of Administration which determines the fiscal sufficiency of all bonds to be issued by the State or its agencies. No such bonds may be issued unless such bonds have first been so approved by the Board of Administration composed of the Governor, Comptroller and State Treasurer. The State Board of Administration staff also serve as trustee on most of the debt outstanding.

Compared to Michigan, Florida is more centralized for administration of debt policy but has less than modern and adequate constitutional and statutory provisions for debt issuance. Given the new environment of federal regulations, taxable public debt, foreign market borrowings and a continuing move toward negotiated sale of more complex debt offerings, constitutional and statutory limitations will have to be addressed with forward vision. Also, it is important to note that Florida is not authorized to issue revenue or tax anticipation notes as a remedy during difficult economic times as in Michigan and other states. Since recent recessions have not affected Florida's economy to the degree they have in other states, short-term borrowing has not been considered a necessity. Of greater concern to Florida is current and future infrastructure needs due to rapid population and economic growth.

Michigan's economic growth peaked during the 1950s and the 1960s when the auto industry flourished in this country. Florida is now experiencing a major growth period which is anticipated to continue through the year 2000. One has to recognize the growing tourist industry, especially the Disney World complex, along with other factors of Florida's growing service, finance, insurance, real estate and trade industries.

Florida's main challenge is to maintain its quality of life given its conservative tax policies and rigid legal construction of financing options. As a leader in growth management legislation and regulations, Florida must now invest in the necessary infrastructure to maintain the quality of life and environment in a growth state. Debt policy and administration are key elements in resolving the backlog of unfunded capital needs estimated at $30 billion with an additional $15 billion of estimated need over the next 15 years.

NEGOTIATED SALES VS. COMPETITIVE BID SALES

State and local tax-exempt bonds are marketed by one of three methods:

(1) competitive bid;

(2) negotiation; or

(3) private placement.

Competitive bid sale, which is the most common, involves a rigid but simple award of bonds to the lowest bidder on a predetermined date, at a specified time, as stipulated in the formal notice of sale. Negotiated sale involves the deliberate selection of firms by an issuer to jointly prepare legal and marketing documents for timely introduction to institutional and retail buyers when market conditions are most opportune. Private placement of bonds involves a closed transaction between issuer and buyer, or experienced investor, that is typically limited in scope and results in reduced issuance cost and limited circulation of the debt.

You may recall that Michigan issues a much higher percentage of revenue bonds than Florida which issues mostly full faith and credit backed bonds. Michigan also sells most of its debt by negotiated sale whereas Florida sells most of its debt by competitive bid sale. This is due to several factors including historical timing of programs, economic conditions, and legal or constitutional requirements. Most states have constitutional and statutory provisions that require the sale of general obligation or full faith and credit bonds by competitive or public bid sale. This is traditional in the legal construction of constitutions as an attempt to keep all transactions bona fide and arms length.

Michigan created most of its currently active bonding programs since the late 1960s when revenue bonds and negotiated sale came into focus because of economic and sociopolitical reasons. Negotiated sales are more cost effective and efficient when you have volatile market conditions, complicated security, large issues, credit problems, and first issues for new programs. In an environment of taxpayer resistance revenue bonding programs can be legislated and implemented without the political hardships of unpopular voter referendums for needed capital finance programs. In recent years, Michigan has experienced every criteria for reliance on negotiated sale of revenue bonds. One market limitation with revenue bonds is the fact that commercial banks are prohibited from underwriting most types of revenue bonds by the Glass-Steagall Act of 1933.

Florida has recently passed legislation which authorizes the sale of refunding bonds by negotiated sale because of the complex structuring of such debt to comply with current federal arbitrage regulations and rigid procedures for computer verification of numbers by independent agents. The use of negotiated sale involves the retention of a management team to structure and sell bonds for a fee and expenses known as the underwriting spread. Total spread usually consists of a management fee, takedown or sales concession, underwriters' risk, and expenses. Such fees should relate to the amount of work involved and marketing cost plus a reasonable margin for risk. Most public sector administrators are suspicious of fees associated with a negotiated sale and therefore prefer avoiding them by competitive bid sale if possible. In most instances, however, a competitive bid contains components of expense, concessions and risk that are not negotiated by the issuer.

Since the merits of a competitive versus negotiated sale have been debated in length, and will continue to be so, I will not belabor the issue here. Needless to say, with today's complex structure of debt due to changing markets, diversified types of issuance, and ever increasing regulations, I sense that the growth in negotiated sales will continue even with more conservative issuers such as Florida. Private placements with mutual funds may increase on a state by state basis depending on the local benefits of tax-exempt bonds combined with the reduction in federal tax exemptions for many types of state and local debt. Private placement can significantly reduce costs of issuance and purchase for sophisticated sellers and buyers of debt.

PRICING BOOKS

One way to limit the uncertainty or suspicion associated with a negotiated sale of debt by sophisticated investment bankers is to request a pricing analysis subsequent to the pricing and sale of bonds. Such analysis in form is known as a pricing book. A *pricing book* is an extra task for underwriters in which they must demonstrate the worth and value of their service to an issuer. Typical contents of a pricing book include analysis of market supply and demand at time of sale; comparison of spread components with other like deals; listing of firms participating in the pricing of bonds; and final allocation of bonds to firms compared to orders or participation formulas.

Most competent underwriters will expand upon the basics of a pricing book to include key elements of rating agency presentations; issuer credit analysis; and historical analysis of the current issue compared to previous like issues on the basis of cost and form. This affords the senior book running manager and other senior structuring managers an opportunity to demonstrate their worth and knowledge in structuring deals.

I have also found that pricing books are an extremely valuable file document for answering questions presented by interested legislators, cabinet officials, state administrators, auditors, news reporters and others. Since the underwriter's name is on the pricing book, they benefit from expanded circulation of this document. Therefore, a well priced and competitively structured negotiated sale can be analyzed in detail and leave everyone involved with a positive "gut" feeling about the deal. I have worked with several underwriters in the development and scope of pricing books and cannot overstate the administrative and sociopolitical value of this document.

BOND PURCHASE CONTRACT

An additional document that is unique or peculiar to a negotiated sale is the Bond Purchase Contract or Agreement. After the successful pricing of a bond issue, underwriters' counsel submits a draft of the contract to the issuer and the senior underwriting managers for negotiation of liabilities of the underwriter and issuer. In reading the document, it appears that the issuer is ultimately liable for every aspect of disclosure and structuring of the bond issue and that the underwriter and counsel have only committed to a good-faith deposit and receipt of the bonds if the world stops and and no subsequent events take place during the marketing period from pricing to delivery.

The document proudly proclaims that the underwriters shall have the right to cancel without penalty the agreement to accept delivery of the bonds under any one of several and various circumstances that, in the sole discretion of the underwriter, materially and adversely affect the marketability of the bonds such as:

–Any action of the United States Congress, President, Treasury Department, Internal Revenue Service, Securities and Exchange Commission, etc.

–Any war involving the United States shall have occurred or any calamity or crisis on any financial market shall have occurred.

–Any order, decree or injunction of any court of competent jurisdiction, or any order, ruling, regulation or administrative proceeding by any governmental body or board having an effect on the issue.

–Any adverse and material change in the state's finances or any litigation pending of material consequences.

These examples are just a sample of the type and form of "market-outs" for the underwriters. My concern is that such conditions are rather global in perspective and are not reasonable, practical, or controllable by the issuer. Therefore, why is the issuer paying a fee to retain underwriters for structuring, marketing skills and risk taking when the Purchase Contract clearly specifies that the issuer is at risk for everything? During debate over the issues, I have been assured that the underwriters have made a sizeable good-faith offering and that they risk losing the State as a future client if they don't deliver. Therefore, the Purchase Contract is a temporary document of limited term and consequences and should not interfere with successful completion of the transaction. Needless to say, I feel the negotiated Purchase Contract needs to be further developed and refined before it can be recognized as a reasonable and pertinent or viable document in a negotiated sale.

Typically, with a competitive bid sale the Notice of Sale and Bid Form contain the parameters for structuring, delivery, and the respective responsibilities of issuer and buyer with a specified good-faith offering. The winning bidder accepts the bond issue at face value based upon the contents of a Preliminary Official Statement, Notice of Sale, and Bid Form as is. Thereafter, on the date of closing, the issuer delivers appropriate legal documents, certificates, and bonds. The purchaser provides payment for the balance due and takes possession of the bonds. Given their limited involvement, underwriters are still capable of marketing the bonds without the benefit of a Purchase Contract with a competitive bid sale.

Although I am extremely supportive of a negotiated sale when it provides needed professional access to the market and contains risk, I question the value of the Purchase Contract to the issuer. It can be perceived as more of a liability than an asset to the process.

SUMMARY

At this point, I would like to conclude with a few comments on the Chapter's perspective. In the previous pages, I have attempted to give the reader a sense of the character and mission of state debt issuers. State government is more sizeable and more rigidly constructed than municipalities for purpose of debt issuance. In an environment of federal regulations, growing competition and more restrictive financial and reporting standards, all issuers will have to be future oriented and structurally flexible. Quality of issuance is, and will continue to be, more important than conservative legal and administrative construction of authority for issuance. That is, the structure and timing of debt issuance should complement the economic forces of supply and demand and be directed toward receptive markets either domestic or foreign.

States that have struggled, in an economic sense, such as Michigan generally have expanded upon debt policy and options for issuance. Other states that have more diversified economies are also compelled to expand and develop debt policy because of infrastructure growth management needs that have to be financed in the face of restrictive regulations and, continuing reductions in federal programs for state and local capital finance needs.

CHAPTER *19*

Overview of Public Authorities and Special Districts

James Leigland
Institute of Public Administration

Government corporations at the state, inter-state, and local levels, constitute the fastest growing, least well understood form of American government—one that is mysterious to many state and local public officials, as well as to members of the investment community. Known across the country as authorities, districts, banks, services, systems, agencies, commissions, boards, associations, areas, companies, corporations, and the like, these entities participate in public works provision in a variety of ways: they build and run bridges, tunnels, tollroads, dams, ports, airports, railroads, and mass transit facilities.

A VARIETY OF PURPOSES

These entities provide essential services, including water supply, sewerage, irrigation, reclamation, and solid waste disposal. Over the last two decades, bond banks, development authorities, and the like have increasingly come to administer a wide array of loans and subsidies to other governmental units engaged in public works provision.

This chapter discusses the defining characteristics of state and local government corporations, and explores some of the available evidence on the nature and extent of the role played by these entities in public finance. (School districts are discussed separately in another

375

chapter.) The final section of this chapter summarizes some of the overall costs and benefits to state and local governments of using the corporate form for the provision of government services.

ESSENTIAL CHARACTERISTICS

The essential characteristic shared by the vast majority of public authorities, special districts, and other similar entities, is corporate status. The separate legal identity provided by incorporation allows such an entity to conduct various kinds of business—including borrowing and revenue retention—"in its own name." Although these corporations are wholly owned by units of regular government, in a technical legal sense the parent government is no more liable for the activities of its corporate subsidiary (unless special promises have been made) that are shareholders of public, private-sector corporations.

This legal personality makes possible, and often necessary, the consideration of these entities as things different and separate from regular government agencies. It also provides these entities with the fiscal and administrative independence and flexibility said to be necessary for the conduct of "business-like" functions of government.

Attempts to use "special district" or "public authority" as generic terms typically invoke empirical characteristics that conflict with the ways in which these terms actually are used in at least some states. Nevertheless, the public administration and public finance literature traditionally has defined public authorities as corporate entities with appointed boards, which raise money in the private money markets, but may not tax. Some authors add that authorities are by definition self-supporting. Special districts, on the other hand, are said to be smaller entities, have democratically elected boards, make little use of the money markets, and raise money through taxation to pay for services that tend not to be self-supporting.

Many entities, called "authorities" and "districts," exhibit these characteristics, but many others—including many of the largest and most powerful state and local government corporations—cannot be categorized so easily. Thousands of governmental entities, formally identified as "special districts," issue general obligation bonds and/or revenue bonds. Sixteen states allow entities formally identified as "authorities" to levy taxes (see Table 19.1).

TYPES OF STATE AND LOCAL GOVERNMENT CORPORATIONS

There are literally hundreds of different kinds of government corporations active at the state and local level—some individual states alone

TABLE 19.1
Selected Examples of Authorities that May Levy Taxes

Florida:	Regional Water Supply Authorities may levy property taxes. Central Pinellas Transit Authority may levy property taxes with voter approval.
Georgia:	Metropolitan Atlanta Rapid Transit Authority may levy sales taxes.
Illinois:	Regional Transportation Authority may impose a retail occupation and use tax. Airport Authorities may levy property taxes.
Kansas:	City-county airport authorities may levy property taxes. Joint port authorities may levy property taxes.
Louisiana:	Regional Transit Authority may levy property taxes with voter approval.
Michigan:	Capital City Airport Authority may levy property taxes. Huron-Clinton Metropolitan Authority may levy property taxes within limits permitted by voters.
Minnesota:	Regional Railroad Authorities may levy property taxes. Sanitary Disposal Authorities may levy property taxes.
Mississippi:	Railroad Authorities may levy property taxes.
New Mexico:	Flood Control Authorities may levy property taxes.
North Dakota:	County Nursing Home Authorities may levy property taxes. Regional Railroad Authorities may levy property taxes.
Ohio:	Regional Transit Authorities may levy property taxes upon voter approval. Regional Water and Sewer Authorities may levy property taxes upon voter approval.
Oregon:	Water Supply Authorities may levy property taxes upon voter approval.
Rhode Island:	Warwick Sewer Authority may levy property taxes upon voter approval.
South Dakota:	Regional Airport Authorities may levy property taxes.
Texas:	Metropolitan Rapid Transit Authorities may levy sales taxes upon voter approval. Regional Transportation Authorities may levy sales taxes upon voter approval.
Washington:	Air Pollution Control Authorities may levy property taxes upon voter approval. Metropolitan municipal corporations may levy sales taxes and motor-vehicle excise taxes upon voter approval.

have over a hundred different legal classifications for their public authorities and special districts. There are, however, a more limited number of basic categories of characteristics that may help in distinguishing one kind of corporate entity from another. For example, an entity may be more or less dependent on its "parent" government; it may be a statewide or more locally based corporation; it may perform one of a basic list of functions, and it may use revenue-backed financing or tax-based financing. These categories of characteristics are discussed in the sections to follow.

Inter-Governmental Dependence

There is no sharp dividing line between dependent and independent government corporations. Each one is a subsidiary organization of a parent government. Theoretically, at least, the relationship between parent and subsidiary may be altered at any time by legislative change in the charter that states the powers and responsibilities of the corporation. Inter-governmental dependence ranges between two extremes of highly dependent and highly independent corporations.

Highly Dependent Corporations. In practice, the most dependent corporations are those that rely on parent governments for both leadership and financing. For example, the New York City Transit Authority (NYCTA) is administered by the board of a parent corporation, the Metropolitan Transit Authority. Most of its capital costs have been financed through city and state bond issues. Title to transit properties operated by NYCTA is vested with New York City.

A dependent corporation's board may be made up entirely of officials from some parent government entity or directed in their activities by such officials (e.g., a city council). Financially, the highly dependent corporation typically has no independent power either to tax or borrow, but must be supported by funds appropriated by parent units (either for operating and capital expenses, or to support debt service for moral obligation or "double-barrelled" (financing). Some financially dependent corporations may be able to recommend appropriation levels, or add-ons to the parent government tax rate to cover service costs. Other highly dependent corporations have their budgets developed by outside officials.

Dependent corporations can be used by regular government units to move deficit-ridden enterprise activities, such as mass transit "off budget." Dependent corporations also provide at least a measure of separate and insulated governance (sometimes simply the appearance of separation), and institutionalize segregated fund accounting for enterprise activities.

Highly Independent Corporations. The most independent corporations, on the other hand, enjoy a more complete assortment of freedoms associated with separate corporate status, including the rights to sue and be sued, contract in their own names, obtain and dispose of property, raise and retain revenues (that do not flow through government treasury and appropriation channels), determine the price of services, and finance capital improvements (through borrowing, taxation, fees, and so on). They have their own governing boards and establish their own administrative structure free from many of the rules and procedures that constrain the activities of regular government agencies. Appointed boards made up primarily of private citizens, have not been shown to be more (or less) dependent on parent governments than popularly elected boards.

Inter-Governmental Aid. One useful measure of inter-governmental dependence is inter-governmental aid relative to other revenues. In general, federal aid has played a larger role in special district revenues than in the revenues of any other kind of local government (in 1984, 26¢ for every dollar of locally raised district revenue came from the federal government). Cities were next highest in dependence on federal aid (15¢ for every dollar of local revenue). (See the figures published by the Advisory Commission on Intergovernmental Relations.) And these figures represent a decline from a peak in 1981.

State aid has traditionally been a smaller, but more stable source of assistance—9¢ for every dollar of local revenue in 1984. But more state assistance comes in the form of subsidies for services specifically identified as meeting social objectives and externalities. In addition, unplanned and largely uncounted state subsidies are caused by authority underestimates of costs or overestimation of demand, and by various tax exemptions and land use activities by districts and authorities.

Geographical Scope

Regional Corporations. Regional corporations carry out functions having state-wide or multi-state impacts, or serve areas considerably larger than that of a standard metropolitan area (e.g., river basins). These are the largest and most powerful types of authorities and districts, at least in terms of their impacts on population and territory.

The governing boards of these entities are typically appointed by one or more governors, or by a governor and other regional officials representing people affected by the corporation's actions. Typical of corporations in this category are power authorities, bi-state or regional transportation authorities or districts, river basin commissions, state-wide infrastructure banks, and major highway authorities.

Prominent examples include the Port Authority of New York and New Jersey, the Illinois Regional Transportation Authority, and the Southern California Rapid Transit District.

Metropolitan Corporations. Metropolitan corporations serve heavily urbanized areas that may, and usually do, contain numerous other governmental units, including other government corporations. These entities perform many urban functions and serve a major part of the population or territory of metropolitan areas, both incorporated and unincorporated. Some are authorities or districts that provide transportation, housing, redevelopment services, sewage disposal facilities, water supply systems, and mass transit. Prominent examples of this kind of district include the Sacramento Municipal Utility District, the Greater Chicago Metropolitan Sanitary District, and the Philadelphia Housing Authority.

Urban Fringe Corporations. Urban fringe corporations operate in the unincorporated urban territory adjacent to cities (or have been annexed into metropolitan areas but continue to exist while their debt is paid off by the new "parent" government). These tend to be small entities, almost always calling themselves districts, often with overlapping or coterminus boundaries. They often have small boards directly elected by property owners or taxpayers, small staffs, and rely on property taxes or assessments for revenues. Many also issue bonds. Although dating back to the 19th century, these corporations experienced rapid growth in numbers in the 1940s and 1950s. They continue to be the fastest growing and most controversial type of government corporation.

Rural Corporations. These entities, again usually referred to as special districts, are the most numerous of all types of government corporations. Most of them serve rural communities beyond the urban fringe areas, or provide improvements to agricultural land (or both), and encompass a wide range of potential functions: sewage, roads, irrigation, water conservation, reclamation, drainage, levee, soil, weeds, pests, electric power, and so on. (In some states, such as California, formerly rural districts now serve urban areas.)

Functional Specialization

Single Purpose. State and local government corporations carrying out public works functions as defined for this study are classified according to function by the 1982 Census of Governments into eight categories:

(1) Airports—Construction, maintenance, operation, and support of airport facilities.

(2) Highways—Construction, maintenance, and operation of highways, streets, and related structures, including toll highways, bridges, tunnels, ferries, street lighting, and snow and ice removal.

(3) Natural Resources—Conservation, promotion, and development of natural resources; includes irrigation, drainage, and flood control.

(4) Sewerage—Provision of sanitary and storm sewers and sewage disposal facilities and services.

(5) Sanitation Other Than Sewerage—Street cleaning, solid waste collection and disposal, and provision of sanitary landfills.

(6) Transit—Construction, maintenance, operation and support of public mass transit systems—bus, commuter rail, light rail, or subway systems.

(7) Water Supply—Operation and maintenance of water supply systems including acquisition and distribution of water to the general public or to other local governments for domestic or industrial use.

(8) Water Transport and Terminals—Construction, maintenance, operation and support of canals and other waterways, harbors, docks, wharves, and related marine terminal facilities.

A number of possible single-purpose entities are missing from the Bureau's list, including bond banks and other corporate entities that carry out financing activities such as borrowing and relending to other government entities. Also missing from the Census Bureau list is any mention of what might be called "functional mode." In other words, a government corporation might carry out financing, construction, or operation only, within any given functional area.

Multi-Purpose. Examples of multi-function entities abound. Regional and municipal corporations typically originate as single-purpose entities in one of the functional categories described previously. However, when these entities become successful they grow and often add new functions.

Noteworthy examples of multi-function regional corporations include the New Jersey Highway Authority, which constructed the Garden State Arts Center on land it owned; the Port Authority of New York and New Jersey, which now operates seven marine terminals, four airports, two heliports, two tunnels, four bridges, two bus terminals, the twin office towers of the World Trade Center, and the PATH mass transportation system; and the Massachusetts Port Authority, which operates

Boston-Logan International Airport, the Tobin Memorial Bridge, various port properties, and the Boston Fish Pier.

Urban fringe corporations typically began existence as single-purpose districts, providing water, sewerage, fire, or garbage collection. Beginning in the late 1950s, however, these entities were increasingly given responsibility for providing a large assortment of services. Variously titled "municipal districts," "improvement associations" (Connecticut), "public service districts" (South Carolina), "metropolitan districts" (Michigan), "community service districts" (California), and "municipal utility districts" (Texas), these entities may provide street lighting and sprinkling, fire protection, tree planting and care, sidewalk, drain, and sewer construction and maintenance, police protection, garbage and refuse collection, and water supply. Many are interim local governments for urbanizing land, subsequently annexed into existing city or county governments.

Different types of rural corporations also have a tradition of serving more than one function. Irrigation districts, for example (also called water improvement, water conservation, or reclamation districts), are common in the 17 western states (where most irrigated farming takes place). Their services often include drainage, power development, flood control and water for domestic use. Typically, these districts may make assessments and issue debt.

Primary Revenue Generating and Debt Financing Mode

The matrix in Table 19.2 indicates possible relationships between revenue generation and debt financing. Isolated state studies exist indicating how many state and local government corporations can be classified in each of these cells, according to statutory authorizations. A 1979

TABLE 19.2
Possible Combinations of Revenue Generating Debt Financing Methods

	Revenue Generation	
Debt Financing	Taxes (& other revenues)	Non-tax Revenues
General Obligation Borrowing		**
Revenue-backed Borrowing		
Both		**

**Non-taxing corporate entities such as the New York State Urban Development Corporation, the Illinois Regional Transportation Authority and others, have statutory authorizations to issue "general obligation bonds" backed by the "full faith and credit" of the corporation—which in these two cases refers to any and all project revenues.

survey in Illinois, for example, reported that of the 54 districts and authorities engaged in transportation provision, 37 were authorized to levy property taxes, as well as issue both GO and revenue bonds. Eight of these taxing entities were authorized to issue only revenue bonds. Eight non-taxing entities were authorized to issue only revenue bonds, while one non-taxing entity was authorized to issue GO bonds (secured by any and all corporate revenues).

No studies exist which classify these entities according to primary revenue generation and debt financing methods, but some generalizations are possible concerning revenues and financing.

Tax-Based Financing Corporate taxing entities—the majority of which identify themselves as "districts"—typically may levy taxes limited by rate. Many of these entities issue "general obligation" debt secured by a tax levy, but satisfactory tax collection experience is vital in satisfying investors—there is typically no possibility of an overlevy to allow for delinquent tax payments. Many taxing corporations are authorized to issue revenue bonds, backed by project revenues, as well as general obligation bonds. Such entities may issue revenue bonds payable from gross revenues of the user charge, levying a tax for operating expenses.

Non Tax-Based Financing. Most large corporate entities, whether authorized to levy taxes or not, fund much of their capital improvements through the issuance of revenue bonds. Revenue debt restricts internal financing flexibility somewhat because project revenues are segregated and unavailable for general-fund purposes. Interest costs for revenue debt also tend to be higher because of the somewhat riskier nature of the sources of repayment—revenue bond issues sometimes require "credit enhancements" such as bank letters of credit, surety bonds from insurance companies, municipal bond insurance, or pledges of state financial support for debt service payments. By and large, however, these limitations are more than balanced by the freedoms afforded by this type of financing: it allows debt issuers to bypass statutory or constitutional limits on tax-supported debt, avoid the need to have voters approve "full faith and credit" bond issues (as many government corporations limited by law to tax-based financing are required to do), and is consistent with demands that the cost of public projects be borne by project beneficiaries.

User charges and lease payments are the two traditional types of project revenues used to secure revenue bonds issued by corporations, but other kinds of revenue may also be pledged in support of such. For example, corporate entities in some states may pledge special tax assessments as security. In California, courts have ruled that special assessments are not taxes, and therefore are not subject to the voter approvals and debt limit restrictions that normally affect tax-based financing in that state. Similarly, states such as California and Minnesota exempt tax increment financing bonds from voter approval and debt limits. Tax increment revenues may also be used in support of revenue bond issues in those states, but these bonds now also face significant new restrictions under the Tax Reform Act of 1986.

Government subsidy, particularly federal aid, plays a significant role in the capital financing activities of many kinds of state and local government corporations. For example, the Federal Aviation Administration provides funding to many airport authorities and districts for the development of capital plans, and the Army Corps of Engineers shares responsibility for port development with port authorities and districts. Until the early 1980s, the federal government was committed to providing up to 55% of the total capital costs of qualified communities' sewer systems, under the Clean Water Act of 1982 and its amendments.

In general, federal aid appears to have been concentrated largely on capital expenditures, rather than maintenance and rehabilitation, sometimes leading to serious shortfalls in operating revenues, for example, in sewage treatment plants.

THE CORPORATE ROLE IN PUBLIC WORKS PROVISION

Of the many functional areas in which state and local government corporations operate, perhaps the most important in terms of public borrowing, has to do with the very general area of public works—the construction and maintenance of major public facilities, and the provision of public works-related services. The following sections discuss the roles played by these entities in selected public works sectors, including water supply and waste water treatment, solid waste disposal, and transportation (airports, seaports, mass transit, highways, roads, bridges and tunnels).

Functional Sectors

Special districts and public authorities address the problems of financing the provision of public works in a variety of ways, depending largely upon the particular public works sector in which the entities operate. This section discusses very briefly the contributions to public works by districts and authorities in different public works sectors.

Water and Sewer Districts

Finances. Water and sewer districts are among the financially strongest of all special districts. Like public power utilities they are usually monopolies, typically with almost complete control over rate making. Basic revenue streams are usually derived from user charges and connection charges. Sometimes districts are able to have local ordinances passed to require mandatory connections to the district's system by all residents. In some jurisdictions, water quality standards by the local board of health may in effect require connections. In many cases, sewer charges are based on water usage.

Water districts may exist as rural irrigation or improvement districts, common in the West and Far West, which serve as retail marketers of water obtained from both local and distant sources. They may also act as water wholesale collection systems, involved in the joint development of a common supply of water resources. In these cases, the wholesaler (a district or authority) becomes a borrower on behalf of smaller entities, which contract to assume shares of the wholesaler's operating costs and indebtedness. The largest wholesalers are active in the debt markets, and typically enjoy reputations as strong credits.

Sewer districts range from small rural water districts, to huge regional "wholesale" sewer authorities that construct and operate regional treatment facilities. The latter often provide wholesale treatment services while municipalities operate and maintain local collection systems for commercial, industrial, and residential use.

Water and sewer revenue bonds—especially those issued by districts or authorities with significant operating histories (five years or more)—are considered among the safest municipal investments and are relatively easy to market.

Types and Functions. Today, there are many different types of special water districts—it is almost impossible to generalize about this form of government corporation. Many state laws authorize the formation of several different types of water districts under general law. In addition, many special water districts have their own distinctive and characteristically complex statutory charters.

Most states have both chosen to expand the purposes of existing special water districts and to create new categories of special water districts to serve increasingly large geographic areas and fill a variety of purposes. The new type of district may, in fact, encompass all or part of existing districts (as well as other water supply areas). This results in layers of districts and a patchwork of authority over water in the same area.

"Development districts" constitute a variety of water district that has proliferated over the past 30 years. They are usually created in much the same way as western special water districts—through the petition by a majority of the land owners or, depending on the jurisdiction, by the land owner or owners who own sufficient land to be a majority of the assessed value of the land in the area. This type of district is heavily associated with land development and can most frequently be found on the fringe of urban areas.

Solid Waste Special Districts

Finances. There are a number of distinctly different sorts of solid waste special districts or authorities. The first is the garbage district (though they may operate under other names), which is likely to be a local government taxing district rather than a district with any separate authority. A second form of district, the one much more likely to issue municipal debt, has a resource recovery project as parts of its program.

Garbage districts generate revenues from service charges or benefit assessments; sometimes these revenues are used to pay private firms who contract with the district to provide pick-up services. Waste-to-energy projects may derive a portion of their revenues from the production and sale of energy. Revenue bond financing for new recovery projects must be supported by independent feasibility studies indicating the likelihood of revenues necessary to make the project economically feasible. A number of communities have faced legal problems as a result of their support for waste-to-energy projects undertaken by independent districts or authorities.

Types and Functions. Generally, districts established for the purpose of providing for solid waste management services may be authorized to provide for the collection and disposal of solid wastes and/or authorized to construct, operate and maintain solid waste treatment and disposal facilities, including resource recovery facilities and facilities that burn solid waste to produce energy. They may be established under state law, by ordinance of one or more contiguous municipalities (e.g., in Iowa, Kentucky, Louisiana, Minnesota, Montana, New Hampshire, New Jersey, New York, and Vermont) or on petition of electors (e.g., in Illinois). Approval of the voters may be required (e.g., in Illinois, Louisiana, and Rhode Island). The governing board may be appointed (usually by the establishing body) or elected.

These districts may be known as garbage districts, solid waste management districts, solid waste disposal districts, or regional refuse disposal districts or authorities.

Airport Authorities and Districts

Finances. Airport authorities or districts, like municipal airports, typically derive revenues from terminal rentals and landing fees, usually secured by special contracts, known as "use agreements," with airline carriers. Concessions and other revenues generated by the airport facilities are also secured by these contracts. Airport operators also may receive grant-in-aid planning and development funds from Federal Airport and Airways Trust Funds.

Airline use-agreements have traditionally accounted for most airport revenues, and have secured most airport authority revenue bond issues. In these kinds of financings, the reactions by investors (and the cost of borrowing to the issuer) is based largely on an analysis of the creditworthiness of the airlines involved.

Types and Functions. A survey of airport management structures conducted by the Institute of Public Administration for United Airlines in 1986 indicated that 56 of 130 airport operators across the country were public authorities—by far the largest single category of governmental management. A 1985 survey by United Airlines as to forms of management among the 25 busiest airports, revealed that 11 of the airports are managed by public authorities. The list of airport operators surveyed in 1986 includes entities calling themselves boards, commissions, departments, agencies, authorities, corporations, trusts, and, of course, simply airports. Every conceivable level of government is represented, including bi- and tri-city organizations.

Twenty-three states have passed general enabling laws to allow for the creation of airport authorities or districts, usually by the governing boards of one or more local government entities. In Illinois, a circuit court judge can create airport authorities on petition of voters and after a hearing and local referendum. Florida, Maine, Nevada, Virginia, and South Carolina have all created airport authorities by special legislation.

Port Authorities and Districts

Finances. Over 130 domestic seaports currently provide a variety of port-related facilities in the United States. Most of these facilities, including almost all large port operations, are managed by special districts or authorities. But while most seaports are managed by port authorities, most port authorities are not exclusively concerned with seaports. Some port authorities have no sea or river port responsibilities at all. These entities have traditionally carried out economic development activities in many communities—acquiring land, financing and/or constructing buildings, installing capital equipment, selling or leasing these properties to private businesses, and issuing industrial development revenue bond debt.

Principal revenues from port operations include docking and loading fees, terminal facilities rentals, concessions, and so on. Facilities for handling containerized cargo have become extremely important for attracting and keeping shipping business at most large ports, and many U.S. ports now handle containerized as well as bulk cargo. Smaller ports that handle bulk cargo exclusively have found themselves at the economic mercy of volatile markets for bulk commodities like coal and fertilizer. Ports also derive revenues directly from specialized services and facilities, and indirectly from the increased business in shipping that such specialized facilities often provide.

Port authorities with a variety of different kinds of operations typically find it much easier to carry out capital financing than authorities with seaport responsibilities only. Many of these large, multi-function authorities are now using pooled bond reserving, a technique pioneered by the Port Authority of New York. Pooled reserves involve the establishment of a single common bond reserve fund into which each project's revenues are deposited. All bonds are repaid from that fund.

Types and Functions. The largest and most financially secure port authorities account for most of the port-related revenue bond financing carried out over the last two decades. Those authorities operate port facilities in New York City (the Port Authority of New York and New Jersey), Boston, Jacksonville, Los Angeles, New Orleans, Long Beach, Oakland, San Francisco, Portland (Oregon), Seattle, and Tacoma, Washington.

Highway, Road, Bridge, and Tunnel Districts and Authorities

Finances. Numerous special district governments exist across the country for the construction, management, and maintenance of highways, roads, bridges, and tunnels. These areas of special district activity present tremendous variety in terms of organizational forms and financing techniques. In general, the financing needs—and challenges—in this area are among the greatest faced by all types of local governments.

Over the last 30 years, the primary state source of transportation revenues has been motor fuel taxes. These taxes now account for about half of all state transportation revenues. Today, the revenue sources of authorities and districts that build and maintain highways, roads, bridges, and tunnels may be classified as user charges (other than fuel taxes) such as tolls, and charges on benefiting properties (such as special benefit assessments or tax increments).

Special benefit assessment is a financing technique that is usually applied to road or street improvements, often in unincorporated areas not otherwise serviced by a metropolitan department of transportation (although assessment districts are now being used more frequently in cities). Whereas turnpikes are typically operated by independent districts or authorities, benefit assessment districts are often dependent districts, in the sense that they exist under the administrative and financial control of a parent entity.

Types and Functions. The major toll road authorities account for most of the major toll-supported highway construction, operation and maintenance in the United States. Some "highway districts," such as those in California and Georgia also collect tolls. Toll bridge authorities are used in South Carolina, New York, Vermont, Missouri, New Jersey, Alabama, Pennsylvania, New Hampshire, Arkansas, Colorado, and Virginia.

Road districts, which raise revenues via benefit assessments as well as tax levies in some cases, exist in a large number of states—often as dependent districts that provide services or collect money under the administrative and financial control of parent government entities.

Many independent road districts exist as well, and may be called road improvement districts (Arkansas, Nevada), county paving districts (South Dakota), road assessment districts (Oregon), good road districts (Idaho), etc. Road improvement districts in Idaho, South Dakota, Oregon, and Arkansas may levy property taxes. Most independent road districts may issue revenue bonds.

Mass Transit

Finances. Mass transit is not typically a self-sustaining enterprise activity, and in this sense it is different from the kind of function traditionally identified with public authorities or special districts. Nevertheless, most mass transit passenger miles are travelled on facilities owned and operated by authorities or districts (52% of those miles are travelled in the Chicago and New York City metropolitan areas alone).

The overwhelming source of mass transit revenues is direct operating or capital assistance by federal, state, or local governments. Another form of funding may be from a dedicated sales tax; Atlanta, New Orleans, and Austin use this technique. The New York City Metropolitan Transportation Authority has received budget surpluses from the Triborough Bridge and Tunnel Authority and some of the latter's net revenues have been pledged as security for MTA revenue bonds. In 1984, only $4.4 billion of the $15.9 billion total spent on mass transportation came from transportation operating revenues.

Most transit operating revenues (apart from governmental aid) come from fares, but a small and growing percentage of revenues is derived from the use of a variety of innovative financing techniques that have been experimented with over the last decade, including connector fees, negotiated investment, benefit assessments, joint venture approaches, and so on.

Types and Functions. Table 19.3 ranks the top ten states in terms of total estimated operating costs of urban transit services for 1986. Costs incurred by these states represent roughly two-thirds of all U.S. costs for urban public transportation. In each of these states, public authorities or special districts play primary roles in transit service provision (major operators are indicated).

The legislatures of a number of states have authorized, through enabling legislation, the efforts of local governments to form authorities

TABLE 19.3
Total Estimated Operating Costs for Urbanized Public Transit

State	Total Estimated Operating Costs*	Principal Public Transit Operator
New York	4,057,200,000	Metropolitan Transportation Authority (Various subsidiary and related authorities) Port Authority of NY and NJ (PATH)
California	1,622,236,000	San Francisco Bay Area Rapid Transit District Southern Calif. Rapid Transit District (Various other Transit Districts)
Illinois	994,700,000	Chicago Transit Authority Regional Transportation Authority (Various Mass Transit Districts and Urban Transportation Districts)
Pennsylvania	673,000,000	Southeastern Pennsylvania Transportation Authority (Various Metropolitan Transportation Authorities)
Maryland	577,353,000	Washington Metropolitan Area Transit Authority
New Jersey	499,600,000	New Jersey Transit Corporation
Massachusetts	488,669,000	Massachusetts Bay Transportation Authority
Ohio	267,946,000	(Various Regional Transit Authorities)
Texas	247,300,000	(Various Metropolitan Rapid Transit Authorities)
Michigan	209,450,000	Southeastern Michigan Transportation Authority (Various Metropolitan Transportation Authorities and Mass Transportation Authorities)
	$9,637,454,000	

or districts to provide mass transit services. For example, voters and legislative bodies in any county in Wisconsin may form a "metropolitan transit authority." In Michigan and Indiana, "metropolitan transportation authorities" or "regional transportation authorities" may be created by legislative initiative of participating counties. Cities in Indiana may also create "public transportation corporations." Cities and/or counties in Ohio may create "regional transit authorities." Iowa cities, individually or in partnerships, may form transit authorities. "Local mass transit districts" may be created in Illinois by referendum in one or more of the cities or counties serviced by the district.

Nation-Wide Statistics

Census Bureau Statistics. The latest, most comprehensive figures available on the financial activities of state and local government corporations are those published by the Census Bureau's Census of Governments after its 1982 census. These figures refer to "independent" corporate entities and do not include entities that the Bureau regards as "subordinate" agencies of regular government. Unfortunately, from a public financial point of view, this latter category is of considerable interest, mainly because these entities tend to be corporations created for debt financing, but over which parent governments maintain more control.

Numbers of Entities. According to the Bureau's reports, "independent special districts" carrying out public works provision (transportation, water resources, and waste management) can be found in the District of Columbia and every state with the exceptions of Hawaii and Alaska (although the Alaska Bond Bank Authority does in fact generate investment in these functions). Of the 28,588 special districts counted by the Bureau of the Census in 1982, 10,418 or 36.4%, were districts directly engaged in public works provision. However, 3,089 of these districts are identified as having virtually no expenditures by the Bureau, and are considered inactive for the purposes of this discussion.

Expenditures. Like the number of special districts nationwide, the totals for those involved in public works provision have continued to grow since 1972—although the rate of growth has rapidly declined. From 1972 to 1982, the number of active, single-function districts and authorities of this kind increased by 2,682.

The amount spent by all special districts (regardless of classification) on public works has also grown precipitously over the decade between 1972 and 1982. The rate of that growth has declined but at a much less rapid rate than that of the increase in the numbers of special districts. In 1972, the amount spent by all special districts on public works was $3.63 billion. By 1977, that figure had risen by $3.99 billion (or 110%) to $7.62 billion. From 1977 to 1982, the figure increased by $5.43 billion (or 71%) to a total of $13.06 billion.

In each of the following states, special districts account for at least $300 million in expenditures on public works. Taken together special districts in these states account for $10.26 billion in such expenditures, or 78.6% of all expenditures on public works by districts or authorities in 1982:

1.	California	$ 2,969,200,000
2.	Illinois	1,405,300,000
3.	Pennsylvania	989,800,000
4.	Texas	840,400,000
5.	Massachusetts	782,400,000
6.	Dist. of Columbia	753,000,000
7.	New York	534,600,000
8.	Washington	439,000,000
9.	Georgia	427,300,000
10.	Ohio	425,900,000
11.	New Jersey	396,000,000
12.	Colorado	300,900,000
	TOTAL	$10,263,800,000

Regional Breakdowns. Over the entire period from 1972 to 1982, the Plains states experienced the largest increase in the total number of special districts engaged in public works provision, with 534 (a 78% increase from 1972). The South Eastern states, on the other hand, experienced the largest percentage increase in special districts, with 190% (an increase of 516 districts).

The far Western states experienced the largest increase in the amount spent by special districts on public works provision, with $2.48 billion (an increase of 113%). (Neither Alaska nor Hawaii contributed to this total—California alone experienced a larger increase than that of any other region.) The South Eastern states, however, experienced the largest percentage increase in special district expenditures, with 1148% (an increase of $1.06 billion).

Functional Breakdowns. The number of special districts spending on natural resources (primarily water resources) showed the largest increase, 1,182, from 1972 to 1982. That figure also represents the largest percentage increase, 451%, over that period. The percentage increase in special districts spending on transit is the second highest over this period, at 403%. The number of special districts spending on water transport showed the small increase from 1972 to 1982, both in terms of numbers (39) and percentage (34%).

In terms of amounts expended for different categories of public works over the period from 1972 to 1982, total expenditures for transit (leveraged by federal grants) increased most, with a gain of over $4.68 billion. This also represents the largest percentage increase, at 427%.

Special districts in the Mid Eastern states have spent far more on airports, highways, and transit than have districts in any other region since 1972. The Far Western states have spent more on water transport, water supply and natural resources than any other region since 1972. Expenditures on sanitation and sewerage are somewhat more tightly bunched among various regions.

Capital Expenditures. States are relying less on special districts and authorities for capital expenditures in support of different categories of public works. In six of the eight categories, percentages were higher in 1972 than in 1982, reflecting the fact that state and local capital expenditures for these categories of public works have increased relative to those of special districts.

Revenues. Nationally, categories of revenue "other" than taxes and user charges—primarily inter-governmental aid—have increased by about 6.5 times in the decade. The percentage of such revenues in total revenues for these districts increased from 30% in 1972 to 50% in 1982. The roles of taxes and charges have remained stable over the 10-year period, with a 2.5:1 ratio of charges to taxes over this period.

Debt. The roles of revenue debt and general obligation (primarily tax-secured) debt in the financial activities of these special districts and authorities have changed dramatically. In 1972, the difference between the amounts of outstanding revenue and GO debt was $470.5 million—in favor of GO debt. By 1982, the nationwide total of special district public works-related revenue debt outstanding had increased to 1.9 times that of GO debt—a difference of $6.2 billion.

"Dependent" Corporations. Because the Census of Governments classifies as "subordinate agencies" many entities identifying themselves as districts and authorities, and consequently does not count the financial information relating to those entities in any special district category, the Census information must be supplemented in order to understand accurately the full role of government corporations in any public financial activity. For example, a recent study of government corporations engaged in public works provision used data from Moody's Investors Service to identify specific districts and authorities engaged in public works investment, which are counted as subordinate agencies by the Census Bureau.

The study identified only 237 "dependent" corporations—compared with over 10,000 listed by the Census Bureau as active public works districts—but the debt outstanding accounted for by these units is equal to 62% of the outstanding debt accounted for by the Census Bureau's 10,000. The entities identified averaged $54 million in debt outstanding in 1982, compared with $2.8 million for entities listed by the Census Bureau. All of these entities are considered by the investment community to possess corporate identities for the purposes of borrowing in the capital markets, contract obligations, and asset management.

In 15 states, the outstanding debt totals for these "subordinate agencies" are higher than that for all of the districts defined as independent by the Bureau—New York, Alabama, and Florida are outstanding examples of this phenomenon.

ADVANTAGES AND DISADVANTAGES TO STATES AND LOCALITIES IN USING THE CORPORATE FORM

Advantages

The use of corporate entities for carrying out governmental functions is said to offer several primary advantages over regular, general purpose government, including:

(1) Managerial and budgetary speed, efficiency, and flexibility for enterprise-type government activities and large-scale construction projects;

(2) Increased access to bond markets;

(3) Institutionalized fund accounting segregation for enterprise activities;

(4) Business-like and self-supporting management—facilitates application of user charges to mixed goods;

(5) Separate and insulated governance (insulation from political pressures and special interests)—necessary where full cost pricing and cost recovery have been established as guiding policy;

(6) Allows precise service district lines to be drawn, insuring that beneficiaries pay for services (even if the entity must have a jurisdiction spanning several government units);

(7) Legal clarity—use of an entity that can sue or be sued.

Some of these characteristics of public corporations can be given to line agencies in order to allow them to undertake enterprise-type activities efficiently without giving up executive and legislative controls. For example, regional or local enterprises or separate executive agencies can be created by state governments and administered by representative commissions, inter-governmental boards, or executive directors appointed by and reporting to the governor, mayor or county executive. All of these entities may have special powers designated by statute, without independent corporate status.

Segregated enterprise funds can be administered by executive departments. Such funds can facilitate protected financial integrity, revenue bond borrowing (if provided for by state constitution or statutes), without requiring separate administrative bureaucracies.

However, some of the advantages outlined above can only be achieved by government corporations. Many state constitutions prohibit regular government units from enjoying the sort of insulation from politics (or special interests), legal clarity, adequate access to the bond markets, and other characteristics that only corporate forms can provide. As a practical matter, multi-jurisdictional impacts and business-like management are often realistically possible only with corporate entities.

Disadvantages

Literally thousands of government corporations function efficiently and in an accountable fashion. Yet there are enduring criticisms of what some observers claim to be the abuses of the corporate form in some states. Some of the most significant of these criticisms are discussed below:

(1) *Insulation from community influence*—critics charge that, in spite of sophisticated planning capabilities, large government corporations have generally been less responsive to citizen and community groups than units of regular government.

(2) *Corporations may engage in "back door" financing*—their independent tax-exempt borrowing capabilities are used often to bypass constitutional and statutory limits on public borrowing, including referenda required in many states in support of general obligation borrowing.

(3) *Insulation from broader capital planning*—they tend to try to protect themselves from the most difficult and subsidy-dependent service responsibilities by promoting their isolation from broader interactive planning systems and tradeoffs.

(4) *Negative impacts on state credit and finances*—the credit position of some states, such as New York, is precarious precisely because of huge volumes of outstanding corporation debt; excessive use of government corporations may lead to "creaming," or removing revenue producing activities from government budgets, leaving deficit operations to fall more heavily on taxpayers or appropriations.

(5) *Resistance to change*—state and local officials sometimes find out too late that corporate powers and structure can usually be changed only by statutory amendment—not by executive order. Such changes may also be limited by legal covenants entered into by the corporation for borrowing and other contracts.

(6) *Vulnerability to special interests*—the isolation and independence of government corporations may create pockets of public activity susceptible to narrow special interest control and/or corrupt business practices.

(7) *Broad economic considerations*—slightly higher interest cost makes more expensive the capital improvements funded via revenue bonds, typically used by corporate entities for financing large projects.

Conclusions

Three conclusions have fairly firm grounding in the available evidence. First, districts and authorities have been useful instruments in carrying out government functions, such as public works provision, by increasing access to bond market capital, by timely construction management, and by providing for precise administrative and financial arrangements for services that must be provided in areas not confined to a single regular government jurisdiction. Restrictive aspects of state and local constitutions and law relative to general government financing and procurement increase the attractiveness of the corporate form in these ways.

Second, the primary weakness of the corporate form identified by most state and local government commentators and study commissions is the tendency for authorities, districts, commissions, and the like to remain isolated from broader policy planning frameworks.

Third, officials at all levels of regular government need much better information on the activities and impacts of state and local government corporations in order to arrive at cost-effective policy decisions regarding their use for raising money in the capital markets, constructing and maintaining public facilities, and providing public services.

Part Four

MUNICIPAL MARKET
TECHNIQUES AND INNOVATIONS

CHAPTER 20

Innovations in the Tax-Exempt Market

John E. Petersen
Government Finance Group

State and local governments depend on the securities markets to raise the majority of funds needed for large-scale capital projects and programs, as well as to meet their cash flow needs.[1] Both the financial markets for these securities and the ways they are tapped by governmental borrowers are subject to changes (sometimes rapid and severe) in response to the changing economy, the purposes for which governments borrow, and the tax laws and other laws and regulations that influence the financial environment.

Although seeds were planted earlier in many cases, the rate and scope of changes during the past decade are unprecedented, for it was a period that saw much innovation in the design and marketing of the tax-exempt security.[2] Some of the innovations were fleeting and did not last

---

[1] By the late 1980s, it is estimated over half of all capital outlays of state and local governments were being debt financed and the trend was upward. See John E. Petersen *The Future of Infrastructure,* Washington, DC: Government Finance Officers Association, Government Finance Research Center (1989), Chapter II-2.

[2] The terms "tax-exempt" and "municipal" are used interchangeably to refer to obligations of state and local governments and their agencies and certain other borrowers (namely, 501(c)3 not-for-profit entities) that receive preferential treatment on the interest income of their obligations under the federal tax code. Earlier, useful reviews of

long, but several have proved enduring and have transformed the classic fixed-income debt instrument and the way it is offered to investors. Underlying the innovations was the need to attract new investors during periods of market turmoil, and this meant the introduction of greater flexibility in how investors and governmental borrowers trade off risks and rewards.

The chapter starts with brief descriptions of the municipal bond market, the demand for and supply of municipal securities, and how these intersecting forces interact to cause changes in the design of instruments and the nature of transactions. Next, there is a discussion of how tax-exempt rates are determined and the components of risk, followed by an analysis of how new risk and reward tradeoffs are accomplished in the creation of innovative techniques. Subsequent discussion covers several major categories of innovations in instrument and security design: tax-exempt commercial paper, variable-rates, putable securities, call options, refunding, zeros, and varieties of credit enhancements. None of these topics is treated in depth: the array of options presented demonstrates the vitality and dynamism of a securities market where governments must configure their capital-raising activities to comport with the latest trends in investment demands arising from the private sector. The chapter ends with a prospective on where the market is heading and the implications for governmental borrowers.

THE SUPPLY OF TAX-EXEMPT SECURITIES

The tax-exempt securities market has changed dramatically over the past decade. Figure 20.1 presents a summary of new issues of long-term and short-term tax-exempt securities since 1981. In terms of overall volume, the tax-exempt market exploded with new issues in the early 1980s, with total sales of both short-term and long-term bonds trebling from $81 billion in 1981 to $224 billion in 1985. The passage of the Tax Reform Act of 1986, was a watershed for the municipal market as for many other forms of financial activity that had been boosted by tax policies of the early decade and the growth of the financial markets in general. After 1986, it receded and then resumed a more leisurely pattern of growth

---

the changes in the tax-exempt bond market are found in John Petersen and Wesley Hough *Creative Capital Financing for State and Local Governments*, Chicago: Municipal Finance Officers Association (1983); John Petersen and Ronald Forbes *Innovative Capital Financing*, Chicago: American Planning Association (1985); Ronald Forbes, "Innovations in Tax-Exempt Finance" and John Petersen and Ronald Forbes "The Impact of Tax Reform on the Tax Exempt Securities Market" in J. Peter Williamson *Investment Banking Handbook*, New York: John Wiley (1988).

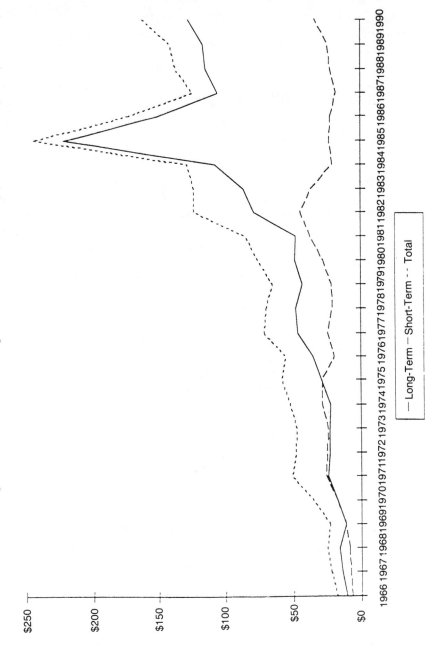

FIGURE 20.1
Volume of New Issues of Long- and Short-Term Municipal Securities—1966–1990 (in billions of dollars)

— Long-Term — Short-Term -- Total

TABLE 20.1
Long-Term Tax-Exempt Bonds by Size of Issue and Number of Issues
(1988 Data)

Par Amount ($ Millions)	Volume ($ Billions)	% of Total $ Volume	# of Issues	% of Total # of Issues
0.0– .9	$ .67	0.6%	1,419	18.7%
1.0– 4.9	7.78	6.8	3,019	39.9
5.0– 9.9	8.32	7.3	1,205	15.9
10.0–49.9	30.94	27.1	1,402	18.5
50.0–99.9	18.82	16.5	279	3.9
100.0 and greater	47.79	41.8	248	3.3

Source: IDD/PSA Municipal Database.

through the remainder of the decade, reaching a level $180 billion in combined volume for the year of 1990.

Understanding the various sectors of the market is important to understanding the innovation that occurred within its boundaries over the past decade. By convention, short-term debt is defined as debt with a stated final maturity at the time of sale of 13 months or less. One of the consequences of the creative financing of the 1980s is that distinctions between long- and short-term debt are blurred as the payment securities have taken on characteristics of both. Thus, the decline in short-term debt issuances in the mid-1980s is partly explained by the substitution of long-term debt with short-term features, and the term "long-term" speaks to the nominal maturity at the time of issuance as opposed to any expectation that its interest payment structure will remain fixed over its lifetime.

The municipal securities market is unique in several respects, not the least of which is that it is very large in terms of the number of issuances and staggering in the number of uniquely identifiable securities outstanding. As is shown in Table 20.1, most new issue tax-exempts are relatively small in size (the average issue size is $15 million, but about half of all issues are less than $5 million). There are approximately 8,000 new issues sold each year and the great majority consist of serial maturities, each of which matures at different times and typically carries different coupons (and maybe other features such as call provisions, as well). As a result, there are an estimated two million separate families of identical (fully fungible) securities outstanding, that are subject to different pricing decisions.[3]

---

[3] The municipal securities market is unique in the respect that issuers are not regulated under the federal securities laws (only the dealers are) and the securities are

For investors, the plethora of individual issues imposes significant information needs in monitoring the changing prospects of their investments. For issuers, the small size of an issue can mean limited geographic appeal in terms of potential investors and relatively high unit costs in bringing it to market. As discussed later, information needs and the desire to reach broader markets have helped stimulate the credit enhancement business. As is also discussed, the great appetite for tax-exempt paper has also meant that major investors will make the effort to seek out and invest in smaller issues and are applying pressure to improve the after-market reporting by these borrowers.

Table 20.2 provides a breakdown of bond sales by use of proceeds over the last decade; these data clearly indicate significant changes in the uses of tax-exempt bond proceeds. During the deluge of tax-exempts in the early 1980s, financing for traditional public facilities (like schools, sewers, and roads) owned and operated by governments declined in absolute terms and in market share. In their place, nontraditional uses that involve the channeling of tax-exempt borrowing proceeds to private projects or persons became prominent.[4] By 1985, over 50% of new long-term issues were sold for nontraditional purposes—including such uses as residential home mortgages, financing of apartments, and industrial or commercial enterprises. Subsequently, borrowing for infrastructure has staged a comeback, because the Tax Reform Act crimped down on

---

not registered by the Securities and Exchange Commission or listed on exchanges, but traded exclusively over the counter. Information flows in the market are matter of considerable concern and debate. The level of detail, frequency, and alacrity with which information flows are determined by market demands, widely observed conventions and the precepts of the antifraud provisions of securities laws as they are thought to apply to state and local obligations. The lack of uniform reporting requirements, such as are required in the registered securities market is thought by some to lead to segmentation and inefficiencies in the market. Others maintain that the market-driven character of information flows is in keeping with the low-risk nature of the great majority of the largely governmental obligations found in the market. See, John Petersen, *Information Flows in the Municipal Securities Market*, Chicago: Government Finance Officers Association (1989).

[4] Nontraditional borrowing has been variously defined but for practical purposes constitutes those forms of private-activity debt that were either terminated or restricted by the Tax Reform Act of 1986. In addition, the interest income on the remaining forms, with certain exceptions, were subject to the application of the alternative minimum income tax. See John Petersen *Tax Exempts and Tax Reform*, Chicago: Government Finance Officers Association (1987) pp. 2–1 to 2–7. The Tax Reform Act of 1986 gutted much of the supply of private activity bonds, which sank to account for less than 20 percent of all bond sales by the end of the decade. However, sales of one nontraditional form (not-for-profit entities, mainly housing and hospital corporations) continue to be important to the tax-exempt market since they are not subject to state volume limits. For a discussion of the operation and impacts of the volume caps on the market, see Dennis Zimmerman, *The Private Use of Tax-Exempt Bonds*, Washington, DC, Urban Institute (1990).

TABLE 20.2
Selected Statistics on Tax-Exempt Yields Relative Yields, and
Breakeven Tax Rate

	Aaa Tax-Exempt Bond Yield	Ratio of Tax-Exempts to Taxables	Breakeven Marginal Tax Rate
1971	5.22%	70.6%	29.4%
1972	5.04	70.0	30.0
1973	4.99	67.1	32.9
1974	5.89	68.7	31.3
1975	6.42	72.7	27.3
1976	5.65	67.1	32.9
1977	5.20	64.8	35.2
1978	5.52	63.2	36.8
1979	5.92	61.5	38.5
1980	7.84	70.6	29.4
1981	10.67	73.4	26.6
1982	10.30	78.8	21.2
1983	8.56	73.8	26.2
1984	9.61	74.9	25.1
1985	8.60	75.6	24.4
1986	6.95	77.1	22.9
1987	7.12	75.9	24.1
1988	7.35	75.7	24.3
1989	6.99	75.5	24.5
1990	6.98	74.9	25.1

Source: Moody's Bond Survey.

the sale of bond issues for nontraditional (private-activity) purpose and also because public policy had moved to emphasize infrastructure spending and its financing by states and localities.[5]

Hand in hand with the changing purposes for tax-exempt borrowing have been changes in the types of borrowers and the types of security pledged to repay debt. Traditional infrastructure projects have been financed by government units that promise the full force of their taxing power as security—the full faith and credit, unlimited-tax, general obligation (GO) bond. In the early 1970s, GO bonds

---

[5]State and local government borrowing and spending for infrastructure purposes where the facilities are owned and operated by governmental entities have surged since their depressed condition of the early 1980s. Because federal aid for construction purposes has stagnated, capital spending has been financed increasingly by borrowing and the tax-exempt bond market has been able to absorb credit demands on favorable terms. See John Petersen, "A Star Amid the Fiscal Gloom," *Creditweek,* Standard and Poor's Corp (February 4, 1991) p. 1.

represented about 60% of all-tax exempt bonds sold. By the 1980s, however the GO bond's share of the market had been eclipsed by that of the limited-liability obligation or *revenue bond,* as it is popularly called. The latter bonds are generally repaid from user charges or from enterprise earnings and do not rely on taxing powers for their security. Securities sold for local utility operations, such as water, sewer, and electric power, are typically revenue bonds.

Throughout the 1980s, the nature of the predominant borrowers changed from the general government to the statutory authority, which is a special-purpose public corporation that usually does not have the power of taxation but does have the authority to float bonds. By the mid-1980s, statutory authorities accounted for over one-half of all long-term tax-exempt borrowing. These entities often are established to accomplish projects and purposes beyond the normal purview of general government activity. Often they are created solely to circumvent debt or expenditure limitations that restrict general units of government. In other instances, the authority has served as a conduit for financing nongovernmental activities in the tax-exempt market (such as in the case of economic development and housing bond authorities).[6]

The growth of nontraditional purposes for borrowing, the rise of the special purposes district and statutory authority, and the wide use of revenue bonds combine to form important background for understanding financing techniques. The transfer of certain financing instruments such as puts, lines of credit, and commercial paper from taxable to tax-exempt markets accompanied the shift of private borrowers to that market. Furthermore, the greater management flexibility typically afforded by the statutory authority has more readily accommodated the sometimes complicated arrangements that creative financing frequently requires.

---

[6] The ascendancy of the revenue bond has several explanations. One has been the need or the desire to finance traditional projects without pledging the power to tax, reserving this power for other services. In other cases, the choice of the revenue bond as a financing mechanism has been based on the belief that those who benefit directly, should be responsible for the repayment. In yet other cases, the limited obligation revenue bond has been the product of political desperation rather than economic inspiration because these bonds typically do not require voter approval and usually are not restricted by various debt limitations. The general idea of creating limited obligations that can circumvent various debt and voter approval restrictions has been extended into a variety of new security forms, including the now ubiquitous tax-exempt lease purchase (sold as bonds with certificates of participation) and a proliferation of special taxing districts (such as the "designer tax" districts created under Mello-Roos in California). For a discussion of the linkage between the rise of the revenue bond and the special purpose authority, see Ronald Forbes, Phillip Fisher, and John Petersen "Recent Trends in Municipal revenue Bond Financing in George Kaufman (ed.) *Efficiency in the Municipal Bond Market,* Greenwich: JAI Press (1981).

INVESTORS AND THE CHANGING DEMAND
FOR TAX-EXEMPTS

The primary appeal of state and local tax-exempt securities is that investors don't have to pay federal or, in many cases, state or local income taxes on the interest income.[7] This characteristic delineates the pool of potential investors as those with higher marginal tax rates. Because of their tax treatments, three major investor groups traditionally supplied the bulk of buying power for the tax-exempt market: commercial banks, property and casualty insurance companies, and higher-income households.

As may be seen in Figure 20.2, the two major institutional investors throughout the 1970s formed the bulwark of demand for state and local obligations. However, except for certain areas of specialized demand, the federal tax code has been altered so as to greatly reduce their importance to the market. A major feature of the municipal securities market over the last five years has been the ineluctable unloading of tax-exempt securities by the commercial banks. Back in the 1960s and 1970s, when the banks were the bulwark of the market, the household sector was the "swing man" that filled the gap in periods of tight credit between the supply of new tax-exempt securities and the cyclical demand of institutional investors. The individual investor was called on only infrequently, in 1966 and 1969 and 1974 to 1975, for example, to pick up the slack. After 1980, however, individual investors and their surrogates—managed bond funds and unit investment trusts—have absorbed the record volumes of new tax-exempts and the traditional institutional buyer faded as major holders of tax-exempts.[8]

The emergence of the household sector as the primary buyers of tax-exempts has been a major factor in the development of new financing techniques. Individual investors are far more heterogeneous in the investment objectives than institutions. Moreover, the small size of their transactions imposes higher processing costs. Individuals are

---

[7] Because of changing tax laws, the statement is subject to numerous complicated caveats. See Petersen *Tax-exempts and Tax Reform*, p. 3.1 to p. 3.12. Since the passage of the Tax Reform Act, state and local income tax treatments have become a more important factor in explaining tax-exempt bond yields. See *Ibid.* p. 3.10.

[8] Commercial bank ownership of municipal bonds decreased by an estimated $136 billion during the years 1986 to 1990, an amount equal to 59 percent of their holdings at yearend 1985. The Tax Reform Act of 1986 sapped an already depressed appetite for municipal bonds on the part of commercial banks.

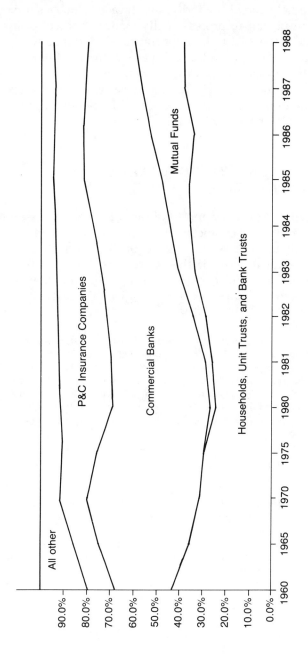

FIGURE 20.2
Trends in Holdings of Municipal Securities—National, State, and Local Issues (1960–1990)

also less likely to have the time or expertise to analyze or to comprehend fully the complex borrowing instruments that are now common.

To help corral the individual investors dollars, tax-exempt funds came into being to professionally manage and select investments. By the end of the 1980s, the importance of the funds was greatly magnified. In the face of a relatively meager supply of new tax-exempts, the funds have greatly concentrated new purchases by the household sector.[9] Consequently, their buying power has placed a premium on the tailoring of issues to meet the needs of a relatively few, highly sophisticated primary market buyers.

DETERMINING THE TAX-EXEMPT INTEREST RATE

As noted, the primary appeal of the conventional tax-exempt bond has been that its interest income is exempted from federal and most state and local income taxes. Therefore, the borrower can offer a lower interest rate than it could if the interest were subject to taxes.[10] Several other considerations can and will influence the interest rate on a particular security. But it is clear that, given the maturity of the debt (the

---

[9] As of the end of the third quarter of 1990, it is estimated that $533 billion (62%) of all tax-exempts were held by the household sector ($349 billion) and mutual funds ($184 billion). Included in the household section's $349 billion are $125 billion of Unit Investment Trusts and $75 billion in bank administered trusts, leaving about $149 held directly by individuals. Author's estimates based on Flow of Funds data and other sources. The holdings of individuals is found as a residual after summing up all the holdings of institutions that report on municipal holdings. The numbers are very rough due to reporting gaps.

[10] The standard analysis starts off that the tax-exempt yield, I_e, is equal to one minus the marginal tax rate, T_m, times the alternative taxable yield, I_t (i.e., $I_e = (1 - T_m)I_t$. For corporations, the top marginal tax rate is 34 percent; for individuals, it was nominally 28% although effectively has amounted to 33% for joint filers with taxable incomes of between approximately $72,000 and $149,000 due the phase out of the benefit of the lowest (15%) bracket (the infamous bubble). Certain bonds issued August 1985 (Alternative Minimum Tax) are subject to the alternative minimum tax for individuals, and all bonds issued after that date are subject to the alternative minimum income tax applied to corporations. Each year subsequent to 1985, there have been relative minor adjustments in the tax treatments which has created a cottage industry of tax lawyers who keep up with these things and leaves mere mortals confused as to what the rules are. Explaining how rates observed in the market are determined by the interaction of general interest rate levels, the need for shelter by sectors and tax structures is more complicated and over the years various explanations have been in vogue. These are reviewed and tested in James Porteba "Explaining the Yield Spread Between Taxable and Tax-Exempt Bonds: The Role of Tax Policy" in Harvey Rosen (ed.) *Studies in State and Local Public Finance*, National Bureau of Economic Research, University of Chicago Press (1986).

period before the principal comes due) and the credit quality (which is largely determined by the ratings conferred by the major credit rating agencies), the rate of return that the investor will require on a tax-exempt security is equal to that available after taxes on a comparable taxable investment. If the two rates are equal on an after-tax basis, investors will be indifferent as to whether they hold a tax-exempt or taxable security. For example, investors in the 28% marginal tax bracket pay 28 cents in taxes on each dollar of added taxable income; for these investors a tax-exempt security yielding a 7% return would be equal on an after-tax basis to a taxable security yielding 9.71%. State and local income taxes can also be important in determining the rate. If the state had a 5% income tax rate (bearing in mind that the state tax is deductible from the federal income tax), the implied taxable equivalent rate would be 10.15.[11]

Table 20.2 presents both the ratio of tax-exempt and taxable interest rates (using AAA-rated corporate and municipal bonds for the comparison) and the inferred marginal tax rates of investors that are on the borderline in terms of holding tax-exempt or taxable securities. Historically, in those periods of high ratios of rates, the participation of the household sector was important. By the late 1970s, household participation began to surge, but the ratio of rates remained reasonably stable. A major reason why this occurred points up another aspect of the relationship: the supply of investable funds seeking tax shelter. During the late 1970s and into 1980 (before the 1981 tax reductions contained in TEFRA), there was a strong inflation-driven growth in the personal income of individual taxpayers and, collaterally, a growth in their desire for tax shelter as they moved into higher tax brackets.

By the 1980s, however, the need to market increasing volumes of new securities to the household sector required dramatic increases in tax-exempt interest rates. In 1981 and 1982, as tax-exempts did battle for investment dollars with other tax preferences, the long-term rate reached the double digit level and the ratio of tax-exempt rates to taxable rates climbed to 79%. The growing importance of the household sector coincided with the most significant reduction in individual tax rates in the past two decades and the creation of many other forms of tax shelters. Thus, the level of tax-exempt rates was driven higher to provide returns equivalent to those on competing tax shelters and on

---

[11] In the case of states and localities with income taxes, the above equation in footnote 10 becomes $I_e = (1 - T_m)(1 - T_{ms})I_t$, where T_{ms} is the marginal state income tax rate. With the lowering of the federal marginal rates, the state's rates have become more significant in determining the differential between borrowers in different states. See Petersen, *Tax Exempts and Tax Reform*, p. 3–6.

taxable investments with a higher after-tax value because of lowered tax brackets.

Subsequent to 1986 and the Tax Reform Act, tax-exempt rates moderated and the ratio of tax-exempt to taxable rates stabilized at approximately 75%, indicating that investors in a 25% marginal tax rate were at the breakeven point. The Budget Resolution of 1990 and the slight upward revision of the individual income tax rates should somewhat improve the market for tax-exempts (meaning that the ratio of rates may fall slightly).[12] Other factors, as will be related in the following discussion, also auger well for the municipal market's capacity and interest rate behavior over the coming decade.

The yield curve for tax-exempts typically has been steeper than that in the taxable market, which means that the short-term market is relatively more favorable for tax-exempt borrowers (the ratio of tax-exempt to taxable interest rates is lower). This is attributable to several factors. A key one is that investors are much more certain about their tax status in the near term than in the distant future. Thus, when investors buy a 20-year bond, they are assuming that they will need shelter for that interval of time (or that their fellow investors will need to shelter income). Second, the workings of the tax laws are such as to foster institutional investment in the short-term securities market because of the deductibility of interest. In the short-term market, this opportunity involves little risk in return for tax-exempt income. Last, very short-term investments that mature quickly expose the investor to relatively little danger of illiquidity through price fluctuations (because the principal returns so quickly), and this is an important attribute for investors who wish to preserve capital value. To these factors are added certain institutional factors arising out of the activities of tax-exempt mutual and money market funds that need short-term investment outlets to "park" their assets.

In subsequent discussions of innovative financing instruments, we will return to the yield curve, focusing on very short-term borrowing; namely, securities that mature as quickly as in a day or a week and that allow the investor the option of specifying when the maturity will occur.

---

[12] The impact of the 1990 federal tax revisions (limitations of deductions for high income taxpayers) was to raise the effective marginal tax rate from 28% to 31.5% in the highest brackets. This will increase the attractiveness of tax-exempt income for truly wealthy that are exposed to the top marginal brackets. See Aaron Gurwitz, *Municipal Market Research*, Goldman Sachs (February 1991) p. 5.

CREDIT QUALITY AND CREDIT RATINGS

An important element in determining the interest rate that jurisdictions must pay on their borrowings is the perceived quality of their credit. Investors always face the risk that borrowers will default; that is, not pay their obligations on time or in full. It is the job of credit analysts to examine transactions and the underlying security of payment and to make determinations as to their relative creditworthiness. Because of the large number of tax-exempt issues and their great diversity, there are companies that make these credit quality assessments, widely followed by market participants. The most influential are Moody's Investor Service, Standard and Poor's Corporation and Fitch Investors Service. The vast bulk of ratings conferred are in the top four major rating brackets, Aaa through Baa (using Moody's notation), which are considered to be "investment grade" ratings.

The significance of the ratings for the cost of borrowing can be seen in Figure 20.3, which plots the differential in yields for 20-year borrowings in the years 1980 through 1990. The differential in borrowing costs between the Moody's prime quality (Aaa) and the lower-medium quality (Baa) has fluctuated between less than one to nearly two percentage points. As may be seen, the risk premia have generally been smaller the past few years. This is because of the relative scarcity of lower-rated paper in the market and the heavy use of credit enhancements, as is discussed below. For example, approximately 35% of all new-issue debt now issued carries the triple-A rating, 26% being the product of credit enhancements.[13] Furthermore, as is also to be discussed, the bulk of outstanding debt is of the highest rating because of the large amount of refunded debt that is backed by escrowed funds.[14] In contrast, only 2 to 3% of new issues represents the lowest investment grade of Baa or BBB.

It is useful to note two things about ratings. First, the company issuing the rating is primarily interested in the strength of the security pledged to the repayment of the debt; the more modest the burden of the debt in relation to the resources pledged to repayment means a higher rating, everything else being equal. Second, although many of the factors that enter into the rating are beyond the immediate control of the borrower (health of the local economy, various constitutional and

---

[13] Aaron Gurwitz, *Municipal Market Research*, Goldman Sachs (February 1991) p. 5.

[14] A product of the massive advance refunding (discussed below) that was done in the past few years is the large supply of triple-A paper in the secondary market. A random sample of 1,000 outstanding debt issues to determine their characteristics recently conducted by Aaron Gurwitz indicates that 21% represent prerefunded issues and that 55% were rated Aaa or Aa, the two highest grades. Gurwitz, *Ibid.*, M2.

FIGURE 20.3
Interest-Rate Spread Between Aaa-Rated and Baa-Rated Municipal Debt Issuances (January 1983–January 1991)

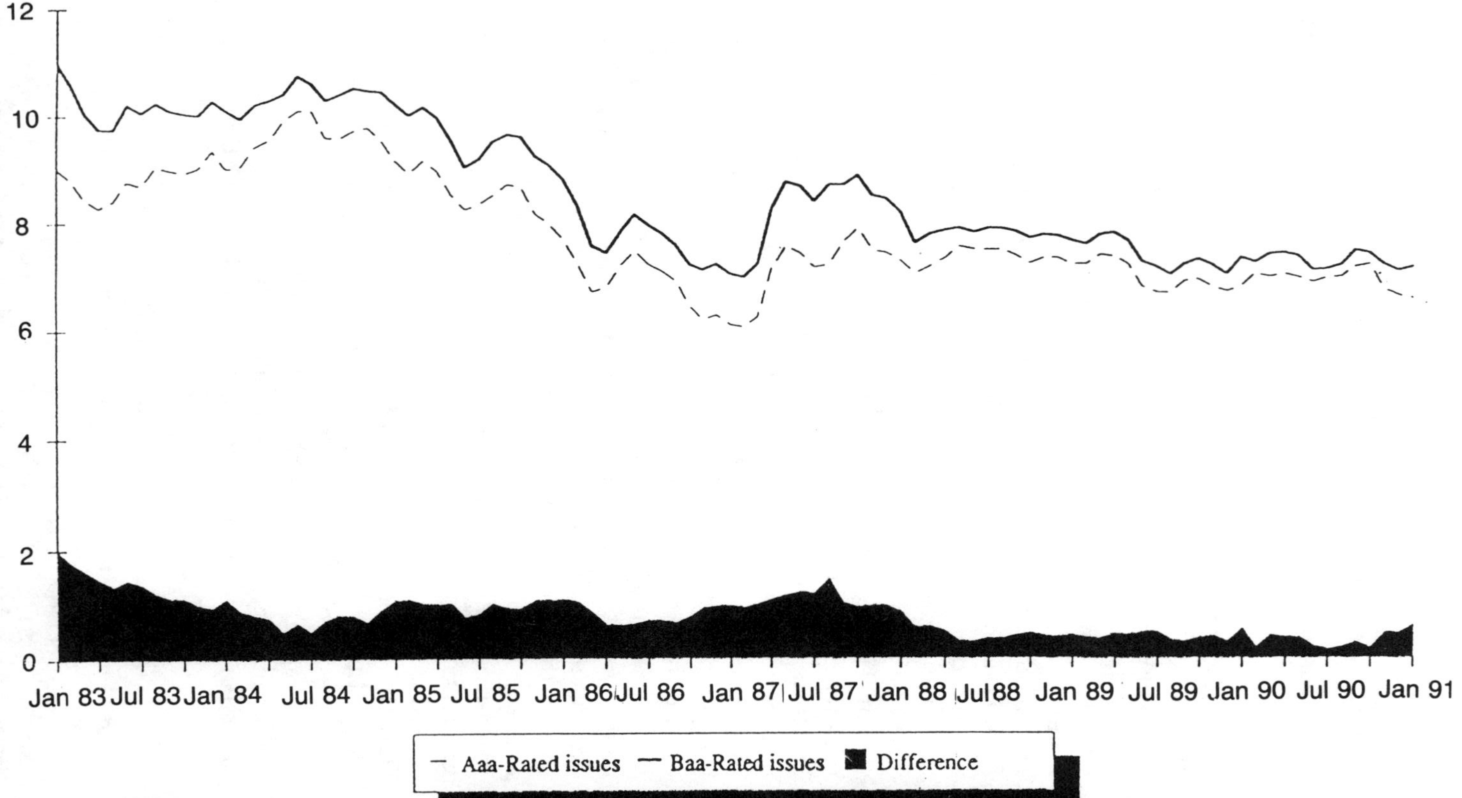

Source: Moody's Bond Record.

state statutory constraints, etc.), borrowers frequently can control or at least influence factors that can enhance or impair the quality of their credit. Designing transactions to strengthen the security pledged and to improve the ratings on them is a major objective in many innovative capital financing techniques.

MECHANICS OF INNOVATION

The preceding overview of the tax-exempt bond market establishes a foundation for examining changes in debt financing techniques. Understanding what is different about these techniques first requires an examination of what is orthodox in the sale of tax-exempt debt and how the methods of borrowing have altered to accommodate changing market conditions and investor preferences.

The traditional package associated with long-term debt is that of an annual cash flow of fixed interest payments (typically paid semiannually) for each maturity with principal due at maturity. The bonds typically have a serial maturity structure, with sets of bonds maturing each year and having their own interest coupon. Thus a 20-year bond would consist of a bundle of 20 distinct security groups ("maturities"), each with its unique price and maturity date. This structure fell from favor with many investors in the early 1980s because of three pervasive uncertainties associated with it: the uncertainty of present values; the uncertainty over future accumulated wealth; and the uncertainty over future value.

The uncertainty over present values is most notable in periods of greater volatility of interest rates, such as that which occurred in much of the 1980s. Yearly variations in interest rates of two to three percentage points between the highs and lows were not uncommon (as contrasted with variations of less than one percentage point a decade earlier). Greater interest rate volatility translates into more uncertainty over market values. With fixed coupon rates, the only way that an outstanding bond can be sold to a new investor to provide a current yield—when market rates of interest have risen—is through a discount in its price, which means a capital loss for existing bondholders.

Regardless of the intended investment horizon at the time of purchase, investors are always watchful of the current market values of their investments. Because of the mathematics of bond pricing and discounting formulas, these price declines are particularly acute on long-term bonds for a given increase in interest rates. However, price changes on short-term securities are far less pronounced even for substantial changes in market rates. Thus, the upward-sloping schedule of interest rates in the yield curve in part reflects the need to compensate investors for the added risks they bear in long-term, fixed-coupon securities.

Some groups of investors have different investment objectives and are less sensitive to fluctuations in prices. For example, they may desire to accumulate financial resources for use at a fixed future date—for retirement of for children's education. For such investors, the stream of semi-annual coupon payments from a long-term bond is not particularly valuable. In the first instance, these semi-annual coupon payments must be reinvested to accumulate, or compound, interest over the planned investment horizon. But the actual interest rate earned on reinvesting the interim coupons will only be known after the fact. Thus the total realized return and future wealth cannot be known at the time the bonds are purchased.

Finally, investors are concerned about the credit quality of their investments. Deteriorating credit quality diminishes the market value of investments and raises concerns over the safety of principal. Investors are especially apprehensive about quality in times of economic downturns and fiscal stress. Certain types of tax-exempts (conduits that depend on underlying asset values or the fortunes of a private enterprise operation) are particularly exposed during periods of uncertainty.

Financing techniques have been designed to alter the traditional risk/reward relationships between borrowers and lenders in a variety of ways and by creating transactions that lower the cost to borrowers. These can be conveniently summarized as follows:

- Shifting interest-rate risk from the lender to the borrower;
- Enhancing the creditworthiness of borrowers by shifting credit-related risks to third parties;
- Increasing the types of returns available to investors beyond those available from the regular receipt of interest income payments or devising instruments and transactions that lower the net borrowing costs to issuers.

These general types of "creative financing" actions can be examined in the framework of the typical yield curve as shown in Figure 20.4, which shows the cost of capital on the vertical axis and the maturity on the horizontal axis. Depicted are two yield curves, one for a lower grade credit (shown as Baa) and one for a prime credit (Aaa). One method of reducing costs is to shorten the maturity, taking advantage of the traditionally lower rates of interest in the short-term markets, as is shown by the movement depicted by arrowed movement 1. The use of short-term market instruments and the adaptation of long-term obligations to take on the characteristics of short-term instruments (variable rates and put options), demonstrate how this shortening of obligations has been performed and its cost implications for tax-exempt borrowers. But it is essential to note that a radical shortening of debt involves risks and costs

FIGURE 20.4
Creative Financing Techniques and Net Cost of Capital

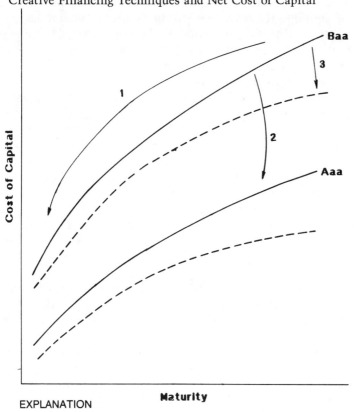

EXPLANATION

1. Move down yield curve (shorten maturity).
2. Enhance credit quality.
3. Employ other economic return and/or lessen net debt service.

to issuers that may offset much of the apparent savings in simple comparisons of the interest costs.

Another move to lower borrowing costs is to improve the credit quality and rating of the obligation. This is illustrated by the shift from the lower grade to the prime yield curve, labeled as movement 2. Credit improvement can be accomplished in two ways: either by the borrowing unit taking steps to strengthen the credit pledged from its own resources or, more commonly, through the use of third-party credit enhancements, such as insurance, guarantees, or various types of credit backstops. Again, the borrower engages in the process of shifting risk from the investor on to itself or to a third party. And, again, this movement usually entails other costs such as insurance premiums or uncertainties as to future financing costs.

The third major movement depicted in Figure 20.4 involves altering the nature of the economic returns to investors and/or lowering the net cost of capital to the borrower. This is illustrated as movement 3, the yield curve found in the conventional securities market is supplanted by one that reflects new, lower costs. Four major varieties of creative financing techniques can create these new, lower-yield curves. The first involves those actions through which the borrower changes the nature of the interest payments to protect the investor against reinvestment risk by, in effect, guaranteeing the reinvestment of interest earnings at a stated rate. An example of its application is found in the original-issue discount or zero coupon bonds. Of course, the borrower assumes the burden of a much larger payment at the end of the investment period and the requisite problems of managing sinking funds or other resources that will be needed to meet the final payment.

The second technique that changes the nature of the economic returns to investors is to design transactions that take advantage of various tax preferences other than the receipt of tax-exempt interest income. Foremost among these techniques has been the design of joint public/private financing whereby private investors—by acquiring ownership interests—have been able to enjoy the benefits of tax preferences such as accelerated depreciation and investment tax credits. Because such preferences are of economic value to taxpaying entities, governments have been able to lower overall financing costs by structuring transactions that contain an equity component and by "selling off" the tax preferences. The opportunity for this type of cost-saving maneuver was virtually eliminated by the Tax Reform Act of 1986.

A third set of innovative financing techniques that can lower the net cost of capital to state and local governments involves the structuring of transactions to take advantage of the opportunity to earn interest through the investment of assets, including the investment in bond proceeds, in taxable securities that yield more than the interest costs of tax-exempt borrowings (a practice called *arbitrage*). While arbitrage techniques for lowering the net cost of capital are of interest in particular transactions, their availability has been greatly curtailed through the most recent federal tax changes.

A fourth technique is that of two or more parties agreeing to repackage their asset and liability cash flows through the use of swaps and derivatives that form synthetic securities. Although standard practice in the corporate market for a decade, swaps represent the latest form of creative financing in the tax-exempt market. Essentially, it involves superimposing the risk/cost curves of another borrower on Figure 20.4 and allowing the two issuers to take advantage of their comparative strengths in different sectors of the market to lower their mutual costs and/or hedge their risks. The use of these techniques are discussed below in greater detail, but most have their origins in the short-term market and the steep yield curve that was a dramatic characteristic of the tax-exempt market in the early 1980s.

While the dollar volume significance of these innovations will wax and wane for technical reasons, the important message is that market professionals on both the buy and sell side became accustomed to tailoring issues to meet specific investment and legal needs.

SEEDBED OF INNOVATION: THE SHORT-TERM MARKET

The best example of creative capital and that which took the market by storm in the mid-1980s was the outpouring of short-term securities and variable-rate obligations to answer the rapidly expanding demands for very short-term, tax-exempt, money market funds. We discuss those techniques first.

The use of short-term debt having a maturity of one year or less has a long history in the tax-exempt market. The traditional forms of such borrowing were *tax* or *revenue anticipation notes* (TANs, RANs) and *bond anticipation notes* (BANs). Tax or revenue anticipation notes are governments' equivalent of working capital loans, and TANs and RANs provide temporary sources of cash to bridge fiscal year gaps between revenue collections and operating outlays. BANs are commonly used to provide interim funds during construction progress. Upon project completion, when final costs are known, BANs are then replaced with long-term bond financing.

These traditional forms of short-term borrowing possess several features common to long-term bond financing. Normally, each note issue carries a fixed interest rate, and each note sale requires a separate borrowing resolution and accompanying sales documentation such as a legal opinion and an official statement. Frequently, a formal competitive bidding procedure is required to award the note issue to underwriters. Not surprisingly, the effort necessary to issue traditional short-term notes has discouraged repeated new offerings with very short maturities of, say, 90 days or less.

The positively sloped yield curve found in the tax-exempt market stimulated the development and growth of a variety of financing techniques designed to lower the cost of borrowing by sliding down the yield curve. New varieties of short-term debt were designed to capture the vast pool of investor funds that seeks to earn tax-free returns without exposure to the interest-rate risks inherent in long-term bonds.

The key distinguishing characteristic of these new instruments was the use of very short-term debt to finance long-lived capital projects. An intentional mismatching between asset life and the maturity of debt used to finance such assets, however, does impose new dimensions of risk on debt management and other innovations came along to hedge these risks.

Early in the 1980s, the tax-exempt commercial paper market, which had languished since its introduction in 1973, made a sudden bound to popularity. These are short-term unsecured promissory notes, with maturities usually of 30 to 60 days, but maybe as short as one day. The maturities are set to coincide with issuer and investor preferences and repayment of the paper is backed up by a credit facility (line or letter of credit) from a commercial bank. For a variety of legal and cost reasons, the tax-exempt commercial instrument was soon supplanted by the variable-rate security.

VARIABLE-RATE SECURITIES AND PUT OPTIONS

Variable-rate securities are found in both the long-term and short-term market. Their chief characteristic is that, instead of a fixed interest rate, the rate is allowed to fluctuate in response to the changing market. In the case of tax-exempt commercial paper, the same effect is achieved by the short maturities that allow investors a close-at-hand option to continue lending at the new rate by "rolling over" their investment (replacing retiring paper with a new loan) or to cash in their loan as it matured. In the case of the variable-rate security, the new rate could be assigned to the outstanding paper without it maturing.

In the early 1980s, variable-rates arose as a new debt instrument that had its yield periodically recalculated to reflect market rates. This instrument had attached the important added inducement of a demand feature that allowed investors to cash in their investment and "demand" repayment. In the long-term market, this characteristic is called *put option*. In either case, this feature greatly enhanced the liquidity of the investor, who, upon short notice, can get back the principal amount of the investment and is not exposed to the risk of capital deterioration found in fixed-coupon obligations. A remarketing agreement backstops the demand features. Also, there is typically need for a liquidity or credit facility to ensure that funds are available if all the securities cannot be successfully remarketed.

Packaging securities to carry flexible rates involves costs. Typically, the letter or line of credit will cost $1/4$ to a full percentage point on the principal amount of bonds covered and the remarketing agent is paid an annual fee on the outstanding balance of 12.5 to 25 basis points. Thus, the cost of accommodating the increased investor liquidity may be 50 to 100 or more basis points on top of the actual interest rate paid. Nonetheless, considerable interest cost savings are possible, if there are wide differences in cost between the rates on short-term paper and long-term debt.

In addition to the interest cost savings, variable-rate issues have other attributes that make them attractive to issuers. First, they are typically convertible to long-term, fixed-rate issues at any interest-adjustment date at the election of the issuer. Thus, should long-term rates drop to a desirable level, the issuer can opt to remarket in the form of long-term, fixed-interest obligations. By the same token, the obligations can be called at any interest-adjustment date at the election of the issuer with no call premium. Last, the underwriting charges on variable-rate demand notes and bonds tend to be smaller ($5 to $10 a $1,000 as opposed to $10 to $15) because they are primarily aimed at large institutional investors.

The disadvantage of the demand bond resides primarily in the interest-rate risk being borne by the issuer. The issuer is unsure from one interest-rate adjustment to the next what its debt service will be. This uncertainty can be hedged to some degree by stating maximums, procuring swaps, or by building in an interest-rate reserve or "guard" fund that can be used to smooth out fluctuations in interest cost. Also, should there need to be recourse to the liquidity facility, the cost of borrowing can escalate sharply because the lending rate is typically pegged to the bank prime rate or higher. Furthermore, there is the risk that the credit rating of the credit facility provider may drop and force a substantial putting back of the issue to the remarketing agent, who then would have to increase rates sharply or make other arrangements for a new backstop arrangement, perhaps under unfavorable market conditions.

While the selection of put bond features can reduce refinancing risks, there is always a chance that bond holders may request early redemption. Because redemptions are made at par, there remains a potential cash-flow risk for borrowers. Issuers need to plan on meeting cash-flow requirements at put dates, and investors and rating agencies will demand safeguards to ensure that put obligations can be met. For many issuers, the size of the maximum potential put will be beyond the reach of their resources. For borrowers, potential sources of cash include standby bond purchase agreements from banks or insurance companies, or remarketing agreements with remarketing agents.

Most commonly, put bonds have carried an irrevocable letter of credit from a highly rated commercial bank as a backup source of cash flow to meet bondholder tenders. These backups require fees, and they also require the borrower to negotiate a reimbursement loan agreement with the lender. While the standby bank could simply hold the tendered bonds as security for cash advanced to meet put requirements, these bonds are likely to have a market value below par (which is why investors put them back). Therefore, reimbursement loan agreements may require new loan terms between borrower and lender based on market yields at the put date—in effect, a refinancing of old bonds. For some borrowers, these loan reimbursements may involve loans at taxable interest rates.

To solve the above problems, investment bankers designed remarketing agreements whereby bonds put for redemption may be redistributed rather than retired. The remarketing alternative has been refined to include conversion options that permit the issuer and the remarketing agent to change the coupon structure from fixed to variable or from variable to fixed at a future put date. These conversion options are also combined with options by the borrower to terminate the put, with advance notice. The termination option, combined with a conversion option to change from a variable rate to a fixed rate, permits issuers to sell fixed-rate, long-term debt at a future date when interest rates have fallen, without the necessity of first calling variable-rate bonds for redemption. These possibilities became extremely important with the passage of the Tax Reform Act in 1986 which put a crimp in the ability of issuers of private-activity bonds to refinance their outstanding debt.

Variable rate securities and put options are most attractive when short-rates are low relative to long rates and when long rates are at what are perceived to be cyclical highs. Thus, the flattening of the yield curve and the general decline in rates has diminished their use as of late, as many issuers have abandoned them to fix-out on the low long-term rates. In 1990, variable rates accounted for about 10% of the volume of bond sales, as opposed to around 20% during the mid-1980s.

CALL OPTIONS

Many government borrowers, even recognizing the advantages of short-term debt in a market with an upward-sloping yield curve, are reluctant to commit themselves to the risks inherent in short-term or variable-rate financing. Instead, they choose to issue long-term, fixed-coupon debt knowing that, while expensive, a ceiling has been placed on future debt-service outlays. Refunding can permit issuers the flexibility to reduce remaining debt-service costs at some future date.[15] The key to refunding is the call option or the optional redemption provision. The optional redemption feature can be thought of as an option contract that is sold by investors to borrowers. The value of this option to borrowers stems from the fact that future interest rates may decline well below the coupon rates on outstanding bonds. In that event, borrowers can exercise the option, redeem outstanding high coupon debt, and finance the redemption with new, lower-cost debt. In effect, the call option enables issuers to buy back their outstanding debt at bargain prices. As an example, a 20-year noncallable bond with a nine percent coupon would command a market price of $134.67 per $100 par value if market rates declined to six percent. A typical call option, on the other hand, would permit issuers to redeem these bonds at a price of $103 per $100 par value. The price of the option is that callable bonds carry higher rates of interest, with yields 10 to 50 basis points higher than on noncallable securities, as well as requiring the payment of a call premium of 2 to 5% of the par value (call premium). The market places the higher premium, the higher the level of rates, anticipating that the higher rates will not be sustained and that the bonds are more likely to be called when rates come down to normal levels.

Issuers can follow two general strategies for exercising the call option when interest rates decline: refundings and advanced refundings. At the end of the call deferment period, usually five to ten years from the sale date of the "old" bonds, issuers may elect to carry out a refunding. A refunding involves the sale of new bonds, the proceeds of which are used to concurrently redeem "old" bonds. Refundings are advisable when interest rate savings can be achieved.

Prior to the first call date, issuers may consider an advance refunding.[16] Advance refunding requires the sale of new bonds, as in a refunding, but the proceeds are not used immediately to redeem outstanding bonds. Instead, proceeds are typically invested in U.S. Government securities and placed in escrow. This escrow fund is used to meet debt-service payments on "old" bonds until the first call date, at which time, the remainder of the escrow fund is used to redeem outstanding bonds. Under the advanced refunding, the "old"

[15] See Lennox Moak *Municipal Bonds Planning, sale and Administration* Chicago: Municipal Finance Officers Association (1982) pp. 321–25.

[16] Federal tax laws over the years, culminating in the Tax Reform Act of 1986, significantly limited the ability to advance refund. Certain types of tax-exempt bonds may not advance refunds at all while others may do so only once. See Petersen (1986) p. 2–9. Nonetheless, most governmental-purpose issuers were able to refund to take advantage of the lower interest rates that prevailed in the late 1980s and 1990. Refundings have been very heavy, amounting to approximately 30% of all bonds sold in the last five years. As a result, there is a preponderance of high grade paper in the secondary market.

bond holders look to the escrow fund for their security (which has been funded by the proceeds from the refunding); under "regular" refunding, bond holders look to the pledged revenue source for their security, which is financed by project revenues (or tax payments, as the case may be). It is possible, if the issuer wishes, to partially refund a bond issue.

THE ZERO-COUPON BOND

The zero-coupon tax-exempt bond (zeros) was spurred by needs to develop broader investor appeal. As noted earlier, the institutional mainstays of this market—commercial banks and property and casualty companies—retreated from the market throughout the 1980s. Individuals have absorbed most of the net new supply of tax-exempts, and, barring dramatic changes in the federal tax code, they will continue to do so in the near-term future.

Long-term zeros may be especially attractive to investors whose objective is the accumulation of future wealth and who also anticipate that their future reinvestment rates may be lower than present coupon rates. The longer the maturity and the higher the coupon rate, the greater will be the importance of the rate of reinvestment in determining final actual return. The zero provides a way to avoid reinvestment risk (although they may be exposed to other risks, such as being called). Zeros can be very attractive investment alternatives to coupon bonds for investors with a long-term investment objective of asset accumulation.[17]

One of the disadvantages to the issuer of zeros is that a much larger par value of bonds must initially be used in order to realize a given amount of net proceeds. Such discrepancies between par value and receipts may be difficult to explain to voters and can cause legal problems in regard to the treatment of indebtedness. The deferral of interest cost until the bonds' maturity can also create uncertainties about the security of the payment and should be planned for through the use of a secure sinking fund.

Compound-interest bonds—also known as capital appreciation, accumulators, and municipal multiplier bonds—are an adaptation of the zeros. Like the zeros, all debt service is postponed until maturity. Unlike zeros, however, the bonds are not sold at an original discount but are sold at par. Meanwhile, the interest component is held by the issuer and compounded at the stated rate so that the investor receives a lump-sum multiple of the principal amount at the end of the holding

---

[17] In the case of tax-exempt securities sold at an original discount, the accretion of interest over the life of the security is tax-exempt. However, capital gains and losses resulting from transactions in the secondary market are subject to regular capital gains taxation.

period. Otherwise, the accumulator operates in much the same way as the discounted zero.

The greatest advantage to the accumulator is a legal one: because most debt limitations (including caps on single-family housing and industrial development bonds) are expressed in terms of the par value of debt, accumulators permit conventional sales that retain the benefit of the locked-in reinvestment return.

Deferred interest payment bonds are especially popular in periods of high interest rates and in current market conditions have become something of a specialty and represent only about 4% of new offerings.

Recent offerings of small-denomination direct issuance (minibonds) have adopted the use of the capital accumulator form of instrument (eliminating the need for issuing semi-annual interest checks) and the use of the put option to provide investor liquidity (in exchange for making the instruments non-transferable, eliminating the need for transfer agents). Reducing the paperwork and the need for outside services makes the costs of raising capital competitive with those in the conventional market (especially if the issuer is done in conjunction with a conventional offering).[18]

HEDGES, REFUNDING ESCROWS, AND SWAPS

The Tax Reform Act of 1986 placed many new and exceedingly complicated restrictions on tax-exempt borrowing in the latter half of the 1980s. Meanwhile, the generally declining interest rate levels encouraged issuers to seek long-term financing, either to lock-in the low rates currently available or to refinance outstanding debt that had been sold in a high-interest rate environment. Accomplishing either one of these objectives under the new restrictions spawned an array of new techniques in the market at the end of the decade.

The 1986 Tax Act, by its restrictions on arbitrage, removed the advantages of delaying bond issuance and quickened the interest of issuers in issuing bonds as a hedge against future increases in the rates of interest. For example, the issuer might have a series of identified projects to be financed and would wish to lock-in the low interest costs or it might simply be speculating that somewhere in the future it might need money and, if so, would have raised low-cost capital. Such

---

[18] Issuers have the option of not selling their bonds to an underwriter for redistribution but of selling them directly to the investing public. Although relatively few have, changes in the technology and instrument design make direct issuance in certain cases. The possibility of direct issuance has not gone unnoticed by investment bankers and probably acts as a curb on spreads. See Lawrence Pierce, Percy Aguila, John Petersen, with Catherine Holstein, *Municipal Minibonds: Small Denomination Direct Issuances by State and Local Governments,* Chicago: Government Finance Officers Association (February 1989).

a borrowing, designed as a hedge against future increases in rates, would have its proceeds placed in escrow at a "restricted" yield so as not to violate the arbitrage restrictions and the various legal and underwriting fees associated with the transaction would be on a contingent basis and only paid when the funds were actually expended as planned. In 1988 and 1989, the Congress passed laws to restrict the practice of such transactions that effectively eliminated the ability of issuers to hedge against future rate increases unless they had projects firmly in mind and ready to go.[19]

The Tax Reform Act also left large volumes of tax-exempt bonds outstanding that were precluded from advanced refunding. In addition, the Act placed constraints on the volume of tax-exempt borrowing that might be done for private-activity purposes by the imposition of state volume caps, which created timing problems for issuances that would exceed to annual limits. The challenge became one of locking in the low rates in the tax-exempt market without issuing tax-exempt bonds. One way this is accomplished is through a device called *refunding escrow deposits* (REDs) in which investors enter into forward purchase agreements to buy tax-exempt refunding issues when the outstanding issues become eligible for call. The investor's money is placed in escrow invested in U.S. Treasuries that are designed to mature just before the maturity of the old bonds to be refunded. Investors are paid from the earnings on the escrowed notes (the interest is taxable) until they come due, at which time the principal is used to refund the old bonds. At that point, the investors become owners of tax-exempt securities.[20]

There are, of course, bets being made in all of this. Investors are betting that rates will go down or maybe that tax rates will rise. On the other side, issuers risk that rates may go down further and that their savings might have been greater had they waited. But in any event, the issuer is locking in a savings in comparison to the coupon rate on the old high-coupon bond.

Another technique used extensively in the corporate and international markets and gaining some acceptance in the tax-exempt market is the use of interest rate swaps. As with escrow deposits, the major impetus for swaps appears to have evolved from the need to accomplish debt management goals (such as changing the nature of the interest rate payment pattern) without resorting to a new issuance (which, as in the case of the advanced refunding, might not be possible).

In the interest rate swap, parties swap their interest payments, which usually involves an exchange of floating for fixed rates. Neither

[19] See Perry Israel "Arbitrage: General and Refunding" *National Association of Bond Lawyers Washington Conference Notebook* (January 12, 1990) Tab II.

[20] For a fuller discussion see *Refunding Escrow Deposits*, New York: First Boston Corporation (1989).

the original obligation nor the principal payments are not effected by the switch. Payments are made on a net basis, with whichever party owning more paying the other the difference. Opinion differs as to whether the swap represents a speculation or a way of obtaining more flexibility in debt management. But, speculation or not, it does offer the possibility to reorganize debt payments without a reissuance.[21]

TAXABLE MUNICIPALS

It once would have been thought to be an oxymoron to use the expression "taxable municipal", but that is no longer the case. Although there were a few early experiments, there emerged in earnest following the Tax Reform Act of 1986 a new class of state and local obligations the interest income on which was taxable under the federal income tax laws. These are bonds sold for purposes that, because of the degree of non-governmental involvement in the transaction, no longer were eligible for tax-exemption or that exceeded the bounds of certain limitations placed by the federal tax code on bonds of that type (such as exceeding volume caps or total issuance costs).[22]

The leading example of taxable financings is the various types of economic development bonds where private firms are aided by state or local governments. Because it is subject to the federal income tax, the taxable security carries higher interest rates than the tax-exempt; but, it may still possess advantages. These arise principally from the fact interest income is exempt from state income taxes, the sponsoring governments may extend certain pledges that improve the creditworthiness of the issue, and the financed improvement may enjoy sales and property tax exemptions.[23]

The taxable municipal market, while growing, is small in comparison to the conventional tax-exempt market, representing only 2 to 3% of total state and local government borrowing.

[21] See *Interest Rates Swaps for the Public Sector*, New York: Morgan Stanley (September, 1990). Swaps can be structured either to hedge liability positions and to better match assets and liabilities or to speculate on where interest rates are headed, depending on how the transaction is structured. In the municipal bond market, swaps can be used to take advantage of the different quality premia charged in the long-term versus short-term market, technical conditions in the market, or tax-driven considerations. Interest-rate swaps are still in their infancy in the municipal securities market, but reportedly, some $24 billion have been done. See William Chew, "Interest Rate Swaps for Municipal Issuers" *Credit Comment*, New York: Standard and Poor's Corp. (December 10, 1990) p. 28.

[22] John E. Petersen "Taxable Bonds At Home and Abroad," *Government Finance Review* (February, 1987).

[23] See *New York's Local Industrial Development Agencies*, Albany: New York State Legislative Commission on state and Local Relations (September, 1989) pp. 41–49.

CREDIT ENHANCEMENTS

The risk of a default—or even the threat of a default—is of primary concern to investors, and events and trends in the state and local government sector have not been reassuring lately as regards default actual and potential.[24] Actually, as was discussed above the risk premia are not as great as they once were, in large part because of the existence of various forms of credit enhancement. Another factor is the large volume of highest grade paper created by past advance refundings that is backed by escrows of U.S. Treasuries.

The growth in credit enhancements is not solely due to deteriorating credit quality. There are two other contributing factors. One has been the growth of the individual investor as the primary buyer in the market. The municipal bond market is distinguished by the large number of issues and the heterogeneous nature of the securities offered. While the larger institutions are able to keep track of the variety of credits and the nuances of their security features, and local institutions (such as local banks) were able to keep track of local conditions, the shift of the market to individual buyers has brought a large number of unsophisticated individual investors to the market. Such investors are generally averse to risk and often do not have portfolios of sufficient size to allow for diversification. Accordingly, a second major reason is that bond underwriters and bond funds have found enhancements not only a useful marketing tool but a protection against accusations of securities fraud to do away with credit risk by buying bond insurance[25]. In many ways, of course, this development has also occurred in the short-term market through letters of credit, which are discussed below.

[24] For example, see Alan Abelson "Municipal Bonds: The New Junk" *Barron's* (October 29, 1990). There has been a general downgrading of credits in the municipal upgraded securities market and in 1990, four times as many credits were downgraded as were up graded by the rating agencies. While general governments have seen declines in rating due to fiscal problems, the greatest risks in the market by far are confined to various categories of private-activity bonds (such as single-family housing, health care, and industrial activity bonds) and a subset of special taxing district bonds that are "governmental" in only the loosest sense of the word. The latter a developer or "dirt" bonds that essentially allow land developers to incorporate as special taxing districts for purposes of selling tax-free bonds for making improvements that are secured on taxes to be collected as the development is completed. Like a lot of real estate, these have not worked out very well in many cases. The bonds were highly speculative, not rated, and paid high rates of interest, but many investors are complaining that they were misinformed and so are homeowners in the struggling districts that are facing huge property tax bills and in many cases are simply walking away from mortgages. See Marj Charlier "Many Tax-Free Bonds Are Going Into Default in Colorado Land Bust," *The Wall Street Journal* (December 7, 1990) p. 1.

[25] John Petersen *Information Flows in the Municipal Securities Market* Chicago: Government Finance Officers Association (1989) p. 2.

The remainder of this section will examine three types of credit enhancements: bank credit supports (which are predominantly, but not exclusively, in the short-term market); bond insurance as provided by private insurers; and state-sponsored credit assistance programs.

BANK CREDIT ENHANCEMENTS

Bank credit supports or facilities, as they are called in the aggregate, come in a great variety, but there are two generic groupings: *lines of credit* and *letters of credit.* The weakest form of bank support is usually found in the line of credit. This type of agreement generally provides only liquidity for the issuer's debt and can be subject to numerous provisions. For example, the line cannot be used if the borrower is in default on its obligation; lines of credit really do not constitute enhancements.[26]

Lines of credit are used primarily in the short-term market for governmental units that are themselves of superior credit standing and that would only need temporary financing to meet financing needs. Banks generally impose two charges on lines of credit—a *commitment fee* and a *draw-down rate.* The commitment fee, which may range from $1/8$ to $3/4$ of 1% of the amount of debt, is like an insurance premium—it is the cost to the issuer of maintaining access to cash at a future date. The drawdown fee is the loan rate charged by the bank when it actually supplies a loan in the future. These loan rates are subject to negotiation. More favorable terms can generally be obtained from banks that maintain deposit relationships with the borrower. Loan fees can range from 75% of the U.S Treasury bill rate to 100% or more of the bank's (taxable) prime rate, with the higher rates required for banks that do not need tax-exempt income, which increasingly the case.

An important form of credit enhancement, rather than liquidity support, is the *letter of credit* (LOC). LOCs are commitments directly between the bank and the investors (or trustees) for the account of the bank's customer, the issuer. In this arrangement, the trustee or investor has direct claims against the bank in the event that debt service is not paid in full and on time. Furthermore, nearly all LOCs are irrevocable and, hence, constitute a direct guarantee of the borrower's obligation by the bank, regardless of subsequent actions by the issuer.

LOC commitment fees are higher than fees for liquidity agreements, ranging from .25 to 1% of the amount of debt. Draw-down on

---

[26] Forbes, "Innovations in Tax-Exempt Financing," p. 378.

loan fees is also higher, reflecting the general level of risk assumed by the lending bank.[27]

Generally, the term of an LOC is shorter than the life of the bonds—terms run from five to 10 years, with provisions included for future renewals at the bank's option. In the event a bank notifies an issuer that it chooses not to renew, the agreement with investors in the "supported" borrowing may stipulate that substitute supports will be supplied or bonds will be subject to mandatory redemption prior to the LOC expiration date. Thus, while investors receive some additional assurances about the safety of their expected future income, the duration of this added safety is uncertain. In the case of long-term obligations or where there might be a weaker form of support, the issue is rated by the rating agencies both on the basis of the bank's credit for the period covered by the irrevocable LOC and on the credit rating of the underlying issuer, since the assumption is made that the LOC may not always remain in effect.[28]

Another concern is the effect of the various contingent liabilities on bank balance sheets. One of the concerns for credit analysts and banks alike is that draw-downs on credit facilities might be systematic; that is, they would all tend to happen at once (e.g., if there were a financial panic in the tax-exempt market that made remarketing impossible). A massive call on bank credit supports or liquidity agreements could present major difficulties for the banking system, as well as catastrophes for individual banks. Credit analysts have looked with concern at the progressive downgrading of ratings on commercial banks. These downgradings have been caused by loan losses, narrowing profit margins stemming from deregulation, and, in some cases, substantial net operating losses.

In addition to credit facilities, banks provide other devices designed to hedge various risks that investors or issuers may encounter. Banks, for a fee, can engineer interest-rate guards (that put maximums on interest rates paid in the case of variable-rate securities); investment agreements (that guarantee the spreads between the cost of borrowed and invested funds); and interest-rate swaps (that convert variable-rate to fixed-rate obligations or vice-versa). These devices can neutralize or hedge various types of risk. The important feature of these devices is the effort to design packages to meet the specialized needs of investors and issuers.

---

[27] Forbes, *Ibid.* pp. 362–63.

[28] In the case of long-term obligations or where there might be a weaker form of support, the issue is rated by the rating agencies both on the basis of the bank's credit for the period covered by the irrevocable LOC and on the credit rating of the underlying issuer, since the assumption is made that the LOC may not always remain in effect.

BOND INSURANCE

Following many of the same impulses of the market that have led to the development of the LOC, the demand for insured tax-exempt obligations has grown rapidly. New issues of insured bonds in 1990 amounted to $33 billion.[29] In contrast to LOCs, which may be ended short of bond maturity, bond insurance is an unconditional promise to pay over the life of the bond issue. The bond insurance companies are typically combines formed by major property and casualty insurance companies with assorted large financial institutions also appearing in the consortiums. They are regulated by the various state insurance commissions.

To be accepted in the market as credit enhancements, insurance companies must be of the highest rating category. At present, there are three major private municipal bond insurance companies: Municipal Bond Investors Assurance Corporation (MBIA); American Municipal Bond Assurance Corporation (AMBAC): and Financial Guaranty Insurance Company (FGIC). The standard bond insurance provides that, in the case of an issuer who fails to make principal and interest payments in full and on time, the insurer will do so. The payments are made according to the original maturity schedule, and such payments continue to be tax exempt.

Premiums are scaled to risk, and the insured borrower's underlying credit quality must meet certain standards to be eligible for insurance. In practice, the borrower must be rated equivalent to Baa or BBB or better by the rating agencies. Premiums range from .25 to 2% of the combined principal and interest due over the life of the issue, depending on maturity and the payment schedule on the premia.[30]

The savings enjoyed by issuers that elect to buy insurance vary depending on the level of interest rates, the relative spreads on interest rates between the grades of bonds, and the particular policy employed. When the premium is paid up-front, the interest cost savings (which

[29] "Quarterly Market Review, December, 1990," Financial Guaranty Insurance Corporation, New York (February 15, 1991)

[30] Generally, insured issues trade at around the rates available on single A to double AA bonds, depending on the underlying pledge and the insurer. Pricing of insurance is an issue and is subject to both regulatory requirements for capital reserves, maintaining prime bond ratings, and intense competition among the companies. For example, the rating services require 10 times as much capital to insure a hospital bond as a state GO. However, premia charged for the hospital will typically only be two or three times as great. The great problem is that there has been little recent experience with defaults to test the adequacy of reserves or the reality of pricing of policies. See, for example, "Municipal Pricing Strategy Called Suicidal To Industry," *Global Guaranty* (November 13, 1990) p. 1.

will occur over several years) need to be examined in present value terms, a practice that has not always been followed.

There has been considerable innovation in the area of bond insurance. Bond insurance has been used to "front-end" LOCs from low-rated or unrated banks, with the bank providing a liquidity agreement and the insurance company providing surety insurance to cover longer-term liquidity and credit risk. Another innovation is the insurance of debt-service reserve. Under this program, the insurer will insure a portion of interest and principal, allowing the issuer to dispense with a debt special reserve.

A final development in the area of insurance has to do with increased competition among insurers. Issuers routinely ask for competitive bids on insurance, as well as having their offerings of bonds bid on an insured and uninsured basis, thereby letting the market determine the cheaper way to borrow.[31]

It is useful to note that the providers of enhancements—commercial banks and casualty insurance companies—were once major investors on their own account in tax-exempt securities. That is no longer the case. Both industries have become more interested in earning fees (which are taxable) than tax-exempt income. Through the institution of the credit enhancement, these intermediaries have been able to capitalize on both their financial flexibility and on their knowledge of the municipal market, while leaving it to the household sector, either directly or through funds, to supply capital. At the same time, the individual investor has been able to buy into the complicated and arcane tax-exempt market with fewer fears about understanding individual credits and less concern for diversification.

STATE CREDIT ASSISTANCE

The simplest and most straightforward form of credit assistance is a state guarantee of local government debt, pledging the state's full faith and credit in support of the local debt. Essentially, this means that the local debt is tantamount to the state's own direct debt in terms of credit quality. While a direct state guarantee provides the greatest degree of credit support and the greatest savings in interest cost (aside from a state giving a direct interest subsidy), it is comparatively rare. In some cases, states cannot extend credit supports to localities because of constitutional restraints. In other cases, the state does not wish to dilute its

---

[31] Thomas McLoughlin and Catherine Holstein "Does Bond Insurance Make Sense?" *Government Finance Review* (December, 1989) pp. 37–38.

own creditworthiness and have its bond ratings threatened. This can happen because a state's direct guarantee counts against the state's debt limitations, and, even if the local debt is currently self-supporting, the guaranteed debt still will represent a contingent liability.

In extending credit assistance, therefore, states generally attempt to insulate their own credit quality by applying certain conditions on local governments that are backed up by a state guarantee.[32]

States have other ways of "softening" the degree of credit support they give to localities. A common technique is a "moral obligation" backing of a borrowing. Under this arrangement, the state is not legally bound to assume responsibility for repayment of loans. Rather, should there develop a deficiency in the debt-service reserve fund, the state governor is required to submit a bill to the legislature that would appropriate the funds to do so. Moral obligations are a weaker form of obligation than a direct guarantee and of less value to local issuers in reducing their borrowing costs. Nonetheless, even in the case where the underlying loans are self-supporting, the obligations still represent a contingent liability of the state.

The most popular form of credit assistance involves the creation of state-sponsored borrowing entities, such as a special-purpose lending authority or a general purpose bond bank, that finance local governments through the purchase of their obligations. The authority collects several local bond issues and consolidates them into a single bond issue that is sold in the national bond market. Typically, such entities have no taxing power and exist solely for purposes of facilitating debt issuance by governmental units. Although the state may provide some direct subsidies to particular types of borrowers or for certain borrowing purposes, the interest rates paid by the lending authority generally form the basis for what the local borrowers must pay.

To enhance the marketability of the lending authority's obligations and lower the costs of borrowing, some form of state-sponsored credit support, such as those discussed above, is often provided so that the authority has a credit rating close to that of the state. In addition, the authority, by pooling smaller issues into a big one, is able to enjoy certain economies of scale, such as lower costs of issuance (printing,

---

[32] For example, a state backup may have prior recourse to the following sources of funds: (1) A lien on revenues of a local project that is financed through the state guaranteed bonds. This might involve certain state requirements on the levies that a locality must make to ensure debt-service coverage. (2) A lien on the general obligation (taxing power) of the local government unit to ensure that sufficient taxes will be raised to meet required debt service. (3) A lien on state assistance payments to the locality so that they are diverted to the repayment of debt if necessary. (4) A lien on a debt-service reserve that is equal to the maximum annual debt service.

legal costs, and the like) per dollar of borrowing and typically lower rates of interest that larger issuances are able to attract.

Most state authorities are geared to financing particular types of projects (such as housing, hospitals, school facilities, economic development, and water and sewer projects), but some are relatively open-ended in the types of projects they can assist. Municipal bond banks, which are designed to finance a broad range of local government functions, operate in a handful of states (including Arkansas, Alaska, Vermont, New Hampshire, Maine, and a new one which has just been formed in Indiana). Generally speaking, the bond banks are especially aimed at helping small governments; most large local government borrowers, if they have sufficient credit quality, prefer to borrow directly on their own.[33]

PROSPECTIVES ON THE MARKET

The municipal market, after a decade of explosive change has settled down for the time being and resumed a more orderly pattern of growth. It however left the 1980s with important legacies that will influence its operation in the future. Aside from the general condition of the financial markets and, from time to time, that of certain classes of borrowers, the enduring theme is the treatment of interest income from the securities under the federal tax code. At present, the treatment is such that several segments have been created that have their particular attributes. Nonetheless, for the most important sets of issuers (governments) and buyers (household) the treatment is predominantly that of full exemption of income. However, the federal tax code remains in an unsettled state. Issuers and other participants would like to see simplifications (especially in the area of arbitrage restrictions) and expansions of purposes that come under the umbrella of governmental purpose, as well as provisions to get the banks back into the market.[34] While there appears no great movement to further restrict use of the tax-exempt market, there are proposals that would increase the competition from other tax preferences, such as the reinstitution of the Investment Retirement

---

[33] For a comprehensive study of credit pooling, see John E. Petersen, et al., *Credit Pooling To Finance Infrastructure,* Chicago: Government Finance Officers Association (1988).

[34] See Anthony Commission on Public Finance, *Preserving the Federal-State-Local Partnership: The Role of Tax-exempt Financing,* Chicago: The Government Finance Officers Association (October, 1989)

Account on a more liberal basis.[35] As it stands, with a minimum of competition from other preferences, each uptick in federal and most state and local income tax rates improves the market for the bonds and lowers the interest cost relative to that paid by other borrowers in the market.

The market for tax-exempt securities is stable and strong, in large part because there is much less competition from alternative preferences than was the case in the early 1980s and it is much less burdened by the supply created by the unfettered issuances of private-activity bonds. Furthermore, the level of indebtedness of governmental issuers borrowing for governmental purposes is relatively low, especially in the case of tax-supported debt. Total tax-exempt debt outstanding including both governmental and private activity bonds has gyrated over the past 20 years when compared to GNP. It fell from 14.2% in 1970 to 12.9% in 1980, peaked at 16.8% at the end of 1985 and subsequently declined to 15% by the end of 1989. Of this, governmental debt, which was equal to 12% of GNP in 1970, stood at 11.7% of GNP in 1989. More significant is the decline of tax-supported debt from 8 percent of GNP to 4.4% at the end of 1989.[36] During the 1980s, there was an unburdening of the tax systems from being pledged to support debt, reflecting the taxpayer revolt and the increased reliance on special districts, user fees, and the use of limited obligations. In the process, of course, the security part of the municipal security became more complicated.

The outstanding debt figures do not tell the whole story and can be misleading. The stock of outstanding debt carries in it the seeds of an exceeding strong tax-exempt market, assuming that there is no major alteration in the federal tax code. It appears that approximately 21% of debt outstanding has been advance refunded and will be maturing in the next five years, when the first call date comes up. In addition, the stock of high coupon bonds (coupon over 8%) that has call dates occurring in the next five years and will be refinanced constitutes another 20% of the outstanding stock. Another 10% has regular scheduled maturities occurring in the next five years. That means that

[35] The President and various Congressional leaders are promoting the revival of a tax-advantaged means of saving for individual investors that would not be as confining as the existing individual investment accounts. Under current law, use of a deductible IRA contribution is limited to those earning less than $40,000 in the case of joint-filers. Others must fund IRAs with taxable dollars, although they can accumulate tax-free until time of withdrawal, which is restricted. The new proposals would both increase the availability of IRAs to higher-income groups and loosen up on the withdrawal penalties. See Albert Creshaw, "Effort Begins to Restore IRA Benefits," *The Washington Post* (March 17, 1991) p. L3.

[36] John Petersen, "Debt is Not the Villain In Fiscal Woe," *Governing* (January, 1991) p. 57.

half of all the bonds now outstanding will either be called in or maturing over the next five years.[37] The implication is that there is a huge hole opening up in tax-exempt portfolios and that unless the new-issue market grows by at least 5%, the dollar volume of outstandings will stagnate through out much of the 1990s, which is a very happy prospect in terms of keeping tax-exempt rates down in relationship to taxables. As tax-exempts become scarce, investors will be increasingly inclined to lockin municipal holdings and will desire long-term call protected paper and will be interested in forward purchase schemes to fill anticipated upcoming holes in portfolio.

Last, despite the current sounds and alarms over credit quality and excepting some of the riskier private-activity and development district endeavors, the prospect is for *yield spreads between bonds* to continue to be compressed. As noted, the overhang of high quality paper will keep the scarcity value of lower-rated issuers high and the institutionalization of household demand through the surrogate of the tax-exempt fund means that they have large portfolios that can absorb risk (and buying power to make and protect their investments). Meanwhile, the activities of the insurers will ensure there is an abundance of Aaa-rated paper. Credit enhancers know that the default statistics for general government shows them to possess infinitesimal risk that does not justify much in the way of credit premiums.[38] Furthermore, in cases where there is risk, they can act in an agency capacity for the market and negotiate as part of writing policies protective covenants that lessen the risk of ever having to fall back on the coverage.

Thus, the innovations have changed the market and there is no doubt that many of them will continue to be important determinants of its behavior. Overall, however, the fundamentals relating to existing federal tax policy, a continuing demand for the securities, the rapidly declining stock of outstanding debt, and the relatively light debt burdens and inherent creditworthiness of all but a few governmental issuers auger well for a market that can do as much financing on favorable terms as the public is willing to permit.

---

[37] Aaron Gurwitz, "Characteristics of Outstanding Municipal Bonds," *Municipal Market Research,* New York: Goldman Sachs (February 1991) pp. M1–M9.

[38] The respective default ratios as measured by the amount of bonds in default as a ratio of bonds outstanding of that type of municipal securities as of yearend 1987 were as follows: conduit (private-activity) securities, 1.2%; governmental securities, including the Easnington Public Power Supply Bonds, "WPPS"), 0.5%; governmental obligations (without WPPS), 0.1%. See Petersen, *Information Flows in the Municipal Bond Market,* p. 78, footnote 70.

CHAPTER *21*

Municipal Swaps*

J. P. Morgan and Co.

The interest rate swap is a relatively new financial product that has exhibited extraordinary growth in its short life. The market originated in the early 1980s as a way for issuers in the taxable market to achieve lower cost funding than was available to them in the capital markets at the time. Today, the outstanding notional on swaps exceeds $2.5 trillion. The presence of dozens of market makers who make prices on interest rate swaps and derivatives ensures fair market pricing and a high level of liquidity. Given the flexibility inherent in swaps and derivatives, these financial engineering tools have many applications beyond simple access to lower cost financing.

Although there are significant differences between the taxable and non-taxable financing products and environments, it is anticipated that the swap market can provide both low cost financing and risk management for tax-exempt issuers and investors as they have for their taxable counterparts. In fact, the need for swaps is greater in the tax-exempt market than in the taxable market because there are fewer financial products available to manage the same exposure to interest

* Reprinted with permission from J. P. Morgan Securities, Inc., 60 Wall Street, New York, NY 10260.

rates. We believe that all potential end-users of the product should be fully aware of the risks and rewards imbedded in the product. It is because of this belief that we write this municipal swap primer.

WHAT IS A SWAP?

An interest rate swap is a contract between two parties to exchange interest payments for a specified period. No principal is exchanged. Typically, one counterparty makes fixed rate payments and the other makes floating rate payments on the "notional" principal amount. Swaps are most typically quoted in terms of the fixed price which a swap dealer is willing to receive (or pay) versus paying (or receiving) a floating rate index. For example, a swap dealer might offer to receive fixed at 6.00% versus paying the rate of the JJ Kenny index.

WHAT ARE SWAP "DERIVATIVES?"

Swap derivatives include swap options, caps, floors, and collars. A swap option is a contract between two parties giving one the right but not the obligation to enter into a new swap agreement or to terminate or shorten an existing swap agreement at some future time at rates agreed upon today.

A swap option gives the buyer utmost flexibility. The buyer can choose to exercise the option when the swap has value. The primary disadvantage to a swap option is that it requires an upfront fee (although JP Morgan will consider imbedding that fee into the swap rate in certain situations). If the option never goes into the money, the fee is a sunk cost that will never result in economic gain. Another disadvantage is that the option buyer has credit exposure to the seller (see below for a discussion of credit risk).

A cap buyer has the right to receive cash payments equal to the difference between the actual level of floating interest rates in the future and the cap level (or "strike rate") agreed upon today if rates go

FIGURE 21.1
Municipal Interest-Rate Swap

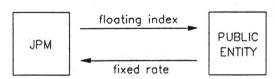

above that level. The cost of a cap is paid upfront and is determined by the maturity, size (notional principal), and strike level. The cap cost is quoted in terms of basis points on the notional amount.

There are several "plusses" to a cap structure for a borrower (or issuer): the borrower benefits from a reduction in rates; the borrower has an upper bound on interest rate exposure; and, in an upward sloping yield curve environment, the borrower benefits from the lower cost of short term interest rates. The "minuses" are that there is an upfront fee on a cap and that the buyer has credit exposure to the seller.

A floor buyer has the right to receive cash payments equal to the difference between the actual level of floating rates in the future and the floor level agreed upon today if rates go below that level. As with a cap, a floor is paid for upfront and the pricing is dependent on maturity, size and strike level.

The benefits of a floor to a lender (or investor) are similar to those of a borrower with a cap: the lender benefits from any rise in interest rates and has a lower return bound in the event that rates fall substantially. Again, there is an upfront fee for this structure and credit exposure to the seller.

A collar is the simultaneous purchase of a cap and sale of a floor. A collar buyer has the right to receive the same cash payments as the cap buyer but is obligated to make the cash payments on the floor. A collar, like a cap, will protect the floating rate borrower from a rise in interest rates. However, the benefit from the decrease in rates is limited by the floor level. A collar is an attractive derivative

FIGURE 21.2
Cap Versus Floating

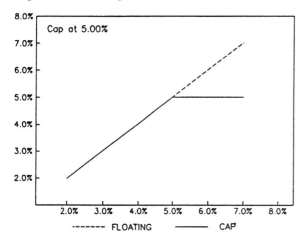

FIGURE 21.3
Floor Versus Floating

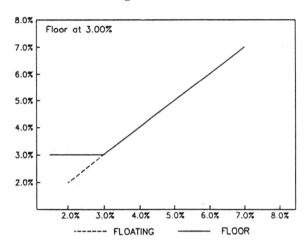

because the premium received from the sale of the floor offsets the cost of the cap. The cap and floor levels can be set at levels resulting in perfectly offsetting premiums: a "costless collar."

The collar will cost less than a cap but will still allow the borrower to set an upper bound on borrowing costs. However, the benefit of the reduction in interest rates is limited by the floor rate. The amount of the credit exposure would be the net amount exposure on the cap and the exposure on the floor.

FIGURE 21.4
Collar Versus Floating

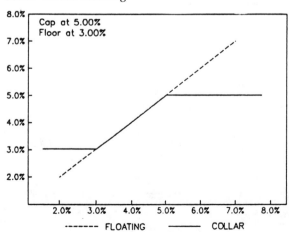

SWAP APPLICATIONS

As mentioned above, swaps were initially developed as a means of allowing issuers to obtain lower cost financing than was available. An issuer could issue in either floating or fixed, whichever was less costly, and convert the debt, if necessary, to the desired form through a swap. Consider the following example: Company A can issue ten year fixed rate debt at 7.15% and floating rate at JJKenny flat. Company B is a better credit and can issue 10-year fixed rate at 6.90% and floating rate debt at JJKenny minus 45 basis points. Company A would like a floating rate liability and Company B would like a fixed rate liability. They can both benefit from a swap as diagrammed below. This synthetic debt can be issued at lower rates than "natural debt" because it arbitrages a market inefficiency between the fixed and floating debt markets.

Swap market makers further arbitrage market inefficiencies by providing two way markets. As a result, companies are not forced to find counterparties that seek to do an exactly offsetting swap from their own. An entity that wanted to pay fixed and receive floating would call a swap dealer for a price.

As the swap market has developed, swaps have been seen not only as a means to achieve lower cost financing, but as financial management tools. Swaps can be tailored to meet any set of cash flows that require hedging.

A common public sector use of a swap as a financial management tool is a synthetic fixout. Consider an issuer with an outstanding floating rate bond that would like to fix part or all of its interest expense. The issuer could do a current refunding or a conversion. These approaches would entail issuance fees and, under certain circumstances,

FIGURE 21.5
Accessing Lower Cost Financing Through Swaps

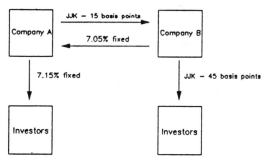

Company A achieves JJK − 5 bp floating rate financing
Company B achieves 6.75% fixed rate financing

FIGURE 21.6
Creation of a Synthetic Fixed Rate Bond

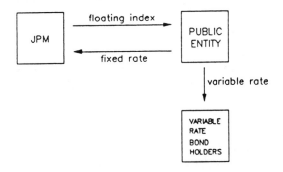

cause the issuer to lose arbitrage benefits that exist under the current issue. An alternative would be to keep the existing bond outstanding and to enter into an interest rate swap in which the issuer pays fixed and receives floating. This approach will achieve the issuer's objective while avoiding issuance costs and restrictive regulations.

Swaps can also be used for asset and liability management. A "prudent" amount of floating rate debt is determined by the asset side of the balance sheet. Interest rate exposure is minimized when floating rate liabilities are equal to floating rate assets. Rather than link a swap with a new or currently outstanding issue, financial managers can utilize swaps to rebalance their portfolios in favor of either fixed or floating rate debt.

FIGURE 21.7
Creation of a Synthetic Fixout

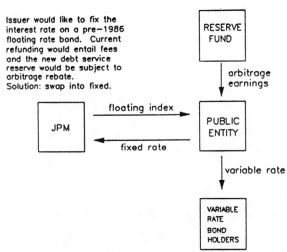

Financial managers can also hedge floating rate debt by purchasing caps and collars and can lock-in a minimum return on assets by purchasing floors.

Finally, swaps and derivatives can be used to profit from taking a view on interest rates. An entity that believes interest rates will rise beyond the market expectation, would want to execute a swap in which it would pay fixed. It would also sell floors and capture a premium believing that it would never have to pay off on the floor.

MECHANICS

The floating rate index that is most commonly used in the taxable swap and derivatives markets is LIBOR. Commercial Paper and Fed Funds are also commonly utilized. The most common tax-exempt floating index is the JJ Kenny Short-term High Grade Index (JJK). JJK is a weekly composite rate for 30-day tax-exempt paper as calculated by Kenny Information Systems, Inc. A specified percentage of LIBOR is also a commonly quoted index.

The frequency of payments in the swap or derivative contract is set to be structured to a variety of frequencies (e.g., monthly, quarterly, semi-annually, etc.). Often, the frequency of payments matches the frequency of the payments of the asset or liability that the contract is meant to hedge.

Payments in the swap are netted. Therefore, rather than the two counterparties each issuing a payment, the net amount is made in one exchange.

Swaps are private transactions that are executed under standard industry documentation. All that is required to execute a swap is the International Swap Dealers association (ISDA) master agreement and a certification that the entity has the legal authority to enter into a swap.

SECONDARY MARKET

Financial managers have added flexibility with swaps and derivatives due to the liquid nature of the secondary markets for these products. After a swap or derivative is entered into, the value of that contract changes as the factors that went into the original price for the contract (such as market rate level and time to maturity) change. For example, consider a case in which Entity X enters into a five year swap in which it pays 6.10% fixed versus receiving JJ Kenny on a notional amount of $100 million. If interest rates rise, the swap will be in-the-money for Entity X because it would be paying what would then be a below market fixed rate. The specific value by which the swap is "in-the-money" can be considered to be equal to what it would cost to replace the swap at the original terms in the then prevailing market. If interest rates rise 50 basis points over the first year, then the in-the-money value of the swap would be equal to the present value of 50 basis points for each of the four remaining years. Using the swap rate as the discount rate, this value would be $1,728,593 (on an HP-12C: n = 4, i = 6.10%, pmt = 50, fv = 0; solve for pv).

The active secondary market ensures that an entity can terminate its position in one of two ways. It can get out of its position with its original counterparty for a fee or a receipt equal to the replacement value of the swap or derivative. This process is called an "unwind." The entity may also "assign" its position. In an assignment, it would be replaced in the contract by an acceptable third party. The party remaining in the swap must agree to the replacement counterparty. This requirement will protect swap counterparties from being assigned those counterparties to whom they do not wish to be assigned to for credit reasons. The stronger the counterparty credit, the more assignable the swap position. Again, the cost or receipt would be equal to the replacement value of the contract.

TAX CONSIDERATIONS

The uncertain tax treatment of specific arbitrage related matters and the potential for changes in the treatment of swap and derivative contracts make it especially important for potential participants in these markets to consult counsel regarding the tax treatment of any contract and its impact on any associated securities. We do not purport to provide adequate counsel regarding tax considerations.

The most important tax issue relates to the integration of the income or expense of a swap executed in connection with the issuance or purchase of a security for purposes of yield calculation. Whether or not this income or expense can be treated as a component of the income, expense, gain or loss from that security can significantly affect yield. Current tax treatment does not require integration. However, there is some evidence that the Internal Revenue Service intends to require integration in at least some swap and derivative applications.

ACCOUNTING ISSUES

As with tax treatment, accounting treatment is uncertain. Potential market participants should consult counsel regarding disclosure requirements. We do not purport to provide adequate counsel regarding accounting issues. The disclosure of swap transactions is under the authority of the Government Financial officers Accounting Standards Board (GASB). In August 1990, GASB issued a comment suggesting that financial statements disclose all swap and derivative transactions as well as the market and credit risk associated with them. The Financial Accounting Standards Board (FASB) has also developed accounting and disclosure guidelines. Industry practice is as follows: any up-front payment made or received is amortized over the life of the swap; if securities are normally carried at cost, swap and derivative positions are carried at cost; if securities are normally marked-to-market, swap positions are marked-to-market.

SWAPS AND THE RATING AGENCIES

The rating agencies recognize the importance of swap and derivative products and their ability to reduce financial risk. They also recognize the potential dangers from the imprudent use of swaps and derivatives. If the products are used to reduce financial risk and credit risks are fully assessed, the rating agencies have indicated that they intend to look upon the use of swaps and derivatives favorably.

LEGAL ISSUES

Swaps and derivative contracts are generally not legally tied to any specific asset or liability. Although swaps and derivatives are often associated with an underlying security or financial transaction, the contracts are completely separate agreements. The issuer retains all the rights and obligations under the asset or liability.

Any public sector entity must establish that it has the legal authority to enter into swap and derivative transactions and that the execution of any particular transaction does not violate constitutional or statutory limitations on incurring debt. Several states include California, Florida, Massachusetts, and Texas have passed legislation allowing certain issuers to execute swaps.

Even in states which have authorized swap transactions, the entering into of swaps is subject to certain conditions, such as that it must be done for bona fide hedging purposes. In states where there is no specific statutory approval for swaps, municipal entities *may* have the power to enter into swap agreements as an adjunct to their general governmental powers. Many market participants will be reluctant to rely on a general grant of governmental power in light of the Hammersmith and Fulham ruling. In that case, the House of Lords held that

U.K. Local Authorities did not have the power to enter into swap transactions and thus swaps entered into with Local Authorities in good faith by market participants could not be enforced against Local Authorities. Although this ruling is not binding in the United States, it has made market participants much more cautious about the issue of power and authority. It should also be noted that, even for entities which have the power to enter into swap transactions, many market participants will require evidence of specific approval of particular transactions.

ISSUES IN SYNTHETIC TRANSACTIONS

Depending on the structure of any given synthetic transaction, there can be several issues involved that all participants should fully understand. They are: counterparty credit risk, rollover risk, basis risk, and market risk.

Counterparty credit risk is inherent in every swap and derivative transaction. Credit risk is the risk that the counterparty will default on the swap. Therefore, credit exposure can be thought of as the replacement value of the swap or derivative product. An entity is at risk only when the swap is in-the-money. On a 20 year $100 million swap where the issuer pays fixed and receives floating, the maximum exposure could be expected to be as high as $55 million. Credit exposure can be effectively managed through careful choice of counterparty and the use of a variety of credit enhancement techniques.

Rollover risk can exist in one of two forms. One type of rollover risk is present when the term of the asset or liability does not match the term of the swap or derivative product. For example, an issuer may have a 10 year swap hedging a 20 year bond. The rollover risk is the risk that the bond issuer may not be able to enter into a new swap at attractive terms when the original swap matures. The other type of rollover risk has to do with the liquidity facilities on the underlying issues. A counterparty that cannot renew its letter of credit on a variable-rate note at an acceptable rate might be forced to fix out the issue which would leave it paying a fixed-rate on the issue and a fixed-rate on the swap.

Basis risk is present when a swap or derivative is used to hedge a particular asset or liability. It is the risk that the index of the swap or derivative will not exactly offset the index on the asset or liability to which it is "matched." Statistical analysis demonstrates that JJK has a very strong linear correlation with national and state indices. Therefore, basis risk is minimal.

Market risk is involved with transactions matched with floating rate paper. In extreme cases, a remarketing agent may be unable to remarket the floating paper. If the issuer has entered into a swap or purchased a cap or collar to hedge his floating rate risk, it will be "over-hedged" if the paper does not remain outstanding. Market risk is a credit risk of the issuer and is not covered in swap agreements.

Through a full understanding of the risks involved in synthetic transactions and careful structuring of these financial products, the risks are manageable. These risks must always be considered in conjunction with the rewards of the synthetic transactions.

CHAPTER 22

The Municipal Interest Rate Swap Market*

Aaron Gurwitz
Goldman, Sachs and Co.

Municipal interest rate swaps provide a means for issuers to reduce capital costs by finessing some of the many pricing anomalies in the tax-exempt market. Growth of the municipal interest rate swap market would have been even faster than it has been were it not for the fact that this financial contract has an appearance of mystery to many potential participants. In fact, there is no mystery once one understands some of the ways in which market anomalies raise an issuer's cost of capital and how interest rate swaps cut through the impediments to cost-effective financing.

This paper is not intended as a "primer" on interest rate swaps. Several such basic descriptions are available.[1] Although we will quickly review the terminology used to describe an interest rate swap, our main purpose is to illustrate how the municipal swap market works by analyzing a complete set of transactions. The transactions involve two municipal issuers and a swap dealer. Under current market conditions, both municipalities can achieve significantly lower borrowing costs

---

*Copyright 1991 by Goldman Sachs.

[1] See, for example, Eileen Baecher, *Swaps and the Derivative Markets*, Goldman, Sachs & Co., January 1991.

than they could have achieved using traditional financing techniques, and the dealer can earn a profit by making a market in municipal interest rate swaps.

A QUICK REVIEW OF THE BASICS

An interest rate swap is a contract between two parties whereby one party (the fixed receiver) agrees to make a series of variable payments and to receive a series of fixed payments. The other party (the fixed payer), makes fixed payments and receives variable payments. The size of the fixed payments is determined by a fixed interest rate multiplied by a "notional" principal amount. The variable payments are determined by multiplying some predetermined interest rate index times the notional principal amount. In general, no principal payments are made either when the contract is initiated or when it is terminated.

Municipal interest rate swaps are interest rate swap contracts in which the floating rate payments are determined by an index of short-term tax-exempt interest rates, and the fixed payment rate is related to the yield on municipal bonds of the same maturity as the swap. The most common floating rate index used for municipal swaps is the J.J. Kenny Index. This index is calculated and reported weekly and represents an average of 30-day tax-exempt rates. The payments made by a municipality under an interest rate swap transaction are not tax-exempt because they are not interest payments. The interest rate swap agreement can extend over whatever period of time the parties agree to. The most common "maturities" for swap contracts range between one and 10 years.

There are several reasons why a municipality would consider an interest rate swap agreement. For one thing, by using interest rate swap contracts, municipal treasurers can quickly alter the characteristics of their liabilities. Suppose the treasurer of a municipality with a fixed rate bond outstanding concludes that interest rates are likely to drop substantially and remain low for about two years. To act on this view, the treasurer could enter into an interest rate swap contract as a fixed receiver, effectively converting the fixed rate obligation into a variable rate liability for the next two years. Likewise, a treasurer with variable rate debt outstanding who is concerned that interest rates might rise sharply for over, say, a three-year period, could use interest rate swaps to effectively convert the debt into a fixed rate liability for the appropriate period of time.

Swaps can also be used to solve very specific liability management problems. Consider a municipality financing a construction project over a two-year period. Suppose the treasurer believes that at 7.25%, 30-year fixed rate debt represents a comfortable cost of capital. However, two-year government bonds yield only 7%, so there will be a "negative arbitrage" loss on the temporary construction investments. This problem can be solved if the issuer enters into a two-year amortizing interest rate swap, in which the notional principal amount of the swap steps down in tandem with the planned construction drawdown, and invests the bond proceeds in a floating rate investment contract.

These examples represent special situations in which swaps may have a use. However, swaps have much broader, more general applications. In fact, all issuers who are legally authorized to do so should routinely consider interest rate swaps as an alternative vehicle for achieving routine financial objectives. Issuers seeking fixed rate liabilities with maturities of 10 years or less should *always* consider issuing commercial paper or other variable rate obligations and entering into a fixed payer interest rate swap contract as an alternative to issuing fixed rate bonds. Issuers seeking to create variable rate liabilities should *always* consider issuing fixed rate bonds and entering into a fixed receiver interest rate swap as an alternative to issuing commercial paper or variable rate demand notes (VRDNs). In general, and subject to the evaluation of some additional, relatively minor risks, the alternative involving the swap will be the right choice if it produces a lower all-in cost of capital.

WHY MUNICIPAL INTEREST RATE SWAPS SHOULDN'T BE POSSIBLE

It is somewhat surprising that issuers should *ever* find opportunities to reduce their cost of capital through the use of interest rate swaps. For several reasons, standard transactions involving the direct issuance of either variable or fixed rate obligations should be more efficient. For one thing, while issuance of a bond involves only two parties—the seller and the buyer—the use of interest rate swaps involves a third party, the swap dealer. The presence of a swap dealer reduces the efficiency of the transaction in two ways. First, the dealer must be compensated for accepting the risks involved in originating and maintaining an open swap contract. Second, the continuing involvement of the swap dealer in the transaction introduces an additional risk to the other parties to the transaction: the risk that the dealer (or other financial intermediary) will be unable to perform under the swap agreement. When a municipality sells a bond to an investor, the only credit risk involved in the transaction is the issuer's ability to service the debt. When a swap is involved, a third party's credit risk is introduced, and this will tend to reduce the efficiency of the transaction.

The second source of inefficiency in a swap transaction relates to the effort involved for the issuer. Bond issuance is a routine transaction from a legal point of view. Interest rate swaps may become routine for municipalities as the market evolves, but at present, entering into a swap transaction for the first time can involve additional legal work, along with efforts to explain an innovative transaction to city councils or boards of trustees. Finally, for the municipal interest rate swap market to work effectively, swaps must make sense not only for one municipal issuer, but for two, and in the opposite direction. Swap dealers are generally unwilling to keep a one-sided municipal interest rate swap position open indefinitely; to do so would involve too much market risk.[2] Dealers, therefore, will be unwilling to enter into an interest rate swap contract with, say, a fixed payer, unless they are reasonably confident of finding another municipality in fairly short order willing to act as a fixed receiver.

Given all of these potential impediments, it is surprising that a municipal interest rate swap market has developed at all. Hence the aura of mystery surrounding this market. Municipal interest rate swaps are possible, however, because the anomalies in the tax-exempt bond and money markets are pronounced enough to overcome all of these impediments and still leave two issuers and a dealer better off than they would have been otherwise.

ONE COMPLETE SET OF ANOMALIES

Our purpose here is not to enumerate all of the anomalies in the municipal market that can create swap opportunities. Instead, we will focus in this section on an example of how two broad market anomalies make a complete, two-sided set of swap transactions both feasible and attractive. In a concluding section we will discuss some other potentially fruitful situations.

Anomaly I Tax-Exempt Money Market Rates for Issuers in High-Tax States Are Particularly Low Relative to Fixed Rates. During the past year, yields on California double tax-exempt 30-day commercial paper (TECP)

---

[2] In this sense, the municipal interest rate swap market is different from the taxable swap market. In the latter, the most common floating rate index is the London Interbank Offered Rate (LIBOR). LIBOR-based obligations are relatively easy to hedge through the use of Eurodollar deposit futures contracts. At present, there are no reliable long-term hedges for obligations based on the J.J. Kenny Index. The only way a municipal swap dealer can reduce exposure to fluctuations in interest rates is to find counterparties willing to take opposite sides of the transaction.

averaged approximately 60 bp lower than the J.J. Kenny Index (Figure 22.1). Over the same period, yields on 30-year Aa-rated California double tax-exempt revenue bonds averaged only 13 bp lower than comparable national paper (Figure 22.2). The differential between the in-state advantage at the short and long ends of the yield curve was even more pronounced in the New York market. New York 30-day TECP yields averaged about 70 bp less than national levels, while AA New York revenue bonds yielded an average of 2 bp *more* than comparable national bonds.

It is not obvious why this differential should exist or why it should persist for so long. One plausible explanation relates the relatively low yields on double and triple tax-exempt money market instruments to the persistent relative steepness of the generic national municipal yield curve. One reason often offered to explain the fact that the municipal curve is persistently steeper than the taxable curve is investor uncertainty about future tax law. Higher yields on longer-term bonds compensate investors for the risk that at some point over the next 10 or 30 years Congress might eliminate tax exemption or expand the alternative minimum tax (AMT) to cover interest on more bonds. Because there is much less uncertainty about tax laws over a

FIGURE 22.1

Yield Spreads: California and New York 30-Day Tax-Exempt Commercial Paper vs. J.J. Kenny Index

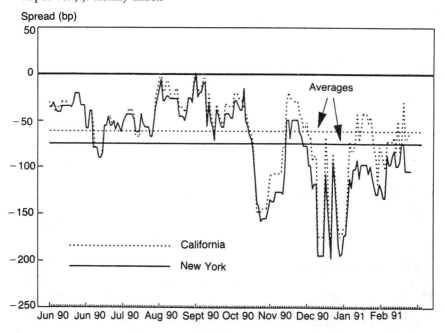

FIGURE 22.2
30-Year Yield Spread: California and New York Revenue Bonds Over Aaa
Insured National Market Paper

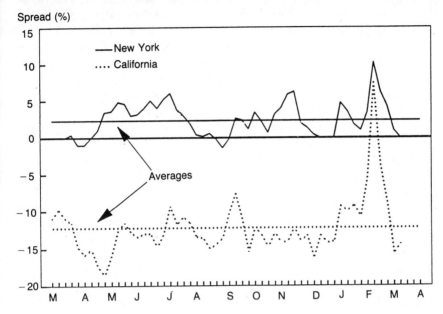

one- or two-year horizon, tax-exempt money market rates do not incorporate such a premium.

The same argument can be extended to the impact of state tax laws. It is highly unlikely that either California or New York will reduce marginal income tax rates during the next 12 months or that in-state bonds will lose their state tax-exemption any time soon. Over the longer term, however, neither marginal tax rates nor the in-state exemption is carved in stone. Investors demand higher yields on longer-term bonds to compensate for this additional uncertainty.[3]

[3] Interestingly, the fact that the relative steepness of the municipal curve is more pronounced in high tax states supports the tax uncertainty hypothesis regarding the shape of the municipal curve. The alternative hypothesis, the "preferred habitat" argument, makes no sense with respect to double tax-exempt municipals. According to the preferred habitat hypothesis, nonfinancial corporate investors tend to buy short-term tax-exempt bonds exclusively. Since corporate tax rates are higher than individual tax rates, yields on the short-term tax-exempts that corporations prefer are lower relative to taxable yields than is the case for longer-term municipal bonds. This hypothesis makes no sense in the case of double and triple tax-exempt bonds, however, because in most states interest on in-state municipals is *not* exempt from state corporate income taxes. The tax uncertainty hypothesis explains both the relative steepness of the national municipal curve and the even more pronounced relative steepness of the double and triple tax-exempt curves.

Whatever the reason, low money market rates in high tax states create an opportunity for issuers to reduce the cost of fixed rate liabilities through the medium of the interest rate swap market. The floating rate index and the fixed rate payment level stipulated under most municipal interest rate swap contracts are based on national market levels. Thus, payments keyed to the J.J. Kenny index will generally be higher than the double or triple tax-exempt payments an issuer in a high tax state must pay on a variable rate obligation.

The fixed rate payment under the interest rate swap might also be higher than what the issuer might pay on a double or triple tax-exempt fixed rate obligation of the same maturity. However, because of the relative steepness of the in-state yield curve, the savings on the floating rate payments more than compensate for the extra cost of the fixed rate payment. In fact, the savings on the floating rate payments can be enough to compensate the issuer for the extra cost of variable rate obligations, including letter of credit (LOC) and remarketing fees. (We will elaborate on this point when we assign numbers to the complete transaction.)

Anomaly II—Tax-Exempt Money Market Rates for Issuers in Low Tax States Whose Bonds Are Subject to the AMT Are Particularly High Relative to Fixed Rates. The second market anomaly is a more recent phenomenon. Over the past 12 months, yields on 30-day "generic" national tax-exempt commercial paper—interest on which is treated as a preference item under the alternative minimum tax (AMT TECP)—averaged 30 bp more than non-AMT levels. This average AMT/non-AMT spread was roughly similar to the comparable spread for long-term bonds. The yield differential between AMT and non-AMT 30-year insured bonds averaged 22 bp over the past 12 months (Figure 22.3).

Recently, however, the AMT/non-AMT spread for tax-exempt money market instruments has widened substantially (Figure 22.4). It is not so much that yields on AMT TECP have risen. Instead, yields on non-AMT TECP have, on occasion, fallen to extremely low levels relative to other money market rates.

The tax-exempt money market has a well-earned reputation as a highly "technical" market. Yield levels on generic national VRDNs, TECP, and so on can fluctuate wildly, even when taxable money market yields are relatively stable. Furthermore, yields on seven-day VRDNs over the past 12 months have occasionally fallen below the after-tax yield on comparable taxable investments. The reason for this performance pattern relates to the peculiarities of the supply and demand balance in the tax-exempt money market. Two dominant groups of investors play a major role in the short-term municipal market: tax-exempt money market funds and nonfinancial corporations. The amount of money these two groups of investors have to put to work in

FIGURE 22.3
30-Year Insured Bond Yield Spreads AMT Over Non-AMT

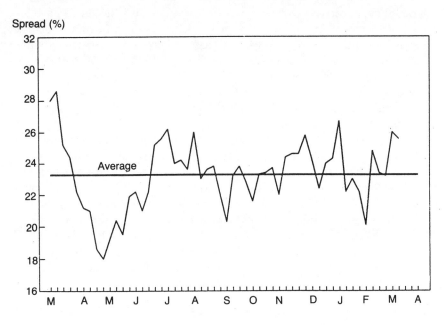

FIGURE 22.4
30-Day Tax-Exempt Commercial Paper Yield Spread AMT Over Non-AMT

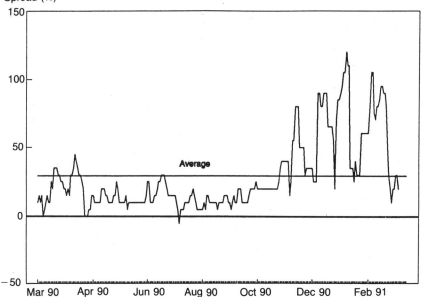

the municipal money market fluctuates substantially over the course of a year. Around the time when quarterly tax payments are due, nonfinancial corporations draw down cash reserves and therefore have less money to invest in the tax-exempt market. Tax-exempt money market funds also tend to experience net cash outflows around tax-payment dates, most notably in the weeks leading up to April 15. Withdrawals also tend to peak during the months of August, when tuition payments are due, and December, around the holiday shopping season. During other months, funds flow into tax-exempt money market funds and corporate coffers.

The aggregate supply of tax-exempt money market instruments is also seasonally volatile. There is typically a hiatus of several weeks between the maturity of one year's issue of New York State Tax and Revenue Anticipation Notes (TRANs) and the sale of the next year's issue. There can be a similar gap between the redemption of one year's State of California Revenue Anticipation Notes (RANs) and the sale of the next year's issue. When such periods of supply scarcity coincide with heavy inflows of cash into money market funds, yields on short-term tax-exempts can fall to extremely low levels relative to taxable money market rates.

On such occasions investors "should" move their cash balances from tax-exempt to taxable money market funds. However, because the amount of money involved is usually relatively small, because of the inconvenience involved, and because, over the course of a year, tax-exempt money market rates will exceed the after-tax yield on a taxable money market fund on average, relatively few investors bother to move their funds as frequently as they might. Corporate cash managers, by contrast, are usually unwilling to accept lower yields on tax-exempts than the after-tax yield on taxable money market investments.

One additional fact will complete the story. Relatively few national tax-exempt money market funds are willing or able to purchase securities that are subject to the AMT. Marketing efforts for these funds focus on providing income that is fully tax-exempt. Even though very few taxpayers are subject to the AMT, most funds have concluded that permitting AMT investments complicates their marketing efforts so much as to be not worthwhile. Most corporate cash managers, however, are much more willing to buy AMT paper. Therefore, at times when tax-exempt money market investments are scarce relative to demand, AMT TECP benefits from this scarcity much less than non-AMT securities. It is on these occasions that the spread between AMT and non-AMT TECP widens substantially. The spread also tends to widen at times when corporations are short of cash but money market funds are not.

These influences have become more pronounced over the last few months, as reflected in the widening trend in the AMT/non-AMT TECP spread. Further, it appears unlikely that the average spread will return to the low levels of several months ago. Tax-exempt money market invest-ments are likely to become relatively scarcer over time. The State of New York is in the process of "bonding out" its annual TRANs issuance. Fur-thermore, the corporate issuers whose tax-exempt obligations are subject to the AMT traditionally have been more willing than municipalities to issue variable rate debt. During 1990, for example, 9.6% of total issuance was variable rate, but 26.8% of AMT issuance came in this mode.

It is important to note that the yield differential between AMT and non-AMT municipal money market instruments is much less pro-nounced for double and triple tax-exempt paper. Tax-exempt money markets in high tax states are so tight that double and tripe tax-exempt money market funds cannot afford to avoid AMT paper. Thus an AMT issuer in a high tax state is more likely to want to be a fixed rate payer in an interest rate swap transaction than a fixed receiver.

THE COMPLETE SET OF SWAP TRANSACTIONS

Figure 22.5 illustrates a complete set of swap transactions that enables two issuers to take advantage of these market anomalies. To motive this transaction, we need an issuer in a high tax state that is seeking to add fixed rate liabilities with maturities between two and 10 years. We also need an AMT issuer not in a high tax state who is seeking floating rate tax-exempt liabilities. Given current specific conditions in the tax-exempt money and bond markets, both of these issuers can expect to do better through the use of interest rate swaps than they could have done by issuing the kind of liability they want directly.

Benefits and Risks for the Fixed Payer

To see why this is so, compare, for each issuer, the net cash flows produced by the swap transaction with the all-in cost of the direct

FIGURE 22.5
Five-Year Municipal Interest Rate Swaps: Two Sides of the Market

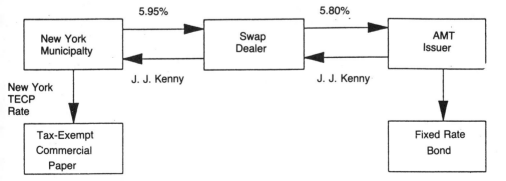

issuance alternative. Suppose that the fixed rate payer in the high tax state could issue five-year debt at a cost of 5.90%. Compare this with the net cost of issuing double or triple tax-exempt TECP and entering into a five-year interest rate swap contract. The net cost will be:

5.95% fixed payments made on the swap

− J.J. Kenny Index, floating rate payments received on the Swap

+ Double or triple tax-exempt TECP payments

+ LOC and remarketing fees.

If we assume that the combined LOC and remarketing fees total 47.5 bp, the net cost of the transaction will be:

$$5.95\% - \text{J.J. Kenny} + \text{TECP} + 47.5 \text{ bp}.$$

We want to know whether this net cost will be greater or less than 5.90%. The answer depends on the average difference between the J.J. Kenny Index and the double or triple tax-exempt TECP rate over the life of the swap agreement. Specifically, the swap will work out better if:

$$5.90\% > 6.425\% - \text{AVG(J.J. Kenny} - \text{TECP)},$$

where AVG(X) indicates the average of X over the period of the swap, or

$$\text{AVG(J.J. Kenny} - \text{TECP)} > 52.5 \text{ bp}.$$

It is impossible to know for certain what the average spread between J.J. Kenny and a specific double or triple tax-exempt commercial paper program will be over the period of five years. The spread depends on market conditions and on how skillfully the TECP program is managed. The J.J. Kenny index reflects weekly average yields on a fixed 30-day maturity, while maturities in a real TECP program can be varied to meet buyer interest. By way of comparison, however, over the past year the J.J. Kenny/TECP spread averaged 61 bp for California issuers and 75 bp in New York. If these relationships persist, therefore, the swap transaction would produce substantial savings for a New York issuer seeking five-year fixed rate liabilities and more modest but still significant savings for a California issuer. For issuers in other high tax states the expected savings will depend on the top-bracket state income tax rate and the technical condition of the local municipal money market.

For the fixed payer, the swap transaction is not the exact equivalent of direct issuance of a fixed rate bond. Specifically, the swap introduces two risks that offset some of the expected savings.

First, the issuer is subject to basis risk. This is the risk that the average spread between the issuer's TECP and the J.J. Kenny Index will average less than the breakeven 52.5 bp over the five-year term of the swap. This could happen for two reasons. First, all short-term interest rates in the issuer's state could rise relative to national market levels. This might occur because of a change in state tax law or because of a heavy volume of in-state short-term or variable rate issuance. Second, the issuer's credit or the credit of the specific LOC bank could deteriorate, raising the fixed payer's TECP rate relative to all other variable rate paper.

The second risk introduced by the swap transaction is counterparty credit risk. The magnitude of this risk is not large because, in the structure we have described, no principal payments change hands. If fixed rate payments on new interest rate swap contracts remain the same or fall, there would be no harm done to the fixed rate payer under the interest rate swap agreement if the counterparty defaulted on its contractual obligation. In that case, the original dealer could simply be replaced with another counterparty offering the same or better terms. Counterparty credit risk is a concern only if market levels for fixed rate payments on municipal interest rate swaps rise. If the original dealer defaulted under these circumstances, the issuer would be worse off because the swap contract could be replaced only at less advantageous terms.

These risks should be taken into account in evaluating the swap transaction. Such evaluations should also take the "upside" risk into account. The swap transaction offers the fixed payer an opportunity to benefit if in-state yields decline relative to national levels or if the issuer's credit quality improves. None of the risks are particularly large, but because they cannot be eliminated, swap transactions that offer minimal expected savings should probably be rejected.

Benefits and Risks for the Fixed Receiver

On the opposite side of the transaction, we have an AMT issuer seeking to create a variable rate liability. In this case, the swap transaction must produce an all-in interest cost of less than:

J.J. Kenny Index

+ LOC and remarketing Fees

+ the average AMT premium over the life of the swap.

The net cost of the fixed receiver swap will be:

> 6.50% fixed rate payments made on the bond
>
> − 5.80 fixed rate payments received on the swap
>
> + J.J. Kenny Index payments made on the swap.

Thus, the net payments made on the swap will be J.J. Kenny plus 70 bp. If we assume that the letter of credit and remarketing fees total 47.5 bp, the AMT issuer will be better off with the swap transaction if the average AMT premium over the life of the swap contract is greater than:

$$70 \text{ bp} - 47.5 \text{ bp} = 22.5 \text{ bp}$$

Again, by way of comparison, the average AMT/non-AMT spread for 30-day TECP over the past 12 months was 30 bp. Based on this statistic, the AMT issuer would be nearly indifferent between the swap and the direct issuance of variable rate debt. However, issuers who agree with our expectation that recent levels of the AMT/non-AMT spread in the money markets are more indicative of future patterns than the 12-month average would opt for the swap over the direct alternative.

The fixed receiver under the swap contract is subject to the same risks as the fixed payer. The swap will turn out to be a bad choice if the generic AMT/non-AMT spread in the short-term market averages less than 22.5 bp over the life of the swap contract, if the issuer's credit quality improves substantially, or if the counterparty defaults at an inopportune time. Observe that the complete set of transactions produces expected debt service cost savings for both issuers. The 15 bp differential between the fixed payer rate of 5.95% and the fixed receiver rate of 5.80 provides the incentive for the swap dealer to bring the two issuers together by making a market in municipal interest rate swaps.

OTHER MARKET ANOMALIES

Our purpose in describing this complete set of transactions was to show how the interest rate swap market can work, not to recommend any specific choices for issuers. Indeed, depending on market conditions, it can make sense for some issuers in high tax states to be fixed receivers and for some AMT issuers to be fixed payers. Nor are the opportunities to save money through the interest rate swap market confined to AMT issuers or municipalities in high tax states.

For example, it can be difficult for lower rated issuers to access the variable rate municipal market. Most variable rate structures require some credit or liquidity support, and under new capital adequacy rules for commercial banks, letters and lines of credit can be very expensive or even unobtainable for weaker issuers. Investors in the municipal bond market, by contrast, may be happy to accept a BBB-rated issuer's fixed rate obligations. In some cases, swap dealers may also be more willing to take on exposure to weaker credits. Because no principal payments are involved, the magnitude of credit risk on an interest rate swap is much smaller than on a letter or line of credit. Even if the swap counterparty requires a letter of credit to guarantee performance under the swap contract, the size of the LOC would be much smaller for the swap than for a bond issue.

Given this anomaly—greater acceptance of weaker credits in the municipal bond market than in the tax-exempt money market—an alternative set of transactions would involve a BBB credit as a fixed receiver and a high-grade issuer as a fixed payer.

Issuers who use interest rate swaps can also benefit from the flexibility of a commercial paper program. The J.J. Kenny Index is reset weekly and represents an average of 30-day tax-exempt interest rates. Thus, at any point in time, this index will not reflect the "best" an issuer can do in the municipal money market. Seasonal variations in the supply of and demand for short-term tax-exempt paper create frequent opportunities for issuers to save on interest expense by issuing commercial paper, or commercial paper mode variable rate obligations, tailored to the specific maturity needs of investors. Thus, issuers who retain the flexibility to set TECP maturities can expect over time to achieve interest costs lower than the J.J. Kenny Index.

One final example: Under international capital adequacy standards, commercial banks are required to maintain equity capital to support all on- and off-balance-sheet credit exposures. For example, a bank must maintain $4 million in equity capital to support a $100 million letter of credit for a corporation. The amount of capital required for any given dollar exposure varies depending on the counterparty. Specifically, a $100 million LOC written for a general municipal government would require only $800 in equity capital. Because less capital is required, the bank should be willing to write an LOC for a municipality for a much smaller fee than would be charged a corporation. If so, issuing variable rate debt would be less expensive, all-in, for a general municipal government than for a corporate obligor. This regulatory "anomaly" creates an opportunity for another complete set of transactions where a general government is a fixed payer and a corporate obligor is a fixed receiver.

CHAPTER 23

The Municipal Bond Futures Contract*

Eileen Baecher
Goldman, Sachs and Co.

The Municipal Bond Index Futures Contract, has become an important tool for investors and dealers in the municipal market. The use of the contract is not yet universal among institutional investors, and the futures market remains highly inefficient. Inefficiencies, in turn, create opportunities for investors in both the taxable and tax-exempt markets, to enhance total portfolio returns and minimal additional risk.

INTRODUCTION

The *Bond Buyer* Municipal Bond Index future has traded on the Chicago Board of Trade (CBT) since June 1985. Despite its five years of history, the structure and pricing of the municipal futures contract are still not well understood by many potential users. This has restricted the growth of the contract to some extent, as both taxable and tax-exempt investors have been unable to properly value the opportunities available in the market. In this report, we will attempt to dispel some of the confusion that surrounds the contract and explain how it

* Copyright 1990 by Goldman Sachs.

can be used for a variety of purposes. We begin by outlining the specifications of both the cash index and the futures contract. We follow this with a discussion of the theoretical pricing of the contract and then give some examples of the use of the contract, in combination with cash municipal bonds and in spread trading against taxable bond futures. Along the way, we will take a look at the historical pattern of some of the relevant variables.

CONTRACT SPECIFICATIONS

Structure

The municipal futures contract is based on the value of the *Bond Buyer* Municipal Bond Index. The contract does not specify a par holding of the underlying index. Rather, the dollar value of one future contract is equal to $1,000 multiplied by price of the future. This differs from the pricing of a Treasury bond or note futures contract, which is based on a stated par value of $100,000. The minimum price change in the future is $1/32$—for example, 90-$2/32$nds to 90-$1/32$nd. Each 32nd has a dollar value of $31.25. The futures trade in the same quarterly cycle as the taxable bond futures contracts: March, June, September, and December. The last trading day of any contract is the eighth last business day of the contract month, i.e., it does not trade during the last seven business days of the delivery month. One of the most important features of the contract is the absence of a requirement for physical delivery of the 40 municipal bonds in the index. Rather, the contract is cash-settled, with a final mark to market against the settlement price.[1] The final settlement price is equal to the average of the means of prices quoted by a minimum of four municipal bond dealer-to-dealer brokers, disregarding the highest and lowest price quotes for the 40 bonds in the index.

The Bond Buyer Index

The index is composed of 40 current long-term municipal bonds that meet the criteria of eligibility listed below:

---

[1] Marking to market is the procedure used on all futures exchanges to maintain the integrity of the contracts. The gains or losses from daily trading activity are calculated after the close of the market each day, and the holder of the position must cover the losses in cash. The money is passed through the clearing house the following day and is credited to those holding a profit on the day's activity. The clearing house serves as the counterparty in all trades and has the right to close positions on which margin calls are not met.

(1) *Size*—Minimum principal value of $50 million except for term housing bonds, which must have a minimum of $75 million.

(2) *Rating*—S&P rating of A− or higher and/or Moody's A or higher (A3 or higher for bonds rated by Moody's using the 1-3 suffix).

(3) *Maturity*—Minimum remaining term of 19 years when initially included in the index.

(4) *Call provisions*—Must be callable, with first call between seven and 16 years and at least one par call date.

(5) *Par issue*—Initial reoffering price between 95 and 105.

(6) *Seasoning*—Bonds must be out of syndicate and eligible for dealer trading in the secondary market at least one business day before inclusion in the index.

(7) *Private placements*—Not allowed.

(8) *Coupon*—Bonds must have fixed semiannual coupon payments.

(9) *Issuer limits*—No more than two term bonds of the same issuer can be included. If more than two are eligible, the larger size and longer maturity bonds will be used.

Index Calculation

The 40 bonds in the index are regularly reviewed, and systematically replaced, to keep the index accurate as a representative benchmark of current long-term municipal bond performance. Twice a month, on the 15th day and the last business day of the month, bonds may be added to or deleted from the index. Any new issue that meets the listing criteria is added to the index. The number of issues is then reduced to 40 by deleting issues that have had their rating level reduced below A−/A or bonds that have an extraordinary redemption clause and a flat price[2] that has risen above 102. A bond may also be deleted if a newly issued term bond of the same issuer is more actively traded than the one currently in the index. If there are still more than 40 bonds meeting the criteria for inclusion, then the least liquid issues— which are generally the shorter-maturity and smaller-size bonds—are removed until only 40 bonds remain in the index.

The continually changing composition of the bonds included in the index could cause a simple average price to change even if the bond yields did not change. Therefore, a *coefficient* is used to smooth the transition and eliminate price jumps that are caused by bond substitution rather than yield changes. When the index composition changes, the

---

[2] Flat price is equal to the present value of the bond minus accrued interest.

coefficient adjusts to maintain a constant index value from the closing on the day before the indexed change to the opening on the day of the change.

The index price is actually a coefficient-weighted arithmetic average of the *converted* prices of the 40 bonds. The converted price is the flat price of the bond divided by its *conversion factor*, which is equal to the price that would make the bond yield 8% to the first par call date, divided by 100.[3] The conversion factor eliminates most of the distortions in nominal price differences caused by coupon level and effectively allows the index price to represent the price of an 8% coupon bond.

The index is calculated using the following formula:

$$\text{Index} = \text{Coefficient} \times \sum_{i=1}^{40} \frac{\text{Bond price}}{\text{Conversion factor}} \times \frac{1}{40}$$

When new bonds are substituted:

$$\text{Coefficient} = \frac{\text{Old index}}{\text{New index price before coefficient is applied}}$$

or

$$\text{Coefficient} = \frac{\text{Old index}}{\sum_{i=1}^{40} \frac{\text{Bond price}}{\text{Conversion factor}} \times \frac{1}{40}}$$

Coefficient Drag

The coefficient adjustment mechanism seems fairly innocuous on the surface, but its use has a subtle effect on the absolute price level of the municipal contract over time. When the market rallies, premium bonds are taken out of the index and replaced with par bonds. The average coupon of the index is lowered, which in turn lengthens the duration of the index. Since the conversion factor corrects for the impact of coupon on price assuming similar yields, the effect of the longer duration is to increase the index price. Thus, to keep the index

---

[3] The municipal bond conversion factors are slightly different from those used for the other CBT contract. For the municipals, the coupon level is rounded to the nearest $1/8$% (rounded up in the case of ties), while for other contracts there is no rounding. Also, the time to maturity for municipals is calculated in complete, three-month increments from the first business day of the quarter following the bond's reoffer date to the first call-at-par date. For other CBT contracts, the term is from the first of the delivery month to the call or maturity date of the bond rounded down to the nearest quarter.

price constant as premium bonds are replaced, the coefficient must be less than 1.0. Conversely, if discount bonds are replaced, the average coupon increases, duration shortens, and the coefficient is greater than 1.0. So far, no surprises. However, because the index changes only every two weeks, the duration of the index can increase only *after* a rally and decrease only *after* a decline. The price change associated with a reversal of a yield change will always catch the index on the wrong side: extending duration after a rally and reducing duration after a price decline. The fact that all of the bonds in the index are callable can intensity this effect considerably. Consequently, the coefficient has a tendency to decline over time and to pull down the index price. This trend appears clearly in Figure 23.1, which plots the history of the municipal contract coefficient.

We can illustrate the drag of the adjustments by using the simplifying assumption that there is only one bond in the index. We will first assume that this is an 8% 20-year noncallable bond and that the index is priced at par. The coefficient and conversion factor are equal to one. Now if the market rallies so that the 8% bond yields 7% maturity, the index price, before bond substitution, will move to 110.68.

$$\text{Index} = (110.68/1.000) \times 1.000 = 110.68$$

FIGURE 23.1
Coefficient History

Coefficient

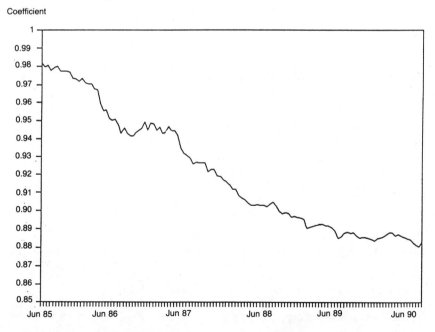

Following this move, a 7% par bond replaces the original 8% bond, and the coefficient equals 0.9972, which maintains the index price from before the substitution.

$$110.68 = (100.00/0.9010) \times 0.9972$$

Next, we assume that the market returns to the 8% yield level. The index price does not just return to par but moves to 99.72, or 0.28% below the original index price. The coefficient at this point is 0.9972 rather than the original 1.0.

$$\text{Index} = (90.10/0.9010) \times 0.9972 = 99.72$$

The 8% par bond will once again become the bond underlying the index, and after substitution, the index price is:[4]

$$99.72 = (100.00/1.000) \times 0.9972$$

The difference between the beginning and ending coefficients reflects the overall lag in the performance of the nominal index caused by the substitution of bonds and its effect on the index duration. Since yield changes are assumed to be normally distributed, the index price will tend to decrease over time because the substitution causes the index duration to lag market movements. This makes price histories of the index difficult to use because, for example, an index price of 100 in January 1990 corresponds to a lower yield level than a price of 100 one or two years later.

CONTRACT PRICING AND USE

Cash and Carry Trades

We define a *cash and carry* trade as the purchase of a deliverable security and the simultaneous sale of that security through the sale of a futures contract.[5] The hedged sale of the security creates a synthetic

---

[4] Note that the coefficient remains at 0.9972 even after the substitution, because the yield level is 8% and the factors will divide exactly once into the bond prices. At other yield levels, the ratio of bond price to factor will not be uniform among bonds of varying coupons.

[5] The cash and carry trade is also called a long basis trade. Selling the cash and buying the future is a "reverse cash and carry" or a "short basis trade."

money market position, beginning with the settlement of the security purchase and maturing on the future delivery date. The rate of return on the synthetic asset is called the *implied repo rate* of the cash and carry and is useful as a measure of the relative value of the futures contract versus the index. If the cash and carry has a return greater than the cost of financing the purchase of the physical security, then there is a potential arbitrage. These arbitrages do appear in the municipal market, although the more common situation is for implied repo rates to be lower than actual financing rates (see Figure 23.2). The difference between the implied and actual rates provides a reasonable measure of the contract's cheapness. The futures price is the selling price; when it is lowered, the holding period return, i.e., the implied repo, declines. Therefore the greater the difference, the cheaper the contract price relative to the spot index.

Creating an actual cash and carry position with the municipal contract is fairly cumbersome, not only because there are 40 individual bonds, but also because the contract does not specify par values of the individual bonds. The future's price is simply multiplied by $1,000 to determine a theoretical market value. Therefore, we cannot specify the true market value of the index without making several assumptions and

FIGURE 23.2
Muni Implied Repo Rate Less Tax-Exempt 45-Day Commercial Paper

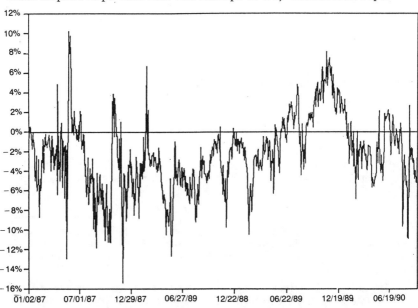

numerous calculations.[6] However, we can calculate a reasonable estimate of the implied repo rate by using two simplifying assumptions:
first, that the index price is the price of a bond with a coupon equal to
the average coupon of the 40 bonds,[7] and second, that this bond can be
found in the market.[8] The return calculation does not require a par
amount to be specified, so by using just the quoted spot index and futures prices, we can find the return on the cash and carry position using the following formula:

$$\text{Return} = \frac{(\text{Index} - \text{FP})(1 - \text{CG}) + \text{Index (CY)}\dfrac{t}{365}}{\text{Index}(1 - \text{TD} \times \text{OI})}$$

where:

$\quad$ FP = Future price

Index = Spot index price

Return = Periodic simple yield

$\quad$ t = Days from settlement to last trading date of contract

$\quad$ TD = Deductible portion of interest paid on financing

$\quad$ OI = Ordinary income tax rate

$\quad$ CY = Current yield of index

$\quad$ CG = Capital gains tax rate applicable to future

Rearranging this return formula, we can determine what a fair value
of the futures contract should be. Like all other futures, which are
standardized forward contracts, the important information includes
the current price, the level of coupon income and the cost of carrying
(financing) the position. In this equation, we use an actual financing
rate ("Repo") as a substitute for the implied financing rate.

$$\text{Future Price} = \text{Index}\left(1 + \frac{\text{Repo} \times \dfrac{t}{360} \times (1 - \text{TD} \times \text{OI}) - \text{CY} \times \dfrac{t}{365}}{1 - \text{CG}}\right)$$

[6] We discuss the assumptions and calculations in detail in the section on synthetic assets.

[7] This price does not include accrued interest, but this omission has a negligible
impact on the return calculation.

[8] This is the assumption used in calculating the total return numbers reported
every month.

The inclusion of tax effects on the price of the future are very important when considering the fair value of the contract.[9] All futures should trade at prices between the arbitrage bounds defined by the executable levels of transacting in the cash and repo markets, recognizing the differences between bid and offered levels. Municipal cash positions are obviously tax-exempt, but futures gains and losses are taxable, and part of the cost of financing may be deductible for some taxpayers. The inclusion of differing tax liabilities drives the range of "fair" values on the municipal contract even wider than for other fixed income contracts.

The cost of establishing a cash and carry determines the upper arbitrage bound, using the borrowing rate in the repo market for the cost of financing, the offered prices of the cash bonds, and the bid side of the futures market. Dealers must use a taxable financing rate and cannot deduct any interest expenses. This means that for the dealer community, the implied repo rate can rise as far as the nominal level of taxable financing rates before arbitrage is possible. Therefore, the upper bound arbitrage level—that is, the future price needed to produce an implied repo rate at which arbitrage is possible—is determined by the level of taxable financing.

The lower arbitrage bound will reflect the level at which "synthetic" municipal bond positions yield more than physical bonds. It is not driven by financing rates in the same way as the upper bound because there is no generally available technique for carrying short bond positions. As discussed below, the synthetic bond return is the combination of the income from a tax-exempt money market investment and the necessary convergence of the future price to the spot index price by each contract's final trading day. All other things being equal, the futures price must be low enough to provide an after-tax return at least equal to municipal bond yields before investors will step in to buy the contract as a substitute for cash bonds. A tax-exempt entity will clearly be able to execute a synthetic using a higher futures price relative to the spot than will a taxable entity. Again, we see that the implied repo rate corresponding to the lower bound price must be a taxable rate.

---

[9] The relevant taxes are the ordinary income tax (for both interest income and expenses) and the capital gains tax. Futures price changes are currently subject to capital gains treatment under the 60% long-term/40% short-term designations. The split is significant only to the extent that short-term losses can only be used to offset short-term gains. Long-term losses can be used to offset either short-term or long-term capital gains. With respect to the financing costs, the deductibility of interest expense on borrowing for purposes of investing in tax-exempt debt is strictly limited under the Internal Revenue Code.

The point of this discussion is that while the contract may appear to be either rich or cheap versus a particular set of tax assumptions, it may become even richer or cheaper because of the tax assumptions valid for the marginal users, which tend to be taxable entities. Goldman Sachs produces a daily report to calculate the fair value range of futures prices based on an input set of tax assumptions. The report can also be used to determine the after-tax implied repo rate, given an input set of spot and futures prices. This information provides a rough indication as to whether the municipal contract is under- or overvalued relative to the cash index. Still, futures arbitragers will generally want to wait until misvaluations are quite substantial before attempting to exploit the cheapness or richness of the contract. Because it is difficult to purchase or sell a portfolio of actual bonds that will reliably reproduce the performance of the index, the return on a cash and carry or synthetic asset trade will also depend on the specific performance of the bonds in the cash position.

Synthetic Assets

As we discussed previously, the formula for the implied repo is actually a simplification of the transactions (and therefore the pricing) needed to execute a cash and carry in the spot market. This is because of the translation of the individual cash bond prices through the factor and coefficient calculations. Remember that the index value, which we used as the dollar investment base for the implied repo calculation, is equal to the coefficient multiplied by the average of actual bond prices without accrued interest, divided by the bonds' individual factors. To physically buy the index would require the outlay of more cash than the index price multiplied by $1,000. Specifically, it would require the sum of the full prices of each bond weighted by the bond's assumed par value used in the index.[10]

Why does this matter? As we stated earlier, the cash and carry trade creates a synthetic money market position; a *reverse cash and carry* is a synthetic municipal bond position. We define a synthetic bond as the combination of a cash equivalent and an instrument that replicates the risk, or price performance, of a physical bond. The futures contract can be combined with a cash (money market) position to synthetically create the *Bond Buyer* Municipal Index. Since the contract has a tendency to trade at the lower end of its fair value range, the synthetic asset frequently appears to be a more attractive way to invest in municipal bonds than simply buying bonds outright.

---

[10] There is no actual weighting of par values in the construction of the index. The individual prices as a percentage of the sum of 40 prices can be used as a proxy.

Synthetic Index Return. Consider a portfolio manager who has $100 million to invest in the municipal bond market. Assume that the manager could purchase the bonds in the index or could use futures to synthetically create the index. The first step in creating the synthetic is to determine the dollar duration of the cash investment—$100 million in this example. The manager then invests the cash in a money market instrument and purchases futures in a dollar-duration-weighted amount. (Alternatively, if he identified the par amount of the index that could be purchased with $100 million, then he could combine the money market asset with the purchase of one contract per $100,000 of the index par value.) On the final trading day of the futures contract, the futures price will converge to the spot price. This convergence will more or less offset the cost of purchasing the physical index at that time. The internal rate of return on this series of cash flows is the return of the synthetic index.[11] More frequently, the return over the term between the spot date and the futures expiration date is used as a measure of the synthetic return. The analysis in either case is based on a static market environment. Absolute changes in yield level will clearly result in a different total return for a short-term holding period.

To determine exactly how attractive the synthetic asset is, the manager must compare it with the cash alternatives; this requires that the two positions be based on the same dollar investment. The return on the physical index is simply its internal rate of return. To determine the net return on the synthetic index, the manager must calculate the after-tax return—netted against the cost of the index—on the combination of a money market investment and the difference between the spot index price and the futures price.

"Quick and Dirty." For simplicity, the synthetic return is frequently compared with the yield on a specific bond instead of the index yield. This allows you to make a very simple estimate of the synthetic asset return by dividing the sum of the tax-adjusted gain from the convergence of the spot index and future prices and the income from the money market investment by the cash invested in the money market. For example, suppose an investor was considering

---

[11] There are several finer points to consider in this analysis: (1) The convergence of spot and futures prices does not take place in a predictable fashion, and cash margin payments may be incurred or received for a slight difference in cash flows. (2) The index comprises bonds with varying maturity and call dates, so the maturity of the portfolio is not a single specific date. This means that the initial investment is not necessarily fully invested over a specific period. (3) The index composition may change prior to the final settlement date, so the full price of the index may be different from the initial estimate.

the purchase of $10 million face value of an 8% bond with a dollar duration of $9,000 per basis point change in yield. The synthetic alternative is to invest the $10 million dollars in the money market—say, a 6.0% tax-exempt instrument maturing on the last trading day of the future contract—and to use the futures contract to bring the duration risk up to that of the physical bond. You can determine the number of contracts needed by dividing the dollar duration of the physical bond by the dollar duration of the future.[12] For simplicity, we will assume that the dollar duration of the contract is $100 per basis point, and therefore 90 futures are used to create the synthetic bond. We can calculate the periodic synthetic return as:

$$\text{Return} = \frac{N \times [\text{Index} - \text{FP}] \times [1 - \text{CG}] + F \times \text{MMkt} \times \dfrac{t}{360}}{F}$$

where:

N = Number of contracts

Index = Spot index price

F = Face value

FP = Future price

CG = Capital gain tax rate

t = Days from settlement to last trading date of contract

MMkt = Money market rate (tax-exempt)

Despite its appeal, this simple calculation has some obvious drawbacks. In the first place, there may be solid fundamental reasons for a difference in the yield of the index compared with the yield of a specific bond. Moreover, there is no assurance that the relative yield performance of the actual bond and the index are well correlated. Yield curve shape, credit, and call features will be different to a greater or lesser extent, and this raises the possibility that the synthetic may underperform the actual on a total return basis.

To Be Precise. The more accurate way to evaluate the return on a synthetic is to compare the yields that would be realized from

---

[12] Dollar duration quantifies the change in the present value of a security resulting from a unit change in yield. The unit change can be a percentage point or a basis point; the magnitude of the change is significant only in that the change must be consistent among all the securities being evaluated. Dollar duration per basis point change is the same measure as the "dollar value of an 01."

(1) actually buying the spot index or (2) investing in the money market and purchasing the bonds at the forward price represented by the future. This involves an estimation of the full price of the index prior to all conversions for futures pricing.

One method of determining a full price for the index is to work with the average coupon of the 40 bonds and the average time to par call dates. The index price is then used as the converted price of a single bond with that coupon and term. For example, if the weighted average coupon of the index is 7.25% with a 15-year term, and the price of the index is 92.5 with a coefficient of 0.886 and a factor of 0.9352, then we can calculate the full price of the index using the formula below:

$$\text{Full price} = \frac{\text{Future price}}{\text{Coefficient}} \times \text{Factor} + (0.25 \times \text{Average coupon})$$

$$= \frac{92.5}{0.886} \times 0.9352 + (0.25 \times 0.0725) = 97.65$$

The full price of the index can be used as a typical bond quote, i.e., as a percentage of par. When multiplied by a face value, this will give the total dollars invested and will allow the calculation of the dollar duration of the index. The (periodic) synthetic return calculation then becomes:

$$\text{Return} = \frac{N \times [\text{Index} - \text{FP}] \times [1 - \text{CG}] + \text{Full price} \times \text{MMkt} \times \dfrac{t}{360}}{\text{Full price}}$$

An even more precise method of determining the full index price requires pricing all the bonds in the index. Market quotes will be flat prices, so the investor has to calculate and add the accrued interest to get a full price. He then estimates a par value of each bond, using the flat price of the bond as a percentage of the sum of bond prices, and multiplies by $100,000. This will give a one-contract par value of the index of $100,000 and a market value of the index equal to the sum of the full prices multiplied by the respective par amounts. The dollar duration of the physical index is equal to the sum of the dollar durations of the bonds in the index; it is used as a measure of interest rate sensitivity.

MUNICIPALS VS. TREASURIES

There are many different reasons for comparing the performance of the municipal bond future with that of the Treasury bond future.

Hedgers might use the Treasury contract because of its greater liquidity or because the municipal future is particularly cheap (sellers) or rich (buyers), relative to the cash index. Traders sometimes take a position in the spread between the two markets on the expectation that one will outperform the other. Regardless of the reason for using Treasury futures with or against municipal cash and futures positions, there are a few points to keep in mind.

Level Effects

The MOB (municipal over bond) spread is the name given to the simple difference between the price of the municipal contract for one delivery month and the price of the Treasury future for the same delivery month. As we discussed earlier, the price of the municipal contract will tend to trend downward over time because of the coefficient drag. Consequently, comparing a MOB spread level from one time period with that of a prior time period cannot provide meaningful information on the relative yields of municipal bonds and Treasury bonds at the different dates.

Additionally, over any given time period, the direction of movement in the MOB spread tends to be strongly influenced by the direction of yield levels. This is because the yields on municipal securities are not as volatile as those on taxable securities. Therefore, as yields in general increase, prices fall further in the taxable market, and the MOB spread widens (becomes more positive or less negative). If yields generally decline, Treasury prices will increase by a greater percentage than municipal prices, and the MOB spread will narrow. Figure 23.3 illustrates the influence of interest rate direction on the MOB spread.

In addition to the differences in yield volatility between the two markets, there are marked differences in convexity between the index and the deliverable pool of bonds that underlie the Treasury bond future. All the bonds in the municipal index are callable and will trade to the call date once the price of the bond exceeds the call price. In a rally, this will tend to limit the upside of the index. While there are many callable bonds eligible for delivery in the Treasury contract, they tend to be delivered only at yield levels below 8.5%.[13] Given that there are no more callable Treasuries being issued and the lowest coupon on a callable is 10.375%, these issues definitely should be trading to call when delivered. When yields are above 8.5%, the noncallable bonds are the most attractively priced bonds for delivery. This shift between callable and noncallable causes a significant duration change in the future. However, the duration shift occurs in a fairly smooth, predictable

---

[13] For more details on this point, see Eileen Baecher and Bruce Petersen, "Which Bond is Cheap?" Goldman, Sachs & Co., *Futures and Options Research,* January 1988.

FIGURE 23.3

Interest Rate Movements and the MOB Spread

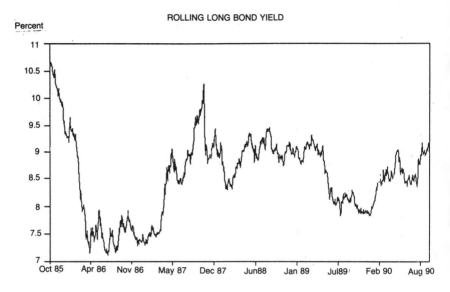

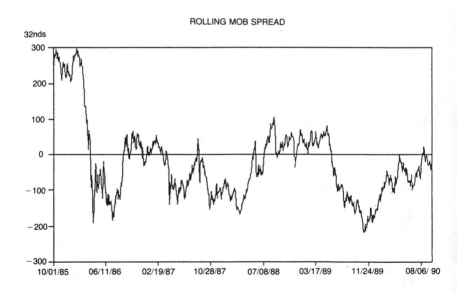

pattern over the yield range of 8 to 9%. The difference in the patterns of convexity between the taxable and tax-exempt contracts means that in quick market rallies, the municipal contract can underperform the Treasury future—a circumstance that exaggerates the effect of yield volatility differences on the direction of the MOB spread.

Hedge Ratios

Hedging requires a portfolio manager to offset the dollar duration of a risky position with a position in a hedge instrument with an equal dollar duration. When municipals are cross-hedged with Treasuries, the hedge ratios must also take into account the volatility difference between the yields on tax-exempt and taxable securities. The process is fairly straightforward. After determining the appropriate number of taxable contracts to offset the dollar duration, the manager multiplies the number of contracts by the percentage correlation between the two types of yields. Although this percentage has fluctuated and will continue to do so because of changes in tax codes, the longer-term average of tax-exempt yield volatility has been between 75% and 80% of taxable yield volatility.

Moreover, as is always the case with duration-matched hedges, the portfolio manager has to monitor and rebalance the positions during periods of high volatility because of convexity differences between the two instruments.

CONCLUSION

The municipal bond futures contract can provide many opportunities for those who are willing to take the time to explore the details of its design. The cash settlement procedure ensures that any cheap or rich contract prices seen during the trading life of the contract will return to fair value by the settlement date. There are important tax implications, but by analyzing future and spot market prices in the context of their own tax exposures, investors should be able to find many profitable uses for the *Bond Buyer* Municipal Bond Index future.

CHAPTER 24

The Valuation of Municipal Forwards^{SM}*

Aaron S. Gurwitz

Arthur M. Miller

Michelle Deligiannis
Goldman, Sachs and Co.

Municipal Forwards^{SM} are contracts stipulating that one or more investors will purchase, at a designated price, tax-exempt bonds with a specified coupon to be delivered by an issuer at some future date. For example, an investor might agree on September 1, 1989, to purchase at par on September 1, 1992, 7.75% coupon bonds maturing in 2019. Contracts involving the forward purchase of more than $500 million in tax-exempt bonds have been entered into since the spring of 1989.

The recent introduction of Municipal Forwards provides opportunities for both issuers and investors in the municipal market. In particular, Municipal Forwards have enabled issuers of pollution control revenue bonds (PCRs) and industrial development bonds (IDBs), who are barred from advance refunding, to "lock in" substantial present value in debt service savings on outstanding high-coupon bonds that cannot be called for several months or years. As the market for Municipal Forwards matures, other uses will be found. For example, during periods when long-term municipal rates are low but short-term taxable rates are lower, issuers funding construction projects would be able to lock in attractive long-term financing rates while avoiding negative arbitrage on bond proceeds.

Because the Municipal Forward market is new and because some of the transaction structures have been complex, the contracts that have been brought to market to date have been priced very attractively from the investor's point of view. However, Municipal Forwards could play an important role in municipal bond portfolios even if the contracts were priced with perfect efficiency. Specifically, forward contracts, such as the Chicago Board of Trade Municipal Bond Index Futures Contract, provide a way in which investors can, in effect, leverage their exposure to the municipal bond market or benefit from aberrations in the shape of the municipal yield curve.

As long as the municipal yield curve is upward sloping, municipal bonds for forward delivery will always be priced to offer a higher yield than otherwise identical bonds for current delivery. For example, in the Municipal Forward contract for the City and County of Honolulu the issuer agreed to sell 7.35% bonds due in 2008 at par 11 months forward. At the time, 2008 Honolulu general obligations for current delivery would have been priced at par to yield something closer to 7%.

The question, then, for both the issuer and the investors was: "Is a 35 bp concession to the current delivery, or 'spot,' rate too high or too low on a bond for delivery 11 months forward?" For the issuer, the 35 bp difference was, in essence, the price it paid for the ability to guarantee the level of present value debt service savings to be realized when the forward bonds were delivered. For the investor, the 35 bp was compensation (1) for the forgone opportunity to earn 7% between the settlement date of the contract and the delivery date of the bonds, since an 11-month tax-exempt investment would have earned only about 5.80% at the time; (2) for the illiquidity of a Municipal Forward contract relative to a cash bond; and (3) for the effort involved in analyzing and purchasing a new product. In this event, both parties agreed that the 7.35% coupon for forward purchase at par was appropriately priced.

The purpose of this month's focus essay is to analyze the valuation of Municipal Forwards and to provide a mechanism for future potential parties to these contracts to decide whether any given difference between spot and forward rates is appropriate. In the body of the essay we analyze the value of Municipal Forwards using direct measures of the cash flows generated by these contracts. In the Appendix, we present methods for evaluating forward purchases using a standard bond calculator, along with a hypothetical example.

ANALYZING MUNICIPAL FORWARDS: COMPARING THE CASH FLOWS

The first step in analyzing a municipal forward contract is to compare two sets of cash flows (see Table 24.1). The first set of flows is that

TABLE 24.1
Equal IRR Cash Flows: Standard Bond for Current Delivery
Versus Municipal Forward Plus a Short Bond

	Standard Standard Bond	Municipal Forward Plus Short Bond
01 Aug 2489	−1,000	−1,000
01 Feb 2490	36.25	31.5
01 Aug 2490	36.25	31.5
01 Feb 2491	36.25	31.5
01 Aug 2491	36.25	31.5
01 Feb 2492	36.25	31.5
01 Aug 2492	36.25	37.3277
01 Feb 2493	36.25	37.3277
01 Aug 2493	36.25	37.3277
01 Feb 2494	36.25	37.3277
	.	.
	.	.
01 Aug 2017	36.25	37.3277
01 Feb 2018	36.25	37.3277
01 Aug 2018	36.25	37.3277
01 Feb 2024	36.25	37.3277
01 Aug 2024	1,036.25	1,037.3277
IRR	7.25%	7.25%
Semiannual Coupon	7.25	7.46554

generated by a bond for current delivery with a 7.25% semiannual coupon and priced at par. The second set of flows is generated by a Municipal Forward contract for purchase in three years combined with a tax-exempt investment that is purchased at par, pays a 6.30% coupon, and matures on the delivery date of the forward bonds. For the present, in order to simplify the analysis we will assume that the bonds for forward delivery are non-callable. Later we will examine the impact of optional call provisions on the valuation of municipal forwards.

As Table 24.1 indicates, both sets of cash flows offer the same 7.25% internal rate of return (IRR).[1] If these cash flows were otherwise equal—specifically, if they were paid by the same obligor and were equally liquid—then an investor would be indifferent between the two. The rate giving rise to the semiannual interest payments for the forward bond that produce the same IRR on the combined short and long positions as on a long bond for current delivery is termed the

---

[1] The internal rate of return is the discount rate at which the present value of the cash flows (receipts and payments) is zero.

forward rate (or the implied forward rate). In this case, the coupon that produces a 7.25% IRR for the combined cash flows is 7.4655%.

LIQUIDITY PREMIUM

In all cases, the actual coupon on Municipal Forward bonds will be at least somewhat above the forward rate. Thus, for example, when the spot rate is 7.25% and the forward rate is 7.47%, the coupon assigned to the bonds for forward purchase at par might be 8.00% or even higher. Part of this additional coupon compensates the investor for the fact that, at present, a Municipal Forward contract is much less liquid than the typical already-issued municipal bond. Evaluating this liquidity premium is a little tricky because the contract is illiquid only until the forward delivery date of the bonds, but the compensation for that illiquidity is built into the coupon of the Municipal Forwards and earned over the entire life of the issue after the delivery date.

To roughly estimate an appropriate liquidity premium for the purposes of our analysis, we begin by observing that the bid-asked spread on some liquid three-year bonds (say, '92 prerefunded issues) is about a quarter-point. The spread on the least liquid three-year paper is about three quarters of a point. Therefore, we can generalize that the municipal market currently demands about a half-point of compensation in the price of a bond for three years' illiquidity. Future valuing this half point concession to the delivery date three years hence at 6.30% produces a .60 point concession. Amortizing this concession over 27-years (the life of the forward bond after the delivery date) at a 7.25% discount rate gives roughly 5.1 basis points (bp) of yield. Thus, an additional five or six bp above the forward rate should be adequate compensation for the fact that the Municipal Forwards will be highly illiquid during the period before the delivery date.

THE THEORETICAL VALUE OF MUNICIPAL FORWARDS

Now the combination of the forward rate (7.47%) and the liquidity premium totals roughly 7.52%. This is the theoretical value of the municipal forward. If the coupon on the forward bonds in our example were set at this level, investors should be completely indifferent between owning the Municipal Forward-short bond combination and owning otherwise identical bonds for current delivery. From the issuer's point of view, the 7.52% rate in this example is the absolute lowest true interest cost (yield to maturity) that could be realized on Municipal Forwards, given the 7.25% estimate of the spot rate, the 6.30% short rate, and a one-half point illiquidity penalty. In practice, of course, the coupon assigned to the forward bonds will have to be above this theoretical rate. Municipal Forwards are, after all a new product, and many investors are required to obtain approval for purchases of innovative investments. Also, although the Municipal Forward-short bond combination would, with a 7.52% coupon, generate the same internal rate of return as a somewhat illiquid but otherwise identical bond for current delivery, the *current* return on the Municipal Forward is lower than that of the standard bond until the delivery date. Thus, investors who are more concerned with current yield than with total return over a long horizon—and there are many of these in the municipal market—would not be indifferent between the two cash flows, even if the forward bonds carried the "theoretically correct" coupon.

Finally, in most of the Municipal Forward transactions executed to date, the investor bears the risk that tax law changes might adversely affect the value of the forward bonds before the delivery date. This risk can be substantial, especially if there is a multi-year lag between the contract settlement date and the bond purchase date, because Congress has, in recent tax legislation, established a practice of "grandfathering" outstanding bonds or existing portfolios when changing the overall treatment of municipal bonds. Forward bonds might not be grandfathered under future tax legislation.

For all of these reasons, the yields to maturity of the forward bonds, evaluated as of the delivery date, is likely to be substantially higher than the theoretical value. The difference between the theoretical value, 7.52% in this example, and the yield to maturity of the forward bonds as of the delivery date will be termed the *additional premium*. Thus, if our hypothetical municipal forwards were to be given an 8.00% coupon and sold at par on the delivery date, the additional premium would be 48 bp. The 48 bp figure is the number investors should look at in deciding whether to buy the bonds. The question would be, does the extra 48 bp provide sufficient compensation for the "hassle" of getting approval of a new product, for the lower current yield during the period before the delivery date, and for the risk of an adverse tax law change?

Issuers should also be aware of the additional premium. In essence, it is the price they pay for locking in the level of rates currently available in the market, and in each case the issuer must judge whether that price is acceptable or too high.

THE IMPACT OF THE YIELD PREMIUMS

It is important to understand how the investor realizes the benefit of these yield premiums—both the liquidity and additional premiums. One way of realizing the benefits would be to sell the forward bonds on the delivery date. Thus, if the spot rate on the issuer's bonds did not change—and recalling that our hypothetical bonds are noncallable—then at the delivery date (assumed to be February 1, 1992) the forward bonds would be worth 108.885 (8s priced to yield 7.25%). Since the bonds would be purchased at par, the investor could realize an 8.885 point gain. Part of this gain, roughly 2.643 points, is compensation for the forgone difference between 7.25% and 6.30% over three years. The remainder, 6.242 points, represents the combination of a .602 point liquidity premium and a 5.640 point additional premium.

Investors such as mutual funds, which mark their portfolios to market on a periodic basis, need not necessarily wait until the delivery date to realize the benefit of these premiums or the compensation for the differential between the long and short rates. As time goes by between the settlement date of the Municipal Forward contract and the delivery date of the bonds, the value of the contract will gradually accrete from zero on the settlement date to 8.885 points just before the delivery date (again, assuming no change in interest rates). That is, as the time remaining before the delivery date diminishes, (1) the cost of forgone interest earnings in advance of delivery declines, (2) the illiquidity premium diminishes, and (3) the elements that contribute to the additional premium becomes less important. Suppose the combined values of all of these yield premiums is 75 bp three years before delivery. If a new Municipal Forward contract were executed one year before delivery and if the spot rate were still 7.25%, the coupon on the new forward bonds might only have to be, say, 7.50%. If so, the outstanding contract would have risen in value, and this increase would be reflected in the net asset value of the portfolio that included the contract. We will discuss below, in more detail, the influences that affect the marked-to-market value of a Municipal Forward.

THE PRICE PERFORMANCE OF MUNICIPAL FORWARDS

Absent an active secondary market in Municipal Forward contracts—which may eventually develop but is not there now—investors who must (or wish to) mark their portfolios to market periodically will have to rely on analytical methods to evaluate these positions. This section outlines our recommended approach to valuing Municipal Forwards in the absence of secondary market prices.

The marked-to-market value of a Municipal Forward contract reflects the following seven elements:

(1) the current spot yield to maturity on the issuer's bonds for current delivery and maturity equal to that of the forward bonds;

(2) the current spot yields to the first and par calls for bonds for current delivery and call dates and prices equal to that of the forward bonds;

(3) the current yield to maturity on obligations of the issuer that mature on the delivery date of the forward bonds;[2]

(4) the characteristics of the forward bonds, including:

coupon,

maturity,

first call date,

first call premium, and

par call date;

(5) the delivery date of the forward bonds;

(6) the liquidity premium on bonds with maturities equal to the delivery date; and

(7) the additional premium on newly issued Municipal Forwards with the same delivery date.

The general approach to valuing an outstanding Municipal Forward is to compute the present value of the cash flows that would be produced if a new buyer purchased the contract in combination with a short-term municipal of (1) comparable credit quality and (2) maturity equal to the delivery date of the forward bonds. The marked-to-market value of the contract is the difference between this present value and par. The discount rate for the present value calculation is the sum of two components:

a) the spot yield to maturity (or yield to call) for long-term bonds of the issue, plus

b) a structure premium.

The structure premium will be defined here as the difference between the spot yield to maturity when the contract was originally priced and the discount rate at which the present value of the cash flows produced by a combination of a short-term tax-exempt investment and the Municipal Forward contract is equal to par. For example, consider the following Municipal Forward contract:

---

[2]Some Municipal Forward contracts have been structured so that the investor receives interest on a escrow account of taxable securities between the settlement date of the contract and the delivery date of the bonds. In such cases, the relevant short rate would be the after-tax yield on the taxables.

Forward Bond Coupon: 8.00%

Settlement: August 1, 1989

Delivery: February 1, 1992

Maturity: August 1, 2019

First Call Date: August 1, 1999

First Call Premium: 102

Par Call Date: August 1, 2001

Initial Spot Long Rate: 7.25%

Initial Short Rate: 6.30%

Initial Spot Yield to Calls: 7.15%

With these values, the combination of a short-term investment in one bond and a Municipal Forward contract to buy one bond produces five semiannual cash flows of $31.50, followed by 27 years of semiannual interest payments of $40 and a final payment of $1,040. The discount rate at which the value of these cash flows is par is approximately 7.67%. Thus, the structure premium is 42 bp. Let us assume that the structure premium remains the same but that all other interest rates rise by 100 bp. That is, the spot long rate becomes 8.25%, the short rate becomes 7.30% and the spot yields to call become 8.15%. In this market, a new purchaser of the outstanding Municipal Forward could produce the cash flow presented in Table 24.2. The discount rates used to compute the present value of these cash flows would be 8.67% in the case of the cash flows to maturity and 8.57% in the case of the cash flows to the calls. We will assume that the marked-to-market value of the Municipal Forward is the difference between par and minimum of these three cash flows (in this case, to maturity), or—$86.66 per forward bond. If yields fall substantially, of course, the discounted present values of the cash flows to one or the other of the call dates will produce the lowest marked-to-market value of the three alternatives.

THE PERFORMANCE OF MUNICIPAL FORWARDS

We can use this methodology to illustrate the impact of various scenarios on the marked-to-market value of a Municipal Forward. In all cases, we will be reporting the "worst case" valuations, based on the minimum of the present values of cash flows to maturity, first call and par call respectively. This approach will tend to underestimate the market value of the forwards the most when the present values are close to the call prices. The hypothetical Municipal Forward on which all scenarios are based is the one described above: the 8% of 2019. In each scenario we

TABLE 24.2
Cash Flows to Maturity, First Call, and par Call for Hypothetical
Municipal Forwards Combined with Short-Term Tax-Exempt Investment

Date	Cash Flow to Maturity	Cash Flow to First Call	Cash Flow to Par Call
01 Feb 2490	36.5	36.5	36.5
01 Aug 2490	36.5	36.5	36.5
01 Feb 2491	36.5	36.5	36.5
01 Aug 2491	36.5	36.5	36.5
01 Feb 2492	36.5	36.5	36.5
01 Aug 2492	40	40	40
01 Feb 2493	40	40	40
01 Aug 2493	40	40	40
01 Feb 2494	40	40	40
01 Aug 2494	40	40	40
01 Feb 2495	40	40	40
01 Aug 2495	40	40	40
01 Feb 2496	40	40	40
01 Aug 2496	40	40	40
01 Feb 2497	40	40	40
01 Aug 2497	40	40	40
01 Feb 2498	40	40	40
01 Aug 2498	40	40	40
01 Feb 2499	40	40	40
01 Aug 2499	40	1,060	40
01 Feb 2000	40		40
01 Aug 2000	40		40
01 Feb 2001	40		40
01 Aug 2001	40		1,040
01 Feb 2002	40		
01 Aug 2002	40		
.	.		
.	.		
01 Aug 2017	40		
01 Feb 2018	40		
01 Aug 2018	40		
01 Feb 2024	40		
01 Aug 2024	1,040		
Present Value	913.343 @8.57%	955.411 @8.67%	942.330 @8.57%
Contract Value	−86.66	−44.59	−57.67

TABLE 24.3
Impact of Parallel Yield Curve Shifts on the
Marked-to-Market Value of Municipal Forwards

Shift in Curve (bp)	Marked-to-Market Value (points)
+300	−21.129
+200	−15.602
+100	− 8.666
−100	5.278
−200	11.071
−300	17.574

alter only one of the determinants of the value of the Municipal Forward, holding the others constant.

Scenario I: Parallel Yield Curve Shifts

As Table 24.1 indicates, the call features of the forward bond tend to suppress performance as interest rates fall. Embedded calls affect the performance of most long-term municipals, but because Municipal Forwards can be used as a leverage vehicle for increasing exposure to the municipal market, the impact of calls on performance will be more important for these contracts than for newly issued bonds. Also, investors have been concerned about call features because the forward bonds are expected to trade at a premium as soon as they are purchased in the future.[3] For these reasons, most of the Municipal Forwards that have come to market to date have carried greater call protection—longer non-refund periods or higher call premiums—than is typical of most newly issued municipals.

Scenario II: Changes in the Shape of the Yield Curve

The value of a Municipal Forward also depends on the relationship between long- and short-term interest rates. In fact, if the yield curve is inverted, then the forward rate is lower than the yield on bonds for current delivery; the investor picks up yield by holding short-term securities and is willing to give up something on the long end in exchange.

---

[3] Under the various tax law limitations, the extent to which IDBs and PCRs can be issued at substantial discounts from par is unclear. Thus, the ability of the issuer to reduce the coupon on the Municipal Forward bond by lowering the purchase price at delivery may be limited.

TABLE 24.4
Impact of Yield Curve Changes on the
Marked-to-Market Value of Municipal
Forwards (Long Rates Held Constant)

Short Rate Change (bp)	Marked-to-Market Value (points)
+300	6.263
+200	4.023
+100	1.784
−100	−2.695
−200	−4.934
−300	−7.174

The impact of changes in the short rate with the long rate held constant
is illustrated in Table 24.4.

Scenario III: Changes in the Structure Premium

Shifts in the structure premium will have the same effect on the value
of the forward contract as changes in the long-term spot rate when the
short rate is held constant. The additional premium can be expected to
diminish over time. Also, if a large number of Municipal Forwards are
sold and a secondary market develops, the illiquidity premium may
diminish. Finally, as new products mature, the market typically demands less of a concession. Table 24.5 illustrates the impact of changes
in the initial structure premium of 42 bp on the value of our hypothetical Municipal Forward contract.

TABLE 24.5
Impact of Changes in the Structure Premium
on the Marked-to-Market Value of Municipal
Forwards

Change in Premium (bp)	Marked-to-Market Value (points)
0 Premium	2.942
−30	1.956
−20	1.144
−10	.340
+10	−1.243
+20	−2.302
+30	−3.445

Evaluating Municipal Forwards Using a Bond Calculator

The results in the body of this report were calculated using standard microcomputer spreadsheet financial functions. These standard functions are useful for illustrating the concepts behind the valuation of municipal forwards. We have also developed methods for approximating the key descriptors of Municipal Forwards (most critically, the forward rate)—and for marking these contracts to market—that can be applied on any standard bond calculator.[4]

CALCULATING THE FORWARD RATE

The Conceptual Approach

To calculate the forward rate and the marked-to-market value we need five items of information:

(1) the *delivery date* of the Municipal Forward bond,

(2) the maturity and call dates of the Municipal Forward bond,

(3) the coupon rate on the Municipal Forward bond,

---

[4]We would, however, urge any investor that intends to hold or trade Municipal Forwards to invest the time to develop the requisite computer software to value these contracts, if only for the sake of convenience and greater certainty of accuracy.

(4) the yield on newly issued long-term bonds of the obligor for current delivery (the *"long rate"*), and

(5) the yield on bonds of the obligor to the delivery date of the Municipal Forward bond (the *"short rate"*).

The bond calculator method derives the forward rate by comparing the following two transactions:

(1) The investor buys a bond of the issuer for current delivery with the same coupon and maturity as the forward bond.

(2) The investor buys a bond of the issuer for current delivery with the same coupon as the forward bond and maturity equal to the delivery date, priced to yield the short rate. On the delivery date the investor buys the forward bond.

The calculation answers the question: "What purchase price for the forward bond would equalize the current present values of these two transactions?" The forward rate is the yield to maturity of the forward bond at that price, evaluated as of the delivery date.

Using a bond calculator, we can compute the current price of the long-term bond purchased in transaction (1) and the current price of the short bond in transaction (2). The difference between the two is the *current* value of the premium or discount on the purchase price for the forward bond that would equalize the value of the two transactions. If, on the delivery date, the investor purchases the forward bond at a price of par plus or minus the *future* value of the premium or discount, the current values of the two transactions will be equal. We can compute the future value of the premium or discount on the forward purchase price by dividing the current value by the price of a zero coupon bond yielding the short rate and maturing on the delivery date.

The Method

The implied forward rate is the coupon rate on the forward bonds that, when combined with the short rate, produces the same internal rate of return to maturity as the obligor's long rate. The steps are as follows:

Step 1. Compute the price today (as a percentage of par) of a bond with a coupon equal to the coupon on the municipal forward bond, at a yield equal to the long rate.[5]

---

[5] If the delivery date of the forward bond is a regular semiannual interest payment date on the forward bond, then the maturity date of the bond being priced should be the maturity date of the forward bond. However, the delivery date of the forward

Step 2. From the result of Step 1, subtract the price today of a bond with the same coupon as the forward bond and maturity equal to the delivery date, priced to yield the short rate.[6]

Step 3. Divide the result of Step 2 by the value of a zero coupon bond (expressed as a decimal) with a maturity equal to the delivery date, priced to yield the short rate.[7]

Step 4. Add 100% to the result of Step 3.

Step 5. Calculate the yield to maturity of the forward bond based on a price equal to the result of Step 4.

An Example

Consider the following information:

Dated Date of the Contract:	August 1, 1989
Delivery Date:	February 1, 1992
Coupon Rate:	7.25%
Maturity:	August 1, 2019
Long Rate:	7.25%
Short Rate:	6.30%

The results of the calculation as of the dated date would be as follows:

Step 1.   Value of the forward bond today.   100.00

Step 2.   Subtract value of a bond with a coupon $-102.166 =$
          equal to the forward bond's and maturity -2.166

---

bond may differ from a semiannual payment date of the forward bond. In that case, the pricing of the hypothetical long bond should be based on a bond with a maturity date equal to the closest date to the actual maturity of the forward bond that corresponds to the semiannual payment date equal to the delivery date of the bonds. For example, if the delivery date of the forward bond is March 1, 1992, and the maturity date of the forward bond is August 1, 2019, the bond being priced in this step *only* should have a stated maturity of September 1, 2019. This adjustment is necessary in order to assure that the semiannual cash flows in this step and in Step 2 coincide. Otherwise, timing distortions will occur.

[6] In principle, we need to know two short rates: (1) the yield on a bond with coupon equal to that of the forward bond and maturity equal to the delivery date, and (2) the yield on a zero coupon bond with maturity equal to the delivery date. If the yield curve is very steep at maturities around the delivery date, these two rates might be different because the two hypothetical securities would have different durations. In practice, however, the two short rates will be very close, and we will assume they are identical.

[7] See footnote 6.

equal to the delivery date, priced to yield
the short rate.

Step 3. Divide by the value (expressed as a decimal)   +0.85635 =
of a zero coupon bond with maturity equal   −2.529 + 100
to the delivery date, priced to yield the short
rate.

Step 4. Add par.   = 97.471

Step 5. Compute the YTM of the forward bond as   7.47%
of the delivery date, based on the result of
Step 4. This is the forward rate.

CALCULATING THE MARKED-TO-MARKET VALUE OF A MUNICIPAL FORWARD

In order to calculate the *worst case* marked-to-market value of an outstanding Municipal Forward, we need the following information:

The Method

• The coupon, maturity and call provisions of the bonds for forward
delivery.
• The delivery date.
• The following four spot yields on the issuer's bonds:
  YTM = the yield to the maturity date of the forward bonds,
  YTD = the yield to the delivery date (the short rate),
  YTFC = the yield to the first call date of the forward bonds, and
  YTPC = the yield to the first par call date of the forward bonds.
• Yield premiums representing the sum of:
  (1) the liquidity premium, and
  (2) the additional premium on the Municipal Forwards.

The method we recommend for calculating the marked-to-market
value is as follows:

Step 1. Compute the price of a bond with the coupon on the forward
bond priced to yield:[8]
  (a) the spot YTM to maturity,
  (b) the spot YTFC to the first call, and
  (c) the spot YTPC to the first par call.

[8] See footnote 5.

Step 2. From each of these results, subtract the price of a bond with coupon equal to that of the municipal forward and maturity equal to the delivery date, priced to yield the YTD.

Step 3. Divide the results of each of these differences by the value (expressed as a decimal) of a zero coupon bond with maturity equal to the delivery date priced to yield the YTD.

Step 4. To the three results of Step 3 add the purchase price of the bonds on the delivery date (usually par).

Step 5. Based on these prices and the coupon on the forward bonds, calculate the following three forward yields:

(a) the forward YTM $= \mathrm{YTM_f}$

(b) the forward YTFC $= \mathrm{YTFC_f}$

(c) the forward YTPC $= \mathrm{YTPC_f}$

Step 6. To each of these yields add the structure premium (P), giving:

(a) $\mathrm{YTM'} = \mathrm{YTM_f} + P,$

(b) $\mathrm{YTFC'} = \mathrm{YTFC_f} + P,$

(c) $\mathrm{YTPC'} = \mathrm{YTPC_f} + P.$

Step 7. Compute the price of a bond with coupon equal to that of the Municipal Forward *as of the delivery date*, priced to yield:

(a) YTM' to maturity,

(b) YTFC' to the first call,

(c) YTPC' to the first par call.

Step 8. Select the minimum of (a), (b), and (c).

Step 9. Subtract the purchase price of the forward bonds on the delivery date (usually par).

Step 10. Multiply by the value of a zero coupon bond with maturity equal to the delivery date, priced to yield the YTD.

The result of Step 10 will be the worst case marked-to-market value of the contract.

An Example

The example will estimate the worst case value of a Municipal Forward contract with the following characteristics:

Coupon:	8.00%
Settlement:	August 1, 1989
Maturity:	August 1, 2019
Delivery Date:	February 1, 1992

First Call Date: August 1, 1999
First Call Price: 102
First Par Call Date: August 1, 2001
Yield Premiums: .528

We will estimate the value of this contract based on the following market yields:

YTM = 7.25%
YTFC = YTPC = 7.15%
YTD = 6.30%

Step 1. Price Based on YTM = 109.123
         Price Based on YTFC = 106.990
         Price Based on YTPC = 106.771

Step 2. Subtract the value of a 8.00% coupon bond priced to yield 6.30% to February 1, 1992:
         Based on YTM = 109.123 − 103.876 = 5.247
         Based on YTFC = 106.990 − 103.876 = 3.1
         Based on YTPC = 106.771 − 103.876 = 2.895

Step 3. Divide by value of zero coupon bond priced to yield 6.30% to February 1, 1992:
         Based on YTM = 5.247/.85635 = 6.127
         Based on YTFC = 3.1/.85635 = 3.636
         Based on YTPC = 2.895/.85635 = 3.381

Step 4. Add the purchase price of the forward bonds ($100.00):
         Based on YTM = 106.127
         Based on YTFC = 103.636
         Based on YTPC = 103.381

Step 5. Calculate the forward yields:
         YTM_f = 7.472
         $YTFC_f$ = 7.559
         $YTPC_f$ = 7.496

Step 6. Add the yield premiums.
         YTM' = 7.472 + .528 = 8.00
         YTFC' = 7.559 + .528 = 8.087
         YTPC' = 7.496 + .528 = 8.024

Step 7. Compute price on delivery date based on each of these yields:

Based on YTM' = 100.00

Based on YTFC' = 100.621

Based on YTPC' = 99.842

Step 8. Select the minimum of these three: 99.842 based on YTPC'.

Step 9. Subtract par:

$99.842 - 100.00 = -.158$

Step 10. Multiply by the value of a zero coupon bond priced to yield 6.30% to the delivery date:

$-.158 \times 0.85635 = \underline{-.135}$

CHAPTER 25

Zero Coupon Bonds— Stripped Zeros*

Alison M. Martier**
Equitable Capital Management Corp.

The Tax Reform Act of 1986 will have many significant effects on the U.S. financial markets. Not only will this legislation influence the general level of interest rates, but it will also alter the relative level of yields on different types of debt instruments. In addition, the Tax Reform Act has generated a new tax-exempt vehicle, the stripped municipal bond. This chapter will focus on this new product, how it is

---

* This chapter was written in 1987, following the implementation of the Tax Reform Act of 1986. At that time, the market for stripped municipal bonds was in its early stages. While the market for originally issued zero coupon bonds has grown over the past few years, the market for stripped zeros has not. There are two reasons for this.

The primary buyer of municipal zero coupon bonds is the individual investor. This investor is seeking ways to save for retirement, finance college educations, etc., and therefore, is purchasing longer maturity bonds. The stripped municipal bond creates securities along the entire maturity spectrum (a bond's coupon payment occurs every six months). Hence, when bonds are stripped a lot of short and intermediate maturity (1 to 15 years) securities are created. There is little investor demand for these maturities.

The second reason that the market for stripped municipals never took off was the lack of liquidity. Each security dealer created its own product and tended to make markets in its own securities. No generic product was created, and a liquid market for the "name brand" stripped zeros never developed.

** Reprinted with permission from the author.

created, marketed, and valued, its advantages and disadvantages, and the outlook for its future.

Prior to the Tax Reform Act of 1986 the "stripping" of coupons from previously issued municipal bonds was not legal. This was unlike the taxable fixed income market, in which there exists a sizable and extremely liquid market for "stripped" securities. The most successful stripped securities in the taxable fixed income market have been based on U.S. Treasury obligations. Treasury bonds long-term call protection and unquestioned credit quality make them ideal candidates for stripping. As a result, the supply of stripped U.S. Treasury securities has grown from nearly zero early in 1982 to more than $225 billion today. The only municipal zero-coupon securities that existed were originally issued zero-coupon bonds. The majority of them were associated with housing issues and therefore carried substantial prepayment risk, which deterred investors.

For the first time, this new law permits interest payments on pre-refunded municipal bonds to be stripped, and allows each component to be sold separately on a discounted basis. Stripped municipal bonds are created by separating the interest payments and the principal payments to be made on an existing municipal bond, so that each payment on the underlying bond is available for purchase as an investment with payment characteristics similar, in most cases, to a zero coupon bond. The underlying securities have been pre-refunded and escrowed to maturity with U.S. Government obligations which ensures the payment of interest, principal, and redemption premium. This also enable the zero coupon receipts to carry the highest quality ratings.

SPECIFICS OF THE NEW LAW

Among the major effects of the tax reform package are the following:

—A reduction in the volume of tax-exempt financing (specifically private purpose funding);

—A substantial cut in the top marginal tax rate on individual and corporate income;

—A reduction in the availability of alternative tax-avoidance and tax-deferral investments;

—A more stringent minimum tax, which includes provisions that would cause the tax-exempt income from certain types of newly issued tax-exempt securities held by individuals and the tax-exempt income of corporations to be subject to tax;

—Elimination of tax preferences available to commercial banks; and

—Elimination of excess arbitrage earnings (leads to less supply).

The following is the text of the technical amendment which permits coupon stripping of tax exempt bonds.

Example: (d) SPECIAL RULES FOR TAX-EXEMPT OBLIGATIONS

In the case of any tax-exempt obligation (as defined in section 1275 (a) (3)) from which one or more coupons have been stripped—

(1) the amount of original issue discount determined under subsection (a) with respect to any stripped bond or stripped coupon from such obligation shall be the amount which produces a yield to maturity (as of the purchase date) equal to the lower of

(A) the coupon rate of interest on such obligation before the separation of coupons, or

(B) the yield to maturity (on the basis of purchase price) of the stripped obligation or coupon,

(2) the amount of original issue discount determined under paragraph (1) shall be taken into account in determining the adjusted basis of the holder under section 1288,

(3) subsection (b) (1) shall not apply, and

(4) subsection (b) (2) shall be applied by increasing the basis of the bond coupon by the interest accrued but not paid before the time such bond or coupon was disposed of (and not previously reflected in basis).[1]

The new law provides that stripped coupons and corpus (principal portion of the bond) which are sold as zero coupon debt instruments, will be treated as if issued at an *original-issue discount* (OID). The accretion of this OID will be exempt from Federal income taxation to the extent that the yield at which the stripped bond or coupon is purchased does not exceed the coupon on the bond as it was originally priced. Each year the tax basis of the security increases at a compound annual rate equal to the coupon on the bond. If the yield on the stripped instrument exceeds that original coupon at the time the investor makes the purchase, the additional gain is taxed as a capital gain when the receipts mature or are sold.

---

[1] *Source:* Amendment to the Internal Revenue Code, Tax Reform Act of 1986.

For example, assume that a typical tax-exempt obligation maturing on January 1, 1989, with a face amount of $10,000 and a 5% coupon is stripped of its semiannual coupons and sold as shown in the following table:

Sale Date	Due Date	Stripped Coupons	Stripped Corpus	Yield	Sales Price	Deemed Issue Price
11/1/86	1/1/87	$250		4.25%	$ 248.42	$ 248.42
	7/1/87	250		4.50	242.87	242.87
	1/1/88	250		4.75	236.86	236.86
	7/1/88	250		5.00	230.44	230.44
	1/1/89	250		5.50	222.47	224.82
	7/1/89		$10,000	5.50	8,898.94	8,992.64

Application of the new stripped coupon rules will produce the following results. Since the original bond coupon is 5% and since all of the stripped coupons from January 1, 1987, through July 1, 1988, were sold at yields of 5% or less, all of the increase in price between the investor's cost and the par value will be tax-exempt original issue discount if the investor holds the bonds to maturity. Investors who buy the coupon and corpus due on January 1, 1989, at a 5.50% yield will have a deemed issue price in those investments for purposes of determining tax-exempt accretion of $224.82 and $8,992.64, respectively, representing the present value of the maturing payment at a yield of 5%.

Accretion in the value of the 1989 stripped securities at a compound annual rate of 5% will be added to the tax basis of the bond and will, therefore, be treated as tax-exempt income. Any amount in excess of the adjusted tax basis realized at maturity or upon sale will be taxed as a capital gain. Thus, an investor who purchased 1989 corpus bonds at $4,449.45 and held them to maturity would have to report $93.70 ($8,992.64 − $8,898.94) in capital gains for the 1989 tax year.

In practice, coupons will be stripped from municipal bonds with original issue yields high enough (high premium bonds) so that no taxable income will result. Among municipal bonds, the ideal candidates for stripping are pre-refunded issues and bonds that have been *escrowed to maturity* (ETMs). Prerefunded bonds and ETMs are backed by escrowed funds consisting of U.S. Treasury securities and have a definite maturity date with no provision for early redemption.

An increasing number of securities dealers have structured stripped municipal transactions. These deals have involved the purchase by the dealer in the secondary market of high-coupon, pre-refunded bonds, which are deposited by the dealer with a custodian, and the simultaneous creation and sale of a separate series of custodial receipts which evidence ownership in the payments stripped from the municipal bonds. It is this receipt that the investor purchase and takes custody of. Coupon receipts are registered, and, depending on how the product is structured, evidence the right to receive either semiannual or annual interest payments. The investor may purchase either a series of coupon payments or payments to specific dates. Principal receipts, also registered, evidence the right to receive principal payments.

These transactions are undertaken by dealers as an arbitrage for their own benefit. A portion of the arbitrage stems from the relatively low price of the premium bonds purchased for stripping, relative to par bonds of comparable term and quality. This spread varies with market factors, including the supply of prerefunded bonds.

Furthermore, the bonds to be stripped are priced to their redemption date, which, by definition, is longer than the dates on which the stripped coupon receipts are due. Given the current positive slope of the municipal yield curve, which influences the pricing of stripped municipals, stripped coupon municipals due in the early years may be sold at a price above acquisition cost. The potential profit to be made by dealers depends on the yield spread between premium and par bonds, yield on stripped municipals, and the stripped municipal program's legal and administrative costs.

As stated earlier, a number of securities dealers have structured stripped municipal products, and have given them various names. Among these are M-CATS (Salomon Brothers), M-BEARS (Morgan Stanley), M-STARS (M Bank, Texas), MRs (Municipal Receipts, Goldman, Sachs), and Municipal Strips.

ADVANTAGES OF THE MUNICIPAL ZERO

The main advantage of a zero coupon issue is the elimination of the reinvestment risk. Because these are zero coupon receipts there is no cash flow to reinvest, so the stated yield to maturity is the actual realized rate of return. To determine the relative value of zero coupons versus coupon instruments it is important to understand the impact on returns on the reinvestment of coupon income. For example, assume that an investor purchases a ten year bond with a 5% coupon at par. At a 5% reinvestment rate, over 21% of the total return on the bond is derived from reinvestment of the coupon income. If the reinvestment rate falls below the coupon rate (i.e., interest rates fall), the effective return would be less than the stated yield to maturity.

The following table presents an analysis of breakeven reinvestment rates—the rates at which the coupon cash flows would need to be reinvested in order to achieve the same returns as zero-coupon instruments.

Maturity	AAA G.O. Yield curve	Probable Muni Zero Curve	Spread	Bond Equivalent Reinvestment Rate
3 year	4.50%	4.70%	20bp	8.20%
5 year	5.00	5.40	40	8.70
7 year	5.60	6.00	40	8.00
10 year	5.90	6.25	35	7.40

Source: Merrill Lynch Capital Markets, Fixed Income Research Department.

The analysis indicates that the elimination of reinvestment risk increases the advantages of zeros over coupon issues in the longer maturities. However, the required reinvestment rate for short-term notes (8.20%) frequently cannot be obtained in the current marketplace. Therefore, even when yield spreads between zeros and coupon securities are narrow, the relative value of zeros over coupons is greater in the shorter maturities.

The table shows that the break-even reinvestment rate for zero-coupon municipals would be approximately 7 to 9% for securities with maturities of three to ten years, at initial spreads of 20 to 50 basis points over the current coupon AAA G.O. yield curve. The coupons from a 10-year 5.90% AAA G.O. priced at par would have to be reinvested at a rate of 8% in order to earn the same amount as a 10-year zero priced to yield 6.4%. If the yield curve remained unchanged or yields declined, the total returns earned from the zero would exceed the returns from the coupon security.

Along with the superior return profile of municipal zeros is the increased price volatility of zero coupons over coupon securities. This is because the zeros have a longer duration. Duration is a measure of the price sensitivity of a bond to changes in interest rates. It can be thought of as a weighted average maturity of both coupons and principal, where the cash flows are discounted by the yield to maturity and weighted by the time periods. Consequently, the duration of a zero coupon security will always equal its maturity, while the duration of a coupon security is shorter than its stated maturity because of cash flows generated from the coupon income. Therefore, it is necessary to compare zero coupon municipals with similar duration coupon municipals when analyzing spread relationships.

Because of this longer duration characteristic, a portfolio manager would want to invest in zeros when he/she is bullish, and would tend to invest in more defensive coupon instruments when he/she is bearish. That is, the superior total rate of return characteristics of the zeros over the coupon securities only holds true in a stable or falling interest rate environment.

Another advantage of the municipal zero receipt is the high quality feature. Because the bonds to be stripped are pre-refunded and escrowed to maturity, the municipal zeros that have been created thus far carry a AAA rating. This virtually eliminates credit risk to the investor.

Finally, unlike the zero coupon municipals issued in the past that have been associated with housing issues, these stripped securities are noncallable, and therefore have no prepayment risk.

USES OF MUNICIPAL ZEROS

Zero coupon municipals have always been attractive to individuals who are saving for retirement. New restrictions on contributions to *individual retirement accounts* (IRAs) incorporated in the Tax Reform Act will expand this source of demand for tax-advantaged investments. However, at the same time, the traditional source of zero coupon municipals—single-family housing finance and advance refundings—will be sharply reduced. The development of the muni-zero product, therefore, comes at a perfect time for individuals who are saving for retirement.

The Tax Reform Act creates another potential use for the municipal zero product. Under the old law, income on assets transferred from parents to children were taxed at the child's marginal rate. Because children's marginal tax rates tended to be very low, many parents bought zero coupon Treasury bonds for their children timed to mature during each year of college. The new law will impose taxes at the parents marginal rate on these Clifford Trusts (trust accounts for children) and other custodial funds for children. Many investors are eager to shift those funds into non-interest bearing tax-exempt bonds. The municipal zero product will be the appropriate investment in cases where Treasury zeros were right under the old law. Furthermore, because these provisions do not "grandfather" previous gifts, there was an incentive for parents before year end 1986 to swap out of zero coupon Treasury bonds in their children's accounts and buy municipal zeros.

Another use for municipal zeros is by corporations to match future balloon liabilities. For example, suppose a corporation's only financial liability was a noncallable zero coupon bond scheduled to mature in five years. If the corporation now has cash on hand, purchasing five year municipal zeros to meet the future payment could be the least expensive way for the corporation to match the liability.

Potential uses of municipal zeros by investors do not have to be confined to the zero-coupon buyer. These securities should be attractive to investors, such as managers of "triple-A rated," intermediate bond funds, who would like to buy pre-refunded bonds but are discouraged by the high dollar price at which these prerefunded bonds typically trade.

VALUATION OF STRIPPED MUNICIPALS

The market value of stripped municipals, like that of all other securities, will be determined by the interaction of supply and demand in the market. However, experience with stripped U.S. Treasury securities can provide some guidance as to how to analyze the value of stripped tax-exempts.

The concept of the *spot yield curve* underlies all analysis of strip pricing and yield. The familiar *current-coupon yield curve* typically represents the yields on par bonds paying semiannual coupon payments and maturing at various points in time. The spot yield curve depicts the yields on zero coupon securities maturing at various points in time. There is a mathematical relationship between any given current-coupon yield curve and a corresponding theoretical spot yield curve. As is always the case with an upward sloping yield curve, the theoretical spot rate curve lies above the current-coupon curve.

As stated previously, the actual prices of stripped municipals will be determined by supply and demand in the marketplace. However, experience with zero coupon U.S. Treasury securities indicates that the actual market yields are, more often than not, very close to what the derived spot rate curve predicts, especially for stripped securities with maturities of ten years or less. If yields on stripped municipals do prove to be close to the theoretical levels, then stripped municipals will be valuable securities for investors with tax liabilities.

SOME SAMPLE OFFERINGS

The following table presents two stripped municipal deals that were issued in late 1986, along with their respective initial offering scales, and the AAA general obligation scale.

Maturity	(10/23/86) AAA G.O.	(1) (10/23) M-CATs	(2) (10/24) MRs
1987	3.90%	4.00%	4.00%
1988	4.25	4.25	4.875
1989	4.75	4.80	5.25
1990	5.00	5.10	5.50
1991	5.20	5.35	5.75
1992	5.40	5.60	6.00
1993	5.60		6.05
1994	5.75		6.10
1995	5.90		6.15

(1) *M-CATS*— (Salomon Brothers), Underlying bonds: $8,971,000 Metropolitan Transportation Authority Facility Revenue Refunding Bonds

coupon: 9 3/4   maturity: 7/1/15

dated: 8/1/85   prerefunded: 7/1/92 @ 102

AAA rated

$7,882,250 Metropolitan Transportation Authority Facility Revenue Refunding Bonds

coupon: 10 3/4   maturity: 7/1/15

dated: 8/15/85   prerefunded: 7/1/95 @ 102

AAA rated

(2) *MRs*— (Goldman, Sachs), Underlying bonds: $16,125,000 Jacksonville Electric Authority, Florida St. John's River Power Park System Revenue Bonds, Issue One, Series Six

coupon: 9 1/2   maturity: 10/1/20

dated: 10/1/85   prerefunded: 10/1/95 @ 102

AAA rated

$7,330,400 Piedmont Municipal Power Agency, South Carolina, Electric Revenue Bonds, Series 1984

coupon: 10 1/2   maturity: 1/1/19

dated: 12/1/84   prerefunded: 1/1/95 @ 103

AAA rated

$24,927,500 Public Utility District No. 1 of Snohomish County, Washington, Sultan Hydroelectric System Revenue Bonds, Series 1983

coupon: 11 5/8   maturity: 1/1/20

dated: 11/1/83   prerefunded: 1/1/94 @ 103

AAA rated

A look at the scale shows that there was strong investor demand for the M-CAT deal, as the yield spreads over the AAA G.O. curve are very narrow. Increased supply, along with changing market conditions, caused the yields on the MR deal to be higher.

Because the product is so new, and the amount that has been issued is relatively small, these securities are currently very illiquid; that is, there is not much of a secondary market yet. This is a temporary disadvantage of this product.

The future for stripped municipal bonds appears bright, however. An increasing number of firms are offering stripped municipal products. For the near-term, the supply of stripped municipals is likely to be determined by market relationships which affect the arbitrage profits to dealers. In addition, issuance costs absorbed by dealers decline with each additional series sold, reducing the yield spread needed to produce an arbitrage profit. Ultimately, investor demand for zero coupon tax-exempt instruments will determine the success of this investment product.

CHAPTER 26

Are Zero Coupon Municipals Congenitally Overvalued?*

Aaron Gurwitz
Goldman, Sachs and Co.

The issuance of zero coupon and other interest-deferred municipal bonds has increased in recent months, both in absolute volume and as a percentage of total issuance (see Figure 26.1). Despite this increase in supply, zero coupon municipals appear to be overvalued relative to coupon-paying tax-exempt bonds. Every term structure of yields on coupon bonds reflects an implicit zero coupon yield curve. Based on the coupon-paying and zero coupon scales for recent new issues, it appears that long-term zero coupon maturities yield between 30 and 40 basis points less than the "correct" theoretical level. Several forces on both the demand and the supply sides of the zero coupon municipal market explain this apparent misvaluation. The stability of these forces suggests that, absent substantial shifts in investor or issuer behavior, this theoretical misvaluation is likely to persist.

THE VALUATION OF ZERO COUPON MUNICIPALS

We can view any coupon-paying bond as a bundle of zero coupon bonds: one "bond" for each semiannual cash flow. Thus, one 7% non-callable

* Copyright 1989 by Goldman Sachs.

FIGURE 26.1
Monthly Issuance of Zero Coupon Tax-Exempt Bonds

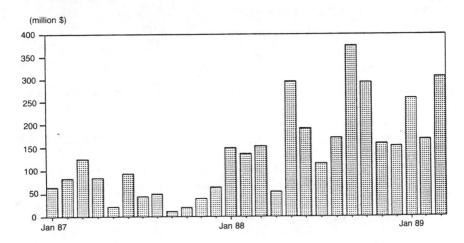

10-year bond can be thought of as a bundle of 20 semiannual $35 zero coupon interest strips and one $1,000 zero coupon principal strip payable in 10 years.

Therefore, we can view the "yield to maturity" (YTM) or "true interest cost" (TIC) of a coupon-paying bond in two ways. The usual way of measuring bond yields is to assume that all cash flows are discounted at the single YTM or TIC. Alternatively, we might assume that each cash flow is discounted at a different zero coupon yield. If the bond as a whole and each of its zero coupon components are all correctly valued in a theoretical sense, then the price of the bond should be the same regardless of whether we use the single YTM or TIC discount rate or the collection of zero coupon rates. Alternatively, if we know the yields on coupon-paying bonds and we assume that the zeroes are efficiently priced, we can compute the implicit yields on the zeroes.

An example may be useful. The simplest case would be a one-year semiannual coupon-paying bond priced at par to yield 6.75% to maturity. Suppose we know that a six-month tax-exempt note yields 6.50%. The question is, what is the theoretically correct value for a one-year zero coupon bond? Note first that the current zero coupon yield will be higher than 6.75%. Because the earlier cash flow is discounted at a lower rate than 6.75%, the later cash flow must be discounted at a higher rate so that the combination will be discounted at exactly 6.75%. We can find the theoretically correct one-year zero coupon yield by solving the following equation:

$$1,000 = \frac{33.75}{(1 + .0325)} + \frac{1,033.75}{(1 + x/2)^2}$$

$$x = .067542.$$

In this equation, the $33.75 figures represent the semiannual coupon payments at a 6.75% rate. The 0.0325 is the discount rate on the first semiannual payment. As expected, the 6.7542% zero coupon discount rate applied to the final principal and interest payment is higher than the YTM or TIC of the bond.

We can extrapolate this method for calculating implied zero coupon interest rates across the entire yield curve. If we knew, for example, that an 18-month coupon-paying bond of the same issuer would be priced at par to yield 6.80%, we could extend the previous example and deduce that the theoretically correct yield on an 18-month zero coupon bond would be 6.8046%. Figure 26.2 depicts the (non-callable) current coupon municipal yield curve as of late March 1989 and the implied (non-callable) zero coupon yield curve. The latter is often termed the theoretical spot rate curve.

In Figure 26.2, theoretical spot rates exceed coupon yields for all maturities. This may be considered typical because the coupon yield curve is upward sloping. However, as Figure 26.3 illustrates, when the

FIGURE 26.2
Recent Non-Callable Coupon Yield Curve and Implicit Theoretical Spot Rate Curve

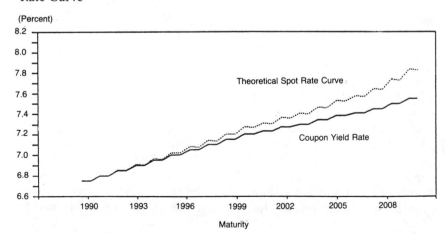

FIGURE 26.3
Downward Sloping Non-Callable Coupon Yield Curve and Implicit
Theoretical Spot Rate Curve

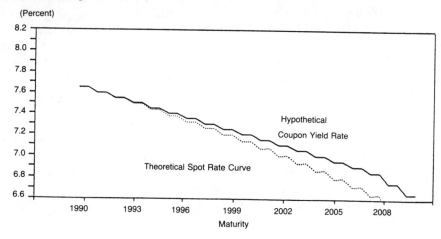

yield curve is downward sloping, theoretical zero coupon yields lie below the coupon curve. Recall from the simple example of a six-month
note and a one-year bond that, when the yield curve sloped upward,
the one-year spot rate had to be higher than the one-year YTM to compensate for the lower discount rate applied to the six-month cash flow.
The same argument applies to the case of a downward sloping curve. If

FIGURE 26.4
Hypothetical Coupon Yield Curve and Peaked Theoretical Spot Rate Curve

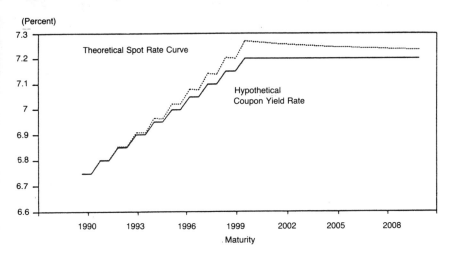

the six-month rate was, say, 7.00% and the one-year coupon YTM was 6.50%, then the one-year theoretical spot rate would have to be 6.49%. Indeed, in the U.S. Treasury bond market, where the yield curve is currently inverted over most maturity ranges, the theoretical spot rate curve and the actual zero coupon Treasury curve are below the coupon yield curve over most ranges.

More generally, the relationship between theoretical spot yields and coupon yields at any given maturity will depend on the slope of the yield curve up to that maturity. The more positive the slope, the higher the theoretical spot rate relative to the coupon yield. With a perfectly flat curve, the zeroes and coupons will have identical yields. If, as in Figure 26.4, the curve is at first upward sloping and then flat, the spread between the theoretical spot rate and the coupon yield will be widest at the point where the curve flattens. This relationship explains the serrated shape of the theoretical spot rate curve. The municipal coupon yield curve is flat over six-month intervals within a single year, and these flat segments affect the shape of the zero coupon curve.

MUNICIPAL ZEROES ARE OVERVALUED

As expected, given the upward slope of the municipal yield curve, market yields on tax-exempt zeroes are higher than the yields on similar maturity coupon-paying bonds. However, at present, as at most times in the past, actual municipal zeroes yield less—sometimes substantially less—than the theoretical spot rates implicit in the coupon curve (see Figure 26.5). In other words, municipal investors appear willing, in the

FIGURE 26.5
Theoretical Spot Rate Curve and Recent Non-Callable Zero Coupon Curve

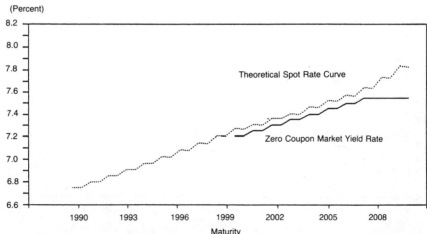

aggregate, to pay more for a payment to be received in, say, 10 years than they would be willing to pay for the same payment in combination with a series of other, previous payments.

The persistence of such misvaluation demands some explanation. It is surprising that investors are willing to pay significantly different prices for the same payment depending on how the payment is packaged. And one would expect that, if there were a persistent excess demand for zero-coupon bonds, existing bonds would be stripped or issuers would take the opportunity to reduce capital costs by issuing more capital appreciation bonds (CABs).

WHY THE OVERVALUATION PERSISTS

The Demand Site

The main reason why investors may be willing to accept a lower yield on zeroes than the theoretical spot rate is the convenience these instruments offer. In particular, investors who are using municipal bonds as a vehicle for college or retirement savings may not want to be bothered with—or tempted to spend—relatively small semiannual coupon payments. The difference between the zero's YTM and the theoretical spot rate might be considered a small price to pay for the convenience of "automatic coupon reinvestment."

Long-term zero coupon bonds are also a more efficient vehicle than coupon-paying bonds for speculation on interest rate moves. The prices of zeroes are more sensitive to interest rate moves than the prices of coupon-paying bonds with the same maturity. In fact, the prices of non-callable zeroes with maturities of about 10 years or more are more sensitive to interest rate changes than the price of any current coupon bond. Therefore, investors who expect interest rates to fall will be attracted to zeroes in anticipation of capital gains.

The value of CABs as a speculative vehicle for bullish investors is diminished because most zero coupon municipals are callable before maturity at a premium to compound accreted value. However, although the embedded call option inhibits price appreciation as interest rates decline it does not eliminate CABs' value as a speculative vehicle. CABs usually offer more call protection than coupon-paying municipals; the latter are typically callable 10 years after issuance at a premium of 102, while the former are more often callable at a 105 premium to compound accreted value after 10 years. Thus, zero coupon municipals may not always be quite as overvalued as they appear; in some cases the difference may merely reflect differences in call protection. For this reason, in our illustrations of the relationship among actual CAB yields, theoretical spot rates and coupon yields we were careful to compare non-callable bonds of all three varieties.

The Supply Side

In the U.S. Treasury Bond market, whenever zero coupon bonds—termed STRIPS—become even slightly overvalued relative to coupon bonds, dealers will buy coupon bonds, strip off their coupons, sell the individual pieces, and make a small profit. This arbitrage prevents actual strip yields from straying too far from theoretical spot rates for very long. This arbitrage was impossible in the municipal bond market until the passage of the 1986 Tax Act, which clarified the tax status of coupon and principal payments stripped from tax-exempt securities. Since the effective date of that Act, some municipals have been stripped. However, the volume of tax-exempt bonds that are appropriate candidates for stripping is small. Two characteristics of most municipal bonds make stripping difficult. First, most tax-exempt bonds with maturities of greater than 10 years are callable before maturity. If a stripped bond is called, the coupons scheduled for payment after the call date become worthless. Thus, callable bonds are not likely candidates for stripping. Second, most municipal revenue bonds are subject to acceleration of principal payments in the event of default. Again, if principal payments are accelerated, the coupon strips become worthless. Thus, investors who hold coupon stripped from most revenue bonds bear a much greater degree of credit risk than holders of principal strips or of unstripped coupon bonds. The most likely candidates for stripping, therefore, are either prerefunded bonds or non-callable general obligations. Given the fact that only long-term municipal zeroes are significantly overvalued (see Figure 26.5), stripping coupon bonds with short or intermediate maturities, such as prerefunded bonds, is not profitable. And non-callable general obligations constitute a very small share of the tax-exempt bond market.

    With the potential for stripping limited, the only likely source of large volumes of new zero coupon municipals would be issuers choosing to come to market with CABs rather than coupon bonds. Some issuers' cash flow patterns dictate the use of zero coupon liabilities. Most issuers, however, are willing to issuer either zeroes or coupon bonds, depending on which structure produces the lowest TIC. When CABs are overvalued, as they are at present, by definition, they produce a lower TIC than coupons. However, the potential supply of CABs is limited by the fact that many issuers are constrained by state law or local ordinance to sell all new issues at close to their par value at maturity. In addition, municipalities that choose or are required to issue bonds through advertised sales are often unable to judge in advance whether CABs or coupons will produce a lower TIC. The recent acceleration in the issuance of CABs reflects, for the most part, the relative overvaluation of these securities. However, it is unlikely that issuers will be able to expand the supply of CABs quickly enough to eliminate the misvaluation of these securities.

IMPLICATIONS

This analysis has significant implications—albeit quite different ones—for both issuers and investors.

Investors should be aware that they are paying a price for convenience and for the responsiveness of zero coupon municipals to changes in interest rates. That price is the difference in yield between the actual CAB YTM and the theoretical spot rate. At present, as reflected in the actual/theoretical spread for non-callable CABs, that price amounts to as much as 40 bp of yield to maturity for 20-year bonds.

Issuers should be aware of the potential for substantial savings in interest costs offered by zero coupon bonds when the demand for these securities is substantial. This is not to say that CABs can always save a great deal of money. Even when zeroes are overvalued relative to the theoretical spot rate, the market's appetite for a particular issuer's CABs may be limited. However, municipalities that cannot, under current state or local law, issue deep discount bonds should consider changing these laws. And municipalities that choose, or are required, to issue through advertised sale should consider giving underwriters the option of including CABs in the issue structure.

CHAPTER 27

High Yield Municipal Bonds

Julie C. Morrone
Lehman Bros.

High yield municipal bonds have found their niche in today's marketplace. Investors' appetite for municipal bonds has been fueled by the elimination of numerous personal deductions under tax code revisions. High yield municipal bonds offer the investor the opportunity to earn tax-exempt income without foregoing yield. With interest on tax-exempt high yield bonds averaging 100 to 200 basis points above A-rated tax-exempt bonds, investors who are comfortable with the risks associated with these securities, consider them an attractive source of income. In order to reduce the risks associated with high yield bonds, retail investors have looked to the bond funds as a means of diversifying their holdings. The number of high yield municipal bond funds doubled in a four-year period, which attests to the popularity of this product. As more bond funds enter the high market sector, competition for performance superiority is fueled. Though the supply of high yield bonds has increased, the demand for such securities continues to outpace the supply.

This chapter is intended to provide a brief overview of the investors, issuers and risks involved in this growing market. The discussion of issuers has been limited to those that are non-investment grade in the primary market. "Fallen angels," bonds which were at one time investment grade, have been for the most part, omitted from this analysis. The bond issues described encompass those having a credit rating of Baa or less by Moody's or BBB– or less by Standard & Poor's or are unrated when accessing the primary market. An issuer may be unrated for several reasons including: a previously issued rating being withdrawn due to insufficient information, or the issuer being ineligible for a rating, or chooses to sell its bond without a rating.

The types of high yield bond issuers vary widely but generally mirror those found in the investment grade market. For purposes of this discussion, they have been divided among the following categories:

—Corporate industrial revenue bond issuers;

—Economic development bonds;

—General obligation bond issuers;

—Special tax/assessment bonds; and

—Revenue bond issuers.

NON-INVESTMENT GRADE INDUSTRIAL DEVELOPMENT BONDS

Corporations are able to access the tax-exempt market by the issuance of industrial revenue bonds or pollution control bonds. Their ability to do so has been virtually eliminated due to restrictions imposed by the Tax Reform Act of 1986 but investors can still purchase these bonds on the secondary market or on the primary market when refunding bonds are issued.

The bonds' ratings reflect the company's creditworthiness and security provisions applicable to that specific bond issue. If a bond issue is secured, for example, a higher rating will be warranted vis-á-vis an unsecured bond issued by the same borrower. From a credit standpoint, the issue is viewed as a corporate bond; however, legally and structurally it is tax-exempt.

UNRATED ECONOMIC DEVELOPMENT BONDS

The Tax Reform Act of 1986 curtailed the issuance of economic development bonds by barring private activity bond issuers from the tax-exempt market. Such bonds can be purchased on the secondary market or on the primary market when a refunding issue is sold. Common examples of unrated economic development bonds include hotel/motel projects, office building and shopping malls projects. The issuance of "qualified" bonds is still permitted for several types of projects including mortgage revenue bonds and parking facilities. Unrated or non-investment grade "qualified" bonds are secured by revenues derived from a "stand alone" project and no municipality or corporation is liable for the debt.

Such financings are often structured as follows: A partnership is formed for the sole purpose of owning the proposed facility. A municipal authority issues the bonds and lends the proceeds to the partnership/borrower. The municipal authority acts only as a conduit in this instance and is not a provider of revenues. The bonds are secured solely by the revenues of the project and often have a mortgage lien on the project. The proceeds of the issue are used for construction costs, issuance costs, administrative costs, capitalized interest and to fund a debt service reserve account. The capitalized interest account is funded in an amount sufficient to pay interest on the bonds during the construction phase of the project. Once construction is completed and capitalized interest is depleted, revenues generated by the project are used to pay interest on the bonds.

Securities issued for such a purpose are very speculative in nature. The following are some of the risks inherent in a project:

—Unanticipated cost overruns in connection with construction of the project may occur. The borrower or contractor may or may not be obliged (depending on the structure of the given financing) to provide additional funds for completion. Even if one of the parties is obligated under the bond documents to pay for cost overruns, it may not have sufficient funds available to do so. As mentioned previously, the borrower is usually a partnership formed for the purpose of owning this project. The partnership may not have other assets and if it does, are not usually pledged to the project.

—Unanticipated schedule delays in connection with the construction may occur causing capitalized interest to be depleted before completion of the project. The borrower or contractor may not be obliged or able to fund the shortfall.

—Once the project is completed, it may not generate sufficient revenues to pay debt service on the bonds. This could be a function of overambitious forecasts during the development stage of the project or a general economic downturn or other unforeseeable events.

—Since no credit ratings were applied for, a secondary market may not exist for the bonds. The underwriter will maintain a secondary market on a best efforts basis only, and can give no assurance that such a market will fully develop or last. The bondholder, therefore, should anticipate having his funds committed for an extended period of time.

—The fair market value of the project may be less than the amount of bonds outstanding. In the event of a default and foreclosure, proceeds may not be sufficient to pay all claims to the project.

According to the *Bond Investors Association* (BIA), $48.7 billion hotel projects defaulted on debt in 1990 which is a decline from $54.8 billion, $83 billion and $145 billion in 1989, 1988, and 1987, respectively. Housing issues fared worse with $781 million bonds defaulting representing 45% of total municipal defaults in 1990.[1] These statistics attest to the speculative nature of this type of project financing.

GENERAL OBLIGATION BONDS

General obligation bonds are issued by municipalities and are secure by the issuers full faith and credit. Debt service is payable from advalorem taxes as well as any legally available monies. General obligation bonds are considered the least risky municipal securities; however, there are numerous non-investment grade and unrated general obligation bonds outstanding. Extensive press coverage has made us well aware of the economic deterioration and declining credit standing of the large inner cities. Though these are the obvious cases, they are not representative of the majority. According to Securities Data Corporation, in 1990 34% of noninvestment grade new issue volume consisted of general purpose/public improvement bonds. Though a more detailed breakdown is unavailable, a good portion of these were issued by small towns and districts.

Among the most speculative general obligation issues in the market are the unlimited tax bonds issued by undeveloped districts. Investors often take false comfort in the full faith and credit pledge. The tax base may consist of a handful of developers (sometimes just one developer) who anticipate developing the raw land and selling the lots to other developers for housing or commercial purposes. The risks involved in such a transaction are numerous:

—The ultimate security for payment of the principal and interest on the bonds depends upon the ability of the district to collect

---

[1] A *default* is defined as nonpayment of debt service or payment made from a draw on the debt service reserve fund.

taxes levied. Developers are under no obligation to develop the property and may sell it at any time. If the developers fail to proceed with development, an excessively high tax rate might have to be levied.

—There is no guaranty that the developers, as taxpayers, will be able to pay such high taxes during the construction phase. The developer is often a limited partnership whose only assets typically are its interests in the project.

—If taxes are high, neighboring districts will seem more desirable to prospective residents.

—Additional debt may have to be issued or completion of the district, again calling for an increase in taxes to fund the debt.

—Growth in the district may be directly affected by the fortunes of the housing industry, which is cyclical and affected by the general business activity in the area, taxes, labor conditions and interest rates.

SPECIAL ASSESSMENT/TAX BONDS

Act 1911 and 1915 Special Assessment Bonds, Mello-Roos Bonds and Tax Allocation Bonds are bonds issued in lieu of general obligation bonds. Such issues are popular in California, where, Proposition 13 limits impose volume constraints on general obligation bond issuance. Act 1911 and 1915 bonds are issued by cities, counties and service districts which are undeveloped, newly developed or proposing redevelopment. Revenues for debt service are derived from non ad-valorem taxes, or special assessments allocated to parcels of land within the district that will receive benefit from the proposed project. The assessments cannot be increased throughout the district for 1911 and 1915 Act Bonds if there is a delinquency on a parcel; however, bondholders have a lien on the property and may initiate foreclosure proceedings.

Under the Mello-Roos Act of 1982, cities, counties, and districts are authorized to form community facilities districts to issue Mello-Roos Bonds payable from a property-related non-advorem tax. The tax may be increased if deficiencies in receipts are realized; however, there is a limit on increases. Mello-Roos Bonds finance a wide range of infrastructure needs for community facility districts that are developing areas where the landowners often consist of real estate developers.

Credit risks associated with Mello-Roos bonds include, failure to obtain all the necessary land use entitlements, developer bankruptcy, construction delays and a housing market slowdown. The risks can be reduced with the imposition of minimum value-to-lien ratios, special tax coverage and fully funded reserve accounts. Also, the level of local government involvement in the planning and evaluation of proposed projects can provide further enhancement. Issuers, investors and government officials' increased participation in this market will serve to establish and refine guidelines in this evolving market. Standard & Poor's and Moody's recently contributed to this effort by establishing criteria for the rating of special assessment and Mello-Roos bonds. In fact, select bond issues for seasoned projects have received investment grade ratings. Since 1983, the issuance of Mello-Roos debt has proliferated in California. New issue volume topped $1 billion in 1990 with no sign of curtailment. The market for Mello-Roos bonds faces challenges in the 1990s; however, most obviously, the slowdown in the California real estate market.

HEALTHCARE REVENUE BONDS

High-yield revenue bonds are issued for a variety of purposes including water and sewer projects, solid waste projects, marine terminals, hospitals, nursing homes, life care centers, electric and power projects, et al. Life care centers and nursing home bonds receive extensive attention since there have been a considerable number of defaults in this relatively young market. These projects are structured on a stand-alone basis and involve considerable construction risk; therefore, any miscalculation in revenue forecast could adversely impact bondholder security. Though a track record of defaults is evident in this sector of the bond market, life care center and nursing home projects continue to be built and receive financing. Demographics confirm the need for additional forms of housing and care for our aging population.

In addition to the construction risk involved in developing a nursing home project, several other risks must be borne. A nursing home's primary source of revenue is Medicaid payments. Any reduction in state and federal medicaid programs will have a considerable impact on a nursing home's revenue stream. Though the nursing home may attempt to increase private-pay revenue to compensate for the deficiency in Medicaid revenues, the benefits of this cost-shifting tactic are limited.

An ever present factor in evaluating a project's viability is the existence of competition which in this case can be in the form of other nursing homes, elderly housing projects or lifecare centers.

Though the inherent risks in a nursing home project are considerable; they are more palatable then those associated with a lifecare center. The construction risk involved in these projects are the same as any stand alone project in that the borrowers in these financings are usually limited partnerships whose only assets are the projects being financed. During the construction phase, interest is payable from capitalized interest funded with bond proceeds. If there are cost or schedule overruns, the parties involved may not be obliged or able to fund the deficiency. Once construction is completed, attaining occupancy within a given period of time, usually 12 to 24 months, is critical to a project's viability.

The fees paid in connection with residing in these facilities—the source of the borrower's operating revenues—are not reimbursable from federal or state subsidies. Residents pay monthly fees from their personal resources. These fees can range from a few hundred dollars a month upward to two thousand dollars a month. In addition to monthly fees, some facilities charge entrance fees as high as $150,000, which may not be refundable upon death. When a new resident enters the facility, he too must pay the entrance fee. The developer depends on the monthly fees and entrance fees to pay debt service on the bonds. Thus, if occupancy is not attained or if turnover is not as high as anticipated, a revenue shortfall may develop.

Hospital bonds can offer the investor the opportunity to earn higher yields without being subject to the amount of risk inherent in nursing home or congregate care facility projects. Hospitals are eligible for investment grade ratings; however, the onset of the prospective payment system in the early 1980's caused many hospitals to fall from the investment grade category due to the deterioration of profit margins. Hospitals are stand-alone facilities; however, construction risk is not a major factor as hospitals generally finance additions and renovations only, with bond proceeds. Construction of a new hospital facility would not be eligible for a rating unless an existing facility guaranteed the debt. This is a very rare occasion though as there are governmental restrictions on building new hospitals and most areas are overbedded. The risks associated with hospital bonds generally relate to the facility's ability to maximize its revenues under Medicaid/Medicare reimbursement guidelines while maintaining costs and market share.

DEFAULTS

Few defaults have been experienced in the hospital sector given the market's size and maturity. According to Standard & Poor's, as of May, 1991, eight issues had defaulted since 1967 affecting $174 million in debt. Hospital defaults are expected to continue given the deterioration in ratings in recent years. As of May, 1991, 6% S&P's outstanding ratings for hospitals were non-investment grade versus 3% in 1983. S&P attributes the defaults to, generally ". . . a competitive service area, exhibited above average utilization declines, high debt burdens, a restrictive payor mix and significant construction and project risk."[2]

According to Bond Investor's Association, the number of defaulted hospital bonds is much higher when nonrated bonds, missed coupon payments and hospitals in a work-out stage are included. BIA has documented 41 hospital bond defaults since 1986. The municipal market in general did not fare well in 1990: A total of $1.8 billion municipal bonds defaulted in 1990, a 78% increase over 1989. The amount was affected however, by defaults in the corporate sector as corporations defaulted on industrial revenue bonds issued. The largest sector of defaults was in housing reflecting the adverse impact of regional economic declines. Housing accounted for 45% of all defaults in 1990 while special assessment districts accounted for 11% of defaults. Downturns in the real estate market and unrealized forecasts are attributable factors to the bonds' demise.

DEMAND

The risks associated with high yield bonds have not deterred demand for these securities. In fact, this sector of the municipal market has grown dramatically in recent years. In 1985, there were 18 tax exempt high yield money market funds with assets of $8.1 billion. In 1987, the number of funds grew to 18 with assets exceeding $13.5 billion. Two years later, the number of funds had grown to 31 with assets of $18.8 billion. This does not include Unit Investment Trusts which had assets of $749 million in 1989.[3] Table 27.1 lists the funds participating in this market and the year they were established.

FUTURE OUTLOOK

The quality of high yield bonds should appreciate as buyers become more sophisticated with the nuances of these financings. Many bond funds have developed expertise in work-outs and default management. Ongoing monitoring and use of legal counsel has become an integral aspect of high yield debt management. Lessons learned from previous errors are serving to strengthen future financings.

Measures to improve disclosure requirements throughout the municipal bond market will have its effect on the high yield market as well,

[2] *Standard & Poor's Creditweek,* May 20, 1991. p. 29.

[3] *Weisinberger Investment Companies Service,* 1990.

TABLE 27.1

High Yield Tax-Exempt Bond Funds*

Fund	Year Established
American Capital High Yield Tax-Exempt Trust	1986
Benham California Tax-Free Fund—High Yield Portfolio	1987
Carnegie Tax Exempt Inc. Trust—National High Yield	1986
Colonial Tax Exempt High Yield Trust	1984
Colonial VIP Trust High Yield Portfolio	1988
Eaton Vance High Yield Municipal Trust	1985
Fidelity California Tax-Free Fund—High Yield Portfolio	1984
Fidelity High Yield Municipals	1977
Fidelity New Jersey Tax-Free High Yield	1988
Fidelity New York Tax-Free Fund—High Yield Portfolio	1984
Fortress High Yield Tax-Free Fund	1987
Franklin Tax-Free Trust—High Yield Fund	1986
GIT Tax-Free Trust—High Yield Portfolio	1982
IDS High Yield Tax-Exempt Fund	1979
Merrill Lynch Municipal Bond Fund	
High Yield Portfolio—Class A	1979
Class B	1988
MFS Managed High Yield Municipal Bond Trust	1985
Olympus Tax-Exempt High Yield Fund	1987
Pacific Horizon High Yield Bond Fund	1984
PaineWebber Classic High Yield Municipal Fund	1987
T. Rowe Price Tax-Free High Yield Fund	1985
Putnam Tax-Free Income Fund High Yield Portfolio	1985
Scudder High Yield Tax-Free Fund	1987
Seligman California Tax-Exempt High Yield Fund	1984
Seligman Pennsylvania Tax-Exempt High Yield Fund	1986
Stein Roe High Yield Municipals	1984
Transamerica Special High Yield Tax-Free Fund	1986
USAA Tax Exempt Fund High Yield	1982
Value Line Tax-Exempt Fund—High Yield Series	1984
Vanguard High Yield Portfolio	1978
Van Kampen Merritt Tax-Free High Income Fund	1985

Tax-Exempt Unit Trust*

Fund	Date Established
American Municipal Trust High Yield Series	1984
Municipal Securities Trust	1983
Prudential Bache Tax-Exempt Unit Trust High Yield Series	1985
Shearson Lehman Bros. Unit Trust High Yield Municipals	1987

*Information derived from the *Weisinberger Investment Companies Service*, 1990.

as underwriters scrutinize these transactions in finer detail. In Colorado, the Governor signed into law a bill requiring annual disclosure reports by special districts and some other issuers in an effort to further regulate their issuance and to enhance bondholders' opinion of the state.

Ongoing legislative changes continue to restrict the issuance of high yield bonds, the diversity of borrowers has not ceased to expand. The issuance of what *The Wall Street Journal* refers to as "junk culture bonds" has proliferated.[4] Civic and cultural groups have ventured into the high yield municipal market to offset eroding city and state government funding. Bond funds are welcoming the opportunity to invest in these bonds since the yields are attractive and the presence of communities strengthens the bonds' creditworthiness. These issues are generally small and are privately placed with sophisticated investors giving the purchaser an opportunity to participate in the structure of the transaction. The bonds are unrated though and are still speculative in nature.

As the high yield market matures, so too are its participants. The efforts of all the parties involved should serve to favorably affect the efficiency and quality of this market.

---

[4] "Junk 'Culture' Bonds Offer Tax-Exempt Twist," *The Wall Street Journal*, May 13, 1991, p. C1.

CHAPTER 28

Taxable Municipal Securities*

J. P. Morgan and Co.

Since 1986, there has been a slow but steady trickle of municipal issuers entering the taxable debt markets. This chapter explores who
those issuers are, why they are using taxable debt, and the investors to
whom they are selling their securities. Moreover, this chapter expands
upon the previous sections of this handbook in discussing the structuring of taxable securities and the additional documentation requirements associated with taxable as opposed to tax-exempt securities.

An important point for municipal issuers to recognize is that their
use of taxable securities introduces them to a group of investors who
have a wide variety of securities from which to choose. In the early
stages of developing this market, the "burden of proof" will weigh more
heavily on issuers than investors. Thus, to achieve the most cost effective

---

financing available, issuers as opposed to investors are more likely to have to make concessions on structure, documentation and marketing.

THE TAXABLE MUNICIPAL MARKET

Overview

The driving force behind the growth in issuance of taxable municipal securities was the Tax Reform Act of 1986. Among other things, the Act established a number of issuance caps that limit the use of tax-exempt financing that benefits private entities. For example, the Act limited a state's ability to issue private activity bonds to the greater of $150 million or $50 per state resident per year. Private activity bonds include, but are not limited to, student loan bonds, certain housing bonds and industrial development bonds. Furthermore, the Act limited certain tax-exempt organizations like universities to a total of $150 million in outstanding tax-exempt debt. Figure 28.1 shows the total taxable municipal issuance by year since 1986, as well as the cumulative taxable issuance between 1982 and 1985, illustrating the significant effect of the Act.

Given the nature of the restrictions mentioned above, it is not surprising that industrial revenue bonds and economic development bonds are the most common type of taxable municipal issuance.

FIGURE 28.1
The 1986 Tax Reform Act Spurred a Significant Growth in Taxable Issuance (Nonetheless, Issuance Since 1986 Has Been Fairly Steady)

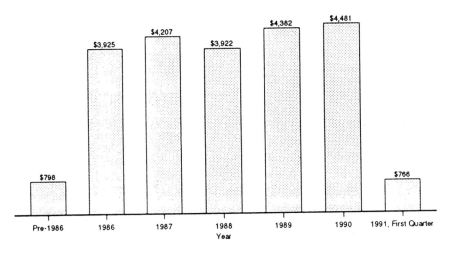

Who Issues Taxable Municipal Bonds and Why?

As previously mentioned, issuers of taxable municipal bonds are either sophisticated issuers of tax-exempt bonds or private entities with experience in the taxable markets. Table 28.1 identifies the top ten issuers of taxable municipal securities since 1986. Issuers use these instruments because tax law prevents them from using the tax-exempt markets.

In short the total municipal taxable issuance is dominated by a number of powerful issuers. Of the total $22.8 billion in issuance, 40% of total issuance has resulted from 10 issuers. Indeed, the top 3 issuers have been responsible for 27% of total issuance.

How Big Is the Market in Which Taxable Municipals Will Compete for Investors?

Municipal issuers need to remember that their taxable securities will be competing for the attention of investors who have, literally, billions and billions of dollars of alternative investment opportunities to choose from. As Figure 28.2 shows, there was approximately $438 billion of non-municipal taxable fixed income issuance in 1990 as opposed to only $4.43 billion of municipal taxable fixed income issuance.

Generally, investors will buy taxable municipal securities because of their attractive yields. The "story" associated with the taxable municipal credit—the extra explanation needed to convince the investor to buy—results in a somewhat higher yield than a comparably rated corporate security. These slightly higher yields may provide additional

Table 28.1

Top 10 Municipal Issuers Taxable Municipal Debt Since 1982
(In Thousands)

Issuer	Total Dollar Amount	# of Issues
Alaska Housing Finance Corp.	$2,585,000	34
City of New York	2,458,000	5
County of Los Angeles, CA	1,100,000	6
Nebraska Higher Ed Loan Prog.	848,600	5
Puerto Rico Housing Finance Corp.	570,000	3
Massachusetts Industrial Fin. Agency	432,760	9
State of Connecticut	403,055	4
Southeast Texas Housing Finance Corp.	339,500	2
Adams County, Colorado	300,000	1
Louisiana Agriculture Finance Auth.	300,000	2
Total	$9,336,915	71

FIGURE 28.2
Worldwide Taxable Fixed Income Issuance (1990)

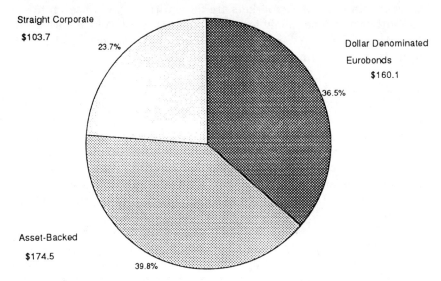

advantage to local or in-state investors, who may not be subject to applicable state and local income taxes, depending on local laws.

Preferential income tax treatment is not, however, a concern of foreign based investors. Thus, yields will be the driving force behind foreign investor decisions with regard to taxable municipals. An important distinction with foreign investors is that issuing in their currency may provide for some lowering of yields, although it does require that the issuer structure hedging programs for exchange rate risk or remain exposed to that risk entirely. This issue will be discussed at greater length in the section on Eurobonds.

BRINGING INVESTORS AND ISSUERS TOGETHER

Structuring

The critical question for taxable municipal issuers is what they will have to do in terms of structuring and documentation in order to get the attention of taxable investors. The traditional structure of a tax exempt deal utilizes both serials and long term bonds. (Serial bonds have stated maturities in consecutive years, paying interest only until maturity, at which time the entire principal amount is repaid. Term bonds, in contrast, have a single stated maturity date, but issuers adhere to a schedule of sinking fund payments that amortize the loan over its life.) Structures in the taxable markets are quite different, with seven to ten year bullets more commonly found. A bullet is simply a loan with a single maturity date. Payments of interest only are due periodically until maturity, at which time the entire principal is due.

Despite these structuring differences, a large number of municipal issuers have chosen to continue adhering to the structuring conventions of the municipal market. Since 1982, the average years to final maturity for a taxable municipal issue has been approximately 19 years. Over half of the issues had more than one term bond as part of the structure. Approximately half of the issues reported having sinking fund payments and call options embedded in the issues. In short, taxable municipal issuers seem to have taken on many of the structuring characteristics of the tax-exempt market. The important question to ask is at what yield?

There is still a relatively small amount of taxable municipal issuance outstanding, approximately $10 billion. Consequently, issuers can structure their issues to appeal to "at the margin" demand for unusual structures. However, once municipal issuers enter the taxable capital markets with any regularity and volume, their ability to attract investors willing to meet their particular structuring needs should diminish.

Municipalities may come to be perceived in a similar light to utilities which are known for their long maturity debt. More important, however, will be the issuer's comfort with matching their structuring requirements with that of the traditional corporate issuer. This is a more likely scenario as investors have more alternatives to invest in than issuers have markets to issue in.

Documentation Requirements for Taxable Municipal Issuance

Current documentation requirements for taxable municipal issuers are not significantly different from that of tax-exempt issues. However, the differences between municipal and private taxable issuers are significant. While corporate taxable issuers can enter the market on very short notice through shelf registrations, it takes the municipal issuer much longer to execute its decision to enter the market, primarily because municipal entities often require legislative or voter approval to enter the market.

At the same time, corporate issuers must submit to more stringent regulatory oversight than municipal issuers. The securities of municipal issuers are exempt from the registration and reporting requirements (but not the anti-fraud provisions) of the federal government.

This eases the disclosure requirements normally faced by corporate issuers. Instead, municipal issuers must follow Municipal Securities
Rulemaking Board guidelines on anti-fraud and disclosure, which are
less stringent.

ISSUING EUROBONDS

One distinct advantage of structuring a taxable municipal issue in a traditional taxable format is that a higher quality issuer can enter the Eurobond market, which can offer less expensive financing than the domestic
markets. Eurobonds are fixed income securities that are issued in the
European market in most of the world's hard currencies.

   During its inception in the mid 1970s, most Eurobond issues
were dollar denominated, owing to the eagerness of U.S. corporations
to tap the dollar surpluses held by OPEC member states. The natural
center of investment for these dollars was London, given the historic
relationship between Britain and the middle-eastern states. Over
time, however, the potential for investing in a wide range of currencies
with limited credit risk opened up the market to a broad range of issuers. Thus the market has become an important part of the global
capital markets.

   Issuers now have a number of different currencies that they can
choose to issue in. Figure 28.3 identifies the currency composition of
the Eurobond market in 1985 and the first quarter of 1991.

   With the rise of non-dollar denominated Eurobond debt have come
the currency exchange opportunities—and risks—that make the Eurobond market attractive to many issuers. An issuer who ultimately
wishes to raise dollars, for example, could take advantage of favorable
exchange rates by issuing foreign currency denominated Eurobonds and

FIGURE 28.3
U.S. Dollars Have Declined as a Percentage of Total Issuance, but the
Dollar Is Still a Significant Presence in the Market

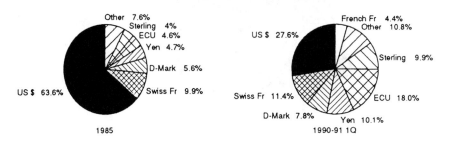

1985

1990-91 1Q

then converting or swapping into dollars, thus achieving a lower cost of capital than could have been achieved by simply issuing in dollars.

Similarly, there are periods when Eurodollar bond issues can be issued more cheaply than in the domestic securities market, due to the changing currency views of investors. While current exchange rates and investor speculation can combine to lower costs on the day of issuance, future coupon and principal payments have to be made in the bonds' denominated currency, thus opening up a currency risk and creating a need for an active hedging program. In the case of a municipal issuer, the hedging tasks would most likely be performed by a financial intermediary, who would bear the currency risk in exchange for a fee.

As in any arbitrage situation, however, it should be noted that hedging not only reduces the potential for downside losses, but also for upside gains. To get the most out of the Eurobond markets, issuers must at times bear currency risks. It should also be noted that many municipal issuers are currently restricted from taking on currency risks and would require special legislative action to enable them to do so.

There are a number of other advantages associated with Eurobond issues. First, the costs of issuance for a Eurodollar issue are somewhat lower as the market for underwriting Eurodollar bonds is more competitive. Second, legal fees and documentation requirements are lower, which is attributable to the more simple Eurobond structure. For example, Eurobond issues usually do not have reserve fund requirements.

Unfortunately, the Eurobond market is currently restricted to a very few large and high quality municipal issuers. Credit quality requirements are high for corporate participants and even higher for

FIGURE 28.4
Eurobond Issuance Evenly Split Between Corporates and
Supranational/Sovereign/Other Government Entities

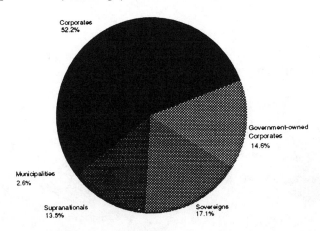

FIGURE 28.5
Institutions Now Represent the Majority of Eurobond Investors, but a
Sizable Retail Investor Base Remains

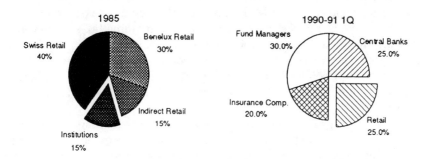

municipals, limiting access to those with AA or better credit ratings.
Furthermore, Eurobond investors are quite liquidity conscious, with
$50 million being approximately the minimum issue size.

Despite these limitations, it should be noted that issuers in the
Eurobond market are not strictly corporations. Figure 28.4 establishes
that the Eurobond market issuance has been evenly split between corporate issuers and non-corporate issuers. Thus, Eurobond investors
are not necessarily averse to investing in non-traditional issuers and
prospects for municipal issuers may improve as the market becomes
more familiar with them.

On the demand side, Eurobond investors prefer very simple structures. The issues are almost exclusively bullet maturities with final maturities of no more than 10 years. In fact, the most popular maturities
are 3, 5, and 7 years. Figure 28.5 shows that investors are evenly split
between institutions and individuals. Importantly, the retail buyers
prefer their anonymity which results in the market using bearer certificates, rather than some type of book-entry system of registration.

The institutional investors are Central Banks, Insurance Companies, Multi-Currency Fund Managers and Pension Funds.

ISSUING MEDIUM TERM NOTES

Taxable Medium Term Note programs (MTNs) have recently been used
by traditionally tax-exempt issuers who have run up against their tax-
exempt issuance caps. Like a commercial paper program, MTNs allow
an issuer to make disclosure for a relatively large total borrowing program, but to issue smaller amounts on an as-needed basis.

The chief advantage of an MTN program is its flexibility. If properly designed, MTNs provide the issuer with the ability to issue varying

amounts of debt at fixed rates or in various floating rate modes in a wide range of maturities. Typically, maturities range from three months to ten years, paralleling maturities commonly seen in the taxable market.

The flexibility of an MTN has special value to a tax-exempt issuer above its tax-exempt cap. An issuer with no remaining tax-exempt capacity can minimize the amount of its taxable debt outstanding by issuing MTNs with maturities that match the redemption dates of its outstanding tax-exempt bonds. Such a strategy allows for the continuing planned replacement of taxable with tax-exempt bonds and a minimization of interest cost.

MTN programs provide a number of other advantages associated with their flexibility. First, they allow issuers to meet smaller than full bond issue size financing requirements on individual borrowings within a program. Second, their flexibility as to the interest rate mode and length of maturity allow the issuer to tailor issues to the market and capture the lowest available rates. Recently, the use of the MTN's flexibility has even been explored in the Eurobond market, in attempts to capitalize on fleeting positive exchange rate conditions.

Of course, there is a downside to the MTN market. Since individual issues are relatively small, investors generally demand relatively high yields to compensate for limited information and liquidity. Hence, MTNs are best suited to issuers who will issue fairly frequently and in fairly large amounts and who can act quickly to capitalize on positive market conditions.

SUMMARY

There is no doubt that states, localities, authorities and private entities will experience sustained if not increased demand throughout the 1990s for the goods and services traditionally financed with tax-exempt debt. So long as the tax-exempt debt volume caps put in place by the 1986 Tax Reform Act remain in force, at least some portion of the need for the new and better mass transit systems, roads, schools, health facilities and environmental technologies so crucial to continued economic success will need to be financed in the taxable markets.

While there have been some preliminary discussions aimed at easing the tax-exempt caps, there is no reason to believe that they will be eased or abolished in the near future. Hence, issuers must learn to use the taxable markets to their maximum efficiency and at their lowest cost. The structuring, documentation and product introductions presented in this chapter should give both issuers and students of municipal markets a good start toward these goals.

Variable Rate Demand Notes

William Dawson
Senior Vice-President
Federated Research Corp.

Over the past 10 years, tax-free *variable rate demand notes* have come from virtual obscurity, a few scattered master notes used in trust departments, to become the dominant short-term tax-exempt note in the marketplace today. How this happened and why is the subject matter of this chapter.

Demand notes are presented from an historical perspective in the first section. These instruments have existed for many years in the taxable as well as tax-exempt markets, but their extensive use in the latter market is relatively recent.

The second section places variable rate demand notes in a conceptual framework. Rather than explain demand notes as a precise legal construct, this discussion conceptualizes the ideas behind the structure in very much the same way the fund managers and investment bankers talked as these new ideas took root. Out of this process, the demand note gained acceptance as a solution to a variety of problems facing issuers and investors.

How and why tax-free money market fund portfolio managers use variable rate demand notes is described in the third section. Here the focus in on how the passage of this investment vehicle from the taxable into the tax-exempt market led to such explosive growth in its usage.

The final section projects some future trends in the use of variable rate demand notes.

HISTORICAL PERSPECTIVE

The first record of a demand note being structured to facilitate the cash management needs of an institutional investor was in 1957. Norman W. Cameron, Jr., then an institutional salesman at Commercial Credit Company and later Vice President Finance, is credited with first developing "master" notes.[1]

In the summer of 1957, Commercial Credit Company, and later that year, General Motors Acceptance Corporation first entered into agreements with the trust department of Mellon Bank such that idle funds of the bank's trust customers could be more efficiently and quickly channeled into a special form of commercial paper known as a master note. Under a *master note,* the funds of many investors (typically the beneficiaries of trusts administered by a bank) are pooled under a single agreement. Technically, a master note is a *variable amount,* variable rate demand note.

Master notes had variable rates typically pegged weekly to one or another short-term money market rate. Initially, Commercial Credit Company used the 90-day commercial paper rate, that is until GMAC made its presence felt by choosing to use the slightly higher 180-day commercial paper rate. In order to establish their presence others were soon paying the highest rate between 30 and 180 days. GMAC, the largest of these programs (at over $3 billion today), later went to a variant of this pricing as well (i.e., the highest of its own 30- to 180-day commercial paper rates).[2]

It is interesting to reflect on the fact that corporate issuers, first finance companies, and later industrial companies, utilities, and bank holding companies, appear to have introduced the concept of a master note directly to the large managers of pooled trust department cash. Clearly these notes offered the issuer (i.e., the borrower) certain advantages over traditional commercial paper; a reduction in transaction costs relative to the continuous offering of commercial paper; the establishment of longer-term relationships with important large clients; and a general expansion of the borrowing capacity of the

---

[1] *The New York Times,* August 9, 1970.

[2] It is my understanding that GMAC has recently changed this practice. In today's market, there is more demand than supply.

issuer. Institutional investors were simply more able and likely to lend, or rather invest, up to their regulatory limit.

The first record of a *variable rate demand note* (VRDN) being issued for purchase outside the trust industry was in 1972. Hamilton Scherer, at the time the Assistant Treasurer of First & Merchants Corp., the bank holding company for First & Merchants Bank in Richmond, Virginia (now part of NationsBank Corp.),[3] negotiated a VRDN between Guardian Mortgage (an REIT) and a corporate client of the bank. The integrity of the demand feature was backed up by dedicated bank lines with a list of approved banks.

By the mid 1970s, as money market funds were just starting to take off, the concept of a master note was already well-entrenched in most large trust departments. Of the total volume of commercial paper outstanding at the end of 1976, $5.2 billion, or a little under 10%, was in the form of a master note or VRDNs.[4] This represented one-fifth of all finance company commercial paper and over 15% of all directly placed commercial paper. While well-known by large institutional investors, the concept was virtually unknown on Wall Street.

That situation changed as the large money market fund groups began to request these instruments. Federated Investors, for example, named its large commercial paper fund, the Federated Master Trust, to capitalize on the popularity of the master note concept. Further it hoped to invest a large percentage of its assets in VRDNs. As investment bankers, spurred on by the Prime taxable money market funds, entered the process, the supply/demand balance was upset as the issuers and fund attorneys struggled with various SEC rules related to eligible instruments in a money market fund and other regulatory problems related to the issuance of VRDNs into a public market. Unfortunately, the regulatory risks were perceived to be mainly on the side of the issuer and, thus, the yields on these notes were driven down. Simply stated, there were more buyers than issuers.

Furthermore, as the rates were driven down, fund managers lost interest. No matter the benefits, the market would have to wait until the regulators caught up to the market and more appropriate yields were re-established. Nevertheless, many of the original notes remained and the dollar volume continued to grow, albeit at a slower pace. The Federated Master Trust did buy some VRDNs.

Familiar with the master note concept, trust departments began to approach tax-free issuers in the mid-1970s. The trust department of Commerce Union National Bank in Memphis, Tennessee (now called

---

[3] Ham Scherer is now Vice Chairman, Whart First Securities Capital Markets.

[4] *Federal Reserve Bulletin*, June 1977, Evelyn M. Howley.

NationsBank of Tennessee), is credited with having established the first tax-free master note in December, 1976, with The Tennessee Housing Authority. Other early notes were established by Larry Pitts, the head of American Fletcher's trust department (now called Bank One, N.A., in Indianapolis), with the Indiana University on June 26, 1978; and Larry Warner and Dennis Weihe at First Kentucky Trust Company with the Kentucky Housing Authority in September, 1978.

The first tax-free VRDN issued through an industrial development authority was issued by the Roanoke Memorial Hospital in 1978 to the First National Bank of Chicago's trust department. Chapman and Cutler was the bond counsel and once again First & Merchants Bank was the placement agent.

Enter the tax-free money market funds. After finally passing the enabling amendments to the Tax Reform Act of 1976, tax-free money market funds first came to market in late 1978. Having established major marketing channels with their taxable money market funds, the early fund groups were faced with a tremendous pent-up demand and a very limited supply of viable tax-free notes. It was difficult then, as it is today, in retrospect to imagine a tax-free money market fund industry of more than $2 or $3 billion given the structure of available securities and the SEC's amortized cost valuation rules under which these funds had to function.

Faced with a major supply problem, tax-free money market funds turned to VRDNs. The Platte River Power Authority issued the first tax-free VRDN offered outside the trust industry. This note was placed with the Federated Tax-Free Trust on November 7, 1980, by Ross Mathews, a vice president at Morgan Guaranty Bank. A close second, on November 21, 1980, was the Nebraska Student Loan Authority also purchased by the Federated Tax-Free Trust. It was placed by Bob Dalton at Kirchner Moore (now part of George K. Baum) and Michael Gort at Smith Barney.

The first tax-free VRDN issued through an industrial development authority and offered outside the trust industry was issued by Copperweld Corp., through the Oswego IDA in Oswego County, New York on March 10, 1981. The note was again placed in the Federated Tax-Free Trust by Andy Kolesar and John Anderson, vice presidents at Pittsburgh National Bank.

The earliest demand notes were all quasi private placements. The first tax-free VRDN offered publicly was issued by the Tucson Electric Authority through E. F. Hutton (now part of Lehman Brothers) on September 20, 1981. This was soon followed by an Alaska Power Authority note issued through Bankers Trust in February 1982.

Unlike earlier VRDNs, the E. F. Hutton *lower floater program* and the Banker Trust TENR program came complete with official statements and, importantly, remarketing agents.

Unlike the earlier tax-free variable rate demand notes which were used primarily as core assets in the funds or as quasi-liquid master notes in large trust departments,[5] these more public deals were truly structured with day-to-day liquidity in mind.

VRDNs greatly expanded the viable supply of tax-free notes eligible for purchase in a money market fund. Demand notes themselves, of course, represented an addition to the viable supply. The use of these notes also allowed a money market fund to purchase longer dated paper while maintaining an appropriately short average maturity.

This was particularly important early in the development of the tax-free money market fund industry because very few tax-free notes were issued under six months. Even a very small percentage of a fund's assets in seven-day VRDNs made a big difference in how far out the yield curve a fund could buy. When this is coupled with the persistence of a very positive yield curve, one begins to understand the critically important part these notes played in the growth of the tax-free money market funds and indeed the tax-free note market.

TAX-FREE VARIABLE RATE DEMAND NOTES

Tax-free variable rate demand notes represented a solution to several problems. In the late 1970s and throughout the 1980s, few banks needed or desired tax-free income. Most were struggling with the problem of how to maintain long term, well established banking relations with tax-free borrowers. Although these relationships were once considered very profitable after taxes, they now represented a net loss. The loss of a bank's ability to deduct the interest cost of carrying tax-free securities, which was part of the 1986 Tax Act, further contributed to the problem.

As discussed briefly above, money market funds had discovered the tax-free note market and were starving for lack of supply. At the same time high taxable interest rates and relatively high individual tax rates had created a great incentive for many high quality borrowers (issuers of debt) to seek out ways of entering the tax-free note market.

The further out the yield curve they ventured, the more inefficient the market. Conversely, the shorter they stayed, the more efficient the market. When one is dealing in millions of dollars, 1 or 2% is very significant. In the early 1980s, tax-free variable rate demand notes often offered a 3 or 4% advantage over long bonds. Notably, the interest cost of

---

[5] Initially, master notes, particularly taxable master notes, were structured and used for liquidity. As time passed they became generally recognized and used as a core asset in STIF funds (short-term investment fund) and money market funds.

these notes moved considerably lower in the remainder of the 1980s as interest rates generally plummeted. Needless to say, the issuers of tax-free variable rate demand notes were to benefit handsomely.

VRDNs appeared to offer benefits to everyone. The issuer received a substantial reduction in his interest costs; the investor gained a large and needed increase in supply; and the banker received large amounts of fee income while maintaining and perhaps enhancing a good relationship with the issuer.

All parties had many reasons to move forward. However, if these notes were to become a reality on a large scale, they had to be structured within the regulatory framework of different agencies of the government; federal, state and local. In retrospect, the most difficult of these regulatory bodies was the Securities and Exchange Commission (SEC). While tax-free municipal securities are, generally speaking, exempt from SEC registration, the SEC does regulate the investment activities of mutual funds, including tax-free money market funds.

Of overriding concern to most shareholders of tax-free money market funds was, and is, their ability to value portfolio securities on an amortized cost basis. A fund's continuing ability to do this is, and was, largely dependent on compliance with an order issued by the SEC. This was later codified into Rule 2a-7 (the amortized cost rules).

The major provisions of the amortized cost rules and their three revisions mandate no security held by the Trust be of more than 13 months (prior to June 1991, it was one year) to maturity, and that the average weighted maturity of the fund's portfolio be less than 90 days (originally 120 days). The maturity of a variable rate demand note is generally defined by whichever is longer—the demand feature or the next interest rate change.[6] The maturity of a simple variable rate note maturing in less than 13 months, however, may be construed for the purpose of calculating the funds average maturity as the date of the next rate change.[7]

Variable rate notes, in general, shortened the average maturity of money market funds using them, stabilized their underlying net asset value and necessarily expanded the available supply of notes.

In theory, a variable rate demand note or "master" note could be established in one of two ways:

---

[6] SEC overview also extends to precisely what will be construed as the maturity for shareholder purposes.

[7] For example: A variable rate note maturing in one year will have a very different effective maturity than will a similar note having the same frequency of rate change but a demand rather than a maturity at the one year point.

(1) the use of a demand feature and a variable rate coupled with a dedicated bank credit facility which the issuer would establish (administrative conduit approach), or

(2) the purchase of a variable rate note or bond with a put or buy-back agreement to a bank (the synthetic approach).

Both approaches offered liquidity and if properly indexed, a market value which approximated cost.

The essence of a variable rate demand note is the three-handed relationship among the investor (a tax-free money market fund, for example), the issuer and the bank (or more generally the credit and/or liquidity support).

The administrative conduit approach allows the investor to make demand for payment upon the issuer which in turn exercises its loan agreement with its bank. The synthetic approach causes the investor to go directly to the bank without involving the issuer. Both solutions offer a variable rate and the integrity of a "demand" feature through recourse to a bank.

One could argue the difference is more one of semantics and legal subtlety than of function. The investor achieves his desired stability of principal and liquidity. However, one might also argue that a third party put or buy-back is a security separate and distinct from the note itself and thus, cannot be used to define the maturity of the underlying note. Unquestionably, the underlying note or bond remains intact. In most cases, it can be technically separated from the combination and even sold.

The SEC's position on this has evolved over time. It is now willing, under limited circumstances, to define the put when properly structured and tied to the bond as a demand payment from the bank. Thus, it is clearly possible for tax-free money market funds to purchase this

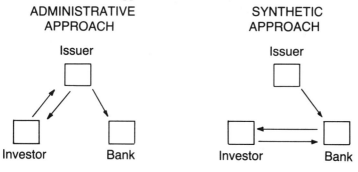

FIGURE 29.1 Relationship Between Issuer, Investor, and Bank—Two Approaches

structure.[8] Very careful structuring makes this approach viable within the constraints of individual prospectuses and recent codifications of the amortized cost exemptive orders issued by the SEC.

Administrative Conduit Approach

Approximately $100 billion in variable rate demand notes using the administrative conduit approach are presently outstanding.[9] This category includes the Banker's Trust TENR program, Goldman Sachs' "Multimode," First Boston's "ACE" program, Shearson Lehman's Money Market Municipal program, which has a variable rate demand mode, Merrill Lynch's "Updates," and most direct placements.

The precise legal structure of a variable rate demand note is somewhat dependent on the nature of the financing and the general quality level of the corporate credit or municipal credit. Typically, a note agreement, an encumbrance certificate, and an opinion of corporate (or municipal) counsel are required in addition to the note itself. When credit enhancement is required, typically an LOC combined with an enforceability opinion and a preference opinion are required. Again, the objective is one of producing a demand instrument that offers tax-free money market funds both a shortened average maturity and assistance in the stabilization of its net asset value.

A substantial body of business practice has evolved over the past several years as to what is an acceptable structure. Initially, a fund's board of directors had to determine the appropriateness or, more to the point, consistency of using variable rate demand notes with their individual money market fund exemptive orders[10] which they had negotiated with the SEC. In July, 1983, the SEC first codified the various amortized cost exemptive orders. Again, the rule has subsequently been revised three times as this market has continued to evolve. The use of a demand feature through the issuer as a means of defining a variable rate note's maturity for a fund's purpose has been clearly endorsed by the SEC in all three revisions of the rule.

The Synthetic Approach

The second revision to Rule 2a-7 of the Investment Company Act (the amortized cost rules) in 1986 clarified a money market fund's ability

---

[8] The put may also be to an insurance company or brokerage firm.

[9] Source: J. P. Morgan Securities, Inc..

[10] Very careful structuring and outside legal advice is highly recommended as this structure presents several potential tax questions.

to purchase what later came to be known as *synthetic variable rate demand notes.* On November 12, 1982, the Daily Tax-Free Income Fund, Inc., offered by the Reich & Tang organization, was the first fund to receive clearance from the SEC to purchase this combination security. It was also the first fund to actively purchase longer-term floating rate tax-free bank loans and attach a put issued by a bank.

Today, this basic conceptual framework has been expanded to include fixed-rate bonds combined with a put, often an LOC and other features. In essence, the investor buys a bond with a fixed or variable coupon, receives the income and pays for these various "bells and whistles" out of that income stream.

In order to comply with the amortized cost rules, several things must be present:

(1) the demand feature or put must be no less frequent than every 13 months;

(2) the end yield to the investor including the cost of credit enhancements and the put must be variable; and

(3) the combined security including the put issuer must be of "high quality."

Needless to say, this is a complicated structure and should not be entered into lightly. Only a qualified municipal bond counsel and/or tax specialist should attempt to structure this kind of security. There are contractual risks and tax risks which only a competent municipal bond counsel is qualified to opine on. Nevertheless, the great efficiency and much lower cost of short-term municipal securities has made this structure possible and indeed profitable to engineer. It is likely this security will work to make the municipal bond market itself more efficient by in effect creating new short-term supply.

Market participants estimate $10 to $15 billion in what I am calling synthetic VRDNs are currently in the market, with $1 to $2 billion rated by rating agencies.[11] Supplemental option bonds, tender option bonds, variable rate trust certificates, variable rate demand custodial receipts, etc., are included in this category.[12]

In summary, VRDNs offered the issuer, the bank, and the investor more attractive positions than they had formerly. As noted above, synthetic variable rate demand notes, however, do not necessarily involve the issuer.

---

[11] IBC/Donoghue's "Money Market Insight," May 1991, Vol. 3, No. 5.

[12] This includes securities initially structured this way.

The *issuer* of classic VRDNs is and was provided essentially long term financing at much lower short-term rates. In fact, most corporate issuers are able to keep these notes on the long-term side of their balance sheets in accordance with the Financial Accounting Standards Board regulations as long as they maintain a back-up credit facility and intend to keep the notes outstanding. A positive long-term relationship was established with large institutional buyers. There was a general reduction in issuance costs. And, finally, a very large new market was opened to the issuer's debt.

The *buyer* as discussed below in greater detail, received many things. First and foremost, VRDNs greatly increased the viable supply of tax-free notes. These notes helped the fund stabilize its NAV, control its average maturity and assure its shareholders a positive after-tax yield when compared to a taxable money market fund. Further, these notes provided a failsafe source of liquidity.

The *bank* received needed fee income. It also maintained and often enhanced its overall banking relationship with the issuer. Finally, the bank became an integral part of a growing new capital market.

It is interesting to note that, in many of the early VRDNs, the interest rate payable to the investor changed in the event the demand feature was exercised. In short, the issuer paid a lower tax-free market rate every day the note's demand feature was not exercised. In the event the demand feature was exercised and the VRDN was not remarketed, the note ended up in the bank which issued the letter of credit. In many cases, the interest rate automatically went back up to virtually the same rate the issuer had been paying or would have paid had he borrowed tax-free from a bank prior to the advent of the VRDNs. As is so often the case in the money markets, all roads lead to the bank. As a practical matter, tax-free VRDNs rarely end up in a bank's lending portfolio. I have never heard of a VRDN going back into a bank for other than very technical legal reasons or credit reasons. That is, despite the fact that certain kinds of VRDNs have been developed for day-to-day liquidity.

USAGE: THE STRATEGY OF USING VRDNS IN A TAX-FREE MONEY MARKET FUND

Tax-free money market funds are themselves variable rate instruments. Indeed, they compete with master notes and VRDNs as short term cash vehicles in trust departments and more broadly in the tax-free market. Nevertheless, tax-free money market funds have been the driving force behind the continuing growth of these investment vehicles.

Properly priced variable rate notes are well-placed in a money market fund. There can be no question that money market funds have added great stability to this market. Indeed, the money funds have had a major role in how these notes are structured and priced. These funds own over half the outstanding tax-free VRDNs in the marketplace today. Thus, how and why fund managers have embraced this concept gives you added insight into the market and its explosive growth.

It can be argued convincingly that a money market fund is advantageously positioned vis-á-vis competitive funds to the extent it has some portion of its coreholdings in variable rate securities. This strategy has at least three reasons to support it.

First, variable rate demand notes can help reduce unusual cash flows into and out of a fund during volatile markets. In particular, variable rate securities will cause a money market fund to reflect rising interest rates more quickly and will not hurt the fund's yield in a constant rate environment. Furthermore, such securities discourage money from entering an individual fund during falling interest rate environments. The fund simply lags the market less. If a fund loses half of its assets as securities mature during a rising rate environment, it must gain 100% of its assets back during a falling rate environment in order to be left with the same assets as it started with. To the extent increased cash flow causes this to happen, the fund lags the market more as interest rates rise than it does when rates fall. As the mathematics buffs say, the fractions don't add. Variable rate securities help reverse this drag on a fund's yield.

Second, in order to maintain the same average maturity, a large core position in variable rate securities necessitates a longer average maturity on the remainder of a fund's assets. This simple dumbbelling at the point of purchase allows a fund to capture the liquidity premium generally demanded of longer dated paper. In fact, it assures a higher marginal rate every day in positive yield curve environments.

Further, by investing a notable percentage of a fund's assets in variable rate securities, transaction costs are reduced and the portfolio manager is in effect given greater flexibility in how the remainder of the fund is invested. If a fund has, for example, half of its assets in variable rate securities, it only invests the remaining half on a daily basis. However, the diversification limits imposed on the fund by the prospectus apply to the whole fund and thus, as a practical matter, effectively double the trader's limits in this example.

This strategy in and of itself will not outperform the results achieved by a portfolio manager capable of perfectly timing the market, but it should give the same portfolio manager a higher yield on his portfolio over the business cycle than he would achieve without it.

Tax-free money market funds could not be managed as a group at anywhere near their present size without VRDNs. While it may be possible to manage a large tax-free money market fund without VRDNs, it is not possible to run tax-free money market funds competitively today without a significant ownership of variable rate notes.

PRICING

Over one-half of the assets of tax-free money market funds as a group, approximately $45 billion, are in variable rate securities. Needless to say, the indices used in pricing tax-free variable rate demand notes are of great importance. Historically, portfolio managers have insisted on three characteristics in variable rate securities which are related to the index:

(1) Integrity against the taxable market (in this way the portfolio manager was in part assured that the fund's yield made sense after taxes when compared to a taxable money market fund);
(2) An assured secondary market (a remarketing agent or when a taxable index was used, a resulting yield that would generally assure a positive carry to market-makers); and
(3) An interest rate which over a period of time approximated the average marginal day-to-day transaction on the trading desk (while the maturity of a variable rate security is normally considered to be the time frame remaining to the next rate change, the rate on a core asset should reflect a point further out on the yield curve).

The first of these bears some comment. Formula-based VRDNs were critical to the early development of this market. In the early 1980s, 50% of prime, for example, was a commonplace formula in privately placed tax-free variable rate demand notes.

Why 50% of prime? This was not a casual percentage of prime. Historically, the prime interest rate has averaged 150+ basis points over 90-day commercial paper interest rates. If you assume 90-day commercial paper to be a good proxy for the gross yield of competing taxable prime money market funds, you begin to understand how a formula like this assured the success of the tax-free money market fund industry.

Example.

10.50%	90-Day Commercial Paper Rate
− .50	Expense Factor of Prime Money Market Fund
10.00%	Prime Money Market Fund Net Yield
× .50	Maximum Tax Rate (early 1980s)
5.00%	After-Tax Break Even Rate

10.50%	90-day Commercial Paper Rate
+ 1.50	
12.00%	Estimated Prime Rate
× .50	Formula Rate
6.00%	Yield on Privately Placed Demand Note
− .50	Expense Factor on Tax-Free Money Market Fund
5.50%	Net Yield of Tax-Free Money Market Fund

Please note in this theoretical example, 50% of prime assured the investor in a tax-free money market fund a 50 basis point yield advantage on an after tax basis versus a prime money market fund.

Today, this market has matured to the point where a periodic review of the index or the equation used against the index is all that is required. Clearly the maximum tax rates on individuals and corporations has changed and will continue to change in the future.

In September, 1988, the Internal Revenue Service issued a notice which prospectively eliminated formula-based VRDNs. The primary topic of Notice 88-130 was the redemption and/or reissuance of tax-exempt bonds. Among other things, a "qualified tender rate," a rate set or indexed periodically by the issue's remarketing agent at a level necessary to remarket the issue at par plus accrued interest, if any, was required of eligible qualified tender bonds (VRDNs). Lacking this, the VRDN may be deemed to have been reissued or to have matured at the next rate change.

Again, the persistence of a positive yield curve within the tax-free note market over a number of years makes the use of variable rate paper particularly attractive in a tax-free money market fund for basically three reasons:

(1) By dumbbelling the fund at the time of purchase in variable rate paper pegged to a point further out the yield curve and in longer dated fixed rate paper, a higher marginal yield is achieved every day with the same resultant average maturity versus a direct purchase on the fixed rate yield curve.

(2) The use of variable rate paper allows a tax-free money market fund to purchase a wider spectrum of securities at different points on the yield curve. This is particularly important in a tax-free money market fund because of the lumpiness of supply.

(3) Variable rate demand notes are an important part of the day-to-day liquidity of the fund. As has been suggested, certain notes are more suited to this purpose than others.

The tax-exempt note market is characterized by high fragmentation and relative illiquidity. These factors contribute greatly to the persistence of a positive yield curve and the appeal of VRDNs.

Originally, a large distinction was made between core asset demand notes and liquidity demand notes. Different indices were, and to some degree still are, used in pricing these securities. However, as the dollar volume in liquidity demand notes grew, the relationship of these vehicles to the taxable market grew closer and closer to the targeted percentages used in the original core notes. While the percentage of a fund in liquidity demand notes (i.e., typically pegged to tax-free indices) versus core asset demand notes (those most often pegged to taxable indices) may be less important today, on average it can have a very dramatic effect over short periods of time. For example, tax-free demand notes tied to the tax-free indices typically have a higher yield in the fall and winter of the year and those tied to the taxable indices are typically higher in the spring and summer. While an experienced fund manager is well aware of this technical factor, prudence normally dictates a good percentage of both securities for liquidity and because of the potential lack of availability at various points of the year.

The persistence of this differentiation between core assets and liquidity VRDNs comes from the dominance of tax-free money market funds in this market and the tendency of portfolio managers to think in terms of portfolio constructs. Portfolio managers look at securities very differently than Wall Street traders, who justify their existence by creating as much volatility and as many transactions as possible. Unfortunately, this subject is beyond the scope of our present discussion.

The year 1986 was a watershed year for tax-free VRDNs. The Tax Reform Act of that year not only changed marginal income tax rates for individuals and corporations, but changed the tax rate of corporations relative to individuals. Prior to 1986 and for many years before, wealthy individuals had the highest marginal tax rate. Thus, prior to 1986, tax-free money market funds which serve primarily individuals were in effect the lowest cost lenders. This all changed in 1986.

Suddenly, tax-free VRDNs made sense to corporations. While the overall supply of tax-free notes to include VRDNs continued to grow, the large national tax-free money market funds gave up market share to corporations and to smaller state-specific tax-free money market funds where tax-free notes still made sense to individuals after state and local taxes were taken into account.

Notably, corporations are not large enough as a group to displace individuals as a group or even to become the dominant investor. Thus, as we move into the future, the individual or his surrogate, the tax-free money market fund, once again, become the marginal investor.

CONCLUSIONS

The tax-free note market is a unique money market for many reasons. Clearly, municipal notes are free from various federal, state and local taxes. Different rules are applied to the registration and ownership of tax-free securities. Further, laws related to arbitrage; the amount of permissible arbitrage and what is or is not a deductible expense are often determining factors in both the dollar volume of new supply and how individual securities are structured. In addition to these and other distinguishing characteristics must now be added the role of financial leadership in the money markets. Rarely have financial markets been as responsive to the needs of investors and in particular large institutional managers of tax-free money market assets than we have witnessed in the past decade.

Unlike the taxable money markets, it is very difficult for brokerage firms or investment bankers to control or even direct the evolution of this market. Notably, brokerage firms have great trouble financing large inventories of tax-free securities. There is no tax-free repo market and without the ability to expense or deduct the taxable interest costs of financing tax-free securities there is great incentive to keep dealer positions small or at least within the confines of the firm's own capital. The investment banker is, thus, much more sensitive and dependent on investor preferences and needs than is true in many other markets.

In this case, the tax-free money market fund represented a dramatic reduction in interest expense and fees paid by the issuer. In a very real sense, these funds not only disintermediated the banks but dramatically lowered the expense of accessing this capital market. Investment bankers, brokerage houses and law firms were all forced to dramatically lower their fees relative to what could be charged on the more traditional fixed-rate bond. Further, the early use of formula-based variable rate demand notes as a basic clearing rate and the insistence of the tax-free money market fund managers that these new VRDNs be properly structured to meet 2a-7 requirements allowed a maximum number of municipal issuers to access this market.

The higher marginal tax rates on individuals versus corporations prior to 1986 and the reversal of these roles since then has clearly effected the dynamics of how interest rates are set on VRDNs. This market is now clearly pricing itself to the marginal new money into or out of it.

There were between $9 billion and $10 billion in tax-exempt notes outstanding in 1986. Well over half of these notes were held by tax-free money market funds. Further, it is estimated that fewer than 15 institutional investors, the majority of which were tax-free money market funds, controlled over 90% of the marginal float on daily transactions in these markets (VRDNs not included). While the market is far less concentrated today and corporations own a material portion of the VRDN market, traditional fixed rate notes are still largely owned by tax-free money market funds as mentioned earlier.

In order for the tax-free money market funds to grow, it was necessary to change the tax-free note market in a major way. It was simply not possible to run large multi-billion dollar money market funds with the supply of tax-free notes originally offered to these funds in the marketplace. New securities had to be created and fund managers had to articulate what they wanted.

The early fund managers were very clear. They maintained that they had great demand for their product, the tax-free money market fund, but there was inadequate supply. Further, the then current structure of tax-free notes severely restricted a money market fund's potential to purchase most new supply directly. If the funds were to realize their potential for growth, they needed a massive new supply far beyond anything contemplated or already in the commercial banking system.

Looking back over the past several years, it is clear tax-free money market funds evolved from taxable money market funds. Tax-free money market fund managers took the concept of a master note or VRDN and successfully adapted it to the tax-free note market. Their success changed the tax-free markets and, in the opinion of this author, are now changing the government and prime money markets.

CHAPTER 30

When to Do a Refunding*

Aaron Gurwitz
Goldman, Sachs and Co.

During the past five years, advance refundings have accounted for more than 45% of municipal bond issues. Over this period municipalities have developed some convenient "rules of thumb" for deciding whether to refund a given bond issue. Typically, an issuer who has no decided views about the direction of interest rates will establish a target level of present value savings, measured as a percentage of the *refunding* bond issue. As interest rates begin to approach the level that will produce that amount of savings, the issuer will begin monitoring the market closely, looking for opportunities to execute the transaction.

Depending on the term of the bonds and the call provisions, setting a present value savings target of 4% or 5% may make a great deal of sense for advance refundings. However, once a bond passes its first call date such rules begin to become less appropriate. As a currently callable bond begins to approach maturity, the interest rate required to achieve any given level of present value savings decreases, slowly at first and then rapidly. Put differently, a call option is a "wasting asset"; its value decreases as it approaches expiration. Trying to squeeze a fixed amount of savings from an aging option may mean that the

---

issuer never realizes any savings at all. In addition, interest rates in the municipal market have been remarkably stable over the past several years. Low market volatility further reduces the chances that any given level of savings will be achieved.

For currently callable bonds, we recommend establishing a schedule of net present value savings under which the required target percentage declines at intervals as the bond approaches maturity and the issuer's call option approaches expiration. Some issuers may wish to adopt "refunding efficiency" (defined below) as an alternative decision rule, although efficiency is somewhat more difficult to measure than percentage present value savings. To the extent that issuers continue to await fixed present value savings targets for current refundings, investors may profit by purchasing slight-to-moderate premium currently callable or soon-to-be callable bonds.

CALL OPTIONS AS WASTING ASSETS

Let us assume that the refunding bonds will have the same maturity as the refunded issue. For two reasons, it becomes more and more difficult to realize any given level of present value savings as the issuer's call option ages. First, if savings are realized over a relatively short period of time, more basis points must be saved per year in order to generate any given level of total discounted savings. In the extreme, assuming no cost of issuance, in order to generate 5% savings at the beginning of the bond's last year of life, the issuer must reduce that year's interest rate payment by 500 bp. Thus, a 7.50% issue would have to be refunded by a 2.50% issue in order to realize net present value savings of 5%. Second, the shorter the time between the refunding and the maturity, the shorter the time over which the issuer must amortize any call premium or the cost of issuing the new bonds.

We illustrate the impact of these two effects in Figure 30.1, which indicates the interest rate that would be required to produce 5% present value savings on the refunding of a 7.50% 30-year bond. In deriving the results, we assumed that the bond was callable 10 years after issuance at a premium of 102, that refunding bonds have the same maturity date as the refunded issue, and that issuance costs were 1%, regardless of the maturity of the refunding bonds.

The chart illustrates the fact that, as the option ages, it becomes more difficult to achieve any given level of present value savings. This general tendency is interrupted at points where the call premium drops from one level to another. As scheduled decreases in call premiums approach, issuers might be well advised to postpone refunding bond issues until after the point that the benefits of the lower

FIGURE 30.1
Interest Rate Required to Achieve 5% Present Value Savings

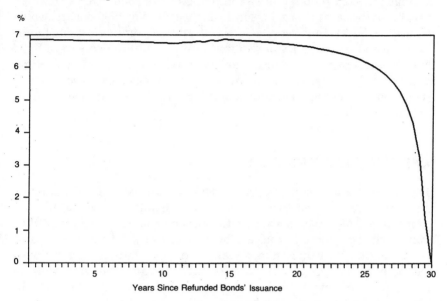

premium can be realized. Also, the upward slope of the municipal yield curve offsets, to some extent, the fall-off in the interest rate level required to achieve 5% savings. Shorter maturity bonds do carry lower interest rates than long-term bonds. Nevertheless, at present the yield curve is not steep enough fully to offset the aging effect on the option value.

A similar phenomenon will occur for serial bonds and shorter-term bonds for which the time period between the first optional call date and the maturity date is less than the 20 years hypothesized in our example in Figure 30.1. For such shorter bonds, a lower refunding rate is required and a constant percentage level of savings may be even more difficult to achieve. For example, a 7.50% bond currently callable at 102 with only three years to maturity would require a 4.55% refunding yield to reach the 5% savings level. For such bonds, a desired savings level less than that for longer-term bonds would be appropriate.

Savings in Constant Dollars

If an issuer were to analyze the savings of a bond that is currently callable—not as a percentage of the refunding par amount but rather in constant (present value) dollars—the required decrease in interest rates to reach the same level of savings is even more dramatic. For example, to reach a 5% level of savings on a 7.50% bond, callable now at par with 18 years to maturity, would require a refunding interest rate of 6.91%; 5% savings in 1992 would require a refunding rate of about 6.87%. However, to achieve the same 5% savings in 1992, measured in 1990 dollars, would require a 6.80% refunding rate—a significantly lower interest rate target.

Given this tendency of required interest rates to decrease, a fixed level of present value savings can prove to be an elusive goal. Rigid decision rules requiring a certain level of savings can prevent the issuer from achieving any savings at all. Some alternative decision rule seems appropriate.

REFUNDING EFFICIENCY

The value of any financial option, including an issuer's call option on municipal bonds, has two components: the intrinsic value and the time value. The intrinsic value is the amount that could be realized by exercising the option. In the case of an issuer's call, the intrinsic value is the net present value savings realized on a refunding. Any option at any point in time is worth *at least* its intrinsic value. The time value of the option reflects the possibility that the intrinsic value may be higher in the future. For an issuer's call option, the time value represents the possibility that greater present value savings may be realized in the future if interest rates decline further.

Options that have no intrinsic value may still have considerable time value. Even when a callable bond is newly issued, the call option has some value. Specifically, if on a 30-year bond the issuer were offered the choice between issuing (10-year, 102) callable bonds at par with a 7.50% coupon or non-callable bonds at par with a 7.25% coupon, the market is placing a 25 bp (3.04 point) time value on the issuer's option. By choosing to issue the callable bond, the issuer would, in effect, be purchasing a call option with no intrinsic value for 3.04 points of time value.

When an issuer executes a refunding, the municipality is realizing the intrinsic value of the option and is giving up the time value. Refunding efficiency is defined as the ratio of the intrinsic value of an issuer's call option (the present value savings) to the total value of the option.[1]

Determining the efficiency of a refunding involves calculating the total value of the issuer's call option. Computing the intrinsic value is relatively straightforward; it is the present value savings the issuer will

---

[1] For a comprehensive discussion of refunding efficiency, see Erol Hakanoglu and Emmanuel Roman, *Issues in Corporate Liability Management: The Refunding Decision,* Goldman, Sachs and Co., April 1990.

realize. Determining the time value of the call option is much more difficult. Even with the help of the computerized options valuation models produced in recent years at Goldman, Sachs & Co. and elsewhere, estimating the value of the option requires assumptions about the future volatility of interest rates. If rates are expected to vary over a wide range in the future, then there is a good chance that at some point the holder of an issuer's option will be able to realize substantially greater savings in the future. If volatility is low, then the chances of realizing substantially greater savings in the near term are also relatively low. Thus, the higher the anticipated market volatility, the greater will be the time value of the issuer's call option and the lower will be the efficiency of a refunding generating any given level of present value savings.

For example, consider a bond with an 8% coupon and 20 years remaining to maturity. Assume further that the bond is currently callable at 102% of par, that the call premium will decline by 1% per year, and that the cost of issuing refunding bonds would be one point. Under these assumptions, the bond could be refunded currently to produce present value savings of approximately 4.6%. This, then, is the intrinsic value of the option. Estimates of the time value of the option depend on anticipated interest rate volatility.

Volatility is measured at an annual rate in percentage terms. A 12% yield volatility indicates that interest rates are likely to remain within a range that is within 12%, up or down, from current levels.[2] So if current yields on long-term municipals are about 7.25%, a 12% volatility projection indicates the expectation that yields will remain in a range between 6.38% and 8.12% over the course of a year. During the mid-1980s volatility was relatively high; between 1982 and year-end 1987 yield volatility on long-term municipal bonds averaged 13%. More recently, volatility has been quite subdued; since January, 1988 the average has been less than 7%.

If we take these figures as brackets around the range of future volatility, then using Goldman Sachs models for estimating the time values of options, the efficiency of refunding this hypothetical issue would be between 49% (13% volatility) and 76% (7% volatility).

Issuers who have a particular view regarding bond market volatility may wish to substitute the traditional present value savings objective with a target defined in term of refunding efficiency. They may, for example, decide to execute a refunding that produces 70% efficiency evaluated at a 9% volatility. Those who do not have strong views about

---

[2] Somewhat more precisely, yield volatility is defined as the annualized standard deviation of periodic percentage changes in interest rates. There is approximately a 67% chance that for the given period, rates will remain within a range of plus or minus one standard deviation from their current value.

likely levels of future volatility may wish to adopt more transparent decision rules that still account for the fact that a call option is a wasting asset and that the municipal market has been remarkably stable.

A TARGET SAVINGS SCHEDULE

Because any given level of present value savings becomes more and more difficult to achieve as a call option ages, issuers who cling to a fixed savings target run the risk of not realizing any savings at all. Municipalities should be prepared to begin reducing their percentage savings targets after the bonds' first call date. For example, suppose the issuer had maintained a 5% present value savings target before the bonds' first call date. It might then make sense to reduce the target percentage present value savings by, say, 50 basis points per year for the next 10 years. If the bonds were still outstanding at that time, then the issuer would execute a current refunding that generated any savings at all over the cost of issuing the refunding bonds.

FIVE PERCENT?

Throughout this discussion we have assumed that the issuer had set an initial target of 5% net present value savings. It is also worthwhile to reconsider this basic figure. As discussed previously, the value of an option depends on (1) the time period between the call date and the maturity date of the bond and (2) the outlook for bond market volatility. The shorter the time between the call date and the maturity date, the lower the value of the option, all else being equal. Moreover, when volatility is high, options have substantial time value; that is, issuers may be giving up a great deal of potential future savings by executing a refunding or an advance refunding in order to realize the intrinsic value of their call option.

   This substantial time value is reflected in the fact that many issuers insisted on achieving at least 4% or 5% present value savings on refundings executed during the mid-1980s. Since then, however, market volatility has declined substantially. Accordingly, the time value of options has decreased, and issuers may have to be satisfied with lower levels of present value savings on future refundings than they were able to achieve during the volatile years between 1984 and 1987. Issuers who, like us, expect that the financial markets of the 1990s will continue to be relatively quiet may want to adjust to that expectation by reducing target savings levels below the traditional 4% or 5%. And for issuers who have current refunding opportunities, an analysis of target savings levels should be made in terms of constant savings dollars, rather than merely on a percentage basis.

IMPLICATIONS FOR INVESTORS

High coupon, nonpre-refunded bonds usually trade on a yield-to-call basis. That is, investors assume that issuers will act to realize the intrinsic value of their call options. To the extent that municipalities do not accept the advice offered in this analysis, then currently callable premium bonds trading on a yield-to-call basis may be undervalued. Investors who purchase a bond on the assumption that it will be called soon can only be pleasantly surprised if the issuer waits to execute a refunding until a (receding) present value savings target is achieved. If issuers act in this way, then investors will continue to earn the high coupon on the outstanding bonds longer than the market anticipated in pricing the bonds, and this will enhance the holder's total rate of return. To the extent that issuers continue to target relatively high present value savings, bonds that are near or past their first call date and are trading at a slight to moderate premium are probably undervalued.

Part Five

CONTEMPORARY PUBLIC FINANCE ISSUES

CHAPTER 31

The Benefits of Fiscal Oversight

Allen J. Proctor
New York State Financial Control Board

Fiscal monitors provide a substantial protection to investors in municipal bonds, a protection which is often underestimated because it frequently accompanies difficult fiscal conditions and lower credit ratings. Fiscal monitors are heterogeneous, and each monitor should be individually investigated to determine the nature and extent of protection offered to holders of bonds of a troubled municipality. Nonetheless, fiscal monitors all share in common the ability to enhance the level of financial disclosure and to apply some degree of additional incentive to municipalities to address their fiscal problems directly and in a timely fashion.

In the next sections, we will briefly discuss the types of fiscal monitors that exist and then provide an extensive discussion of the benefits which fiscal monitors can provide and some effective ways in which to do so. Given its status as one of the oldest and most well-known public fiscal monitors, the New York State Financial Control Board for New York City is reviewed and its applicability as a model for establishing an effective system of fiscal monitoring for other jurisdictions is discussed. Finally, several critical issues facing municipalities over the next decade are reviewed and the contribution of fiscal monitoring to addressing those issues is discussed.

WHAT IS A FISCAL MONITOR?

A fiscal monitor is an independent public or private body that analyzes the finances and operations of government in order to provide alternative perspectives on local fiscal problems and, in some cases, to provide possible solutions. In many cases, this role is provided by local civic groups, which will publish reports and hold public education forums. Fiscal monitors are also created by state governments, often in conjunction with the provision of substantial financial support to a troubled municipality, whether through special taxing authority, credit guarantees, or extraordinary funding. For the state, the fiscal monitor provides a continual oversight to determine that the objectives of its support are being carried out and to provide early warning when state financial guarantees will be called upon.

Fiscal monitors can provide an additional, and impartial, source of information for investors. Even though standards for disclosure in public offerings are quite extensive nowadays, the reports of an independent fiscal monitor can be used to confirm that the municipality's own reports are reasonable and factually correct. The monitor can also provide commentary that enables the investor to know if the municipality is credibly identifying and addressing its fiscal problems as well as implementing solutions in a timely and effective manner. If certain activities that led to past financial problems are prohibited by statute, then the monitor can be an effective reporter on compliance with those statutes and prohibitions.

MOTIVES FOR FISCAL MONITORING

When a municipality encounters severe fiscal problems the initial motive to create a fiscal monitor may be a refined form of finger-pointing. Charges of local mismanagement may emerge, countered by charges that the managers could do their jobs if only the elected officials would heed managers' warnings and make the necessary decisions. Alternatively, one may hear the well-worn charge that traditional urban areas are no longer fiscally viable, which of course would be countered by the charge that urban areas are the only ones with the courage not to run away from the problems of modern society and if the federal and state governments would show similar courage this fiscal problem wouldn't exist.

The reality is that fiscal problems emerge because of operational problems or because of difficulties in acquiring adequate credit on manageable terms. The motives that justify choosing a fiscal monitoring process as the appropriate response are basically three: the need to restore credibility to the budget process; the need to catalyze a laggard decision-making process; or the need to prohibit practices that led to credit impairment.

Restoring Credibility Through Public Reporting and Commentary

The most direct way to restore credibility is to institute public reporting. In a surprising number of cases, basic information, such as the number of employees on the payroll or the amount of an agency's budget paid for with local tax funds, is not made easily available to the public. More than anything else, fiscal monitoring means enhanced public reporting, both factual and analytical. A fiscal monitor's most basic task is to require enough information in a timely and accessible format so that public reports can be an effective mechanism to prompt responsible fiscal management.

An effective report would include detailed estimates of revenues and expenditures for the budget year. These estimates would be reported by type, such as personnel expenses, debt service expenses, other expenses, tax revenues, federal and state grant revenues, other revenues, etc. These estimates would also be reported by intended use, such as by department and/or by program. Depending on the areas in which credibility needs to be enhanced, reports could also be required on monthly operations (planned revenues and expenditures versus actual), cashflow (planned versus actual), and capital budget commitments and expenditures (planned versus actual).

The format of public reports can also be an issue affecting credibility. A format that makes it easy to know both the level of current spending and the change in current spending from the previous, audited fiscal year is essential. If the government doesn't do this well in its own reports, the fiscal monitor's reports can do so. Such reports should also include statements that reconcile current estimates against the previous set of reported estimates. This reconciliation can be especially important in times of fiscal stress because there will be many published statements with multiple interpretations such as "revenues are down," "spending has jumped," "the budget gap is now doubled."

Experience has shown that seemingly contradictory statements usually arise from the use of different bases of comparison. This can easily be standardized, the number of contradictions reduced, and the credibility of public statements enhanced. For example, at the end of each fiscal quarter a report of the status of the current budget can be presented showing changes to annual estimates since the last report, distinguishing changes due to revisions in base estimates of revenues and expenditures from changes due to actions taken to rebalance the budget.

This format makes it clear where the budget has deteriorated, how much it has deteriorated since the last quarter, what actions are contemplated to offset that deterioration, and how much each of those offsetting actions is expected to be worth.

Analogous to the format problem is the issue of applying generally accepted accounting principles (GAAP) to budgeting. This is an area fraught with controversy, but the controversy is primarily a professional debate over fine points. At its most basic level, GAAP is a standardized method of counting that is now the norm for audited financial statements. At the current time, there is no standardized method of counting for budgets.

The credibility of today's budget must be grounded in some way on the reality of the past. GAAP budgets currently provide the only means to reconcile intent (i.e., the budget) with results (i.e., financial statements) and they provide the only means to evaluate how realistically the programmatic and fiscal content of the budget maintains continuity with the fiscal years just completed. Without some form of standardization between financial statements and budgets, the credibility of budget data will remain in doubt. New York City has used GAAP budgeting for over a decade with no serious operational problems. Since GAAP already exists and has an established review process, it is the ideal candidate as a standard for budgeting and accounting. It, or its successors, should become the norm for budgeting nationwide, and certainly for municipalities with credibility problems.

Catalyzing Effective Decision-making

In many cases, problems that could be manageable with quick action become unmanageable when too much time passes without corrective action. One cause for delay is lack of consensus regarding the sources, or at times the existence, of serious problems. Reporting requirements like those discussed above can be effective in prompting public discussion of fiscal problems. Monitors can also play an effective role through their commentary. Their evaluation of the government's diagnosis of its problems provides a second opinion that can prompt consensus if the case is persuasive. On the other hand, anticipation of a critical monitor's evaluation creates a strong impetus for accurate government to undertake a recalcitrant and persuasive self-examination.

A second cause for delay in correcting fiscal problems is the excessive use of superficial actions that may balance current-year budgets without addressing the underlying cause of recurrent imbalance. Examples of such actions are extraordinary asset sales, aggressive debt refundings, temporary deferral of expenses or acceleration of receipts, shifts to long-term financing from pay-as-you-go financing, and changes in pension funding rules, among others. Fiscal monitors are extremely effective in providing the analytical sophistication needed to assess the adequacy and effectiveness of such remedies. Once again, anticipation of criticism by fiscal monitors may in itself prompt governments to moderate their reliance on temporary solutions, particularly those that may aggravate the underlying fiscal problems.

The fundamental approach to budget balance taken by governments may also be affected by the reporting requirements imposed by fiscal monitors. Governments have become adept at cash budgeting techniques that use deferral of expenses or acceleration of receipts to create the illusion of budget balance. The introduction of GAAP reporting will help to reveal the illusion, but one action to discourage the practice is the requirement that the budget be balanced in accordance with GAAP both when the budget is proposed and when the budget year ends. In essence, pure cash manipulations will lose their utility because they do not contribute to closing GAAP deficits.

While GAAP is susceptible to its own set of manipulations, the set is smaller and more difficult to achieve, making GAAP balance in general more indicative of substantive, recurring budget balance than the more common requirement of cash balance. GAAP balance, therefore, is a very demanding requirement. It may be needlessly demanding for a well-functioning government without operational or credit problems. For a government with serious problems that it is reluctant to face, however, GAAP balance requirements compel a greater degree of substantive remediation.

The decision-making process can be further accelerated by requiring that balance be evaluated periodically throughout the year rather than just when the financial statements are audited at the end of the year. This requirement could also mandate a periodic evaluation of the financial results of previously announced actions to balance the budget. This last requirement is an effective way to create accountability, especially if the troubled government is prone to unrealistic hopes that fuzzy notions of "better management" will solve its fiscal problems.

This reporting requirement could also go one step further and require a quarterly action plan to close the re-estimated gap. This is essentially a process of quarterly budget balance. It has been used in New York City and it has been remarkably successful in focusing the government on identifying its fiscal problems and implementing solutions in a prompt and timely manner.

Prohibiting Practices That Can Impair Creditworthiness

If the municipality's problems arise from specific practices, the most effective response can be statutory prohibitions of those practices with simultaneous creation of a fiscal monitor to enforce compliance.

For example, if credit abuse has occurred, specific restrictions on volume, terms, and/or maturities of short-term and long-term debt should be written into statute and bond covenant. If capital financing has led to an unsupportable debt service burden, additional restrictions could be enacted which define what types of capital projects must be financed on a pay-as-you-go basis. This may be particularly useful if the jurisdiction has many types of non-recurring or unpredictable revenues, which are more suitable funding sources for capital projects than for recurring operations.

Sometimes problems have emerged because budgets have been based on arbitrary or unsubstantiated revenue or expenditure estimates. An effective deterrent is to establish personal accountability for the estimates supporting the budget. One possible form would be certification that the revenue estimates are based on reasonable and appropriate assumptions and that the expenditure estimates reasonably reflect the cost of programs. A fiscal monitor would receive the written certification from top government officials. If problems have been especially egregious, criminal penalties could be imposed for false or misleading certifications.

THE NEW YORK CITY MODEL AS A GUIDE TO OTHER JURISDICTIONS

The Financial Emergency Act (the Act) was enacted in 1975 by New York State to govern the fiscal monitoring of New York City. It establishes two fiscal monitors, the Financial Control Board and the Office of the State Deputy Comptroller for New York City. Review and reporting powers are assigned to both fiscal monitors but most powers to enforce the Act are assigned to the Financial Control Board. Some limited review powers are assigned to the Municipal Assistance Corporation, a public benefit corporation of the State of New York. In general, the powers under the Act expire in 2008.

The provisions of the Act are of two kinds, prohibitions of certain borrowing practices and detailed specification of the financial planning process. The Act specifies that oversight and enforcement will rely primarily on submission to the fiscal monitors of quarterly modifications of a rolling four-year financial plan. The minimum content and form of the modifications is specified by the monitors, but the city has, appropriately, taken this requirement and expanded it into a major public media event in which it tells the public in substantial detail the problems the city faces and how the city plans to respond. It is a high profile, highly public process. The fiscal monitors review the city's new plan and analyze its strengths and weaknesses in a series of public reports issued one month later.

The Financial Emergency Act specifies guidelines for what areas fall under the purview of the fiscal monitors. The monitors are specifically prohibited from commenting on the spending priorities of the city. The monitoring process is focused on affordability of spending programs, not on the appropriateness of the spending decisions. The monitors' role with respect to contracts, including labor contracts, is similarly limited to evaluating whether they are costed-out accurately and whether the resources identified to fund the contracts are adequate.

One of the most difficult issues in administering a semi-permanent monitoring effort is the tension created by its two very different roles, that of an observer and reporter of fiscal policy and that of an enforcer of the law. The New York State Financial Control Board functionally separates those roles. Its observer/reporter role is continual and is performed primarily by the staff of the Board under the direction of an executive director. In contrast, its role as enforcer is not continual, but rather can be initiated or retired by the seven-member board according to criteria laid out in state law. Its enforcement powers are restricted to approval or disapproval of an entire financial plan and of all debt issuance, and the city retains significant authority to determine what revisions will be made in order to meet the board's objections. The enforcement role, moreover, is performed primarily at the board level. In this latter role, members of the board rely on their own staffs as well as on the staff of the board for advice in carrying out their functions.

The advantage of such a two-tiered structure is that the monitoring process is not conditioned on crisis. In particular, the monitoring can function after a crisis has ebbed and perform the type of reporting function that is intended to resolve the municipality's problems. Should slippage occur, continual monitoring also serves as an effective early warning system that the enforcement role may need to return. Without such a two-tiered structure it is likely that, once the need for enforcement has ebbed leaving the monitoring function without a potential enforcement role, the self-corrective aspect of monitoring would likely be less effective because ignoring the warnings of the monitors would no longer embody the peril of enforcement.

The effectiveness of the monitoring process in New York is dependent upon the level of public disclosure and the level of sophistication of staff analysis by the monitors. Since the process began in 1975, complete and detailed disclosure has become such an accepted part of financial planning and budgeting that there need be minimal enforcement effort on the part of the monitors. In many ways, the media have used the disclosure mechanism to become an additional, and effective, fiscal monitor. The analytical content of the monitoring process is highly dependent on the interests and capabilities of the staff of the monitors. Because the Act imposes performance criteria for the first year of the financial plan but only disclosure criteria for the outyears, the analytical focus of the monitors has gravitated to the first year and to the achievement of current-year budget balance under generally accepted accounting principles.

In adapting New York's fiscal monitoring process to other municipalities, several factors should be considered. First, New York City has enormous media coverage. Monitoring focused on disclosure has succeeded in New York in part because media coverage created a strong incentive for the city to embrace the disclosure process. Without similar extensive media coverage, consideration should be given to focusing more on compliance than does the New York model. A municipality that is reluctant to disclose its financial plan in sufficient detail to be useful, or to provide adequate documentation to allow a monitor to verify the reasonableness of the plan's underlying assumptions, can seriously compromise the effectiveness of the monitoring process.

Second, the Financial Emergency Act was designed to deal with a financial crisis and the need to maintain the confidence of the credit markets. For this reason, much of the compliance language of the law deals with prohibitions on certain uses for short-term borrowing, escrow procedures for debt service, and requirements for external auditing of financial statements. The law was not designed to respond to budget problems. In fact, it is rather unsophisticated in situations where spending requirements overwhelm revenue availability, requiring simply that the city balance the budget promptly and put debt service and legal mandates before all else. After the initial 1978–1982 plan was completed, it was not anticipated that there would be a need for future multi-year budget workouts. Thus, the necessary flexibility for future workouts is not specified under the law so that its permissibility is subject to a wide range of legal opinions.

Third, the law was written before there was widespread experience in financial planning for localities. Therefore, it focused on defining what planning was and on specifying the disclosure mechanism for disseminating financial plans. The law did not consider the issue of what constitutes good or thorough planning.

This omission is particularly consequential for the outyears of a financial plan in which the critical factors are forecasting judgment and methodology. In the first year of the plan, the distinction between good judgment and forecast accuracy is not significant because accuracy is much more objective and public disclosure of financial data is often sufficient to reveal egregious errors and to prompt appropriate responses by the government. In contrast, the hallmark of a good outyear financial plan is quality of analysis and judgment rather than accuracy of forecasts. In particular, the purpose of a multi-year financial plan must ultimately be to evaluate the financial implications of program decisions, to identify conflicts in program priorities, and to identify the agencies and individuals accountable for carrying out the actions necessary to resolve those conflicts. The New York model does not currently address these areas.

If the 1990s turn out to be a decade of slow economic growth with strong social and infrastructure needs, a monitoring and planning process of some kind would be enormously helpful for municipalities seeking to avoid continual fiscal problems. First, a fiscal monitor can enhance the process by adding credibility to statements of fiscal condition. Second, with sufficient enforcement powers, a fiscal monitor can establish accountability within the municipality for adhering to a workout plan. Third, a fiscal monitor can increase public confidence by providing an objective and comprehensive source of financial and operational information and by establishing sufficient controls for payment of debt service to sustain the confidence of the credit markets. The New York model has successfully provided all these benefits.

FUTURE DIRECTIONS IN GOVERNMENT OVERSIGHT

After the immediate pressures of the current recession have ended, municipalities will be ready to stabilize their services and maintain order in their finances. In the 1980s, the role of the federal government was sharply redefined and reduced. At the same time, a vast array of social problems and a renewed public awareness of the need for adequate public infrastructure sharply expanded the responsibilities of municipalities. Municipalities were able to cope with both changes and carry out an expanded role then because of the unprecedented length of the economic recovery which, with few exceptions, extended to most parts of the country and produced the tax revenues needed to fund these multiple roles. The current recession, however, has scaled back those revenues, revealing the conflict between traditional notions of local taxing authority and the wide range of local spending obligations that are now commonplace.

The resolution of this conflict requires a careful reexamination of all the roles municipalities currently fulfill. Such an examination must look beyond blaming federal aid policies or the current recession. Rather, municipalities must evaluate what roles are critical for them to perform and what roles should be left to the private sector, the state government, or the federal government. They must then assess the ability of the local economy to support those roles on a long-term, stable basis.

Some fortunate municipalities will discover that their problems are truly cyclical; that is, the economic recession is the primary problem and it is temporary. However, the majority will conclude that resources are short and that better management and planning are essential to fulfillment of their primary roles.

Almost all governments will have to undertake two basic steps. First, most governments will need to seek ways to accommodate the rising demand for municipal services within the tight constraints imposed by the local tax base of the 1990s. This effort will entail bringing their budgets into structural balance. Second, they will need to adopt some form of rigorous multi-year financial planning, which is the most effective way to facilitate the establishment of the goals, policies, and procedures needed for governments to surmount these challenges effectively.

Structural Balance

Structural balance describes the situation in which the structure of the revenue budget and the structure of the expenditure budget are sufficiently complementary that each is similar in size and grows at roughly the same rate over time. Different revenue and expenditure structures will respond to economic expansions or recessions at different rates so that, at different points in an economic cycle, differently structured budgets may have larger or smaller deficits and surpluses than others. If a municipality's finances are structurally balanced, however, over time the surpluses will offset the deficits. Without structural balance, deficits will be persistent and will overwhelm any surpluses created in years of exceptional economic strength.

Expenditures can be restructured in several ways. The locality can change the types of services it provides, such as scaling back on capital spending or shifting some expenses to the state or federal government. It can also change the cost of existing services such as by raising productivity, including containing growth in the cost of personnel benefits; reducing manpower requirements for services, including consolidation of functions; or changing procedures to allow more management flexibility to tailor service delivery to changing service demands. Of course, a locality can also change the amount of existing services (e.g., reduction of hours of service, frequency of service, or scope of service).

Revenues can also be restructured in several ways. The locality can change the types of revenues in a way that generates a tax base that grows more rapidly, for example, through the elimination of caps and other restrictions on growth of the real property tax, expansion of resident and non-resident personal income taxes, or elimination of consumption taxes that tend to exhibit little growth. It can also try to enhance stability through reduced reliance on highly volatile taxes such as corporate income taxes or real estate transfer, capital gains, or mortgage recording taxes. Lastly, and perhaps most commonly, a locality can change the size of taxes through rate or base increases.

Functionally, a structurally balanced budget requires more than that revenues be sufficient to fund expenditures. The budget must also have a sound structure that is functionally viable over time. For revenues, viability means that the revenue structure assists, or at least does not harm, the economy that generates those revenues. For expenditures, viability means that all legally required services are provided and an acceptable level of fundamental local services can be sustained over time without recurrent need for substantial changes such as personnel layoffs, temporary cancellations of programs, or tax increases. In other words, the value and purpose of structural balance is to minimize large waves of hiring that are reversed with layoffs and to minimize large tax cuts that are reversed with subsequent tax increases. Because of the abstract nature of structural balance, the analytical resources and reports of fiscal monitors can be critical in sustaining public understanding and support of a sound restructuring effort.

It should be evident that a financial plan that is structurally unbalanced is more likely to require sizeable annual deficit reduction programs. To minimize the disruption of continual deficit reduction, good financial management should seek to enhance its ability to anticipate in what areas of the budget gaps may emerge and to take prompt action when gaps do emerge. Two critical ways to do this are to establish a thorough analysis of the potential risks to revenue and expenditure estimates and to undertake extensive contingency planning of how to respond should those risks materialize. Risk analysis and contingency planning are perhaps the most significant contributions a fiscal monitoring process can make to local financial management.

Risk Analysis

Since any budget or financial plan is a set of estimates, it is a certainty that some revenue estimates and expenditure estimates will be wrong. Risk analysis attempts to identify what may go wrong, when one should know, and what one will then do. Risks in revenue estimation are familiar to many and therefore do not need further discussion. Risks in expenditure estimation are less familiar. Chronic risks in budgets include the estimates for growth in demand for government services. Oftentimes, important risks exist in estimating future growth in the social services caseload and in the possibility that personnel cutbacks will result in backfilling through unbudgeted overtime. Major unanticipated expenses can also arise from litigation. Risk analysis in this area seeks to anticipate settlements or judgments, when they might occur and how much they might be.

Contingency Planning

When risks materialize in the midst of a fiscal year, the primary brakes that a government can apply are on hiring and purchasing. A contingency plan is a series of budget cutting actions crafted before the need for implementation exists. The advantage of preparing plans in advance is to provide time to design a plan that produces the necessary budget savings while preserving long-term policy goals and sustaining fundamental services as well as possible. Of course, establishment and adequate advance funding of a rainy day fund or tax stabilization reserve is a longer-term form of contingency planning that is an important supplement to shorter-term budget cutting plans.

In general, a reasonable contingency plan would provide for reductions comparable in magnitude to historical mid-year slippage in the budget. A contingency plan would develop a sizeable attrition program in advance that identified which departments and job titles were likely to yield attrition and what the dollar savings reasonably could be. It would also include an approval process for granting exemptions to a comprehensive hiring freeze since some exemptions must always exist in order to avoid breakdown in the provision of government services. In terms of purchasing, a contingency plan would work out in advance detailed plans to cancel spending authorization and would evaluate any problems that would arise from across-the-board reductions in spending, with exemptions to avoid these problems.

Thorough contingency planning would allow prompt action to maintain budget balance and, hopefully, would avoid disruption of basic, fundamental services. While it would not provide the degree of stability of basic services that a structurally balanced budget and plan would provide, contingency planning ideally would allow a more orderly and less erratic budget reduction effort than could be produced without advance planning.

Multi-Year Financial Planning

Fiscal monitors have an essential role in fostering a multi-year financial planning process and maintaining its integrity and usefulness in facilitating reliable and stable provision of government services. Sustained effort, or stability in basic services, means avoiding not only sharp spending reductions during economic downturns but also sharp expansions when the economy is growing rapidly and tax revenues are yielding budget surpluses. To achieve all this requires thorough financial planning, a meticulous approach to fiscal management, and the ability to restrain spending and set aside surpluses in good times for use in maintaining basic services in difficult times.

Unfortunately, despite these benefits, one of the most difficult tasks in governmental fiscal management is developing and adhering to the commitments of a multi-year plan. In an urban environment, the demand for services will always exceed the ability to provide these services so that there is a constant competition for resources. This competition makes it difficult for any particular service to maintain a high priority claim over resources year after year, particularly if the costs of the effort are immediate while the benefits may emerge several years later. In the current environment, for example, there is a critical need for numerous, concrete initiatives to raise worker productivity. In general, such initiatives can take up to a year to develop and can generate additional costs for several more years before producing significant cost-savings three or four years after initiation. These types of programs are very vulnerable in an environment of large budget cutbacks.

Multi-year plans are also difficult to uphold because they are effectuated by a budget appropriation process that commonly deals with one year at a time. A multi-year undertaking that is initiated in one adopted budget could be cancelled in any successive adopted budget. Thus, legally, the financial commitment has at most a one-year horizon. In such a setting, continuation of existing programs or initiation of new programs that will be completed or brought up to speed within one budget year has a clear advantage because results will be available by the next budget adoption debate. The inherent difficulty of sustaining financial commitments over a multi-year framework is, of course, compounded when elections change the legislature or administration.

Despite these difficulties, financial planning offers the potential for an early warning system of eventual conflicts between program decisions and funding. In periods of tight budgets, new programs are often stretched out over several years or are initiated late in the fiscal year to minimize current-year costs. Obviously, the total costs of a new program then will not emerge until several years later. The affordability of a new program can be evaluated, therefore, only by placing it in the context of future budgets. Only through a comprehensive planning process can a latent financial conflict be identified and resolved before it becomes a current year budget crisis.

Tying Management Planning to Financial Goals

The fiscal pressures of the 1990s are likely to place tremendous pressure on municipalities to maintain their responsiveness to new problems while not expanding their claim on resources. In order to achieve this daunting assignment, management planning must take on an urgent priority. It is possible that capital spending needs will lead to increased debt service that must be accommodated with lower spending elsewhere. To achieve this without deterioration in other basic services, municipalities will need extensive productivity efforts that seek to *maintain* service levels with *fewer* resources.

Productivity is difficult to achieve in general and virtually impossible to achieve if programs are assembled and designed to deal with only immediate budget problems. Certainly savings can be achieved from an effort that occupies only a few months of the year. Major restructuring of service delivery or elimination of excessive overhead costs, however, more often requires substantial lead times to design and implement workable management plans to achieve those objectives. If the work force is governed by civil service rules or collective bargaining agreements, productivity from more flexible task assignment or changes in work rules will require legislation or negotiation. A multi-year management plan is beneficial not only to make sure ample time is allowed for implementation but also to provide the context for identifying the future service benefits that warrant procedural changes today. Such information can be critical in dealing with a skeptical legislature, civil service commission, or labor union.

Thus, multi-year financial planning can be an empty promise if management plans are not closely linked to their financial plans. Where the financial plan is the government's commitment to the public, the management plan provides the promise of the bureaucracy to fulfill that commitment. For example, a commitment to achieve a five percent reduction in refuse collection costs is incomplete without a plan detailing how departmental management plans to achieve those savings, which personnel are responsible, and when interim goals will be achieved.

As with financial plans, fiscal monitors can be beneficial in overseeing management plans. The professional expertise of a fiscal monitor can be a fairly efficient mechanism for evaluating the viability of a management plan and the reliability of the financial results tied to that plan.

Monitors and Multi-Year Planning

Fiscal monitors can provide oversight and commentary on three areas that require effective discipline on the part of government if the planning process is to be realistic. First, they will provide commentary on the reliability of the municipality's estimates of revenues. Second, they will opine on the reliability of the estimates of the costs of spending programs. Third, since most plans that show a shortage of resources will also show a series of corrective actions to bring spending into line with revenues, fiscal monitors can provide effective oversight of progress on those corrective actions and, where progress is lagging, an analysis of the consequences of delay.

Multi-year planning brings government decision making into the realm of socio-economic forecasting. So much judgment is involved in the forecasting process that the "second opinion" afforded by monitors becomes critical to the credibility of the planning process. Fiscal monitors provide a disinterested pool of professional expertise that can provide the public with reasonable assurances that the government's plans are backed with careful analysis and responsible estimates of costs and benefits.

CHAPTER 32

Municipal Bond Insurance*

Michael E. Satz
Chairman and Chief Executive Officer
Capital Re Corporation

Joan Russell Perry, Ph.D.

Municipal bond insurance provides credit enhancement of investment grade debt obligations issued by or on behalf of the states and their political subdivisions. The nationally recognized rating agencies, importantly Standard & Poor's Corporation (S&P) and Moody's Investors Service, Inc. (Moody's), each assigns a rating to insured municipal bonds which reflects the claims-paying ability rating of the insurance company. The claims-paying ability of the majority of the municipal bond insurance companies is rated AAA and Aaa by S&P and Moody's, respectively, and therefore the municipal bonds insured by those companies are rated triple-A.

Municipal bond insurance indemnifies the insured against nonpayment by the issuer of principal and interest when due on the insured municipal bond. The insurance lowers the municipal issuer's cost of borrowing in the public debt market. The borrowing costs of the municipal issuer are lowered to the extent that the insurance premium is less than the difference between the yield on the triple-A insured bonds and the yield which otherwise would be required to sell the bonds without insurance on the basis of their uninsured credit rating. In the

---

* Reprinted with permission from the authors.

context of a credit enhanced sale into the public debt market, municipal bond insurance:

(1) Simplifies the explanation attendant to the complex security structure of an underlying municipal credit in order to facilitate its sale in the public market;

(2) Normalizes certain types of obligations which customarily trade at a discount to their apparent market value;

(3) Expands the potential market for infrequent issuers or relatively small bond issues; and

(4) Diversifies and thereby expands the potential market for frequent issuers or relatively large bond issues.

From the perspective of the insured bondholder, municipal bond insurance:

(1) Provides increased protection against transient and ultimate loss;

(2) Supports liquidity for the insured bond issue in the secondary market; and

(3) Reduces exposure to price volatility in the secondary market which may be caused by periodic changes in the underlying credit quality of the insured bond issue.

Municipal bond insurance is a financial guaranty in the form of a surety regulated under the insurance laws of the various states. The policyholder is the insured bondholder. In the event of nonpayment by the issuer, the municipal bond insurance company pays the principal and interest on the insured bonds in accordance with their original payment schedule (without regard to redemption, acceleration or other advancement of maturity). Moreover, the insurer will pay any deficiency in the debt service which is due if a prior payment by the issuer is determined to be a preferential transfer, voidable under Federal bankruptcy law, and a court orders the disgorgement of such payment. The municipal bond insurance policy does not insure against the nonpayment of principal or interest caused by the insolvency or negligence of the trustee or paying agent for the bonds. Upon payment by the insurer, the insurer becomes subrogated to the rights of the bondholder to the extent paid and, as a result, may be empowered to direct remedies and is entitled to any recovery which is thereafter realized. The municipal bond insurance policy is unconditional, irrevocable and is not subject to cancellation by the insurer.

There is an exception to the general disclaimer of the insurer's liability for payments due upon redemption, acceleration or other advancement of maturity. The insurer is liable for any redemption which is otherwise mandatory under the express terms of the insured bonds, such as payments which become due upon the application of mandatory sinking fund installments. The operative premise is that the insurer should be required to make any such payments which are within the reasonable expectation of the bondholder as a contractual obligation of the issuer, giving effect to the enhanced credit quality of the insured bonds.

The insurance protection under a municipal bond insurance policy, or any payment under such policy, does not affect the federal tax-exempt status of the interest on the insured bonds. A municipal bond insurance policy is exempt from the registration requirements of the Securities Act of 1933.

The municipal bond insurance business was founded in 1971 with the formation of the American Municipal Bond Assurance Corporation (the predecessor of AMBAC Indemnity Corporation, AMBAC). The Municipal Bond Insurance Association (the predecessor of Municipal Bond Investors Assurance Corporation, MBIA) entered the business in 1974. There are currently five companies active in the municipal bond insurance business, four of which dominate the insured market.

Applicable state regulation requires that municipal bond insurance can be conducted only in a monoline form (i.e., the insurer may only insure financial guaranty and specified related risks). Accordingly, each of the municipal bond insurers is organized as a monoline insurance company.

The municipal bond insurers are organized to reflect the importance of underwriting, or credit analysis, to their financial results. Unlike traditional property and casualty insurance, with respect to which underwriting generally is premised on actuarial analysis, the underwriting of municipal bond insurance is a function of the analysis of transactional credit risk. Exposure (insured principal and interest) to capital is typically maintained at a ratio in excess of 100-to-1, reflecting the fact that risk is underwritten on a transactional basis to a "no-loss" expectation.

The products which fall under the general ambit of municipal bond insurance include:

(1) new issue insurance—the insurance of all or a portion of a bond issue upon its original issuance;

(2) insurance of unit investment trusts—closed-end investment portfolios which include the bonds of various issuers;

(3) insurance of mutual funds—open end managed investment portfolios containing the bonds of various issuers;

(4) insurance of individual portfolios—the insurance of personal holdings which remain insured so long as they remain in the individual's insured portfolio;

(5) secondary market insurance—the insurance of outstanding bonds trading in the municipal bond marketplace; and

(6) debt service reserve fund insurance—the insurance of only the reserve fund component of a municipal bond issue.

Additional insurance products which have been developed by the municipal bond insurance industry include the insurance of municipal interest rate swaps, insured municipal equipment lease programs and the insurance of bank deposits of municipal funds.

The municipal bond insurance industry has matured, with real limits as to its future revenue growth and as to its potential for profitability. Although municipal bond insurance premium continues to increase in the aggregate, the boundaries of the industry's growth are being tested within the municipal bond market, with the penetration of insurance exceeding 30% of total new issue volume. Consequently, municipal bond insurers are expanding into non-municipal financial guaranties, applying the same concept of market intermediation through credit enhancement as that inherent in the insurance of municipal bonds. Furthermore, the U.S. domestic municipal bond insurance and reinsurance companies have been instrumental in fostering European market acceptance of financial guaranty insurance and proving its value. The market for financial guaranty insurance is developing currently in conjunction with the evolution of the global capital markets.

THE PARTICIPANTS

History and Structure

Municipal bond insurance is a conceptual derivative of financial guaranty insurance. In its first developmental stage, financial guaranty insurance was subsumed within traditional product lines, and as such can be dated to the 19th century. While generally requiring the occurrence of a specified event for a claim to be incurred, rather than being directly linked to a payment default, the insurance coverage performed as a financial guaranty; the event which would give rise to the claim necessarily reflected the credit quality of the obligor whose performance was subject to the coverage. The coverage commonly took the form of surety, but it was in substance a financial guaranty. The lack of specialized resources and particularized focus inherent in this approach was responsible for the early negative reputation of the financial guaranty insurance business.

Financial guaranty insurance was recognized as a distinct subset of surety with the formation in the United States of the first municipal bond insurance company. A regulatory extension of mortgage guaranty insurance, municipal bond insurance constituted the first form of financial guaranty insurance to be treated as a fully separate product line. It was in the context of municipal bond insurance that financial guaranty insurance acquired the analytical principal which directs the product toward the provision of a financial value which is discrete from the value implicit in the redistribution of risk characteristic of the majority of traditional insurance products.

Throughout the 1970s and into the early 1980s two companies were involved in underwriting municipal bond insurance. When AMBAC, the industry founder, issued its first policy in September, 1971, it was a monoline insurance company and a wholly owned subsidiary of MGIC Investment Corporation, an insurance holding company primarily engaged in the mortgage guaranty insurance business. MBIA, originally an association comprised of multiline property and casualty insurance companies, was organized in 1974. In the period from 1983 to 1986, Financial Guaranty Insurance Company (FGIC), Bond Investors Guaranty Insurance Company (BIG) and Capital Guaranty Insurance Company (CGIC) entered the business. In 1989, BIG was acquired by MBIA, its insured portfolio 100% reinsured by that company. In 1990, Financial Security Assurance, Inc. (FSA), a financial guaranty insurance company organized to insure non-municipal debt obligations, commenced activity in the municipal bond insurance business.

Other financial services companies have made cameo appearances as financial guarantors in the municipal bond market, including finance companies, property and casualty companies, and domestic and foreign banks. Furthermore, companies have selectively participated by specializing in the insurance of particular bond types. A number of these former participants are no longer active because of rating downgrades or the inability to comply with the regulatory requirement that the municipal bond insurance business be conducted in a monoline form. Table 32.1 sets forth the principal municipal bond insurers and their respective ownership.

During the past several years, while the demand for municipal bond insurance has been expanding (see Figure 32.1), a number of changes have taken place in the ownership structure of the companies dedicated to providing financial guaranty insurance.

As shown in Table 32.1, the ownership of municipal bond insurance companies is generally dominated by single large institutional investors and/or characterized by public ownership. Insurers have

TABLE 32.1
Ownership of Municipal Bond Insurers

	Percentage
AMBAC Indemnity Corporation (AMBAC)	
Public	50.3%
Citibank, N.A.	49.7
Capital Guaranty Insurance Company (CGIC)	
Fleet/Norstar Investors	40.0
Constellation Investments, Inc.	27.5
United States Fidelity and Guaranty Company	17.5
Safeco Corporation	10.0
SIBAG Finance Corporation	5.0
Financial Guaranty Insurance Compnay (FGIC)	
General Electric Capital Corporation	100.0
Financial Security Assurance (FSA)	
U.S. West Financial Services Inc.	90.0
Tokio Marine & Fire Insurance Company	9.9
Municipal Bond Investors Assurance Corporation (MBIA)	
Public	32.9
The Aetna Casualty and Surety Company	27.2
The Fund American Companies, Inc.	23.6
CIGNA Corporation	11.6
Credit Local de France, CAELCL S.A.	4.7

been typically owned by small groups of private corporate investors, including investment banks, property and casualty insurance companies, and utilities, as well as other non-financial companies. An increasing concentration of ownership accompanied by access to the public equity market appears symptomatic of the successful maturation of a municipal bond insurance company.

Ratings

S&P and Moody's rate the claims-paying ability of municipal bond insurance companies. Prior to 1984, only S&P rated such companies. While from 1971 to 1979 the claims-paying ability of AMBAC was rated AA by S&P, municipal bond insurance has become exclusively a triple-A product. As a touchstone for the triple-A rating, S&P and Moody's model the ability of a municipal bond insurance company to withstand both the financial stress of a systematic, economic decline associated with a depression and the financial stress of discrete losses unrelated to such a decline. The rating agencies consider many factors, including the insurer's capitalization, future access to capital (ownership),

FIGURE 32.1
Volume of New Long-Term Municipal Bond and Insured New Municipal Bond

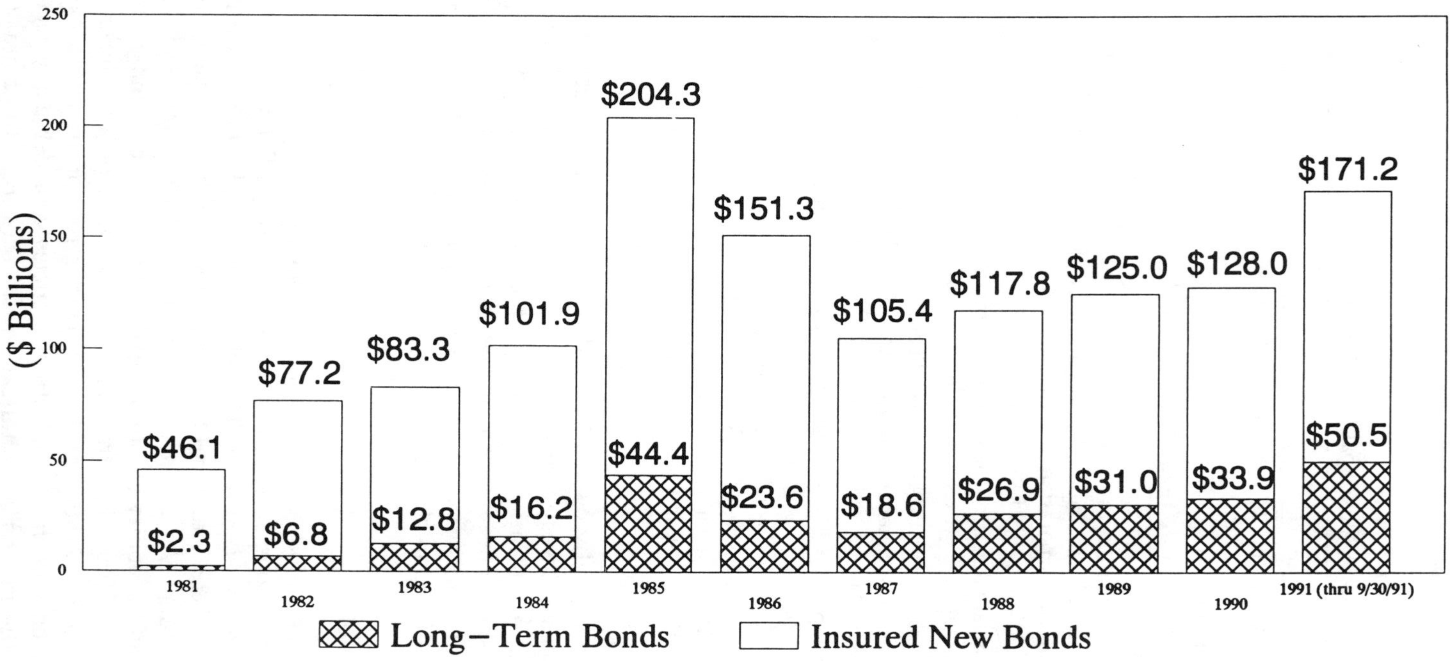

projected cash flow, the quality and diversification of the insured portfolio, and investment portfolio quality. Further, underwriting process
and criteria, management and certain administrative factors are taken
into account in analyzing claims-paying ability. The claims-paying ability of FGIC, AMBAC, MBIA and FSA is rated triple-A by S&P and
Moody's. CGIC is rated AAA by S&P, but is not rated by Moody's. In
addition, Duff & Phelps, Inc. and Fitch Investors Service, Inc. have assigned triple-A ratings to the claims-paying ability of certain municipal
bond insurers, but to date such ratings have been of lesser importance
in determining the trading value ascribed by the capital markets to the
municipal bond insurance offered by each insurer.

There are significant differences in the approach of the rating
agencies in assessing the claims-paying ability of municipal bond insurers. Larger bond issues or recurrent bond issues with large cumulative
exposure represent an important segment of the municipal bond market
and can be highly profitable to the insurers because of economies of
scale. However, from the rating agency perspective, the insurer's exposure to any such single risk is a potential threat to the insurer's financial integrity, and is therefore limited by the rating agencies. S&P's
limitation is stated as a percentage relationship of the insurer's capital
and surplus to the par amount of the retained exposure of the insurer
(net of reinsurance) to any single risk. The limiting percentage is dependent on the bond type, with a general disregard of credit quality as it
may vary within the investment grade assignation. The limiting percentage reflects the potential maximum loss expectation for each bond
type as determined by the rating agency, and the percentage relationship to capital and surplus reflects assumptions as to ability of the municipal bond insurer to earn back any such loss over a two year period.
Further, in applying a depression scenario to an insured portfolio as a
measure of capital adequacy, S&P has published capital charges by bond
type, as a percentage of annual debt service insured, to parallel differing risks of default, both as a matter of probability and severity (see
Table 32.2).

In connection with the rating agency's overall assessment of the
capital adequacy of the insurer, Moody's generally limits an insurer
with respect to its net retained exposure to any single risk by projecting a "shock loss" involving the default of the insurer's larger single
risks in a depression scenario. The extent of the "shock loss" is adjusted to reflect bond type, but not credit quality. While Moody's dif-
ferentiates the risks of default among bond types for the purpose of
assessing an insurer's capital adequacy (unlike S&P, giving effect to
credit quality), the rating agency has not published such information,
implicity deemphasizing bond type as a surrogate for risk and creating resistance to the trend toward a differentiated pricing structure.

TABLE 32.2
Capital Adequacy Guidelines

Category*	Capital Charge (%)
Bond Market Sector	
Municipal:	
General Obligation	
States	3%
Cities and counties	10
Schools—elementary & secondary	4
Special districts:	
Post secondary education	10
Nonutility	12
Utility	17
Health Care	
Hospitals	30
Hospital systems (three or more hospitals with geographic dispersion)	20
Hospital equipment loan program	25
Health maintenance organization (HMO)	30
Clinic Practices closely affiliated with hospital	30
Nursing Home	30
Nursing Home system (three or more homes with geographic dispersion)	20
Life care center	35
Life care center system (three or more centers with geographic dispersion)	25
Utilities	
Public power agency (substantial nuclear or other proj. risk)	40
Public power agency (little or no nuclear or other proj. risk)	15
Water, sewer, electric & gas systems (revenue secured)	12
Solid waste disposal to energy or landfill (revenue secured)	35
Solid waste system (with landfill and/or waste to energy facility)	25
Solid waste transfer stations, trucks (no landfill/waste to energy facility)	15
Housing	
State agency single family	10
Local agency single family	20
Insured multifamily	6
Noninsured multifamily	20
Collateralized letters of credit	8
Special Revenue	
Colleges and universities	
Public:	
General obligation—unlimited:	
Tuition and fee pledge	9

TABLE 32.2 (*continued*)

Category*	Capital Charge (%)
General obligation—limited:	
Tuition and fee pledge	10
Auxiliary enterprises	15
Private:	
General obligation	25
Auxiliary enterprises	35
Municipal pooled common bond fund	25
Guaranteed student loans	10
Airports	12
Airports—limited tax backed	10
Ports	18
Ports—limited tax backed	14
Parking revenue	25
Toll roads—five-year operating history	20
Toll roads—less than five-year operating history	30
Bridges—five-year operating history	25
Bridges—less than five-year operating history	35
Tax-supported debt:	
Sales tax—local	15
Sales tax—statewide	8
Gas tax—local	18
Gas tax—statewide	12
Gas & motor vehicle registration—local	15
Gas & motor vehicle registration—statewide	10
Tax allocation	25
Guaranteed entitlements	10
Special assessments	30
Hotel/motel tax	25

Nevertheless, a result of this general agreement that risk can be differentiated by bond type, and as to relative risk among broad categories of bond types, is that the utilization of capital by the insurer can be determined on a transactional basis and therefore price can accurately reflect the cost of capital.

The rating process is coordinated at S&P by personnel experienced in the analysis of corporate credits and at Moody's in the analysis of municipal credits. One may speculate as to the impact of this organizational disparity on the analysis applied by each of the rating agencies to evaluate claims-paying ability. To date, Moody's has emphasized "hard" capital and has required that an insurer maintain a larger capital base, relative to its exposure, than has S&P. S&P has permitted the insurer greater flexibility to employ alternate forms of capital (e.g., investor commitments, credit facilities, etc.), with somewhat greater emphasis on the insurer's available cash flow.

The rating agencies' standards are different from those applied by the insurance regulators. The rating agency evaluates the municipal bond insurance company's ability to pay claims continuously during a period of general economic catastrophe. By rating the claims-paying ability of an insurer triple-A, the rating agency is expressing its expectation that the insurer will remain solvent under any and all foreseeable circumstances, including that of the most severe economic distress. Insurance regulators traditionally have applied standards intended to provide reasonable protection to the policyholder. The regulators are not concerned with assuring the continued financial viability of an insurance company throughout a period of economic depression, but rather the ability of the insurer to remain solvent and pay its claims during normal economic periods. Therefore, while few insurance companies are rated triple-A with regard to their ability to pay claims, companies not so rated may be considered solvent and responsible participants in the insurance market, warranting the confidence of both regulators and policyholders.

The Depression Scenario

Since the beginning of the municipal bond insurance business concern has been expressed over the insurers' operating leverage. The fundamental economics of municipal bond insurance companies have been developed with the goal of both leveraging and structuring the insured portfolio to survive an economic depression. The landmark research of Dr. George Hempel on municipal defaults during the Great Depression of the 1930s[1] is a touchstone for the insurers, the regulators and the rating agencies for the development of depression scenarios in order to assess capital adequacy. According to Dr. Hempel's findings, at the depths of the Great Depression of the 1930s, 16% of the cumulative annual debt service on outstanding municipal bonds was in default. By the end of the seventh year of the Depression the default rate had decreased to 6%.

Significant changes in the municipal bond market have occurred since the 1930s. Municipal bond insurance companies now insure a range of municipal bonds that are not fully analogous with that studied by Dr. Hempel. A considerable portion of the defaults during the Great Depression were attributable to obligations which would not be of investment grade quality and, consequently, unqualified for insurance by

---

[1] Doctoral Thesis: "The Postwar Quality of Municipal Bonds," The University of Michigan, 1984.

municipal bond insurers. Furthermore, a substantial part of such defaults were attributable to the issuer's inability to repay because the funds were on deposit in banks which failed. This risk has been significantly reduced through regulatory reform.

The above factors generally imply a result as to the expected default rate more favorable than that in the Great Depression. However, greater risk may now be found in the diversification of the municipal bond market through the introduction of complex municipal financing structures and techniques, the proliferation of revenue bond financing, and the advent of project financings and financings secured by corporate credits. In evaluating risk, this new municipal market should be contrasted with the general obligation bonds which comprised the large majority of the municipal bond market in the 1930s. This has led the insurers and the rating agencies to increasingly differentiate risk by bond type, while creating uncertainty as to the projected impact of the "next" depression on the municipal bond market.

In this regard, it should be noted that in a more recent study of municipal default, Robert Godfrey[2], Director of Research and Business Development for MBIA, while concluding that the rating agency perception of the risks of default were conservative and, therefore, their assessment of capital adequacy may overstate the capital requirements for insurers, also questioned the legitimacy of bond type, geography and related factors as significant elements of default risk and proposed balance sheet strength, degree of leverage and the behavior of the revenue stream relied upon to pay debt service as the primary determinants of default.

Management and Organization

Municipal bond insurance companies typically operate at statutory risk to capital leverage ratios of between 100-to-1 and 200-to-1. For this purpose, *risk* is defined as aggregate insured unpaid principal and interest (net of reinsurance and qualified collateral or net aggregate exposure). Statutory capital is equal to policyholders' surplus plus contingency reserve. Thus, net aggregate exposure may be one to two hundred times statutory capital. In any business leveraged in this manner, underwriting, or the analysis of credit quality, must be management's primary focus. The insurers' internal organization reflects the importance of the underwriting function.

None of the companies employs more than approximately 300 individuals. Although a significant proportion of the professional staff are

---

[2] "Risk Based Capital Charges for Municipal Bonds," JAI Press Ltd., 1990.

credit analysts, the combined labor pool is small, and not homogeneous. The prior employment experience of the underwriters in the insurance companies range from government to academia, commercial banking, the rating agencies, investment banking, institutional portfolio management and the legal profession. The underwriting groups are usually formed around expertise in certain areas of municipal finance including health care finance, taxed-backed and general obligation bonds, utilities, education and housing. Most of the municipal bond insurers have an extensive in-house legal staff to assist in the qualification of bonds for insurance.

The marketing, underwriting and pricing functions are not allocated uniformly. Underwriters may perform marketing/sales functions, or marketing may be separated from underwriting. Nevertheless, the negotiation and structuring of an insured municipal bond transaction is often a complex task. The underwriters, marketing personnel and attorneys in each company generally work as professional teams, and the distinct aspects of their separate functions often become blurred.

Pricing has evolved as a product of a sophisticated analytical process. Insurers employ pricing models which guide the pricing decision. The models describe transactional profitability. In addition to the "objective" decision resulting from the model, pricing is also a function of extant competitive forces and market conditions. Responsibility for pricing may be a marketing function, within the control of underwriting, or directed by an interdisciplinary committee.

The marketing function is primarily a service and information function. The municipal bond insurance business is limited by external factors, including the total volume of the municipal market, interest rate levels, the relative complexity of financings offered in the market, the ability of the rating agencies to service demand on a timely basis, and legislation which may affect the tax-exempt status of the interest on municipal bonds. These externalities control demand and define the potential maximum penetration for the insurance product.

Market Share

Although market share has proven to be a dynamic factor, with the maturation of the industry a rough equilibrium in market share has been reached. In the late 1970s when AMBAC was rated AA by S&P and MBIA was rated AAA, MBIA dominated the insured new issue market. In 1979, the year in which AMBAC obtained its AAA rating, MBIA insured two-thirds of an insured new issue market aggregating $700 million in principal amount.

From 1983 to 1987, demand for the insurance product increased dramatically in concert with increasing emissions in the municipal bond market, with $43.4 billion of new issues insured in 1985. It was during this period that additional companies entered the business offering a full range of municipal bond insurance products (see Figure 32.2). Market share was redistributed, and at year-end 1986, AMBAC, FGIC and MBIA had shares of 27%, 28% and 37%, respectively, of the insured new issue market. An aggressive marketing effort by BIG significantly improved its penetration of the insured new issue market in 1987, at which time all of the major municipal bond insurer's had AAA/Aaa claims-paying ability ratings.

Industry penetration into the new issue market continued to increase. By 1990, over 26.5% of the $128 billion new issue market was insured. Concomitantly, competition intensified and pricing declined dramatically from 1987 to 1990, leveling thereafter. AMBAC, MBIA, and

FIGURE 32.2
Municipal Bond Insurance Timeline

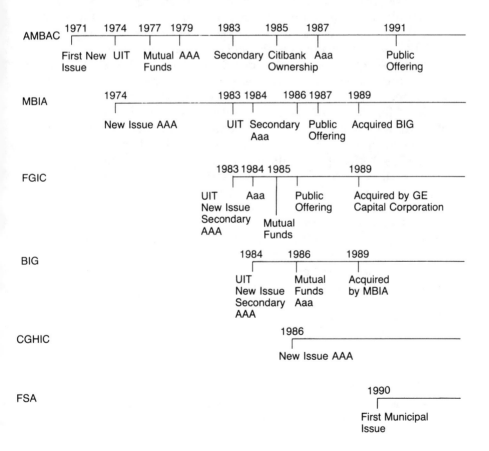

FGIC alternated as the leader in market share, with MBIA and AMBAC generally emerging as the more dominant market participants. FSA effectively entered where BIG departed. Currently, although competitive pressures still remain, none of the insurers is actively differentiating itself by consistently offering materially lower pricing. Underwriting standards have been maintained despite the competition for market share, reflecting in part management discipline and in part the concentrated oversight of the rating agencies. It can be expected that over time market share will be a function of an insurer's pricing policies, and its internal strategies involving the necessary balance between generation of net income and return on equity.

REGULATION

Municipal bond insurance is a type of surety which is regulated under the insurance laws of the various states. In 1971, the New York Insurance Department became the first state regulatory body to specifically regulate municipal bond insurance as a distinct insurance line. California, Florida, Illinois, Wisconsin and New Jersey subsequently enacted separate municipal bond insurance regulation as part of their respective insurance codes. These regulatory schemes recognize municipal bond insurance as a unique surety insurance product which requires special regulatory standards. In other states, municipal bond insurance falls generally within the broad category of surety or credit insurance, but the corresponding regulations may be incomplete or inappropriate in the context of municipal bond insurance. In 1989, New York replaced its municipal bond insurance regulations with a comprehensive financial guaranty insurance statute. California followed with a similar statutory scheme, which was enacted in 1990. The New York and California laws and the NAIC Model Act (discussed below) have become the industry standards and all require that financial guaranty insurance be transacted in a monoline form.

While specific provisions vary, the laws governing municipal bond insurance, whether in the form of administrative regulation or legislation, typically include provisions for

(1) limiting the insurer's exposure with respect to obligations issued by a single entity and secured by a single revenue source, or single risk;

(2) restricting the insurer's aggregate exposure to some multiple of statutory capital;

(3) establishing and maintaining special reserves (including the contingency reserve and case basis loss reserves);

(4) allowing the insurer to reduce exposure to the extent of qualified reinsurance; and

(5) filing and reporting requirements.

Aggregate risk and exposure to any single risk are independently regulated. Single risk exposure is limited to a fixed percentage of statutory capital (equal to policyholders' surplus plus contingency reserve). For municipal bonds, the New York[3] and the California laws limit the average annual debt service to all exposures secured by the same revenue source to 10% of the policyholders' surplus plus contingency reserve. Furthermore, the insured unpaid principal amount of any single risk is limited to 75% of policyholders' surplus plus contingency reserve. The aggregate exposure of an insurer is also limited in relation to its statutory capital. The ratio of aggregate unpaid insured principal and interest (net of qualified reinsurance and collateral) to statutory capital may not exceed stated levels. Historically, a 300-to-1 risk to capital ratio has been applied to municipal bonds under state insurance law.

The contingency reserve is a loss reserve established to protect policyholders against the extraordinary losses which may occur during a period of economic catastrophe such as a depression. The contingency reserve is unique to the financial guaranty insurance and mortgage guaranty insurance. These monoline insurance classes are the categories of insurance products which are underwritten to a standard of "no loss" on a transactional basis, but for which it is expected that losses will be incurred on a portfolio basis coincident with economic cycles. Although the statutory methodologies differ, the amount required to be deposited in the contingency reserve is generally a function of both premiums earned (or written) and actual exposure underwritten (or outstanding). Deposits into the reserve are made before any interest or dividends payments on the insurer's corporate obligations. As of December 31, 1990, the amounts on deposit in the contingency reserves for the major municipal bond insurers were as follows: MBIA $261.1 million; FGIC $114.5 million; AMBAC $228.2 million, FSA $37.2 million and CGIC $9.6 million.

Case basis loss reserves are established at the time a monetary default on the insured obligation appears imminent. The general funding principle for case basis loss reserves presupposes that municipal bond defaults are transient and the insurer's liability cannot be accelerated. For transient type defaults, the reserve is established in an amount equal to the scheduled debt service for the next succeeding three years. If the default is likely to be permanent in nature, the reserve is generally

---

[3] Domiciliary state for MBIA, FSA, and FGIC.

funded in an amount equal to principal amount of the ultimate net loss. Deductions from case basis loss reserves are allowed for the time value of money. Therefore, the nominal reserve amount is discounted to calculate the actual present value of the amount to be reserved.

Under the New York and California laws, reinsurance may qualify to reduce the reported statutory exposure of the municipal bond insurance-company. Usually, for the reinsurance to qualify the reinsurer must itself be:

(1) a financial guaranty insurance company licensed as such in the applicable jurisdiction, or

(2) multiline reinsurance company otherwise licensed which

    (a) maintains a minimum policyholders' surplus in a prescribed amount,

    (b) establishes and maintains the required special reserves for a financial guaranty insurance company, and

    (c) complies with special aggregate limits on exposure which are half of those applicable to a financial guaranty insurance company, or

(3) an unlicensed reinsurer which satisfies certain express standards and appropriately collateralizes its reinsurance obligations.

Under general property and casualty insurance laws, reinsurance ceded qualifies for financial statement credit if the reinsurer is an authorized reinsurer in the applicable jurisdiction or the reserves attendant to the reinsurer's liability are appropriately collateralized.

In those states which specifically regulate financial guaranty insurance, policyholders of financial guaranty insurance companies are denied access to the insurance security funds, or state guaranty funds, established to provide a monetary resource against the insolvency of insurance companies within such jurisdictions. Generally, the policy forms and premium rates (prices) are required to be filed with and approved by the insurance departments of the various states in which the insurer will use such forms and rates.

In 1986, the National Association of Insurance Commissioners (NAIC) adopted a model law for the regulation of financial guaranty insurance, of which municipal bond insurance is a subset (the NAIC Model Act). The NAIC Model Act, which is not effective without further legislative or regulatory action in the individual states, was the first comprehensive regulatory scheme which contained a requirement that municipal bond insurance must be underwritten only by a monoline form. Therefore, under the New York and California laws and the NAIC Model Act, the monoline requirement means that municipal bond insurers may only be licensed to write a single product line, financial guaranty and related insurance, and are prohibited from writing any other insurance products.

The complement to a monoline insurance company is a multiline insurance company, which has been the customary corporate format for insurance underwriting in the United States. The stated regulatory purpose of the monoline requirement is the necessity of isolating financial guaranty insurance from other insurance products through the forced segregation of capital. As a result, the multiline insurer's financial integrity would be protected from losses incurred in connection with the financial guaranty business and the "traditional" policyholders would not be at risk to the financial guaranty insurance business. However, the nature and extent of financial guaranty risk are subject to significant debate. On an historical basis, municipal bond insurance has not been shown to involve any greater risk than other insurance products. Indeed, municipal bonds have been and are a permissible investment for multiline insurance companies. Recent events may even indicate that the reverse is more likely to be true. The traditional property and casualty insurance lines are more susceptible to catastrophic loss than is the municipal bond insurance line. Nevertheless, as reflected in the NAIC Model Act, the direction of regulation is to mandate a monoline structure for any insurer writing municipal bond insurance.

As previously indicated, all current participants in the municipal bond insurance industry are monoline insurance companies. Therefore, assuming that the monoline requirement does not extend to reinsurers (as is the case in the New York and California laws and NAIC Model Act), the municipal bond insurance industry will remain unaffected by the monoline issue. However, it should be recognized that as an adjunct to the greater comfort which the monoline requirement may provide to the regulators, there has been established a significant and arguably unnecessary barrier to entry into the municipal bond insurance business.

ASSOCIATION OF FINANCIAL GUARANTY INSURORS

The Association of Financial Guaranty Insurors was established in April 1986 as a trade association for the financial guaranty insurance industry. The stated purpose of the Association, as set forth in its corporate charter, is

(1) to provide a forum for the discussion of problems of common interest to its members and communicate those concerns to legislators and insurance commissioners, purchasers of financial guaranty insurance and the financial community;

(2) to serve as a medium for the collection and dissemination of information;

(3) to promote the efficient conduct of the business of financial guaranty insurance;

(4) to develop and promote financial guaranty insurance as an integral and respected element of the credit market; and

(5) to foster a reasonable and orderly regulatory environment responsive to issuers and holders of debt obligations and to the providers of financial guarantees.

The Association includes within its membership all of the major participants in the U.S. domestic financial guaranty insurance industry: AMBAC, CGIC, Capital Markets Assurance Corporation, Capital Reinsurance Company, Connie Lee Insurance Company, Enhance Reinsurance Company, FGIC, FSA, and MBIA.

While the promulgation of the NAIC Model Act served as an impetus for its formation, the Association has been active not only in the area of pending state regulation, but with respect to Federal tax legislation and other Federal regulatory matters. Other Association efforts have been directed at the Government Finance Officers Association disclosure guidelines for the public offering of municipal bonds, the development of statutory accounting standards, the reporting of statistical information concerning the industry, and the education of the credit market as to the financial viability of the industry and the value of its insurance product.

STATUTORY AND GAAP
ACCOUNTING CONTRASTED

A municipal bond insurance company is required to file with the insurance department in each state in which it is licensed annual financial statements prepared in accordance with statutory accounting rules prescribed or permitted in the company's state of domicile. Those municipal bond insurers which are publicly traded companies also provide quarterly and audited annual financial statements, to both their investors and the Securities Exchange Commission, which are prepared in accordance with generally accepted accounting principles (GAAP).

Statutory accounting is concerned with the protection of the policyholder (the insured bondholder), while GAAP accounting is directed toward the investor (the stockholder). The principal differences between statutory and GAAP accounting relate to the treatment of the contingency and loss reserves, and the recognition of acquisition expenses. Statutory accounting mandates the establishment of a contingency

FIGURE 32.3
Statutory Accounting

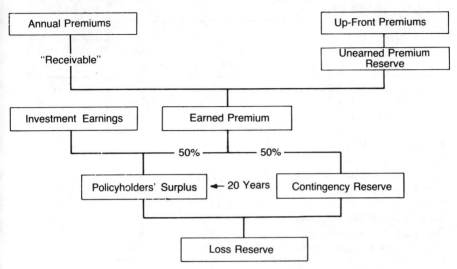

*Contributions to the contingency reserve may reflect a percentage of the insurer's exposure rather than 50% of earned premiums, whichever is greater.

reserve funded in accordance with the applicable regulation. GAAP does not recognize the statutory contingency reserve. However, some insurers have recently established (without an audit exception) "contingency" type GAAP credit reserves for prospective losses on a portfolio basis. GAAP permits acquisition expenses to be amortized over the life of the insured bond issue to which such expenses relate. Conversely, statutory accounting requires the recognition of all underwriting expenses in the year in which such expenses are incurred. As a result, GAAP accounting would normally generate greater pretax income *per annum* than statutory accounting (see Figure 32.3). The methodology for earning premium may also differ under GAAP and Statutory accounting principals.

The rules of statutory accounting are specified under applicable insurance regulation; GAAP accounting provides greater flexibility to the insurer to adopt accounting policies along a continuum of reasonableness, albeit subject to audit. As a result, significantly different levels of pretax GAAP income can be validly derived from the same statutory income statement. The following hypothetical income statement contrasts approaches to GAAP accounting which, in their recognition of earned premium, treatment of reserves and recognition of expenses (including the treatment of ceding commissions relating to reinsurance arrangements) act to either defer reported pretax GAAP income or optimize reported pretax GAAP income on a current basis:

TABLE 32.3

Triple-A Insurance Company Hypothetical Income Statement
(Dollars in Millions)

	Statutory	GAAP (Deferral of Income)	(Otimization of Income)
Direct Premium Written	$100.0	$100.0	$100.0
Quota Share Ceded	(25.0)	(25.0)	(25.0)
Facultative Ceded	(1.0)	(1.0)	(1.0)
Excess of Loss Ceded	(4.0)	(4.0)	(4.0)
Net Premium Written	$ 70.0	$ 70.0	$ 70.0
Increase (Decrease) in			
Unearned Premium Reserve	(35.0)	(35.0)	(21.0)
Net Premium Earned[a]	$ 35.0	$ 35.0	$ 49.0
Contingency Reserve	$ 17.5	—	—
Underwriting Exp. Incurred	35.0	35.0	$ 35.0
Reinsurance Commission	(6.5)	(6.5)	(6.5)
Deferred Acquisition Expenses[b]	—	(5.0)	(11.0)
Case Basis Losses	2.0	2.0	2.0
Credit Reserve[c]	—	10.5	.0
Total Underwriting Charges	$ 48.0	$ 36.0	$ 19.5
Gain (loss) from Underwriting	(13.0)	(1.0)	29.5
Net Investment Income	$ 30.0	$ 30.0	$ 30.0
Pretax Income	$ 17.0	$ 29.0	$ 59.5

[a]Statutory accounting and GAAP accounting may recognize earned premium on the same basis, commensurate with the actual reduction in the potential liability of the insurance company for the payment of principal and interest (i.e., as the insured debt service is paid by the issuer). Alternately, GAAP accounting may recognize earnings on a more accelerated basis, reflecting the reduction of risk as a corollary to the passage of time (rather than as a reflection of the actual payment of debt service) and incorporating a concept of weighted average life with respect to the exposure of the insurer.

[b]GAAP accounting which acts to defer pretax income may provide for the deferral of underwriting expenses net of reinsurance commissions. GAAP accounting which acts to optimize pretax income on a current basis may provide for the deferral of 50%.

[c]A GAAP credit reserve is a loss reserve, but it is not established in connection with a specific payment default (unlike a case basis loss reserve). A GAAP credit reserve is an actuarially based loss reserve intended to create an identity between expected losses in the insured portfolio and the premiums that earned over the life of the insured portfolio.

REINSURANCE

Reinsurance is a transaction whereby the reinsurer agrees to indemnify the primary insurance company against part or all of a loss which the latter may sustain under a policy which it has issued. Municipal bond insurance companies utilize reinsurance to

(1) increase insurance capacity;
(2) satisfy applicable regulatory and rating agency standards;
(3) augment financial strength; and
(4) manage risk exposure.

As described previously, state insurance laws and regulations as well as the rating agencies impose minimum capital requirements on municipal bond insurance companies, limiting the aggregate amount of insurance which may be written and the maximum size of any single risk which may be insured. Depending on the perceived quality of the reinsurers, the rating agencies have permitted a municipal bond insurance company to reduce its exposure to the extent of its reinsurance arrangements for the purpose of measuring capital adequacy. Moreover, if the reinsurers are qualified under applicable regulation, the exposure of a municipal bond insurance company can be reduced for statutory purposes through its reinsurance arrangements. Therefore, reinsurance allows the reinsured to increase its capacity to write new business by reducing the insurer's gross liability on an aggregate and single risk basis while continuing to comply with applicable limitations. Furthermore, every primary company is actively engaged in managing the risk of its insured portfolio based on internal underwriting criteria and portfolio management guidelines. Reinsurance is instrumental to achieving those portfolio risk management goals. Reinsurance is increasingly being employed to stabilize financial results and diversify the capital base of the primary municipal bond insurers.

There are two major kinds of reinsurance, treaty and facultative. Treaty reinsurance requires the reinsured to cede and the reinsurer to assume specific classes of risk underwritten by the ceding company. Facultative reinsurance is the reinsurance of part or all of a single policy subject to a separate negotiation for each cession. It offers the option of accepting or rejecting the individual risk submission generally as distinguished from the obligation to cede and accept as a treaty reinsurer. Insurers generally will seek facultative agreements when treaty exclusions preclude the cession or inclusion of a particular risk or when capacity of the treaty program is insufficient for a given risk (e.g., when policy limits are in excess of treaty limits).

The generic types of reinsurance are proportional and non-proportional. Proportional includes:

(1) quota share reinsurance whereby the assumed risk is a fixed percentage of the reinsured's risk;
(2) surplus share reinsurance whereby the percentage of risk assumed is a multiple of the reinsured's net retention up to a stated maximum; and
(3) variable quota share whereby the percentage of assumed risk increases with the size of the risk up to a stated maximum.

Non-proportional reinsurance includes risk assumption per risk and per occurrence in excess of a reinsured's retention, subject to a specified limit. Another type of non-proportional reinsurance is stop loss or aggregate excess of loss reinsurance.

Quota share treaty agreements provide for the reinsurance of a predetermined fixed percentage of all business written by the insurer and defined within the terms of the agreement. For example, in a 10% quota share reinsurance treaty, the reinsured assumes 10% of the debt service liabilities on each municipal bond issued insured during the treaty term and 10% of premium is transferred to the reinsurer. If a loss occurs, the reinsurer pays the reinsured its 10% share of the loss and establishes loss reserves for its proportionate share of exposure. The insured bondholder, as the policyholder, would make claim directly to the municipal bond insurance company. The obligation of the reinsurer for payment is only to the reinsured municipal bond insurer.

Surplus share reinsurance agreements are in essence variable quota share reinsurance agreements. Rather than establishing a predetermined fixed percentage, the municipal bond insurer may agree to prorate premiums and losses in excess of a specified level of exposure. To illustrate, the municipal bond insurer may agree to cede all exposure in excess of $60 million, to a maximum cession of $40 million. The actual percentage which is ceded in any one case will vary according to the size of the insured bond issue. Once the percentage has been established, premiums and losses are apportioned on the basis of such percentage.

Under proportional reinsurance agreements, a percentage of ceded premiums is paid by the reinsurer to the municipal bond insurance company as a ceding commission, to compensate the insurer for acquisition and servicing expenses.

Non-proportional reinsurance divides the risk between the reinsured and reinsurer in a different manner. For example, excess of loss reinsurance provides coverage of losses exceeding a specified level. The reinsured retains a first loss position which must be satisfied before the reinsurer must make payment. Excess of loss reinsurance is, in effect, an insurer's insurance policy against catastrophic losses, on either a single risk (per risk excess) or portfolio (aggregate excess) basis.

A municipal bond insurance company can use unqualified reinsurance exclusively for internal risk management. However, this is an expensive alternative for the insurer since regulatory and rating agency credit would not be permitted.

Worldwide reinsurance capacity for municipal bond insurance has historically been extremely limited. This scarcity gave impetus to the creation of specialized financial guaranty reinsurance companies such as Capital Reinsurance Company (Capital Re) and Enhance Reinsurance Company (Enhance). The claims-paying ability of Capital Re and Enhance is rated AAA by S&P. In 1990, 22% of the municipal bond insurance market was reinsured, reinsurers assuming $134.5 million in direct premium from the primary insurers. In 1990, Capital Re and Enhance accounted for 77.6% of ceded municipal bond reinsurance. Capital Re had the larger market share as measured by gross premiums written.

The number of reinsurance companies which comprise the qualified municipal bond reinsurance market is expected to remain small. As a result, risk syndication has become increasingly important. Through the development of innovative retrocessional programs, Capital Re has become the major syndicator of municipal bond insurance risk, developing additional capacity in the international market for this specialty insurance line.

THE INSURERS' EVALUATION OF CREDIT QUALITY

Credit Quality

A municipal bond insurer evaluates an issuer's ability to pay its debt obligations on an issue-by-issue basis. Although the rating agencies and the investors in the municipal market also analyze credit quality, different considerations are necessarily brought to bear by a municipal bond insurer. Unlike a rating agency which may withdraw or change a rating or an investor who may sell into the secondary market, a municipal bond insurance company cannot unilaterally cancel its policy and thereby readdress its risk. A municipal bond insurance company's liability is necessarily long-term and its credit decisions are made in light of this extended commitment. The average life of the insured portfolios of the municipal bond insurers approximates 15 to 17 years.

Credit quality is only one of several considerations for an investor. Other factors may include whether a municipal bond is over or undervalued in relation to its inherent credit quality (or nominal rating), the potential payment of sinking fund installments to cushion and increase value, consideration of supersinkers or other elements of financial structure, and probability of refundings or optional calls. These investment considerations are inapplicable to the municipal bond insurers' underwriting analysis. A municipal bond insurer's decision to insure is fixed on whether the bonds will be paid on a timely basis. Once made, the decision to insure is a commitment for the life of the bonds.

The insurers' underwriting criteria for evaluating credit quality differ by bond type and include economic, financial, managerial, sociopolitical, and structural factors. For, example, general obligation bonds (i.e., bonds secured by the issuer's full property taxing power) are not structured to include debt service reserve funds. Indeed, such reserves are often not permitted under applicable state statutes and are discouraged under Federal tax law. However, the insurers' underwriting criteria would not prevent qualification for insurance based on the absence of a debt service reserve fund. On the other hand, typical underwriting standards would require a student loan revenue bond issue or project-related revenue bond financing to have a debt service reserve fund as a precondition to insurance.

Underwriting criteria vary among the municipal bond insurers and are subject to periodic revision. In spite of such variations the essential requirement remains that the insurers maintain insured portfolios of at least investment grade quality as determined by the rating agencies (BBB- by S&P and Baa3 by Moody's). Investment garde credit quality generally indicates an expectation that an issuer will pay debt service when due. At the marginal investment grade level, "BBB-" or "Baa3", there may be some uncertainty as to the timeliness of payment or there may be features otherwise considered speculative in the long term. On an historical basis, the likelihood of default increases dramatically for securities which are below investment grade. There can be and has been limited disagreement between the insurers' credit analysts and the rating agencies as to whether or not a certain municipal bond issue should be considered investment grade. The insurance of bonds which were not considered investment grade by the rating agencies when insured has been minimal. An insured bond's credit quality may deteriorate over time with a consequent reduction in rating. However, the volatility of credit quality on a portfolio basis, given an insured portfolio of any size, should be quite low during normal economic cycles.

Bond Types

The municipal bond insurers provide coverage on a variety of bond types (see Table 32.2). With the industry's maturation, the insured portfolios of the major municipal bond insurers are now comprised of municipal bond general obligation (or tax-backed revenue) bonds, hospital revenue bonds, utility revenue bonds, housing revenue bonds and bonds of other miscellaneous security types. There are, in fact, few types of public purpose bonds (municipal bonds) which are unacceptable to all major insurers if their repayment is appropriately secured. However, the rating agency capital requirements for municipal bonds secured by corporate obligors have increased the cost of the insurance companies so as to make insurance of such bonds price prohibitive.

Credit Oversight

The insured portfolio of each major municipal bond insurance company contains thousands of bond issues. As a result, effective portfolio management and control requires a disciplined and highly organized credit oversight and monitoring process. Each company has approached this aspect of the business somewhat differently. MBIA has established a separate credit surveillance department consisting of over twenty professionals. This approach is followed by FGIC. AMBAC leaves the responsibility of credit oversight to the several underwriting groups. Most insurers have developed credit review and classification systems which result in placing the insured bond into a certain category according to its payment performance and outlook. Credits which are experiencing unique financial problems are targeted for exceptional review and oversight. Extremely troubled issues are usually referred for special remedial action.

Credit oversight is a dynamic process. The insurers are constantly reviewing and monitoring their insured portfolio for credit instabilities and adverse changes. Reports and updates on individual credits, industry segments, regional economics and other portfolio oversight topics are frequently researched and prepared. The larger insured obligations are put on regular review schedules, which usually include a site visit and extensive discussions with the officials responsible for the obligor's finances.

Portfolio Management

In a mature municipal bond insurance company considerations relating to the management of the insured portfolio are weighed when deciding whether to offer insurance on a particular bond issue. Generally, the insured portfolio should be diversified by bond type, size, geographic location and scheduled debt service payment dates. Although geographic diversification protects against natural disasters and other geographically correlated risk, including local economic factors, apparent geographic concentration may be ameliorated by the introduction of other security enhancements which are not geographically centered. For example, Federal Housing Administration insurance or primary mortgage insurance of local single-family housing bonds, and fire and casualty (earthquake) insurance written by a company not physically located near the source of repayment of the insured bonds, may mitigate geographic concentration.

Diversification by bond type is also a desirable portfolio management goal. For example, concentration in a specialized bond type such as hospital revenue bonds may produce acute vulnerability to economic downturns in the health care industry.

Size distribution (i.e., the amount of principal insured for each single risk) is a somewhat more subtle, but nevertheless worthy, object of portfolio management. Relatively small bond issues or small portions of large bond issues (under $10 million from the insurer's perspective) require essentially the same credit analysis as larger bond issues. Since smaller issues account for only a modest differentiation in the fixed costs of the insurer, they suffer from diseconomies of scale. However, larger bond issues (particularly in the $100 million range) pose greater risk to the insurer. Larger bond issues increase the insurer's potential for a shock loss involving the substantial dilution of cash flow available to pay present and future claims and the reduction of capital and surplus available to establish loss reserves. To mitigate against this potential, an insured portfolio can be managed to include a preponderance of smaller bond issues. More stringent credit standards can be applied for the insurance of larger bond issues or a special reserve can be established on a GAAP basis to cushion earnings against the trauma of extraordinary shock losses. Reinsurance can be utilized to reduce an insurer's exposure to larger bond issues either on a proportional, per risk excess or aggregate risk excess basis. The major municipal bond insurers have adopted one or more of these precautionary measures.

Insured portfolios are also managed for diversity in terms of the credit quality of the municipal bonds insured (i.e., the actual public ratings or private ratings provided by the rating agencies or other internal estimates of credit quality). Periodic examinations of an insured portfolio on the basis of underlying ratings can demonstrate the volatility of credit quality over time and highlight the non-investment grade portion of the insured portfolio. In an insured portfolio of any size, however, any such examination can mask important disparities. For example, although a hospital revenue bond and a general obligation bond may have the same underlying rating, it is not at all certain that the likelihood of a payment default or the projected term or intensity of a payment default is the same. Quality distribution by bond type must also be examined to define volatile segments of the insured portfolio and establish appropriate monitoring procedures.

THE BENEFITS OF INSURANCE AND ITS PRICE

Although municipal bond insurance has been described as "sleep" insurance for investors, a variety of other reasons exist for its purchase by issuers, by portfolio managers, by dealers in the secondary market, and by sponsors of unit investment trusts and mutual funds. These capital market participants benefit from the price advantage that the triple-A rating provides. As a matter of Federal tax law, the cost of the insurance necessarily compares favorably with the consequent yield advantage. Additionally, insurance provides significantly greater liquidity for bond issues in the secondary market, for the bonds of unknown or infrequent issuers, for small blocks of bonds and for bonds with complex security structures. Marketability is also improved by insuring portions of large issues in order to appeal to retail investors. In certain instances, insured bonds provide a less expensive triple-A rating relative to the increasing scarce "natural" triple-A. The benefits to each participant exceed the insurance cost.

Municipal bond insurance premiums are usually quoted in terms of a percentage of the total principal and interest payable during the stated life of the bond issue. For example, a premium of .60% is .60% times the total principal and interest due on the bonds to maturity. Expressed in terms of basis points (each basis point equals $1/100$ of 1%), the .60% nominal insurance premium is equal to approximately 180 basis points, or approximately 15 basis points per annum (assuming a market multiplier of three as the relationship between the total principal and interest on the bonds to their maturity and the principal of the bonds).

Municipal bond insurance companies derive price from considerations relating to cost, profitability, market conditions and competition. Costs normally reflect rating agency capital requirements, acquisition expenses, and servicing costs (administration, data processing, reporting, credit oversight and remedial management) associated with the insured bond issue over its nominal life. For example, hospital revenue bonds require complex and experienced credit analysis and must be monitored frequently since the security source is a proprietary business enterprise. The insurers dedicate disproportionate (as measured by insured volume) analytical resources to health care. Hospital revenue bonds require more rating agency capital for the insurer on a comparative basis. Therefore, the price for insuring a hospital revenue bond should be, and has been, higher than for insuring a general obligation bond, which requires less rating agency capital support and involves lower acquisition and servicing costs.

Both general and company-specific considerations relating to a targeted, or desirable, level of profitability are involved in pricing. The key variables affecting the profitability of a mature municipal bond insurance company are losses, the return on its investment portfolio, and expenses. Although profitability might be considered of interest only to the investors in the insurance companies, policyholders should be interested in an insurer's profitability as a requisite to an insurer's ability to attract (and retain) quality reinsurance, to increase retained earnings and to incentivize future capital investment. While prices for new issue insurance have deteriorated, there is wide recognition that a minimum price, or floor, must be maintained if the municipal bond insurers are to preserve their ability to attract new capital investment by sustaining a favorable return on invested capital.

Considerations for pricing related to market conditions include interest rate levels and the projected yield spread between the insured and uninsured bond issue. Competition from other insurers bidding to insure the same bond issue can prompt many questions, real and illusory. (Does the competition have the capital capacity to insure the bond issue? Does the competition normally target this type of bond issue for insurance? Is the competition able to qualify and price the bond issue within the applicable time constraint?) Furthermore, an emphasis on market share requires aggressive pricing.

Pricing for secondary market insurance is similar to pricing for new issue insurance and is tailored to the municipal bonds to be insured. Pricing for the insurance of portfolio products (unit investment trusts and mutual funds) is calculated to produce the same level of profitability to the insurer as new issue insurance. In general, premiums for new issue and secondary market insurance are paid in full at the time the insurance policy is issued, although annual premium methodologies are becoming more widespread.

The pricing of the municipal bond insurance product has become more sophisticated in recent years. All of the factors described above have been incorporated into transactional profitability models developed by each of the major insurers. These models are useful guides in determining potential profitability levels and sensitivities to price adjustments. However, notwithstanding the underlying "science" of this approach, the ultimate pricing decision remains a result of the competitive viscera and negotiation.

THE USEFULNESS OF INSURANCE— LOSS EXPERIENCE

The goal of a municipal bond insurer's underwriting process is to minimize losses. Municipal bond insurance is underwritten to a no loss standard. On a portfolio basis, however, it is expected that losses will be incurred. A paid loss ratio of 10% of earned premiums has been commonly assumed for the purpose of financial projections. To date, MBIA, AMBAC, FGIC, and FSA have had paid and incurred losses, which in the aggregate have been nominal in relationship to total premium volume. The municipal bond insurers have paid all claims in full and on time.

A payment default on an insured bond does not necessarily constitute an ultimate loss to the insurer. In the general obligation, tax-backed and municipal revenue bond sectors, including utilities, defaults normally represent a cash flow deficiency on the part of the issuer. The issuer is unable to pay debt service when due. However, payment defaults on these municipal bond types historically have been transient and recoverable. The loss is typically minimal after salvage. Salvage has approached 100% and has generally exceeded 90%. The insurers' real peril is a funding risk rather than a risk of ultimate net loss, and therefore the financial stress experienced by the insurer is one of liquidity.

Some insured municipal bond types such as health care (hospital, nursing home, and related enterprises) bonds are susceptible to some risk of ultimate loss. Since these obligations are usually supported solely by the revenues of a discrete health care enterprise, failure of the enterprise may result in a permanent inability to pay debt service. It should also be noted that extraordinary circumstances have caused permanent losses in more traditional municipal bond types. A case in point is the default of the Washington Public Power Supply System on bonds issued to finance its No. 4 and 5 nuclear plants. In taking unprecedented action, the courts invalidated the "take or pay" contracts which had provided for a purported absolute obligation on the part of various municipalities to make payments in amounts sufficient to pay the debt service on the bonds. (In the case of the Washington Public Power Supply System, despite legal invalidity, salvage of 30% to 40% of principal is expected.)

An important feature of municipal bond insurance is that the insurer's payment liability cannot be accelerated. The insurer guarantees the payment of principal and interest only in accordance with the bond's original payment schedule. Without the possibility of acceleration the threat of shock loss to the insurer is blunted. Normally, when a payment default occurs or is otherwise perceived to be imminent, a statutory case basis loss reserve is required to be established. Although statutory reserving policy has yet to become standardized, the amount of the reserve is generally equal to the present value of the debt service due on the insured bonds in the next succeeding three years. In the rare instance when a permanent total loss can be anticipated, the case basis loss reserve established will equal, on average, the principal insured or an amount equal to anticipated par amount of the ultimate net loss. The interest component of the loss is addressed by not applying a present value factor to the case basis reserve. Additionally, since the insurer's liability cannot be accelerated, the insurer is afforded time to work-out the credit problem in an orderly manner.

Proven methods have evolved

(1) for monitoring deteriorating credits,

(2) for working with problem credits to prevent payment defaults,

(3) for administering and paying claims, and

(4) for recovering salvage on claims paid.

Some of the insurers have established remedial management (i.e., work-out) departments or teams to handle the most seriously troubled credits. A few of the methods employed in addressing credit problems prior to a payment default include the managed refinancing of the bonds, obtaining outside financial assistance for the issuer and paying for independent financial and management studies and encouraging the issuer to make suggested changes. Occasionally, separate insurance agreement are entered into between the insurer and the obligor on the bonds which incorporate key financial performance indicators, which if violated require the funding of debt service and other reserves, or the retirement of the debt.

As mentioned previously, municipal bond insurance companies are required as a regulatory matter to establish contingency reserves against losses during periods of economic catastrophe. The contingency reserve must be funded by setting a percentage of earned or written premium in accordance with applicable regulation. Typically, the contingency reserve will compound slowly over the first decade of an insurer's operations, and may appear undersized in relation to insured principal when an insured portfolio has grown rapidly.

BASICS OF THE EVALUATION OF A MUNICIPAL BOND INSURANCE COMPANY

In evaluating a municipal bond insurance company from the policyholders' perspective, a number of fundamental elements must be considered both separately and in combination including:

(1) the form and quality of the insurer's capitalization;

(2) the insurer's capital base relative to its exposure (i.e., leverage);

(3) the insured portfolio's quality and diversification;

(4) the composition and performance of the investment portfolio;

(5) capacity to pay present and future claims as a function of cash flow;

(6) available claims paying resources (equal to policyholders' surplus, contingency reserve, unearned premium reserve, case basis loss reserves, reinsurance and other supplemental capital facilities);

(7) subjective willingness to pay claims when due;

(8) access to capital for growth;

(9) financial performance;

(10) ownership structure and commitment; and

(11) management.

Financial Indicators

Since statutory accounting provides generally uniform standards of reporting for all municipal bond insurance companies, and because statutory financial reporting is designed to describe the level of policyholders' protection, the statutory financial statements are best utilized for individual and comparative analysis of the municipal bond insurance companies. Below is a list of financial indicators which may be utilized to evaluate protection to policyholders.

Financial Strength

—Statutory Capital (Policyholders' Surplus and Contingency Reserve)

—Claims Paying Resources (Policyholders' Surplus, Contingency Reserve, Unearned Premium Reserve, Case Basis Loss Reserves and Supplemental Credit Facilities)

—Net Statutory Income (Including Net Earned Premium and Net Investment Income)

—Admitted Assets (Including Cash and Investments)

—Qualified Reinsurance

—Net Exposure (Insured Unpaid Principal and Interest, Net of Reinsurance and Collateral)

—Net Insured Annual Debt Service (Current and Succeeding Year)

—Net Insured "Weighted" Average Annual Debt Service

—Average Life of Insured Portfolio

—Annual Expenses

—Net Exposure/Statutory Capital

—Net Insured Principal/Statutory Capital

—Net Exposure/Funds Available to Pay Claims

—Net Insured Annual Debt Service/Statutory Capital

—Net Insured Annual Debt Service/Pretax Statutory Income

Investment Portfolio

—Average Life of Investment Portfolio and Largest Single Investment Risk (excluding United States Government and Agency Obligations)

—Overlaps with Larger Single Risks in Insured Portfolio

—Quality Distribution

—Investment Mix (Fixed Income Securities, Equities etc.) and Duration

Selected Ratios Utilized by Rating Agencies and Market Analysts

—Net Insured Principal of Largest Single Risk/Capital

—Unearned Premium Reserve/Net Exposure

—Net Income/Net Insured Annual Debt Service

—Expense Ratio (Net Underwriting Expense/Net Premiums Written)

—Paid Loss Ratio (Net Losses Paid/Net Earned Premium)

—Incurred Loss Ratio (Net Losses Incurred/Net Earned Premium)

—Combined Ratio (Expense Ratio plus Incurred Loss Ratio)

—Assets/Net Exposure

Capital

Capital is, by definition, a cornerstone to the financial strength of a municipal bond insurer and fundamental to any evaluation of the quality of its claims-paying ability (see Figure 32.4). Capital includes policyholders' surplus and the contingency reserve (statutory capital), reinsurance and supplemental capital facilities. If preservation of the triple-A rating is an objective, attention must be paid to the insurer's ability to pay claims without invading capital. Although several of the insurers have

FIGURE 32.4
Industry Comparison (Total Qualified Statutory Capital—9/30/91)

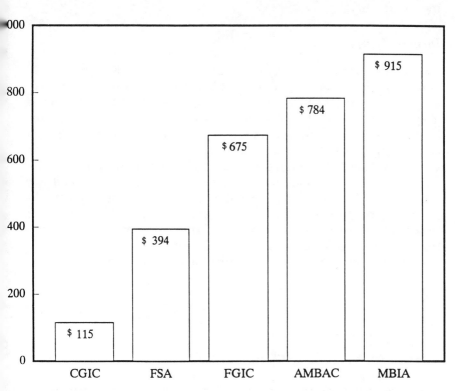

established special GAAP loss reserves and supplemental capital facilities to provide liquidity or substitute aggregate capital, the primary defense to an invasion of its capital base, upon the occurrence of losses, is an insurer's cash flow from its insured portfolio (earned premiums) and investment portfolio (investment income).

Cash Flow

The cash flow of an insurer consists of investment income, premiums earned from the unearned premium reserve, and annual premiums, if any. The nominal runoff (e.g., the expiration of insured exposure) of the insured portfolio provides a basis to predict earned premiums. The prepayment or other refunding of insured bonds, to the extent that the insurer's exposure is thereby reduced, would accelerate such earnings. Annual premiums are not reflected on an insurer's statutory balance sheet. Furthermore, as historical deposits into the contingency reserve reach the end of the statutory holding period (generally the 20th anniversary), such deposits will be released from the reserve and may significantly enhance unassigned surplus, thereby contributing to liquidity.

Insured Portfolio

The quality and diversification of the insured portfolio become increasingly important as a municipal bond insurer matures. The average credit quality of the insured portfolio, its volatility over time, its geographical distribution, its balance among bond types, and its quality by bond type are indicators of the strength of the portfolio should adverse changes in the general economic climate or any of these areas occur. The size distribution of the insured portfolio (the proportionate number of relatively small bond issues) is an indicator of the ability of the municipal bond insurer to withstand multiple losses. Attention should be paid to the number, type and quality of large (over $100 million) bond issues in the insured portfolio. The projected runoff of the insurer's exposure (see Figure 32.5) provides a context to dimension the relationship among exposure, capital and cash flow.

FIGURE 32.5
Annual Runoff of Insured Principal and Interest*

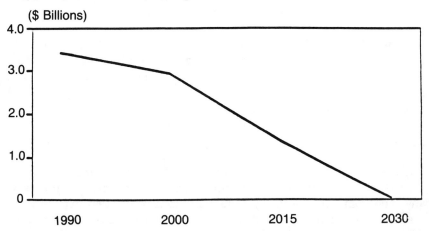

*A mature municipal bond insurance company should have a runoff schedule for its insured portfolio which reflects the graph. Under the rules of statutory accounting earned premiums will be commensurate; under GAAP accounting earned premiums may be accelerated in relation to runoff depending on the accounting policy which is adopted by the insurer. The above is without regard to refundings.

Investment Portfolio

The size, performance and composition of the investment portfolio must be considered. The investment portfolio should limit the block size of municipal investments, should minimize any duplication of risk with larger bond issues in the insured portfolio, should contain high quality investments, should be tailored to the term of the insurer's liability, and should have appropriate liquidity.

Ownership

Ownership structure, and the quality and commitment of institutional investors, are also important. Municipal bond insurance is capital intensive, and the ability of insurers to generate capital internally and to obtain additional investment is critical to the business. In times of financial stress the maintenance by a municipal bond insurer of its triple-A rating may depend on its ability to attract capital. Some investors may be more able than others to provide capital, and even able investors may not be willing to invest additional capital in the insurer if alternative investments appear more attractive. Sustained capital commitment is a corollary of the expectation of sustained profitability.

Management

The quality of management is extremely important yet difficult to evaluate. Nevertheless, such an evaluation, while subjective, is important in that municipal bond insurance is credit driven; it is a business in which long term profitability, if not financial viability, is determined, to a great degree, by today's underwriting decisions. Indices which may be applied to an evaluation of management are the experience and education of the senior personnel, the longevity and continuity of service, and reputation.

An insurer must have a significant presence in the market to optimize its flexibility in managing its future (i.e., the size, type and quality of municipal bonds it is given the opportunity to insure). No matter how it is quantified, market share should be stable or improving over time. However, as discussed, if an insurer is managed to maximize market share, standards of credit evaluation and prices may each be lowered so as to materially increase the probability of losses and impair financial solidity. Finally, intelligent monitoring of the municipal bond insurance industry is vital. The insurers will respond to the informed expectations of the market, and this responsiveness should support the maintenance of the financial integrity of the municipal bond insurance companies and their retention of the triple-A claims-paying rating.

CHAPTER 33

Letter of Credit-Backed Bonds

Abraham Losice
Standard & Poor's Corporation

Since 1979, thousands of municipalities, corporations, municipal authorities, and not-for-profit entities have issued bonds that are supported by *letters of credit* (LOC). The credit risk for these financings is based on an irrevocable obligation by a bank to provide for payment of the debt in the event that the obligor does not pay. Issuers can borrow at a more advantageous rate by obtaining credit enhancement from a bank LOC. The following discussion will describe the features and credit risks of LOC-backed bonds and the structure known as *put bonds*.

The banks that are active in this market are those that can lend high ratings for the bonds. The decision of a bank to offer an LOC is a credit decision similar to extending a loan. The bank prices an annual commitment fee for the LOC. Terms for reimbursement are established. These terms generally require immediate reimbursement for LOC draws. Draws which are not immediately reimbursed carry interest rates at a spread over the prime rate, similar to loan rates. Since they are taking the full credit risk, the banks also secure their reimbursement with collateral and guaranties.

Initially, the LOC market was dominated by domestic U.S. banks. In the mid-1980s, foreign banks became major players. These banks issued LOCs through U.S. branches of their banks. Aggressive pricing on the part of foreign banks in conjunction with higher credit ratings led to their majority position in this market. Subsequent drops in credit ratings worldwide have led to a currently balanced distribution of LOC providers.

Typically, a bond transaction is issued by a municipal entity which serves as a conduit. The bond proceeds are loaned to the underlying obligor, which is the entity that bears the responsibility for repayment of the debt. Issuance through a municipal entity can earn tax-exempt status for the bonds and lower debt service for the underlying obligor. The companies that are the underlying obligors are mostly unrated or low rated companies. To gain access to the capital markets and even lower debt service, these bonds can be credit enhanced with letters of credit which cover full payment of principal and accrued interest. Highly rated banks provide letters of credit in exchange for an annual commitment fee and a reimbursement agreement with the underlying obligor.

Bondholders should look to conclude that the only credit risk is the risk of the bank honoring draws on its LOC. The bondholder should be insulated from any bankruptcy, default, or lack of performance by the obligor. By issuing an irrevocable LOC the bank takes the risk of the obligor's performance. The following are the risks and concerns associated with making this conclusion.

PREFERENCE CONCERNS

Payment of debt could be recaptured from bondholders as an avoidable preference in the event of the filing of a petition under the U.S. Bankruptcy Code with respect to the issuer, the borrower, any general partner or guarantor of the borrower. Under the Code, a trustee in bankruptcy may set aside, or recapture, certain payments on account of debt made within a certain period of time prior to the filing of a bankruptcy petition. The appropriate preference period varies from 90 days, under the federal statute, to one year in the case of a payment made to or for the benefit of an insider.

There are several ways to deal with possible preference problems. It begins with the choice of payment structure. The three basic structures are:

—Direct pay;
—Prioritized direct pay; and
—Extension.

Each payment structure has its own special analytical concerns.

In a *direct pay structure,* the first source of payment to bondholders, is funds drawn under the LOC. The LOC must specifically state that the bank will pay with its own funds. Since banks do not file for bankruptcy under the Bankruptcy Code, LOC money is inherently preference proof.

The *prioritized direct pay structure* is similar to direct pay. Bondholders are paid with LOC funds as the secondary source if the trustee does not hold sufficient preference-proof funds. Preference proofing entails providing the trustee with funds at least 91 days before a payment date and certifying that the depositor has not filed for bankruptcy within that period. The 91-day period is based upon the Code's use of a 3-month preference period. For transactions in which an insider provides a guaranty of either bond payments or reimbursement payments to the bank, the preference period is extended to one year.

Insurance proceeds are often used as a payment source for redemption following damage to the project. If the insurance policy is written directly to the trustee, then the insurance proceeds can be considered a preference-proof source of payment. If the insurance policy is written to the underlying obligor, and the underlying obligor receives the payments from the insurance company, the insurance proceeds must be held for the preference period before they may be paid over to bondholders.

The *extension structure* is the least common payment structure. In this structure, bondholders are paid first with nonpreference-proof funds. Since this structure could allow for the disgorgement of bond payments following a bankruptcy, the LOC is sized to cover the maximum amount of preference payments in addition to its coverage of principal and accrued interest. Upon a bankruptcy filing, the LOC is drawn upon to establish an escrow fund for the preference risk. To protect bondholders from the consequences of a bankruptcy following a final payment, the LOC expiration date must extend beyond the duration of the appropriate preference period. Following the conclusion of such period, if the trustee does not receive evidence of no bankruptcy, the LOC shall be drawn upon to establish an escrow fund.

Variable rate demand bonds which use remarketing proceeds as the initial source for purchase price payments also raise preference concerns. The remarketing proceeds that can be used as a payment source to tendering bondholders must be restricted. These proceeds may not include funds from the issuer, the company, any general partner, or guarantor.

CREDIT-CLIFF ISSUES

Bondholders try to determine the probability of the full and timely payment to the bondholder until final maturity, or such time as the bonds are paid in full. Credit cliff events (i.e. events which lead to a termination or reduction of the amount or level of credit support prior to such time) therefore are important factors in the analysis of these structures.

LOC Expiration

Structures allowing for the expiration of the outstanding LOC prior to maturity are a common potential credit cliff. Most bonds have 20 to 30 year maturities, while the letters of credit supporting them rarely have terms beyond 7 years. The bondholder faces the possibility of having purchased an LOC-backed bond issue, but being left holding unsupported bonds. To prevent such a scenario, an extension of the LOC or a substitute LOC must be executed prior to expiration of the existing LOC. Any alternate LOC must meet the requirement for rating maintenance. If there is no LOC extension or substitution prior to LOC expiration, then it is necessary to take out the bondholders through a mandatory redemption or a mandatory tender. Bondholders may be given the option of retaining their bonds. To affirm their intent to retain the bonds, they must acknowledge, in writing, their understanding of the rating consequences. In the case of mandatory tenders, undelivered bonds should be deemed tendered.

LOC Substitution

A similar concern arises upon the provision of a substitute LOC. The possibility of a substitute LOC from a lower-rated bank undercuts the integrity of the issue. To avoid such a scenario, any substitution of the LOC must be accompanied by written certification from the rating agency that the provision of the substitute will not in and of itself result in a reduction or withdrawal of the then current rating on the bonds. Alternatively, a substitution may be executed without certification of rating maintenance if existing bond holders are taken out via a mandatory tender or redemption at or prior to the date of substitution. Retention options may be offered with the same stipulations as outlined above.

Nonreinstatement

Another potential credit cliff arises from provisions in the LOC or the reimbursement agreement which allow the bank to declare an event of default under the reimbursement agreement or non-reinstatement of interest coverage under the LOC following a draw for interest. Any notification from the LOC provider to the trustee of these events should be deemed an event of default under the terms of the indenture, leading to a mandatory and immediate acceleration of the bond maturity. Such an acceleration should be structured so that the LOC has sufficient interest coverage to cover all interest until it ceases to accrue. Any waiver of these events of default should be contingent on written evidence of the LOC provider's renewed willingness to support the deal and the reinstatement of interest coverage in full.

Timeliness of LOC Draws

It is important to synchronize the trustee's draw instructions under the bond indenture with the payment terms of the LOC, to ensure that the LOC is drawn upon to provide for full and timely payment. In the case of bonds supported by both a facing and a confirming LOC, the bonds are entitled to the rating of the higher rated bank if structured in the following manner. The trustee's draw instructions must leave sufficient time to draw upon the confirming LOC in order to provide full and timely payment in the event the facing bank fails to honor a draw on its LOC.

Conversion

Conversion from one interest rate mode to another can also give rise to credit concerns if the LOC either expires on conversion or has insufficient interest coverage for the new mode. The provision of a substitute LOC with sufficient interest coverage and certification of rating maintenance, or a take out via a mandatory redemption or tender, can adequately address this concern.

LETTER OF CREDIT

An LOC must be only for a sum certain with a definite expiration date. Other limitations within an LOC are its terms for draws and its terms for reinstatement. There are also specific turnaround times for the bank to honor an LOC draw. All of these terms are reviewed in conjunction with the structure of the bond to conclude that the LOC offers full coverage for the transaction.

The formula to calculate the required amount of LOC coverage is the following:

Principal—The principal portion must equal the current outstanding amount of bonds.

Premium—The amount corresponding to the largest premium applicable to a mandatory redemption.

Interest—The interest portion shall be an amount equal to the maximum amount of days of interest that could accrue calculated at either:

1. the actual rate for fixed rate bonds; or
2. the maximum rate for floating rate bonds.

For purposes of calculating the interest rate of the LOC, the appropriate length of the calendar year, 360 day or 365/6, must correspond with the basis of calculation within the bonds.

A leading concern in structuring an LOC-backed issue is establishing the amount of days of interest coverage in the LOC. The LOC must cover the maximum amount of interest that can accrue in the worst case scenario.

For direct pay and prioritized direct pay transactions the same worst-case scenario would apply. In this case, the trustee draws on the LOC for full coverage of the longest interest period. Following the draw, the LOC bank sends notice of non-reinstatement of interest coverage at the latest possible time in accordance with the terms of the LOC. The trustee then accelerates the issue, and interest ceases to accrue at the latest time in accordance with the indenture. The calculation of interest coverage should also consider delays in notices or payments caused by non-business days. In extension transactions, where non-preference proof money is the first source of payment to the bondholder, the worst case scenario concerns the consequences of the company's bankruptcy. In addition to coverage for accrued interest, the LOC must also cover the maximum amount of interest that can be disgorged from bondholders if it were deemed a preferential transfer. Most transactions of this type have individual features. The factors to consider in calculation of interest coverage are:

(1) schedule of loan payments;
(2) timing of notice of bankruptcy;
(3) events of default;
(4) grace periods;
(5) acceleration schedule; and
(6) the applicable preference period.

THE TENDER PROCESS

A similar analysis is applied to the payment of purchase price as assessing the likelihood of full and timely payment of regularly scheduled principal and interest. If remarketing proceeds are the first source of funds to be used for tenders and LOC funds are the second, the trustee should be instructed to draw on the LOC in an amount equal to the total purchase price due to tendering bondholders less the amount of the remarketing proceeds on hand prior to the draw time deadline established in the LOC. It is important that the trustee only consider proceeds actually on deposit as opposed to proceeds which are expected to be received. If the trustee were to draw on the LOC on the basis of expected proceeds and any expected remarketings were to fail, a shortfall in total funds available to pay tendering bondholders would exist. This would jeopardize the timeliness of the payment. In most instances, it would be too late to make a second draw on the LOC to make up the shortfall and still make timely payment of purchase price. There can be reliance on expected proceeds which reflect an unconditional guarantee from the remarketing agent to deliver remarketing proceeds regardless of whether expected remarketings are successful or not.

Since the tender process often involves several different parties (trustee, tender agent, remarketing agent), proper coordination of the flow of information and funds among the various participants is necessary to ensure full and timely payment of purchase price to bondholders. In some deals payment of purchase price to bondholders is made by the tender agent rather than the trustee. If the LOC is written to the trustee, and the trustee is instructed by the indenture to make draws on the LOC, the trustee must be instructed either to transfer the moneys received from an LOC draw to the tender agent, while allotting adequate time for the tender agent to pay bondholders prior to the close of business on the purchase date, or to direct the LOC bank to pay all proceeds of a tender draw directly to the tender agent. Another acceptable option is to have the LOC Bank authorize, and the indenture instruct, the tender agent to make all tender draws directly, without involving the trustee. Remarketing proceeds must also be transferred from the remarketing agent to the party paying purchase price in adequate time for payment to be made to bondholders prior to the close of business on the tender date. All notices must be given or confirmed in writing.

PURCHASE PRICE REINSTATEMENT

Any time all or a portion of tender price is paid from proceeds of a drawing on the LOC and the LOC coverage amount reduces upon honoring of the draw, the concept of purchase price reinstatement is an important factor. Bonds that are purchased with LOC moneys are generally held as pledged bonds and must not be released to the new purchasers until the trustee has received written confirmation from the

LOC bank that the LOC has been reinstated to its full amount of coverage for the bonds in question; otherwise, bondholders could be exposed to credit-cliff risk by holding bonds that are not supported by the LOC.

REMARKETING DISCOUNT

Most put bonds only allow the bonds to be remarketed at par. On some transactions, the remarketing can be at a discounted price. To insure full payment to tendering bondholders, the discount must be limited to the amount of LOC coverage specifically for remarketing discounts.

EXPIRATION OF THE PUT OPTION

The bondholder should be insulated from the performance of the issuer or the underlying obligor. Events of default due to bankruptcy or technical default by the issuer or underlying obligor should not lead to the expiration of the put option, as that would be inconsistent with the short-term nature of the transaction.

OPTIONAL REDEMPTIONS

Certain transactions are structured where payment of premium or principal associated with an optional redemption is not covered by the LOC. For such event, the trustee shall not send out a notice of redemption to the bondholders unless:

(a) there are sufficient preference proof funds on hand prior to the giving of such notice; or

(b) such notice will be conditional and contain language to the effect that the redemption will be rescinded in the event there will not be sufficient preference proof funds on hand prior to the scheduled redemption date.

TRUSTEE'S ROLE

In LOC-backed transactions, the trustee is obligated to fulfill its fiduciary responsibilities. Bondholders rely on the trustee to follow the terms of the bonds and to draw upon the LOC in accordance with its terms. Terms of the deal must be drafted in a clear and unambiguous manner to gain that reliance on the trustee.

VARIABLE RATE PUT BONDS

At the beginning of the 1980s, interest rates were taking a steep climb. Businesses, small and large, were facing difficulties in raising capital. Interest rates were making many projects uneconomic. To get bank loans borrowers were facing prime rates of 20%. Interest on investment grade bonds were lower, but even the capital markets were demanding historically high rates for the relatively few creditworthy companies. How could a company raise capital when it meant locking in such high rates for a long-term project? The key to entry to the capital markets was credit enhancement. The vehicle to address high rates was and is variable rate put bonds.

The solution came in 1981. The firm E.F. Hutton developed the *lower floater*. This structure filled a need and became popular immediately. As the title suggests, it featured an interest rate which adjusted in this case monthly. Along with the floating rate came a put option for the bondholder. This meant that once a month the bondholder had the option to sell his bond at par back to the issuer. The issuer also holds an option. His option is to choose the time when to convert the bonds to a fixed rate of interest till maturity. Those are just the basics to this structure. Before the details of operation are discussed it is important to understand the advantages for the two sides to this deal—the issuer and the bondholder.

The issuer has a number of obstacles to face when raising capital for a long-term project. To attract investors the issuer has to satisfy their concerns of the issuer's creditworthiness. While this is true on any financing it is especially true on a long-term bond as the bondholder is stuck in the deal till maturity—20 to 30 years away. The market demands that the issuer pay a premium for holding the principal so long. This is known as the liquidity premium since the bondholder is stuck in an illiquid position, bears longer credit risk, and misses the opportunity for other uses of his funds. It is most readily apparent in the upward slope of the normal yield curve. The way for the issuer to reduce this premium is to give liquidity back to the bondholder. E.F. Hutton did it monthly in their original structure. Currently, the most popular put option is one where the bondholder is able to choose to put any business day with 7 days notice. With this structure the liquidity risk is only seven days. For the issuer it means he/she can take advantage of interest rates at the lowest end of the yield curve. It means the ability to fund a long-term project by simulating short-term financing.

For the bondholder, put bonds mean the ability to get out of the deal whenever he/she pleases. If the bondholder is an institutional investor, there is an advantage: A bond that can be tendered any day with 7 days notice can be treated as a 7 day maturity when the fund reports its average maturity.

One of the leading issues in choosing the time to go to market is to try to time interest rates. Trying to figure when interest rates are right is an uncertainty facing all issuers. There are times when the issuer is certain that rates are wrong. With projects waiting to be started and issuers confident that they can, in the long-term, be done economically, the issuers look to get to market immediately. The lower floater helps the issuer do that. Rates can go up, rates can go down. When they float down low enough the issuer can lock in the low rates by converting the bond to a fixed interest rate till maturity. Some deals target this rate from the start with a drop-lock rate. It is still possible to mistime interest rates, however much of the risk is eliminated. Importantly, it gives issuers a greater opportunity to raise capital for projects when the projects need to be done.

While issuers are concerned that interest rates are too high, bondholders are concerned about investing when interest rates are too low. They have natural concerns that interest rates will rise and that they will suffer investment or opportunity losses. Even when rates fall the bondholder can't lose his bargain if the issuer offers the bondholder an opportunity to keep his investment at par. It is also effective call protection. This eliminates much of the investors interest rate risk.

An important side effect of the liquidity of lower floaters is the group of investors that it attracts. Many of the institutional investors, pension funds, and portfolio managers, put high value on liquidity and only invest short term. By offering a put option, especially on investment grade bonds, the issuer increases the demand by developing a wider pool of potential investors. The increase in demand can be effective both in selling out the issue and in lowering the cost of debt service.

Once floating rate bonds were developed with Hutton's lower floater, it was only a short time before other firms got involved with their own versions. Investment bankers were also creating different structures based on different indices for the floating rate and timing of the put option. The index was basically to keep the bonds trading at par. Most bonds give this responsibility to a remarketing agent who would reset the rate at all remarketing dates to keep the bonds trading at par and sell out all the bonds. Some issues allow conversion to different floating rate modes. The timing for resetting the rate and remarketing is established at the wishes of the issuer. He could choose what was most advantageous off the yield curve. This opportunity was created with multi-modal bonds. These are bonds that can convert between modes where the bonds float weekly, monthly, quarterly, semi-annually, annually, or multi-annually. Two special developments were the daily rate mode and the commercial rate mode. The daily rate, when the bondholder may put on any day, is technologically difficult since it demands a structure that can operate a put option all within the course of one business day. When used it takes advantage of the absolute lowest end of the yield curve. The commercial paper mode, just like commercial paper itself, features interest periods from one to 270 days. This allows the issuer and remarketing agent the ability to customize the maturity for each of their investors. It attracts a similar market as commercial paper and simulates it well.

In understanding the operation of variable rate transactions it is important to note two sides, the appearance of the terms in the legal documentation and the workings in real life. For this case, we will discuss a transaction fully supported for principal, interest, and purchase price by a letter of credit (LOC) from a high-rated bank. This would mean that the bondholder is not concerned about the performance of the issuer. The only credit risk for the bondholder is the risk of the bank performing in a full and timely manner on its LOC.

Coverage under an LOC is only a finite dollar amount. With LOC interest coverage limited, the floating rate on the bonds must be equally limited. It is common to see maximum floating rates of between 12 and 15%. There are two factors in the choice. The issuer and remarketing agent want the most flexibility to keep the bonds trading at par. This would lead them to choose an out of sight number. It is tempered, though, by the cost of the credit enhancement.

Interest payment dates are closely matched to interest rate mode. Daily, weekly, and monthly bonds usually pay interest on the first business day of each month. This is usually calculated based on a 365-day year. Modes that are semi-annual or longer pay interest semiannually based on a 360-day year. The commercial paper mode is a bit different. It pays interest at the end of each period when the investment is either rolled over or paid off in principal.

When the bondholder wants to exercise his put option, he would give notice to the trustee and the remarketing agent. In the most common case, he would have his bond purchased at par 7 days later. Throughout that week the remarketing agent would be trying to line up purchasers and would be adjusting the rate to attract them. On the business day before the purchase date, he would notify the trustee if he lined up a purchaser. On the purchase date, he would report to the trustee, by the latest time for an LOC draw, if he has received sufficient remarketing proceeds to purchase the bonds. If he has, then that is the source for full payment at par to the tendering bondholder (the issuer is usually not involved as a source for payment). If not, then the trustee conducts an LOC draw for timely payment on the purchase date. When the LOC is used for purchase price, it reduces the coverage to the extent of the draw. Coverage is reinstated automatically following reimbursement. The remarketing agent continues to try to remarket the bonds following an unsuccessful remarketing. When the remarketing agent does find a purchaser, he would take the proceeds, send it as reimbursement to the LOC bank, wait to receive notice of LOC reinstatement, and only then deliver the bonds to the new holder. The new bondholder would want to be sure that he has full LOC coverage.

That is how a 7-day put works in theory. All the terms concerning LOC draws and reinstatement satisfy the bondholders credit and liquidity concerns. In actuality the LOC is nearly never used. When notice of a put comes, the remarketing agent tries to sell the bond that day as a secondary market transaction. Many bonds are held in the name of the bondholder's broker. These bonds are often resold to other clients of that broker and it would not appear as a change of ownership in the eyes of the authenticating agent. In this way most bonds are not sold in accordance to the terms of the bond documents. Assuming purchasers are not lined up or that they are but their money is not delivered in time, LOC draws are still hardly used. While it is not his legal obligation, almost invariably the remarketing agent will put up the money and purchase the bonds. This is a frequent occurrence. He/she can place the bonds in his inventory and keep up his image as a firm that supports its deals and is a completely successful remarketing agent.

CHAPTER 34

The Role of the Financial Advisor

William W. Cobbs and Wesley C. Hough
Public Resources Advisory Group

Annette L. De Lara
The School Board of Dade County

The complexities of financing the needs of state and local government increased significantly from 1970 to 1990 as the tax-exempt securities market underwent several transformations: from the staid and steady character of the early 1970s through a period of explosive growth in volume and product until 1985 to the smaller and more restrictive market of post-tax reform. In the midst of this environment stands the government unit with a need to finance efficiently its infrastructure renewal and expansion needs.

DEVELOPMENTS IN THE TAX-EXEMPT MARKET

From 1970 to 1985, there was an 11-fold increase in the volume of tax-exempt securities issued. The growth of the municipal bond market was largely fueled by the use of tax-exempt debt for non-traditional purposes. By 1984 supply had grown to $101.9 billion from $17.8 billion in 1970, then surged to $204.3 billion in 1985 as issuers went to market with financings which would lose tax-exempt status under the Tax Reform Act of 1986. Accompanying the growth in volume was a shift from general obligation debt to revenue bonds. As seen in Table 34.1, revenue-supported debt increased from 34% of the total

TABLE 34.1
General Obligation vs. Revenue Supported Debt ($s in thousands)

	General Obligation Supported Debt	Percent	Revenue Supported Debt	Percent	Total Volume
1970	$11,803,081	66.5%	$ 5,958,564	33.5%	$ 17,761,645
1975	15,003,410	51.2%	14,322,820	48.8%	29,326,230
1980	16,347,134	34.7%	30,786,321	65.3%	47,133,365
1985	55,285,705	27.1%	148,994,903	72.9%	204,280,608
1989	37,627,844	30.6%	85,408,704	69.4%	123,036,548

Source: The Bond Buyer.

tax-exempt market in 1970 to 69% in 1989, with most of the shift occurring between 1970 and 1980. In many instances, special agencies and authorities were created to issue this debt.

The increase in volume being driven by a demand for tax-exempt capital, as opposed to increased investor demand for tax-exempt securities, also spurred the development of different financing structures to attract new buyers. For example, during the relatively high interest-rate period of the early 1980s, variable-rate instruments were developed to lower the cost of borrowing and satisfy investor appetite for money market securities. This period also saw the creation of a number of financing alternatives, such as capital appreciation bonds, tender option bonds and tax-exempt commercial paper, to target the particular needs of certain institutional and individual investors. These changes altered the nature of the capital formation process by increasing the involvement of other parties including engineers, attorneys, and occasionally, private partners.

The tax-exempt securities market changed again with the Tax Reform Act of 1986. In addition to sharply narrowing the range of projects eligible for tax-exempt status, numerous restrictions and conditions were placed on issuers. The capital project needs of communities did not change, but their access to tax-exempt capital was curbed and, for many types of projects, eliminated. Tax law revisions have continued and so has the need for capital. Thus, issuers now have to evaluate a much broader range of options prior to deciding on a plan for financing capital improvements.

The increased complexity of municipal finance due to intricate financing structures, the technical nature of many projects, the multiplicity of financing alternatives and the restrictive regulatory environment have combined to cause more and more issuers to rely on outside advisors for guidance through the debt management procedure. Debt issuance is no longer a routine function. The tasks of analyzing debt affordability, reviewing alternatives, monitoring market trends, tracking the evolving regulatory requirements and screening new products are so highly specialized that even the largest and most sophisticated issuers frequently retain an outside financial consultant.

The financial advisor's responsibilities may be extremely broad—advising the client on an ongoing basis regarding the funding requirements for a long-range capital improvement program—or may be limited to the successful completion of a single transaction. In either instance, the financial advisor advises the client on the appropriateness of the financing structure, assists in obtaining credit ratings, and advises on the timing, marketing and fairness of the pricing and terms of the sale. Financial advisors often provide additional services, such as advising on financial feasibility, investment strategies, and the development of fiscal policies.

TYPES OF FINANCIAL ADVISORY FIRMS

Financial advisory services are provided by three types of firms: investment banks, commercial banks, and independent financial advisors. Investment banks generally offer financial advisory services as a sideline to underwriting and trading tax-exempt securities. Commercial banks with public finance departments may offer advisory services as an offshoot of their other financial services. Independent financial advisors serve strictly as financial consultants and do not underwrite or trade securities. Table 34.2 indicates the composition of the 50 top financial advisory firms, based on the dollar volume of transactions for 1989.

The principal public finance activity of investment banks is the buying and selling of municipal securities for clients and for their own portfolios. Many of the major investment banks maintain municipal securities research departments as a part of their trading operations. The resources of an active trading desk and municipal market research support can provide insight into investor reception of particular credits and structures and can be helpful in making decisions of timing, marketing, and initial pricing. One risk of having an investment banking firm serve as a financial advisor is an over-reliance upon the firm's trading desk, as each firm has a different client base and an accurate read of the market requires a broad range of information. The investment banker as financial advisor must be committed to representing the issuer as aggressively as possible during negotiations even though, in another transaction, they may be a member of an underwriting syndicate with the same firms and be dependent upon the good will of the senior manager for bond allocation, which creates the potential for a conflict of interest.

TABLE 34.2
Top 50 Financial Advisory Firms 1989

Category	Number	Percentage
Investment Banks	28	56%
Independent Financial Advisors	29	38%
Commercial Banks	3	6%

Source: Securities Data, Inc.

Commercial banks provide issuers with a full range of banking and investment services and can serve as an issuer's advisor in the sale of securities. For many governmental units which sell small amounts of debt on an infrequent schedule, the established relationship with the commercial bank may make it practical to obtain debt issuance services as a part of the overall banking contract. There are limitations imposed by the lack of concentration in the area of public finance, however, as many smaller commercial banks do not actively trade securities but simply execute transactions upon the instruction of their trust department. One particular advantage regional commercial banks can offer is familiarity with the issuer's circumstances and an interest in maintaining a long-term relationship which may permit the bank to commit resources to the municipal issuer at a level above that which could be justified by other types of financial advisors. The major money market banks which now underwrite negotiated as well as competitively bid securities more resemble investment banks in the provision of financial advisory services. Consequently, the same advantages and caveats apply.

Independent financial advisors serve only as financial consultants and do not participate in the underwriting or trading of securities. Independent financial advisory firms fall into two major categories—those with a national client base and those which focus on specific types of financings or particular regions of the country. As the provision of financial advice is the focus of independent financial advisory firms, their orientation is often broader than advice on the mechanics of the sale of bonds and can include ongoing participation in a governmental unit's capital planning and credit rating. To monitor market reception of particular issues and credits, independent financial advisors must maintain contact with municipal bond trading desks. Strong contacts are developed and maintained by frequent presence in the marketplace; therefore, independent financial advisory firms with clients that are frequent issuers are more familiar with market activity. Since these firms do not participate in the securities market, there is no potential difficulty in representing the client as aggressively as possible through the negotiations with underwriters.

The financial advisory activities of investment and commercial banks are regulated by the Municipal Securities Rulemaking Board (MSRB). Rule G-23 of the MSRB regulates the conditions under which an investment bank or commercial bank may serve on a transaction as an underwriter and financial advisor. The rule makes a distinction between competitive and negotiated sales but is designed to protect the issuer from any possible conflicts of interest. Participation of the financial advisor as an underwriter in either type of sale requires the "informed consent" of the issuer. In a negotiated sale, the financial advisor must first resign from its formal advisory role and disclose in writing to the issuer any potential conflict of interest which may arise from the change in roles.[1] In a competitive sale, the financial advisor must receive written permission from the issuer to submit a bid. Some states have an outright prohibition on this practice and, in general, it is not considered to be in the best interest of the issuer. Because independent financial advisors neither underwrite nor trade securities, their activities are not regulated by the MSRB.

DUTIES OF THE FINANCIAL ADVISOR IN THE SALE OF SECURITIES

The principal role of the financial advisor is to orchestrate the debt issuance process to ensure that it is completed in a timely and cost-effective manner. The financial advisor is often the first outside consultant that a governmental agency will hire in the development stage of a new borrowing program. One of the initial tasks of the advisor is usually to evaluate the funding needs of the project and the resources available to the issuer to repay any debt to be issued. In this instance, a primary responsibility of the financial advisor is to recommend a financing plan that will result in the most favorable cost of capital for the issuer. The advisor should determine that the individual debt issue fits into the issuer's long range capital needs and that the maturity schedule and interest payments mesh with the existing obligations of the issuer. As a consultant whose focus is the overall financing of a specific project, the advisor can provide an objective assessment of the optimal blend of capital, including non-debt sources

---

[1] According to the MSRB, "the Board continues to believe that there is a prima facie conflict of interest when a municipal securities professional acts as both financial advisor to the issuer and purchaser of the issuer's securities in a negotiated sale . . . ."

such as governmental grants and pay-as-you-go financing, if appropriate. The financial advisor not only brings expertise in the capital formation process, but also provides support to the limited resources a finance officer may have available to devote to the financing. These duties usually include the following:

Assist in Selection of Members of the Financing Team

A public offering requires the participation of many parties: bond counsel, financial printer, bond trustee, paying agent, bond registrar or bond depository and, in the case of a negotiated sale, underwriters. The financial advisor is often requested to assist the issuer in the procurement of these specialists. Certain types of financings require an expanded group of professionals including independent certified public accountants, consulting engineers or other feasibility consultants. Project revenue supported bonds, for example, may require a report and opinion from a recognized consulting engineer that the project can be completed for the amount budgeted and that project revenues will be sufficient to meet operating costs and debt service requirements. Other types of financings, such as tax increment bonds and sales tax revenue bonds, require the services of a qualified consultant to make projections of revenues. The financial advisor should not be the party who supplies these studies; rather the advisor should use its experience to assist in the selection of the consultants and oversee their contribution to the financing process.

If the securities are to be sold through a negotiated sale, in which case the underwriting team is selected prior to the bond sale, the financial advisor usually assists the issuer in the selection. The selection of underwriters for a negotiated sale is frequently accomplished through a *request for proposal* (RFP) process. The financial advisor assists the issuer in defining the selection criteria and evaluating the responses. Factors to be evaluated might include a firm's experience and performance with similar financings, a firm's distribution and sales capabilities, the team to be assigned to the financing, and proposed fees and expenses. The type and size of the financing and the overall tone of the market should be considered in determining the size and composition of the underwriting team. For example, if the issuer is offering $200,000,000 of municipal utility revenue bonds, the financial advisor may recommend a senior manager with extensive experience in similar financings supported by an underwriting group comprised of both national and regional firms with a mix of institutional and retail base. Such a recommendation should be based on the advisor's opinion that the team composition will result in an efficient distribution of securities to get the best price for the issuer. The advisor may also recommend that the issuer conduct interviews with a limited number of firms to clarify items in their proposals and to see personally how the team members appear to work together.

Once the selection process is completed, the advisor should serve as the liaison between the issuer and the financing team to ensure that the interests of the issuer are well-articulated and observed throughout the financing. The advisor often has the lead role in organizing finance team meetings and takes responsibility for setting agendas, assigning tasks, establishing schedules and monitoring the issue's progress. In a negotiated sale, the advisor may be requested to oversee the senior manager's coordination of the underwriting group. For instance, an issuer may want the bonds to be distributed among members of the management group including regional, retail or minority firms in a pre-determined manner, such as a specific percentage of bonds allocated. In this case, the financial advisor would work with the group to develop an agreement among underwriters to document bond retention, allocation and other matters so that the issuer's intentions are carried out.

Coordinate the Rating Process

As examined elsewhere in this book, the rating process for municipal securities consists of analysis of a number of demographic, economic, financial, and management factors. Financial advisors are experienced in the credit rating process and can assist the issuer in the preparation of a clear, concise presentation on the financing. The advisor can make the task of both the issuer and the rating analyst easier by structuring a presentation that focuses on important credit factors. The advisor may provide the rating analysts with a financial ratio analysis that compares the issuer's credit quality to that of other comparable issuers or may prepare a comprehensive debt affordability analysis to demonstrate the ability of the issuer to afford the new debt. Such analysis may be helpful in demonstrating the potential for a higher rating or to validate an existing rating. For certain financings, the advisor may arrange for the rating agencies to make a site visit to allow the analysts to observe the economic environment and management style of the issuer.

In the days preceding release of the rating, the advisor serves as the liaison between the issuer and the analyst to answer any questions and to resolve any concerns regarding the issuer, the project or the financing. Upon release of the rating, the advisor will provide the information to potential bidders, investors, the press and others who should be informed.

Assist in Preparation of Offering Documents

The offering or official statement is the principal document that represents the issue and the issuer to potential investors and must adequately and accurately disclose all information necessary to make an informed investment decision. Just as important as the information included in the offering statement is the information that is omitted; the advisor, together with all other financing team members, must take care that pertinent information is not left out of the document and that all facts are fully disclosed. The advisor assists in the completion of the document and often arranges for its printing and timely distribution to bidders and major institutional investors.

The offering statement is usually developed in two phases. A preliminary offering statement is prepared prior to the sale, describing the issue, its terms and security, and the issuer. For a competitive sale, the financial advisor assists the issuer and bond counsel in drafting the offering statement, while in a negotiated sale the financial advisor also works with the senior managing underwriter and its counsel. A final official statement, containing the terms of the sale, including interest rates, maturity amounts and redemption provisions, is prepared immediately following the sale of the securities.

The Securities and Exchange Commission (SEC), in its Rule 15(c)2-12, has promulgated specific requirements to which issuers and underwriters of municipal securities must adhere. Although the Rule places primary responsibility for adequate disclosure on the underwriter, the underwriter is reliant upon the issuer to supply accurate and timely information. Specifically, these compliance requirements are that a preliminary official statement be available sufficiently in advance of the date bids are due on the securities, that the preliminary official statement be "deemed final" by the issuer prior to its release and that only minor changes may be made to the offering statement between the preliminary and final stages. It is the financial advisor's responsibility in a competitive sale to facilitate the underwriter's ability to comply with this rule. Although the SEC places the burden of compliance with the Rule on the underwriter, it is clear that issuers who prefer to sell their bonds through competitive sale must facilitate compliance with these requirements.

The advisor also arranges for the printing of the notice of sale in publications to satisfy all legal requirements and to inform the financial community of the upcoming sale. For a competitive sale, the financial advisor prepares the notice inviting bids which sets forth the terms of the securities and the conditions for award to the lowest bidder. This document must meet the specific condition of the market, as well as comply with state and local restrictions. Features such as early redemption provisions, permissibility of discount bid, the range of permitted interest rates, and the structure and amount of each principal maturity must be clearly described in the notice. In addition, the bid form must be clear and easily completed given the time constraints of a competitive sale.

Determine the Economies of Credit Enhancement

For certain issuers and under certain market conditions, the advisor may determine that credit enhancement such as a guarantee from a municipal bond insurer or letter of credit bank is advantageous or even necessary for market access. In such cases, the credit rating of the guarantor generally is substituted for the credit rating of the issuer. The selection of a credit enhancement provider should be done by a request for bid process. The advisor prepares and distributes a summary of the financing to prospective providers and recommends the selection of one or more on the basis of their bid cost to guarantee the debt service.

Generate Interest in the Securities

In a competitive sale the financial advisor performs many of the functions that an underwriter performs on a negotiated sale with respect to pre-sale marketing of the offering. The advisor must place the issue before all potential bidders and investors in order to maximize the competition for the offering. The financial advisor serves as the issuer's liaison with the investment and commercial banks expected to bid on the securities and maintains the issue's visibility before these potential bidders. Depending on market conditions and investor interest, the advisor may attempt to increase the number of bids to be received by actively contacting syndicate members to learn of their interest in the issue. A syndicate with significant excess participation in the days preceding the sale may be a candidate for splitting to form two or more syndicates. In other instances, the advisor may concentrate on the several syndicates that it knows will be bidding to answer all questions of the senior managers and their management groups.

If the financing is the first sale of bonds for the issuer, the return to the market after a long absence or if there is important information to relate, such as improved financial performance or a change in political leadership, the advisor may recommend one or more informational meetings with potential bidders, institutional investors and other parties prior to the sale. These meetings are typically held in the major national financial centers and in the regional financial center of the issuer's home state. Such meetings provide an opportunity for the issuer and its advisor to present the positive aspects of the upcoming sale and to address any concerns over the transaction.

In planning a competitive sale, the advisor should ensure that the bidding syndicates are able to utilize all available options to structure a competitive bid. These may include the flexibility to structure maturity amounts to create one or more term bonds out of several serial maturities, to create capital appreciation bonds, or to bid a deep discount on the bonds. The financial advisor may also pre-qualify the issue for municipal bond insurance in the secondary market so the lead manager can purchase the insurance for one or more maturities if the underwriter determines that the ensuing credit rating will result in a sufficient reduction in interest costs to offset the price of the insurance.

Evaluate and Negotiate Financing Terms

One of the financial advisor's primary responsibilities is to provide the issuer with an independent informed judgment as to the appropriateness of the financing terms offered on the day of sale. Such judgment is based on the advisor's knowledge of the credit quality of the issuer and its relative standing in the market, rates afforded comparable issues, the overall tone of the market, interest rate levels and costs of issuance for similar credits.

In a competitive sale, the actual interest rates and underwriting expenses to be paid by the issuer are established through the bidding process as set forth in the notice inviting bids. At the scheduled date and time, competing syndicates submit bids to purchase the securities. The financial advisor oversees this process, including the bid opening, checking each bid for compliance with the provisions outlined in the notice inviting bids and performing an independent review of the effective interest cost of each bid to determine the winning bid. The advisor recommends the award to the firm or syndicate of firms that has provided the bid which will result in the lowest overall cost of funds to the issuer. The advisor often appears before the issuer's governing body to recommend the award and compare the bids received to other issues concurrently in the market.

In a negotiated sale the terms (interest rates, reoffering yields, call features and the underwriters' compensation) are established through a negotiation between the issuer and the senior management group. The financial advisor represents the issuer in the negotiation process with the sole objective of obtaining the most efficient financing cost. The advisor should prepare a pricing book several days in advance of the sale to provide a basis for making pricing decisions. The pricing book contains information on comparable issues in the market and an update on recent market trends, including the expected demands of investors interested in the particular offering and recommended initial levels for all financing terms so that the issuer can make informed decisions during the negotiation process. The senior managing underwriter initiates the pricing process by recommending an initial interest rate and reoffering scale for the issue, along with the components of the gross underwriting spread, or discount. The advisor should compare these recommendations with its own findings and discuss possible modifications with the issuer. Once the issuer is satisfied that the initial terms are appropriate, the underwriting group is permitted to begin taking orders for the securities.

During the pricing of the bonds, the advisor monitors the market reception of the issue. The advisor maintains frequent contact with the issuer and schedules periodic conference calls to evaluate the sale. During the calls, revisions to the terms of the financing are considered in view of investor reception and overall market conditions.

Depending on the market factors and the size of the issue, this process can take one to two days. Once the issuer is satisfied with the terms of the sale and the underwriting group is prepared to underwrite the bonds, the advisor recommends to the issuer whether or not to accept the offer. On many occasions, the financial advisor can so improve the terms offered that its fee is more than offset by the savings in interest rates and transaction costs.

Review Results of Sale

Following any sale of securities, the financial advisor monitors the market reception and reoffering yields for several days as an indicator of the fairness of the pricing and how well the offering is received by investors. The advisor tracks the unsold balance of the issue held by the syndicate members on a periodic basis. In addition, the advisor compares the terms of the sale to other comparable issues in the market to provide a basis of evaluating the competitiveness of the rates the issuer received. The advisor should prepare a report for the client that analyzes the sale as measured by market absorption, level of bids compared to other issues in the market, market conditions and underwriting spreads. The advisor may be requested to prepare a post-sale analysis of the sales performance of the underwriting team members. This type of follow-up analysis assists the issuer in planning its future financings and in determining the composition of future financing teams.

Assist on Closing

The bond closing takes place one to three weeks after the bond sale. During this interim period the advisor participates in the completion of a number of critical tasks so the ultimate transfer of funds from the purchaser of the securities to the issuer and the transfer of the securities from the issuer to the purchaser is completed smoothly. First, the official statement must be finalized, printed and delivered to the purchaser within seven business days after the sale in order to comply with SEC rules. Next, the bond resolution, trust indenture, other legal documents and legal opinions must be finalized. Finally, the advisor arranges for the transfer of funds and for the investment of the proceeds, subject to arbitrage restrictions, to ensure that they are available when needed for the project or program being financed.

ADVISORY ASSISTANCE BEYOND DEBT ISSUANCE

The duties of a financial advisor may encompass a broader scope than the issuance of securities at any particular time. Although the advisor's primary responsibility is to assist in the successful execution of a financing that will result in the most favorable cost of capital to the issuer, the advisor should ensure that the debt issue fits into a comprehensive capital plan. The pressures of a pending bond sale do not create the best environment for development of a financing strategy. The long-term interests of the issuer will be better served through a plan of finance that gives consideration to the financing of all the issuer's future capital needs. The terms of each individual bond sale, including restrictions in the bond indenture covering such areas as the ability to issue additional indebtedness, rate covenants and redemption provisions, have long-term implications for an issuer's ability to manage its fiscal operations and meet future financing needs. The financial advisor that has first prepared a long-term plan of finance can ensure that the issuer's overall objectives, as well as short-term financing needs, are well-served by any particular bond issue.

As part of the long-term plan, the advisor may be charged with determining the amount and types of obligations that the issuer is projected to be able to afford, given the financial resources expected to be available to service any debt. After an examination of projected revenues and expenditures, including debt service payments, the financial advisor might determine that the original plan of finance would probably produce inadequate debt service coverage. To correct this situation and thereby improve the project's feasibility and the bond issue's creditworthiness, the advisor would develop a series of alternatives for the issuer to consider. These might include reduction in the project's cost and the size of the bond issue or, more likely, changes to the financing schedule or in the type of issue. For example, the total amount of the financing and the resultant debt service, might be reduced by funding the projects through several bond sales over a period of time rather than through one sale at the start of construction, reducing the amount of capitalized interest included in the use of proceeds. Similarly, capitalized interest might be reduced by issuing variable rate demand obligations during the construction period and switching to fixed rate bonds upon completion of the project.

Early involvement of the advisor can also facilitate an issuer's ability to integrate a particular type of financing into its current budgetary and cash management practices. A revenue bond financing for a water and waste water operation, for example, may necessitate the creation of a separate enterprise fund and the preparation of historical financial statements and projected results of operation before revenue bonds can be issued. In addition, revenue bond indentures often require new funds and accounts to be established and it is important that these fit into the existing structure of the issuer. Because this groundwork can take at least a year, an issuer must be made aware of requirements sufficiently in advance of the need for funds to accomplish the financing on schedule. An experienced advisor can oversee these efforts prior to actually assembling the financing team. In addition to benefiting from the advisor's knowledge and experience in similar situations, the issuer will save the expenses of bringing a financing team together earlier than necessary.

The financial advisor also keeps the issuer informed of new developments in municipal finance and the impacts on the issuer's specific situation. The development of new capital markets instruments was extensive in the 1980s and issuers current with the latest market developments were at a competitive advantage when it came to raising capital at the lowest cost. Equally important is an issuer's ability to respond quickly and decisively to changes in federal legislation that may either restrict the eligibility of projects or instruments that may be used or directly impact the financial operations.

For example, in the first few months of 1987, immediately following the effective date of the 1986 Tax Reform Act, many issuers were effectively locked out of the market while they struggled to decipher the various arbitrage rebate and reporting requirements. Issuers able to develop quickly a plan responding to the changes were prepared to enter the market in a period of extremely low volume and thereby obtained attractive interest rates. Financial advisors played a key role in disseminating information to issuers to aid in compliance with the new laws.

An active advisor will keep the issuer informed of market conditions even when not in the market with a specific financing. The advisor may track the reoffering rates for the issuer's securities in the secondary market and advise the issuer of particular investor interest or disinterest in their securities. The advisor also should monitor the market for opportunities to refinance a client's outstanding debt at lower interest rates or under more attractive terms.

An advisor's experience may be especially valuable in assisting an issuer having budgetary troubles by developing fiscal policies to address the concerns of rating agencies and potential investors. The advisor can provide insight into the market's expected response to an issuer's fiscal stress, assist in preparation of a plan to address these problems and develop a program to inform investors and the credit-rating agencies of the steps to be taken by the issuer. A well-planned program in which the budgetary difficulties are acknowledged, identified, and addressed can have a significant impact in defraying any potential negative effect on the cost of borrowing.

The financial advisor can also be an objective source of information in what is often a highly politicized environment. The advisor is frequently asked to appear before the governing body of an issuer in connection with a particular financing or to discuss other matters. The advisor may be asked to provide its opinion on the desirability of establishing financial policies to enhance the issuer's credit or market reception. In developing a long-term strategy, the advisor may be helpful in building a consensus among an issuer's political leaders that will be critical to successful implementation of the plan of finance. Prior to a specific financing, the advisor may be useful in explaining the recommended structure for the financing and provide a resource to the governing body to make informed decisions.

CONCLUSION

Municipal finance has changed in the past two decades. Chief finance officers of governmental units are now more like their corporate counterparts in their need to be current with the latest financing vehicles. A financial advisor provides an informed voice in the increasingly complex financing process. As the issuer's representative, the advisor can make a valuable contribution to the smooth implementation of the financing. In addition, the issuer receives an objective opinion as to the plan of finance and the terms and conditions of the issue.

The financial advisor's activities range from responsibility for a single financing to the creation of an overall debt management strategy. In any case, a main function of the advisor is to help the government entity achieve the most efficient cost of funds on the debt issued. The tasks involved in this function include the development of financing plans, assistance in selection of the financing team, preparation of documents, generation of interest in the securities to be offered and evaluation and negotiation of financing terms. Frequently, the advisor can negotiate rates and costs of issuance that provide significant savings to the issuer.

In other instances, the advisor takes on a wider range of tasks, including the development of long range financing strategy and the analysis of financial feasibility. This function is essential to the issuer in developing financing alternatives, assuring the affordability of a project and securing the issuer's overall financial objectives.

CHAPTER *35*

Information Flows in the Municipal Bond Market: Disclosure Needs and Processes

John E. Petersen
Government Finance Group

The municipal securities market is a large and varied sector of the financial markets. States, their local subdivisions, and the many derivative and accompanying authorities and districts enter the new-issue market with thousands of offerings each year. According to one recent estimate, there are 58,000 governmental units that may issue debt in a given year. There are approximately 1.5 million separately identifiable municipal securities outstanding (representing in the vicinity of 150,000 separately identifiable issuances).[1] Issues range in size from less than one hundred thousand to several hundred millions of dollars and in purposes financed from curbs and sidewalks to high-technology waste treatment facilities.

Despite the volume and diversity—or more properly, because of it—the municipal securities market has developed patterns and pro-

[1] The figures are based on CUSIP number assignments on outstanding tax-exempt debt. Since most municipal securities are sold in serial-maturity form, the 1.5 million number refers to individual maturities that are fully fungible in other respects, and the 150,000 issues refers to an estimated average of 10 years of maturity per issue. Based on remarks of Gordon Wooton at February 1988 seminars, "Informing the Municipal Bond Market: Disclosure Guidelines and Practices," and contained in the *Seminar Notebook*, GFOA, February 1988 (Hereinafter, *Disclosure Seminar Notebook*) Tab VI.

tocols for providing information to the participants in the securities market, including that ultimate recipient, the final investor. The details of these patterns will vary, depending on several factors such as the nature and size of the offering and type of issuer. Nonetheless, the commonalities are more important than the exceptions: the municipal market is undergirded by a large and complex flow of information that accommodates its daily business.

This chapter consists of two parts. The first describes the process, the players, and the documents involved in the disclosure of information concerning municipal securities transactions. It commences with a description of the new-issue marketing process, moving from pre-sale to the time of award and the closing on the issue. Next, it discusses the post-issuance disclosure process, stressing the reporting practices and market services that are intended to keep investors up-to-date on their holdings. It is important to note that the subject is approached from the context of market practice. That is, disclosure is described as an information-providing process integral to the ongoing operation of the market. The section's purpose is primarily descriptive: It does not attempt to prescribe a set of abstract standards or to sort out legal problems, but rather, describe how things have been done in market.

The second part deals with current developments and issues regarding information in the market. The last year and a half has been a busy one on the municipal disclosure front, a period during which all of the important actors and their associations have gotten involved. The second section briefly discusses the regulatory context of disclosure and the role of the GFOA Disclosure Guidelines, summarizes complaints with current municipal disclosure process, and concludes with a review of the municipal disclosure initiatives recently proposed by the Securities and Exchange Commission.[2]

---

[2] There is substantial activity on the municipal securities disclosure front, for reasons outlined in the remarks of Robert Baker, et al., in *Disclosure Seminar Notebook*, Tab 1. The GFOA Task Force on Municipal Disclosure in its report accompanying the recent revisions to the GFOA *Disclosure Guidelines for State and Local Government Securities* (Chicago: Government Finance Officers Association, 1988), called for continuing study of current reporting, distribution of official statements and information regarding security descriptions. See remarks of John Petersen, *Disclosure Seminar Notebook*, Tab II. The Municipal Securities Rulemaking Board has asked the U.S. Securities & Exchange Commission (SEC) to create a central repository under SEC rulemaking powers, suggesting issuers be responsible for filings. The GFOA in a separate letter to the SEC suggested that dealers might make such filings under rulemaking powers already possessed by the MSRB. For copies of the correspondence, see *Disclosure Seminar Notebook*, Tab VI. In September of 1988, the SEC published for comment the concept of a central repository, asking for suggestions as to its sponsorship, structure, and operation. *Report of the Securities and*

DOCUMENTS AND PROCESSES

New-Issue Team

The heart of the information-providing process before and through the time of a bond issuance is a team, a team that may consist of various participants that develop the documentation accompanying the offering of a security for a particular issuer. This notion of a team forming the "inner circle" of those that actually structure the issue and those in the "outer circle" that receive and use the information they provide is captured in Figure 35.1, which is taken from an earlier edition of a rating agency document. How the team works together—the steps by which new issues of municipal securities are brought to market—are well known in general, although documented in often anecdotal and prescriptive fashion.[3] Depending on the markets, the size of the issuer, the type of sale employed, the use of proceeds, and other variables, the players and procedures will differ in detail.

Generally, early in the process the issuance team is formed. The composition of the team differs depending on the nature and size of the issuance and the type of sale that will be employed; and, within the team, assignments as to disclosure responsibility will vary from deal to deal. Typically, at a minimum, the team consists of the governmental issuer (usually represented by a chief financial officer), bond counsel (a specialist in municipal securities law), and a financial advisor and/or the underwriter (acting in the capacity of a financial specialist to assist in the transaction). If it has been decided that the sale will be negotiated, the underwriter is selected by the issuer prior to the sale and becomes a member of the team. Depending on the size and nature of the transaction, the team may also contain other specialists, such as an engineer or other project-related consultant (who opines on the feasibility of the project if the issuance is to be secured by project-generated revenues), an auditor (who opines on the financial reports of the issuer), and, perhaps, an attorney representing the underwriter, if the transaction is a negotiated one. Also sometimes joining the team will be a credit enhancer or a counsel for a credit enhancer. The function of these professionals is to structure the issuance and to assist the issuer in the

---

Exchange Commission on Regulation of Municipal Securities, Washington, D.C., September 22, 1988 (Report on Regulation). The Report contains as Attachment B, SEC Release No. 26100 which was reprinted in the Federal Register.

[3] A recent and thorough discussion is found in Virginia Horler, Guide to Public Financing in California, San Francisco: Packard Press 1988, pp. 180–218. A view of the issuance process from the perspective of the underwriter and trader is given in Wilson White, The Municipal Bond Market—Basics, Jersey City, New Jersey; The Financial Press, 1985.

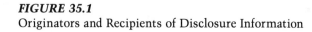

FIGURE 35.1
Originators and Recipients of Disclosure Information

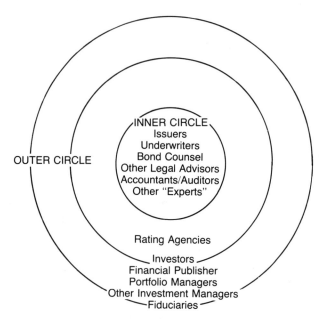

marketing of the offering including the production and dissemination of the offering-related documents.

Figure 35.2 provides a complicated, but essentially accurate, depiction of the parties producing information and the flow of such information throughout the new issue market. Generally, there is a timeline during which documents are produced and several echelons of recipients (financial services, dealers, the financial press) of such information ultimately culminating in the final investor. We will return to the flows of disclosure documents presently; but first, we examine the participants on the issuance team. The potential composition of the team, the inner circle, is depicted at the lower left hand corner of Figure 35.2. Among those listed are lawyers, engineers, auditors, the financial advisor and, depending on the nature of the method of sale, the underwriter. The presence of the underwriter is displayed in relief in Figure 35.2, since it will not be present in the team in the case of a competitive offering until the sale is consummated, but will be present during the presale period in a negotiated transaction. In terms of actual management of the issuance process and informing the market of a pending sale, the assignment of duties within the team can be distributed in a variety of ways. Table 35.1 provides an example of such an allocation of the responsibilities among

FIGURE 35.2
Information Flows: New Issue

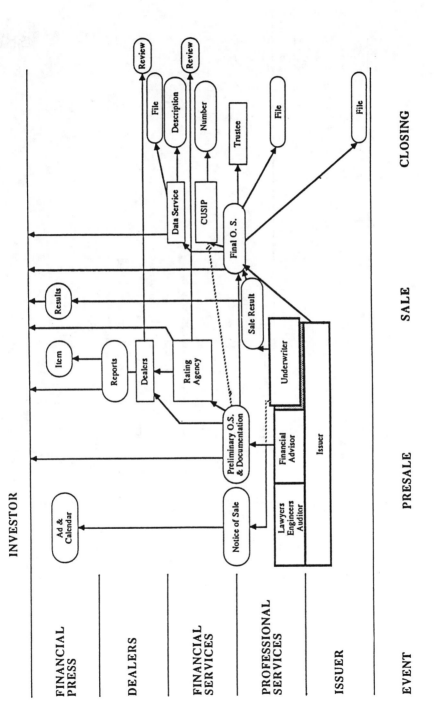

Table 35.1
Bond Schedule

City of
Proposed Bond Sale Schedule

Revised Draft (4/17/87)

Legend: CC—City
FA—Financial Advisors
BC—Bond Counsel

Date	Days Until Closing	Activity	Responsibility	
			Primary	Secondary
Mon—March 9	108	Make assignments of OS mark-up	FA	
Fri—March 13	104	Send marked-up copy of last O.S. (proof of cancelled Note Sale)	FA	CC
Thu—April 9	77	Organizational Meeting:	FA	
		• Decide on issue structure	CC/FA	
		• Use of in-house or financial printer	CC	
		• Arbitrage-rebate and related concerns	BC	
Mon—April 20	66	Meet with typesetter to obtain price quote (or FA sends out RFP for financial printer)	CC	
Tue—April 21	65	Send Hard copy of OS mark-up to City		
Fri—April 24	62	Send hard-copy mark-up of O.S. to typesetter	CC	
		Send rating agency presentation outline to City		
Wed—April 29	57	Receive and revise first draft of O.S.	FA	CC
Mon—May 4	52	Corrected first draft of O.S. returned to typesetter	CC	
Wed—May 6	50	Develop RFP for bond printing	FA	
		Mail RFP for bond printing	FA	
Thu—May 7	49	Receive and revise second draft of O.S.	CC	FA
		Determine final issue size and structure	FA	CC
		Develop notice of sale and bid form	FA	CC
Mon—May 11	45	Corrected second draft of O.S. returned to typesetter	CC	

		Notice of sale sent to City's printshop	BC	
Thu—May 14	42	Receive and revise third draft of O.S.	CC	FA
		Receive and revise draft of notice of sale	CC	FA/BC
		Draft presentation narrative/graphics	FA	
Wed—May 20	36	Receive final plates of O.S.	CC	CC
		Send proofed plates to city's printshop	FA	
		Send City mailing labels & Final rating agency document	FA	
		Apply to DTC for eligibility certification	CC	CC
May 18–22	38–34	Proposed timeframe for meeting/field visit with S&P	FA	
Thu—May 21	35	Rating meeting with Moody's (proposed) (and with S&P if the site visit is not accepted)	FA	
		Send draft legal opinion and bond copy to bond printer	CC	BC
Wed—May 27	29	Receive O.S. (200 copies) from printshop	CC	
		Mail O.S. and draft legal opinion to rating agencies with rating request	FA	CC
Tue—May 26	30	Advertise and mail O.S. to underwriters	CC	
		Award bond printing contract	CC	
June 8–9	17–16	Conduct analysis of comparable bond sales	FA	FA
Wed—June 10	15	Bid opening/Bid verification/Award	FA	CC
		Deposit good faith check of winning syndicate	CC	
		Review and revise first proof of bond	BC	CC/FA
		Return corrected first proof of bond to printer	BC	
Thu—June 11	14	Determine bond yield for arbitrage purposes	BC	FA
Tue—June 16	9	Review and revise final proof of bond	BC	CC
		Prepare nonlitigation certificates & other documents	BC	CC
		Complete revisions to final official statement	FA	
		Final O.S. (200 copies) from printshop	CC	
		Provide registration instructions to registrar	CC	Purchaser
Thu—June 25	0	Deliver set of final O.S.s to winning underwriter	CC	
		Prepare official bond sale transcript	BC	
		Conduct Delivery/Closing	BC	CC/FA

team members and the timing of activities in the case of a recent competitive issuance. According to this schedule, disclosure activities begin three months before the sale and three and one-half months before closing. In the case of this sale, duties are split among the issuer, bond counsel, and financial advisor. A detailed listing of sale-related responsibilities with associated dates and responsible parties is presented in Table 35.1.

Disclosure Roles of Participants

The disclosure roles of the participants in the municipal bond market are flexible. This arises from the unique regulatory framework of the municipal securities market are flexible, a subject discussed in more detail in subsequent sections. Issuers typically look to local and state laws, custom, and professional standards such as the GFOA *Disclosure Guidelines* for guidance in the process. Underwriters and financial advisors rely on the same sources with added structure regarding their duties provided by the rules of the Municipal Securities Rulemaking Board (MSRB). Bond Counsel and other experts also rely on the customary way of doing things, as well as their professional standards. All participants must be attuned to their responsibilities as implicit in the anti-fraud provisions of the federal securities acts. For this reason, they also pay attention to legal opinions and federal agency actions especially those of the Securities and Exchange Commission (SEC).

The following commentary discusses the typical roles of team members that might be involved in a sale, distinguishing between the competitive and negotiated sale.

Issuer. The issuer assembles the team of experts to assist in the structuring of the transaction and the provision of materials. These participants may be selected in a variety of ways and may be engaged on an issuance-by-issuance basis or for an interval of time. Smaller and infrequent issuers are as a practical matter very reliant on the expert team, the chore of which will usually be formed by a financial advisor, bond counsel, and in the case of a negotiated transaction, the underwriter and its counsel. The issuer, in some cases, may take the lead in producing the official statement and other sales-related documents. More likely, however, the issuer officials' job, aside from selection of the team, is two-fold:

(1) to provide basic information to be incorporated into the disclosure document; and
(2) to review that document and to attest to the veracity and comprehensiveness of the information contained therein.

Financial Advisor. Financial advisors (FAs) evidently are used in 60% of all issuances (based on the last two years of bond sales data).[4] FAs may carry on a variety of functions. When an FA firm is employed, it almost always will be in charge of the development of the official statement and the dispatch of other presale documentation to the market.[5] In those sales where a financial advisor is not present, usually negotiated sales or direct placements, that coordinative function will be carried out by the underwriter. Bond counsel or the issuer itself may also play the coordinative role in competitive sales, where there is no financial advisor.

Underwriter. In the negotiated sales, where there is no separate financial advisor, the underwriter typically will take on the role of managing the information flow to the market in connection with the sale. As discussed below, this function may be performed by special legal counsel (underwriter counsel) that handles the details. In those cases where the underwriter also serves as the financial advisor, it is subject to special MSRB rules to avoid or disclose potential conflicts of interest between the two roles.[6]

Bond Counsel and Other Lawyers. In both negotiated and competitive sales, bond counsel may perform numerous duties, but its traditional responsibilities revolve around opining on the legality of the issue, its tax status, and sundry legal documents such as the form of the bond and the transcript of the bond sale. The additional roles of bond counsel in preparing transactions for market and their corresponding responsibilities as regards to disclosure are extensive, flexible, and subjects of professional debate.[7] In negotiated transactions, the bond counsel's role may be supplemented by the underwriter's counsel, which typically has primary responsibility for the assembly of the disclosure documents and the provision of a disclosure letter that opines on the

---

[4] Calculated from data supplied by Municipal Securities Data Inc. by the Government Finance Research Center.

[5] John Petersen and Pat Watt (eds), *The Price of Advice,* Chicago: Government Finance Officers Association, 1986, p. 20.

[6] Municipal Securities Rulemaking Board (MSRB) Rule G-23. Under this rule, a firm can both act as FA and bid on the bonds if they are sold at a competitive sale and the issuer approves. While G-23 allows a firm acting as FA to resign from its advising role and to participate in an underwriting, this practice is prohibited by a stricter California law (Sec 53591 of the Code).

[7] For an up-to-date discussion of the roles of bond counsel, see Section on Urban, State and Local Government Law, *Disclosure Roles of Counsel in State and Local Government Securities Offerings,* Chicago: American Bar Association (1987), pp. 8–25.

adequacy and accuracy of disclosures. As the term implies, the client of the underwriter counsel is the underwriter. Issuer's counsel may be involved in the preparation of disclosure information, but the role is usually limited to opinions regarding the organization and good standing of the issuer, various procedural matters, and the existence of pending litigation.[8] Other counsel, such as that of a credit-enhancing entity, where an enhancement such as bond insurance or a letter of credit is involved, or that for a private beneficiary, as in the case of a conduit borrowing where the ultimate security is based on a private party's credit, may get involved in the transaction.

Other Experts. A bevy of other experts may be involved in the production of various "expertised" sections of the disclosure documents, namely: auditors (providing audit reports) and engineers and market analysts (providing feasibility studies and engineering reports). These additional experts are likely most important in various revenue-supported and private-activity transactions. Another important player in a transaction may be the provider of a credit enhancement, which may be represented by its own counsel. The underlying documents generated in conjunction with such studies, reports, or the provision of additional credit backing (the insurance policy, letter of credit, and the like) may be included in part or in whole in the official statement or incorporated by reference, with their availability noted. The GFOA *Disclosure Guidelines* note the importance of identifying experts and obtaining their permission to have their products included in the official statement.[9]

Disclosure Documents

A number of important documents and other informational items are generated before and at the time of sale of a new issue municipal security by the issuer or other members of the issuance team. As was shown in Figure 35.2, information supplied by the issuance team is digested by numerous recipients, which, in turn, add other elements to the information flow (such as the opinions of the rating agencies or the security descriptions of the data base providers). These derivative and secondary flows of information provided by the financial services industry, acting as members of the "outer circle" that intermediate information, will be discussed subsequently.

---

[8] *Ibid.*

[9] *Disclosure Guidelines for Offerings of State and Local Government Securities,* Chicago: Government Finance Officers Association, January, 1988, (Hereinafter, *Disclosure Guidelines*) Procedural Statement 9, p. 93.

Notice of Sale. An essential document in the competitive sale, the Notice of Sale is an official publication by the issuer that describes the terms of sale of a planned new offering of securities. The document, which can vary greatly in length and detail depending on custom, law, and circumstance, normally contains the date, time and place of the sale; the amount of the issue; the nature of the security; information concerning the official statement and delivery of bonds; the legal opinion; method of delivery; and, in the case of competitive issuances, a copy of the official bid form. Figure 35.3 is an example of a one-page Notice of Sale. Others may run to several pages.

The Notice of Sale typically serves as the basis for an official advertisement for the offering, which typically is printed in *The Bond Buyer* and in local newspapers. Figure 35.4 presents an excerpt of such an advertisement as it appeared in *The Bond Buyer*, indicating the availability of the complete Notice of Sale and the bidding form.

Official Statements. The official statement is the document (or documents) prepared in conjunction with sales of state and local government securities to provide information to prospective purchasers of the securities. Although other terms such as "prospectus" or "offering circular" are sometimes used in reference to the official statement, it is important to distinguish the fact that the document is "official" in the sense that it has the approval or authorization of the issuer thereby making it the issuer's document and that it is a "statement," a direct exposition of information concerning the offering.[10]

A requirement of the official statement is to provide a complete and accurate written statement that presents information in such a manner as not to misrepresent or omit any material fact that the investor needs in making an investment decision. Guidance as to those items to be considered for inclusion in the official statement is provided by the GFOA Disclosure Guidelines for Offerings of State and Local Government Securities, contained in the volume *Disclosure Guidelines for State and Local Government Securities* (*Disclosure Guidelines*).[11] The *Disclosure Guidelines*, since their introduction in 1976, have enjoyed wide acceptance as regards the content of official statements, a fact evidenced by the growing uniformity and completeness of official statements.[12]

---

[10] Joseph Daly, *A Guide to Official Statements*, New York: Law & Business, Harcourt Brace/Janovich, 1982, p. 1.

[11] *Disclosure Guidelines*, Guidelines for Offerings of State and Local Securities, pp. 17–54.

[12] See, for example, Robert Lamb and Stephen Rappaport, *Municipal Bonds*, New York: McGraw Hill, Second Edition, 1987, pp 230–232, and *Disclosure Guidelines*, p. 7.

FIGURE 35.3
Bond Advertisement for City of Cambridge, MA.

NOTICE OF BOND SALE

$3,360,000

City of Cambridge

Massachusetts

General Obligation Bonds

Sealed bids will be received by the City Treasurer of Cambridge, Massachusetts, at City Hall, First Floor, Office of the City Treasurer, in Cambridge, Massachusetts, on

JUNE 25,1986

until 11:00 A.M. E.D.S.T., at which time they will be opened and announced for the purchase of $3,360,000 general obligation bonds. The bonds are dated July 1, 1986 and will mature in serial amounts on July 1 in each of the years 1987 to 1997. Interest will be payable semiannually on each January 1 and July 1, beginning January 1, 1987. The bonds are not subject to redemption prior to their stated maturities. The bonds will be awarded on the basis of the lowest true interest cost (TIC) to the City.

The approving legal opinion of Messrs. Palmer & Dodge, Boston, Massachusetts, Bond Counsel, with respect to this issue shall be furnished to the successful bidder at the expense of the City. the legal opinion will be printed on the back of the bonds and will state that the bonds constitute valid and legal binding general obligations of the City. Additional information, including the Official Notice of Sale and the Preliminary Official Statement may be obtained from the undersigned at city Hall in Cambridge, Massachusetts 02139 (617) 498-9030 or from the City's Financial Advisor, Michael P. Buckley, Assistant Director, Government Finance Research Center, 1750 K Street N.W., Washington, D.C. 20006 (202) 466-2013.

/s/ JAMES P. MALONEY, JR.
City Treasurer

FIGURE 35.4
Bond Advertisement for School District of Charlotte County, Fl.

SUMMARY NOTICE OF SALE

$37,000,000

School District of Charlotte County
Florida
General Obligation Bonds, Series 1988

Sealed Bids will be received and considered at the Office of Robert L. Bedford, Superintendent of Schools, School District of Charlotte County, Florida, 1016 Education Avenue, Punta Gorda, Florida 33950, on

FEBRUARY 17, 1988

until 11:00 A.M., E.S.T., at which time they will be publicly opened and announced, for the purchase of all, but not less than all, of $37,000,000 School District of Charlotte County, Florida General Obligation Bonds, Series 1988 (the "Bonds").

The Bonds will be dated as of March 1, 1988, with semiannual interest payable March 1 and September 1, commencing September 1, 1988. The Bonds will be issued in book-entry form and will be registered in the name of Cede & Co., as nominee for the Depository Trust Company (DTC), New York, New York. The Bonds will mature on March 1 in the years and the amounts as follows:

YEAR	AMOUNT	YEAR	AMOUNT
1989	$ 810,000	1999	$1,745,000
1990	875,000	2000	1,885,000
1991	940,000	2001	2,035,000
1992	1,020,000	2002	2,200,000
1993	1,100,000	2003	2,375,000
1994	1,190,000	2004	2,565,000
1995	1,285,000	2005	2,770,000
1996	1,385,000	2006	2,990,000
1997	1,495,000	2007	3,230,000
1998	1,625,000	2008	3,490,000

Certain of the Bonds are subject to redemption prior to maturity as described in the Official Notice of Public Sale.

The Bonds will be payable solely from and secured by a prior lien upon and pledge of the proceeds of the levy and collection of a direct annual tax, without limitation as to rate or amount, upon all taxable property within Charlotte County, Florida sufficient to pay the principal of and interest on the bonds as they become due.

The Bonds are being offered for sale subject to the unqualified approving opinion, as to the legality and exclusion of interest on the Bonds from gross income for federal income tax purposes, of Nabors, Goblin, . . .

Source: The Bond Buyer.

As was displayed in Figure 35.2, in practice there frequently will be two iterations of the official statement: a Preliminary Official Statement (POS) and a Final Official Statement (FOS).[13] As the term implies, the POS is a pre-sale document that is distributed by the issuer and its agents to elicit interest in and provide information about the forthcoming sale. Typically, the POS is made available to all who request it and sent to potential underwriters (in a competitive sale), the rating agencies, and, perhaps, major institutional investors before the scheduled sale. Dealers, in return, may provide the POS to potential investors. The important thing to recognize is that the POS is a "draft" document and subject to amendment and completion prior to, at the time of, and subsequent to sale and prior to delivery of the final version. In the case of the competitive sale, the POS will typically be distributed one to two weeks before the sale of the bonds, as is shown in Table 35.1. Figures 35.5 and 35.6 are the cover sheets of a Preliminary and Final Official Statement, respectively, from a recent competitive offering.

Once the bonds are awarded, certain information may be added or appended, which is usually supplied by the underwriter and gives the terms of the sale, and the POS, so modified, is delivered by underwriters to investors. Note that when the issuer itself makes no changes to the POS after the sale, the POS "automatically" becomes the FOS.[14] According to MSRB Rule G-32, the FOS is to be delivered by the dealer (if provided by the issuer) to the buyer at least by the settlement date. Relatedly, the underwriter or financial advisor is to make the FOS available to dealers at least two days before settlement. If an FOS has not been prepared by or on behalf of the issuer, the underwriter, under the same MSRB rule, is to so disclose that fact to the customer and to send a POS if one was prepared.

In the negotiated sale, the procedures often are the same, except the existence, timing, and distribution are more flexible, as in the case of the notice of sale that was discussed above. The rules of delivery of information in the negotiated sale, as promulgated by the MSRB, are the same as for competitive offerings, except that they also require that the underwriter supply, in addition to or a part of the FOS, information concerning the underwriting spread, fees for distribution, and initial offering prices.

Offering Circular. An offering circular is a summary document frequently prepared by an underwriter providing information about

---

[13] *Disclosure Guidelines*, Procedural Statement No. 2, p. 81.

[14] The rules of the MSRB are contained in the *MSRB Manual*, April 1987, Commerce Clearing House (CCH). See also remarks of John Gardner, et al., *Disclosure Seminar Notebook*, Tab IV, for a summary of those rules most relevant to disclosure.

FIGURE 35.5
Preliminary Official Statement.

PRELIMINARY OFFICIAL STATEMENT DATED JUNE 24, 1987

NEW ISSUE

Moody's Investors Service, Inc:
Standard & Poor's Corporation:
(see "Ratings")

In the opinion of Bond Counsel, interest on the Bonds will be exempt under existing statutes and court decisions from all present Federal income taxes except as set forth in the section herein "Tax Exemption," and from taxation by the Commonwealth of Virginia.

$12,170,000 General Obligation Bonds, Series 1987

COUNTY OF LOUDOUN, VIRGINIA

Dated: July 1, 1987   **Due: July 1, as shown below**

The Bonds will be issued as fully registered bonds in denominations of $5,000 and multiples thereof. The Bonds will bear interest from July 1, 1987. Interest on the Bonds will be payable on July 1 and January 1, commencing January 1, 1988, by check or draft mailed to the registered owner of record on the registration books of the County maintained by the Registrar. Principal of the Bonds will be payable at the corporate trust office of the Registrar, which is First American Bank of Virginia, McLean, Virginia. The Bonds will be issued for the purpose of paying for various improvements, as more fully described herein under " Authorization and Purpose of the Bonds."

The Bonds will constitute valid general obligations of the County of Loudoun, and the full faith and credit and unlimited taxing power of the County is irrevocably pledged to the payment of the principal of and the interest on the Bonds.

The Bonds maturing on or before July 1, 1997 are not subject to redemption prior to their stated maturities. Bonds maturing on or after July 1, 1998 are subject to redemption prior to their stated maturities at the option of the County as more fully described herein under "Description of Bonds-Redemption."

AMOUNTS, MATURITIES, INTEREST RATES, AND PRICES OR YIELDS

Year	Principal Amount	Interest Rate	Yield or Price	Year	Principal Amount	Interest Rate	Yield or Price
1988	$610,000	%	%	1988	$610,000	%	%
1989	610,000			1999	610,000		
1990	610,000			2000	610,000		
1991	610,000			2001	610,000		
1992	610,000			2002	610,000		
1993	610,000			2003	610,000		
1994	610,000			2004	610,000		

FIGURE 35.5   *(continued)*

Year	Principal Amount	Interest Rate	Yield or Price	Year	Principal Amount	Interest Rate	Yield or Price
1988	$610,000	%	%	1988	$610,000	%	%
1995	610,000			2005	610,000		
1996	610,000			2006	610,000		
1997	610,000			2007	580,000		

(Plus accrued interest)

The Bonds are offered for delivery when and if issued, subject to the approval of validity by McGuire, Woods, Battle & Boothe, Richmond, Virginia, Bond Counsel, and to certain other conditions referred to herein. It is expected that the Bonds in definitive form will be available for delivery in New York, New York, Washington, D.C., or Richmond, Virginia, on or about July 29, 1987.

Dated: June   , 1987

This is a Preliminary Official Statement and the information contained herein is subject to correction and change. The securities described herein may not be sold nor may offers to buy be accepted prior to delivery of an Official Statement in final form. This Preliminary Official Statement shall not constitute an offer to sell or the solicitation of an offer to buy.

FIGURE 35.6
Final Official Statement

NEW ISSUE   Moody's Investors Service, Inc: Aa
                                 Standard & Poor's Corporation: A+
                                 (see "Ratings")

In the opinion of Bond Counsel, interest on the Bonds will be exempt under existing statutes and court decisions from all present Federal income taxes except as set forth in the section herein "Tax Exemption," and from taxation by the Commonwealth of Virginia.

$12,170,000 General Obligation Bonds, Series 1987
COUNTY OF LOUDOUN, VIRGINIA

Dated: July 1, 1987   **Due: July 1, as shown below**

The Bonds will be issued as fully registered bonds in denominations of $5,000 and multiples thereof. The Bonds will bear interest from July 1, 1987.

FIGURE 35.6 (continued)

Interest on the Bonds will be payable on July 1 and January 1, commencing January 1, 1988, by check or draft mailed to the registered owner of record on the registration books of the County maintained by the Registrar. Principal of the Bonds will be payable at the corporate trust office of the Registrar, which is First American Bank of Virginia, McLean, Virginia. The Bonds will be issued for the purpose of paying for various improvements, as more fully described herein under " Authorization and Purpose of the Bonds."

The Bonds will constitute valid general obligations of the County of Loudoun, and the full faith and credit and unlimited taxing power of the County is irrevocably pledged to the payment of the principal of and the interest on the Bonds.

The Bonds maturing on or before July 1, 1997 are not subject to redemption prior to their stated maturities. Bonds maturing on or after July 1, 1998 are subject to redemption prior to their stated maturities at the option of the County as more fully described herein under "Description of Bonds-Redemption."

AMOUNTS, MATURITIES, INTEREST RATES, AND PRICES OR YIELDS

Year	Principal Amount	Interest Rate	Yield or Price	Year	Principal Amount	Interest Rate	Yield or Price
1988	$610,000	6.00%	4.20%	1998	$610,000	6.40%	6.45%
1989	610,000	6.00	4.75	1999	610,000	6.60	100
1990	610,000	6.00	5.00	2000	610,000	6.80	100
1991	610,000	6.00	5.25	2001	610,000	6.90	100
1992	610,000	6.00	5.50	2002	610,000	7.40	NR*
1993	610,000	6.00	5.70	2003	610,000	7.40	NR
1994	610,000	6.00	5.85	2004	610,000	7.50	NR
1995	610,000	6.00	100	2005	610,000	7.50	NR
1996	610,000	6.20	100	2006	610,000	7.50	NR
1997	610,000	6.30	100	2007	580,000	7.50	NR

(Plus accrued interest)

*Not Reoffered

The Bonds are offered for delivery when and if issued, subject to the approval of validity by McGuire, Woods, Battle & Boothe, Richmond, Virginia, Bond Counsel, and to certain other conditions referred to herein. It is expected that the Bonds in definitive form will be available for delivery in New York, New York, Washington, D.C., or Richmond, Virginia, on or about July 29, 1987.

Dated: July 28, 1987

an issue expected to be offered for sale. It is often used to promote interest in the sale and is used to advertise the securities. In some cases where a financial advisor is employed a similar summary of key information may be sent to potential underwriters and investors. An example of an offering circular is provided in Figure 35.7. The important distinction is that the offering circular typically is not "the" official document of the issuer, but rather an informational piece that may be put out by another member of the issuance team.

CUSIP Number Applications. An important and universal use of the POS and FOS is in the obtaining of CUSIP numbers, as is required under MSRB Rule 34. Dealers and dealers acting as financial advisors are required to make application to the MSRB or its designee (currently the CUSIP Service Bureau, which is managed by Standard & Poor's Corporation), for the assignment of a CUSIP number no later than the date of award of the bonds or signing of the bond-purchase agreement. According to Rule G-34, in applying for the CUSIP number, municipal securities dealers are to provide eight items of information describing the issue. The purpose is two-fold:

(1) to assure a unique identification number is affixed to each municipal bond issue (or maturity) that differs in its terms and security; and

(2) to provide information that dealers may use in making confirmations to customers in compliance with MSRB Rule G-15.

As noted, different CUSIP numbers have been assigned to approximately 1,500,000 issues which essentially comprise the "known universe" of municipal securities.

The needed information for CUSIP number assignments, according to MSRB dictum, is to be provided by the submission of a Notice of Sale, the POS, legal opinion, or "similar documentation" reflecting the required information. Generally, POSs are sent to the CUSIP Service Bureau prior to the sale, with a FOS to be sent after the sale. The obtaining of CUSIP numbers is practically universal (such numbers are required by MSRB as a prerequisite to trading a security), and it is evident that the CUSIP Service Bureau should receive copies of virtually all official statements either prior to or soon after the sale of securities.

Sale Results. Immediately after a sale, the results are published in *The Bond Buyer*, the trade journal of the municipal securities market. Results are typically reported by the issuer's financial advisor or the underwriter. *The Bond Buyer*, using its listing of sales, follows up on advertised sales to obtain the results. Examples of recent results of sales

FIGURE 35.7
Offering Circular

FOR SERIES OF 1988B MINIBONDS

NEW ISSUE

In the opinion of Bond Counsel, under existing statutes and court decisions and subject to conditions described herein "Tax Exemption" interest on the Minibonds (1) will not be included in gross income for Federal income tax purposes, (2) will not be an item of tax preference for purposes of the Federal alternative minimum income tax imposed on individuals, and (3) will be exempt from all taxation by the Commonwealth of Virginia. Such interest may be included in the calculation of a corporation's alternative minimum income tax and may be subject to other Federal income tax consequences described in the section herein "Tax Exemption."

$2,000,000

City of Virginia Beach

General Obligation Public Improvement Bonds, Series of 1988B "Capital Appreciation Minibonds"

The $2,000,000 General Obligation Public Improvement Bonds, Series of 1988B (the "Minibonds") will constitute valid general obligations of the City of Virginia Beach, and the full faith and credit and unlimited taxing power of the City is irrevocably pledged to the payment of the principal of and the interest on the Minibonds.

Dated: May 11, 1988   **Due:** May 11, 1991

The Minibonds will be issued by the City of Virginia Beach as fully registered Minibonds and are being sold as Minibonds and will be issued in denominations of $500 and integral multiples thereof. Principal and interest payments will be made on May 11, 1991, when the Minibonds are due.

AMOUNTS, MATURITIES AND INTEREST RATES

Year	Principal Amount	Interest Rate
1991	$2,000,000	5.50%

The Minibonds are offered for delivery when, as, and if issued subject to the approval of validity by Hunton & Williams, Richmond, Virginia, Bond Counsel, and to certain other conditions referred to herein. It is expected that the Minibonds in definitive form will be delivered at the expense of the City to successful applicants, on or about May 11, 1988.

FIGURE 35.8
Sales Results

Results of Competitive Bond Sales

Compiled by Mary Stoever, Assistant Manager,
Susan Manzetti and Joanne Montalvo

ARIZONA

Somerton, Ariz. — $700,000 — Certificates of participation (Municipal Financing Program). Series 2, dated Jan. 20, 1987, were purchased on Jan. 20, 1987, by Rauscher Pierce Refsnes, Inc.

ARKANSAS

Mountain Pine Sch. Dist. No. 46 (Garland Co.), Ark., Jan. 18 — $625,000 — School bonds were purchased by Dean Witter Reynolds, Inc.

Results of Negotiated Bond Sales

Compiled by Ethel Chamberlain, Assistant Manager,
and Diane Williams

CALIFORNIA

Bay Area Government Association (Berkeley and Los Altos) Calif. — $4,515,000 — Certificates of participation, dated June 1, 197, were purchased through negotiation on June 16, by Kelling, Northcross & Nobriga, Inc.

Pajaro Valley Unified Sch. Dist. Calif. — $5,000,000 — 1987 Tax and revenue anticipation notes, dated July 1, 1987, were purchased through negotiation on June 26, by Ehrlich-Bober & Co. Inc.

COLORADO

Colorado Springs, Colo. — $13,325,000 — Hospital revenue bonds. Series 1987, dated Oct. 1, 1987, were purchased through negotiation on Oct. 13, by Dain Bosworth Inc.

FLORIDA

Nassau Co. Sch. Dist., Fla. (Fernandina) — $2,145,000 — Certificates of indebtedness (Bank Qualified). Series 1987, (MBIA Insured), dated May 1, 1987, were purchased through negotiation on April 30, by Trust Company Bank, Atlanta.

Source: The Bond Buyer.

for competitive and negotiated sales are contained in Figure 35.8, taken from *The Bond Buyer*. In addition, filings of sales results are made with the Public Securities Association (the records being maintained by Interactive Data under contract), with the MSRB (under Rule A-13, an underwriting information form must be filed for the purpose of calculating dues, which must contain the top page of the Official Statement), and with the U.S. Treasury (using Forms 8038 and 8038G or 8038GC) for purposes of tax compliance (the degree, if any, of public access to such information is unknown at this time). Finally, the results of major new-offering sales will be evidenced by "tombstone" advertisements frequently taken out by the winning underwriting firms in national circulation newspapers, typically *The New York Times* or *The Wall Street Journal*, and trade journals. Figure 35.9 provides an example of a tombstone.

Financial Services Publications

Thus far, the information provided to the market before and at the time of a new issue sale has been that originating from and under the control of the issuer and its issuance team members. But it is important that the market gets additional information fed into it. Much of the issuer's information is digested by and restated by various financial service firms, often with summaries of key information and opinions as to the investment quality and supplemented by other information, by various financial service firms. In the municipal securities market, the role of these translators and opinion makers is especially important because of the great number and variety of municipal issuances. In this section, we review the numerous services that render opinions on and summarize the information provided by issuers for purposes of informing the market.

Rating Agencies. The rating agencies—Moody's Investor Service, Standard & Poor's Corporation, and, in a supporting role, Fitch Investor Service—play a vital part in the municipal bond market. For a fee, each of the agencies, based on information supplied by the issuer and their own research, provides ratings of the securities being offered. There are nuances to exactly what the ratings mean and how they should be interpreted, but essentially they speak to the credit quality, the likelihood that bonds will pay interest and principal in full and on time. In the process of creating categories of comparable credits, they classify groups of bonds from prime quality down to those that are in default.

In the case of each rating agency, applications for ratings are typically made by the issuer or its agents prior to the sale of new issues (if application is not made and ratings are in effect for outstanding parity issues, these may either be withdrawn or rated without request). The details of how the agencies arrive at their ratings need not detain us here

FIGURE 35.9
Tombstone

$1,006,500,000
North Carolina Eastern Municipal Power Agency
Power System Revenue Bonds, Refunding Series 1987 A

The Bonds are dated March 1, 1987, due January 1, as shown below, and are subject to redemption prior to maturity, as described in the Official Statement.

In the opinion of Bond Counsel, under existing law and regulations, interest on the 1987 A Bonds is excluded from gross income for federal income tax purposes and will not be treated as a preference item in calculating the federal alternative minimum tax imposed on corporations and taxpayers other than corporations. See "Tax Exemption" in the Official Statement for a description of certain other provisions of law which may affect the federal tax treatment of interest on the Bonds. In the opinion of Bond Counsel, under existing laws of the State of North Carolina, the 1987 A Bonds, their transfer and the income therefrom (including any profit made on the sale thereof) are free from taxation by the State of North Carolina or any political subdivision or any agency of either thereof, excepting inheritance or gift taxes.

$ 10,940,000 7   % Serial Bonds due January 1, 2000—Price 100%
$ 12,500,000 7.10% Serial Bonds due January 1, 2001—Price 100%
$ 9,180,000 7.20% Serial Bonds due January 1, 2002—Price 100%
$ 30,000,000 7.30% Term Bonds due January 1, 2004—Price 100%
$ 71,175,000 $7^3/8$% Term Bonds due January 1, 2007—Price 100%
$199,780,000 $7^1/2$% Term Bonds due January 1, 2015—Price 100%
$422,925,000 $7^1/4$% Term Bonds due January 1, 2021—Yield 7.50%
$100,000,000 $7^1/4$% Term Bonds due January 1, 2022—Price 100%*
$150,000,000 $4^1/2$% Term Bonds due January 1, 2024—Yield 7.30% +

(Accrued Interest to be Added)

---

*FGIC Insured Bonds
+Original Issue Discount Bonds

The 1987 A Bonds are subject to the approval of legality by Wood Dawson Smith & Hellman New York New York Bond Counsel. Certain legal matters in connection with the 1987 A Bonds are subject to the approval of Poyner & Sprull Rocky Mount North Carolina, North Carolina counsel to Power Agency and Brown & Wood, New York, New York, counsel to the Underwriters

---

FIGURE 35.9   (*continued*)

Smith Barney, Harris Upham & Co.
Incorporated

Merrill Lynch Capital Markets   Salomon Brothers Inc.
The First Boston Corporation   Dillon, Read & Co., Inc.
Carolina Securities Corporation   First Charlotte Corporation
Interstate Securities Corporation   J. Lee Peeler & Company, Inc.
                    Wheat, First Securities, Inc.

March 26, 1987

---

and are covered elsewhere.[15] In the case of all the agencies, after analysis by assigned specialists, the rating is subject to review by a committee, communicated to the applicant (which may be the issuer, an underwriter, advisor, or investor), and then released to the media. Both of the major agencies continue to review ratings throughout the life of an obligation as long as information is regularly supplied. If the required information (annual financial reports, budgets, capital plans, etc.) is not supplied, the rating is withdrawn and the withdrawal is noted in the agencies' publications.[16]

The reach and importance of the rating agencies, especially Moody's and Standard & Poor's, is best evidenced by the preponderance of issuances that carry ratings. According to information provided by Securities Data Inc., for the period of January 1, 1985 through January 25, 1988, 93% of all issuances by dollar volume (some $490 of $527 billion) carried a rating by one or both of the two major agencies. (See Figure 35.10.) In terms of size of issue, those with ratings predominated among the larger issues (only 3% dollar volume of those issues in excess of $100 million did not carry a rating from Moody's or Standard & Poor's. See Figure 35.10). In terms of numbers of issues, over 76% carried ratings by one or both of the two major agencies, with the bulk of those issues that were unrated being of less than $5 million in size. (See Figure 35.11.)

---

[15] The rating agencies regularly publish their own explanatory volumes. See recent editions of *Moody's on Municipals: An Introduction to Issuing Debt*, New York; Standard & Poor's *Credit Municipal Ratings*, New York; and *Introduction to the Municipal Division*, Fitch Investor's Service, New York. In addition to these volumes, the agencies frequently publish special analyses of how particular types of issuers and transactions are evaluated from a credit perspective.

[16] Moody's estimates that 200 to 300 ratings are dropped a year because the issuers either issue new debt, but do not request a rating, or do not supply sufficient information for a review of the outstanding debt. This would represent 1 to 2 percent of ratings in effect.

FIGURE 35.10
Bond Ratings and Amount of Bond Issuances

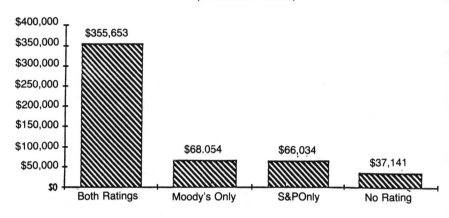

(A) January 1, 1985 to January 25, 1988
(in millions of dollars)

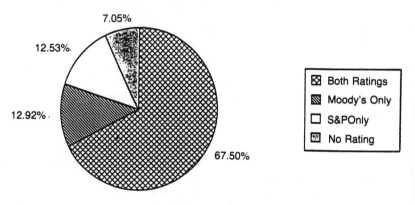

(B) Bond Ratings and Amount of Bond Issuances
January 1, 1985 to January 25, 1988

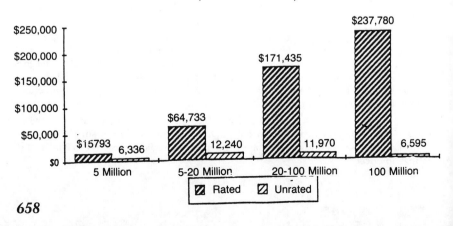

(C) Dollar Amount of Rated Issuances Versus Unrated Issuances
January 1, 1985 to January 25, 1988
(in millions of dollars)

FIGURE 35.11

Number of Bond Issuances by Ratings

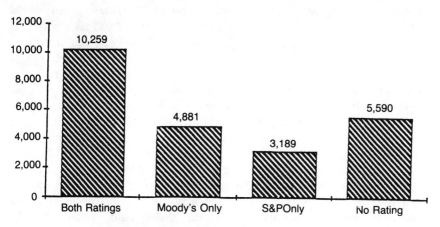

(A) January 1, 1985 to January 25, 1985

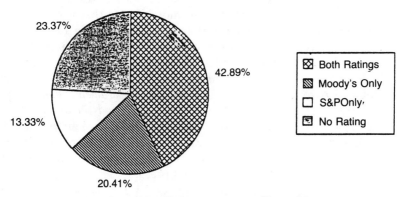

(B) Percentage Composition of Bond Ratings
January 1, 1985 to January 25, 1988

**Number of Rated Issuances versus Unrated Issuances
January 1, 1985 to January 25, 1988**

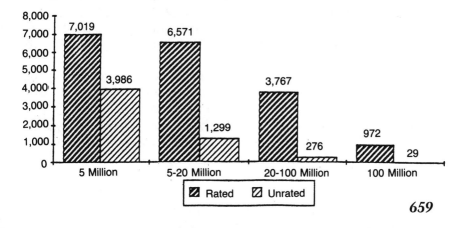

In addition to the ratings directly conferred on the issuances, it is important to take into consideration those issues that were reported as enhanced by some form of credit support. Considering only those issues that were "unrated," analysis indicates that 2,933 issues (52% of unrated issues) amounting to $28.6 billion (77% of the dollar volume of unrated issues) were not benefited by a credit enhancement. Since a security with a credit enhancement typically trades on the rating of the enhancing entity, this means that only about 10% of the number of issues and 2% of the dollar volume of issuances did not enjoy a credit rating from the two major agencies either directly or indirectly. The absence of any ratings was typically found in small issues, the average size for issues neither rated or enhanced being $1 million.

The rating agencies have large arrays of publications and services that inform participants of changes in ratings. Even announcements that they are reviewing ratings typically are widely reported in the financial press, especially for larger, widely-held issues. A brief overview of their services and publications follows next.

- **Moody's Investor Service:** Moody's publishes a *Municipal Credit Report* on each issue of $1 million or more in size that it rates. The reports are also issued when outstanding ratings are reviewed. The reports supply key information and the rationale for ratings. Moody's *Municipal and Government Manual*, which contains information on the ratings of approximately 20,000 municipal borrowers, is published annually. Also available are *Municipal and Government Manual Supplements* (published twice weekly), *Municipal Bond Survey* (published weekly, giving all new and revised ratings and news on upcoming issues), and *Moody's Bond Record* (published monthly, giving all bond and note ratings in effect). In addition to these documents, Moody's releases information to the financial press.

- **Standard & Poor's Corporation:** Standard & Poor's (S&P) publishes numerous periodicals that provide their ratings and a description of the credits. *CreditWeek* is published weekly and gives all new ratings and ratings withdrawn. A feature of the S&P Service is *CreditWatch*, which highlights potential changes in credits both in tabular form and with write-ups. In addition, S&P publishes a bi-monthly volume, S&P's *Municipal Bond Book*, that lists ratings changes, provides rating rationales on selected issues, and lists all outstanding ratings (approximately 10,000 ratings are in effect), with summary statistics (including the issuer's six-digit CUSIP number).

- **Fitch's Investor Service:** Fitch's performs its service on a more limited scale than the two larger agencies, rating an estimated 500 to 600 new issues a year. The results are reported in the intermittent publication of *Municipal Credit Analysis,* which discusses each issue or issuer separately, much in the fashion of Moody's credit reports.

Data Base Information Services. Several firms provide continuing information on new-issue and outstanding bonds. The role of the CUSIP Service Bureau was discussed earlier. The CUSIP numbers are fundamental to identifying and tracking securities throughout their life. In the event that the securities are altered so that they are no longer fungible with those having the existing CUSIP number, then dealers are required to apply for a new CUSIP number, according to MSRB regulation (Rule G-34). As noted above, the CUSIP Service Bureau generates security descriptions to be used in confirmations, to comply with Rule G-15. A brief explanation of these and the information incorporated in the security description is found in Figure 35.12. In addition, Standard & Poor's Corporation markets a more complete security description data base that is available as a printed publication with weekly updates.

Information is also provided by several firms maintaining electronic data bases. Usually the day after the sale of bonds, Kenny Information Systems and Securities Data Inc. will place summary information in their data bases, which are accessible by computer modem. The Kenny system's main data base, MUNIBASE, reportedly has information on 1.3 million outstanding issues and performs $7^1/2$ million changes in the data based each year, which are carried out by a staff of 100 persons. Both Kenny and Securities Data Inc. subscribe to CUSIP and the appearance of an issue in the CUSIP file not previously carried will trigger the entry of issues into their files. Reportedly, CUSIP, Kenny, and perhaps other firms regularly cross-check their files to see if issues have been assigned CUSIP numbers and if descriptions agree. Under its contract with the MSRB, the Service Bureau is required to place documents it receives for purposes of assigning CUSIP numbers in a room for public inspection and use by other users.

Interactive Data of the *Investment Dealers Digest* (IDD) also maintains data files for outstanding issues, reaching back into the original Investment Bankers Association new issue files of the 1960s (which IDD maintains under contract to the Public Securities Association, the PSA). Last, Moody's also offers electronically-delivered information on municipal debt, including a new issue calendar, listings of recent ratings activity and condensed versions of the credit reports. While an examination has not been exhaustive, it is useful to compare the items the services collect based on their sales literature. Table 35.2 provides a partial listing of the information carried by the above firms on their files. Data are updated as needed over the life of the issue.

As is true with all data bases, information can be "sliced" and "diced" to perform various functions, with different prices for the

FIGURE 35.12
Municipal Bond Description Service—Rule G-15

This rule requires, among other things, that brokers and dealers in municipal securities shall give or send to customers written confirmations which includes, if applicable, the following description of the securities for each transaction:

A. Required—Fixed at Issuance

1. Name of Issuer
2. Dated date and first coupon date
3. Interest Rate (discount rate, where applicable)
4. Maturity Date
5. If the securities are limited tax
6. If the securities are revenue securities
7. If the securities are
   a. Callable
   b. Puttable
8. On revenue securities, the type of revenue (if necessary to materially complete description)
9. Names of any parties other than the issuer obligated with respect to debt service (if necessary to materially complete description)
   a. Corporate Obligors
   b. Federal Guarantees
   c. Letters of Credit
   d. Insurance
10. If securities are available only in fully registered or book-entry form
11. Statement of the interest payment cycle on non semi-annual periodic interest securities
12. If the securities are original issue discount securities
13. If the securities are floating or variable rate securities
14. If the securities are "stepped coupon" securities

B. Required—Fixed Post Issuance

1. Statement that securities have been
   a. Called
   b. Pre-refunded
   c. Escrowed to Maturity
   d. Defaulted
2. Redemption date and price of securities which have been
   a. Called
   b. Pre-refunded
   c. Escrowed to Maturity
3. Secondary market security enhancements:
   a. Insurance
   b. Letters of Credit
   c. Puttable (Dates & Prices)

TABLE 35.2
Municipal Bond Information Available from Financial Data Services

Descriptive Information	Securities Data	Kenny Information	Moody's Credit	Interactive Data
Total Principal Amt.	x	x	x	x
Name of Issuer	x	x	x	x
Title of Issue	x	x	x	x
Date of OS				
Type of Issue	x	x	x	x
Date of Obligations	x	x	x	x
Interest Payment Dates	x	x	x	x
Date from which Interest Paid			x	
Identification of Special				
Interest Features	x		x	
Denomination of Securities			x	
Description of Security or				
Source of Payment	x	x	x	
Identification of Trustees,				
Registrars and Paying Agents	x		x	
Redemption Features	x	x	x	
Put Features	x	x	x	x
Maturity Date	x	x	x	x
Tax Status	x	x	x	
Credit Enhancement	x	x	x	
Book Entry Registration				
Identification of Repository		x		
Identification of Counsel	x	x	x	
Ratings	x	x	x	x
Designation as New Issue			x	
Date and Delivery of Issue	x	x	x	
Purpose of Issue	x	x	x	x
Relevant Legal Features			x	
Relation to Other Securities			x	
Contact Personnel			x	
Description of Enterprise	x	x	x	
Debt Structure			x	x
Debt Service Schedule			x	x
Overlapping Governmental				
Debt			x	
Historical Data			x	
Yield	x	x	x	x
Call Date	x			x
Coupon Date	x	x		x
Original Discount Price				x
CUSIP	x	x	x	x

different assemblages and scope of data. An example is provided by the types of information that can be derived from Kenny Information Systems, ranging from CUSIP number identification through current price quotes (see Figure 35.13).

Repositories. In addition to the publications and listings of key items, two firms retain official statements in repositories that make copies available for purchase. *The Bond Buyer*, using its microfilming facility, Munifiche, provides copies of official statements on both a subscription and individual basis.

Reportedly, OSs for virtually all issues sold since the late 1970s exceeding $1 million in size are available from *The Bond Buyer*. Securities Data Inc. also retains official statements that are available in hard copy for a charge. It has collected over 25,000 official statements for issuances since 1980, initially collecting those for issues over $5 million, but recently (since 1985) collecting all it can acquire.[17] The Investment Dealers Digest also maintains a data base of official statements, starting as of 1985.

Officials statements are available from Investment Dealers Digest and Securities Data Inc. for $30 to $40 a copy. *The Bond Buyer* microfilm copies are available for 50 cents per page and a minimum change of $20.00 per official statement.

Both *The Bond Buyer* and Security Data obtain OSs on a voluntary basis from underwriters, dealers, bond counsel, and FAs. However, there is an enforcement mechanism at work because the contributors are also data users. The industry rankings of firms (which is important for competitive reasons) depends on their reporting information in full and timely fashion.[18]

Recently, Securities Data Inc. was acquired by the International Thompson Organization, which owns *The Bond Buyer*, and the two OS repositories are in the process of being pooled. While an inventory of the combined coverage of the merged repositories evidently remains to be done, Securities Data Inc. estimated that they had OSs on file for about 80% of all issuances and 95% of the dollar volume of publicly traded bonds sold since 1980, and they actively pursue missing sales and items. Supplementing those holdings with *The Bond Buyer* files should increase the coverage of the repositories.

Those transactions that are not accounted for by OSs (and where firms may have difficulty in getting full security descriptions as used in the data base systems discussed above) reportedly fall into

---

[17] Remarks of Joseph Kelly, *Disclosure Seminar Notebook*, Tab VII.

[18] *Ibid.*

Data Base Description

CUSIP Scan—Identifies the CUSIP number using the characteristics of the bond.

Enter bond description: CA, CALIF, 550, 93

130618EP2*	6	1-74	CALIFORNIA ST	5.500	6	1-93		N
130618JE2*	6	1-79	CALIFORNIA ST	5.500	6	1-93		N
130618MZ1	8	1-79	CALIFORNIA ST	5.500	8	1-93	PUT-M	N
130618NA5	8	1-79	CALIFORNIA ST	5.500	8	1-93	UNIT-	N
130774DZ2*	5	1-72	CALIFORNIA ST UNIV REV	5.500	11	1-93	HSG S	C

CUSIP Inquiry—Provides full description of bond identified above.

Enter CUSIP number: 130618MZ1

| 130618MZ1 | 8 | 1-79 | CALIFORNIA ST PUT-MERRITT-TOPS -REG- | 5.500 | 8 | 1-93 | UNIT- N |

PUT LOC - MAR MID SER AC   CA

OPT PUT 4- 1-86 100.000 1 TIME

NOTIF DATES: 90 THRU 30 DAYS B4 PUT

*SECURITY CUSIP #130618JH

*UNIT CUSIP #130618NA

CUSIP Inquiry—Provides full description including called bond data.

Enter CUSIP number: 011830SHO

| 011830SH0 | 12 | 1-81 | ALASKA ST HSG FIN CORP MTG REV 2ND SER | 11.250 | 12 | 1-12$ | N |
| AA/ A+ | | | SNGLE FAM SPL @ A. T. LOC - CRCKR NAT | | | | AK |

OPT PUT 12- 1-86 100.000 & EA YR

NOTIF DATES: 60 DAYS B4 PUT

MAND SKG FUND BY LOT BEG 12- 1-97

DTD 12-01-81 1ST CPN 06-01-82

*** DTC ELIGIBLE ***

*** MSTC ELIGIBLE ***

CALLED BOND DATA: TYPE	DATE	PRICE	REF DATE
P	12-01-85	100.000	11-12-85
P	12-01-84	100.000	11-07-84

Mini-Universe Evaluation—Provides current prices for selected issues (available to J.J. Kenny customers.)

Enter CUSIP number followed by $:499746FQ3$

| 499746FQ3* | 9 | 1-75 | KNOXVILLE TENN ELEC REV SER L N/C | 7.000 | 9 | 1-86 | N |
| AA/ AA | | | | | | | TN |

*** DTC ELIGIBLE ***

QUOTED AS OF 1/28/86 YLD = 6.22 $100.427

Source: Kenny information systems, Kenny group, 55 Broad Street, New York, NY 10004 (212) 530-0925.

the categories of private placements, locally sold issues (not reported in the financial press), and local hospital, nursing home, and housing issues, and industrial development bonds.[19] Also, the floods of new issues that occurred in late 1985 and the summer of 1986 generated by impending tax legislation led to logistical problems in obtaining OSs and recording data.[20]

Costs of Information Services. Information provided by the rating agencies and data base services entails costs, which may be borne by various participants in the market. Issuers typically pay fees for the ratings and, in competitive transactions, for the costs associated with the printing and distribution of official statements. In the case of negotiated offerings, these expenses may be paid by the underwriter. Ratings range in cost from a thousand dollars for small, uncomplicated issues to several thousands of dollars for large, complicated issues. Official statement printings costs vary greatly, but a charge of $5,000 to $10,000 for a print run of 1,000 copies is a reasonable approximation, with the marginal costs of $1 to $2 per added copy. (This figure does not include the costs of writing and editing the texts or of distribution.)

A systematic job of collecting the prices of various financial information services has not been attempted, but the following items provide examples of what it costs in 1988 to stay informed under the existing information system.

For example, Standard & Poor's weekly *CreditWeek* costs $1,300 a year and its bi-monthly *Municipal Bond Book,* $700 a year. The *Municipal Bond Description Service,* published weekly, costs $1,400 annually, as does a subscription to the *Daily Bond Buyer.* Obtaining copies of individual official statements from a repository costs $30 to $40 per document or $0.50 per reproduced page. Subscriptions to receive copies of all new OSs of particular categories or regions are available from *The Bond Buyer* for several hundred dollars a year. Connect time on electronic data bases runs about $175 per hour, although lower rates for heavier usage are available. CUSIP numbers cost $70 per issue, and subscriptions to the hardcopy CUSIP manuals (with supplements) are $1,350 per year. There are approximately 3,000 CUSIP subscribers.

As the above indicates, the information system in the municipal bond market tends to work on a wholesale basis (large quantities of information going to a limited number of subscribers) and is geared toward dealers, traders, major institutional investors, and trust

---

[19] Remarks of Gordon Wooton, *Disclosure Seminar Notebook,* Tab VII.

[20] Remarks of Joseph Kelly, *Disclosure Seminar Notebook,* Tab VII.

departments. After the initial sale and the receipt of the OS, individual investors are likely to be largely reliant on the information that is filtered through to them from the financial information services industry by way of their dealer representative or such information that they may obtain directly from the issuer.

Secondary Market Information

The post-issuance or secondary market in municipal securities is as far-flung and diverse as the primary markets, ranging from well-known issues that trade frequently and for which there is a reasonably continuous market (and, not surprisingly, lots of information) to small issues that never have nor ever will be traded after their initial distribution. The market is practically exclusively over the counter—there being hardly any listing or trading at the exchanges—and there is no electronic marketplace to capture the latest trades. The exact size of the municipal secondary market is unknown, but it has been estimated at one to two times the size of the new issue market in ordinary times.[21]

Generally, dealers buy securities into inventory (rather than act as brokers) and resell them at a markup. Except for the well-known dollar bonds, prices are quoted in yield. Because of the variety and number of municipal securities, the trader in municipals has some special information needs. The most widely circulated trading information is found in the *Blue List*, published daily by Standard & Poor's, which lists bonds offered and offering prices or yields. Typically, over $1 billion worth and 12,000 separate issues are listed daily. It is available both in published form or through computer on-line services (the Blue List Ticker). *The Bond Buyer* also provides a ticker service (also available through computer on-line services) named MuniFacts that gives both primary and secondary market pricing information. In addition to Munibase, the firm of J. J. Kenny has a wire service (Kenny Wire) that goes to several hundred dealers listing securities that are looking for quotes.

The above media, along with various pricing services (which provide estimates of bond prices on most recent actual trade results and/or estimates based on previous price relationships) form the basic market-derived information as to prices at which securities are being offered or traded.

Dealer Disclosure. Pricing information is vital to dealers, not only in the daily conduct of their business but also, supposedly, in

---

[21] *Fundamentals of Municipal Bonds*, Public Securities Association, New York, 1987, p. 79.

conforming with MSRB rules regarding the confirmation of transactions, suitability of investment, fair dealing, and to avoid running afoul of the anti-fraud provisions of the federal securities acts.

But while the price to be paid for the security is an important disclosure, it is only one of the items to be incorporated into the confirmations of sales either to other dealers or customers. As the market has become more complicated, the confirmation has increasingly taken on the character of a disclosure document. The requirements for confirmations are covered by Rules G-15 (customers) and G-12 (dealers) of the MSRB. Rule G-15 requires that in a transaction in municipal securities with a customer, a municipal securities dealer shall give the customer a written confirmation of the transaction containing the following information:

> (E) description of the securities, including at a minimum the name of the issuer, interest rate, maturity date and if the securities are limited tax, subject to redemption prior to maturity (callable), or revenue bonds, an indication to such effect, including in the case of revenue bonds the type of revenue, if necessary for a materially complete description of the securities, and in the case of any securities, if necessary for a materially complete description of the securities, the name of any company or other person in addition to the issuer obligated, directly or indirectly, with respect to debt service or, if there is more than one such obligor, the statement 'multiple obligators' may be shown.

The security description services discussed above are generally relied upon to provide the content used to identify the issues on confirmations. As noted, security description files are organized by CUSIP numbers.

Adequate description of securities in confirmations is not the only or, perhaps, the most important informational needs of traders and dealers. Fulfillment of Rules G-17 (Fair Dealing) and G-19 (Suitability of Recommendations) may be interpreted to mean that a dealer cannot recommend purchase or sale of securities without reasonable knowledge or inquiry into the information about the security or the issuer.[22]

Issuer Disclosure. The role of issuer-generated information in the secondary market is one that has received limited attention in the past.[23]

---

[22] See Deborah Carter, "Disclosure in the Secondary Municipal Securities Market" in *Disclosure Seminar Notebook*, Tab IV.

[23] Robert Doty in his paper "State and Local Government Securities Disclosure: Can Perfection be Achieved" (contained in *Disclosure Seminar Notebook*, Tab VI, surmised that secondary market disclosure has received little attention to date because there has

In 1985, the SEC considered the possible imposition of current reporting disclosure requirements for municipal issuers. It rejected them on the basis that the costs of a periodic reporting requirement were not justified with respect to seldom traded issues and that frequent issuers already disclosed through new-issue information.[24]

A large-scale survey of market participants in late 1984 was conducted at the outset of the *Disclosure Guidelines* revision process to identify disclosure problem areas. It showed secondary market concerns were a relatively low priority (18th out of 22 topic areas in importance).[25] A subsequent survey done in 1985 by the National Federation of Analysts identified frequent difficulty in obtaining information in the case of tax-exempt health care, housing, and industrial development bonds, but seldom in the case of general government obligations and traditional public-purpose utility bonds; nor did any governmental-purpose issuers refuse to supply information.[26]

At present, it appears secondary market disclosure practices are determined by the size of the issue, the frequency of their issuances, and the nature of the borrower. Issuers may use a variety of documents and media to disclose on a recurring basis. Frequent issuers may fulfill that function by the regular production of new issue official statements, which not only informs new investors, but up-dates existing owners of debt as well. Furthermore, issuers produce annual financial reports that are distributed to the financial information services, especially the rating agencies, and to others, such as analysts and investors, that request them.

For most governments, unless they are frequent issuers or large enough to justify specialized reports to bondholders, the key document for current reporting to the financial markets is or should be the *comprehensive annual financial report* (CAFR). While their format and detail may vary somewhat, the content of the CAFR is well established, consisting of audited general purpose financial statements, individual

---

been relatively little demand by investors for continuing credit information. For example, the *Bond Buyer* attempted to include annual reports in its Munifiche system and found there to be insufficient demand to justify the service (pp. 14–15).

[24] U.S. Securities and Exchange Commission, Report in Response to Congressional Inquiries Relating to Government and Municipal Securities Regulation, Letter of Chairman John S.R. Shad to Hon. Timothy Wirth, Chairman, Subcommittee on Telecommunications, Consumer Protection and Finance, Washington, D.C., March 12, 1985.

[25] John Petersen and Michael Buckley, "GFOA/NABL Survey Identifies Concerns of Municipal Market Regarding Disclosure Practices," *Municipal Analyst Forum*, National Federation of Municipal Analysts, July 1985, pp. 1, 9.

[26] "Results of Survey on Adequacy of Disclosure of Credit Information for Tax Exempt Bonds," National Federation of Municipal Analysts, September 1985, p. 3.

fund statements, which include footnotes and are accompanied by introductory and statistical sections.[27] The CAFR provides ample opportunity to provide the information needed by analysts and investors. Because the documents are comprehensive, having several objectives other than just informing investors in a government's securities, CAFRS are not inexpensive to produce and often, given the large number of accounts and schedules contained, are very bulky documents.

An example of the kind of debt-related disclosure information that can be provided in the CAFR is illustrated in Figure 35.14. It should be noted that the commentary shown, drawn from the introductory sections' letter of transmittal, is accompanied by extensive statements, schedules, and notes covering every aspect of the entity's financial operations and condition. The standards of CAFRs are established by the *Government Accounting Standards Board* (GASB). While not all states and localities are required to prepare financial statements following *generally accepted accounting principles* (GAAP), the great majority of those of financial significance are.[28] The use of GAAP is strongly urged by the GFOA Disclosure Guidelines. Results reported elsewhere indicate that a large (70 percent) and growing percentage of local governments are required by state law or local to prepare their financial reports in conformance with GAAP. In addition, most are audited annually according to generally accepted auditing standards by an independent auditor.[29]

Some large issuers also produce periodic special reports to bondholders to inform them of trends and developments, a practice that is easier since the advent of registered bonds. Such reports, which are intentionally in very summary for (sometimes referred to as popular reports), may be released annually or quarterly and contain informal (unaudited and aggregated) financial information and brief commentary regarding recent events of interest. The scope of potential interest in such reports means they are typically limited to larger general government or major utility issuers. An excerpt from such a report by a major electric utility issuer is shown in Figure 35.15.

The municipal market's evolution toward more flexible financing vehicles (which allow for the restructuring, repricing, or refinancing of outstanding debt) and the substantial decline in interest rates (which

---

[27] Authoritative guidance to state and local government financial reporting is provided by *Government Accounting, Auditing and Financial Reporting*, Government Finance Officers Association, Chicago, 1988. The GFOA also publishes a series of financial reporting books to provide examples of reporting techniques in specific areas (*Financial Reporting Series*).

[28] *Report on Regulation*, p. 20.

[29] Municipal Finance Officers Association, *Surveying the States*, Chicago, Illinois, 1984, pp. 19–25.

FIGURE 35.14

Excerpt from Milwaukee Metropolitan Sewerage District 1986
Comprehensive Annual Financial Report

| | Comparative Revenue Schedule | | | | | |
| | 1986 | | 1985 | | Increase | Percentage |
	Amount	Percent of Total	Amount	Percent of Total	(decrease) over 1985	Increase (decrease)
Nonoperating revenues:						
Tax levy	$69,307,449	89.4%	$70,312,038	91.4%	($1,004,589)	(1.4%)
Interest earned on restricted assets	6,726,179	8.7%	4,271,135	5.5	2,455,044	57.5
Capital charges— communities outside the District	2,153,917	2.8	2,368,974	3.1	(215,057)	(9.1)
Other	(667,558)	(0.9)	7,652	—	(675,210)	(8824.0)
	$77,519,987	100.0%	$76,959,799	100.0%	$ 560,188	0.7%

Expenses

District expenses for the year 1986 amounted to $50,084,871. This represented
a decrease of 1.8% from the 1985 total of $50,989,494. A comparative
breakdown of the expenses by type is shown on Exhibit B-1.

Increases in salaries and wages due to management merit increases and in
accordance with collective bargaining agreements were more than offset by
increased capitalization of salaries and wages to various construction projects.

Energy costs for natural gas and fuel oil decreased 20.9% over 1985
primarily because of more favorable rates for natural gas, and the continued
efforts of the plant energy management program.

Solids waste disposal costs were reduced by 21.7% or $536,170 in 1986.
Approximately $300,000 of that reduction can be attributed to lower hauling
costs of Agri-Life to farmland because of a new hauling contract that
became effective at the end of 1985. Reduced hauling of Agri-Life to Jones
Island as a result of construction problems experienced at both plants early
in the year accounts for the balance of the lower costs.

Property, plant, and equipment

As of December 31, 1986, total property plant and equipment amounted to
$1,194,646,262 before accumulated depreciation of $107,119,622. Additions
during 1986 total $191,516,542 with deductions of only $1,387,902. All fixed
assets are recorded at cost. Depreciation is provided using the straight-line
method over estimated useful lives of five to one hundred years depending
on the specific assets. A summary of fixed asset changes and related
depreciation expenses by major account classification is shown in Note 10 to
the financial statements.

FIGURE 35.14 (continued)

Debt administration

General obligation indebtedness outstanding at December 31, 1986, amounted to $248,980,000. Included in this amount is $183,500,000 of general obligation bonds sold by the District. The remaining balance represents $65,480,000 of outstanding bonds issued by Milwaukee County on behalf of the District. In accordance with legislation adopted in 1982, the District became obligated to annually pay to Milwaukee County amounts sufficient to pay principal and interest on bonds issued by Milwaukee County on behalf of the District which remain outstanding at December 31, 1983. Prior to this legislation, the District could not issue bonds and relied on Milwaukee County to issue bonds for its capital improvements.

The following tabulation presents general obligation bonds issued by the District:

Date of Issue	Amount	Average Life in Years	Effective Interest Rate	Interest Cost per Borrowed Dollar
April 19, 1983	$ 41,500,000	10.203	8.2030	82.4 cents
July 19, 1984	$ 32,000,000	8.964	9.2985	83.1 cents
May 1, 1985	$110,000,000	7.950	8.4903	67.7 cents

The District's bonds continue to have the same ratings which they carried for the past four yesrs. These ratings are as follows

	Moody's Investors Service	Standards & Poor's
General obligation bonds	Aa	AA

Several useful indicators are shown to reflect the current District debt position:

Year	General Obligation Bonds Outstanding	Percentage of Bonded Debt to Equalized Value	Bonded Debt Per Capita	Ratio of Debt Service to Operating Expenses
1986	$248,980,000	1.22%	$271.97	61.0%

Exhibits B-8 to B-13 in the statistical section of this report present more detailed information about the District's debt position.

FIGURE 35.15
Excerpt from a Summary Current Report

Massachusetts Municipal Wholesale Electric Company
Statements of Financial Position
March 31, 1988 and 1987
(Unaudited)
(Dollars in Thousands)

| | March 31, | |
	1988	1987
ASSETS		
Electric Plant		
In Service	$ 388,627	$ 386,934
Accumulated Depreciation	(62,158)	(48,351)
	326,469	338,583
Under Construction	673,130	582,317
Nuclear Fuel-net of amortization	40,415	36,483
Total Electric Plant	1,040,014	957,383
Special Funds	318,493	305,374
Current Assets		
Cash and Temporary Investments	14,454	11,976
Accounts Recievable	10,178	5,143
Unbilled Revenues	7,736	7,534
Inventories	7,949	7,237
Prepaid Expenses	1,858	1,811
	42,175	33,701
Total Special Funds and Current Assets	360,668	339,075
Deferred Charges		
Amounts Recoverable in the Future Under Terms of the Power Sales Agreements	111,763	116,103
Unamortized Debt Discount and Expenses	40,996	39,857
Other	888	945
	153,647	156,905
	$1,554,329	$1,453,363
LIABILITIES		
Long-Term Debt		
Bonds	$1,459,950	$1,261,445
Notes	—	1,928
	1,459,950	1,263,373
Bond Anticipation Notes Payable	—	110,000

FIGURE 35.15 (continued)

Other Current Liabilities		
Current Maturities of Long-Term Debt	13,118	10,906
Notes Payable	199	162
Accounts Payable	35,004	23,488
Accrued Expenses	46,058	45,434
	94,379	79,990
Total Notes Payable and Other Current Liabilities	94,379	189,990
	$1,554,329	$1,453,363

Source: Massachusetts Municipal Wholesale Eelctric Company.

set off a large wave of refundings) combined to confuse analysts and disappoint many bondholders. The major problem that gave rise to many customer complaints was the exercise of the extraordinary call by issuers that called in bonds prior to their otherwise stated optional call date. This activity occurred typically because the rapid decline in interest rates that occurred in 1985 through 1987, which made it uneconomic to lend out the original borrowed proceeds for their intended purposes. Owners of high-yielding, long-term debt found their holdings suddenly called and cashed in, with much lower interest earning alternatives for their money. The disappointment was even greater had they bought the debt in the secondary market at a premium and it was called at par. To what extent the unhappy outcomes were products of insufficient disclosures, and by whom, has not been determined.[30]

[30] The biggest disclosure headache the MSRB evidently had to contend with was the exercise of extraordinary calls by issuers in 1985 and 1986 as interest rates tumbled downward. Evidently, security descriptions used failed to indicate the possibility of such calls, leading to bonds being traded at a premium in the secondary market and then called at par. According to various MSRB interpretations (for example, MSRB Interpretation of February 18, 1983 by Donald F. Donahue), extraordinary redemption provisions, while they should be disclosed, would not effect the computation of yield on price, which would be the first date an issuer could exercise a voluntary call of the entire issue.

Alarmed by the rise in extraordinary calls, the MSRB proposed amendments to Rule G-15 requiring dealers to obtain and provide to customers on request complete written information. Commentators indicated that only the issuer official statement could provide that data and they would have compliance problems because of the difficulty and cost of obtaining official statements in the secondary market. See Letter of MSRB Chairman James Hearty to SEC Chairman David Ruder, December 17, 1987, pp. 8–9, *Disclosure Seminar Notebook*, Tab VI.

FIGURE 35.16
Secondary Market Offering Circular.

This Secondary Offering Circular amends and supplements certain information contained in the Offering Circular dated August 13, 1986 prepared in connection with the issuance of the Certificates. The Offering Circular is contained in its entirety in Part II hereof, and constitutes an integral part of this Secondary Offering Circular.

NOT A NEW ISSUE

$1,145,000
State of Florida
Acting by and through the Comptroller of the State of Florida
Adjustable/Fixed Rate Certificates of Participation, Series 1986
(Consolidated Equipment Financing Program)
Evidencing Undivided Proportionate Interests of the Owners Thereof
in an Adjustable/Fixed Rate Master Lease Purchase Agreement

Date of Original Issue: August 13, 1986   Due Date: August 15, 1994

Conversion Date: July 1, 1987

On August 13, 1986, $475,000,000 aggregate principal amount of State of Florida, Acting by and through the Comptroller of the State of Florida, Adjustable/Fixed Rate Certificates of Participation, Series 1986 (Consolidated Equipment Financing Program) (the "Certificates") were issued, each Certificate evidencing an undivided proportionate interest in an Adjustable/ Fixed Rate Master Lease Purchase Agreement dated as of August 1, 1986 (the "Lease") by and between the State of Florida (the "State") acting by and through the Comptroller of the State of Florida (the "Comptroller") and Public Leasing Corporation of Florida (the "Lessor"). The Lessor irrevocably assigned certain of its rights under the Lease, including the right to receive Basic Rent Payments (as defined herein) from the Comptroller, to Sun Bank, National Association (the "Agent"), and pursuant to an Escrow and Paying Agent Agreement (the "Agent Agreement") the Lessor authorized the Agent to issue the Certificates. Proceeds of the Certificates were to be used to (i) finance the acquisition of Equipment (as defined herein) for use by the State or its agencies, (ii) refinance certain Prior Use Equipment (as defined herein) previously acquired by the State or its agencies, (iii) fund a Reserve Account and (iv) pay the costs associated with (a) the original issuance of the Certificates, and (b) the conversion of the interest rate with respect to portions of the Basic Rent Payments and the Certificates evidencing same from an adjustable rate of interest (an "Adjustable Rate") to a fixed rate of interest (a "Fixed Rate"). Pursuant to the terms of the Agent Agreement and the Lease, the Interest Portion of Basic Rent Payments due under the Lease as represented by the Certificates in an amount equal to $1,145,000 (the 11 "Converted Certificates" or "Fixed Rate Certificates") is being converted from an Adjustable Rate to a Fixed Rate on July 1, 1987 (the "Conversion Date").

Another problem is found in outstanding bonds that are remarketed subsequent to their issuance, by which time the information contained in the official statement becomes stale. One solution has been the use of a secondary market offering circular that amends and supplements the original official statement.[31] Figure 35.16 illustrates such a secondary market offering circular.

The GFOA *Disclosure Guidelines* devote a section to current reporting by issuers, providing guidance on the types of information to be considered for periodic reporting and events that might warrant an immediately disclosure.[32] The *Disclosure Guidelines* also suggest the usefulness of a two-part official statement, one part which contains information on a specific offering and the second, an information statement regarding the issuer that may be updated periodically.[33] The Procedural Statements provide advice as to how information should be disseminated and encourage issuers to keep lists of those requesting periodic and episodic reports. Submission of these items, when such disclosures are made, to a central repository is particularly stressed.[34] However, as the *Disclosure Guidelines* note, the metes and bounds of optional disclosure documents for the secondary market and their efficient distribution need further examination.[35]

ISSUES AND INITIATIVES

The preceding section presented the mechanics of disclosure in the context of providing information in the municipal securities market. Those processes collectively are the product of historical custom, assorted state and local laws, municipal dealer self-regulation, various professional standards, and the participants' perceptions of their exposures to the federal securities laws and those of the states as well. The information gathering and dissemination processes, after suffering stresses in the mid-1970s arising out of the New York City financial crisis, evidently served the municipal market well through the end of that decade. But, under the pressures of rapid growth, recurring disruptions, and relentless innovation in the markets, municipal disclosure practices came in for increasing criticism. Practices that suited the needs of traditional

---

[31] Remarks of Hyman Grossman, *Disclosure Seminar Notebook,* Tab I.

[32] *Disclosure Guidelines,* Guidelines for the Timely Provision of Information on a Continuing Basis, pp. 57–76.

[33] *Ibid.,* p. 61.

[34] *Ibid.,* Procedure Statement No. 8, pp. 91–92.

[35] *Ibid.,* p. 9.

borrowers selling conventional instruments did not fare as well in the hurly-burly of the early 1980s.

Although the roots of concern reach back into the earlier years, several events that occurred and studies undertaken over the past two years focused attention on the adequacy and timing of information flows in the municipal market, culminating in three important initiatives being proposed by the Securities and Exchange Commission.[36] In this section recent developments in municipal disclosure are reviewed. It commences with a review of the current municipal securities regulatory framework and the recent revisions to the GFOA Disclosure Guidelines. There follows a recapitulation of the major criticisms of the current disclosure process, and the Securities and Exchange Commission's recently proposed initiatives for improving that process.

The Regulatory Framework

The regulatory situation of municipal securities is unique. The offer and sale of municipal securities are subject to the antifraud provision of the federal securities laws and similar laws at the state level.[37] However, municipal securities are expressly exempt from the registration and periodic reporting requirements of the federal securities laws, which is also typically the case under state securities laws. Because of these exemptions, a different, more flexible and less rigorous standard of negligence has usually been applied to governmental issuers with respect to the antifraud statutes.

Although municipal issuers and securities are not subject to the registration and reporting requirements, those brokers and dealers who deal in municipal securities are subject to direct regulatory requirements. By virtue of the 1975 Amendments to the Securities Acts, the Municipal Securities Rulemaking Board (MSRB), an industry self-regulatory body, has rulemaking authority over industry practices. Rules of the MSRB must be approved by the Securities and Exchange Commission (SEC), and their enforcement is carried out by the SEC and other securities and bank regulatory bodies. The regulatory authority of the MSRB and the SEC are expressly restricted with respect to municipal securities issuers so as to prohibit the requiring of the

---

[36] Recent developments in municipal disclosure are discussed at length in Robert Doty, *Life After WPPSS: Issuer Disclosure in the State and Local Government Securities Market,* Packard Press, Philadelphia, 1988 (Hereinafter, *Life After WPPSS*). See also, Robert Fippenger, *The Securities Law of Public Finance,* The Practicing Law Institute, New York City, 1988.

[37] *Report on Regulation,* pp. 13–16.

filing of documents or information before a sale (SEC and MSRB) or the requiring that a document be furnished to prospective purchasers (MSRB). These constraints reflected the interests of intergovernmental comity, the absence of fraud, and the low-risk nature of the municipal security.[38]

Although not subject to direct regulation, governments and government officials have reason to be concerned about the securities laws and their liabilities under them. The official statements that they produce in conjunction with sales of securities are, in fact, the issuer's documents. They play a pivotal role in providing information about the issuer and issuances so that investors can make informed investment decisions. Accordingly, issuers must take care that they provide full and accurate disclosure in these documents. To fail to do so may mean running afoul of the federal securities laws, not to mention state statutes and common law. Recent legal decisions, principally associated with the Washington Power Supply System, have spotlighted the application of these laws to municipal securities issuers.[39]

As a consequence of this regulatory structure, the municipal bond market has relied to a great extent on market pressures and the exposures of participants to the antifraud provisions to develop suitable disclosure practices, a situation often termed as voluntary disclosure. A key to the development of appropriate disclosure practices has been the existence of the GFOA *Disclosure Guidelines for State and Local Government Securities*. First released in 1976, the *Disclosure Guidelines* were rapidly accepted as providing authoritative guidance and demonstrably improved official statements. The municipal market, recovering quickly from the New York City crises, performed well through the end of that decade. In addition, the widespread improvements in financial reporting by state and local governments implementing generally accepted accounting principles helped sustain confidence in the market.

The 1980s were to usher in several new challenges for disclosure. The expansion of private-activity and conduit bonds, growing complexity of municipal bond deals, increasing reliance of individual investors, intense pressures created by threats to tax exemption, highly volatile interest rates, and default by the Washington Power Supply System, all

---

[38] Remarks of David Ruder, Chairman, Securities and Exchange Commission, *Disclosure in Municipal Securities Markets,* October 23, 1987, *Disclosure Seminar Notebook,* Tab VI, pp. 11–12.

[39] See Doty, *Life After WPPSS;* Chapter 1. Doty concludes that the system of voluntary disclosure has been replaced by a judicially imposed mandated system of disclosure for issuers that applies not only to original offerings but perhaps to the secondary market as well, pp. 1.

placed strains on traditional marketing processes and reactivate concerns about disclosure.

In January 1988, after three years of research and review, a thoroughly revised edition of the GFOA *Disclosure Guidelines* was released. The *Guidelines*, which had been most recently revised in 1979, followed the same approach as its predecessors, containing recommendations regarding the contents of official statement documents, the contents of continuing disclosure releases, and procedures to follow in making disclosures. However, the suggestions, which had previously been contained in two free-standing texts, were integrated into one volume, with stress placed on the on-going nature of disclosure as an integrated process. Several areas of disclosure were introduced and existing items were treated in greater detail, to reflect market practices and needs. In particular, more guidance was provided regarding credit enhancements, bond calls and prepayments, original discount issues, variable-rate and multi-modal interest payments, put options, defeasance of funds, and several procedural items relating to when, how, and to whom information should be supplied.[40] The Municipal Disclosure Task Force of the GFOA in its report accompanying the *Disclosure Guidelines*, also proposed that the idea of a central repository, the submissions of information to which is repeated suggested throughout the *Guidelines*, be studied and that such an effort should involve all market participants.[41]

A Summary of Disclosure Concerns

A series of seminars on the subject of municipal bond market disclosure, at which the latest edition of the GFOA *Disclosure Guidelines* was introduced, served as a forum for examining the roles of the various participants in generating and disseminating information in the market.[42] The seminar sessions provide a point of departure for determining what is collectively known—and not known—about the existing disclosure process in the municipal securities market, its inadequacies, and how it might be improved. The following summary presents the major areas of concern identified at the seminars and elsewhere,

---

[40] *Ibid.*, Chapter 3.

[41] Report of the Task Force on Municipal Disclosure, Government Finance Officers Association, dated October 28, 1987, *Disclosure Seminar Notebook*, Tab II.

[42] *Disclosure Seminar Notebook*, cover page. The seminars were held in San Francisco (February 12, 1988), Washington, D.C. (February 26, 1988), Chicago (February 29, 1988), and New York (June 6, 1988) and were sponsored by the Government Finance Officers Association; American Bar Association, Section on Urban, State, and Federal Law; National Association of Bond Lawyers; and the Public Securities Association. Approximately 550 individuals attended the four seminars.

along with observations on the sources of difficulties and possible solutions with minimal changes to the existing regulatory framework.

Availability of New Issue Official Statements. The great preponderance of new municipal offerings evidently have official statements that are provided by issuers in conjunction with bond sales, but there is concern that there are issuances where such documents either do not exist or were not delivered by the managing underwriter to other syndicate members, dealers, or customers. Recent statistics on this score from a survey done by the *Public Securities Association* (PSA) indicate that this problem is largely focused on small-issue private-activity bonds.

In June 1988, the PSA published the results of a national survey of dealers and dealer banks regarding disclosure. The results indicated that the content and sufficiency of state and local government disclosure documents were rated satisfactory to excellent by 94% of the respondents. Small issue industrial development bonds and other conduit bonds performed not as well as government-purpose issues and, generally, smaller issues received lower scores than larger ones. Financial information was found to be satisfactory or excellent by over 90% of the respondents. The soft spots amid the generally clean bill of health were in the timeliness of receiving official statements (discussed next) and the availability of information in the secondary market (where, again, conduit issues received the lowest score.)[43] In addition, the PSA respondents indicate that official statements are prepared 84% of the time (to their knowledge), in new issuances; however, the statistical method used undoubtedly led to an understatement of the frequency of preparation.[44]

Unfortunately, the PSA survey did not shed much light on the nature of "missing" official statements. The extent to which Rule G-32 requiring deliveries of FOS's (or an affirmative statement to the effect that there will be no FOS) is followed is not known, but would appear to be a problem.[45] The MSRB has recordkeeping requirements

[43] Public Securities Association, *Municipal Securities Disclosure Task Force Report: Initial Analysis of Current Practices in the Municipal Securities Market*, New York, 1988. (Hereinafter, *PSA Task Force Report*).

[44] A relatively large percentage of the PSA survey respondents (21%) indicated that they estimated official statements to be prepared in 74% or less of new-issue sales. This is a great variance in the opinion of those that actively participate in the market and probably reflects the limited exposure of those respondents. The actual percentage is probably in the range of 90 to 95% of the issuances and a higher proportion of the dollar volume. See *PSA Task Force Report*, Table 4.

[45] Letter of MSRB Chairman James Hearty to S.E.C. Chairman David Ruder, dated December 17, 1987, *Disclosure Seminar Notebook*, Tab VI, pp. 7–8.

(Rule G-8 and G-9) that require records of the distribution of OSs. But, because of its inability to enjoy better enforcement of its rules by the National Association of Securities Dealers and the bank regulatory agencies, the MSRB has indicated it is uncertain as to both the magnitude of or the causes for the absence of an OS at the time of original offering.[46]

The actual existence of an OS at or about the time of original offering appears to be much less of a problem than that of the timing of its delivery (which is discussed below) and is a problem likely restricted to small issues.[47]

Timing of Official Statements. Another complaint has to do with the availability of sufficient information prior to sale and of changes occurring between the preliminary and final version of the OS before the latter document is delivered at closing.[48] The availability problem was borne out by the results of the PSA survey. Industry respondents in 44% of the cases indicated the timely availability of documents (preliminary and final) was less than satisfactory or poor, and 33% of the time, official statements were not furnished to dealers in new issue transactions until after the settlement. Not surprisingly, such problems were greater in negotiated transactions than competitive ones.[49] Timing appears to be a problem in certain negotiated transactions, where POSs either may not be distributed or distributed only in sketchy form and where the parties, still in the process of negotiating the transactions, may modify terms and conditions up to the point of sale.

Changes between the POS and FOS may be an inherent problem in negotiated transactions, where major motivations in using that form of sale are flexibility in market timing and the tailoring of issues to primary investors' needs. Such timing problems, however, would seem to be largely related to structuring and pricing the transaction, rather than involving the underlying factors relating to descriptions of the issuer or its creditworthiness.

The problems of late delivery of OSs were likely compounded by the change in the MSRB's G-32 requirements from the earlier requirement that OSs, if available, be sent at the time trades were confirmed to the present requirement that FOSs be delivered at time of settlement. While this step, taken in 1985, was meant to economize on

---

[46] *Ibid.*, p. 8.

[47] *Ibid.*, footnote 11, p. 5.

[48] Letter of National Federation of Municipal Analysts to the GFOA Task Force on Municipal Disclosure, dated August 11, 1987.

[49] PSA Task Force Report.

paper flows, it may have unwittingly de-emphasized the production of earlier, more complete official statements.

The MSRB, noting OS delivery problems stemming from dealers not complying with G-32, has suggested that the adoption of more stringent requirements might be needed: "These might include prohibiting settlement by managers and other dealers of transactions with customers on new-issue securities for which an official statement has been authorized except on delivery of the final official statement."[50]

Adequacy of Contents. Most observers applaud the comprehensiveness of the GFOA *Disclosure Guidelines* and endorse the guidance they contain.[51] But, some commentators lament that official statements show too little standardization: not only come in a variety of sizes and formats, but may be written in murky and ponderous prose or give insufficient detail and emphasis to important aspects of the transaction.[52] Although complaints regarding the presentation of financial data and the abbreviated discussions of credit enhancements have been noted, the major problems appeared to be in the absence or tardiness of such information needed for making complete security descriptions.[53] Furthermore, these shortcomings appeared greatest in the description of callability, put options, and the operations of variable-rate securities.[54]

As discussed in the preceding part, security descriptions used for confirmations in trading and sales to customers are derived from financial service firms using official statements and other sales-related information and are of particular usefulness in the secondary market. While problems of completeness of description may very well exist, what is not known is the extent to which they are attributable to there being (1) no OS, (2) an inadequate OS, (3) a late OS, (4) errors in

[50] *MSRB Reports*, "New Issue Disclosure Requirements", March 1987, p. 2.

[51] It should be noted that the *Disclosure Guidelines* indicate that their use "may not be appropriate" for disclosure involving private-purpose conduit bonds "where debt service is dependent upon payments by a private entity involved in the offering" (p. 19). Chairman David Ruder of the S.E.C., in a speech to the Public Securities Industry on October 23, 1987, renewed the S.E.C.'s previous recommendations that these bonds no longer be exempt from the disclosure provisions of the Securities Acts. *Disclosure Seminar Notebook*, Tab III.

[52] Such variety is not necessarily bad and is a byproduct of flexibility offered by the existing legal status of municipal market disclosure. See Doty, *op. cit.*, pp. 5–6.

[53] See, for example, the remarks of Bert T. Edwards, *Disclosure Seminar Notebook*, Tab IV.

[54] Remarks of Angela Desmond at the GFOA Disclosure Seminar in Chicago, February 29, 1988.

the writing of the security descriptions, or (5) failure of securities sales people to understand and/or disclose the information contained in the description. Furthermore, it may be that investors do not read or cannot understand the disclosure information sent to them. Again, looking at the absence of quantitative data as to where the gaps and delays in the information chain occur, it is difficult to determine who among numerous suspects is the culprit. It should be noted in passing that there is an inherent tension between presenting in summary fashion an "adequate" description of a security and presenting the "comprehensive" description of an instrument with complicated maturity and interest payment features.[55]

Central Repository. Both the MSRB and the GFOA have viewed with favor the use of central repositories for official statements. An initial difference, however, is found in the method of implementation. The MSRB has suggested that the SEC mandate that those state and local government issuers preparing OSs file them with the repository. The GFOA has recommended voluntary submission on the part of issuers. It has noted, further, that dealers under existing law could be required to make such filings, were Rule G-32 to be amended to that effect.[56]

The means of implementation and details of how a central repository might work are subjects for research that exceed the boundaries of this study. However, how a repository might contribute to improved information flows and remedy certain disclosure problems noted above is worth summarizing.[57] First, it is evident from the foregoing discussion that most, if not virtually all, OSs should be centrally collected, if not always in timely fashion, by the CUSIP Service Bureau, where CUSIP numbers are assigned in conformance to Rule G-32. Also, two existing private repositories, those of *The Bond Buyer* Securities Data Inc., and *Investment Dealers Digest* have extensive, if not universally complete, libraries of official statements. Furthermore, the rating agencies and private data-base services have collected masses of OSs and the MSRB itself requires the submission, where available, of cover sheets from OSs (used in the calculation of fees to conform to Rule A-13). These existing aggregations of OS submissions suggest that a logical first step would

[55] See Letter of MSRB Chairman James Hearty to S.E.C. Chairman David Ruder, dated December 17, 1987, *Disclosure Seminar Notebook*, Tab VI, p. 8.

[56] See *Ibid.*, pp. 9–12, and Letter of GFOA Executive Director Jeffrey Esser to S.E.C. Chairman David Ruder, dated December 18, 1987, *Disclosure Seminar Notebook*, Tab VI.

[57] For an outline of discussion points relating to a central repository, see remarks of John Petersen, *Disclosure Seminar Notebook*, Tab VI.

be to inventory and cross-check against CUSIP numbers all existing OSs contained in repositories. Next, steps should be taken to see that OSs currently submitted for other purposes, once they have fulfilled those other immediate needs, are preserved. Such preservation would require an industry-wide cooperative effort, but is a logical precursor to the definitive formation of a repository.

Second, the central and timely collection of OSs could be fostered by a modification to Rule G-32 requiring that any OS (either POS or FOS) received by an underwriter be promptly submitted to the MSRB or its designee. One possible alternative would be to integrate the requirement with the assignment of CUSIP numbers under existing Rule G-34. Thus, the OS could be sent to the CUSIP Service Bureau and CUSIP could certify the receipt of the document. The CUSIP agency could then, as a matter of contract, distribute the OSs to a repository. This would greatly facilitate the recordkeeping as regards both the availability and timing of OSs. By the same token, the non-existence of an OS should be a matter of record and in itself would appear to be a material fact to be disclosed in transactions.[58] The compelling argument for placing any requirement for submission on the underwriter is that party, as the securities professional, is operationally positioned to know the requirements, procedures, and effectuate the actual transmission of documents.

Third, the MSRB's original proposal for a mandatory central repository envisaged a system of submission of OSs by issuers in computer-readable (digital) form, thereby accommodating the electronic transfer of information.[59] A similar approach is that used by the SEC's Edgar project for electronic filings by a limited number of volunteer corporate entities, electronically filing standardized SEC forms. Clearly, under a system of sending OSs to a repository, there is nothing inconsistent with the option of making submissions on an electronic basis. But, it appears that the municipal market, with its multiplicity of official statements of varying length and organization, presents particular obstacles to electronic standardization. The bulk of the SEC's depository activity (under contract to Bechtel Corporation, which provides the service to the SEC

---

[58] Rule G-32 states that a broker dealer shall not sell any new issue municipal security unless it delivers to the customer, no later than at the settlement of the transaction, a copy of the final official statement or, if no final official statement is prepared, a written notice to that effect. If a preliminary OS is made available, then that shall be sent to the customer with a notice that no final OS is being prepared. The non-existence of a final official statement is not a required disclosure in confirmations under existing Rules G-12 or G-15.

[59] See letter of MSRB Chairman James Hearty to SEC Chairman David Ruder, dated December 17, 1987, pp. 9–11.

in exchange for commercial use of the information) continues to consist of copying paper submissions on to micro-fiche records.[60] As already noted, firms in the private sector have seen it worthwhile to provide such a repository service in the municipal bond market.

Advances in technology may make the debate over form of submission moot.[61] At present, there is no reason not to start to collect "hard copies" of official statements and purposefully develop incentives for those that submit materials in forms readily useful for electronic storage and transmission.

Fourth, sundry legal questions may be present in the submission, but it is difficult to see them as being sufficiently novel or towering as to obstruct the creation of a repository. Typically, the underwriter is already in the position of transferring OSs (albeit, the issuer's document) to investors and others and it is not at all clear why the transmission of a copy to a repository would in some way increase, lessen, or otherwise rearrange existing legal liabilities.[62] A collateral but separate concern is that of information contained in the OS becoming stale and misleading subsequent users as to its freshness in subsequent years. That concern seems to be intrinsic to the provision of any official document produced as a specific date. But, to the extent that there is a problem of using dated documents to meet certain future disclosure needs, it might be lessened by having a repository where standard industry-wide practice could make sure that users were notified that the documents on file spoke only of the date as which they spoke.

[60] The arrangement with Bechtel has not been without problems, both in terms of operations and the monopoly implications of centralizing market information flows. See Sandra Sugawara, "Seemingly Perfect SEC Deal Stirs Controversy for Bechtel," *The Washington Post*, Washington Business, October 31, 1988, p. 1.

[61] Rapid advances in optical scanning techniques may obviate the need for more uniform type faces and formats for official statements. Millions of pages can be stored and transmitted electronically. However, to be of use, the contents need to be indexed and, typically, printed in hard copy for final users. Careful thought needs to be given to the technology so that sophisticated and expensive technologies do not inhibit effective participation by smaller firms (or issuers).

[62] The American Bar Association, in commenting on the central repository proposal of the MSRB, noted that filing requirement for OSs could be accomplished under G-32, concerning broker/dealer disclosure duties and that the SEC could provide a safe harbor rule "establishing that a party does not undertake any legal responsibility for the contents of a document solely by transmitting it to a central repository." Letter of James K. Cheek and Robert S. Amdursky of the American Bar Association to David Ruder, Chairman of the Securities and Exchange Commission, March 30, 1988, p. 5. *Disclosure Seminar Notebook*, Tab VI.

A fifth and final observation relates to continuing information needs in the market. The OS document (and related documents emitted at the time of the original sale), while important, is but an initial link in the chain of facts and figures needed to keep the market informed. Certain items disclosed in the original OS will be of lasting value (such as the description of the security), while others will fade in importance over time (such as the financial data). Thus, while retaining the complete contents of the entire OS is desirable, there are some parts that, practically speaking, will be of much greater continuing usefulness than others.

The market already acknowledges this distinction by the selectivity shown by financial information services in extracting and digesting certain informational items. Whatever may be the current imperfections, those private firms that produce security descriptions and build data bases perform the function of distillation and compression of information suitable for organized access and economical transmission in fulfilling disclosure needs (as incumbent in Rules G-15 and G-12) and to support analytical and trading decisionmaking. Such data, as has been discussed above, are frequently combined by information providers with data taken from other sources regarding prices, ratings, called bonds, and so forth, to fulfill the informational needs of their customers. Adding in a record of where the OS resides and, someday, having the capability to transmit it electronically is but part of a massive web of data that may be drawn together with the proper economic incentives.

In view of the multiplicity of uses and sources of data in the informational network of the market (of which the original OS document is but a part), it would appear especially worthwhile to envisage the services of a repository as part of this larger information system. How the existing system might be better integrated and the recovery and transmission of various informational items perfected are timely topics for consideration. For example, practicality suggests that for transactions after the initial offering, the longer-term need is for improved security descriptions. Such descriptions would be more complete than those now found in present G-15 requirements, but more accessible and economical to transmit and use than the entire OS, the usefulness of which (but not the bulk) declines over time. Establishing priorities, recognizing the variety of suppliers and users, and ascertaining the varying significance over time of informational items should, if not precede, then accompany and guide the nature and pace of improvements of information flows in the municipal markets.

It does not strain the credulity to envisage a system where the various bits of information could be electronically assembled into a network where users could gain access to various specialized services that now must be contacted individually. Users could select from a menu what information they desired and then, using the CUSIP number or a security description, access at a charge, these items they needed, as well as note those that were not. Being able to quickly and economically determine what was known and unknown about a particular issue or issuer, given the needs or perceptions of that particular information user, would appear to be the ultimate disclosure tool.

The SEC Municipal Disclosure Initiatives

Recent disclosure developments have occurred against the backdrop of the SEC's investigation of the Washington Public Power Supply System's (WPPSS) default on $2.25 billion in revenue bonds issued to finance two nuclear plants. The bond defaulted in 1983, and the subsequent SEC investigation had been accompanied by massive private litigation. In addition to its investigation of WPPSS, the SEC and other federal and state agencies were investigating other possibly fraudulent offerings in the municipal market. Furthermore, in December 1987, the Municipal Securities Rulemaking Board sent a letter to the SEC discussing disclosure problems and suggesting the creation of a central repository and an SEC mandate that issuers file their official statements and related disclosure documents.[63]

On September 22, 1988, the SEC released its long-awaited report on WPPSS. This was accompanied by a report on regulation of municipal securities containing a set of initiatives designed to improve disclosure in the municipal securities market. The report on regulation consists of three parts: a proposed new rule (Rule 15c2-12) concerning the review and distribution of official statements by underwriters; the Commission's legal interpretation of the disclosure obligations of underwriters; and a request for comment on the MSRB's proposal to establish a central repository for official statements.

The SEC's initiatives are aimed at dealers and underwriters but represent a new thrust at improving and standardizing disclosure practices that will have implications for state and local governmental issuers. The SEC, while acknowledging improvements in governmental accounting and the valuable contributions to disclosure by the GFOA and others, believed additional regulatory measures were needed to improve disclosure practices. It decided to exercise its existing authority over municipal dealers to promulgate interpretations and rules designed to prevent "fraudulent, deceptive, and

---

[63] Letter of MSRB Chairman James Hearty to SEC Chairman David Ruder, dated December 17, 1987, *Disclosure Seminar Notebook*, Tab VI.

manipulative" practices. Specifically, it proposed a four-part rule to require that underwriters of issues exceeding $10 million in size would need to obtain and review a "nearly final official statement" before bidding for or purchasing the offering. The proposed rule would require that the underwriter contract with the issuer, or its agents, to obtain sufficient copies of official statements to make them available to purchasers (complying with MSRB rules) and to provide copies to "any person" requesting one promptly upon request.

The SEC, reacting to what its investigations had shown to be less than universal recognition of underwriter's disclosure responsibilities in municipal offerings, also provided an interpretation of applicable legal standards governing reviews of issuer disclosures. The interpretation, while specifically directed at underwriters, has had an impact on issuers of all sizes.[64] It establishes requirements that underwriters must form a basis for believing issuer disclosures and, in doing so, should examine disclosure documents, check for omissions or inaccuracies, get explanations for discrepancies, and, depending on a variety of factors, use other information sources available to them.

Last, the SEC requested comment on the proposal by the MSRB to establish a central repository to collect information concerning municipal securities. As discussed above, the MSRB proposal calls for mandatory submission by issuers of official statements and other documents to a repository where information, perhaps in electronic form, would be obtainable at a fee.

A summary of the three initiative and their implications for issuers is given in Figure 35.17. Because the legal interpretation is immediately effective, has the broadest reach, and forms the logical basis of the other initiatives, it is examined next.

Interpretation. The SEC's interpretation of the legal standards applicable to municipal underwriters, based on judicial decisions and administrative actions, emphasizes that underwriters have a responsibility to have a "reasonable basis for belief" in the truthfulness and completeness of the key representations made in any disclosure documents used in an offering.[65] This is based on the view that the underwriter, as a securities professional, implies a recommendation about the securities it reoffers. The interpretation attempts to provide a basic,

---

[64] Immediately after the release of the SEC initiatives, underwriters began to show greater concerns about disclosures. See Vicky Stamas, "Maine Bond Bank Calls SEC's New Disclosure Proposals Prohibitive for Small Bond Issuers," *The Bond Buyer*, November 17, 1988, p. 1.

[65] *Report on Regulation*, p. 29.

FIGURE 35.17
Summary of SEC Municipal Disclosure Initiatives

The Securities and Exchange Commission in the September 28, 1988, Federal Register published three initiatives regarding the municipal securities market: a legal interpretation of municipal underwriter disclosure responsibilities, a proposed rule governing the timing and distribution of disclosure documents, and a proposal for a central repository for disclosure documents. The SEC requests comments on the interpretation, proposed rule, and central repository proposal by December 27, 1988. The initiatives and their implications for municipal issuers are summarized below.

SUMMARY OF INITIATIVE	*IMPLICATIONS FOR ISSUERS*

Interpretation

- SEC interprets that federal securities laws require that underwriters must have a reasonable basis for believing the truthfulness and completeness of key representations made by issuers in their official statements. At a minimum, underwriters must obtain and carefully review official statements and other disclosure documents.
- In negotiated underwritings, the review can be expected to be more intensive than in the case of competitive sales and underwriters may not depend solely on the representations of the issuers.
- The extent of the review will depend on the reliance on officials and others knowledgeable in the deal, the nature of the underwriting commitment, the role of the underwriter (manager or syndicate member), type of securities (governmental general obligation or revenue bonds or private activity), past familiarity with issuer, maturity of obligation, presence of credit enhancements, and the type of sale.
- In the review, underwriters should apply knowledge such as prior experience with issuer, secondary market trading, and research their firm has done.
- Underwriters must follow up on errors or omissions of key facts in disclosure documents and receive credible and complete explanations.

- The completeness and accuracy of the content and the timeliness of the distribution of official statements are even more important than before.
- Official statements, as a practical matter, will be required by underwriters in all underwritten offerings to protect against possible securities laws violations.
- Underwriters must receive statements in time to read them carefully. Underwriters must clear up with issuer any inaccuracies or omissions, which means they need to provide the names and numbers of those who can answer questions.
- The level of underwriter review necessary will depend on several factors, but can be expected to be more thorough for negotiated, private-activity and revenue-secured offerings and those of first-time issuers.
- In negotiated transactions, underwriters unable to rely solely on the representations of the issuer may need to investigate and verify data with other experts.
- Issuers will need to be sensitive to key disclosure items and be prepared to explain inconsistencies and omissions.

TABLE 35.17 *(continued)*

Proposed Rule (15c2-12)

- The rule would require that firms acting as underwriters on municipal offerings of more than $10 million comply with four new requirements:

  1) Obtain and review, before bidding for or purchasing an offering, a "nearly final" official statement that is complete except for certain information unavailable before the sale.
  2) Send a copy of preliminary official statements supplied by issuers promptly to potential bidders and buyers upon request.
  3) Contract with issuers to obtain within two business days of the sale sufficient copies of the final official statement to meet MSRB rules and to furnish copies to anyone upon request.
  4) Send one copy of the final official statement in a timely manner to anyone who requests it.

- The rule would apply only to brokers and dealers who are directly covered by SEC regulation.
- The rule requires that before bonds can be underwritten, there must be an official statement, defines what is a "nearly final" official statement, specifies when the statement is to be prepared, and says that final official statements must be available in sufficient quantity to supply single copies to anyone that requests them.

- As in the case of the interpretation, more attention and resources may need to be given to preparing official statements.

- The rule, in effect, will require issuers to prepare official statements for bonds that are underwritten. Direct issuances by governments to the public are not subject to the rule.
- Certain transactions that have been done before official statements were available may not be possible.
- The nearly final official statement requirement will mean that virtually all of the contents of the statement will need to be made final before the sale
- A final official statement will need to be prepared and sent quickly after sale; more copies may be needed.
- A preliminary official statement, along with underwriter's information regarding the sale, may suffice as the final official statement.
- The issuer or its agent will need to contract with underwriters to supply sufficient copies of official statement for ongoing (secondary market) use.
- Distribution of the official statements, preliminary and final, will be an underwriter's responsibility in both the primary and secondary market.

Central Repository

- SEC requests comment on the MSRB proposal for a central repository for official statements and other disclosure-related materials.
- Information would be centrally available in a central location to interested parties and would be available, for a fee, shortly after sale of an offering.
- Among questions to which responses are sought are:
  —Is a central repository necessary?
  —Should it be created by industry or mandated by the SEC?

—Should submission be mandatory or voluntary?
—What information should be submitted?
—In what forms should information be received and sent?
—Should there be periodic disclosure reporting requirements?

- Repository will make disclosure documents available nationally from a central place, perhaps relieving issuers of maintaining old official statements.

TABLE 35.17 *(continued)*

• Deposit of documents may be either mandatory or voluntary. The MSRB proposal calls for mandatory submission by issuers enforced by the SEC rule. GFOA has suggested that underwriters could be required to make submissions, and that submission by issuers be voluntary.	expand into receiving periodic reporting from issuers. Soon, reporting might be mandatory for either underwriters or issuers. —How should the repository be financed?
• Repository could be of use in both new issuances and secondary market transactions.	• Financing of the repository could be by charges levied on design issuers, or other users, or some combination of the above.
• Initially and principally aimed at official statements, a repository might	

flexible framework as to the efforts required of underwriters in both negotiated and competitive underwritings.

At a minimum, underwriters are to review official statements carefully and professionally for possible inaccuracies and omissions. The interpretation does not prescribe specific procedures for review. Rather, it states that the formulation of a reasonable basis depends on such things as:

(1) reliance on issuer officials and others knowing about the deal;

(2) type of underwriting arrangement;

(3) role of the underwriter;

(4) type of securities offered;

(5) past familiarity with issuer;

(6) maturity;

(7) the absence or presence of credit enhancements; and

(8) the nature of sale (competitive or negotiated).

For example, the frequency of issuance and history of the issuer are of prime importance in the review process: any first time project or borrower deserves more scrutiny than those with established track records.

Importantly, the SEC recognizes the difference between the competitive and negotiated sale, and attempts to affirm good market practice in both cases. Basically, the interpretation states that in the negotiated sale, the underwriter typically has a greater responsibility for disclosures and role to play in disclosure process since it is involved in the design of the issuance and the preparation of the official statement. In the case of the competitive offering, the Commission recognizes that the underwriter arrives on the scene after the issuance has been structured, has a less intimate relationship, and, correspondingly, that there is a lower level of review responsibility. In a normal competitive offering of an established issuer, an underwriter will meet its obligation if it reviews the official statement and receives from the issuer a "detailed and credible explanation" concerning any aspect that on its face or on the basis of information available to the underwriter appears to be inadequate.[66] Since in a negotiated transaction the professional review cannot rely solely on the representations of the issuer, there may be the implication that such may be possible in competitive offerings—unless the underwriter has other information available or sees deficiencies in the official statement (such as the lack of independently audited financials).

The SEC notes that effectuation of the proposed new rule, discussed next, would facilitate the minimum review requirement by requiring that underwriters obtain and read official statements prior to bidding on or buying the offering.

One worry is that the review requirement will have a chilling effect on competitively bid transactions where, unlike many negotiated offerings, underwriters generally do not employ securities counsel. Adding another lawyer to the transaction would obviously add to the cost of offering bonds. That possibility depends on how such terms as "key factors" and "review in professional manner" are operationally defined and, accordingly, what standards of negligence prevail.

Most competitively bid transactions, notwithstanding the unique WPPSS debacle, are "garden variety" deals involving established governments that possess solid revenue sources. If the desire is not to burden the traditional market, the reviews by underwriters will be appropriately flexible and "vanilla deals" will continue to flow unimpeded. But underwriters must take care to examine disclosure documents to make sure they understand the deal and can honestly inform their customers about the transaction.

Proposed New Rule. The proposed rule would standardize for municipal issues in excess of $10 million the disclosure process with respect to the timing of printing and delivering of official statements. Also, the newly defined, "nearly final" official statement would be required to contain information in final form except for specified items

---

[66] *Ibid.*, Attachment B, p. 57. Underwriters cannot ignore information from other sources than the disclosure documents. Previous underwriting, secondary market trading, and the underwriter's research department are reservoirs of information available to them in their review.

related to the pricing and size of the securities sold. Underwriters will be required to send preliminary official statements prepared by issuers upon request and to enter contracts with the issuer or its agents to ensure sufficient copies of final official statements to send a copy to anyone requesting one.

Before discussing the individual parts of the rule, it is useful to examine the proposed scope of its coverage. Unlike the legal interpretation discussed above, which applies to all underwritings, the proposed rule would be limited to issuances in excess of $10 million. The desire evidently is to balance the increased costs that may be caused by added review and more documents with the benefits of providing enhanced investor protection. According to figures provided in the SEC report, the $10 million minimum means only 25% of all municipal issuances are affected but 86% of the dollar proceeds would be covered.[67] Other than that balancing of costs and benefits, the dollar cutoff is arbitrary. The SEC in its report asked for comments on the rule's coverage.

The Public Securities Association and the Municipal Securities Rulemaking Board both have called for a lowering of the threshold to $1 million, arguing that the rule's requirements should be universal except for the smallest issuers.[68] However other commentators found it unreasonable on antifraud grounds to assert that all issuances over $10 million need the governance of the rule while those of less than $10 million do not. The GFOA and other issuer groups believe that a case based on patterns of abuse has not been demonstrated by the SEC, and argue that governmental obligations should be exempted from the rule's requirement or, if there were to be a threshold for them, it should be no lower than $25 million.[69] Aside from the massive failure of WPPSS, the evidence from defaults and SEC enforcement actions indicates that the use of proceeds and type of bond are the critical features in assessing risk. Traditional governmental-purpose bonds already demonstrate high levels of disclosure and low levels of risk. Conversely, it is the typically

[67] *Ibid.*, Attachment B, p. 20.

[68] Letter to Jonathan Katz, Secretary, Securities and Exchange Commission, from Austin Konen, Chairman, Municipal Securities Division, Public Securities Association, dated December 23, 1988 (hereinafter, PSA Comment Letter). Letter to Jonathan Katz, Secretary, Securities and Exchange Commission, from John Rowe, Chairman, Municipal Securities Rulemaking Board, dated November 28, 1988.

[69] Letter to Jonathan Katz, Secretary, Securities and Exchange Commission, from Jeffrey Esser, Executive Director, Government Finance Officers Association, dated January 12, 1989 (hereinafter, GFOA, Comment Letter). See also, Letter to Jonathan Katz, Secretary, Securities and Exchange Commission, from National Governors' Association, *et al.*, dated January 13, 1989.

smaller conduit private activity bonds that have shown the greatest gaps in disclosure and risk of default.[70]

The Commission report in a footnote indicates that it still favors requiring the registration of private-activity conduit bonds and acknowledges that, as a breed, they appear to be dying off because of recent tax law changes.[71] Given the Commission's concerns and their higher historical propensity to default, it has been argued that the rule's coverage should depend on type of security and that offerings of private-activity conduit bonds, whatever their size, should abide by the rule. Because such an approach would embrace those tax-exempt issues, large and small, that represent greater credit risks, it would provide the greatest potential for more investor protection.

In addition to the threshold, the SEC requested comment on exemptions from the rule. The questions of threshold and exemptions are intertwined since the lower the threshold, the greater the need to consider exemptions, especially in the case of smaller issuers. In the short-term market, for example, loans are made from local banks that require a minimum of disclosure documentation. Also, reofferings involving a few sophisticated investors would appear logical candidates for exemption. Several suggestions have been made regarding exemptions, including not having the rule apply where the securities are in denominations of $100,000 or larger (and cannot be broken down), are reoffered only intrastate, or where the sale is certified to be made to sophisticated investors at a limited sale who certify they will either hold the securities or resell only to other sophisticated investors.[72]

---

[70] Based on Federal Reserve Board statistics, it is estimated that at year-end 1987 there was $195 billion in conduit securities (and other private-activity obligations) outstanding, and $529 billion in governmental obligations. The respective default ratios by type of issues are:

Conduit securities	1.2%
Governmental obligations (WPPSS included)	0.5%
Governmental obligations (without WPPSS)	0.1%

(See GFOA Comment Letter, pp. 7–8.)

Conduit bonds are obligations where the governmental entity does not own or operate the facility or program financed by bond proceeds and is not responsible for the payment of debt service on the bonds other than from revenues derived from the financed facility or program. (*Ibid.*, p. 5.)

[71] *Ibid.*, Attachment B, p. 13.

[72] Letter to Jonathan Katz, Secretary, Securities and Exchange Commission, from James Creek, *et al.*, American Bar Association, dated January 26, 1989, pp. 15–16 (hereinafter, ABA Comment Letter); and Letter to Jonathan Katz, Secretary, from Paul Maco, Chairman, Special Committee, National Association of Bond Lawyers, dated January 31, 1989, pp. 8–15 (hereinafter, NABL Comment Letter).

Taken together, the remaining four substantive parts of the proposed rule standardize a process for distributing preliminary and final official statements. The first requirement of the proposed rule, comporting with the legal interpretation, says that dealers cannot buy obligations without first obtaining and reviewing an official statement. One of the questions to arise is just how preliminary or "nearly final" the official statement must be.[73] In the case of bonds issued in competitive sales, where the official statement is used in soliciting underwriting bids, a preliminary official statement is typically complete except for the items enumerated.

As was discussed earlier in this report, the preliminary official statement is well established in the competitive market but is a more tenuous concept in the negotiated market. In the negotiated transaction, the concept of the nearly final official statement may lead to problems, since important features of the transaction, which is being tailored to meet investor desires, are not known until the last minute. This is especially so with fast-moving "wire deals" that seek to take advantage of favorable market conditions where the underwriter's commitment to buy has preceded the production of an official statement. The extent to which these deals will still be possible depends either upon exemptions or an expansion of the items that need not be final in the nearly final official statement.

Could items other than those enumerated by the SEC, were they specifically indicated as being supplied later, be omitted from the nearly final official statement? Such items might consist of the identification of the registrar, trustee, or credit enhancer, and certain information typically supplied by the issuer or experts after the sale are items that are usually contained in the final official statement. For example, could a major issuer announce on an annual basis a financing program, create an official statement that covers issuer description and basic security features and then supplement it with the details of each transaction as part of the final official statement which is supplied after the sale? Or, can bonds of large, well-known issuers be sold on the representation of the issuer that nothing has changed that will materially affect the credit? Besides these issues relating to the timing of information as discussed above, it is unlikely this requirement will be an impediment to issuers so long as the definition of an underwriter's "reasonable basis for belief" in information is itself reasonable.

---

[73] The SEC defines an official statement as complete except for the following information: the offering price, interest rate, selling compensation, amount of proceeds, delivery dates, other terms of securities depending on such factors, and the identity of the underwriter. *Ibid.*, Attachment B, p. 68.

The second substantive requirement is that dealers send preliminary official statements supplied to them by issuers to potential bidders or investors promptly, upon request. Again, this appears to be a codification of existing good practice in the competitive market where notices of sale indicate the availability of preliminary official statements to prospective buyers. However, the distribution function is typically in the hands of the issuer or its financial advisor since the identity of the underwriter is not known until the actual sale. The SEC commentary indicates that there may be changes required in the preliminary official statement and that underwriters would need to notify investors of any such changes prior to their investment decision and provide copies of an amended final statement. This process is already suggested for issuers by the GFOA *Disclosure Guidelines*.[74]

Where the issuer's preliminary official statement does not undergo change in key representations, the SEC requested comment on excusing dealers from the requirement that a final official statement also be provided to those investors. This would comport with present practice where the issuer's preliminary official statement is supplemented by underwriter-provided information regarding the pricing of the issue and the name of the underwriter (as is currently required under MSRB rules) and, so amended, is considered the final official statement.[75]

The third requirement of the proposed rule is that underwriters contract with the issuer or its agent to obtain copies of the final official statement within two business days after a final agreement to purchase the securities for sufficient numbers of official statements to conform with any MSRB rules on prospectus delivery as well as the satisfying of a fourth requirement regarding on-going availability. Among the more pertinent questions is whether two days are sufficient time to produce the official statement. In most cases that may be possible, but other legal procedures may present problems for some issuers.[76] Also, for smaller issuers the requirement may increase the costs of printing and limit the number of printers that may bid on the job.[77] The key concern of when the final official statement is to be delivered to the investors (as opposed to when it is obtained by the underwriter) is a matter the SEC has left to the MSRB to determine.

---

[74] *Disclosure Guidelines*, p. 83.

[75] This would also agree with procedures recommended in the *Disclosure Guideline*, p. 81.

[76] PSA Comment Letter, pp. 15–19.

[77] GFOA Comment Letter, p. 10. Most commentators have suggested that a 5-day turnaround for the FOS would be more realistic.

The fourth requirement is that the final official statement be sent in a timely manner, upon request, to any person. The SEC indicates that this need can be satisfied by an agent acting on behalf of an issuer; the agent could be a printer, the syndicate manager, or a repository, such as discussed below. The thrust of this paragraph of the rule is to speed up the process of completing the final official statement, to ensure sufficient copies for initial distribution, and to assure the continuing availability of the official statement in the secondary market.

The Commission, aware of the rule's continuing burden, asked for comment on what added costs will be entailed and the desirability of charging for copies. Most respondents have suggested that a reasonable charge would be appropriate, that submission of the official statement to a repository capable of fulfilling ongoing requests should relieve underwriters of further responsibility, and that the responsibility to provide statement should be limited to the life of the obligation (or some shorter period).[78]

A Central Repository. Last, the SEC asked for comment on the need for a central repository for official statements and its sponsorship and nature of operation. The basis for discussion is the proposal by the MSRB. Setting aside other issues, a major advantage to the repository would be in meeting on-going requests for official statements stemming from the secondary market, especially were the proposed rule adopted. Clearly, it might be operationally advantageous for underwriters and issuers to refer requests for official statements to a repository rather than to keep them on hand for years. Firms go out of business and governments change—and both lose files. The repository could act as collection point and as a library for current reporting information, a function also supported in the GFOA *Disclosure Guidelines.*[79]

While all respondents could see advantages, the details of the repository concept sparked major debate among the respondents to the SEC. The debate reflected concerns about the mandatory nature of submissions, who would operate the facility the implications of a potential monopolization of information services. The PSA in its response called for the mandated submissions to come from issuers and, pushing

---

[78] For example, see ABA Comment Letter, pp. 22–23. There is an associated legal problem with continuing provision of the official statement, that of "staleness" of the information. It has been suggested that the SEC establish reasonable standards for discharge of the duty and recognized that submission to a central repository would provide protections to underwriters in this respect. *Ibid.*, p. 23.

[79] PSA Comment Letter, pp. 20–24. The PSA suggestion went well beyond the MSRB proposal and brought a strong reaction from the GFOA regarding its conflict with the Tower Amendment. See GFOA Comment Letter, Appendix.

beyond the MSRB's original concept, argued that the mandate should extend to the issuer's POSs. The PSA also pushed for the repository having the capability of distributing disclosure documentation during the underwriting process, a concept it called Automated Disclosure Documentation Retrieval System (ADDRS).[80] Other commentators were more guarded in embracing the repository and, while acknowledging the usefulness of centralized information, were concerned about over-centralization of the process and the role of the private sector in its sponsorship and operation.[81]

The GFOA, which has long acknowledged the desirability of issuers voluntarily submitting their disclosure documents to a repository supported in its comments to the SEC the establishing of standards for repositories. It also noted that the private sector already performs many repository functions and should continue to have the opportunity to operate the repositories. It also insisted that any submission requirement should not fall on issuers, it being more efficient to regulate dealers in the process.[82] Above in this report, it has been argued that a repository could be created by MSRB rules within the existing regulatory framework. Furthermore, a nearly complete collection of official statements of issues in excess of $1 million is already in existence at the private repository run by the Bond Buyer/Securities Data Inc.[83] How the existing framework of information flows, which is a product of market demands for data rather than regulatory fiat, will compete with or compliment a centralized source remains to be determined.

Conclusion. The consideration of the SEC report, the proposed rule and other initiatives takes place in the context of a relatively quiet but intensely competitive municipal bond market. The volume of new offerings is steady as are interest rates, and both are much lower than the hectic period of three years ago. The condition of the market is hardly one of lack of investor confidence. In fact, the municipal bond market has performed very well and the greatest problem is lack of supply of new issuances. Concerns about credit quality are subdued; the interest differential between highest and medium-grade bonds has shrunk to very low

---

[80] Letter to Jonathan Katz, Secretary, Securities and Exchange Commission, from J. Kevin Kenny, dated December 27, 1988. Kenny suggested that experienced business in the private sector be allowed to operate as repositories under guidelines established by the SEC or MSRB and that there should not be a single repository.

[81] *Disclosure Guidelines*, p. 91.

[82] GFOA Comment Letter, pp. 12–15.

[83] Letter to Jonathan Katz, Secretary, Securities and Exchange Commission, from Robert November, Executive Vice President, *American Banker—Bond Buyer,* dated December 23, 1988.

levels.[84] For these reasons, the timing of the debate on regulation of municipal securities is fortunate. In this atmosphere, a reasoned consideration of the initiatives and their implications should be possible.

The heart of the SEC initiatives may well be the process that develops under the underwriter's reasonable review process and what legal standards of liability evolve. In the negotiated transactions, the process and corresponding standards would appear not to cause any major disruptions. In the competitive market, which is populated by many small conventional government issuers, attempts to over-complicate the disclosure process could make their issuances costly and inhibit issuer access to the marketplace.

The proposed rule, which creates a process for disclosure, and thereby a standard procedural framework for implementing the interpretation, has been subject to a lengthy critique and, no doubt, will be modified substantially before it is implemented. The debate over the proposed rule illustrates one disadvantage of specific regulatory requirements: almost every rule begets subsequent rules to clarify or define what the first one failed to contemplate. Bearing that in mind, several commentators have urged caution in either applying the rule too broadly or having it be too specific.[85]

Caution in regulating the market is warranted. It would be ironic and unfair if the multitude of honest, efficient, and straight-forward governmental borrowers were to face escalating costs and restricted markets because of the failings of one large power bond and the speculative issuance of a limited number of conduit bonds. The disclosure problems involving certain private-activity bonds and innovative transactions, driven by prior tax considerations and a high-interest rate environment, are solving themselves as times change and bonds retire. Most of the damage grew from pressures and laxities that are receding into history. The municipal market is steadier, smaller, and wiser. The extent to which that market becomes more regulated as a legacy of its learning process, however, remains to be seen.

Subsequent to the writing of this chapter, the SEC promulgated Rule 15(c)2–12, which is similar to the proposed rule described above. The MSRB adopted new rules to effectuate the SEC rule, including the establishing of a central repository. These and other changes are described and reflected in the 1991 edition of the GFOA Disclosure Guidelines.

[84] GFOA Comment Letter, p. 2.

[85] The National League of Cities found the proposed rule misdirected, rigid, and costly to implement. It proposed that the Commission defer action on it until a better case were made for its need. Letter to Jonathan Katz, Secretary, Securities and Exchange Commission, from Alan Beales, Executive Director, National League of Cities, dated January 30, 1988.

CHAPTER 36

Responsibilities of Bond Counsel

Michael Ettlinger
Orrick, Herrington & Sutcliff

John Koehane

The prevailing conception of the duties of an attorney is that of an advocate who assumes an intentionally biased role to advance a particular interest or cause. In most instances, this is an appropriate portrayal. In fact, the very underpinnings of the Anglo-American legal system essentially compel the assumption of such an adversarial role to counter a potentially omnipotent adversary who is embracing a conflicting interest. Most observers have distinguished the role of bond counsel from that of the adversary counsel, choosing to characterize the role of bond counsel as independent. As such, bond counsel acts, in effect, as a legal auditor in the transactions in which it is involved.

HISTORICAL REFERENCE

The presence of bond counsel in municipal transactions is the result of an historical imperative. Indeed, while history has mandated bond counsel's primary function to be that of a "legal auditor," it exists manifestly in an ever-evolving state; it is being further redefined by the Securities and Exchange Commission and court decisions and through self-regulation within the municipal securities industry. Much change has resulted in response to abuses related to municipal financings as well as to a greater understanding of market variables. To understand and appreciate the role and attendant responsibilities of bond counsel, it is necessary to examine its origin and subsequent evolution.

Evolution of the Need for Bond Counsel

The settling of the American frontier in the latter part of the nineteenth century was dependent upon the success of extending rail and transport inland. After obtaining legislative authority, numerous states, counties and cities issued bonds to build and maintain thousands of miles of railroad tracks. In many cases the risks inherent in building a railroad proved insurmountable and their realization led to a surge of railroad bond defaults. In an attempt to avoid paying their obligations, the defaulting issuers claimed that the bonds were invalidly issued. The reasons most often cited were that the railroad projects exceeded prescribed geographic areas and that the bond debt was larger than statutorily permissible. Such actions jolted the investment community, which could no longer rely on legislative declarations that bonds were valid. As a result of the use of such technical defenses by issuers, investors came to reject municipal bonds as investments. Some other guaranty or evidence of integrity was required.

Independent Role of Bond Counsel in Issuing Its Opinion

The entrance of bond counsel to oversee bond transactions was seen as a solution to the railroad bond defaults which had crippled the municipal bond market. If investors could be assured that, in the opinion of an independent attorney, the bond issuer could not take refuge in constitutional or statutory loopholes to avoid repayment of debt, municipal bonds would be recognized as safe investments. The basic task of bond counsel was to identify and examine the various constitutional and statutory requirements for the issuance of municipal debt and, when satisfied of the issuer's compliance therewith, to issue an opinion stating that the bonds were validly issued. Bond counsel did not (and does not today) provide an economic assessment of the issuer's ability to repay debt, nor does it analyze the credit of the issuer. Nonetheless, assurance of an opinion by bond counsel as to validity boosted investor confidence, thereby enhancing the marketability of the bonds. This practice spread quickly and, by the turn of the century, the opinion of a recognized bond counsel became an integral part of a municipal bond issue.

Increased Complexity of Bond Counsel Role
Due to an Increase in the Variety of Financings

The early years of bond counsel's existence were relatively simplistic when compared with the more intricate and sophisticated tasks undertaken by bond counsel today. A more complex financial market and an ever-changing tax regulatory scheme justify a bewildered investor's increased reliance upon the expertise of bond counsel both to determine the structure of a municipal financing and to effect legal compliance with such structure. Further, the entrance into many transactions by entities other than issuers, such as entities that provide credit enhancement, suggest that there is a broad range of other parties who place direct reliance upon bond counsel's expertise.

From its inception, bond counsel has had an implied responsibility towards bondholders. This can be rationalized upon the basis that the services of bond counsel were directed originally towards the making of investment decisions by prospective bondholders. However, although some explicit standards now exist, the legal responsibilities of bond counsel towards bondholders has never been clearcut. Responsibilities, if any, towards other parties involved in bond transactions are similarly nebulous but secondary to that of bondholders. In certain instances it would be possible theoretically to analogize the responsibilities of bond counsel to those of counsel in the more highly regulated registered public offering context of corporate securities transactions. However, due to the limited amount of litigation in the municipal securities area and the intrinsic differences of registered public offerings, any such comparisons or analogies to be drawn would be speculative at best. Undoubtedly, future developments will be instrumental in helping to more specifically elucidate the legal responsibilities of bond counsel.

THE RESPONSIBILITIES OF BOND COUNSEL—ILLUSTRATED BY THE LEGAL OPINION

Introduction

The issuance of a legal opinion, otherwise referred to as an approving or validity opinion, represents the ultimate disposition of the responsibilities of bond counsel. It is the predicate action for every bond issue. The responsibilities of bond counsel can be understood best by evaluating the process that bond counsel must typically undertake prior to rendering such an opinion. The legal opinion, as the end result of bond counsel's efforts, consequently is rendered at the end of the financing—the closing—and should reflect the favorable resolution of the various tasks performed and inquiries made by bond counsel throughout the financing.

Analysis of Legal Authority. Although the legal opinion may address several items, the bond issue is void *ab initio* if bond counsel is not satisfied that proper legal authority exists for the transaction. Depending upon the particular circumstances, a finding of proper authority can be based upon various sources of explicit or implied authority for the issuance of the bonds. Often it is based upon an interpretation of a combination of various regulations and pronouncements that have at least an ancillary connection with the proposed bond issue. These include statutes and other regulatory provisions, judicial decisions, administrative pronouncements and constitutional provisions. These items vary based upon the very ideosynchratic nature of every bond issue, including, among other things, the locale of the issuer and the type of project to be financed. For example, a waste-to-energy financing may have a host of more complex tax requirements than a hospital financing, in which bond counsel may focus more specifically on third party reimbursement issues.

Depending upon which sources are operative in any particular case, bond counsel must take whatever unique formulation exists to form its opinion as to the ultimate authority for the bond issue. Clearly, the most preferable situation arises when explicit statutory authority for the issue exists. However, often this is not the case or, even when such explicit authority does exist, it may be tempered by other independent conflicting or modifying provisions. Bond counsel must decide how to resolve such conflicting provisions.

In addition to the more intricate analysis detailed above, which may require bond counsel to reconcile very specific or obscure provisions, bond counsel must continue to acknowledge the role of constitutional and statutory provisions, such as home rule statutes, and other sources such as charters that may provide a general underlying basis for the issuance of bonds by a governmental entity. Bond counsel has often found authority for bond issues based upon such general authority. The renowned treatise written by Judge John Dillon in the late nineteenth century which introduced what is commonly called the "Dillon Rule" addresses directly the breadth of power to be enjoyed by municipal corporations and has been applied often to justify the issuance of bonds on the basis of a general grant of authority. It has been and is considered today to be a fundamental tenet of municipal bond law. The "Dillon Rule" declares that a municipal corporation possesses express powers, powers necessarily or fairly implied in or incident to such express powers and powers indispensable to the purposes of the corporation.

When bond counsel is brought "into the circle" in the initial stages of a financing it must be in a position to advise the parties responsible for selecting the ultimate structure of the issue as to the existing statutory or constitutional language that controls. When adequate or appropriate constitutional or statutory provisions for the contemplated financing do not exist, bond counsel often will draft proposed legislation within constitutional constraints and appear before legislative committees to aid in its enactment. Only in an extremely rare instance, if at all, would an amendment to a state constitution be suggested.

Issuer's Bond Authorization Process. Once the statutory framework is intact and bond counsel is satisfied that the transaction has an irrefutable legal foundation, bond counsel will ensure that the issuing governmental body take the appropriate steps to validly authorize and issue the bonds. Generally, the governing body of the issuer, such as the board of trustees or directors of a municipal authority or the county supervisors or city council of a municipality, as an initial step, should adopt a resolution that the issuer may thereupon proceed with the financing, indicating its intended purpose. Such a resolution will likely include a finding that the financing is necessary to achieve a stated goal of the community. Often the proceeds of a financing will be used to construct a necessary or beneficial project or to expand an already-existing project. Another common reason for proceeding with a financing is to achieve a present value cost savings, typically through a refunding, on debt service payments expected to be made on an outstanding bond issue. The board, via the resolution, usually delegates the practical responsibilities required to complete the bond issue to other staff members of the municipality. Therefore, this resolution should set constraints for the issue to prevent the actual transaction from deviating unreasonably from that which had been contemplated originally by the board. Such deviations, then, would require that the board be reapproached for their approval and, hence, would leave untarnished its ultimate control over the financing. Typical constraints include specifically earmarking bond proceeds for certain purposes, specifying maturity provisions and limiting the dollar amount of the financing.

Once board approval has been obtained, bond counsel should work with the issuer and issuer's local or general counsel to obtain any required regulatory approvals and to hold any required hearings. Concurrently, all other aspects of the financing should be taking form. Among other things, appropriate parties should be initiating title searches (where a mortgage to real property is part of the security for the bonds), performing "number runs" incorporating prevailing interest rates (to ensure that during the course of the financing the transaction continues to be beneficial economically and, hence, justifiable), conducting "due diligence" examinations (to identify as early as possible any matters potentially harmful to the financing) and exploring opportunities to obtain, if deemed necessary to market the bonds, municipal bond insurance or other forms of credit support. While each party tends to its individual responsibilities, the working group as a whole should conduct meetings, several if necessary, to tailor the bond documents to the transaction as agreed upon.

Often, during the time period when a bond transaction is taking shape certain elements will change, depending upon a variety of factors, both foreseeable and unforeseeable. For example, a foreseeable change of circumstances such as a change in interest rates may occur which could render the transaction economically impracticable. Instead of abandoning the financing, the borrower might prefer to alter the schedule of principal and interest payments to make a rise in interest rates less burdensome. Bond counsel must be certain that any such changes in the structure of the financing will not jeopardize or compromise the earlier constitutional, statutory and regulatory compliance. Unforeseeable changes will require a similar process to exact such compliance. A major rating agency, in light of a changing business environment, may require an issuer to agree to additional or more restrictive covenants or impose upon certain institutions more stringent financial coverage ratios. Bond counsel must determine, as before, whether such changes are permissible.

Bond Documentation. Bond documentation is based usually upon one of two common structures for bond issues: bond resolution or trust indenture format. Each is designed to govern and accomplish similar, if almost identical, objectives. The subtle differences between the two approaches surface in the greater degree of control vested in the trustee in the indenture scenario. Nonetheless, each establishes the parameters and the structure for the issue by providing for the funds and accounts which will house bond proceeds (e.g., the construction fund account and the reserve fund) and by providing for a pledge of, among other things, assets, revenues, or property as security for repayment of the bonds. Each format also establishes the other material terms of the bond issue, including:

a) general terms of the bonds such as medium of payment, date, authentication and transfer;

b) redemption provisions;

c) ability to issue additional bonds;

d) establishment of additional funds, including the debt service fund, and the application thereof;

e) general covenants of the issuer;

f) rights and responsibilities of and other matters affecting the bond trustee;

g) provisions for supplemental or amendatory resolutions or indentures;

h) remedies upon default; and

i) defeasance and discharge of the lien created by the bond resolution or trust indenture.

Often the bond resolution or trust indenture is intended to be a general document applicable to all future bonds to be issued by the issuer. When this is the case, bond counsel must then prepare a supplemental resolution or indenture, as the case warrants, to establish the specific provisions for each such future financing of additional series of bonds. All future series of bonds will be bound by the general terms of the bond resolution or trust indenture and the respective supplemental resolution or indenture must set specific provisions which abide by the parameters originally established by the bond resolution or trust indenture.

Depending upon the nature of the security and other specifics of the transaction, bond counsel will draft or review other documents as may be required. In particular, bond counsel would prepare an escrow deposit agreement to provide for the deposit of moneys into an escrow fund to effect a refunding. Bond counsel would also assist in the implementation of a liquidity facility which would more likely necessitate a review of the attendant documents including a letter of credit, remarketing agreement and reimbursement agreement.

Bond Sale Pursuant to a Purchase Contract. When the bond documents accurately reflect the contemplated transaction, the issuer and underwriter may schedule the bond sale pursuant to the terms of a purchase contract. Most importantly, the purchase contract specifies the purchase price to the underwriter, which is the principal amount of the entire bond issue less a pre-negotiated discount to the underwriter, commonly called the *spread*. But it also sets forth much more; in fact, it sets the stage for the remainder of the transaction. Thus, the issuer and the underwriter must refer to the terms of the purchase contract to determine the ramifications of many issues that may arise from the time of the sale until the closing for and ultimate delivery of the bonds. Although the purchase contract is drafted usually by underwriters counsel, bond counsel must carefully scrutinize its terms lest the issuer become bound by some undesirable terms. The most common provisions of the purchase contract include the following:

a) The purchase price to the underwriters (which may be comprised of many underwriters that form a group of managers or a syndicate), which is usually the principal amount of the bond issue less a discountfactor, plus accrued interest on the bonds from the initial date of the bonds through the date of the closing.

b) Time and place of the closing and the procedure for the delivery of the bonds.

c) Good faith deposit. Concurrent with the execution of the purchase contract, the underwriters will deliver to the issuer a check in the amount of approximately one to two per cent of the principal amount of the bond issue to indicate their anticipated performance, in good faith, of their obligations pursuant to the purchase contract. Should the issuer ultimately fail to deliver the bonds or elect to terminate the obligations of the underwriters, generally the issuer must return the deposit to the underwriters. However, if the underwriters fail to accept and pay for the bonds upon tender by the issuer, then the issuer generally will retain the deposit as full liquidated damages. If the bonds are delivered and accepted as expected, then the deposit will be applied towards the purchase price or canceled upon the underwriters' payment of the full purchase price.

d) Documents to be delivered by the issuer to the underwriters at the time of execution of the purchase contract; typically, these include the offering or official statement (usually in preliminary form), the issuer's resolution approving the bond issue and accepting the form of reasonably complete bond documentation and an auditor's *comfort letter* relating to changes in the issuer's financial situation since the date of its most recently available audited financial statements. In a *conduit financing*, in which the issuer merely lends bond proceeds to finance the project of a different *end user*, such as a hospital or a university, a comfort letter relating to such an ultimate beneficiary will be required.

e) Representations of the issuer—as to its due organization and existence; that appropriate action has been taken to authorize the issuance of the bonds which, upon delivery, will be valid obligations; that the issuer is not in default on any outstanding obligations; that the offering documents are accurate (this may be certified to in several ways of varying tenor and specificity); and that there is no material litigation pending or threatened against the issuer.

f) Representations of the underwriters to make a bona fide public offering of the bonds at not more than the public offering prices set forth in the official statement.

g) Closing conditions of the underwriters' obligations. These requirements of the underwriters must be satisfied at or prior to the delivery of the bonds, or the obligations of the underwriters will be terminated. The most important closing conditions require the provision or evidence of the following:

(1) a *bring-down* of the issuer's representations made at the time of execution of the purchase contract, affirming their continued veracity to the closing date;

(2) that the issuer's approving resolution was validly adopted and remains valid, binding and in full force and effect;

(3) that the bonds have been duly authorized, issued, executed, attested and authenticated in accordance with the resolution and any other applicable documents and constitutional, statutory and regulatory provisions;

(4) the appropriate legal opinions of the various attorneys in the transaction;

(5) consents of various parties such as a feasibility consultant or an auditor to the inclusion of their reports in the offering statement;

(6) a *no arbitrage* or other relevant tax certification;

(7) a *bring-down* of the auditor's comfort letter; and

(8) evidence of the ratings received on the bonds.

The above items may vary significantly from transaction to transaction. In addition, depending upon the structure of the transaction, the subject matter of the transaction and the regulatory scheme under which it falls, several additional items may be required by the underwriters.

h) Events permitting the underwriters to terminate their obligations—commonly referred to as *underwriters' outs*. These differ from, and are in addition to, breaches or derelictions by the issuer of duties imposed by the purchase contract. They include generally unforeseeable events such as legislation introduced which would change the nature of the Federal tax exemption on the bonds to be issued so as to materially impair their marketability, action taken to require registration of the bonds with the SEC, a suspension of trading in securities on the New York Stock Exchange, a national bank moratorium, a national emergency or war.

Contents of the Legal Opinion

Valid and Binding Obligations. The threshold question addressed by bond counsel's opinion relates to the validity, or legality, of the obligations. Bond counsel's conclusion as to such validity is to be determined through the already identified process of analyzing existing constitutional, statutory and regulatory provisions to establish the requisite authority and, when required, by drafting new legislation.

The approving opinion must state that the issuer has been duly created and is validly existing. It must state further that the bonds are valid and binding obligations of the issuer enforceable in accordance with their terms and the terms of the applicable resolutions or indentures. Due to the possibility of exceptional and unforeseeable circumstances, it has been the practice of bond counsel to make such statements subject to bankruptcy, insolvency and other laws affecting the rights of creditors generally. Nevertheless, bond counsel's approving language conveys a message that the security for the obligations is adequate to the extent of its compliance with all applicable laws (although bond counsel generally makes no representations regarding the financial sufficiency of the security). Most bonding statutes contain certain requirements or tests for the underlying security and, accordingly, bond counsel may render its approving opinion only if such tests are satisfied. However, as limited by the exclusionary language stated above, the obligation to pay debt service on the bonds remains subject to bankruptcy laws and, consequently, bondholders might not be accorded priority status in the event of a bankruptcy by the issuer of the bonds.

The basis for bond counsel's opinion should be manifest from an examination of the record of proceedings for the transaction. The record of proceedings, usually formally memorialized in bound legal transcripts, should contain the operative documents of the bond issue from its initial authorization by the issuer through the ultimate delivery of the bonds. However, the notion that this "examination" entails a *de novo* evaluation of documentation by bond counsel is perhaps somewhat misleading. The role of bond counsel has changed from the early days such that now bond counsel generally is responsible for approving the succession of steps requisite to the proceedings rather than for merely performing an after-the-fact review at the time of the closing for the bond issue. This is a more logical application of bond counsel's services. Contemporaneous or near contemporaneous participation in the entire proceedings is likely to avoid a defect that would void a bond sale. Thus, by the time that a complete record of proceedings is available (generally at the preclosing or closing), absent extraordinary circumstances, bond counsel should have approved all of the proceedings of the financing, making the "examination" of the record of proceedings a perfunctory task. With respect to the status of the issuer, the final record of proceedings should include, among other things, the following:

a) Evidence of the legal existence of the issuer. In the past, investors were often defrauded when bonds were issued by non-existent governmental entities.

b) Evidence of the authority of the issuer to issue obligations.

c) Evidence of the performance of proper procedures for the authorization and issuance of the bonds, including adoption of resolutions, ordinances and referenda and compliance with notice and other requirements for such actions.

d) Evidence of certain security being pledged, such as a mortgage or an interest in personal property or a lien on anticipated revenues or receipts.

Evidence of the various items described in a. through d. above may take the form of actual executed documents or copies of such documents certified by an authorized official of the issuer. The actual documentation will vary depending upon the structure and complexity of the financing. In addition, a plethora of documentation regarding the end user (if other than the issuer), the efficacy of the project to be financed and the marketing of and other financial considerations and information concerning the bond issue should be included.

Unqualified and Qualified Opinions. The approving opinion should not be rendered matter-of-factly. Bond counsel is expected to render its approving opinion only after undertaking and completing a thorough review of the financing. Then, bond counsel should render such only when it is clear that an approving opinion is warranted under the circumstances. Generally, an approving opinion takes the form of an "unqualified" opinion, which means that, after, careful investigation, bond counsel has not identified any potentially problematic circumstances which could threaten the validity of the issue.

An unqualified opinion generally is necessary to market the bonds successfully. Due to the very essence of bond counsel's role, bond counsel must anticipate and appreciate the great reliance that investors will place on its opinion. Within the market arena, investors are assumed to make their investment decisions on the basis of an approving opinion. Its mere issuance constitutes notice to them that there is no questionable aspect of the bond issuance. When questionable circumstances arise, therefore, such an unqualified opinion is clearly inappropriate and would serve to deprive a potential investor of notice of material information that must be disclosed to allow for and informed and reasonable investment decision.

Because the rendering of a legal opinion is uniquely within the domain of bond counsel, the discretion to determine what shall constitute a questionable circumstance material enough to influence the rendering of such opinion lay there as well. There are but few choices when troublesome or previously unencountered circumstances arise. After careful deliberation, bond counsel may decide either that no approving opinion may be rendered or, if less severe circumstances exist, that a "no merit" or a "qualified" opinion is warranted. Bond counsel clearly should refuse to render an approving opinion if there has been a defect in any portion of the authorization or issuance proceedings for the bonds. Once such a defect has been identified, the analysis is over; no approving opinion will emerge but the parties may attempt to rectify any shortcomings indicated by bond counsel.

The more challenging situation occurs when the appropriateness of a "no merit" or a "qualified" opinion must be adjudged by bond counsel. Occasionally, before the completion of bond issuance proceedings, an interested party files a lawsuit challenging the validity of the bonds on one or more grounds. This may be distinguished from the scenario discussed earlier in which the issuer or end user is faced with a pending lawsuit the subject matter of which is something other than a direct challenge to the legality of the bond issue. In that case, the presence of such a lawsuit will not invalidate the bond issue but, depending upon the severity of the potential consequences, may compel disclosure to investors via the respective complement of offering documents. Here, however, regardless of how frivolous the bond validity lawsuit may be, bond counsel may be, bond counsel must put investors on notice that there has been a direct attack upon the issuance of the bonds.

Because of the outcome of any lawsuit is speculative, bond counsel must be careful especially not to risk an ultimately incorrect conclusion as to validity in the midst of what is a threat to the very essence of the bond issue. Thus, notice to the investor of this type of lawsuit must be accomplished through the legal opinion, the most communicative annunciation of the bond issue. However, bond counsel must make an assessment of the merits of the action and its probable outcome. If bond counsel believes that the action is frivolous or that there is no reasonable basis for the claims being asserted it may render a "no merit" opinion. This is an acceptable opinion for most investors as it is intended to convey that the claims do not affect bond counsel's conclusion as to the validity of the issue. On the other hand, when bond counsel believes that there is some reasonable basis for the claims it must disclose this and render such a "qualified" opinion which does not speculate as to the outcome of the lawsuit. A "qualified" opinion effectively kills a bond issuance because investors may not wish to take a risk when such material legal uncertainties exist. In either situation, due to the great reliance which the public places upon bond counsel's opinion, bond counsel must be extremely conservative in handling any questionable circumstances that may arise during the course of the financing.

Tax Exemption. Once the issue of validity has been laid to rest bond counsel's opinion typically addresses the tax-exempt status of the bonds. Since the advent of the federal income tax in 1913, interest on municipal bonds has been exempt from federal income taxation. This feature enables municipal issuers to market bonds to investors at a discounted interest rate in comparison to other types of bonds. The exemption has been qualified and circumscribed repeatedly by Congress, so that the tax-exempt status of each individual bond issue warrants careful attention by bond counsel. In light of the most recent changes to the Internal Revenue Code, in order to render a legal opinion that a bond issue is tax-exempt, bond counsel must analyze or evaluate the anticipated use of bond proceeds, the percentage of funds to be applied to costs of issuance, the yields which will be obtained on the investment of bond proceeds and the identity of the ultimate beneficiaries of the bond issue. Facilities which at one time were eligible for tax-exempt financing, such as sports arenas, are no longer eligible or are eligible on a much more restricted basis. Other facilities, such as waste removal sites, have been accorded tremendous importance over the past several years and are now considered to be a valid public purpose for the issuance of public debt.

It can be expected that Congress and the U.S. Treasury Department will continue to mandate further changes in the tax treatment of municipal bonds in the future. In addition to the tax exemption requirements of the Internal Revenue Code, bond counsel must be cognizant of the regulations promulgated under the Internal Revenue Code and of revenue rulings and letter rulings of the Internal Revenue Service which reflect its case-by-case pronouncements and, hence, create its own body of substantive law. Because of the great complexity inherent in the determination of tax exemption as well as the frequency of a changing legal climate, many bond counsel firms delegate the task to a core of tax specialists.

With respect to tax exemption, the opinion of bond counsel must be adapted to comply with a changing legal environment. It no longer directly states that the bonds are unequivocally "tax-exempt" [as it customarily stated prior to the enactment of the Tax Reform Act of 1985 (the "1985 Act")] but states that interest on the bonds may be excluded from gross income, depending upon the satisfaction of a set of particular conditions. The practical effect of bond counsel's opinion is to confer any such exclusion (or "exemption" prior to the enactment of the 1985 Act) upon the holders of the obligations. However, as a result of the 1985 Act, an unequivocal opinion is no longer possible. Bond counsel's opinion has been complicated further by treatment of tax exemption with a mandatory regard for the application of an alternative minimum tax, a tax surcharge on Social Security benefits and certain other qualifications. As a result, the extent of tax exemption, if any, may now be at issue also and may depend upon what entity is the holder of the obligations. In addition to federal tax exemption, bond counsel usually determines whether an issue may be exempt from income taxation in the state in which the issuer is situated.

Securities Act of 1933 Exemption and Trust Indenture Act of 1939 Exemption. Since 1933, bond counsel has been required to analyze the standing of municipal obligations with attention to the federal securities statutes. The Securities Act of 1933 (the "1933 Act") establishes requirements for registration of securities. It specifically exempts from its onerous registration requirements any security issued by the United States, any territory, state or political subdivision thereof. However, exemption of municipal obligations from registration requirements does not necessarily exempt the obligations or bond counsel from other requirements of the 1933 Act or from the Securities Exchange Act of 1934 (the "1934 Act"), including the anti-fraud provisions, particularly if any such exemption would serve to undermine either statute's objective of fair dealing in securities transactions. Bond counsel often adds to its opinion that the trust indenture or bond resolution is exempt from qualification under the Trust Indenture Act of 1939.

Negative Comfort on Disclosure Documents. In addition to the foregoing declarations that bond counsel traditionally includes in its approving opinion, bond counsel is often requested to render an opinion which addresses the accuracy of the disclosure document, usually the official statement in a public offering, which describes the transaction and is circulated to prospective investors. The preparation and ultimate adequacy and accuracy of the official statement is clearly the province and task of underwriters counsel. However, in light of the close working relationship between bond counsel and underwriters counsel, parties to the transaction often expect that some "comfort" will be given by bond counsel as well with respect to the accuracy of the official statement. Such comfort is understandably somewhat less potent than that traditionally expected from underwriters counsel, the most superior arbiter concerning disclosure matters. Indeed, bond counsel may likely present a non-affirmative opinion, considered "negative comfort," to the effect that nothing has come to its attention that the official statement contains a material misstatement or omission. The use of such language is not the result of mere semantic convenience or coincidence; it is the result of the municipal industry's self-regulatory scheme which has emerged with reference to the specific requirements prescribed for transactions that fall more squarely within the purview of the SEC and the 1933 and 1934 Acts.

In order to provide negative comfort, bond counsel theoretically need not take an active role of inquiry or investigation (stating that "nothing has come to [bond counsel's] attention" indeed suggests a passive role) more expansive than that exercised to arrive at an approving opinion. This stems from bond counsel's primary role of approving the legality of the transaction rather than monitoring the disclosure agenda being employed to market the transaction. However, the scope of bond counsel's responsibilities is always subject to revision (and, in all likelihood, expansion) administratively, legislatively and judicially.

In this light, as a precaution in an uncertain regulatory environment that includes the ongoing Washington Public Power Supply System litigation, bond counsel will usually make some further inquiries to justify any statement to be made regarding disclosure documents. Underwriters counsel, on the other hand, must undertake a thorough investigation because the accuracy of the disclosure document is its primary responsibility. The investigation is usually referred to as a "due diligence" examination. The scope of such an examination will depend upon the context of each individual transaction and will differ, as noted, depending upon whether it is being performed by bond counsel or underwriters counsel. Further, even if bond counsel is not required to provide any negative comfort regarding disclosure, bond counsel, at a minimum, will generally make an inquiry constituting somewhat less of a due diligence inquiry merely to provide justification for its approving opinion. Difficult, and as yet unanswered, questions have arisen concerning bond counsel's responsibility to uncover disclosure issues during this more limited due diligence process. The notion of due diligence will be discussed more thoroughly later on.

Basic Procedure Involved in Arriving at Legal Opinion

  (i) Documentation required by bond counsel.
 (ii) Examination of relevant constitutional and statutory law (including enabling legislation).
(iii) Determination of other necessary statutory/regulatory compliance.

Before ultimately rendering its legal opinion, bond counsel will be deluged by a wealth of information about the issuer, the end user, the obligations, the item to be financed and any other matters that it deems necessary. Bond counsel must determine its threshold level of comfort before it renders its approving opinion; no other party to the transaction may dictate this. However, other parties to the transaction may dictate other standards to be applied or requirements to be applied with respect to some other vital aspect of the transaction, such as the provision of a liquidity facility.

Such additional requirements are generally inapposite to, and thus will not affect in any way, bond counsel's decision to render its legal opinion unless they identify, whether inadvertently or tangentially, issues material to the approving opinion. In fact, they often concern items of importance to the business, non-legal, features of the transaction. However, even if there is no deleterious effect on bond counsel's opinion the introduction into the equation of such extrinsic factors could disrupt or quash some other vital portion of the transaction, rendering impracticable or impossible an otherwise viable financing. From a legal standpoint, the financing would likely remain possible to complete. Consequently, as is often the case in today's business environment, an appropriate substitution or remedy for the failed structure may, as a practical matter, not be readily available within the given time frame, allowable costs or other constraints governing the transaction.

The above scenario illustrates the importance of the careful coordination of all elements of a bond issue. Bond counsel must accept the leadership position in doing so. Thus, to begin the dual role of coordinating the transaction while garnering the requisite details to render a validity opinion, bond counsel must attempt to understand the parameters of the financing—simply, what all of the parties, particularly the issuer, can and cannot do.

After bond counsel has discussed and considered the contemplated transaction with the issuer, bond counsel will typically require the issuer and other parties to provide certain documentation. Much of this documentation is standard and will form a portion of the record in every transaction. The issuer's articles of incorporation and other organizational items fall into this category. However, depending upon the complexity or other unusual aspect of the financing, bond counsel is free to and should request additional information that bears upon the idiosyncratic realities of each individual deal. In addition, bond counsel must maintain an anticipatory focus for identifying and examining the relevant constitutional, statutory and regulatory requirements, including enabling legislation and applicable tax laws for the transaction. Similarly, bond counsel must advise the parties of any additional statutory or regulatory compliance which may be necessary before completing the transaction. Often, depending upon the requirements, local counsel to the issuer or general counsel to the end user, as the case may be, will assist the issuer in effecting such compliance. For example, general counsel to the end user should provide assistance in the filing of a certificate of need application which is often necessary in hospital transactions.

Importance of Due Diligence in Bond Counsel Role. The investigation discussed above establishes the crucial framework for bond counsel's strategy for the remainder of the financing. Bond counsel is equipped now to determine to what extent a supplemental due diligence investigation should be undertaken. The concept of due diligence in municipal securities transactions is derived from the 1933 Act. Exemption of municipal securities from registration under the 1933 Act does not preclude the application of the federal securities statutes' anti-fraud provisions which give rise to the concept of due diligence. Although this concept may be applied with respect to bond counsel, it is essentially and traditionally has been primarily applicable to underwriters counsel in the context of the preparation of the offering statement and the resulting disclosure items within (although, as mentioned, bond counsel may be expected to render a disclosure opinion, thereby extending its potential accountability pursuant to the federal securities statutes and for which a well-designed and executed due diligence examination may be necessary). The underlying notion is that the responsibilities of the parties can be limited by the facts which they discover during the course of a reasonable investigation.

In the analogous area of corporate securities to which the federal securities statutes are applicable, the 1933 Act explicitly states a defense for an underwriter or other party (potentially liable) for misleading registration statements concerning corporate securities. It is a defense if such party had, after reasonable investigation, reasonable ground to believe and did believe that the included statements were true and that there was on omission to state a material fact or necessary to make such statements not misleading. This standard, although not directly applicable to municipal securities exempt under the 1933 Act, has prompted parties to a transaction, at the very least, the underwriter and its counsel, and often, bond counsel (as mentioned previously), to undertake a similar due diligence examination for municipal issues as well. This is especially true when bond counsel is giving a disclosure opinion and, hence, may be held to a higher standard of investigation.

But even when no such opinion is contemplated, bond counsel could conceivably uncover facts which should put it on notice that further investigation may be warranted. Thus, even if bond counsel does not perform such and official due diligence investigation, the documentation which bond counsel reviews for the purpose of rendering its approving opinion or its privity to information discoursed during the financing could charge bond counsel with an obligation beyond the mere determination of the legal sufficiency of the bond issue.

For example, certain items such as a financial feasibility study or an auditor's report or management letter are often debated among a financing's working group, including bond counsel, and will almost always contain information regarding the issuer or end user that describes some shortcomings or potential shortcoming of the entity as well as suggestions for improving financial performance. Such items should always be examined with care by all parties.

In order to render its approving opinion, bond counsel must tread across a broad range of issues which arise during the course of the financing. Arguably, this is why bond counsel's role in putting together the official statement has, in recent years, increased in importance. Bond counsel's qualitative assessment of the deal in reaching its legal opinion is often inseparable from the considerations involved in formulating an accurate official statement. Further, bond counsel's general expertise in the area enables it to make the more narrow judgment as to the items which are material for disclosure purposes. It is this expertise of bond counsel, perhaps, which may help to extend its responsibility to the more substantive aspects of the official statement. As a theoretical matter, in municipal issues, there is no legal requirement under the federal securities laws that there be an official statement. However, as a practical matter, the official statement may be the only effective way to establish that information that had been provided to a bondholder was accurate and not misleading. Thus, in the same way that an official statement may be used offensively to allege that bondholders have been defrauded, the official statement may be used defensively to assert that no such fraud existed. What remains is a question of fact as to which clearcut standards generally do not exist.

Much of what underwriters counsel will review will be items which will enable underwriters counsel to evaluate whether statements contained in the offering document are accurate (as opposed to bond counsel's evaluation of the legal basis for the issue) and complete so that an investor who reads such a prospectus may make an informed investment decision. For example, assume that bond counsel has concluded that a particular issue is valid and is willing to render an approving opinion to that effect. As part of the due diligence examination, underwriters counsel may have uncovered a lawsuit against the issuer or the end user, the unfavorable outcome of which could pose a serious threat to the issuer or end user's available moneys to repay the obligations. This fact would not affect bond counsel's conclusion in rendering its legal opinion. However, it would be material with respect to any economic representations regarding the issuer or end user's economic viability and, ultimately, the prospective ability to repay the debt. Clearly, then, the due diligence standard is directed towards items germane to disclosures made to the public which is presumed to form an economic assessment of the bond issue.

A due diligence examination underscores a complex process. The underlying purpose of the examination is to discover any factors that might pose a threat to a bondholder's security interest for repayment of the obligations. This comprises a plethora of concerns involving bond counsel or underwriters counsel's sphere of influence which could range from a question as to the legality of the pledge of revenues pledged for repayment of the obligations to certain financial, economic or demographic factors or assessments that may affect an issuer's ability to realize amounts sufficient to pay debt service. In the former instance, bond counsel must refuse to give an approving opinion if the pledge is invalid. In the latter instance, the lack of confidence in the issuer's ability to make debt service payments is an economic assessment which concern must be disclosed in the official statement, but does not in and of itself invalidate the issue under any legal doctrine. Instead, if such a concern is adequately disclosed, rating agencies, bond insurers and prospective bondholders will be in a better position to evaluate the credit of the issuer and the corresponding investment risks. At such point, market influences such as the downgrading of the ratings on the obligations and the discount at which they must be sold results within this now presumably informed marketplace. Thus, in the event that the exposed investment risks come to fruition, the parties to the financing may have a defense to allegations of fraud, assuming that adequate disclosure is found to have been made.

Although the major "due diligence" efforts likely will be conducted by underwriters counsel, bond counsel should be well-apprised of the procedures which underwriters counsel is expected to follow. The minutes of the issuing entity must be examined. This exercise is intended to bring to light any potentially adverse circumstances which have been debated by the board of directors or any committee thereof which could have an unfavorable effect on the marketability of the bonds or the ability of the issuer to pay its debt obligations. Examination of the issuer's litigation files will determine whether there is any pending or threatened lawsuit which could also adversely affect the issuer's ability to repay the obligations. The examination may also include a review of the major contracts and leases to which the issuer is bound, an inquiry as to the labor/management relations of the issuer, and any other pertinent materials which will vary depending on the nature of the issuer and, often, the contents of the minutes (e.g., accreditation reports for a hospital or university or an engineer's report for a power plant).

Necessity of Test Case or Validation Proceeding. When required, bond counsel may be enlisted to supervise a procedure called *validation*, a test case, of sorts. Validation is a judicial proceeding by which the issuer seeks to obtain a determination as to the validity of the obligations. This step may be necessary when the prospective financing presents a novel or difficult legal question that bond counsel is unwilling to resolve singlehandedly. Further, more complex situations may prompt the market to require additional assurances that the issue's validity will be upheld if subsequently attacked.

The complexities inherent in the duties of bond counsel make bond counsel the most logical arbiter of the efficacy of a test case or a validation proceeding. Nonetheless, the decision to pursue a test case may be influenced by other participants in the transaction who may have had a vital role in arriving at the transaction's complex structure. The element of bond counsel discretion is less evident in those states which have statutory provisions which mandate validation proceedings for virtually all bond issues in such state (indeed, bond counsel, in many instances, may have drafted such statutes). The interests of future holders of such obligations are further protected by such guaranteed judicial scrutiny.

Special and Increased Participation of Bond Counsel

Advice as to Alternative Financing Techniques. When structuring a bond transaction, whether it be an initial issuance, a refunding, a reoffering, or other contemplated transaction, bond counsel should be involved from its inception. Even where the anticipated transaction is considered to be relatively straight-forward, such as the release of escrowed funds of a completed financing, bond counsel has the specialized knowledge to determine precisely what unusual measures, if any, may be necessary. One of bond counsel's significant roles has been to draft legislation prescribing the general bonding provisions of many states as well as enabling legislation covering most facets of an issuing entity's powers and operation. Bond counsel, almost intuitively, should be in a position to explore and evaluate present and future alternative financing techniques in light of existing and evolving regulatory schemes, which are often the reflection of bond counsel's input.

Determination of the Entity Which Is to Serve as Issuer, Subsequent Creation of Such Entity or Legislative Grant of Additional Powers to Such Entity. When the end user of proposed bond proceeds has been identified, bond counsel must determine whether there already exists an available entity to serve as issuer for such bonds. If not, bond counsel must consider whether any particular issuing entity may properly exist for the purpose of issuing such bonds. Thus, if bonds may be issued for the benefit of such an end user, bond counsel may be required to initiate a process to create an issuing entity or to effect a legislative grant of additional powers to an existing issuing entity which although is not yet vested with the requisite authority, is the most advantageous alternative.

Other Tasks of Bond Counsel Relating to the Structuring of the Transaction. The determination of the structure of a bond issue evokes a two-fold purpose: first and foremost is to provide an iron-clad security structure for the bondholders, towards whom bond counsel has an implied responsibility and, second, is to provide as much flexibility for the issuer and end user in using the proceeds, tempered by the consideration that the bonds will be outstanding for a long time and, hence, many unforeseeable events may transpire. However, any flexibility so reserved must not diminish the quantity or the integrity of the security accorded the bondholders. Some of the most critical issues and provisions for the structuring of a bond financing (any of which may or may not be statutorily or constitutionally affirmatively sanctioned in any individual case) include decisions as to:

a) selection of variable or fixed interest rate bonds or a combination thereof;

b) redemption terms;

c) the composition of the security, such as a lien upon revenues and a pledge of a mortgage;

d) the ability of the proposed issue to constitute bonds on a parity with the issuer's outstanding bonds and whether additional parity bonds may be issued in the future;

e) liquidity facilities, including letters of credit;

f) the procurement of municipal bond insurance;

g) inclusion of a "put" option for bondholders;

h) remarketing options for bonds tendered pursuant to a "put" arrangement; and

i) the advantageousness of removing the lien of old security documents through a defeasance.

Of course, in each case above, assuming that state law permits the various structures, bond counsel must also address the question of federal and/or state tax exemption in order to determine if such permitted structures will be viable for the stated purposes of the financing.

Drafting of Bond Documents. After the parties have agreed upon the initial structure of the financing, bond counsel must prepare documentation in conformity therewith, with special emphasis upon the security for the obligations. Many issuers have found it to be beneficial to retain the same bond counsel on a long term basis because, over time, bond counsel may develop a special familiarity with the issuer. This can result in a more simplified documentation process for the transaction and lower fees for the issuer. The inclusion of the following documents by bond counsel is standard for most bond transactions: trust indentures, bond resolutions, loan agreements (which may include the pledge of a mortgage as additional security) relating to the lending of the bond proceeds from the issuer to the end user in a conduit financing, documentation relating to the tax-exempt status of the bonds, including an arbitrage certificate which sets forth the expected and, where relevant, the historical uses of the tax-exempt proceeds and closing documentation which relates to the ability of the various parties to the transaction to act in their respective official capacities and to the accuracy of the statements made in any disclosure documents, particularly the official statement. Other documents relating to credit providers, such as liquidity agreements or letters of credit, are generally drafted by the credit providers and their counsel and are subject to the approval of bond counsel.

Interfacing with Issuers or Lessees, Credit Providers, Rating Agencies and Others. When the primary documents for a bond financing have been drafted, bond counsel must then interface with all other principals and their counsel to ensure that each segment of the transaction is in accord with the complete transaction. In the more simple transactions, this task generally involves the issuing entity, the underwriters, the end users and all respective counsel. In more complex financings, however, bond insurers and other credit providers, lessees of a given project and other interested parties also may become involved. In either case, if the financing is to be marketed to the public, rating agencies, most frequently Standard & Poor's Corporation and Moody's Investors Service, Inc. may be potent factors in casting some of the ultimate terms of the financing.

While the ability of an issuer to issue municipal obligations is controlled essentially by the constitutional and statutory provisions already discussed, those provisions often merely set parameters for bond financings and within such parameters many terms stand subject to debate. Discussions and disagreements among the various parties to the transaction often concentrate on the available options within such parameters. For example, an economic consideration of importance to the various parties might revolve around the decision to prohibit the issuer's optional redemption of the obligations until a certain date. A less economic but more structural consideration might concern a decision to prohibit the issuance of additional bonds in the future on a parity with the present issue. It is the role of bond counsel to determine how any of these provisions would comport with the constitutional and statutory requirements for the issue. Even if they appear permissible for the present time, bond counsel must extrapolate as to their effect over the expected life of the obligations and conclude whether the security for the bonds might be diluted. If so, such provisions must be stricken from the transaction if the security is susceptible of falling below the controlling constitutional or statutory thresholds. If the adoption of such provisions poses no danger of violating constitutional or statutory parameters, the potentially negative effects of such provisions may be a relevant disclosure item for purchasers of the obligations.

Flexible Financing Techniques. At the same time that bond counsel may be attempting to add flexibility into a financing structure or to design a structure which will provide flexibility for the future, there exist a host of financing constraints which will serve to qualify the implementation of such flexibility. In particular, federal and state constitutional and statutory provisions usually contain certain limitations which may impede the ability to utilize certain flexible financing techniques. In any event, it is bond counsel's ongoing responsibility to identify the limitations and to guide the parties through the often very narrow course to effect compliance with any such applicable limitations or regulations while preserving the transaction's flexibility. Indeed, certain limitations ultimately may make a financing illegal or impractical or economically unfeasible.

Clearly, bond counsel must counsel the parties that such a possibility exists. Bond counsel's attempts to build flexibility into a transaction must take on a prospective approach, anticipating the limitations within the context of the applicable parameters. Certain limitations not present at the outset of a financing may become applicable at some point after issuance of the obligations. Bond counsel should attempt to explain to the parties how such contingencies may affect the transaction. Some of the more common limitations include:

a) interest rate limitations;

b) restrictions on negotiated sales;

c) use of out-of-state trustees;

d) debt ceiling limitations;

e) choice of available financing documents or methods such as loan agreements, leases or installment sales;

f) need for governmental approvals such as certificates of need (in hospital financings) and plans for doing business (in student loan financings); and

g) restrictions on use of proceeds to pay various costs.

Relationship with and Division of Labor (Disclosure and Other Underwriting Documents) with Underwriters Counsel and Potential for Similar Securities Law Treatment. Perhaps the most dynamic relations in a municipal financing exists between bond counsel and underwriters counsel. This is in large part a practical outgrowth of the negotiations conducted to arrive at the terms of the transaction and to accurately portray such terms to potential investors. As a result, there is often great overlap in their tasks. For example, the official statement, as the end product of the underwriters counsel's labors in a public offering is really the *issuer's* document, over which bond counsel legitimately should retain a degree of control. In addition, by viewing a bond transaction in a wholistic manner, few tasks of the financing may be accomplished where bond counsel and underwriters counsel to maintain such a detached sense of autonomy. This is exemplified by the necessity to coordinate the due diligence examination of each counsel. However, this view also explains a more esoteric spirit which enables both counsel to participate in the development of new financing techniques.

The close relationship of bond counsel and underwriters counsel forces the question of whether or not bond counsel may be charged additionally with the duties and responsibilities of underwriters counsel for its limited capacity in helping to disseminate information to the public. For all of the progress made in recent times by the municipal industry, the explicit duties and responsibilities of bond counsel remains somewhat cloudy. In fact, this has become one of the industry's most heated and timely debates in light of recent bond defaults. One may choose to speculate that its resolution will center on the analogies which may be drawn from other securities transactions, particularly with respect to the duties ascribed to counsel there. However, until legislative or judicial pronouncements provide further clarification, bond counsel must continue to pay homage to the fundamental tenets which have enabled the municipal industry to flourish in the past while mindful of the industry's need to adapt to changing environments in the future.

CHAPTER 37

The Future of Infrastructure Needs and Financing

John E. Petersen
Government Finance Group

Catherine Holstein
Export Technology

Barbara Weiss*
The Government Finance Research Center

EXECUTIVE SUMMARY

Infrastructure, the facilities that provide transportation, water supply, waste disposal, and other basic services is vital to the economic well-being of the nation. In this country, the building and maintaining of public works is largely the responsibility of state and local governments. Until very recently, however, the need to replenish and expand public works has been ignored. As governmental responsibilities expanded and revenues became pinched, infrastructure has repeatedly lost out in the increasingly intense struggle for public attention and funds. The result of neglect has been a prolonged deterioration in the condition of the public's existing stock and shortage of new capital to meet the needs of growth. By the early 1980s, the infrastructure was wearing out faster than it was being replaced so that there was less of it for each person and firm to use as each year passed.

- Because there is no one definition of what constitutes infrastructure, much less universally accepted standards as to what the level

---

* Note: The views expressed in this paper are those of the author and do not necessarily represent those of the Government Finance Officers Association.

of such investment should be, measures of infrastructure needs are usually somewhat judgmental and frequently controversial. But by whatever yardstick applied, the declining level of infrastructure capital stock that occurred in the 1980s became viewed as a serious problem by experts. As their warnings have been underscored both by dramatic happenings such as bridge collapses and flash floods, day-to-day aggravations of traffic congestion and airport delays, the public and political leadership have begun to take note.

- Using studies of infrastructure needs that focus on the core functional areas of facilities . . . highways, bridges, and other transportation; wastewater treatment and solid waste; and water supply and conservation . . . it is estimated that total state and local government spending on fixed investment, which currently is at an annual level of $80 billion needs to be increased anywhere from $10 to $70 billion a year to replace existing capital stock, meet performance standards, and handle new growth. The biggest claimant on infrastructure spending funds has been and will be highways, roads, and bridges, with water and sewerage requirements close behind. Regionally, needs will vary, with replacement and upgrading being more important in the older areas of the nation and new facilities of primary concern in the South and West. On the other hand, some areas that have been heavy demanders of capital financing in the past, such as public education, appear to require less attention in the future because of a changing demographic profile.

- The sources of funds to finance infrastructure have fluctuated in importance over the years. A rapid growth in federal aid, which peaked at supplying over 40 cents out of every dollar spent on infrastructure, displaced the share of financing from the own-sources of state and local governments (current revenues and long-term borrowing) through the 1970s and much of the 1980s. Recently, the decline in federal aid has led to a resurgence in the funding provided by borrowing in particular. Moreover, states and localities, faced with taxpayer resistance and desiring not to raise taxes, have increasingly relied on user charges and fees. Given the tightness in budgets at all three levels of government, it is evident that borrowing will be called upon as the primary source of infrastructure funding.

- Because of the impacts of the 1986 Tax Reform Act, which greatly reduced the purposes for which tax-exempt borrowing may be undertaken, the size and scope of the tax-exempt securities market will be increasingly determined by infrastructure financing requirements. While state and local governments continue to face legal and institutional impediments in accessing the credit markets (some of which were created by the Tax Reform Act), much flexibility has been developed in the use of special districts, limited liability obligations, and leasing.

- Where borrowing can be undertaken, the debt burden situation of state and local governments viewed in the aggregate is generally favorable. By the global measure of debt outstanding as a percent of GNP, governmental purpose debt is well below historical levels, especially in the case of that which is tax-supported. Moreover, the tax-exempt market itself, except when there are overt threats to tax-exemption, appears to have sufficient capacity to handle easily increased volumes of borrowing as might be required.

- Over the next decade, state and local governments, no matter what their ardor for more infrastructure spending, will face considerable financial constraints in increasing their levels of capital spending. Federal aid for capital spending purposes is of primary significance. Because of the bleak outlook for federal finances, projections call for only a one percent a year increase in such aid. This means that states and localities will need to finance an increasing share of their capital spending from their own sources.

- While borrowing can be expanded greatly, an increase in the revenues for debt service will act as an effective constraint on how much can be borrowed and how quickly borrowing levels can be increased. Likewise, the portion of capital spending that can be financed directly from current revenues (without resorting to borrowing) will be constrained. Reviewing historical evidence, it appears that a 6 to 8% rate of annual growth in own-source revenues is achievable, but higher rates most likely are not sustainable over a prolonged period of time. Projections of future levels of infrastructure spending, whatever may be the hypothesized need, must be examined against realistic assumptions regarding the impacts of effective constraints.

- Combining projections with constraints indicates that a level of infrastructure spending equal to approximately 2% of GNP and, hence growing at the same rate as GNP, constitutes a credible scenario. Assuming a 4% rate of inflation and GNP growing at a little over 6%, such a scenario produces annual capital outlays on the order of $154 billion, approximately twice the level of spending that occurred in 1987.

- The changing mix of financing patterns will affect the growth in borrowing demands. Again using the 2% of GNP target for capital spending, the share of total funds raised for that purpose from long-term borrowing will increase from 55% (1987) to 70% in 1995. It is projected that new capital borrowing of $127 billion will need to be undertaken annually for infrastructure purposes by 1995. Assuming that other tax-exempt borrowing (primarily that done for private-activity purposes) continues as allowed under existing laws, an added \$38 billion in annual borrowing would be accomplished. This brings total projected tax-exempt borrowing to \$165 billion, approximately twice the current volume of new-capital bond sales.

- Economic recessions have and will continue to alter state and local capital spending patterns. Were a recession to occur over the period 1989 through 1990, such spending and related financing requirements would likely take a dip as projects were cancelled or delayed and funds shifted to other uses. Were recession of the nature and duration of that experienced in 1982–1983 to occur in 1989–1990, it would reduce annual capital outlays by \$6 billion to \$8 billion below the values projected that assume smooth growth.

- Popular support for infrastructure will continue to grow as public awareness of the human and financial costs of public works deficiencies are recognized and publicized. The use of user charges and special districts designed to finance improvements from the resources of beneficiaries will continue to grow in significance. Of special political importance will be the coalitions at the state and local levels of those parties that stand to benefit by improvements (developers, homebuilders, contractors) with governments to rally popular support for projects needed to permit them to proceed.

The past few years have seen much discussion about the "crisis" in public infrastructure. In a nutshell, the problem is that the nation's stock of public capital goods has not kept pace with economic and social needs. In growing areas, new development is handicapped by a lack of adequate facilities. In declining areas, the dilapidated condition of public facilities is an impediment to restoring economic vigor. Overcrowded jails, congested highways, polluted waterways and leaky water mains are all taken as manifestations of the crisis.

THE INFRASTRUCTURE CHALLENGE

Identifying the physical dimensions of the needs for public capital spending is itself no small task and often controversial. But, measuring need is only a first step in doing something about the situation. The larger and much more difficult chores are to figure out how the needed improvements are to be financed, and who, ultimately, will pay for them.

What Is Public Infrastructure?

Defining just exactly what public infrastructure is and how much infrastructure there should be presents difficult technical problems.

However, at the risk of oversimplifying, a sensible measure of the aggregate investment in domestic infrastructure is found in the capital outlays made by state and local governments for public works. A good working definition is found in the National Income Account's measure of that spending done for government equipment and structures which it calls fixed capital investment.[1] Others examining the topic have taken a more limited view which considers only such public works as transportation- and water-related public facilities.[2] But the essentialness and economic character of such items as jails, schools, and solid waste facilities argue that a more inclusive definition is useful in most applications.

Focusing on the spending of states and localities in the definition creates problems as regards comprehensiveness, since the federal government and the private sector also make outlays that contribute to, or substitute for, meeting the public's infrastructure needs. But, in our nation's economic system, the latter's roles as direct providers of capital services used by the general public are relatively minor, at least for the present. Because state and local governments provide by most measures 90% of the infrastructure spending, we will be talking about the fixed investment spending (structures and equipment) of these governments for the greatest part.[3]

State and local governments are big spenders on capital goods (gross fixed investment was an estimated $76 billion in 1987). But, they are not as big spenders as they should be or would like to be. Those wishing to assess the adequacy of capital spending need to remember that for most governments, capital outlays are episodic, and performance needs to be viewed over a period of years.

Examining capital outlays in any one year is unsatisfactory from a normative standpoint, since it fails to account for the fact that an investment made in any one year provides services over time to changing cadres of users. Also, capital improvements last several years, and one is typically interested in the "bricks and mortar" that are put in place each year to serve each citizen. Thus, it is desirable to adjust annual expenditures for growth in population, changing prices, and to

[1] Government equipment and structures are physical assets that, were they owned by the private business sector, would be counted in fixed business capital, plus equipment and facilities that have no counterpart in the business sector. See John C. Musgrave, "Government-Owned Fixed Capital in the United States, 1925–1979," in *Survey of Current Business*, March 1980, p. 33.

[2] U.S. Congressional Budget Office, *Public Works Infrastructure: Policy Considerations for the 1980s*, U.S.G.P.O., Washington, D.C., April 1983.

[3] Only in the area of highways and conservation does federal direct spending account for much infrastructure used for peacetime purposes.

sum them into a stock of capital. The capital stock is not static; it physically depreciates over time, becomes obsolete, and, ultimately, is retired from service. Thus, a stock of capital needs to be constantly replenished to keep from shrinking.

Let us examine the annual expenditures on gross fixed investment between 1950 and 1987 as defined in the national income accounts.[4] Figure 37.1 illustrates that, in real per capita terms, state and local government investment peaked in 1968 and was in decline up until the last couple of years. Until the late 1970s the level of annual investment, nonetheless, was sufficient to offset the depreciation and retirement of facilities and add to the total capital stock per person. By 1979, however, the real per capita amount of publicly owned capital stock began to decline, as is displayed in Figure 37.2. The measurement of the real value of public capital stock is admittedly crude, and declines in certain areas or for some purposes are not necessarily bad. However, a precipitous fall in public capital stock does constitute a reason for worry. Moreover, most observers contend that at present levels, the amount of capital stock is far below that which is needed, as we will discuss below.

The aggregate capital spending and stock figure discussed above mask the capital spending patterns for the individual functional categories of capital. In Table 37.1 another perspective is given of the capital spending patterns of state and local governments, this time focusing on the growth rates of real aggregate (not per capita) spending by function. Cyclical patterns that reflect both the changing demography and fiscal circumstances of state and local governments are evident. Throughout the 1950s, for example, highway spending (largely propelled by federal grants for the interstate system) grew rapidly. In the early 1960s, conversation and water supply were the favored categories, followed by other buildings and hospitals in the latter part of that decade.

By the 1970s, real spending on all types of structures, with the exception of sewers (driven mightily by federal construction grants), began to decline. The malaise spread to virtually all forms of capital spending in the late 1970s as fiscal stringency, high rates of inflation, and taxpayer resistance all took their toll on capital spending levels. In the early 1980s, only highway spending (spurred by the passage of

---

[4]Other definitional and data problems emerge regarding what is included as capital spending (for example, governments include land acquisition as part of capital spending but the National Income Accounts do not), and esoteric points surrounding the measurement of capital's condition, the role of maintenance spending, appropriate depreciation techniques, and the like. While of interest in many applications, these issues are secondary to our concerns, which to do with broad contours of financing of state and local capital spending.

FIGURE 37.1
Gross Fixed Capital Formation per Capita (1950–1987)

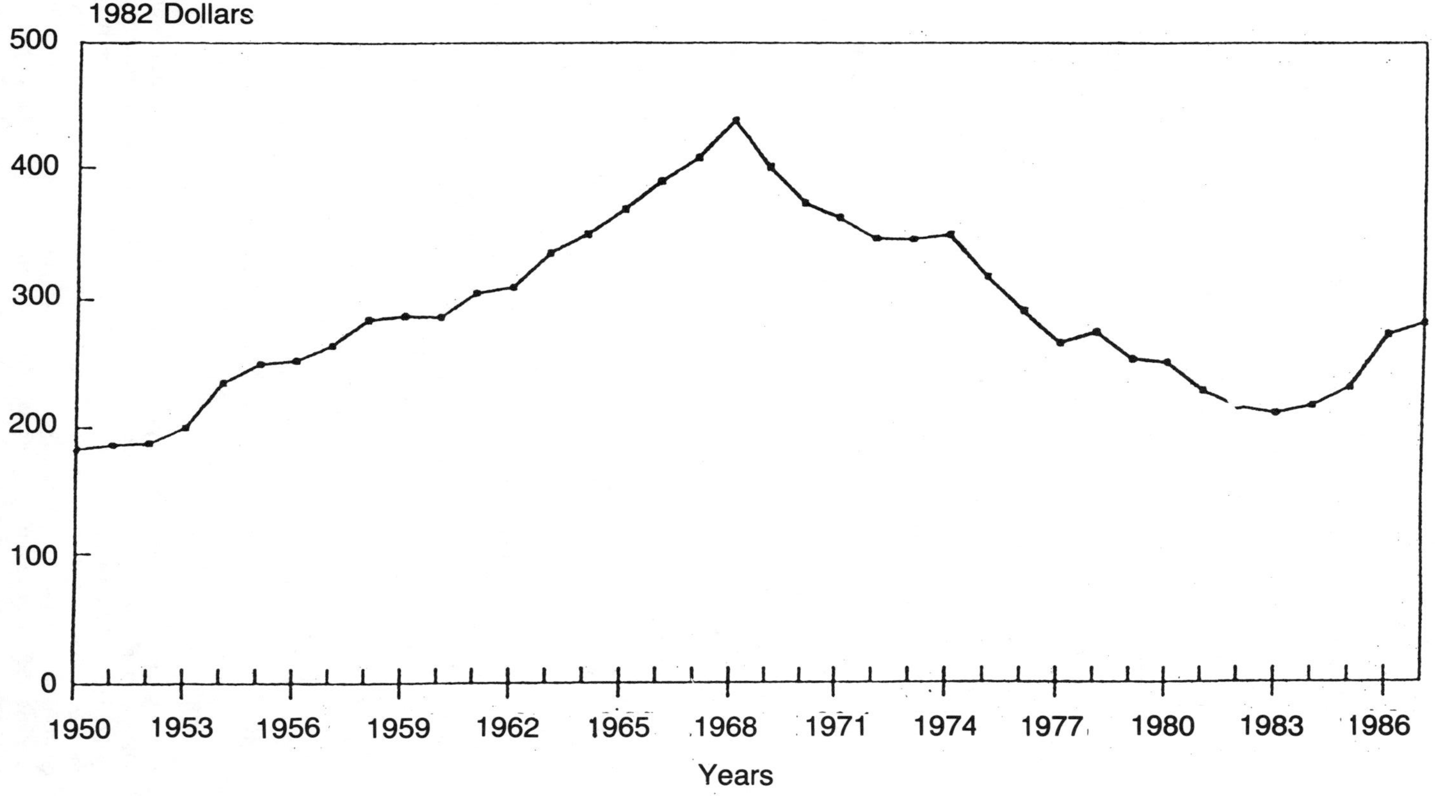

Source: Government Finance Research Center.

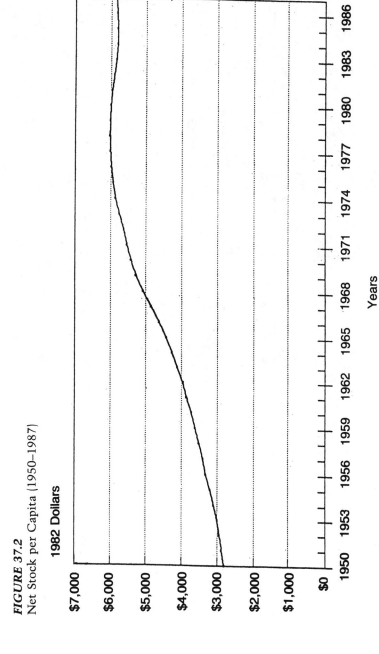

FIGURE 37.2
Net Stock per Capita (1950–1987)

1982 Dollars

Source: Government Finance Research Center.

TABLE 37.1
Growth Rates of State-Local Capital Outlays By Functional Category, 1950–87 (In Constant Dollars)

					Period Annual Averages			
	1950–54	55–59	60–64	65–69	70–74	75–79	80–84	85–87
Construction[1]	8.4%	4.7%	6.4%	2.9%	-1.4%	-5.1%	-1.8%	7.2%
Education Bldgs.	12.3	-0.9	6.7	3.0	-1.9	-11.0	-8.8	10.9
Hospitals	-7.5	3.9	0.7	9.0	2.2	-13.2	-1.4	-4.0
Other Bldgs.	4.3	2.3	6.0	13.6	6.1	-6.8	1.9	11.2
Highways	10.6	6.7	5.0	0.3	-6.5	-7.6	5.5	3.5
Conservation & Development	0.0	6.1	17.4	-0.7	-10.3	-4.8	-5.5	11.8
Sewers	5.6	7.8	8.2	0.0	12.3	2.2	-5.3	4.0
Water Supply	6.0	-2.4	11.8	-1.2	-3.6	0.1	-5.6	14.0
Equipment	7.6	-8.1	7.5	13.3	7.6	-3.2	6.3	9.2
All Structures & Equipment	8.3%	3.6%	6.4%	4.0%	0.0%	-4.8%	1.5%	7.7%

[1]Including construction not separately classified.

Source: Advisory Commission on Intergovernmental Relations, Bureau of Economic Analysis, and Bureau of the Census.

the federal highway tax in 1982 and increased state fuel taxes) staged much of a comeback.

The period 1985 through 1987, for which numbers are just becoming available, have witnessed a sharp recovery in nearly all forms of capital spending by state and local governments. The uptick is due primarily to recovery from the recession of the early 1980s and hit the sector hard.[5] Furthermore, there has been notoriety given to infrastructure needs in the popular press. Recent bond election results tend to confirm that the popular mood is positive towards capital spending once more.

Spending for Future Needs

The above results—depicting a decade-long, prolonged decline in real capital stock that is starting to reverse itself—makes a prima facie case that public capital spending needs are not being met. The costs of inadequate or worn out infrastructure are perceived to be large, although they are difficult to quantify, because they are widely spread throughout society and the economy. Aside from the annoyance and inconvenience experienced by ordinary citizens in their daily lives, studies have documented that transportation productivity is impaired (increased operating costs due to fuel use, repairs, and time loss), pollution levels increase to unhealthy levels, and environmental changes cause dislocations as the quality of life deteriorates. Recent evidence has been presented that the deterioration in public capital has dampened the productivity of private capital investment to the detriment of long-run production.[6] History and international comparisons indicate that there is a complementary relationship between public and private capital. That is, if the public sector capital stock sinks too low in relation to that in the private sector, the latter will find its production (and level of investment) shrinking.[7]

Several recent studies have attempted to quantify what infrastructure spending should be. "Needs" studies are intrinsically difficult and debatable because they require the setting of a desired level, which is usually determined by engineering or other standards.

[5] Laura Rubin, "State and Local Government Finance in the Current Expansion," *Federal Reserve Bulletin,* February 1988.

[6] David Alan Aschauer, "Government Spending and the Falling Rate of Profit," *Economic Perspectives,* Federal Reserve Bank of Chicago, May/June, 1988.

[7] Rebuild America Coalition, *Making America's Economy Competitive Again,* Washington, D.C., September 1988.

As there is no uniform standard by which analysts and governmental bodies define infrastructure, national studies of the status of the public capital stock or aggregate estimates of future needs are invariably based on different assumptions and encompass varying public works components. Nonetheless, three major studies have provided estimates of needs for major categories of infrastructure: The Association of General Contractors (AGC), the Congressional Budget Office (CBO), and the Joint Economic Committee (JEC).

AGC Study

The Associated General Contractors of America released a study in 1982 entitled, "Our Fractured Framework: Why America Must Rebuild."[8]

The AGC study focuses on projecting the minimum level of capital investment required to meet (then) currently identifiable needs and did not include estimates for possible future infrastructure demands. In the absence of an existing inventory of the nation's public works, a valid measure of the condition of the present public works system, and a generally accepted gauge of the investment needed for repairs and replacement, the AGC Task Force surveyed available literature and studies addressing infrastructure needs and contacted over 100 cities, states and organizations to produce its estimates.

The AGC survey produced an estimate of capital investment required to meet identifiable needs in excess of $3 trillion. This estimate was determined by examining required capital needs for 17 functional areas. Unlike the other studies, the AGC report adopted a broad definition and included functional areas such as educational facilities, prisons, post offices, and multi-family and low-income housing, in its measure of public works. This broad definition resulted in aggregate estimates significantly higher than the other national studies. In addition to its broad scope, the AGC's method of estimating required capital investment using engineering standards as a cost basis resulted in an inflated needs estimate.

JEC Study

The Joint Economic Committee of the U.S. Congress in conjunction with the Graduate School of Public Affairs at the University of Colorado

---

[8] The report provided estimates of infrastructure needs; however, state and local government-owned capital was not separately considered in the analysis. To supplement the November report, a special AGC Infrastructure Task Force was employed to present total government-owned fixed investment needs, as well as possible solutions to the infrastructure crisis. This report, *The Infrastructure Crisis: An AGC Update*, was released in May, 1983.

conducted a study released in February 1984 called "Hard Choices: A Report On The Increasing Gap Between America's Infrastructure Needs And Our Ability to Pay For Them." The study's main purpose was to develop an aggregate estimate of national infrastructure needs and revenues available to meet those needs through the year 2000. The Joint Economic Committee used data gathered from 23 states representing five geographic regions as a sample from which to construct a national needs figure. As stated by the JEC, this national figure could only be used as a base for which to develop a more inclusive estimate of needs, due to the high degree of variation among the states' definitions of needs.

Individual case studies for the 23 states were provided by sources in each state. The JEC study focused on only four major functional categories in its definition of needs—highways and bridges, other transportation, drinking water, and wastewater treatment. The resulting national needs estimate of $64 billion per year was substantially lower than the AGC study, which is partly attributable to its narrower definition of public works and focus on the state and local sectors.

CBO Study

Over the past five years, the Congressional Budget Office has produced a series of studies of infrastructure needs and the federal role in meeting them. From these studies, estimates of infrastructure spending needs can be developed for those categories where there is federal program interests.

The CBO defines infrastructure as those publicly provided services that underlie commercial activity: highways, aviation, mass transit, waste treatment, and water transportation.[9] The CBO definitions are close to those of the JEC. Unlike the AGC study, the CBO definition of public works does not include the functional areas of public housing, prisons, hospitals, schools, and hazardous waste treatment facilities.

According to the CBO, the plight of the nation's infrastructure has reached a critical level. However, it foresees not just more capital spending, but also better allocations of resources and the adoption of programs requiring charges to end-users as remedies. The Congressional Budget Office currently estimates that $427 billion of capital investment would be required through the year 2000. This figure is slightly lower than the estimate of the JEC due to the statement of needs as being a function of the price and quality of the service delivered and not as absolute values.[10]

[9] Congressional Budget Office, *New Directions For The Nation's Public Works: A CBO Study,* August 1988.

[10] Congressional Budget Office, *New Directions,* p. 2.

TABLE 37.2
Comparison of Annual Capital Investment Requirements and Actual
Capital Outlays (in billions of 1982 dollars)

Infrastructure Category	AGC Study	CBO Study	JEC Study	Actual Outlays[1] 1985–1986
Highways and bridges	$ 62.8	$27.2	$40.0	$23.4
Other transportation (mass transit, airports, ports, locks, waterways)	17.5	11.1	9.9	8.0
Drinking water	6.9	7.7	5.3	4.5
Wastewater treatment	25.4	6.6	9.1	5.7
Total	$112.6	$52.6	$64.3	$41.6

[1]Figures include approximately $2 billion in direct federal capital spending, the rest being state and local government expenditures.

Source: National Council on Public Works Improvement, *Fragile Foundations: A Report on America's Public Works,* February 1988, and U.S. Bureau of the Census, *Governmental Finance, 1985–1986.*

Comparing Needs Estimates

As described previously, the estimates have been derived for various time frames and for different groupings of public works. In order to compare them, they have been converted into annual spending levels that should occur between 1989 and 2000 (a 12-year interval) and have been stated in constant (1982) prices. Also, they have been adjusted to encompass the same functional groups of infrastructure, since the three studies did not cover the same categories of spending.

As may be seen in Table 37.2, the annual spending estimates range from over $100 billion to $52 billion (in 1982 dollars) for the four major categories shown. By comparison, actual capital spending levels as of fiscal year 1986 (also shown in 1982 prices) was about $42 billion, which is shown in the final column of Table 37.2. Thus, depending on whose estimates of needs one uses, the shortfall of annual spending as of 1986 was $10 to $70 billion. To the extent these four categories represent only about half of all capital spending by states and localities (for example, education, community development, sanitation functions are omitted), the capital spending gap is undoubtedly greater.[11]

[11]U.S. Bureau of the Census, *Government Finance,* Washington, D.C., 1987.

Needs by Functional Category

Aggregate needs are of interest in measuring the overall level of spending and financing that will be needed. But it is on the level of the individual governments deciding on individual functions that spending decisions most likely will be made.

Highways and Bridges. Aggregate capital investment needs are by far the greatest in the areas of highways and bridges—vital components of infrastructure for the economic health of the private and public sectors of the economy. While the United States has an extensive network of highways and bridges, their overall condition has deteriorated in the past decade. Examining bridges alone, in December 1984, the Department of Transportation identified 140,808 or 25% of a total 575,045 bridges as structurally deficient. The Department estimated costs for replacement and repair in excess of $47 billion through the year 2000.[12]

A *prima facie* case for this need is illustrated in Figure 37.3. As shown, capital spending has been declining since the late 1960s, while the number of miles travelled has increased at a rapid rate, inferring that the nation's highway network exists mainly as a result of past and not recent investment. Consequently, capital requirements for the years ahead will be mostly for upgrading, rehabilitation, and maintenance of existing roads and bridges as opposed to constructing new roads.

Major highways are unique in nature in that they are mainly operated and built by state and local governments with much of the construction funded by the federal government. However, as need for new construction declines and maintenance management increases, the role of the federal government may diminish to the point that federal aid will be disbursed only to those activities of national significance.

Recent analysis by the Congressional Budget Office indicates that while to fix all deficiencies would cost about $35 billion, total spending of $25 billion on highways would make better economic sense and that much of that outlay should go into maintaining existing standards.[13] New construction should be focused on urban areas that are currently subject to congestion. The highest levels of urban traffic congestion are reportedly found in the highway systems of Alabama, California, Connecticut, Georgia, Massachusetts, New Jersey, New York, Pennsylvania,

---

[12] National Council on Public Works Improvement; *Defining the Issues: A Report to the President and the Congress,* September 1986, p. 26.

[13] Congressional Budget Office, *New Directions,* p. 14.

FIGURE 37.3

Comparison of Total U.S. Capital Spending for Roads and Bridges and Vehicle Miles of Travel

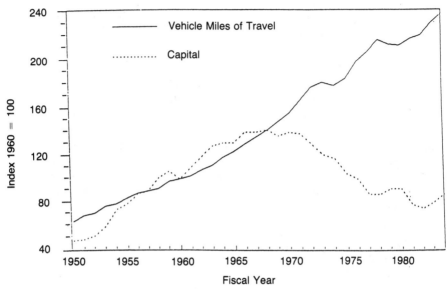

Fiscal Year

Source: Apogee Research Inc. from U.S. Federal Highway Administration data.

and Texas.[14] Overall, annual capital spending of $25 to $35 billion on highways and bridges in current (1988) dollars is a reasonable prospect for spending, with increasing emphasis on urban systems.

Public Transit. Highways and bridges are not the only components of the nation's transportation network that are likely to be major demanders of capital. The areas of public transportation such as bus and subway systems will require a large amount of investment to repair and rehabilitate dilapidated systems and to build new transit to relieve traffic congestion, a responsibility residing primarily with local jurisdictions. For mass transit systems, investment will be needed for fixed as well as moving stock. Many older subway systems require substantial investment for new trains, as well as for improved tracks and ventilation systems. Other cities need capital to build entire new public transportation systems.

Mass transit has been heavily aided by the federal government (obligations for federal aid ran at $2.5 billion for capital grants and $860

[14]Congressional Budget Office, *New Directions*, p. 5.

million for operating assistance in 1987) and is very controversial. Much less of the aid is going to major projects and much is being scattered inefficiently among medium and small cities. Furthermore, buses, rapid rail, and street cars carry only 15 percent of all commuters, and there is reportedly overcapacity on many of the newer systems.[15] Nonetheless, major urban areas suffering highway congestion are likely to continue building light rail alternatives or to continue experimenting with high-speed bus systems. Total capital spending of $4 to $6 billion a year on mass transit (with $2.5 billion in federal capital aid continuing) appears to be a reasonable estimate for annual levels.

Water Supply and Distribution. Traditionally, responsibility for water supply and distribution has been mixed among local governments and privately owned utilities (which represent about 20% of all systems). Major water distribution problems in coming years will be the replacement of deteriorating systems in older urban areas. Many large cities are experiencing declining water quality and pressure due to old and leaky pipes. Needed expenditures to replace or clean and line existing pipes are estimated to run $4 to $6 billion on an annual basis. The quantity of water conserved through the replacement and repair of malfunctioning water mains may be sufficient to offset increased demand stemming from population growth in older areas. It is clear, however, that in areas of rapid population growth where there is a seasonal variation in the level of precipitation, such as the western region of the country, new sources of supply and storage systems will have to be established. According to the Congressional Budget Office, new growth will engender an added requirement of $4 to $6 billion in annual capital needs.[16]

Municipal water systems will experience increased operating expenses while needing higher levels of investment in order to comply with the 1986 Amendments to the Safe Drinking Water Act. The Amendments called for the determination of maximum levels of, and standards required to monitor, a number of pollutants which pose a health threat. They also require municipal water systems to follow set guidelines pertaining to filtration and disinfection of these contaminants. Unlike other functional areas, there are little or no federal funds available to meet water supply requirements. Water users will carry the burden of the costs for compliance to the new standards. However, of all municipal services, water supply has the soundest basis in terms of employing user charges.

---

[15] Congressional Budget Office, *New Direction*, Chapter II.

[16] Congressional Budget Office, *Public Works Infrastructure*, p. 132.

Wastewater Treatment. Since 1972, massive federal involvement in the wastewater treatment area has driven state and local spending patterns. Currently, states and localities are trying to comply with the July 1, 1988 secondary wastewater treatment regulations issued by the Environmental Protection Agency (EPA), which require that wastewater treatment plants meet certain standards or that a capital improvement program be implemented, if needed, to meet these standards. For many municipalities, this will mean expanding plants to meet sewage flows and upgrading existing technology. According to the EPA, total capital spending on sewerage facilities to handle existing population will need to be $60 billion. (See Table 37.3.)

In the past, federal and state grant programs have contributed a large part of wastewater treatment financing. However, many of these programs are ending. The 1987 reauthorization of the Clean Water Act called for the phasing out of the construction grant program and its extinction by the year 1991, leaving states and localities to bear the full cost of wastewater projects. To aid the transition, the federal government provided seed money for *state revolving-loan funds* (SRF). To participate, states must provide 20 cents for every dollar contributed to its SRF by the federal government. These capital grants, which are currently being used to help localities comply with the July 1, 1988 secondary wastewater treatment regulations, will eventually be available for funding other pollution control programs.

TABLE 37.3
Costs of Wastewater Treatment Facilities Needed to Meet Clean Water Act Requirements for the 1986 Population, by State

State	Total Cost (Millions of Dollars)	Total Cost per Capita (Dollars)	Basic Cost (Millions of Dollars)	Basic Cost per Capita (Dollars)
United States	60,222	250	32,992	137
Alabama	445	110	338	83
Alaska	112	210	94	176
Arizona	477	144	443	133
Arkansas	232	98	197	83
California	4,632	172	2,810	104
Colorado	72	22	68	21
Connecticut	1,041	326	413	130
Delaware	48	76	26	41
District of Columbia	245	391	245	391
Florida	2,352	201	1,439	123
Georgia	599	98	438	72

TABLE 37.3 (continued)

State	Total Cost (Millions of Dollars)	Total Cost per Capita (Dollars)	Basic Cost (Millions of Dollars)	Basic Cost per Capita (Dollars)
Hawaii	208	196	120	113
Idaho	118	118	87	87
Illinois	2,732	236	1,012	88
Indiana	1,485	270	395	72
Iowa	595	209	552	194
Kansas	367	149	288	117
Kentucky	1,140	306	574	154
Louisiana	796	177	526	117
Maine	267	228	186	159
Maryland	642	144	516	116
Massachusetts	3,733	640	2,053	352
Michigan	3,016	330	1,566	171
Minnesota	903	214	473	112
Mississippi	393	150	331	126
Missouri	925	183	768	152
Montana	39	48	21	26
Nebraska	120	75	85	53
Nevada	95	99	83	86
New Hampshire	735	716	306	298
New Jersey	3,290	432	2,167	284
New Mexico	56	38	33	22
New York	11,451	644	3,154	177
Nor+h Carolina	921	145	608	96
North Dakota	15	22	15	22
Ohio	3,096	288	1,994	185
Oklahoma	268	81	226	68
Oregon	727	269	345	128
Pennsylvania	1,453	122	844	71
Rhode Island	346	355	92	94
South Carolina	446	132	379	112
South Dakota	58	82	49	69
Tennessee	869	181	627	131
Texas	2,088	125	1,863	112
Utah	288	173	262	157
Vermont	144	266	69	128
Virginia	792	137	431	74
Washington	2,069	464	1,199	269
West Virginia	856	446	468	244
Wisconsin	1,107	231	808	169
Wyoming	24	47	23	45

Note: Basic cost excludes costs of rehabilitation or replacement of sewers, new collector sewers, and combined sewer overflows.

Source: Congressional Budget Office, using EPA and Census data.

Solid Waste. Environmental concerns regarding solid waste disposal have heightened recently due to the declining capacity of many landfill sites. According to the National Council on Public Works Improvement, approximately 450 tons of solid waste are generated by Americans each day, of which 95% is disposed of at sites nearing full capacity.[17] In addition, new site locations are increasingly difficult to place into operation as a result of the numerous tests and studies which must be completed prior to site selection and widespread public opposition to locations.

Many of the procedures regarding the implementation of new facilities and regulations governing existing sites are translating into enormous cost increases for solid waste disposal. A decade ago, municipalities were paying only $3 or $4 per ton of solid waste for disposal in an open dump site. However, with more restrictive guidelines regarding the environmental impact of disposal sites, costs have risen to $20 per ton for disposal at sanitary landfills and as much as $30 to $50 per ton for disposal at waste-to-energy sites. Reportedly, there are more than $18 billion in such projects being planned, although low energy costs and the Tax Reform Act of 1986 severely lessened their attractiveness.[18]

Although waste-to-energy facilities have become a popular method of disposal in recent years, there will not be sufficient capacity to meet waste disposal demands throughout the next decade without use of traditional sanitary landfills. The National Council on Public Works has estimated that by the year 2000 waste-to-energy facilities will have the capacity to process 20% of the projected waste stream or 32 billion tons of waste, with the remaining 80% disposed of in sanitary landfills.

Responsibility for solid waste disposal has historically resided with local governments. Involvement on a state and federal level has mainly been limited to serving as regulators. Spending on solid waste facilities, currently at $600 million, should increase to $1 billion to keep up with needs.

Airports. Domestic airports are currently in a period of rapid expansion as they respond to the deregulation of the airline industry, increased ridership, and new routing techniques (Hub and Spoke). Traditionally, airports and airlines have funded projects through airport fees, which carriers pay on an annual basis, but it is evident that

---

[17] R.W. Beck and Associates, *The Nation's Public Works Report on Solid Waste*, National Council on Public Works Improvement, Washington, D.C., May 1987.

[18] J. R. Laing, "The Rebuilding of America," *Barron's*, November 14, 1988, p. 9.

this resource will not be able to meet such large capital investment as demanded by the airport expansion plans. Overall, spending on all airports to meet new capacity needs and to bring them up to recommended standards is estimated at $24 billion or $2.5 billion a year over the next decade.[19]

Hazardous Waste. Hazardous waste management is a growing public concern, although many facilities are owned and operated by the private sector. It is estimated that U.S. industries generate more than two tons of hazardous waste per year for each person in the country and that costs associated with disposal exceed $100 billion.[20] National Council on Public Works Improvement studies indicate that the costs for disposal are too high for private sector businesses that generate the waste to bear alone. The public sector will have to start sharing the burden as demonstrated by the creation of Super Fund, but reliable estimates of the publicly borne costs eventually may not be available.

Needs by Region

Aside from the functional categories needs discussed above, there remains the question of where, geographically, the capital spending takes place. In this regard, there are two types of spending to keep in mind—that for replacement of existing facilities (or to upgrade them to meet mandated levels) and that needed to meet the demands of growing or relocating population.

As was indicated, highway expenditures—if spent efficiently—will be focused on the urban metropolitan areas where congestion is worst. These are also the areas where mass transit monies will be in the greatest demand. Wastewater clean-up, on the other hand, is less sensitive to growth needs and more to existing populations, the natural environment and engineering concerns. Here, New England, the Northeast, the Northwest, and the Middle West find major burdens looming ahead, although growth is slower than elsewhere.

Projections of population growth provide the best overall indicator as to where capital spending driven by expansion will tend to occur. As has been widely noted, the nation has seen major growth occurring in the sunbelt region —the southern and southwestern areas. A list of the 10 most rapidly growing states in shown in Table 37.4.

[19] Congressional Budget Office, *New Directions*, p. 72.

[20] J.C. Walter, et al., *Impact of Global Climate Change on Urban Infrastructure*, the Urban Institute, Washington, D.C., November 1988.

TABLE 37.4
Projected Percentage Change in Population 1980–2000

	1980–1990	1990–2000
U.S. TOTAL	10.3%	7.1%
Regions		
Northeast	2.9	2.4
Midwest	1.5	−.3
South	15.8	11.0
West	21.1	13.7
FASTEST GROWTH STATES		
New Hampshire	24.1	16.7
Georgia	22.0	19.4
Florida	31.5	20.3
Texas	24.5	14.1
New Mexico	25.3	20.5
Arizona	38.0	23.1
Utah	21.6	12.1
Nevada	34.4	21.1
California	23.1	15.0
Alaska	43.4	19.2

Source: U.S. Bureau of the Census, *Current Population Reports*, p. 25.

Florida, New Mexico, Arizona, and Nevada are slated for the most rapid growth over the next decade. If the southern-western tilt in population continues as projected, 62% of the population will live in the South and West by 2010, as compared to 48% in 1970. Only one rapid growth state, New Hampshire, is not in the South or West. Also, the midwestern states are generally slated to lose population.

These projections suppose that two essentially environmentally problems can be solved and solving these will likely involve capital spending of substantial proportions. First, for the southern states, water supply presents substantial problems. In the case of Florida, pumping of fresh water has led to subsidence and saltwater intrusion. Also the high water tables present problems for waste disposal. In the Southwest, water supply is limited to support residential growth, unless substantial cutbacks are made in agricultural use (which is the likely result). As noted, municipal water supply seems to be well established as a self-supporting function with heavy use of user charges, which bodes well for supporting future spending.

A second, and more difficult to quantify, challenge is that found in the "Greenhouse Effect." This is the global warming trend that, if not retarded, will lead to a large public facility needed to keep coastal public places habitable. Recent studies indicate that the resulting heating and rising water levels (due to polar melting) will have impacts on economic activity and infrastructure spending needs.

These impacts will not be evenly split. A recent study projects at least $600 million in added capital spending in Miami-Dade County to adjust to rising water levels and temperatures. New York City, looking to the year 2030, will require several billions in spending to protect its water supply. Other cities, such as Cleveland, would find their costs little changed, as the climate warms.[21]

Demographic projections also provide insights to the service demands of selected parts of the population. Public education, for example, is sensitive to the demand for facilities derived from changing levels of enrollment. For the decade 1990 through 2000, the population in the age group 5 to 17 years old (the age group with greatest significance for primary and secondary education) is estimated to grow at 7%, a little less than total population growth. However, the projected growth is concentrated in the South and West. In fact, the growth in school-aged population is centered in Florida (22% increase), California (16.5%), Arizona (24%), Georgia (17.5%), and Texas (10.5%). These five states account for over two million of the larger school-aged population, or over two-thirds of the total national increase.

Conversely, most of the states in the north central region will see no change or even decline in that 5 to 17 year age group—and in public school enrollments.

It might be noted that the next age cohort, the 18 to 24 years group, reflecting the "baby bust" of the early 1970s is projected to be smaller in 2000 than in 1990. This should mean a continuing low-level demand for new, higher education facilities in all areas of the country and pressure to eliminate excess facilities.

Looking Ahead: The National Council's Report

The National Council on Public Works final report, issued early in 1988, provides the most recent and comprehensive evaluation of the nation's public works. Its principal finding is that the current level of spending on infrastructure is insufficient to meet the demands placed on America's public works for the years ahead.[22] To meet these requirements, the Council recommends:

---

[21] National Council on Public Works Improvement, *Fragile Foundations: A Report on America's Public Works*, 1988.

[22] National Council on Public Works Improvement, *Defining the Issues, Report to the President and Congress*, September 1986.

- A national commitment, shared by all levels of government, the private sector and the public.
- Clarification of the respective roles of the federal, state and local governments in the construction and management of infrastructure.
- Steps to improve the performance and efficiency of existing facilities.
- A rational capital budgeting process at all levels of government.
- Strong incentives to ensure adequate maintenance and adopt new technologies.
- More rigorous and widespread use of less capital-intensive techniques for delivering services and meeting service needs.
- Financing of a larger share of the cost of public works by those who benefit from services.
- Removal of unwarranted limits on the ability of state and local governments to use tax-exempt financing.
- Additional support for research and development to accelerate technological innovation and for training of public works professionals.

When it came to the overarching subjects of how much spending should be done and by whom, the council was vague. First, relying on the belief that infrastructure spending return to the level of GNP it represented in 1960 (2.3%) it called for a doubling in spending. Second, it stressed increased efficiency in the use of infrastructure especially through application of the user-pay principle. Third, it called for removal of legal barriers that inhibit states and localities from greater use of tax-exempt bond financing.

What was conspicuously absent from the Council's report was any federal role, other than that implied in re-examining the tax code in the aftermath of the 1986 Tax Reform Act.

In the absence of any federal initiative, infrastructure needs will be identified and financed by state and local governments, primarily relying on their own financial resources.

Developing realistic expectations of the extent of such financial resources and the ability and ardor of governments to expend them are the next concerns of this report.

FINANCING INFRASTRUCTURE: PAST, PRESENT, AND FUTURE

Who will pay the tens of billions of dollars needed to build and rebuild public works? What to do about increasing investment in infrastructure opens up the intertwined questions of which levels of government are responsible and have the resources to support increased spending. Before examining those issues, however, it is useful to review briefly from what sources state and local infrastructure spending has been financed in the past.

When viewed as a whole, state and local government capital outlays can be financed from three sources:

- Borrowing in the credit markets;
- Current revenues from a government's own sources; and
- Federal government aid.

Based on estimates developed by the Government Finance Research Center, the period of the last 30 years has seen these alternative sources of funds fluctuate greatly in importance.[23] Table 37.5 provides for the period 1955 through 1986 annual estimates of the dollar amounts, and, in Figure 37.4, the relative importance of these sources of funds, in financing capital spending.

In the 1950s, before the dramatic growth in the state and local sector, capital spending by these governments was largely financed by long-term bond sales. During the 1960s, federal aid for public construction grew, as did contributions from current revenues, and the importance of borrowed funds diminished. The 1970s saw a dramatic rise in the importance of federal aid as a source of capital funds and, late in the decade, a sharp decline in contributions from current revenues, as this source of funds came under the pressure of taxpayer revolts and recessionary conditions. In the 1980s the trend has been one of diminished federal aid and a growing reliance on debt financing. It appears that financing from current revenue sources is near the bottom of a trough, accounting for only a little over 15% of capital spending.

For reasons to be discussed below, it is evident that federal grants are unlikely to grow with any vigor, and very likely will decline in real, per capita terms. Financing from current revenues will be difficult to expand rapidly, if at all, in the near future, (although certain "non-debt" variants may present interesting, if limited, alternative means of financing). Last, the debt financing option appears the most promising one, although as we shall see, it has many uncertainties attached to it. Next, each of these will be discussed in turn.

---

[23] See John Petersen and Arthur Gitajn, *Projections of State-Local Capital Stock Requirements*, Government Finance Research Center, Washington, D.C., May 1985.

TABLE 37.5
Sources of Funds for State and Local Government Fixed Capital Formation

	(Aggregate Amounts in Bilions)			(As a Percent of Fixed Capital Formation)		
Year	Fixed Capital Formation	Federal Grants	Debt Financed	Current Receipts	Federal Grants	Debt Financed	Current Receipts
1955	10.3	0.8	5.3	4.2	7.8%	51.5%	40.8%
1956	11.6	1.3	5.3	5.0	11.2%	45.7%	43.1%
1957	12.9	1.8	5.3	5.8	14.0%	41.1%	45.0%
1958	13.9	2.3	5.8	5.8	16.5%	41.7%	41.7%
1959	14.3	2.8	6.5	4.9	19.7%	45.7%	34.6%
1960	14.3	3.3	6.7	4.3	23.1%	46.9%	30.1%
1961	15.5	3.7	6.9	5.0	23.7%	44.3%	32.0%
1962	16.3	4.0	7.0	5.3	24.5%	42.9%	32.5%
1963	18.0	4.3	7.8	5.9	23.9%	43.3%	32.8%
1964	19.5	4.7	8.6	6.2	24.1%	44.1%	31.8%
1965	21.4	5.0	9.5	6.9	23.4%	44.4%	32.2%
1966	23.8	5.4	9.9	8.5	22.7%	41.6%	35.7%
1967	26.0	5.8	11.2	9.0	22.3%	43.1%	34.6%
1968	28.5	6.2	12.6	9.7	21.8%	44.2%	34.0%
1969	29.2	6.6	13.3	9.3	22.6%	45.5%	31.8%
1970	29.8	7.0	14.3	8.5	23.5%	48.0%	28.5%
1971	31.5	7.8	17.1	6.7	24.7%	54.2%	21.1%
1972	32.2	8.5	19.2	4.4	26.5%	59.7%	13.8%
1973	34.7	9.3	19.3	6.1	26.8%	55.6%	17.6%
1974	41.2	10.1	18.2	12.9	24.5%	44.2%	31.3%
1975	42.5	10.9	19.4	12.2	25.6%	45.6%	28.7:%
1976	40.4	13.5	19.3	7.6	33.4%	47.8%	18.8%
1977	39.6	16.1	20.5	3.0	40.7%	51.8%	7.6%
1978	46.6	18.3	21.5	6.8	39.3%	46.1%	14.6%
1979	49.4	20.0	22.0	7.3	40.5%	44.6%	14.9%
1980	54.0	22.5	21.2	11.2	41.0%	38.6%	20.4%
1981	53.0	22.1	19.9	11.0	41.7%	37.5%	20.8%
1982	51.5	20.5	25.6	5.5	39.8%	49.6%	10.6%
1983	51.5	20.5	27.2	3.8	39.8%	52.8%	7.4%
1984	59.4	22.7	30.2	6.5	38.2%	49.2%	12.6%
1985	64.0	24.8	33.2	6.0	38.8%	51.9%	9.4%
1986	76.0	26.2	38.2	11.6	34.5%	50.3%	15.3%

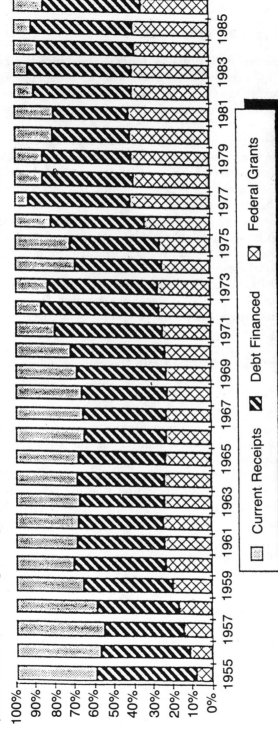

FIGURE 37.4
Sources of Funds for State and Local Government Fixed Capital Formation (1955–1986)
(As a Percent of Fixed Capital Expenditures)

Source: Government Finance Research Center.

Federal Aid for Capital Spending

As was depicted in Figure 37.4, federal assistance has been of major importance in financing state and local capital spending. The importance, of course, has varied by functional category. Federal assistance has been of greatest importance in the areas of highways, sewer, and transit.

There is little question that federal assistance has had a pervasive effect on both the types of capital spending state and local governments have undertaken and the way in which it has been financed. For the recipient governments, the often generous matching grants have greatly lowered capital costs and have tended to skew state and local budgets toward those project areas where federal assistance was available.[24] Also, the federal funds have substituted for funds that in many cases might have been raised by the states and localities themselves.[25]

A particularly graphic example of this substitution phenomenon is present in the case of federal wastewater facility construction grants. Capital spending by the recipient local governments dropped dramatically in response to the rapid uptick in federal wastewater assistance in the early 1970s. Partially in recognition of the diseconomies and distortions built into the original Clean Water Act, the federal matching percentages and funds available to municipal wastewater treatment have declined dramatically and the entire program is being shifted to making loans.[26] Similarly, the Army Corps of Engineers public works programs in water control and transportation have been shifted from 100% federal expenditures to state and local matching requirements.

As has been already noted, the most recent information indicates that federal aid in general, including that for capital assistance, has slowed down markedly and, by all indications, will continue to decline in significance.[27] Fiscal austerity at the federal level will continue to make the prospects for grants to help states and localities bleak until new revenue sources are found.

---

[24] U.S. Congressional Budget Office, *The Federal Budget for Public Works Infrastructure Management*, U.S.G.P.O., Washington, D.C., July 1985, pp. 7–8.

[25] U.S. Congressional Budget Office, *Federal Policies for Infrastructure Management*, U.S.G.P.O., Washington, D.C., June 1986, pp. 80–86.

[26] John E. Petersen, *Financing Clean Water*, First Boston Corporation, New York, 1985.

[27] "Gramm-Rudman-Hollings: Fiscal Armageddon for State and Local Governments," *Public Sector Review*, Touche Ross, Washington, D.C., January 1986.

Financing from Current Revenues

As was displayed in Figure 37.4, current revenues from state and local governments' own sources in the 1950s contributed as much as 50% of all funds to capital spending. But this source of funds has receded in importance steadily over the years, although it can be of major importance in particular functional areas and at certain levels of government. A leading example has been in the area of highways, streets, and roads, where fuel tax revenues are often used directly by states or passed on to localities for capital spending. Local governments often use current revenues, some of which are earmarked for such purposes, to pay for their recurring and smaller capital outlays. Studies done by the U.S. Joint Economic Committee have documented that cities of all sizes on average financed about 40% of their general government capital spending from current revenue sources, either currently collected or accumulated in carry-over balances from previous fiscal years.[28]

A problem in the use of current revenues for major expenditures is that, except for very large units, the amounts available in any given year are relatively meager. Conventional wisdom among finance officials is that capital spending is one of the first items to be reduced when fiscal condition weakens because capital expenditures can be more easily delayed than can operating costs. Officials say that the level of capital expenditures from current revenue is determined simply by seeing what will be left over after operating expenses have been met. The downtrend in capital spending and the pinched use of current receipts, demonstrated in the early 1980s, would seem to verify that conclusion.

Furthermore, attempts to accumulate funds in a "savings account" in the form of growing fund balances not only postpones the receipt of the benefits of the desired expenditure, but requires a political discipline that can seldom be sustained.

There is an abundance of public finance literature, both academic and applied, that argues for and justifies borrowing as the preferred method for aligning benefits and costs over time. In the case of capital facilities, fiscal austerity at the local government level caused either by economic recession or taxpayer resistance has sent them searching for alternative revenue sources.[29]

---

[28] John Petersen and Deborah Matz, *Trends in the Fiscal Condition of Cities: 1983–1985*, U.S. Joint Economic Committee, Washington, D.C., May 1985, pp. 12–13.

[29] See Roger Gordon and Joel Slemrod, "An Empirical Examination of Municipal Financial Policy", in Harvy S. Rosen (ed.), *Studies in State and Local Public Finance*, National Bureau of Economic Research, New York, 1986, pp. 53–82.

Historically, a major source of local revenues has been the property tax. The growth of this source has been legislatively constrained in recent years by the enactment of laws such as Proposition 13 in California and Proposition 2-1/2 in Massachusetts. As a result of such legislation, governments frequently have had to reduce the level of long-term capital investment financed out of current revenues. One expert on infrastructure finance writes:

> To meet the needs that have been documented in recent studies, state and local governments would have to increase all taxes by about 40%. This would be constitutionally or legally impossible in many states, and politically impossible in all.[30]

This point is reinforced by a 1985 study by Touche Ross & Co. that surveyed state and local government officials on the preferred ways of financing capital investment. The study indicates that financing infrastructure through increases in local taxes is consistently the least attractive of alternatives available to public officials.[31]

A major change in public finance has been the shift to user fees to lessen the burdens of general taxation, especially that of the property tax. Among the new "user-charge" forms of revenue is that of the impact fee, which has increased greatly in importance especially in areas where development precedes growth in the tax base. The linkage between impact fees and capital spending is particularly tight in view of the fact that needed improvements in infrastructure are usually the legal nexus for the imposition of such fees.[32]

The term *impact fee* is used rather loosely to refer to a number of approaches. A 1988 survey of 43 communities throughout the United States to determine the extent to which they were using impact fees showed that respondents included developer fees, cost-recovery mechanisms, negotiated exactions, linkage programs, inclusionary zoning and tax increment financing within the general term impact fee. That survey revealed that 31 of the 43 communities surveyed had or were in the process of imposing developer fees and that 21 of them used negotiated exactions (contributions in lieu of fees).[33]

---

[30] Roger Vaugh, *Rebuilding America: Financing Public Works in the 1980s*, Vol. 2, Washington, D.C.: Council of State Planning Agencies, 1983, p. 4.

[31] Touche Ross & Co., *Financing Infrastructure in America*, Chicago, Touche Ross & Co., 1985, p. 1.

[32] John Petersen, et al., *Non-debt Financing of Public Works*, Government Finance Research Center, Washington, D.C., June 1986.

[33] Cynthia Angell and Charles A. Shorter, "Impact Fees: Private Sector Participation in Infrastructure Financing" in *Government Finance Review*, October 1988, p. 20.

A large, but unknown, amount of capital facilities are not bought outright by governments but rather are "given" to them through dedications made by private developers. Such exactions are frequently required as a condition for many types of planned development. The nature, location, and amount of facilities to be dedicated to use by the general public are part of the negotiations surrounding rezonings and the approval of site plans. Projects of this nature may in fact be financed by special districts through the sale of tax-exempt bonds, but the security provided often is the credit of the developer, and the payment of principal and interest is reflected in higher sales prices and rental rates, rather than in governmental collected tax receipts and user charges. Such techniques have been heavily employed in certain states and are best suited to rapidly growing areas. Developer fees and exactions, usually given for capital improvement purposes, already exceed $1 billion annually in California alone and could produce as much as $15 billion annually were they employed nationally.[34]

In considering the obtaining of capital services through the use of current revenues, it should be noted that many financing techniques have been developed to procure the services of capital goods without purchasing the facilities outright or resorting to what is legally defined as borrowing. Leading alternatives are the leasing (or the installment purchasing) of facilities from other governmental units or the private sector, or entering into service contracts whereby an entire service (as opposed to simply the use of facilities) is procured.[35] The basic idea is that a government can enjoy capital services without actually taking ownership of property or "borrowing" as defined by state law. Because of these devices, the underlying capital spending (and often the underlying borrowing) do not show up as governmental capital outlays but rather as a current operating expenditure. The extent of this behavior is unknown, but it probably amounts to the equivalent of several billions in capital outlays each year.[36]

Debt Financing and Related Techniques

Going into debt to finance capital outlays has historically been the means to raise the large amounts typically needed to finance major capital expenditures. It has also been one of the most circumscribed of governmental activities since the ability of one legislature to bind the

[34] John Petersen, *et al., Non-debt Financing of Public Works*, Government Finance Research Center, Washington, D.C., July 1886.

[35] *Ibid.*, p. I-12.

[36] *Ibid.*, p. I-15.

actions of future generations is a potent power and one that can be abused.

The prospects for increasing the debt-financing of public works are bright from the perspective of the needs and the lack of financing alternatives, but whether governments are willing to borrow and on what terms and conditions governments will be able to borrow are key issues in doubt.

The willingness of governments to borrow is critical because there are manifold institutional barriers, such as debt limits and referendum requirements, to selling bonds for infrastructure, especially if they are tax-supported, general obligation bonds. The typical form of regulating general obligation bonds has been through state-imposed caps on debt levels and/or referenda requirements, while constraints on revenue bonds usually have taken the form of prohibitions on types or usage.

Debt Limitations. Municipalities in 44 states face direct constitutional or statutory limits on the amount of general obligation debt they are allowed to engender.

These limits, related to some percentage of a municipality's real property levels, in practice have little impact, as municipalities generally maintain levels of indebtedness far below the cap.[37] Local officials do not consider state debt limits to be a major constraint on borrowing; in 1986 only 3.8% cited them as a major barrier to their borrowing programs.[38] The existence of debt limits is partly psychological. Credit analysts involved in municipal issues have demonstrated a desire to retain the limits even while acknowledging that the limits are seldom tested. The importance to creditors of the limitations' existence increases as the general credit of a municipality decreases, even though the troubled city is not near the legal debt cap. For cities with strong financial resources, the analysts favor retention of the limits because removal would introduce a potential source of volatility into the market.[39]

Statutory interest rate limits are also used to control municipal debt in 40 states.[40] The relevance of this limit is questionable due to

[37] John Petersen, et al., Constitutional, Statutory and Other Impediments to Local Government Infrastructure Financing, Washington, D.C., Government Finance Officers Association, 1987, p. 40.

[38] Ibid., p. 41.

[39] New York State Legislative Commission on State-Local Relations, New York's Limits on Local Taxing and Borrowing—Time for a Change?, Albany, New York State Legislature, 1983, p. 119.

[40] Petersen, et al., Constitutional and Statutory Impediments, p. 42.

states' willingness to adjust the limits as needed to respond to the credit market.

Referendum Requirements. Another major form of control of general obligation debt are the referenda requirements on local indebtedness. Voter approval of bond issues is generally required in 42 states. The impact of this constraint is strongly felt by local officials who believe more capital expenditures are needed: more than one-third consider referenda requirements as the major restraint to indebtedness.[41] As a result of these requirements, municipalities have found several methods to issue debt without voter approvals, including:

- Allowances of general obligation debt issuance to certain levels without referenda;
- Issuances of nonregulated revenue bonds for activities previously financed by GO bonds; and
- Shifting the cost of capital construction forward to developers while rebating the cost through tax incentives or abatements.

Analyses and surveys conducted for the National League of Cities have led to recommendations for reducing referendum requirements, allowing local officials to indebt their cities without voter approval. This position is strongly opposed by creditors, who have shown in surveys that they consider the existence of the referendum requirements to be the most desired constraint on government debt, especially as the general financial health of a municipality declines.[42]

Tax and Expenditure Limitations. Tax and expenditure limitations have had a detrimental effect on all forms of local government spending, including capital spending, especially when the latter is financed by current revenues. In the face of legislated revenue restrictions, governments have tended to postpone capital spending. Although borrowing may appear to constitute a method of avoiding certain revenue-related limitations, restrictions on future revenue-raising powers tend to reduce the reliability of prospective debt service. More directly, they have negated the ability of governments in many states to make the traditional "full faith and credit" pledge of property taxes, unlimited as to rate or amount, in support of debt. Less directly, but of substantial importance, is the impression left by the

[41] Michael Pagano, *How the Public Works: Major Issues in Infrastructure Finance,* Washington, D.C., The National League of Cities, 1986, p. 16.

[42] New York State Legislative Commission, p. 151.

TABLE 37.6

Restrictions on State and Local Government Tax and Expenditure Powers (October 1985)

States	Overall Property Tax Rate Limit	Specific Property Tax Rate Limit	State-Imposed Limits on Local Governments					Limits on State Governments
			General Property Tax Levy Limit	General Revenue Limit	Limits on Expenditure Limit	Assessment Increases	Full Disclosure	
Total Number	12	31	22	6	6	7	14	18
Alabama	CMSA	CMSB						
Alaska	CMSD		CMD					Const. A
Arizona			CMA			CMSA		Const. A
Arkansas		CMSB	CMSA¹					
California	CMSA					CMSA		Const. A
Colorado		CSB	CMB		SD		CMSA	Stat. D
Connecticut								
Delaware		SD	CA¹					
Washington, DC							C	
Florida	CMA	CMSB					CMSD	
Georgia		SB						
Hawaii							CD	Const. A
Idaho		CMSB	CMSA				CMSA	Stat. A
Illinois		CMSB	CMSA				CMSA	
Indiana			CMSA				CMSB	
Iowa		CMB ³						
Kansas					SD	CMSA		
Kentucky	CMSB	CMSA	CMD				CMSA	
Louisiana		CMSD	CMSA¹					Stat. A
Maine								
Maryland				CMA		CMD	CMD	
Massachusetts		CMSA	CMSA					
Michigan	CSB	MB	CMSA	MB				
Minnesota		CMSD	CMSD		SD			
Mississippi		CMSB	CMSA	CMSA			CMSA	Const. A

756

State	1	2	3	4	5	6	Const./Stat.
Missouri	CMSB					CMSA	Const. A
Montana	CMSB						Stat. A
Nebraska	CMSB			CMSA[5]		CMSD	
Nevada	SB	CMD					Stat. A
New Hampshire							
New Jersey		CD	MSD				
New Mexico	CMSB	CMSA			CMSA		
New York	CMSB	CMSB			CMA[2]		
North Carolina		CMSA					
North Dakota		CMSD[1]					
Ohio	CMSB						Stat. A
Oklahoma	CMSB				CMSA		
Oregon	CMSB	CMSB					Stat. A
Pennsylvania	CMSB[4]	M					
Rhode Island		M				M	Stat. D
South Carolina							Stat. A
South Dakota	CMSB						
Tennessee	CMSD					CMSA	Const. A
Texas	CMSB					CMSA	Const. A
Utah	CMSB						Stat. A
Vermont						CMD	
Virginia		CMSD	SD				
Washington	CMSD	CMSD					Stat. A
West Virginia	CMSB						
Wisconsin	CMSB						
Wyoming	CMSA						

C—County   M—Municipal   S—School District   Const.—Constitutional

B—Enacted before 1970   D—1970 to 1977   A—1978 and after   Stat.—Statutory

---

[1] Limits follow reassessment.

[2] Applicable to only New York City and Nassau County.

[3] Only for selected districts (fire, Library, Cemetery, etc.).

[4] Jurisdictions with home rule charters are not subject to limits.

[5] Expires December 31, 1984.

Source: ACIR staff compilation based on surveys of state revenue departments, October 1985.

adoption of limitations that retroactively affect the ability of governments to meet outstanding obligations. Major downgradings followed the adoption of such limitations in California and Massachusetts, and the cost of borrowing and market access were adversely affected.

State limitations on revenues and expenditures generally occur as:

- Restrictions on local property taxes of the California Proposition 13 and Massachusetts Proposition 2-1/2 genre;
- Limitations on the total amount of property taxes that a local government can collect through its annual property tax levy; and
- Limitations on local government spending, which may or may not include spending for debt service on all or selected types of debt obligations.

The nature and extent of tax and expenditure limits is charted in Table 37.6, which shows on a state-by-state basis the dates enacted and the application to county, municipal and school districts within the state.

The political limitations on local government debt financing surface at the polls on election days, when bond referenda are put before the voters for approval. The history of voter approvals and rejections of proposed bond issues maps out like a roller coaster, with sharp dips and ascents the most salient feature. During the 1950s and early 1960s, approval rates ran in the range of 60 to 85%. The decade following 1968 showed wild gyrations from 33 percent approval to no more than 63% receiving the "yes" vote. The trend since the late 1970s has been on the upward slope, although not without its setbacks, to an 80 to 90% approval rate. Figure 37.5, based on data from *The Bond Buyer*, depicts this history.

As will be discussed later, the growth in tax-exempt financing occurred in areas typically not related to infrastructure borrowing and almost universally these programs were financed by revenue bonds. Where infrastructure is needed and governments wish to borrow, the revenue bond (which depends on non-tax sources for security) has been relied on because its use is not as constrained. But selling either tax-supported or revenue-supported debt usually involves a pledge to raise taxes or charges to repay the debt, something which is never politically easy to do.

Credit Market Access. Access to the credit markets can also present problems. The past several years have been turbulent and confusing for both the issuers and buyers of governmental debt, as a result of widely fluctuating financial markets and the equally unpredictable twists and

FIGURE 37.5
Bond Volume Approval Rates (1955–1988)

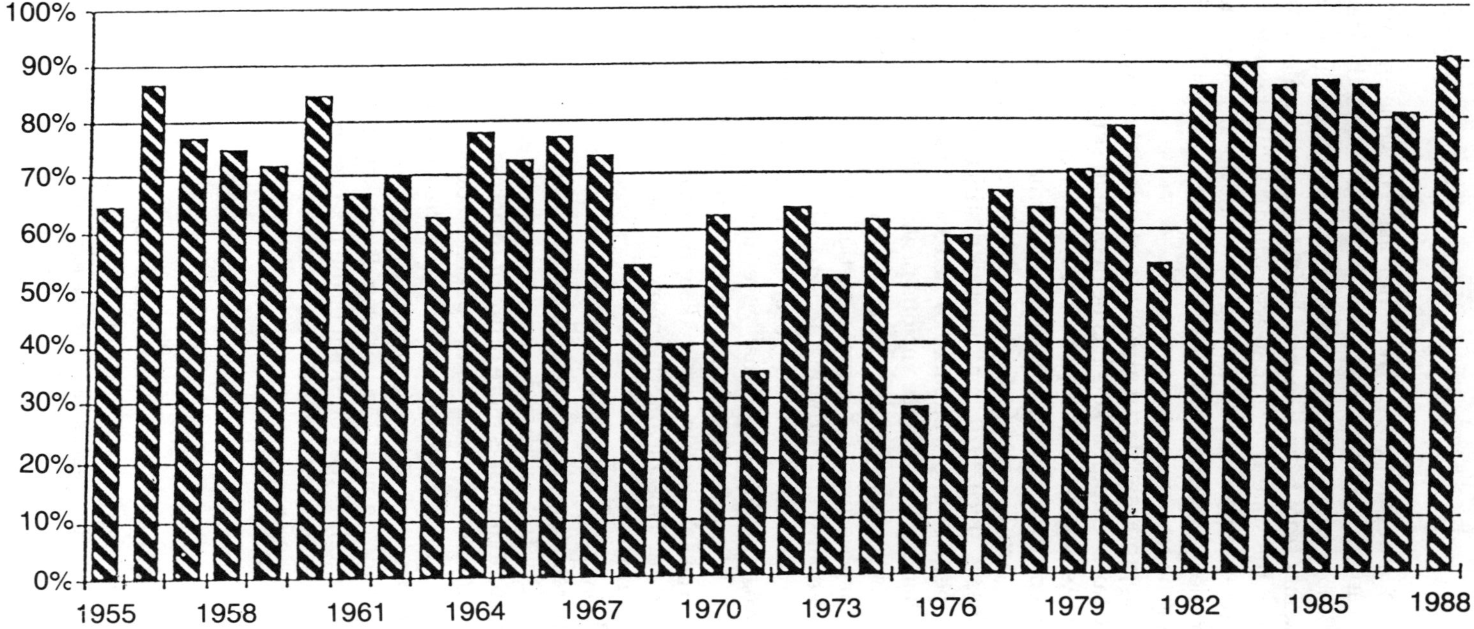

Source: The Bond Buyer.

turns in federal tax policy. The latter aspect, while important to all forms of capital financing, has been especially so in the case of state and local obligations, the vast majority of which pay interest income that is exempt from federal income taxes (and usually also exempt from the taxes in the state where they are issued). While tax exemption has been of great importance in saving state and local governmental borrowers money over the years, that feature has also cost the U.S. Treasury foregone tax revenues.[43]

The appropriate starting point is to calculate how much financing in the tax-exempt markets has been done to support infrastructure spending. As has been widely observed, only a minority of tax-exempt long-term borrowing over the past few years has been targeted for this purpose. Figure 37.6 sets forth the trends in tax-exempt borrowing for selected years since 1970, making the distinction between that borrowing done to support publicly owned facilities (traditional borrowing) and that done to finance various private-activity (non-traditional) uses, such as business facilities or residences that are owned and operated by nongovernmental private parties. Another distinction to be made is that between borrowing done to raise new capital and borrowing which represents refundings of outstanding debt. According to Figure 37.6, by 1985 traditional governmental purposes constituted only 37% of the total borrowing for new capital.[44] Subsequent to the passage of the Tax Reform Act of 1986, the share of traditional borrowing has grown. This means the market is more devoted to financing infrastructure.

The dividing line between public and private purposes is important in appreciating the role of borrowing in supporting state and local capital facility financing and why, as we shall see in the next section, the tax-exempt market is more difficult to access. The large quantity of borrowing for non-governmental purposes added to the supply of tax-exempt securities, drove up the cost of borrowing under most market conditions, and led to lost federal tax revenues.[45] As a result, the Tax Reform Act took aim at the tax-exempt market and placed severe restrictions on it. It is the condition of the tax-exempt market as a mechanism for raising funds for infrastructure spending that we will turn to in the next section.

[43] Michael Pagano, *How the Public Works: Major Issues in Infrastructure Finance,* Washington, D.C., The National League of Cities, 1986, p. 16.

[44] New York State Legislative Commission, p. 151.

[45] Michael Pagano, *How the Public Works: Major Issues in Infrastructure Finance,* Washington, D.C., The National League of Cities, 1986, p. 16.

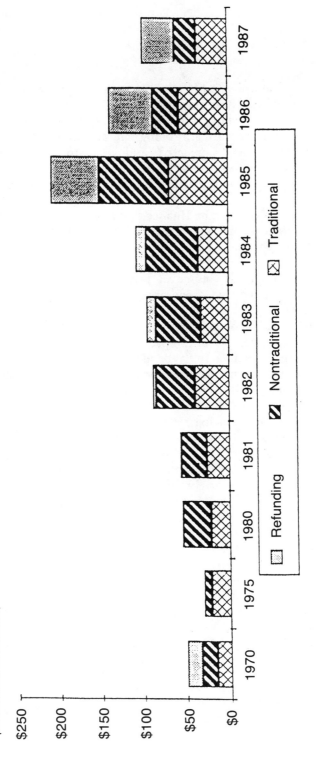

FIGURE 37.6
Volume of New Long-Term Tax-Exempt Debt by Traditional and Non-Traditional Purposes (1970–1987)
(In Billions of Dollars)

Tax Exemption, Tax Reform, and
Financing Infrastructure

The Tax Reform Act affected the tax-exempt market in a myriad of ways. To detail those provisions and explore the pathways of the impacts is a major chore that has been undertaken elsewhere.[46] Furthermore, the impacts are still being felt, as market adjustments continue to take place and legislative and regulatory fine tuning continue apace. But, the major impacts and their implications for infrastructure financing can be summarized by the following highlights.

- **Fewer projects can be financed on a tax-exempt basis because of the restraints placed on borrowing, especially that involving private-activity bonds.**

The issuance volume of private-activity tax-exempt bonds has been greatly reduced. Generally, these are bonds that finance projects where more than 10% of the debt service is paid by those benefiting from facilities not available to the general public. Also, obligations where more than 5% of the proceeds are loaned to private parties are considered private-activity bonds.

Several factors account for the slump in private-activity financing, including the tighter definitions on what constitutes private-activity bonds, what their proceeds may be used for, the disallowance of tax-exempt financing for uses that once were permissible, and the institution of state-by-state caps on the volume that may be sold. For example, those private-activity bonds that are restricted by state borrowing caps (which accounted for approximately $50 billion worth of borrowing in 1985) are limited in the aggregate to a little over $13 billion as the caps have twisted into place by 1988.[47] Deals involving nongovernmental use of facilities or loans are much more complicated to arrange and more costly to undertake and now represent a declining share of the market.

In terms of infrastructure financing (as opposed to other uses of borrowing proceeds) the impact of the tighter restrictions on private-activity bonds has had several harmful effects. Overall, the tighter restrictions have greatly hampered public/private cooperative financing

---

[46] For an overview, see Penelope Lemov, "The Municipal Bond Market After Tax Reform: It's a New Way of Doing Business," *Governing*, March 1988, pp. 42–49. Detailed discussion of the Act's provisions and their early and anticipated impacts is found in John Petersen, *Tax Exempts and Tax Reform: Assessing the Consequences of the Tax Reform Act of 1986 for the Municipal Securities Market*, Government Finance Officers Association, Chicago, February 1987.

[47] John Petersen (February 1987), Chapter 2.

arrangements. Such arrangements have been of particular significance in the case of solid waste (waste-to-energy facilities); airports, ports, and terminals; industrial pollution control; and parking, stadia and convention centers. Five particular restrictions limit the use of private-activity bonds:

(1) The use of tax-exempt proceeds may not be allowed at all (as in the case of industrial pollution control, stadia and parking facilities). In other words, private-activity bonds cannot be sold on a tax-exempt basis.

(2) Even where they are allowed to be sold on a tax-exempt basis, the private-activity bonds are very limited by the state caps which means that they must compete (economically and politically) with each other for allocations.

(3) The interest on private-activity bonds, as a class, is subject to the application of the *alternative minimum tax* (AMT), which drives up their interest costs.

(4) Rates of depreciation on privately owned facilities and equipment financed by tax-exempts is slower, having longer depreciable lines.

(5) Cost of issuance (legal fees, underwriting costs, etc.) have been limited to 2% of the proceeds for private-activity bonds.

The complete or partial loss of tax-exempt financing for many privatization alternatives has limited the scope of financing options open to local governments. Such options had offered cooperative efficiencies, such as jointly meeting public and private construction needs to the cost advantage of both. In addition, the availability of tax exemption to states and localities represented a leverage factor for the public sector in its dealings with the private sector, especially in growing areas. The more liberal uses formerly afforded tax-exempt borrowing permitted governments to finance private sector needs on advantageous terms. This cost-savings potential made private firms and developers willing partners in addressing the needs of communities for infrastructure. For example, the tax-increment bond, which pledged future tax revenues to the repayment of bonds, was a widely used means of financing community development and land acquisition. The tax-increment bond legally lives on as the *qualified redevelopment bond* (QRB), but severe new restrictions on its operation have made it practically unusable as a tax-exempt instrument. For example, QRBs must be secured by taxes at the same rates as in comparable areas and special charges cannot be imposed on redeveloped areas.

Because of the tight restrictions and caps, governmental programs and projects that require or desire private involvement are slowly moving to the use of a new form of municipal security, the taxable bond, the interest income on which, as the name implies, is subject to the federal income tax.

- **The municipal market is fragmented and complicated by the varying tax treatments for different classes of bonds.**

The new federal income tax exposures created by the Tax Reform Act fragmented the formerly homogeneous market (as regards to federal tax treatment) into subdivisions, where rates of taxation depend on class of municipal security, the nature of the investor, and when the bond was acquired. Table 37.7 provides a summary of the variety of tax rates that now apply to various "tax-exempt" securities. The marketplace reflects these different tax exposures in the differing interest rates carried on various types of bonds. For example, those bonds that are potentially subject to the individual *alternative minimum tax* (AMT bonds) carry interest rates that are 25 to 50 basis points higher than those found on bonds not subject to that tax. Conversely, bonds issued by governments that expect to borrow less than $10 million a year (called *bank qualified bonds*) allow certain tax advantages to banks and, resultingly, enjoy interest rates 25 to 50 basis points lower than other

TABLE 37.7
Summary of Tax Rates on Income from Municipal Securities Under Various Provisions of the 1986 Tax Reform Act

Investor Group and Type of Tax	Class of Municipal Security	
	Governmental[1]	Private Sector[2]
Individual Regular Income[3]	0.0%	0.0%
AMT	0.0%	21.0%
Corporation Regular Income	0.0%	0.0%
AMT		
Preference Income	0.0%	20.0%
Excess Book Income[4]	10.0%	10.0%
Property and Casualty Companies:		
Regular Income	5.1%	5.1%
AMT		
Preference Income	11.5%	20.0%
Excess Book Income[5]	11.5%	20.0%

[1]Governmental and 501(c) (3).

[2]Not included are those private activity bonds that are fully taxable.

[3]Not including tax on social security income prorated to tax-exempt income.

[4]Not including the 0.12 percent Super Fund tax on excess book income exceeding $2 million.

[5]Bonds acquired before 8/8/86 are taxed at 10% under the excess book income.

bonds. In 1987, approximately $20 billion in AMT bonds were issued and $7 billion in bank qualified securities. Another market instrument has evolved, taxable municipal securities, and in 1987 approximately $5 billion were issued to finance purposes (involving governmental entities) no longer having access to the tax-exempt market.

- **Few opportunities remain to earn arbitrage income by investing bond proceeds.**

Perhaps the most pervasive effect of the Act was to place strict limitations on the opportunities of issuers to earn arbitrage income by borrowing tax-exempt and investing the proceeds on a taxable basis. In its heyday, arbitrage activities substantially increased the level of borrowing and made much of it relatively interest-intensive. Taking dead aim at what the Congress considered an abuse of tax exemption, the Tax Reform Act squashed arbitrage-driven borrowing by shortening the period of unlimited arbitrage earnings from three years to six months, by disallowing the cost of issuance as a reduction in available funds for purposes of calculating yields, and by placing severe constraints on the definition of short-term deficit financing. Perhaps most pernicious was the universal requirement that issuers keep track of their investible proceeds and rebate any profits to the Treasury.[48]

The impact of the arbitrage restrictions have been fairly substantial for issuers. Although the arbitrage opportunities are not as lucrative as they once were, arbitrage profits could be used to lower the costs of borrowing or to decrease the amount borrowed by as much as 5 to 10%. The new restrictions have all but eliminated the possibilities for arbitrage and have increased the administrative burdens of governmental borrowers.

- **Governments have lost the financing flexibility of advanced refunding.**

Because of limitations placed on the practice of advanced refundings, governments are permitted only once to refinance outstanding bonds (which remain outstanding but are backed by escrowed proceeds from the second issuance) in order to achieve interest savings. Even where advanced refundings are permitted, new issuances must not go beyond the term of the first call date in the original bond issue. As was

---

[48]Joseph Magnus and John Petersen, *Arbitrage Rebate Requirement*, Research Bulletin, Government Finance Research Center, Government Finance Officers Association, Washington, D.C., January 1988.

shown in Figure 37.6, refunding bonds (most of which were advance re-fundings) were a major source of supply to the municipal market when interest rates dropped and multiple refinancings were a means of low-ering subsequent debt service costs.

- **More burdensome procedures surround the issuance process.**

The Tax Act mandated more paper work of those involved in the market. All tax-exempt transactions must now be regularly reported to the Internal Revenue Service. Records must be kept to record earn-ings on investments and to make rebates of profits, if necessary. Re-strictions have been placed on the costs of issuance of private-activity bonds. Because of the various tax implications, bond dealers are re-quired to disclose to customers that different bonds have different tax implications.

- **Institutional investor demand for tax-exempts has evaporated and that of the individual investor, buying directly or indirectly through tax-exempt funds, reigns supreme.**

In part, due to the change in the taxation of banks and also con-tinuing a decade-long trend, the demand for tax-exempt securities has gone into a dramatic decline. As Figure 37.7 displays, the major insti-tutional investors, commercial banks and property and casualty in-surance companies have become disinvestors in tax-exempts (the banks alone have seen fit to let their municipal portfolios shrink by $50 billion during 1986 and 1987). This means that individual in-vestors, either purchasing directly in the market or by buying shares of mutual funds or unit trusts, are dominant in the market.

Efforts to Relax Restrictions

Efforts are underway to roll back or at least alleviate the burdens and constraints of sundry provisions in the Tax Reform Act and some may be successful. Recently, a special commission was formed by Congress-man Anthony of Arkansas to examine the multitude of impacts that Tax Reform has had on state and local governments.[49] The Anthony Com-mission is still at work, reviewing the entire issue of federalism as af-fected by the Tax Act. Specific targets for redress are withdrawing the application of the Alternative Minimum Tax to tax-exempts, loosening

---

[49] *Draft Report to the Anthony Commission on Public Finance on Tax Issues from Task Force 4*, Government Finance Officers Association, Washington, D.C., April 11, 1988.

FIGURE 37.7
Buyers of Tax-Exempts (1980–1987) (Net Flows in Billions of Dollars)

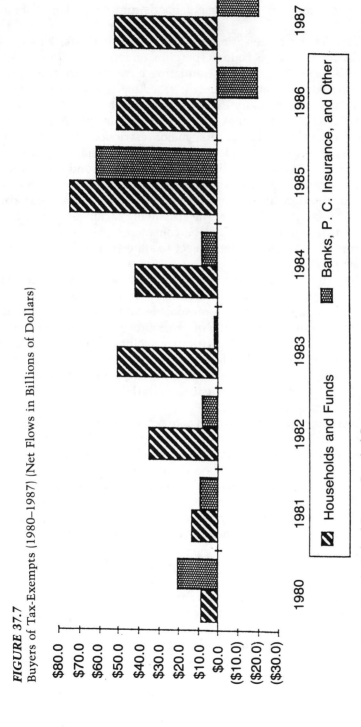

Source: Flow of Funds, Federal Reserve Board of Governors.

the arbitrage restrictions, and forestalling the pending sunsetting of small-issue industrial development bonds and single-family housing bonds.

Remedies have been proposed to remove particular barriers presented by the federal tax code to spending on infrastructure. A comprehensive package dedicated to stimulating infrastructure spending has been proposed by Senator Domenici. Based on the recommendations of the Private Sector Advisory Panel on Infrastructure, the Domenici bill calls for, among other things, the creation of an infrastructure bond that would be exempted from three major restrictions of the Tax Reform Act. Such bonds would include those issued for sewerage facilities, solid waste and hazardous waste disposal, water supply, and other facilities required of public agencies for compliance with environmental standards (this could include a mass transit system, for example). In particular, these bonds, whatever the financing arrangement used for infrastructure bonds, would not be considered private-activity bonds and accordingly would not be subject to state volume limits nor to the Alternative Minimum Tax.

The arbitrage requirements for infrastructure bonds would be eased to permit a temporary investment period of three years, so long as funds were taken down at a reasonable rate, and would exclude reserve funds from the definition of gross proceeds for purposes of calculating arbitrage. Last, infrastructure facilities would be placed in the seven-year depreciable life category (instead of the 15- to 20-year classes in which they are now placed) and those financed by tax-exempts would be granted 10-year lives (rather than the 24- to 50-year life now assigned).

The substance of the changes is to make investment in these forms of infrastructure more attractive and greatly broaden the opportunities for public/private cooperation without sacrificing tax exemption. Similar proposals for all municipal bonds have been proposed. For example, the Government Finance Officers Association has recommended that the arbitrage restrictions be eased for governmental bond issues of less than $25 million in size and permit issuers to keep arbitrage earnings from investment so long as they were devoted to project spending.

Fiscal Capacity and the Burden of Debt

A basic question is that of the capacity of states and localities to sustain increased indebtedness. Assessing this has to do with the burden that increased indebtedness will place on revenue-raising mechanisms of governments and, ultimately, the underlying tax and revenue bases of these governments. While there are no perfect measures of these capacities, analysts have typically relied upon such measures as gross national product (at the national level), personal income (at the state level), and full-market value of real property (at the local level) to calculate debt burdens.

Examining the debt burdens of state and local governments requires care. This is especially so as of late because so much nominal "municipal" debt is, in fact, claims against underlying obligors that are household, not-for-profit corporations, or for-profit corporations. The latter two classes of tax-exempt debt do not represent "governmental obligations" since, as revenue bonds, they are conduits of nongovernmental debt. The Federal Reserve Board makes these distinctions among the types in its calculation of outstanding liabilities and these separations are useful in estimating trends in the debt burdens represented by governmental-owned-and-operated facilities.

Table 37.8 presents the historical record of debt outstanding and debt burden as measured by outstanding tax-exempt debt for all purposes (including private activity and by governmental purposes) as a percentage of GNP. As may be noted in the lower panel of Table 37.8, the burden of debt by this measure rose in the 1980s and then declined in recent years. In 1987, total tax-exempt debt equalled 16% of GNP. However, the debt for governmental purposes came to 11.7% of GNP. That amount is significant when viewed against the higher percentages observed in the 1960s and 1970s, when state and local governmental-purpose debt was over 14% of GNP.

There has been a shift from general obligation tax-supported to revenue-supported debt. It is estimated that general obligation tax-supported debt has declined as a percentage of GNP from 9% in the 1960s to about 4.5% at present. This reflects, in part, the changes discussed earlier in this chapter regarding the philosophical tenor of the taxpayer revolt and the rapidly growing use of special districts and user charges. Because benefits are perceived to be focused on certain groups that should pay for them, the scope of the underlying credit pledged as security is also constricted.

Two conclusions are evident. First, tax-exempt debt outstanding is now dropping as a percentage of GNP, primarily because outstanding private-activity debt is starting to decline. Second, governmental-purpose debt burdens are relatively low, especially with respect to tax-supported debt, compared to recent history. Unlike federal and corporate debt, state and local indebtedness has not grown with respect to the sector's financial resources.

FUTURE SPENDING PROJECTIONS AND THEIR IMPLICATIONS

The first section of this chapter presented a range of estimates for infrastructure spending to reach "desired levels." The second section of

TABLE 37.8
Tax-Exempt Debt Outstanding by Responsible Sector (in Billions of Dollars)

Year	Total	Governmental Purpose				Private Activity
		Total	G.O.	Revenue	Short-Term	
1965	$100	$100	$ 62	$ 38	$ 6	*
1970	144.4	144	80	64	13	*
1975	223.9	215	126	89	19	$ 9
1976	239.6	226	130	96	15	14
1977	263.0	238	138	100	12	16
1978	291.3	256	143	113	12	36
1979	321.5	273	145	128	13	49
1980	351.9	289	147	142	15	63
1981	374.6	294	150	144	16	80
1982	428.4	325	160	165	22	104
1983	484.6	360	163	197	21	125
1984	522.2	386	166	220	18	154
1985	658.4	450	176	274	19	208
1986	689.2	493	190	303	23	196
1987	723.7	529	201	328	29	194

Tax-Exempt Debt Outstanding by Responsible Sector (as a Percentage of GNP)

Year	Total	Governmental Purpose				Private Activity
		Total	G.O.	Revenue	Short-Term	
1965	14.23%	14.23%	8.79%	5.43%	0.78%	*
1970	14.22	14.22	7.88	6.34	1.31	*
1975	14.01	13.42	7.88	5.54	1.16	0.59%
1976	13.45	12.67	7.30	5.37	0.81	0.78
1977	13.21	11.93	6.93	5.00	0.58	0.78
1978	12.95	11.36	6.36	5.01	0.54	1.59
1979	12.82	10.88	5.78	5.10	0.52	1.94
1980	12.88	10.59	5.38	5.21	0.55	2.29
1981	12.27	9.64	4.91	4.72	0.52	2.63
1982	13.53	10.25	5.05	5.20	0.69	3.28
1983	14.23	10.57	4.79	5.79	0.63	3.66
1984	14.36	10.60	4.56	6.04	0.48	4.23
1985	16.83	11.51	4.50	7.01	0.48	5.33
1986	16.25	11.63	4.48	7.15	0.54	4.62
1987	15.99	11.69	4.44	7.25	0.65	4.29

the chapter focused on how capital improvements have been financed in terms of the historical sources of funds and the techniques by which they are tapped. In this section, we will employ an accounting model to tie together the infrastructure needs, desired levels of annual expenditures on capital goods, implied sources of funds, and the implications for the volume of future borrowing by state and local governments.

The focal point of the analysis is on yearly capital spending and the resulting accumulation of capital stock, since it is the perceived needs for structures and equipment that drives the investment decisions of governments.

The desire for investment, however, will always be tempered by the financial resources that can be mustered to pay for improvements. Furthermore, most capital spending takes several years to evolve, as the projects are planned, contracts let and construction put in place. Weather, fiscal squeezes, labor actions, and shortages can all extend project completion times. Thus, whatever may be the desired level of capital stock and improvements to that stock, the yearly rate at which they may be realized may be constrained.

In the following projections, numerous simplifying assumptions have been made and these are summarized in Appendix 37.1 of this report. Capital spending by state and local governments is measured by the National Income Accounts concept of gross fixed investment, as was discussed in the first section. It will be recalled that definition embraces spending on structures, plant, and equipment. Thus, the terms capital spending, gross fixed investment, and infrastructure spending are used synonymously.

The infrastructure investment and needs figures and the definitions of financing sources are compatible with the needs estimates discussed in that section. The general approach used is to establish target values for the year 1995 (in terms of either real capital stock per capita or levels of capital spending) that comport with the major studies of needs that were discussed.

Projection Scenarios

Four scenarios have been selected as bases for projections:

- *Fixed Per Capita Case:* This case assumes that investment takes place which is only sufficient to maintain real stock per capita fixed at its 1987 level ($5,846 per capita in 1982 prices).

- *2% of GNP Case:* Annual capital outlays are fixed at 2% of GNP. This would mean that capital spending grows at the same rate as GNP, after moving up from the 1987 ratio of 1.8% of GNP. This case aligns fairly closely with that recommended by the National Council on Public Works Improvement.

- *CBO Target Case:* Real Net Capital Stock grows at the rate needed to reach the target level indicated by the Congressional Budget Office study.
- *JEC Target Case:* Real Net Capital Stock grows at the rate needed to reach the target level indicated by the Joint Economic Committee study.

In each of the above cases, the projection period extends from 1988 to 1995, using the 1987 figure as the initial known value for capital spending. Each of the above scenarios, once the spending is calculated to meet the target, produces a series of annual capital outlays and capital stock figures. Each scenario, if it is to be realized, subsumes the underlying financing required to support the spending that would take place, a concern we take up later.

For each of the four cases we have constructed a spreadsheet which quantifies the relationships between spending and financing for the period 1984 through 1995, which are contained in Appendix 37.1. It should be noted that the results are presented in current dollar terms (not in constant 1982 dollars). Initially, we have assumed that the prices for capital goods (the price deflator) will increase at an annual rate of 4.2% between 1987 and 1995 and that GNP, again expressed in current dollar terms, will grow at 6.3% annually. If one were to assume faster or slower rates of growth in prices or of economic activity as measured by GNP, the projections of capital spending and required financing would change accordingly. After presentation of the initial results, there is also a presentation of a scenario where a recession occurs during the years 1989 and 1990.

Assessing the overall realism or feasibility of the projection requires a similar projection of the financing sources and the implications.

In Figure 37.4, the historic record of financing was presented. In the projections, the same basic separation of sources has been used. We have separated out the financing sources used to fund outlays by:

- Current revenues from our sources;
- Federal grants used for capital purposes; and
- Long-term borrowing.

For the projections, the shares of the three sources in financing any given year's capital outlays have been calculated using the following major assumptions:

- Current revenues are assumed to finance 15% of capital outlays. The reasoning is that current revenues will return to representing a somewhat higher share of support than was the case in the mid 1980s.

Greater use of user charges impact fees for new development may push this level higher. However the need to meet increasing debt service requirements will limit the availability of current receipts for direct spending.

- Federal grants for capital spending are forecasted, in accordance with CBO projections, to remain virtually constant in current dollar terms. While it is possible that federal aid may increase more rapidly, that outcome is unlikely given the current and foreseeable fiscal situation of the federal government. The assumed rate of growth in capital grants is only 1.3% per year for the period 1988 to 1995.

- Borrowing proceeds have been calculated as a residual. That is, after the contributions of current revenues and federal grants to capital spending are subtracted, the remainder of the capital outlays are assumed to have been borrowed in the long-term markets. It should be noted that funds from borrowing represent take downs of bond funds as opposed to a given year's actual borrowing. (See Appendix 37.1.) How borrowed funds for infrastructure are related to total long-term borrowings in the tax-exempt market is discussed later.

Results of Projections

The results of the four projections assuming constant rates of growth in GNP are depicted in Figure 37.8, which shows projected paths of capital expenditures. Table 37.9 summarizes the implied levels of capital spending by 1995, the implied annual rates of growth between 1987 and 1995 in spending, and what spending in 1995 would be as a percent of GNP in that year.[50]

The range in implied annual growth rates in spending is from 5% (Fixed Per Capita Case) to 12.8% (JEC Target Case). Recently, as was noted in Table 37.1, capital spending by state and local governments in various categories has reached double digits, as the spending caught up from the depressed levels of the mid 1980s. Looking further back into history, sustained growth of 8 to 10% in capital spending is not unheard of for substantial periods of time. A 9% annual rate of growth in capital spending occurred between 1960 and 1968, and 7% between 1970 and 1978.

However, the credibility of such projections must be judged by their implication for financing sources. Is a doubling or more of annual capital spending over the next eight years realistic, given the expected capacity of sources to support such spending?

---

[50] The growth pattern shown in annual spending is smooth, which in reality will not occur. The impact of a recession on the projections is presented in the following notes.

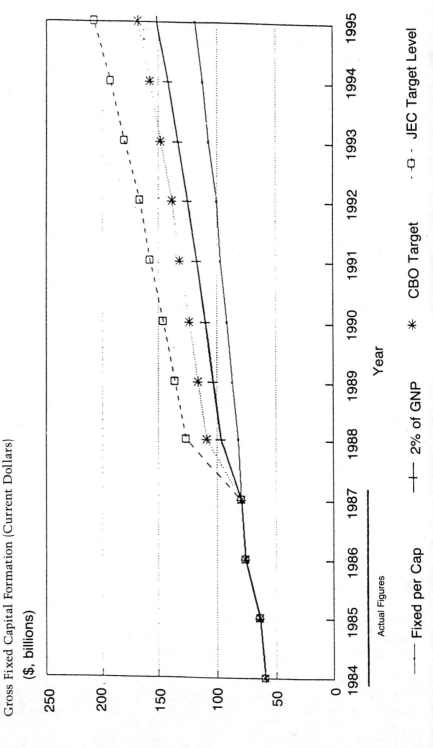

FIGURE 37.8
Gross Fixed Capital Formation (Current Dollars)
($, billions)

Actual Figures

Year

—— Fixed per Cap ———+——— 2% of GNP ———*——— CBO Target ·-□-· JEC Target Level

TABLE 37.9
Actual Capital Outlays and Projected 1995 Levels Under Four Scenarios:
Outlays in Billions of Dollars Annual Growth Rates, and Percent of GNP

	1987 Actual	1995 Projections			
		Fixed per Cap	2% of GNP	CBO Target	JEC Target
Outlays	$79.4	118.5	154.1	168.2	207.5
Growth Rate	—	5.1	8.6	9.8	12.8
As Percent of GNP	1.75	1.56	2.00	2.22	2.74

Source: GFRC, Appendix A.

The answer to that question will depend jointly on the willingness
and ability of states and localities to call upon their own sources of
funds, current revenues and borrowing, to pay the bill. Because federal
aid is projected as having essentially no growth during the period, the
contributions of governments will need to go up at a rate faster than
does total capital spending, since they must finance a larger share of
total costs.

Table 37.10 again shows capital spending levels as projected for
1995, this time breaking them down among the three financing sources.
Scanning the results shows own-source resources having to grow at between 6 and 16% annually, with the higher growth rates required, the
greater the capital spending projection. Judging by historical standards,

TABLE 37.10
Actual 1987 and Projected 1995 Shares of Financing Under Scenario
Projections: Billions of Dollars Annual Growth Rate Shown in Parentheses
(1987–1995)

	1987 Actual	1995 Projections			
		Fixed per Cap	2% of GNP	CBO Target	JEC Target
Total	$79.4	118.5	154.1	168.2	207.5
	(—)	(5.1)	(8.6)	(9.8)	(12.8)
Current Revenues	9.4	13.8	18.8	21.2	27.4
	(—)	(4.9)	(9.0)	(10.7)	(14.3)
Borrowed Funds	47.3	78.2	106.3	120.4	153.8
	(—)	(6.5)	(10.7)	(12.4)	(15.9)
Federal Grants	23.8	26.5	26.5	26.5	26.5
	(—)	(1.3)	(1.3)	(1.3)	(1.3)

Source: GFRC, Appendix A.

sustained growth in current revenues as a source of capital spending in excess of 8% a year appears unlikely. And while funds raised by borrowing may grow briefly at higher rates, the consequent growth in debt service burdens, which also impact on future current revenues, would appear to present intermediate to longer-term barrier to achieving higher targets.

From a sustainable-level perspective—especially given our federal "no-growth" aid assumption—it would appear that the 2% of GNP capital outlay target is the most realistic of the four scenarios presented. This result would be reinforced (and perhaps capital spending might be pushed higher) were federal aid for capital spending to grow. For example, were federal aid to grow at 4.3% (the same rate as the price level) federal grants would amount to $32 billion by 1995. This would make another $5 billion available to support added spending or, if substitution occurs, for reducing the burden on state and localities' own sources.

Implications for Borrowing

The above projections have important implications for the volume of borrowing by state and local governments in the market. However, the relationship between one year's borrowing and capital spending is an easy one to formulate. To translate the demand for borrowed funds into annual borrowing volumes requires smoothing and assumptions as when the proceeds are used for spending purposes.[51] Also, not all borrowing done in the municipal bond market is for purposes of financing capital outlays by state and local governments.[52] Thus, to estimate total volumes of borrowing, it is necessary to estimate also the non-governmental, private-activity borrowing. Last, the projections do not take into consideration borrowings for refinancing outstanding debt (refundings and advanced refundings), which do not lead to new spending.

The estimated levels of borrowing are shown and displayed in Figure 37.9. Shown there for each capital spending level is a derived volume of borrowing. The dollar volumes shown are for new capital; refundings when they occur will add to total sales.

---

[51] We assume borrowing in any given year creates funds that are taken down in equal installments the year it occurs and the following two years. Thus, debt applied is derived from present period borrowing and that occurring in the previous two years. We assume that 90% of proceeds are used for capital purposes.

[52] See Section II above for a discussion of borrowing for non-governmental purposes. Money spent from the proceeds of private-activity bonds are generally not counted as spent by state and local governments by the statistics gathering bodies because the governments seldom own the facilities.

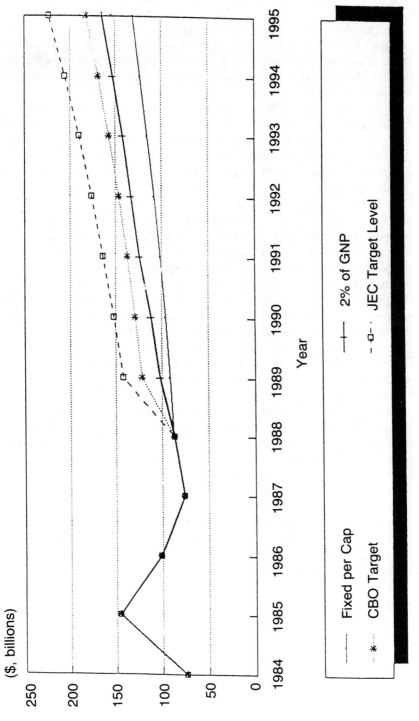

FIGURE 37.9
Total New Issue New Capital Borrowing

(\$, billions)

Year

Legend:
— Fixed per Cap
— 2% of GNP
* CBO Target
-□- JEC Target Level

Source: Government Finance Research Center.

The dollar volume of borrowing will, in any year, exceed the amount of borrowing applied to capital spending in the same year because of two reasons: Only 90% of borrowed proceeds lead to capital outlays and borrowing is done in advance of the take-down of bond funds for spending purposes.

According to the projections, new capital borrowing would range from $130 billion (fixed per cap case) to a high of $225 billion (JEC case). The preferred projection, derived from the 2% of GNP scenario projection estimates a level of $165 billion in new capital borrowing by 1995, of which $127 billion would be governmental purpose and $38 billion in private-activity bonds.

In examining the total new capital borrowing volumes, it is important to remember that we assume that the existing federal tax treatment of municipal securities will remain in place throughout the projection period. If so, then the numbers correspond to new-capital borrowing in the tax-exempt bond market. Were the tax laws to be tightened with respect to private-activity bonds, either in terms of the types of securities that may be sold on a tax-exempt basis or the state-by-state volume limitations, then a proportionate share of borrowing would be shifted to the taxable securities market. Currently, taxable municipal bond sales are at approximately $3 billion a year and continuing growth is likely as the existing volume caps and restrictions of the use proceeds lead more states and localities to enter that market.

Likewise, the new-capital volume figures do not include refundings, which have been very important to total bond market volumes over the past few years. High levels of municipal refundings have been induced by lower interest rates and special situations arising out of the tax law changes. Therefore, we assume that refundings will be less significant in the future; but even in more normal periods of time, they should be expected to add several billions to the annual financing totals. Based on recent analysis, it would appear that a level of approximately $25 billion in refundings could be expected for 1989, bringing total new issue tax-exempt borrowing to approximately $125 billion for that year.

Impact of a Recession

As has been discussed, the credibility of the projections must also be tested by "what ifs" when growth fails to be smooth and events intervene. One unfortunate event that is likely to occur over the next eight years is an economic slowdown or a recession. Were there to be repetition of the 1981–1982 recession for the period 1989 and 1990, growth in capital spending would undoubtfully be derailed, especially in the

FIGURE 37.10

Gross Fixed Capital Formation (Current Dollars)
($, billions)

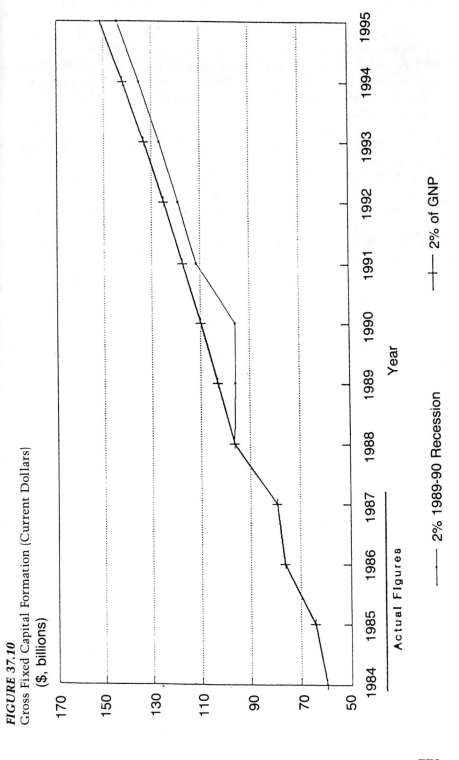

Year

Actual Figures

—— 2% 1989-90 Recession   —+— 2% of GNP

absence of a federal aid program to promote countercyclical behavior on the part of states and localities.

Figure 37.10 depicts a recession scenario overlaid upon the 2% of GNP case used in the above projections. Were governments to follow the same pattern of response as they did in the early 1980s and were the projected recession to mirror that period in its intensity and duration, capital spending would drop by a maximum of $8 billion by 1990 below projected amounts assuming smooth growth. As Figure 37.10 illustrates, recovery would occur by 1991; but, there would be a "loss" in the capital stock accumulated and both annual outlays and borrowing would be fractionally lower throughout the remainder of the period than had there been sustained growth. Under our formulation, long-term borrowing would also be affected as a downturn in spending levels would reduce borrowing needs.

Methodology

The **four** tables included here in Appendix 37.1 are taken from a model developed by the Government Finance Research Center. GNP forecasts (Row 1) were obtained from the CBO August update: *Economic Outlook and Update*. Real Gross Capital Stock (Row 3) is defined as the value of equipment and structures currently in service before deduction of losses through depreciation.[1] Real Net Stock represents the value of the gross stock less accumulated depreciation. Depreciation (Row 8) is calculated using the straight line method, assuming equipment is 7.45% of gross stock with an average life of 15 years, and structures are 92.55% of gross stock with an average life of 51.9 years. Stock removed from service is calculated as one percent of year-end total gross stock in the preceding year.

Gross fixed capital formation (Row 10) is calculated as the difference in Real Net Stock from the current and preceding years plus depreciation. Current own source revenues (Row 14) are assumed to be 15% of total own source revenues. This approximates the proportionate contribution from that source made during the 1980s. Debt applied to fixed

[1] John C. Musgrave, "Fixed Reproducible Tangible Wealth in the United States, 1984–1987," *Survey of Current Business* (August 1988), p. 84.

781

capital (Row 15) is the residual of gross fixed capital formation after the removal of federal grants and current own source revenues.

Governmental purpose borrowing projections are calculated assuming borrowing applied to current-year, fixed capital is 90% of the combined average of governmental purpose borrowing in the current year, and the following two years. An assumption of 90% was used to compensate for the portion of total new issue borrowing which is not used for the formation of new capital.

Within the calculation of governmental purpose borrowing, $7 billion was subtracted from governmental purpose borrowing in 1986 to compensate for borrowing which would not be used for new capital purposes.

The recession scenario used for 1989 through 1990 roughly mirrors the recession of 1981 through 1983. Real GNP falls by one percent from 1988 to 1989 and then grows by one percent from 1989 to 1990. It then resumes a 2.1% growth rate for the remainder of the period. Because state and local capital spending is sensitive to changes in GNP, we show it declining during that period by two percent in 1989, remaining steady in 1990, and then growing with GNP.

Financing Volume 1986- 1995
Holding Real Net Stock per Capita at 1987 Level

					Projections					
	1986	1987	1988	1989	1990	1991	1992	1993	1994	1995
GNP 1982 Dollars	3759.2	3867.0	3993.2	4101.0	4195.3	4291.8	4390.5	4491.5	4594.8	4700.5
GNP Current Dollars	4240.30	4536.70	4811.79	5146.76	5479.09	5845.46	6234.55	6651.93	7089.00	7577.20
Real Gross Capital Stock	2333.7	2378.1	2422.9	2466.8	2511.2	2556.3	2601.8	2646.2	2691.1	2737.4
Real Net Capital Stock	1406.9	1426.0	1431.9	1452.7	1464.6	1477.5	1481.6	1500.3	1511.4	1522.5
Population	241.6	243.9	246.1	248.3	250.5	252.7	254.6	256.6	258.5	260.4
Real Net Stock per Capita	5823.26	5846.66	5846.66	5846.66	5846.66	5846.66	5846.66	5846.66	5846.66	5846.66
Deflator	112.8	115.7	120.5	125.5	130.6	136.2	142	148.1	154.3	161.2
Depreciation	53.21	54.22	55.24	56.24	57.25	58.28	59.32	60.33	61.37	62.41
Stock Removed from Service	23.34	23.78	24.23	24.67	25.11	25.56	26.02	26.46	26.92	27.37
Gross Capital Formation 1982 $'s	65.16	68.62	68.10	69.10	70.12	71.14	70.43	72.03	72.48	73.52
Gross Capital Formation Current $'s	76.20	79.40	82.06	86.73	91.57	96.90	100.01	106.67	111.84	118.51
Grants for Capital Investment	26.2	23.8	25	24.8	23.7	24.5	25	25.5	26	26.5
Total Own Source Revenue Financing	50.0	55.6	57.1	61.9	67.9	72.4	75.0	81.2	85.8	92.0
Current Own Source Revenue Financing	7.50	8.34	8.56	9.29	10.18	10.86	11.25	12.18	12.88	13.80
Debt Applied to Fixed Capital	42.50	47.26	48.51	52.64	57.63	61.54	63.76	68.99	72.96	78.22
Debt Applied to Fixed Cap as a % of GNP	1.002%	1.044%	1.008%	1.023%	1.053%	1.053%	1.023%	1.037%	1.029%	1.032%
Gross Capital Formation as a % of GNP	1.797%	1.756%	1.705%	1.665%	1.671%	1.658%	1.604%	1.604%	1.577%	1.564%
Total New Issue Borrowing	100.97	76.17	87.00	91.32	95.69	101.44	107.33	114.53	121.97	130.57
Governmental Purpose	70.97	45.17	59.00	63.32	67.09	71.24	75.43	80.73	86.17	92.37
Private Purpose - Capped	20.00	20.00	17.00	15.30	14.00	14.10	14.20	14.30	14.40	14.60
Private Purpose - Uncapped	10.00	11.00	11.00	13.30	14.60	16.10	17.70	19.50	21.40	23.60

Depreciation calculated as equipment 7.45% of Gross Stock and structures (92.55% of Gross Stock depreciated over 51.9 years)
GNP forecasts from CBO August Update: Economic Outlook and Update
Grants— Federal Budget— Special Analysis
Current Own Source Revenues calculated as 15% of Total Own Source Revenues

Financing Volume 1986 - 1995
Gross Fixed Capital Formation at 2% of GNP

					Projections					
	1986	1987	1988	1989	1990	1991	1992	1993	1994	1995
GNP 1982 Dollars	3759.2	3847.0	3993.2	4101.0	4198.3	4291.8	4390.5	4491.3	4594.1	4700.5
GNP Current Dollars	4260.38	4526.70	4811.81	5116.76	5479.06	5845.42	6234.51	6651.89	7049.76	7577.16
Real Gross Capital Stock	2333.7	2378.1	2422.9	2481.9	2546.0	2615.3	2690.2	2771.1	2858.3	2952.3
Real Net Capital Stock	1406.9	1426.0	1440.4	1461.3	1500.7	1537.4	1578.8	1625.2	1677.1	1734.4
Population	241.6	243.9	246.1	248.3	250.5	252.7	254.6	256.6	258.5	260.4
Real Net Stock per Capita	5823.26	5846.66	5852.94	5913.59	5990.52	6083.86	6201.13	6333.77	6487.63	6660.68
Deflator	112.8	115.7	120.5	125.5	130.6	136.2	142	148.1	154.3	161.2
Depreciation	53.21	54.22	55.24	56.58	58.35	59.63	61.33	63.18	65.17	67.31
Stock Removed from Service	23.34	23.78	24.23	24.82	25.46	26.15	26.90	27.71	28.58	29.52
Gross Capital Formation 1982 $'s	65.46	68.63	83.18	88.97	94.71	101.84	107.77	114.99	122.55	130.98
Gross Capital Formation Current $'s	76.20	79.40	96.24	102.94	105.58	116.91	124.69	133.04	141.80	151.54
Grants for Capital Investment	26.2	23.8	25	24.8	23.7	24.5	25	25.5	26	26.5
Total Own Source Revenue Financing	50.0	55.6	71.2	78.1	81.9	92.4	95.7	107.5	115.8	123.0
Current Own Source Revenue Financing	7.50	8.34	10.69	11.72	12.58	13.46	14.95	16.13	17.37	18.76
Debt Applied to Fixed Capital	42.50	47.26	66.55	66.41	75.55	78.85	84.74	91.41	98.43	106.23
Debt Applied to Fixed Cap as a % of GNP	1.022%	1.044%	1.258%	1.250%	1.332%	1.344%	1.359%	1.374%	1.380%	1.403%
Gross Capital Formation as a % of GNP	1.797%	1.754%	2.000%	2.000%	2.000%	2.000%	2.000%	2.000%	2.000%	2.000%
Total New Issue New Capital Borrowing	100.97	76.17	87.00	108.22	115.24	123.59	132.58	142.38	152.95	164.72
Governmental Purpose	70.97	45.17	59.00	79.92	86.84	93.39	100.68	108.58	117.15	126.52
Private Purpose - Capped	20.00	20.00	17.00	15.00	14.00	14.10	14.20	14.30	14.40	14.60
Private Purpose - Uncapped	10.00	11.00	11.00	13.30	14.60	16.10	17.70	19.50	21.40	23.60

Financing Volume 1986—1995
1995 Real Net Stock Per Capita at CBO Target Level

						Projections				
	1986	1987	1988	1989	1990	1991	1992	1993	1994	1995
GNP 1982 Dollars	3759.2	3847.0	3993.2	4101.0	4195.3	4291.8	4390.5	4491.5	4594.8	4700.5
GNP Current Dollars	4240.30	4526.70	4811.79	5146.78	5479.09	5845.46	6234.35	6651.93	7089.80	7577.20
Real Gross Capital Stock	2333.7	2378.1	2422.9	2488.6	2555.8	2624.6	2695.1	2765.3	2837.8	2911.3
Real Net Capital Stock	1406.9	1426.0	1460.6	1496.0	1532.1	1569.0	1604.7	1641.8	1679.0	1716.9
Population	241.6	243.9	246.1	248.3	250.5	252.7	254.6	256.6	258.5	260.4
Real Net Stock per Capita	5823.26	5846.66	5935.18	6025.04	6116.25	6208.85	6302.86	6398.22	6495.15	6593.49
Deflator	112.8	115.7	120.5	125.5	130.6	136.2	142	144.1	154.3	161.2
Depreciation	53.21	54.22	55.24	56.74	58.27	59.84	61.45	63.05	64.70	66.38
Stock Removed from Service	23.34	23.78	24.23	24.89	25.56	26.25	26.95	27.65	28.31	29.11
Gross Capital Formation 1982 $'s	65.86	68.62	89.89	92.11	94.38	96.69	97.18	100.14	101.90	104.32
Gross Capital Formation Current $'s	76.20	79.40	104.31	115.59	123.25	131.70	137.99	148.30	157.23	168.17
Grants for Capital Investment	26.2	23.8	25	24.8	23.7	24.5	25	25.5	26	26.5
Total Own Source Revenue Financing	50.0	55.6	83.3	90.8	99.6	107.2	113.0	122.8	131.2	141.7
Current Own Source Revenue Financing	7.50	8.34	12.50	13.62	14.93	16.08	16.95	18.42	19.68	21.25
Debt Applied to Fixed Capital	42.50	47.26	70.82	77.18	84.62	91.12	96.04	104.38	111.54	120.42
Debt Applied to Fixed Cap as a % of GNP	1.00%	1.04%	1.47%	1.09%	1.56%	1.55%	1.50%	1.56%	1.57%	1.58%
Gross Capital Formation as a % of GNP	1.79%	1.75%	2.25%	2.26%	2.25%	2.25%	2.21%	2.22%	2.21%	2.21%
Total New Issue New Capital Borrowing	100.97	76.17	87.00	121.04	128.25	137.10	146.29	157.13	168.54	181.54
Governmental Purpose	70.9	45.17	59.00	92.74	99.65	106.90	114.39	123.33	132.74	143.34
Private Purpose — Capped	20	20	17	15	14	14.1	14.2	14.3	14.4	14.6
Private purpose — Uncapped	10.00	11.00	11.00	13.30	14.60	16.10	17.70	19.50	21.40	23.60

Financing Volume 1984 - 1995

1995 JEC Target Real Net Stock Per Capita

	1986	1987	1988	1989	1990	1991	1992	1993	1994	1995
						Projections				
GNP 1982 Dollars	3759.2	3847.0	3993.2	4101.0	4195.3	4291.8	4390.5	4491.5	4594.8	4700.5
GNP Current Dollars	4240.30	4526.70	4811.79	5146.76	5479.09	5845.46	6234.55	6651.93	7089.80	7577.20
Real Gross Capital Stock	2333.7	2371.1	2422.9	2503.4	2586.5	2672.3	2760.9	2850.4	2943.4	3038.7
Real Net Capital Stock	1406.9	1426.0	1475.5	1526.5	1579.2	1633.6	1687.8	1744.3	1801.9	1861.3
Population	241.6	243.9	246.1	248.3	250.5	252.7	254.6	256.6	258.5	260.4
Real Net Stock per Capita	5823.26	5846.66	5995.38	6147.88	6304.27	6464.63	6629.07	6797.69	6970.61	7147.92
Deflator	112.8	115.7	120.5	125.5	130.6	136.2	142	148.1	154.3	161.2
Depreciation	53.21	54.22	55.24	57.08	58.97	60.93	62.95	64.99	67.11	69.28
Stock Removed from Service	23.34	23.78	24.23	25.03	25.87	26.72	27.61	28.50	29.43	30.39

Gross Capital Formation 1982 $'s	67.55	68.62	104.70	108.13	111.67	115.32	117.10	121.51	124.72	128.76
Gross Capital Formation Current $'s	76.20	79.40	126.17	135.71	145.84	157.06	166.28	179.96	192.44	207.46
Grants for Capital Investment	26.2	23.8	25	24.8	23.7	24.5	25	25.5	26	26.5
Total Own Source Revenue Financing	50.0	55.6	101.2	110.9	122.1	132.6	141.3	154.5	166.4	181.0
Current Own Source Revenue Financing	7.50	8.34	15.18	16.64	18.32	19.88	21.19	23.17	24.97	27.16
Debt Applied to Fixed Capital	42.50	47.26	85.99	94.27	103.82	112.68	120.08	131.29	141.48	153.81
Debt Applied to Fixed Cap as a % of GNP	1.002%	1.044%	1.787%	1.832%	1.895%	1.928%	1.926%	1.974%	1.996%	2.030%
Gross Capital Formation as a % of GNP	1.797%	1.754%	2.622%	2.637%	2.662%	2.687%	2.667%	2.705%	2.714%	2.736%
Total New Issue Borrowing	100.97	76.17	87.00	142.25	152.01	163.69	175.95	190.21	205.38	222.54
Governmental Purpose	70.97	45.17	59.00	113.95	123.41	133.49	144.05	156.41	169.58	184.34
Private Purpose - Capped	20.00	20.00	17.00	15.00	14.00	14.10	14.20	14.30	14.40	14.60
Private purpose - Uncapped	10	11	11	13.3	14.6	16.1	17.7	19.5	21.4	23.6

Depreciation calculated as equipment (7.45% of Gross Stock depreciated over 15 years) and structures (92.55% of Gross Stock depreciated over 51.9 years)

GNP forecasts from CBO August Update: Economic Outlook and Update

Grants - Federal Budget - Special Analysis H

Current Own Source Revenue calculated as 15% of Total Own Source Revenue

CHAPTER *38*

Emerging Borrowing Priorities—Financing Infrastructure

Stephen Peters
Shearson Lehman Bros.

Stephanie Smith Lovette
Sutro and Co., Inc.

K. Tina Choe
Shearson Lehman Bros.

In the past decade, a new word, *infrastructure,* has entered the political vocabulary, reflecting a growing concern over the adequacy of the nation's public capital plant. The terminology, infrastructure, describes the physical framework that supports and sustains virtually all economic activity: the nation's transportation and mass transit, water and wastewater systems and public buildings.

Infrastructure allows for the daily movement of people, the distribution of goods throughout the economy, and the improvement of the quality of life by providing a cleaner, safer environment. Infrastructure can be directly linked to the United States' growth and competitiveness in international markets and can effect the competitiveness of individual states, localities and business firms. In addition, public infrastructure constitutes a significant sector of the nation's economy; total spending on public works for capital improvement, operation and maintenance was $95 billion dollars in 1989.[1]

Despite infrastructure's importance and economic benefits, there has been a significant decline in the levels of real capital investment resulting in the deterioration of existing capital facilities. The level of

---

[1] J. M. Laderman, "New Streets Paved with Gold," *Businessweek*, October 16, 1989, pp. 92–93.

capital spending on public works investment has declined from 2.3% of GNP in 1960 to 1.1% in 1985. The United States now ranks 55th among nations in infrastructure capital investment.[2] Continued poor maintenance has caused sufficient deterioration in structures to pose public health and safety risks.

Infrastructure deterioration is evident; pavements on the interstate highway system are cracked and rutted, there have been extensive water main failures in the northeast, water shortages are facing the west, dams have burst in the mid-west and ground water aquifers are being depleted in the southwest, bridges in older cities have been closed. All of these factors indicate some neglect of the public responsibility to maintain capital facilities.

The infrastructure problem is national in scope although there are sub-national differences. In older industrialized areas, aging facilities need substantial rehabilitation or replacement. In comparison, growth areas face a diminution of their quality of life unless existing infrastructure is expanded to accommodate the needs of new residents and businesses. Both areas have trouble funding infrastructure projects. The condition of U.S. infrastructure would be a concern even if the problems of deterioration or disinvestment were not found in all states. The economies of various regions and states are so interdependent that some negative impacts are observable if any part of the nations basic infrastructure functions poorly.

To exacerbate the situation, infrastructure decision making is highly fragmented and complex. Infrastructure decision makers include the federal, state, and local governments, the private sector and the voting public. Local governments (including municipalities, counties, and special districts) have primary responsibility for the construction, upkeep and operation of transportation, and water and sewer facilities. Which type of local government has responsibility and which type of financing is employed depends on state law and historical patterns of development. State governments have direct responsibility for parts of the highway system and the regulation, coordination and financing of infrastructure. The federal government plays a crucial role in financing infrastructure and its regulations influence both patterns of investment and standards of service. In addition, the federal government has played a direct role in the construction of water supply and inland waterway projects.

Heightened concern over finances and fiscal scarcity has caused a shifting of responsibility between federal, state and local governments.

---

[2]*America's Infrastructure: Preserving Our Quality of Life*, Rebuild America Coalition, December 1989, p. 1.

There has also been a shifting of funding responsibility away from the general public to the private sector and direct beneficiaries. These changing conditions have raised questions about the degree infrastructure should be funded out of current revenues or through long-term debt instruments. The changes in the federal tax system have lent greater urgency to adjusting existing financing tools and exploring new means to supply the funds needed for essential public works improvement.

FINANCING OF INFRASTRUCTURE

Traditionally, public infrastructure has been financed by all levels of government on a pay-as-you-go basis. Since World War II, governments have increasingly turned towards the private sector to provide needed sources of capital for certain types of projects. The key feature of municipal securities is their tax-exempt status. Bondholders are not required to pay federal tax on their interest income and are often exempted from state and local taxes as well.

There are two types of municipal securities; general obligation debt secured by the full faith and credit (taxing power) of the issuing entity, and revenue bonds which are secured by the user fees or service charges paid by the users of the service. In 1991 the total new issue tax exempt debt was $164 billion dollars, 65% of that figure was revenue bond debt. The growth of revenue bond financing can be traced to several factors; the constitutional debt limitation of most State and local governments, and the taxpayer revolts in several States limiting increases in property taxes, the primary source of local revenue. Revenue bond obligations rarely constitute a direct debt of the municipality or the state. Due to debt limitations, many localities are issuing revenue bonds for projects that have a separate source of income, like user fees, while keeping general obligation debt to fund projects that do not have an alternative source of income.

Municipal debt can be rated by one or more of three major rating agencies; Standard & Poor's Corporation, Moody's Investor Services or Fitch Investor Services. These companies provide a rating system to compare different municipal issues, and assist investors in determining the quality of different debt issues. The rating agencies play a very important role in the municipal bond market since many bond purchasers are sensitive to these ratings. For example, many retirees look to invest in only Aaa/AAA bonds and many trust departments are restricted to purchasing only A or better issues.[3] As a result, the bond

---

[3] Priscilla Hancock, *Overview of the Municipal Bond Market* (Lehman Brothers Handbook), Summer 1991, pp. 2–4.

rating is a primary factor in determining the saleability of the issue and, therefore, the interest rate a municipality will have to pay to bondholders. To enhance a credit rating, an issuer can use bond insurance, thereby increasing the security and rating on the financing.

The organizational system for developing and delivering water is complex and varies tremendously by state and region. Water may be supplied by the public or private sector. Public sector providers include municipalities and water districts. Private sector providers include private utility companies and rural cooperatives. Individuals also supply their own water from ground or on site surface water facilities.

Direct responsibility for water delivery generally rests with local governments, but state governments become involved in a variety of areas; including right of way issues, interstate compacts regarding rivers and lakes and interbasin transfers. In the arid regions state governments act as master planners and adjudicators of water disputes.

The federal government has a long standing history of being involved with the development of water resources in the West as a tool for economic development. The Army Corps of Engineers undertakes water projects to control flooding, improve water transit and develop water supplies. The Farmers Home Administration helps finance small rural water systems. The Federal Safe Drinking Water Act of 1974 mandates inspection of public water supplies and treatment if any of several contaminants are found.

WATER

Water supply and distribution generally consists of four elements; source, storage, treatment, transmission. These four elements are defined as follows:

(1) *Source*—Water may be drawn from surface or groundwater sources. The infrastructure includes facilities related to well site or surface water development and watershed protection.

(2) *Storage*—Storage facilities are needed if the water flows vary over time in quantity or quality or to provide pressure for the water distribution system. Infrastructure costs includes site acquisition and development; construction repair or rehabilitation of improvements; construction or repair of reservoirs, standpipes or elevated tanks.

(3) *Treatment*—Is required to improve water quality.

(4) *Transmission and Distribution*—The system designed to bring water from the initial source of supply to the storage and/or treatment facility and then to the final user. The infrastructure includes a

system of aqueducts, pipes, valves, pumping stations, meters and hydrants.

Future Needs

Water problems fall into several areas:

- Deterioration of Old Water Distribution Systems in Urban Areas
- Inadequate Sources of Supply and Storage Facilities of Urban Systems
- Overdrawing of Underground Aquifers
- Development of Additional Storage Capability to Maintain Population Growth and Agricultural Economies of the Arid Western States
- Contamination of Existing Groundwater and Surface Supplies
- Rehabilitation of Dams to Assure Public Safety
- Improvement of Water Treatment Facilities

It is estimated that an investment of $103.7 billion is required to address the above areas and meet the nation's water needs until the year 2010.[4]

Estimated Sources of Funds

There have been ongoing discussion and legislation at the national level to reduce government spending on water resources and move closer to a market doctrine for water. The Congressional Budget Office has stated that marketable water services are generally heavily subsidized, under-valued and over consumed. However, it is difficult to implement a pure market doctrine for water because it has been traditionally treated as a public utility and there are legal constraints to changing this catego-rization. For example, the use of the prior appropriation doctrine in the Western states and the riparian rights doctrine in the Eastern states would severely limit the use of pure market doctrine.

Traditionally, water systems have been financed by the govern-ment on a pay-as-you-go basis or by general obligation bonds. Due to the shifting of water system financing from the Federal government to the local level, many municipalities are looking at new alternatives for financing water projects. Some of the alternatives being considered are levying new user fees, dedicating specific fees for water and private market financing. There are several constraints on private financing including; limited authority to levy user fees, statutory prohibitions

---

[4] *EPA 1988 Needs Survey*, Environmental Protection Agency, February 1989.

or ceilings on debt financing and regulated interest on state bonds. In addition, the 1986 Tax Reform Act severely limited tax exempt financings where private parties were involved in the construction or operation of the facility.

The solution to some of these problems is to create sub-state entities not bound by State debt prohibitions. Several municipalities, including New York City, have created special water authorities which allow them to issue bonds without interfering with City or State bonding limitations. In addition, western states have been using Special Districts, extending over several political jurisdictions, to assist in allocating resources and avoiding state debt limitations. It is expected that as the constraints on municipal finance tighten water system spin offs will occur more frequently.

Credit and Marketing Considerations

The main credit and marketing considerations for new water systems are the usage charges and connection fees, estimates of the number of people that will hook up to the system and limitations on rate setting. Credit rating agencies analyze the service area including wealth indicators, customer growth rates and leading users. Other review factors include the management of the system in terms of billing procedures, enforcement of mandatory system hook ups, and the extent of federal and state participation in the capital program. In recent years, the stability and output of the water source have also been important considerations, as more states face drought conditions and the over allocation of water supplies.

WASTEWATER TREATMENT

Sewage collection systems and wastewater treatment facilities are necessary for the protection of public health in urban areas. However, municipalities have often ignored the ill consequences of raw sewage discharge into waterways and ground water supplies. The concern over water pollution increased during the 1960s and 1970s. Due to this concern, many localities invested in treatment plants to replace individual septic and cesspool systems and outdated sewer systems. The passage of the Federal Water Pollution Control Act Amendments of 1972 marked the adoption of a national commitment to improve water quality. The federal government mandated that all municipal wastes be treated at the secondary level or better. At the same time, it committed billions of dollars to a Wastewater Construction Grant Program.

Estimated Need

The Environmental Protection Agency (EPA) has been actively involved in assessing wastewater needs since the passage of the Clean Water Act (CWA). Every two years, the EPA publishes a needs survey outlining the investments that will be needed to comply with the federal law. These estimates include those facilities for which a water quality or public health problem could be documented in accordance with the 1986 survey requirements. The EPA survey reports on two needs areas:

(1) Current Needs—The estimate of the cost of providing treatment service to the 1988 population for abatement of existing pollution control problems.

(2) Design Year Needs—The estimate of the cost of addressing all treatment for populations projected to be in place in the year 2008.

The 1988 survey estimated a cost of $67.9 billion to address the current needs category and $83.5 billion for the design year category.

The 1988 survey evaluated 15,591 facilities and found that 10,835 of the facilities surveyed had documented water quality or public health problems. In addition, 39 states and territories submitted separate estimates for needs that did not meet the established documentation criteria provided by the EPA. The cost for these projects exceeded $15 billion.

The 1988 survey was limited to facilities that were eligible for federal financing.

Financing Alternatives and Federal and Local Role

Wastewater collection and treatment systems are generally a local government responsibility. Some treatment facilities are municipally controlled, but in many areas a special district covering a broader geographic area is responsible for the facility. States have the responsibility for administering the federal water quality laws and construction grant programs. Some states also play a role in financing wastewater and treatment facilities. Local governments are generally responsible for investment in wastewater treatment facilities; however, the Clean Water Act states that lack of compliance with certain areas of the law can lead to a moratorium on future development.

Under the pre-1987 CWA, the federal government would pay up to 55% of the construction costs to renovate an existing plant to treat wastewater to a secondary level. The state or locality was expected to pay for the other 45% of the cost. The 1987 amendments to the Clean Water Act shifted the financing of treatment facilities from federal construction grants to state revolving loans. The state revolving fund can be used to provide assistance for constructing publicly owned water treatment works, for implementing a management program, and for developing and implementing a conservation and management plan. This revolving fund will be used to make loans, refinance existing debt, guarantee financial obligations, earn interest and pay administrative costs. The state revolving fund program was intended to give state's flexibility in the types of projects that could be funded. Congress allocated $18 billion for water pollution control through 1994, including $9.6 billion for existing projects and $8.4 to capitalize the revolving funds.

Prior to the 1986 Tax Reform Act, some wastewater treatment plants were built by private companies and financed by public industrial revenue bonds. The advantage to the municipality was that the plant was usually built in a more timely and cost effective manner than with municipal procurement. The advantage to the private company was the ability to use accelerated depreciation and investment tax credits. In addition the private company usually obtained a 25-year contract to operate the plant for the municipality. The 1986 tax law disallowed the use of accelerated depreciation and severely limited the use of revenue development bonds.

Credit and Marketing Considerations

Wastewater treatment facilities can be funded through general obligation bonds, system or project based revenue bonds or a hybrid of several financing tools. In general the rating agencies analyze four aspects of the program; the economic base of the service area, legal characteristics of the issuer's program, the issuer's administrative structure, and the issuer's financial condition.

TRANSPORTATION

The Intermodal Surface Transportation Efficiency Act was passed in 1991, which provides for the federal funding of our nation's roads, bridges and mass transit systems. As in other areas, the federal government has increasingly transferred transportation funding responsibilities to the state and local level. Combining their new fiscal responsibilities with the need to perform new and rehabilitative construction, municipal bonds are a method in which state and local governments and authorities can raise the necessary capital to service the public's needs. It is anticipated that the issuance of municipal bonds in the area of transportation will increase in the future tieing more closely costs and revenues to their direct beneficiaries.

HIGHWAYS AND BRIDGES

Highways and bridges are a major component of the nation's transportation system. Their effective functioning is essential to the United States' economic performance. Inferior and deteriorated roads not only increase the cost to the user through greater fuel usage and accelerated vehicle depreciation, but also the economy through lost productivity and potential investment capital. The hours spent in traffic jams could be used to manufacture more products; the money spent on additional fuel could be invested in the U.S. economy. It is estimated that the cost of congestion in the nation's 39 largest metropolitan areas totalled $34 billion in 1988. America's highway and roadway system is 3.9 million miles and serves 187 million vehicles per year. In 1989, $65 billion dollars was spent on this system, including the capital, maintenance and operating costs incurred at all levels of government.[5]

The financial responsibility for constructing highways is shared by federal, state and local governments. Federal funds are utilized generally on a matching fund basis for capital maintenance projects on the National Highway System (NHS). The Surface Transportation Act has given the states greater flexibility in utilizing federal funds. With the current recession impacting the availability of funds in many states, this will assist some states which have been experiencing difficulties meeting the matching requirements necessary to receive the federal aid. Beyond the construction stage, state and local governments have the responsibility for the operations and day-to-day maintenance of the roads. In 1989, $75.6 billion was spent by all levels of government for highway programs (inclusive of all capital and non-capital expenditures). Federal funding through the Highway Trust Fund declined from 24.8% in 1980 to 22.5% in 1989, whereas, local funding increased from 25.7% to 27.4% during the same period. States' contributions have remained unchanged at 50%. In 1989 the Federal-Aid Highway system (the predecessor to NHS) consisted of 851,714 miles or less than 22% of the total U.S. roads; however, this system carried more than 80% of all highway traffic.

The Act divides the former Federal-Aid Highway system into three parts; the NHS and the Surface Transportation Program. The newly created 155,000 mile NHS will be comprised of the Interstate System which consists of 44,849 miles of controlled access highways and carries 22% of all traffic. The remaining 110,151 miles on this system will include principal urban and rural arterials and the Defense

---

[5] U.S. Department of Transportation, Federal Highway Administration, *Status of the Nation's Highways and Bridges: Conditions and Performance, 1991, Introduction and Executive Summary*, July 3, 1991, pp. 3–5.

Highway Network. The Surface Transportation Program replaces the former primary, secondary and urban classifications into a flexible block grant funding system. The states can increase their funding to these roads by transferring their unused portions of the NHS and bridge programs. The roads under this new program comprise of main roads important to interstate, statewide and regional travel, secondary and feeder roads linking farms, distribution outlets and smaller communities, and routes serving all activity in urban areas. This system carries 59% of all traffic and consists of approximately 450,000 miles.

The United States has one of the world's largest stock of highway bridges (bridges that span more than 20 feet), 577,296 in all. Of these, 275,749 are part of the federal-aid system.[6]

Future Need

Between 1980 and 1988, travel on the U.S. road system increased at an average rate of 5% per year. By the year 2005, highway travel is expected to exceed 3 trillion vehicle miles. The Federal Highway Administration projects that by the year 2000, 41,000 miles of interstate, 334,000 miles of arterial roads and 636,000 miles of collector roads will require capital improvements to maintain serviceability.

In 1900, 134,072 (130,224 not on the federal-aid system) bridges have been labelled structurally deficient, which is defined as bridges that are restricted to light vehicles, closed or required to undergo immediate rehabilitation to remain open. In addition, 91,756 (80,396 not on the federal-aid system) bridges have been designated as functionally obsolete. Functionally obsolete is described as no longer meeting the usual design criteria for the system of which it is an integral part. These statistics translate into 39% of all highway bridges possessing major structural deficiencies.

In 1989, the federal government estimated the cost of eliminating the backlog of highway deficiencies at $400 billion. By ignoring needed repairs recognized in 1987, the public sector added an additional $8 to $12 billion to the backlog estimate. Looking ahead, the American Association of State Highway and Transportation Officials estimated in 1988 annual capital investment requirements to be $58.5 billion to meet future transportation needs. Capital expenditures at that time for all levels of government totalled only $31 billion. At this funding level, there is an annual shortfall of $27.5 billion.[7]

---

[6] *Ibid.*, pp. 13–14.

[7] Rebuild America Coalition, *America's Infrastructure: Preserving Our Quality of Life*, December 1990, p. 13.

The above figures show the seriousness of the problem. Unless a concerted effort is made on the federal, state and local level, America's highway infrastructure will face serious problems in the following decades. The lack of funding for highway infrastructure can lead to death and injury for motorists and greatly increased annual transportation costs. However, funding for highways and bridges has been slowing down and in some areas decreasing in the past 10 years. This decrease has been due to:

- The near completion of the interstate system—As the interstate system nears completion after 35 years, federal capital funds are decreasing since state and local governments have the responsibility for operating and maintaining roads.
- Financing of roads through the in-elastic gasoline tax—Most states and the federal government rely on gasoline tax revenue to finance capital improvements for highways. These taxes are ususally levied on a per gallon basis. After the oil embargo of 1973 and the rise in gasoline prices, Americans switched to more fuel efficient automobiles and moderated their gasoline consumption.

The Surface Transportation Assistance Act of 1982 increased the gasoline tax from four cents to nine cents per gallon with a one cent set aside for mass transit. Despite the increase in the gasoline tax, the federal share of the total national highway program decreased by 11% from 1980 to 1989.[8] In 1990 the federal motor fuels tax was increased to 15 cents per gallon, however, 50% of the increase was allocated to reduce the nation's deficit.[9]

Much of the capital needed for highway and bridge repairs and rehabilitation must be financed by state and local governments because of their traditional responsibility for maintenance and operations and cutbacks in federal funding. States and localities are beginning to finance their own rehabilitation and repair needs. In 1989 bond issues contributed 7% of total public sector financing of highways and 9% of state and local financings of highways. The greatest contributions came from user charges (motor fuel taxes, motor vehicle taxes and tolls) which accounted for 60% of public sector financing of highways.[10]

[8] *Ibid.*, p. 17.

[9] Richard Berke, "House Democrats Reach Accord on Transport Bill," *The New York Times*, June 27, 1991, Section A, p. 20.

[10] *Status of the Nation's Highways and Bridges: Conditions and Performance*, p. 17.

Credit and Marketing Considerations

The shortfall in highway financing can be funded in a variety of ways. Localities are experimenting with many different types of financing vehicles, including the capital markets. The capital market allows a locality access to better rates and quicker access to funds than a pay-as-you-go program. Many states do not consider revenue bonds general debt, therefore, most bond issues are not hampered by constitutional debt limitations.

General highways are funded from a combination of governmental appropriations and user fees, including the federal gasoline sales tax. Other user fees include vehicle registration and license fees, motor fuel taxes, taxes or fees on trucks, development fees and special sales taxes.

Development fees are a fairly new trend. Fees are levied on developers who are building new areas or are adding to an existing area thereby increasing traffic volume. Development fees are only useful in growing areas with high desirability. In low growth areas developers are not usually willing to pay the extra costs, since they are less likely to be able to charge higher prices for their development in comparison to previously built projects. In addition, the levying of development fees usually requires proof that the specific project is increasing traffic (the nexus test). It is difficult to establish nexus in older built out areas.

Toll financing is another alternative that allows direct user fees. Tollroads are more expensive to build and operate than non tollroads. However, tollroads can be built faster and are better maintained than highways funded by state highway taxes. Obtaining financing for new toll road projects is very difficult because of the unreliability of projected traffic counts and the competition from non toll projects. The Congressional Budget Office stated in its report on tollroads that only 10% of the existing urban mileage on the interstate system could meet the market test to be a self-supporting tollroad.[11]

Originally, tolls have not been allowed on highways which were built using Federal money. However, the 1987 Highway Act has allowed tolls on an experimental basis in nine states. The Surface Transportation Act has extended this ability to all fifty states.

The rating agencies look to the economic base of the surrounding economy, relative importance the state places on highway construction and maintenance, and source of repayment in determining a bond issue's rating. Highways which have a dedicated source of

---

[11] *Toll Financing of US Highways*, Congressional Budget Office, December 1985.

revenue (i.e. specific taxes) are considered to have a high level of support from the state.

MASS TRANSIT

There are approximately 1,800 public mass transit systems in the United States; 800 are located in cities with populations of over 50,000 and 1,000 are in smaller cities and rural areas. Transit systems generally consist of bus service, light or heavy rail service, van or carpool service or a combination of several types. Transit systems are funded by federal, state and local governments. Transit operations are funded 44% by fares, 47% by state and local governments and 8% by the federal government. Capital costs are funded 80% by the federal government and 20% by state and local government.

Estimated Needs and Future Sources of Funds

It is estimated that at least $90.8 billion in capital investment is required for mass transit between 1992 to 1997, or over $15 billion per year. This figure includes:

- $22.7 billion (25%)—new and modernized bus and rail facilities
- $30.1 billion (33%)—construction of new fixed guideway starts and extensions
- $20.3 billion (22%)—vehicle purchases and rehabilitation and expansion of current service
- $17.7 billion (19%)—other capital uses, including computer systems, and fare collection and communication systems.

Sources of Funds

The funding of mass transit is changing due to the shift away from dependence on federal funding to more local self-sufficiency. The main source of federal funding has been through the Urban Mass Transit Administration (UMTA) which recently has been renamed the Federal Transit Administration (FTA).

Funding decisions are made on proof of need and the local financial support for the system. Ridership figures and local sources of revenue are the criteria generally used. Systems with dedicated taxes or fees do very well under this new criteria. Unfortunately, it is very difficult to get political support and consensus on the local level for transit projects. Voters seem to be willing to fund new light rail systems, but not improvements in existing systems.

The private sector has been involved in mass transit in several ways including; special benefit assessments, transit impact requirements, corporate payroll taxes, leasing and sale of development rights or existing facilities and employer sponsored transit pass programs. Privatization of services has been tried on a small scale in several transit districts. For example, Dallas and Houston, Texas contract out to a private bus company to operate several suburban express bus routes. Santa Fe, New Mexico's transit system consists of taxi service contracted out to local companies. To date, there is not one mass transit system that is completely privately owned and operated.

Credit and Marketing Considerations

There are three types of financing used for mass transit; general obligation bonds, net revenue bonds and specific tax pledges. Mass transit bonds are secured with many of the same revenue sources as highway bonds; special sales taxes, user fees (fares), development fees and the one cent federal gasoline tax. The main credit concern is that there is a dedicated source of revenue to secure the bonds. In general farebox revenue and operating subsidizes are not enough security for the rating agencies. New York City is the only transit district that has been able to issue bonds backed solely by operating subsidizes and fare revenue.

The rating agencies evaluate the economic viability of the service area and the competitive position of mass transit. The mass transit industry's history of deficit operations and its labor intensive nature are always a credit concern. When evaluating a new system the area's traffic pattern and congestion levels are measured. New systems rarely achieve their projected ridership. In evaluating an older system the agencies evaluate ridership patterns and assess changes in the patterns subsequent to a fare increase. In both new and established systems management is carefully evaluated for creativity in marketing and maintenance programs and good labor relations and productivity.

AIRPORTS

There are 780 commercial airports in the United States, served by scheduled airlines, commuter airlines, and air taxi operations. In addition, there are 2,379 general aviation airports. Airports are generally run by local jurisdictions with minimal state government involvement. The federal government is responsible for safety and air traffic control through the Department of Transportation (DOT) and the Federal Aviation Administration (FAA). The federal government also assists in the financing of capital improvements through the collection and distribution of the Airport and Airway Trust Fund.

The aviation industry has changed dramatically since deregulation in 1978. Prior to deregulation the Federal government was involved in every aspect of the industry including route and fare setting. Since deregulation the industry has been free to conduct business with very few federal mandates.

Several changes have occurred since deregulation which have increased the number of airline passengers. The hub and spoke concept, which has been adopted by numerous airlines, has eliminated a significant number of point-to-point flights and has increased the number of shorter flights passengers must board. This has been a major source of increased congestion at airports. Secondly, the proliferation of discount fares as airlines competed for passengers travelling for leisure. However, the level of discount fares is expected to decline as the airline industry undergoes its current trend of consolidation.[12]

The managers of large airports were faced with huge capital investment needs and a changed business climate. Traditionally capital needs were met by issuing airport revenue bond issues secured by long-term use agreements with the airlines serving the airport. These use agreements were generally negotiated to run with the life of the bond. After deregulation, airlines were no longer willing to sign long-term use agreements because use agreements equalized rates across all air carriers. In addition, airlines wanted to be able to move into new markets without being saddled with long-term agreements. Investors' attitudes on the security of airport use agreements also changed as many carriers encountered financial difficulties.

Estimated Needs and Future Sources of Funds

There were 278 million air passengers in 1978, by 1988 the figure had increased to 455 million. It is estimated that the number of air passengers will reach one billion by the year 2000. In 1986, 16 airports were designated by the FAA as "very congested." This figure is expected to increase to 58 "seriously congested" airports by the year 2000. The Airport Operators Council estimates ten new airports are needed to handle the present and future air traffic volume. Current plans to expand and enlarge existing airports will only accommodate 25% of expected air travel growth.

The Federal Aviation Administration prepares an airport plan on a systematic basis. The plan covering 1986 to 1995 identified $24.3 billion in capital investment needs, approximately two-thirds of which

---

[12]Standard & Poor's Corporation, *S & P Municipal Finance Criteria*, 1989, p. 47.

is necessary to increase the capacity of existing airports. The remaining funds are needed in the areas of system maintenance and improvement.

Credit and Marketing Considerations

Prior to deregulation, most capital financing was based on airline use agreements. As previously stated, use agreements were less popular with the industry and investors after deregulation. The rating agencies recognized the changes and started to develop new rating strategies. The rating agencies now use passenger demand, instead of use agreements, as the key analysis tool for airport revenue bond financing. The measure of passenger demand is the number of emplanements and the type of airport. Passenger emplanements are the number of people that embark and disembark at that airport. In addition, the rating agencies rate airports on the type of passenger demand they generate. Airports are categorized as hub or airline home based airports, destination or origination airports, connecting airports, regional airports and commuter airports.

Use agreements are still used by the airline industry, but today's agreements are generally shorter in length. The rating agencies analyze existing use agreements for two reasons. An use agreement provides extra security for the bondholder and an airport's management and collection history regarding the use agreement gives an indication of airport fiscal and managerial practices.

MUNICIPAL LEASING

Municipal lease-purchase financing, often called *municipal leasing*, is a contractual agreement that government uses to acquire facilities and equipment. Municipal leases are much like other leases, payments are made in installments over time and the lease payments are secured. The security for municipal leases is the lease revenues (i.e. the annual governmental appropriations for the lease payments). In addition, many are secured by the equipment or facility that is being leased. There are two types of lease-purchase financing; leasing of individual equipment or several pieces of equipment using a master lease, and building leases. Municipal leasing provides many benefits to a governmental entity including:

- 100% financing of the equipment and related expenses so the governmental lessee does not have to pay a cash down payment.
- Financing over time which allows the government to pay for the equipment or facility over its full useful life.

- Leases are outside of the traditional governmental debt limitations since the transaction is subject to annual appropriation. Debt is not created so voter approval for municipal leasing is usually not required.

Lease-purchase financing is used for facilities that are essential to the continued provision of government service. A *certificate of participation* (COP) is an undivided interest in a stream of annual appropriated lease payments from the municipality.

The issuing entity issues COPs or bonds and uses the proceeds to finance projects. The security for the COPs or bonds are the annually appropriated lease payments. Ownership of the equipment or building is held by the issuing entity of an appointed trustee, but the municipality has the exclusive possession, custody and control of the equipment or building and is responsible for its maintenance. If the governmental lessee determines the use of the equipment or building is no longer needed it can terminate the agreement through non-appropriation. The problems with exercising the non-appropriation option are outlined in the credit consideration section.

The total appropriations are equal to the purchase amount so at the end of the bond term the equipment or building ownership reverts to the municipality.

Equipment and Master Leasing

Master leasing and regular equipment leasing are structured similarly. In a regular equipment lease there is only one piece of equipment on the lease; under a master lease several pieces are purchased under one (master) lease. Master leasing provides cost reduction in several areas:

- Less expensive than the rate charged by private leasing companies; and
- Lower administrative costs by reducing the number of lease payments and in the refinancing of existing higher interest leases.

The mechanics of master leasing is as follows: The municipality identifies its future equipment needs and potential purchases during a specified time period. The equipment being financed can be new, equipment under existing lease agreements, which have a buy-out option, or equipment purchased outright in the past for which the municipality prefers to be reimbursed for and pay over time. The municipality is responsible for identifying the equipment that will be purchased and the issuer is responsible for acquiring the equipment with the revenue produced by issuing bonds or COPs. The financing structure is based on the useful life of the equipment purchased. Any debt related to a piece of equipment will be retired prior to the end of the equipment's useful life.

Capital Facilities Leasing

A capital facility lease purchase is used for governmental facilities like office buildings, schools, prisons or courthouses. Capital facility leasing is structured similarly to equipment leasing. The government body enters into a lease agreement with another municipal entity. This entity can be another government or a duly empowered body like a public authority. Often the lessor is simply an entity created by the government to issue bonds in its behalf. The reason for this is that lease payments are considered tax-exempt if they are divided into principal and interest and the lessee and the final owner are both public entities. Prior to construction of the facility, the government enters into a lease-purchase agreement with the lessor providing for lease payments by the governmental body. The issuer then issues bonds or COPs and sells them to investors. The investors provide the construction funds with their security being the government appropriated lease payments. At the end of the lease period the facility ownership reverts to the government.

Credit and Marketing Considerations

The rating for a certificate of participation (COP) is based on the municipality's general obligation bond rating since the rating agencies are analyzing at the municipality's ability to pay. The certificate of participation is generally rated one step lower then a general obligation bond. A well secured lease purchase revenue bond usually costs one quarter to one half of a percentage point more in annual interest costs than a general obligation bond. A lease purchase revenue bond has higher issuance costs than a similar general obligation bond issue.

As previously stated, COP obligations contain a non-appropriation clause allowing the municipality to stop appropriating funds for the lease without penalty. A non-appropriation of funds would have the same effect on the market as a bond default. The fear of lowering their credit rating and losing access to the capital markets keeps cities from exercising the non-appropriation clause.

Due to the provision for non-appropriation, the security provided to the certificate holders in the event the government unit ceases to make lease payments is a critical element to the COP rating. In general, the COP holders have a security interest in the facility or equipment under lease. If the government does not appropriate funds for the lease the trustee can rent, lease, or dispose of the property and the payments will be used to pay the COP holders. The ability to grant a security interest is not universal, in certain states this feature is prohibited by law.

BIBLIOGRAPHY

America's Infrastructure: Preserving Our Quality of Life, Rebuild America Coalition, December 1990.

A Guide to Innovative Financing Mechanisms for Mass Transit, An Update, Department of Transportation, December 1985.

APTA Survey of Transit Capital Needs, 1992–1997, Advance Summary of Findings, American Public Transit Association, October 1990.

Aschauer, David Allen, "Infrastructure: America's Third Deficit," *Challenge: Magazine of Economic Affairs,* Volume 34, No. 2, March–April 1991.

Berke, Richard, "House Bill Carries Something for All," *The New York Times,* July 26, 1991, Section A, p. 13.

Berke, Richard, "House Democrats Reach Accord on Transport Bill," *The New York Times,* June 27, 1991, Section A, p. 20.

Berke, Richard, "Senate Approves Bill to Overhaul Transportation," *The New York Times,* June 20, 1991, Section A, p. 6.

"Bridge Repair Gets High Priority." *Automotive News,* October 2, 1989, p. 14.

Current Cost-Sharing and Financing Policies for Federal and State Water Resources Development, Congressional Budget Office, July 1983.

Defining the Issues, A Report to the President and the Congress, National Council on Public Works Improvement, September 1986.

Federal Budget for Public Works Infrastructure, Congressional Budget Office, July 1985.

Hancock, Priscilla. *Overview of the Municipal Bond Market, Lehman Brothers,* Summer 1991.

Hard Choices, A Report on the Increasing Gap Between America's Infrastructure Needs and Our Ability to Pay for Them, Joint Economic Committee, February 1984.

Highway Statistics 1989, U.S. Department of Transportation, Federal Highway Administration, 1989.

"Highways/Tollroads Credit Review," *Standard & Poor's Creditweek,* March 19, 1990.

Laderman, J.M. "New Streets Paved with Gold," *Businessweek,* October 16, 1989, pp. 92–93.

Lehman Brothers, "Financing Water and Wastewater Facilities, Alternative Approaches."

"More Federal Money Than Ever, but States are in Trouble," *Engineering News Record,* Vol. 226, No. 4, January 28, 1991, pp. 44–46.

New Directions in Transportation, A Private Sector Report on Transportation Capital Needs, 1987–1996, American Transportation Advisory Council, October 1985.

"Our Crumbling Infrastructure," *Nation's Business,* August 1990, pp. 16–24.

S & P Municipal Finance Criteria, Standard & Poor's Corporation, 1989.

"Tax Reform's Effect on Municipal Issues," *Standard & Poor's Creditweek,* February 26, 1990, p. 20–21.

The Intermodal Surface Transportation Efficiency Act of 1991, The American Road & Transportation Builders Association, December 18, 1991.

Transit 2000: Executive Summary, American Public Transit Association, November, 1989.

Transit 2000: Managing Mobility: A New Generation of National Policies for the 21st Century, American Public Transit Association, November 1989.

"Transportation on the High Road," *The New York Times,* July 6, 1991, Section 1, p. 20.

Toll Facilities in the United States, U.S. Department of Transportation, Federal Highway Administration, February 1991.

Worldwide Airport Traffic Report, Calendar Year 1989, Airport Operators Council International, 1989.

CHAPTER 39

Environmental Finance: New Directions and Opportunities

William B. James, C.F.A.
Prudential Securities Incorporated

This chapter is divided into two sections. Section one discusses two recent examples of significant municipal environmental finance programs: the State Revolving Fund established under the 1987 Amendments to the Clean Water Act of 1972 and the emissions trading program established under the 1990 Amendments to the Clean Air Act. Specific detail is provided on each of these two programs. Also included in this section is a discussion of various types of market-based economic incentives for the control and reduction of various types of environmental pollution.

Section two of this chapter provides a discussion of the recent activities of the USEPA-sponsored Environmental Financial Advisory Board. The activities of this Board, as confirmed by the recommendations of its recently published reports, underscore the importance of this Board in acting as a catalyst for positive changes in municipal environmental finance initiatives.

TWO EXAMPLES OF MARKET-BASED MUNICIPAL ENVIRONMENTAL FINANCING PROGRAMS

The passage of the amendments to the Clean Water Act in 1987 (the "1987 Act") and to the Clean Air Act in 1990 (the "1990 Act") represent new directions and opportunities in municipal environmental finance in the United States. The State Revolving Fund ("SRF") Program that was established under the 1987 Act incorporated a new approach to the funding of municipal wastewater treatment projects. Under the 1987 Act, the funding of the construction grants program originally established in 1972 was eliminated in 1990. The 1987 Act provided for a transition to the SRF Program. The SRF Program incorporates a "capitalization" grants approach which grants, along with the required 20% state match, are deposited into the State's SRF to be used to make loans and provide other forms of financial assistance to municipal wastewater construction projects. The 1990 Act incorporates a market-based approach for the control of air pollution. Title IV of the 1990 Act focuses on the reduction of acid rain through an emissions trading program for investor-owned utilities. Title I of the 1990 Act encourages a market-based emissions trading program that may be implemented by states for the control of air pollution.

Provided below are details on these two market-based municipal environmental finance programs. Both programs represent a redefinition of who is responsible for meeting the costs of the environmental mandates established by federal regulation. They also represent a shift in the role of state governments from a largely passive role to a somewhat more active role in municipal environmental finance. Also, the continued reduction of all types of Federal grant programs has shifted the responsibility of the cost of continued environmental finance compliance to state and local governments. The increasing financing burden placed on state and local governments for environmental finance has been exacerbated by the ever-increasing costs of these environmental compliance programs.

For the SRF Program these challenges have been converted into opportunities for states to implement new and innovative environmental finance solutions to their wastewater environmental financing problems. The emissions trading program established under the 1990 Act represent another new and significant challenge and opportunity for states to implement new and innovative approaches to the funding of environmental projects for the control of air pollution.

The State Revolving Fund Program Established Under the Federal Water Quality Act of 1987

The State Revolving Fund and Its Significance. The SRF is significant for several reasons. First, it represents a significant change in how the funding of wastewater construction costs occurs in the United States. Specifically, it shifted from the use of construction grants (established under the original Clean Water Act of 1972) to a capitalization grants program for the funding of a loan program to be initiated by a state's SRF Program. Additionally, all federal construction grants were phased out in federal fiscal year 1990. There was a transition at the point to the exclusive funding of the capitalization grant program. The SRF capitalization grant program is scheduled to be phased out in federal fiscal year 1994 unless it is reauthorized. The authorization amounts for the SRF capitalization grants program was established at $8.4 billion in the 1987 Act. Federal appropriation amounts have averaged about 78% of the authorized amounts. The State Revolving Fund also requires a minimum 20% state match of the federal capitalization grant amounts.

The Types of Financial Assistance Permitted Under the SRF Program. There are several types of financial assistance which may be provided from the state's SRF. One permitted use is to make loans for qualified publicly owned wastewater treatment facilities, for example, secondary treatment, advanced treatment, infiltration/inflow correction, replacement/rehabilitation of sewers, new collector sewers, new interceptor sewers and combined sewer overflow projects. Loan interest rates may range from 0% to current market interest rates. SRF funds may be used for the purpose of refinancing existing debt obligations in which such debt was incurred and construction commenced after March 7, 1985 (the introduction date of the 1987 Act). Also, the SRF may guarantee or purchase insurance for local debt obligations. The SRF may also be used as a source of revenue or security for SRF obligations. (It is under this provision that states have issued leveraged bonds for their SRF Programs). Loan guarantees for sub-state revolving funds is also a permitted use of SRF funds. Lastly, the SRF is permitted to use up to 4% of the capitalization grant for administrative purposes.

What Are the Needs for SRF Funds? According to the EPA's *1988 Needs Survey*, $83.0 billion is needed through 2010 to construct SRF-eligible wastewater treatment and collection system projects. These amounts do not incorporate the costs associated with new funding eligibilities, replacement needs and new enforceable requirements under the 1987 Act (e.g., non-point source control, sludge disposal, estuary protection and stormwater projects). A recent update of wastewater treatment needs by the Association of State and Interstate Water Pollution Control Administrators (ASIWPCA) indicates that these needs now total $137.8 billion.

Total Funds Available in the SRF. A recently completed EPA survey indicates that for the 1988-1989 period approximately $28.7 billion has been made available to meet SRF-eligible needs. There has been a significant gap—the *funding gap*—for the funding of wastewater treatment needs in the United States. Using the EPA's *1988 Needs Surveys* estimate of needs—$83.0 billion—it is obvious that there still exists a "funding gap" between the estimated needs of $83.0 billion and what has been funded to date; this translates into a $54.3 billion "funding gap." Using ASIWPCA's estimate of needs—totalling $115.4 billion—versus what has been funded to date—$28.7 billion—there is an even larger remaining "funding gap" of $86.7 billion.

SRF Implementation Status. To date, all 50 states and Puerto Rico have established an SRF and have received at least one capitalization grant. Through September 30, 1990 (the latest available data) a total of $2.8 billion in federal capitalization grants have been awarded. The key structural and operating aspects of the SRF Program are as follows. First, the method of obtaining the required 20% state match have included state appropriations, state general obligation bonds, SRF revenue bonds and the pledging of SRF loan repayments. Fourteen states have used some form of bond leveraging to maximize SRF funding amounts. The types of financial assistance provided have included: loans (74%); purchase of refinance of existing obligations (12%); leveraging (12%); and, administrative costs (2%). The interest rates on the loans have ranged from 2 to $5^1/2$%. One-third of the states vary the interest rates depending on the ability of the loan participant to repay the loans. The types of projects expected to be funded include: wastewater treatment projects (69%); wastewater collection (28.5%); non-point source and collection (1.9%); and estuarine activities (0.6%).

Issues Associated with the Implementation of the SRF Program. Certain issues have been identified that have impacted the implementation of the SRF Program. First, the amount of the capitalization grants for the SRF Program that the federal government has appropriated has been significantly less than the authorized amounts (on average, 22% less). The effect of this has been not only less funding but also less certainty and confidence in the availability of funding by the federal government, now and in the future. There has been some difficulty in providing SRF assistance to economically distressed communities due to the inability of these communities to repay loans. Next, the application of the federal "cross-cutters" (i.e., the federal laws and authorizes regulating the use of federal monies/grants) has added significantly to both administrative complexities and project costs. The use of the federal letter of credit (LOC) for the payment of the capitalization grants to the states has added both complexity and costs to the program. Not only has there been a loss of potential interest earnings for the SRF by using the LOC as a payment mechanism, but there has also been the slowness of payments of the capitalization grants to the states. Lastly, the statutory restrictions on the availability of SRF funds for administrative costs (limited to 4%) has provided inadequate funds for these costs on a long-term basis (since the federal capitalization grants are due to expire in 1994). Another issue associated with the SRF Program has been the fact that land is not an eligible cost under the SRF Program. The effect of this is that municipalities must obtain separate financing for the costs of land. Lastly, due to the requirement of a "dedicated source of revenue to cover loan repayment," it has been difficult to fund non-point and estuarine activities under the SRF Program.

The Emissions Trading Program Established Under the Clean Air Act of 1990

Under the Clean Air Act of 1990 (the "1990 Act"), significant changes were accomplished relating to the USEPA's approach to the reduction of air pollution throughout the United States. Under Title IV of the 1990 Act, a market-based approach to the reduction of acid rain is being implemented. This acid rain program addresses the pollution control measures which must be undertaken by investor-owned utilities through an emissions trading program. Title I of the 1990 Act sets forth general provisions and definitions relating to state and federal implementation plans for the control of air pollution. The use of economic incentives is expressly allowed for in the general state implementation plans and in the general provisions relating to non-attainment measures.

In 1987, the EPA promulgated revised National Ambient Air Quality Standards (NAAQS) for particulate matter (PM) which replaced total suspended particles (TSP) as the indicator for PM with a new indicator called "PM-10" (i.e., particulates with a aerodynamic diameter of less than or equal to a nominal 10 microns). To date, the EPA has designated 16 areas as "non-attainment for PM-10" and has notified the governors of these states of this determination. Under this designation, these 16 areas must meet certain milestones to avoid being redesignated as a "Severe Non-Attainment PM-10 Area." If so designated, an area would be subject to severe economic and regulatory restrictions, including severe restrictions on manufacturing expansions and additions.

A proactive strategy that may be implemented by an non-attainment area is the implementation of a marketable emissions trading program as permitted (and encouraged) by the 1990 Act.

The Clean Air Act of 1990: General Provisions. The United States Environmental Protection Agency (the "EPA") is in the process of developing rules for economic incentive programs pursuant to Section

182(g)(4)(B) of the Clean Air Act Amendments of 1990. The EPA must promulgate economic incentive program rules within two years after enactment of the Amendments (by November 15, 1992). The EPA currently intends to publish proposed rules in April 1992 and promulgate final rules in November 1992.

Pursuant to Section 182(g)(4)(B) of the Clean Air Act Amendments of 1990, the EPA must publish rules for economic incentive programs. One of the options that may be implemented by a state is, the use of economic incentive programs in certain cases. An economic incentive program is mandated upon the failure of a state to submit a compliance demonstration or to meet applicable milestones for reasonable further progress in extreme ozone non-attainment areas, and is identified as an option upon such failure in serious and severe ozone non-attainment areas. An economic incentive program is also mandated upon the failure of a state to submit a milestone demonstration, to meet a required specific emission reduction milestone or to attain the standard in serious non-attainment areas.

The 1990 Act requires that economic incentive programs adopted by states be consistent with the EPA's economic incentive program rules. The economic incentive programs must be "nondiscriminatory" and consistent with applicable law regarding interstate commerce. The economic incentive program rules are to include "model plan provisions which may be adopted for reducing emissions from permitted stationary sources, area sources, and mobile sources," as well as guidelines which specify how revenues generated by the plan provisions shall be used.

The 1990 Act also broadly encourages innovation through the use of market-based approaches, not only in the Title IV acid rain program, but also in Title I general provisions and definitions for state and federal implementation plans. The use of economic incentives is explicitly allowed for in the general state implementation plan ("SIP") provisions and in the general provisions for non-attainment area SIPs. Economic incentives are also allowable in federal implementation plans (FIPs).

The EPA intends to encourage the development of economic incentive programs which increase flexibility and stimulate the use of less costly strategies, as well as provide incentives for the continued development and implementation of innovative emission reduction technology and strategies beyond those specifically mandated through state and federal standards and regulations.

Types of Economic Incentive Strategies Considered. The economic incentive programs may include "State established emission fees or a system of marketable permits, or a system of State fees on sale or manufacture of products the use of which contributes to ozone formation, or any combination of the foregoing or other similar measures," as well as "incentives and requirements to reduce vehicle emissions and vehicle miles traveled in the area, including any of the transportation control measures." Other sections of the 1990 Act refer to ". . . other control measures, means, or techniques (including economic incentives such as fees, marketable permits, and auctions of emissions rights)" . . . and ". . . economic incentives (including marketable permits and auctions of emissions rights) concerning the manufacture, processing, distribution, use, consumption, or disposal of the [consumer or commercial] product."

One broad category of economic incentive programs is based on marketable emission limits. As with all types of economic incentive programs, a wide range of variations in this category exist that could be incorporated as a part of a state implementation plan. Emission sources may achieve their permitted emission limits either directly, or by purchasing emission credits from other sources. Credits may be purchased from other sources in the program, or (in some regulatory program designs) from other sources which participate in the system. Allowing sources with lower cost abatement alternatives to trade emission credits to sources facing more expensive alternatives reduces the overall cost of meeting a given total level of abatement (the "bubble" concept).

A second category of programs is based on the use of emission fees. An emission fee program establishes and collects a fee on emissions, providing a direct economic incentive for emitters to decrease emissions to the point where the cost of abating emissions equals the fee on emissions.

A third category of programs is based on the provision of information. For instance, a labelling program on certain types of products could provide consumers with information at the point of sale about the pollution characteristics of various products. This can provide an incentive for consumers to choose less polluting products.

Many other types of economic incentive programs have been designed or implemented that fall outside of these three general categories. Examples include: old car buy-back programs; motor vehicle trip reduction measures and other transportation control measures; public awareness campaigns; capital grants for technological innovation or implementation; some sort of credit for early reductions; and, adjustments in building codes or zoning ordinances.

Applicability. The economic incentive program rules will apply to any economic incentive program adopted by a state. For example, the schedule for serious, and severe, ozone non-attainment areas missing a reasonable further progress milestone may leave as little as six months for the economic incentive program to operate prior to the next milestone. Consequently, the time available to develop, implement and achieve emission reductions in an economic incentive program will be extremely limited if the state waits until a milestone failure occurs to initiate the selection of an economic incentive program. Also, only one year is available to an extreme ozone non-attainment area prior to the date by which the next milestone is to be met.

As a result of these mandated time schedules, the EPA is encouraging states to voluntarily initiate development of an economic incentive program as soon as they determine that a milestone failure is likely, or that such a program could be advantageously included as part of their SIP. States are encouraged to consider inclusion of economic incentive programs, where appropriate, in the SIPs due three or four years after enactment. Submittal at that time would be more likely to allow for sufficient time to develop, implement and evaluate the effectiveness of the program. The EPA currently intends to apply these economic incentive program rules to evaluate any economic incentive programs voluntarily submitted by States as part of the new or revised SIPs.

Characteristics of the Emissions Trading Program Established Under the 1990 Act. Provided below is a description of the key characteristics of an emissions trading program. To date, such a program has not been implemented in municipal environmental finance.

Tradeable Permits. Sources would receive tradeable emission permits. Each permit initially would entitle a holder to emit a fixed and determined amount of emissions. Such permits would have specified emissions limits. The commodity (*i.e.* a unit of emissions) will be fungible and definite.

Broad Market. The market system for emissions trading would include all source categories. Tradeable permits would be eligible for use, sale or lease within and among all sources and source categories. In addition, a broad market is necessary to allow implementation of the lowest cost emission reduction methods. Emission reductions can be achieved at a cost lower than that anticipated for most large stationary sources through the application of traditional "command and control" techniques by allowing such sources the flexibility to meet emission reduction requirements by identifying and implementing control techniques and mechanisms from previously uncontrolled, less controlled and less expensively controlled sources.

Emissions Baseline. All sources would be assigned an initial emissions baseline based on actual emissions during a representative period of years. Emissions would be measured on an annual basis for trading purposes. The permitting authority would be empowered to set a separate daily peak emissions level that takes into account a source's operating variability to ensure against significant adverse localized impacts.

Declining Emissions Entitlement. The emissions entitlement associated with each tradeable permit would periodically decline by fixed percentage amounts based on what is required to attain the applicable national ambient air quality standard by the applicable attainment date. The declining balance would be the same for all source categories, including mobile, consumer product and other sources.

Notice to Permitting Authority. As required by the 1990 Act, the permittee would submit an initial compliance plan, pursuant to which the permitting agency would record the applicable annual emissions allowance level and, if appropriate, peak daily emissions level (taking into account a source's projected operating variability). The permittee would submit regular progress reports and certify, on at least an annual basis, that facility emissions are in fact no greater than the allowance level. Permittees who trade allowances or who wish to obtain additional allowances by virtue of one or more innovative control strategies would be required to provide advance notice to the permitting authority.

Since facility emission allowances are determined at the initial stage, there would be no need to quantify emissions prior to each trade. Thus, the emissions trading program significantly streamlines the trading process. The permitting agency would continue to require and monitor that records adequate to assure compliance with facility or system-wide emissions limits are kept and to enforce compliance with such limits.

Certainty of Entitlement. The marketable permits must have a predictable value to assure the development of an efficient market and to motivate companies to invest in emission reduction strategies to the greatest possible extent. The emissions allowance associated with each tradeable permit would be treated as an entitlement, subject only to the declining value of the emission allowances attached to each such permit which is required to attain applicable ambient air quality standards.

The permitting agency, after providing the public with notice and an opportunity for comment, would be authorized to make equal adjustments to the value of allowances for all sources if necessary to "get back on track," if improvements in methods of quantifying emissions show that the initial allowances or subsequent credit determinations (in the case of innovative strategies) do not allow the non-attainment area to meet reduction commitments. Adjustments for other reasons should not occur.

Prior Shutdown Credit Policy. Once historic emissions baselines are established and reflected in tradeable permits, the prior shutdown policy should be withdrawn. Withdrawal is necessary to promote the efficient functioning of an emissions trading market.

Intrasource Trading. Tradeable permits would be assigned to facilities and groups of facilities under common ownership rather than to specific units or discrete operations. Therefore, there would be no individual emissions limit for a specific unit. Emissions limits would be monitored and enforced on a facility-wide or system-wide base (the bubble concept).

Non-Traditional Sources. Several possible strategies exist to bring mobile, area and other non-traditional sources into an emissions trading policy. One strategy would distribute emissions allowances at some efficient point of a product chain and require that distributors hold or secure the necessary allowances for any products (i.e., cans, solvents, fuels) distributed in a given year. The allowances would be no different from and fungible with permits for stationary sources and would be eligible for trading across source categories.

Other Examples of Economic Incentives

In the past, the EPA has made significant progress in protecting the environment. Such improvements were made through the use of "command-and-control" regulation which was based on the promulgation of uniform, source specific emission or efficient limits backed by the use of enforcement actions. A complete dependence on this command-and-control approach will not, by itself, achieve completely all environmental goals. This is due to the reality of the types of environmental problems facing environmental protection (e.g. ozone duplication). Economic incentives achieve these goals since they can influence rather than dictate actions. This approach may characterized as a "marketplace" approach.

Recently, the EPA published a report on "Environmental Incentives: Options for Environmental Protection." A variety of market-based measures to promote environmental goals were discussed in this Report. These include:

(1) *Creation of markets*—Creation of tradable government-issued privileges to discharge pollutants to use scarce environmental resources;
(2) *Monetary incentives*—Methods to change market incentives, including direct subsidies, reduction of subsidies that produce adverse environmental effects, fees, and taxes;
(3) *Deposit/refund systems*—Programs to discourage disposal and encourage central collection of specific products;

(4) *Information disclosures*—Actions to improve existing market operations by providing information to consumers; and

(5) *Procurement policies*—means by which the federal government uses its own buying power to stimulate development of markets (e.g., for recycled products).

The criteria used to evaluate the merits of incentive-based policies include:

- Is the environmental problem the result of some externality?
- How significant is the resulting environmental problem?
- Which jurisdiction (local, state, or federal government) can most effectively address the problem?
- Will an incentive-based approach help maximize net social benefits?
- Will a particular incentive-based policy be effective?

In this EPA Report there was provided a list of potential applications of a wide range of incentive approaches which include:

(1) Municipal Solid Waste Incentives
   a) Volume-based Pricing of Municipal Waste Services
   b) Incentives to Recycle Scrap Tires
   c) Deposit/Refund System for Lead-Acid Batteries
   d) Credit System or Deposit/Refund System for Used Oil
   e) Other Municipal Solid Waste Incentive Applications

(2) Global Climate Change Incentives
   a) Fee on Carbon Content in Fossil Fuels
   b) International Trading of Greenhouse Gas Emission Rights
   c) Incentives to Encourage Electricity Conservation
   d) "Sipper/Guzzler" Rebate/Fee to Encourage Purchases of More Fuel-Efficient Vehicles

(3) Water Resource Incentives
   a) Changes in the Pricing of Water
   b) Deposit/Refund or Tax/Rebate System for Pesticide Containers
   c) Reduction of Federal Subsidies Encouraging Development in Coastal Areas

(4) Multi-Media Incentives
   a) Local Fees on Volatile Organic Compound Emissions from Major Sources

b) Market Incentives to Reduce Consumer and Commercial Use of Solvents

c) Deposit/Refund System for Chlorinated Solvents

d) Labeling of "Environmentally Responsible" Products

e) Marketable Permit or Surcharge System for Lead

f) Charge on Toxic Release Inventory Releases

g) Reduction of Federal Subsidies Encouraging Use of Virgin Materials

h) Federal Procurement Policy Initiatives.

THE ENVIRONMENTAL FINANCIAL ADVISORY BOARD: A CATALYST FOR CHANGE

The Board was established in 1989 by the EPA to provide authoritative analysis and advice to the EPA Administrator regarding environmental issues to assist EPA in carrying out its environmental mandates. The Board is focusing on environmental finance issues at the Federal, state, and local levels, particularly with regard to their impact upon local governments and small communities. The Board's goal is to address the capacity issue of state and local governments to carry out their respective environmental programs under current federal tax laws and various federal mandates. The Board is endeavoring to increase the total investment in environmental protection by facilitating greater leverage of public and private environmental resources to help ease the environmental financing challenges facing our country.

The Board is assigned the role of providing advice on the critical environmental financing issues facing our nation, consistent with current federal tax laws. Objectives consistent with this role include:

- Reducing the cost of financing environmental facilities and discouraging polluting behavior;
- Creating incentives to increase private investment in the provision of environmental services and removing or reducing constraints on private involvement imposed by current regulations;
- Developing new and innovative environmental financing approaches and supporting and encouraging the use of effective approaches;
- Identifying approaches specifically targeted to small community financing;
- Assessing government strategies for implementing public-private partnerships, including privatization and operations and maintenance issues, and other alternative financing mechanisms; and

- Reviewing governmental principles of accounting and disclosure standards and how they affect environmental programs.

Members of the Board were selected on the basis of their professional qualifications and diversity of perspectives and backgrounds that will enable them to provide advice and guidance to the Administrator on environmental financing issues. The Board consists of a group of independent experts drawn from all levels of government, including elected officials; the finance and banking community; business and industry; national organizations; and academia.

To date, the Board has published three reports: the "Incentives for Environmental Investment: Changing Behavior and Building Capital"; "Small Community Financing Strategies"; and, "Private Sector Participation in the Provision for Environmental Services." A fourth report is to be finalized shortly (i.e., "Public Sector Options to Finance Environmental Facilities"). The following is a summary of each of these reports.

A Description of the Board's Reports

Incentives for Environmental Investment: Changing Behavior and Building Capacity. This report recommends three basic strategies in order to change the nature of the debate on environmental finance. These are:

a) to strengthen and institutionalize an environmental finance capacity within EPA which, in turn, will serve as a guide for the international community;

b) to assist state and local governments to self-finance all environmental infrastructure; and

c) to reduce the costs of environmental protection through the creation of new economic and market-based incentives.

The key proposals discussed in this report are as follows:

a) exclude bonds used to finance public-purpose environmental facilities from state volume caps;

b) eliminate the currently imposed restrictions on costs of issuing tax-exempt, private-activity bonds used to finance environmental facilities;

c) exempt interest earned on bonds issued to finance public-purpose environmental facilities as a tax preference item for the purpose of calculating the alternative minimum tax on personal and corporate tax returns; and

d) allow advance refundings of tax-exempt, private-activity bonds used to finance environmental facilities.

One other board proposal is to enable issuers of tax-exempt bonds to earn interest on bond proceeds without penalty over a reasonable period of time for construction of environmental facilities, provided that excess interest earnings (earnings above the bond yield) are used exclusively to reduce the size of the bond issue.

In addition to the proposals, the Board has reviewed the following fundamental approaches to reducing pollution that merit the EPA's attention:

a) imposition of economic penalties, such as effluent fees, to reduce the volume or toxicity of discharges;

b) use of economic incentives, such as tax or other credits for investments in waste-reducing technologies or activities, to promote pollution prevention; and

c) removal or biases in current policies that inhibit waste reduction.

Small Community Financing Strategies for Environmental Facilities. In this report, the Board examines three financing strategies from small communities:

a) Improving coordination among small community financial assistance programs;

b) using bonds banks to improve access to the bond market for small communities; and

c) improving financial assistance to small communities under the SRF Program.

This report describes the types of financing problems faced by small communities. These include:

a) lack of access to capital can constrain or defer investment in new or expanded environmental facilities;

b) capital costs of facility construction can exceed the financial capability of many small communities; and

c) some low-income and/or very small communities may not be able to afford the costs of operating an environmental facility properly.

Underlying these financing problems are a number of factors that characterize small communities. These include:

a) higher unit costs because small facilities lack the economies of scale that can be achieved by larger facilities;

b) an inadequate customer base to set user charges that support the full cost of providing environmental services;

c) a low credit rating makes it difficult to issue debt or raises the interest costs of debt financing;

d) higher fixed costs of small bond issues (e.g., legal and underwriters fees) for those small communities that can obtain debt financing; and

e) Lower household incomes, which reduces the ability of community residents to pay increased user charges, regardless of facility size.

The Board examined programs that provide financial assistance to small or low-income communities or rural areas for environmental infrastructure projects. These programs include financial assistance programs administered by federal agencies, by state agencies where a federal program is administered at the state level, and a federally chartered financial institution, CoBank, which plays an important role in rural areas. These sources of financial assistance to small communities are listed below.

- State Revolving Fund (SRF) Program. The SRF is administered by the states and funded by capitalization grants from EPA and state matching funds. SRFs primarily award loans to local governments for construction of wastewater treatment facilities.

- Water and Waste Disposal Loan and Grant Program. This program is administered by the Farmers Home Administration (FmHA), U.S. Department of Agriculture. The FmHA Water and Waste Disposal Program provides loans, grants, and loan guarantees primarily for water and wastewater systems that serve rural areas or communities under 10,000 population. The 1990 Farm Bill created the Rural Development Administration (RDA) and requires transfer of the FmHA Water and Waste Disposal Program to the RDA.

- Public Works and Development Facilities Grant Program. Administered by the Economic Development Administration, the U.S. Department of Commerce, this program awards grants to finance construction of public works and development facilities (including water and wastewater facilities) to promote long-term economic development.

- Community Development Block Grants (CDBG)/Small Cities Program. The CDBG/Small Cities Program is funded by the Office of Community Planning and Development, U.S. Department of Housing and Urban Development. Administered principally by the states, CDBG/Small Cities funds provide grants for activities that benefit low-income communities. These grants can be used to construct public facilities such as water and wastewater systems.

- Partners for Environmental Progress (PEP) Initiative. PEP is new initiative of the U.S. Army Corps of Engineers that will provide financial assistance for market feasibility studies to help small communities find ways to privatize environmental services.
- Appalachian Regional Commission (ARC) Supplemental Grants. ARC's supplemental grants program provides grants to supplement other federal grants to fund community development facilities such as water and wastewater systems.
- CoBank, the National Bank for Cooperatives. CoBank is a federally chartered and regulated financial institution that received expanded authority under the 1990 Farm Bill to finance water and wastewater systems in communities under 20,000 population.

This report also proposed two actions: a) make public statement highlighting the financial services and programs available to small communities in complying with environmental mandates; and b) convene a roundtable of small community financial assistance programs. The agenda of the roundtable should address these needs:

a) ways and means to effect improved coordination among small community financial assistance programs;
b) coordination of small community financial assistance programs with EPA's geographic initiatives;
c) mechanisms to promote pollution prevention;
d) collection and exchange of more detailed information about small community environmental facility needs for all media;
e) mechanisms and incentives to encourage private sector participation;
f) Improvements in technical assistance and outreach efforts;
g) EPA should provide technical assistance on the establishment and use of bond banks; and
h) EPA should identify barriers to effective bond bank operations and develop strategies to overcome those barriers.

Additionally, the Board recommends that the EPA explore the financial, legal, and administrative feasibility of creating a regional or multi-state institution to facilitate issuance of tax-exempt bonds by small communities.

The Board has identified four general problems faced by small communities under the above described SRF Program:

a) small communities may not gain priority under the SRF if they must compete directly against larger communities;

b) small communities may not find affordable financing using SRF loans for construction of wastewater treatment facilities;

c) small communities may not seek SRF funds because they lack the ability to document needs and meet application requirements; and

d) even if SRF financing for capital costs was available, some small communities may not be able to afford the operation and maintenance expenses costs of a wastewater treatment facility.

The Board recommends that the Administrator should consider seeking legislative changes to the SRF Program to improve financial assistance to small communities. Additionally, the EPA should also actively encourage states to give more attention to small community needs in their current SRF programs.

The Board has concluded that taking action to target a portion of financial assistance directly to small communities is an important step in addressing small community environmental facility needs. The first two actions presented below represent two alternatives for targeting financial assistance directly to small communities. These two actions are: a) create a small community set-aside under the SRF Program; or b) create a new revolving fund exclusively for small communities covering wastewater treatment, drinking water, and solid waste management.

A third action to improve the affordability of SRF loans for small communities is to extend the SRF loan term beyond 20 years for small communities. Extending the SRF loan term would increase the affordability of SRF financing for small communities by lowering annual debt service. Lower annual loan repayments would especially benefit those small communities in weak financial condition. The SRF also may benefit by reducing potential loan problems, such as late payments or defaults.

Other actions recommended in this Report include:

a) vary interest rates based on ability-to-pay or other measures of economic need;

b) provide supplemental state grants for hardship cases;

c) allow subsidization of principal for loans made from the repayment stream;

d) mitigate federal requirements for small communities;

e) provide guarantees for small community debt; and

f) provide technical assistance to small communities.

Private Sector Participation in the Provision for Environmental Services. The Board has developed the following strategies for the Administrator's consideration to increase private participation in providing environmental services.

Stimulate the Creation of Public-Private Partnerships. The first strategy is for EPA to continue to expand its efforts to forge new links between the public sector and private partners. Through demonstration projects, development of a privately funded development fund to finance the formation of public-private partnerships, technical assistance and expert advice to local governments and recognition for successful partnerships, and encouragement of voluntary private sector projects to finance environmental facilities or projects.

Evaluate Implications of Increasing Flexibility of Federal Grant Policies. The actions that would increase EPA's flexibility in applying federal grant regulations include:

(1) provide, on a case-by-case basis, waivers that allow facilities to define public ownership of facilities as majority public ownership of assets or as public control over financial and operational decision-making;

(2) through waivers, include reinvestment in EPA-approved facilities in the definition of compensation to the federal government for grant-funded assets;

(3) provide explicit regulatory definition of the period of federal interest for grant-funded real property as a facility's design life; and

(4) define and sanction acceptable encumbrance of grant-funded real property through case-by-case waivers.

Encourage Modification of State and Local Laws that Constrain Private Investment. The EPA can use the experiences of these states, along with other model statutes to develop the ability to provide technical assistance to states and localities that are seeking to increase the flexibility of their financing options.

Encourage Full Cost Pricing. This strategy would encourage full cost pricing is twofold: first, to encourage the most efficient use of resources possible; and, second to provide to private sector with accurate indications of the potential revenues from an investment, to encourage the highest level of private funding possible.

Reduce Risks Associated with Private Investment or Operation of Public Facilities. The EPA should encourage different approaches to risk pooling and risk sharing to limit potential investors' exposure to liability from environmental investments.

Public Sector Options to Finance Environmental Facilities. In order to significantly improve public finance strategies in support of environmental programs, the Board reviewed the following actions in this Report.

Regular Inventory of Environmental Protection Costs. The Board first considered the availability of current data on the public costs of meeting environmental mandates for wastewater, drinking water, and solid waste infrastructure. Cost data for drinking water and solid waste initiatives are not collected in a comprehensive way or on a recurring basis, as they are for wastewater facilities. Such data would provide a valuable tool to assess the financial impact of mandates, evaluate financing strategies, and measure progress toward environmental goals. The Report therefore urges EPA to undertake a regular comprehensive inventory of the public sector costs of environmental protection.

Improvements to the SRF Program. The Board supports seeking administrative and statutory improvements in the current SRF program as a near-term priority. If further federal funding is made available, the Board also supports channeling such funds to the current SRF program, as it has served as a successful mechanism in providing assistance for wastewater investments.

However, the Board generally does not support the creation of set-asides within the SRF to target national priorities. Separate accounts that assign a particular funding priority to a subset of programs can be rigid and unresponsive to state needs and priorities. In contrast, the Board supports the establishment of set-asides based on the recipient group targeted and type of assistance offered, such as set-asides for small system projects. This support is based on a need for hardship grants, which are not included in SRF types of assistance, and the difficulty that small local governments have in competing for financial assistance. A multimedia small community set-aside is further justified by the need for such grants to finance water supply and solid waste management in these communities.

In addition, the Board feels that the impact of the Clean Water Act equivalency requirements and cross-cutters should be evaluated if further federal funds become available.

Expansion of the SRF Program. The wide variety and magnitude of public health and environmental needs for physical facilities argue for additional flexibility in the SRF for assisting multimedia eligibilities. In response to this need, a second approach was endorsed by the Board for the delivery of further federal assistance, if such assistance is made available. This approach involved an expansion of eligibilities for the SRF program. The Board strongly supports the allocation of additional federal appropriations for environmental financing to the SRF program, which has been proven effective.

A Federal Alternative to the SRF. The Board does not support the creation of alternative federal grant mechanisms for capital assistance such as the Clean Water Fund, as proposed in the Senate bill reauthorizing the Clean Water Act. In terms of eligibilities, the Clean Water Fund is duplicative of the SRF and reintroduces a large-scale federal categorical grant program. The Board believes that the SRFs should remain as the principal mechanism to deliver continued federal funding should it be made available.

Environmental Trusts. The Board considered national and state environmental trusts, to serve both program and capital assistance functions. A trust could serve a valuable capital formation function in many states, not only to assist the SRF, but also other state financing programs. The Board believes a properly designed trust could perform these functions with fee revenues and certain other authorities independent of annual federal appropriations. Given the uncertainty of future federal funding, a trust could play a particularly important complementary role in building state capacity and financing multimedia environmental infrastructure.

The Board recognizes that state environmental trusts and fee systems have been established by the states and shares the concern that federal actions not disrupt current state initiatives in this regard. The federal role in expanding the use of state trusts should be one of active encouragement through a number of incentives, but without penalty for nonparticipation.

Although the trust concept has several major concerns, the Board believes that the potential inherent benefits warrant a cross-program evaluation by EPA and careful consideration by federal and state policy makers. As part of the trust evaluation, the Board recommends that EPA examine the state trust concept as an alternative to the national trust, supported by fee revenues. The evaluation should stress the advantages and limitations of linking the state trust with the SRF and should include incentives and sources of revenue. The evaluation should also consider modifying the SRF itself to accommodate the broader multimedia functions of a state trust. The latter becomes particularly advantageous if eligibilities are expanded for the SRFs.

Environmental Fees. Environmental fees should play a broader role with respect to assisting state programs, than has heretofore been the case. National and state fee systems may be used as the primary revenue sources for existing state programs or environmental trust funds. Either way, they should be viewed as a potentially significant source of additional, supplementary revenue to help states meet the increasing demands placed on their capacity to manage environmental issues and meet state needs and priorities. Any proposal to implement a national fee system by itself, or in support of national or state trusts, should be carefully evaluated for potentially duplicative or disruptive effects on existing state fee systems.

In many cases environmental programs cannot be totally dependent for funding on fee-based revenues. The strength of state programs is enhanced by the use of a diversity of funding sources, including state and federal appropriations. The Board does not suggest that fees be adopted as a means of eliminating or reducing other existing sources of funding support.

The Board further recommends that EPA support, through technical assistance and cooperative agreements, any current state efforts to create environmental fees and trusts as public finance strategies for meeting environmental needs.

CHAPTER 40

Privatization in a New Key*

Aaron Gurwitz
Goldman, Sachs and Co.

Private sector firms have always played a major role as contractors in the construction and operation of public capital facilities. These contracts have generally been structured on a fixed fee basis, occasionally with some limited incentives for superior performance and some limited penalties for poor performance. In almost all cases, the public sector, users of the facility, or bondholders have borne the major risks inherent in infrastructure investments: that projects would fail to provide the anticipated public benefits or that project revenues would fall below expectations.

Recently, however, state and local policy makers in the United States and central government officials in the United Kingdom have begun to consider a new, more active role for private firms in the provision of public infrastructure facilities. Specifically, governments have begun to solicit proposals from private sector entities that are willing, *at their own financial risk,* to design, construct, and operate public capital facilities. To date, most of the proposals have involved the construction of toll roads and bridges. But the approach may also be applied to other types of facilities, such as airports or mass transport.

This chapter explores this new variety of privatization. We conclude that the relative financing costs of public and private sector ownership depend on how we evaluate the risks borne by the public sector when it owns an infrastructure facility. We believe that if this public equity stake in projects is evaluated correctly, then the financing costs of the two approaches are quite similar. Although the availability of "free equity" to publicly owned projects does create an apparent cost saving, other advantages of private ownership, not incorporated in traditional cost-benefit analysis, might easily outweigh any slight financial disadvantage of taxable financing. Private ownership does, however, raise some important basic public policy issues regarding the regulation of monopolies and the use of eminent domain. These questions are serious enough to suggest that private ownership may have applicability as a way of expanding and improving our public infrastructure only under certain circumstances. The essay concludes with a discussion of the circumstances in which private ownership makes the most sense as a public policy tool.

RECENT POLICY INITIATIVES

The largest privately owned infrastructure project in the world today is, of course, the Channel Tunnel. Indeed, the fortunes of private ownership as a policy initiative seem to rise and fall with the performance of the "Chunnel" stock on the London Stock Exchange and the Paris Bourse. The uncertainties of this particular project notwithstanding, the ability of a private sector company in the immediate aftermath of the October 1987 stock market collapse to raise equity capital to finance a large, risky capital project was impressive—enough so to start both private entrepreneurs and public officials thinking about other applications of the Chunnel approach.

Worldwide numerous private initiatives are under various stages of discussion. In the United States, one special purpose company, the Virginia Toll Road Corporation, has been authorized to proceed. However, relatively few of these projects will succeed unless private ownership becomes public policy in a systematic way.

At present, in addition to the Virginia project, two major broad-based public policy initiatives in this direction are under way. In the United Kingdom, the government has proposed formal mechanisms by which private sector entities would be able to submit unsolicited proposals for toll road development and obtain the public sector's approval for the project. Public sector participation in the project would be restricted to *limited* use of eminent domain. Private developers would retain full title to the facility for a specified period of years, after which ownership would be transferred to the public sector. The government's proposals are now under consideration in Parliament.

The major U.S. policy initiative along these lines was enacted by the California Legislature as AB 680 and became law in August 1989. The law authorizes the State Department of Transportation (CalTrans) to select four demonstration projects that would be privately developed and operated. The Act contains few specifics and generally allows CalTrans a great deal of flexibility in specifying the terms of agreements, regulating the private sector firms, and using eminent domain. CalTrans's requests for proposal have stimulated a great deal of interest.

COMPARATIVE COSTS OF PUBLIC AND PRIVATE FINANCING

The debate over whether the public or the private sector is best suited to undertake any given task has always been a central issue in economic thought. The purpose of this essay is not to try to resolve this debate but to highlight some of the issues involved in private ownership of infrastructure projects in the United States today. One of these questions involves the relative costs of public and private financing under a tax law that permits tax-exempt financing in the first instance and forbids it in the second. Our analysis indicates that the apparently obvious answer—that access to tax-exempt interest rates creates a strong bias in favor of public ownership—is not quite correct. To be sure, a public sector entity borrowing in the municipal market will pay a lower nominal interest rate than a private entity borrowing in the corporate market. However, if the private sector borrower is profitable, and therefore taxable, the relevant borrowing cost will not be the before-tax rate on corporate bonds, but the effective *after-tax* interest cost. As Figure 40.1 indicates, the average yield on current coupon A-rated municipal revenue bonds has, in fact, been higher over the past three years than the average yield after a 34% federal tax rate on newly issued A-rated industrial corporate bonds.

Despite the fact that after-tax interest cost per dollar borrowed might be slightly lower for the private sector, the overall *explicit* financing cost is probably lower for the public sector for two reasons. First, and less important, most start-up infrastructure projects will not realize profits until several years after the facility goes into operation. Thus, private sector infrastructure entrepreneurs will not realize the benefits of the deductibility of interest expenses while the project is under construction and during the first years of operation. The larger negative cash flow in the earlier years reduces the internal rate of return from the private sector's point of view.

FIGURE 40.1

Yields on A-Rated Municipal Revenue Bonds and on A-Rated Industrial
Corporate Bonds Before and After Corporate Taxes
(Corporate Tax Rate = 34%)

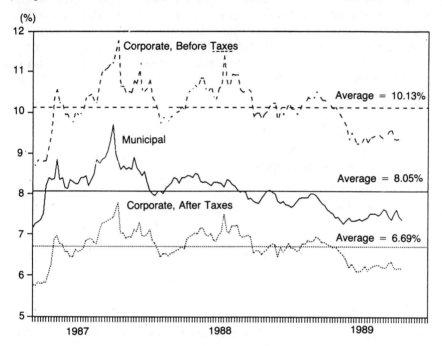

The "Cost" of Equity

Second, although the private sector has a lower effective borrowing
cost once taxes are taken into account, the public sector is able to borrow a larger proportion of project costs. Lenders generally demand a
substantial equity contribution from private sector borrowers. By contrast, lenders in the municipal market are willing to rely on a public
sector pledge to raise revenues, along with a relatively small debt service reserve fund, and to lend the full cost of an infrastructure project. Thus, the "cost" of equity, usually measured as a "normal" rate of
return, is explicitly included in the private—but not the public—sector's total financing cost.

To illustrate the impact of the different treatment of equity under the alternative forms of financing let us consider a single project
costing $100 million. Assume that as a publicly owned project, the fa-
cility could be fully financed in the tax-exempt bond market at an all-
in cost of 8.05% (the average A-rated revenue bond yield since early
1987). Assume further that (1) if the facility were privately owned, in
order to achieve the same credit rating bondholders would demand a

10% equity stake and (2) in order to attract equity investors, the project must produce an expected 15% return on equity after corporate taxes. With a 34% corporate tax rate, this means that project revenues must generate a 22.73% before-tax return on the portion of the project financed by equity. Suppose, finally, that the project will be profitable and taxable from the first year and that 90% of the financing can be obtained in the corporate bond market at an all-in before-tax cost of 10.13% or an after-tax cost of 6.69% (the average since early 1987). Under these assumptions, the all-in after-tax capital costs of the alternatives would be:

Public Ownership		8.05%
Private Ownership		
Borrowed Funds	$6.69 \times .9 = 6.02$	
Equity	$22.73 \times .1 = 2.27$	
Total		8.28%

As noted, any delay in the profitability of the project, as would be likely, would further impair the relative attractiveness of the private alternative.

The Public Equity Stake

These explicit capital costs, however, are misleading from a public policy point of view. Bondholders are willing to forego an up-front equity contribution to infrastructure development projects from the public sector only because there is a reliable, explicit commitment on the part of a government or a government agency to bear a substantial part of the economic risks inherent in the undertaking. In the case of a facility financed through general obligation borrowing, the risk that the economic costs of the project will exceed its benefits is borne by the general taxpayer. Likewise, taxpayers benefit if benefits exceed costs.

For projects financed by revenue bonds and secured by the issuing authority's covenant to charge fees sufficient to maintain a specified debt service coverage ratio, the equity stake is, in effect, provided by those potential users of the facility who are willing to pay the highest tolls. To see why this is so, consider the case of a toll bridge. Suppose there are two and only two mutually exclusive groups of potential users of the bridge: one group who will use the facility if the toll is $5 per trip or less and another who will use the bridge if the toll is $2 per trip or less. Suppose further that the number of $5 users is sufficient to provide adequate debt service coverage, even if no $2 commuters use the facility. Assume finally that the Toll Bridge Authority aims to maximize revenues, that there is no congestion, and that there is no way to discriminate between $5 users and $2 users. In this example, therefore, the $5 users bear the equity risk. If there are enough $2 users so that the lower toll would produce sufficient debt service coverage, then the price is set at $2 and the $5 users get a clear benefit equal to $3 per trip. If there aren't enough $2 drivers, then the price is set at $5 and the $5 users get no benefit. Finally, bondholders bear the risk that the number of $5 users will fall lower than what is needed to support debt service.

In this simple example the $5 users bear no cost if they alone generate sufficient revenues to meet debt service requirements. A trip is worth $5 to them, and that is exactly what they pay. In most cases, however, bond covenants require authorities to charge fees sufficient to meet operations and maintenance expenses *and* to produce a debt service coverage ratio of more than 1.0. Any excess coverage can be thought of as an equity contribution by the users of the facility who are willing to pay the highest tolls.

Valuing the Public's Equity

Thus, regardless of whether the project financing is secured by a general obligation pledge or a revenue bond covenant, there is, in effect an equity investment either by taxpayers or facility users, even when the facility is publicly owned. When we compare all-in financing costs, as in the example above without accounting for this public sector equity contribution, we are treating the willingness of taxpayers or facility users to bear these risks as a free good. While it is clear that some value should be placed on the public's willingness to bear these risks, it is quite difficult to assign a monetary value to this "equity contribution." For purposes of this discussion it is not necessary to derive a precise value for this element of a publicly owned project's capital structure; it will be sufficient to offer some observations with respect to whether the public's equity commitment will add more or less than private stockholders' investments to the overall effective all-in cost of capital.

The easiest case to analyze is that of a publicly owned facility financed by revenue bonds. If we assume that, for any given credit rating, bondholders will demand the same degree of protection in the corporate and municipal markets, then the effective equity contribution will be the same whether the project is privately or publicly owned. And if we observe further that toll road users should receive the same return on their "equity" contribution as stockholders would, then both the magnitude of and the expected return on the equity contribution should be the same under both forms of financing.

The analysis of taxpayers' equity contribution through a general obligation pledge is somewhat more elusive. Nevertheless, the fact that most state constitutions impose severe restrictions on the full faith and credit pledge suggests that this security should be used only to finance projects offering the highest expected rate of return. Thus, when we compare private financing with general obligation financing, we should assume a substantially higher return on equity in the latter case.

All of this suggests that if we evaluate the public's equity contribution to infrastructure projects correctly and if the project is profitable immediately, then the all-in effective (after-tax) financing cost of private ownership could be somewhat lower than that of public ownership. To be sure, the higher explicit (before-tax) interest rates paid by private sector borrowers do make net cash flows more negative before the project construction phase and the first years of operation. However, this relatively small bias against private sector ownership could be corrected through the tax law by expanding the permissible "private purpose" uses of tax-exempt financing to include transportation projects. Alternatively, the tax depreciation schedule for such projects might be shortened to compensate for the bias.

THE NONFINANCIAL BENEFITS AND COSTS OF PRIVATE OWNERSHIP

Given that the financial costs of public and private ownership are roughly comparable, the choice between the two approaches can turn on other issues. Advocates of private ownership argue, not without justification, that investors with their own capital directly at risk and focused intensively on a single project rather than a city- or state-wide infrastructure development program might have a stronger incentive and the wherewithal to push projects to completion quickly. Private investors might be particularly likely to pick the economically "right" projects, to try to expedite approvals, to demand rapid completion of construction at low cost, and to maintain and operate the facility efficiently. Selective use of private ownership could also help alleviate pressures on overburdened public works departments.

Private ownership is, however, problematic in several respects. For one thing, private ownership of an essential capital facility creates a private monopoly. Even when alternative routes are available, unregulated toll road owners will still be able to charge the revenue-maximizing monopoly price as long as alternative routes are few enough so that demand is relatively inelastic. The potential for abuse of monopoly power can be controlled by regulating tolls through a public utilities commission or, as has been proposed in California, through the Department of Transportation. However, rate regulation itself introduces some economic distortions; the opportunity to earn a regulated, "normal" rate of return may not be sufficient to provide the incentives for superior performance discussed in the previous paragraph.

What is perhaps more important, development of almost any transportation project is difficult—often impossible—without resort to the governmental power of eminent domain. Without this power, a single property owner can extract nearly the full economic benefit of an infrastructure project. In fact, both the U.K. and California proposals envision limited use of eminent domain to support private sector project development. The right of condemnation is one of the most fundamental attributes of sovereign power, and its use in support of a private sector business initiative raises questions of fairness.

APPROPRIATE APPLICATIONS

Given the fiscal pressures on state and local governments as a result of taxpayer revolts and reduced federal aid payments—and given the rough equivalence of the financing costs of public and private ownership—this new type of privatization probably does have a role to play in upgrading our public capital infrastructure. However, the problems involving monopoly power and the use of eminent domain suggest that this public policy tool will be applicable only under certain circumstances. Among the types of projects that seem to offer the most appropriate applications for private ownership are the following:

- *Riskier Projects.* An aggressive program of infrastructure development will include some projects whose immediate payoff is particularly risky, requiring a relatively large equity stake. If private sector entrepreneurs are willing to take this risk, the public sector should consider accepting the offer.

- *Projects that complement other private sector developments.* For example, toll road projects that improve access to a new real estate development might properly be viewed as the responsibility of the developer.

- *Projects not requiring use of eminent domain.* If private infrastructure developers are able to assemble all of the project right-of-way without resort to eminent domain, then one of the major objections to this form of ownership would be eliminated.

- *Facilities with Close Substitutes.* If users of the facility have several reasonably good alternatives, then demand for the services of the facility will be more elastic and the danger of excessive monopoly power will be diminished. Thus, for example, privately owned express lanes along a freeway right-of-way would offer relatively little opportunity to charge monopoly prices because the more crowded free lanes and local streets would remain available as substitutes.

CHAPTER 41

The Ongoing Battle: Almost 70 Years of Assaults on Tax-Exempt Municipals*

Joan Pryde

Railing against the excessive volume of tax-exempt bonds, the legislator warned Congress that "very few taxpayers realize the danger and cost of this rapidly growing evil." Was it Rep. Brian J. Donnelly, D-Mass., who has riled the market several times in the past few years? Wrong. Rep. Fortney Stark, D-Calif., enemy of the industrial development bond? Think again. Maybe House Ways and Means Committee Chairman Dan Rostenkowski, D-Ill., who presided over the passage of major curbs on tax-exempt bonds in 1986? Not even close.

Those words were spoken long before any of those three legislators were born. They were part of a statement made in 1920 by House Banking Committee Chairman Louis T. McFadden. Rep. McFadden would later become famous as the author of legislation to prevent interstate banking. But on that day 72 years ago, he was more interested in making sure state and local governments lost what he considered their unfair financial advantage over private business. "The most immediate and efficient remedy will be legislation to tax all and to abolish these special privileges of tax exemptions," he was quoted as

---

* Reprinted with permission from the Bond Buyer, One State Street Plaza, New York, NY 10004-1549.

saying. Happily for issuers and underwriters of municipals, Rep. Mc-
Fadden never got his wish.

Anyone who thinks assaults on tax-exempt bonds began in the
1980s, or even the 1960s, would be surprised to learn that for most of
this century supporters of municipal finance have been forced to fight
to keep the tax exemption intact.

IN THE BEGINNING . . .

The debate originally was over whether tax-exempt bonds should exist
at all. Through the years, major political and business figures like
Franklin Roosevelt, Andrew Mellon, Robert Morgenthau, Cordell Hull,
and Wright Patman argued in favor of their elimination. In the 1950s,
the debate changed, revolving instead around how to restrict the municipal tax exemption to make sure state and local governments were
using it to forward so-called "public purposes"—and not just to help
private businesses or to make money by investing in taxable securities.

As the debate changed, so did *The Daily Bond Buyer's* coverage.
Up to the 1960s, the paper published long opinion-laden accounts of
the discussion in Washington over whether tax-exempt bonds were
worthwhile. But as Congress approved more and more restrictions on
issuance of municipal bonds, the paper carefully tracked the lawmakers' deliberations and gave detailed descriptions of bills that were approved. The first time in this century that Congress scrutinized the
municipal bond tax exemption was during debate on the 16th Amendment to the Constitution—proposed in 1909 and finally enacted four
years later—which permitted the federal government to impose an income tax.

The amendment contained what was to some proponents of tax-
exempt bonds a troubling phrase: Congress may extract taxes "from
whatever source derived." At the time, the legislators involved agreed
they did not mean to imply Congress should tax municipals. But those
four little words would come back to haunt bond proponents again
and again over the next few decades.

Debate over the phrase, in fact, was sparked in 1918, just five
years after the 16th amendment was added to the Constitution,
when Congress considered imposing a surtax to pay for the costs of
World War I. *The Daily Bond Buyer,* in fact, reported on August 10,
1918, that the House Ways and Means Committee had approved a
plan to include municipal bond interest in a war tax. The proposal
never became law.

"The much-discussed question of the taxation powers conferred
upon Congress by the 16th Amendment is thus revived, and is,

presumably, to be once more argued pro and con throughout the country," the newspaper said, adding that tax-exempt bonds probably would find protection from this assault in the judicial system. "The consensus of opinion is that the courts would not uphold Congress in an attempt to tax bonds of states or municipalities, just as it refused to sanction efforts made in the past to levy such taxes," the paper said.

THE NEED TO GUARD EXEMPTION

But the debate must have continued, because only a week later the paper printed verbatim the texts of statements made in 1910 during debate over the 16th amendment by Gov. Hughes of New York and Sen. Elihu Root of New York, both proponents of municipal bonds and keen on preserving tax exemption.

At the time, Sen. Root had said he saw no cause to worry that the phrase "from whatever source derived" could be construed as allowing a tax on municipals. But Gov. Hughes felt it necessary to spell out why it was important to safeguard the municipal exemption. "To place the borrowing capacity of the state and of its government agencies at the mercy of the federal taxing power would be an impairment of the essential rights of the state, which as its officers, we are bound to defend," Gov. Hughes had said in 1910. "We cannot suppose Congress will not seek to tax incomes derived from securities issued by the state and its municipalities," he continued. "It has repeatedly endeavored to lay such taxes, and its efforts have been defeated only by implied constitutional restriction."

Later that month, the newspaper reported that the Investment Bankers Association of America—a group that would in later years spawn the Securities Industry Association and the Public Securities Association—was advising municipal bond issuers to fight attempts to restrict the municipal tax exemption.

A lawyer for the investment bankers group reportedly sent a letter to a group called the National Association of City Comptrollers containing "advice to the municipalities to the effect that they take a more active part in the situation in Washington opposing . . . the general assertion of the power to tax state and municipal bonds without a further constitutional amendment."

It was at this early stage that lawmakers began to see inequities where corporations that were heavily in debt also held large amounts of tax-exempt bonds. The Ways and Means bill, in fact, included a provision that, according to the daily, required that "any individual or corporation paying interest on indebtedness which would naturally be deducted from gross income is only permitted to deduct the amount of such interest 'in excess of interest received free from taxation under this title.'" Decades later, the Internal Revenue Service and Congress would make further attempts to curb the ability of firms to borrow to buy tax-exempt debt.

A hint of some of the arguments for taxing municipals appears in an editorial in the newspaper on September 3, 1918. The editorial took pains to state that "all municipals are not owned by millionaires" and insisted that the amount of revenue the federal government would collect from the tax could not compare with the loss in revenue that would be experienced by state and local governments.

"What kind of a bargain would this be?" the newspaper asked. "What possible excuse could be offered for a tax that destroys in wealth more than it derives in revenues?"

SHELTER FROM THE NEW INCOME TAX

One of the things that may have been galling bond opponents was the fact that municipal securities had become a safe haven for taxpayers trying to avoid the income tax, then only seven years old. The daily noted on August 23, 1920, that in September 1913, "a concerted buying movement on the part of municipal bond dealers" had set in, and, within a few weeks, "private investor demand for municipals was fast cleaning the dealers' shelves."

It did not take long for the legislative assault on bonds to revive. In December 1920, Rep. McFadden proposed an amendment to the Constitution that would have allowed taxation of interest on newly issued municipals. In offering his amendment, Rep. McFadden called municipal bonds a "rapidly growing evil." He was not alone. Surprisingly enough, even some state officials agreed with him, as the newspaper reported on February 16, 1921.

"The tax-exempt bond has become a serious problem in America," said George Lord, a state legislator from Michigan. "It has brought about the withdrawal of an appreciable amount of the nation's financial resources from active business."

The Treasury Department joined the act that same year, with Secretary Andrew Mellon writing to the House Ways and Means Committee and calling the increasing outstanding volume of tax-exempts "an economic evil of the first magnitude" because it diverted capital from private enterprise. Mr. Mellon estimated that about $10 billion of tax-exempts were outstanding at the time.

But a few months later, in December, President Harding was telling Congress it should not rush into approving a constitutional amendment against tax-exempt bonds. "Such a change in the Constitution must be very thoroughly considered before submission," he said.

Rep. McFadden's amendment was never approved. But the idea surfaced again 13 years later. On February 10, 1933, Sen. Cordell Hull of Texas offered an amendment even more sweeping, because it would allow taxation of outstanding, as well as newly issued, municipal bonds.

But bond traders apparently were not worried. "In municipal bond circles, the general reaction to the Hull proposal is that there is so little chance of its success that it is worth but slight considerations," the daily reported.

THE MARKET PANICS

But the market did panic in December, when the Senate suddenly added to its version of the National Industrial Recovery Act—a cornerstone of President Franklin Roosevelt's New Deal legislation—a provision to tax interest on newly issued tax-exempt bonds. Traders calmed down a few days later, when the provision was dropped during a conference between House and Senate lawmakers to resolve differences in the two versions of the legislation.

Proposals to tax municipals seemed to be coming from all sides. That same month, the newspaper mentioned in passing that Sen. Ashurst had proposed another constitutional amendment to tax interest on municipals, and in January 1934, Sen. Augustine Lonegran, D-Conn., introduced legislation to end the tax exemption for municipals. The different approach taken by those two initiatives indicated there continued to be a difference of opinion as to whether Congress had the power to tax municipals or if the Constitution would have to be amended before such a tax could be imposed.

The plethora of proposals was beginning to wear on the municipal market in 1934. "The municipal business has slowed down because of the uncertainty as to the outcome of certain developments which are occupying so much attention in municipal circles," the newspaper reported on March 12. Once again, the proposals were unsuccessful, and things seemed to quiet down for a few years. But as World War II loomed, President Roosevelt appeared once again to seize upon taxation of municipal bond interest as a new source of revenue.

Treasury Secretary Robert Morgenthau sent legislation to Congress in 1941 to tax interest on newly issued bonds, saying it was important to eliminate "the inequitable tax exemption on interest from [municipal] government securities."

In that same year, the paper printed an impassioned defense of tax-exempt bonds by Austin J. Tobin of the then-called New York Port

Authority and an official with the Conference on State Defense, which the newspaper described as a group composed of mayors, corporation counsels, state attorneys general, and other local officials "who have united to resist federal interference with their local fiscal affairs."

Mr. Tobin argued that only a small fraction of outstanding state and local bonds were held by the wealthy, which he defined as those individuals making more than $5,000 a year. He told the Independent Bankers Association later that year that federal tax challenges "are threatening the very existence of the states as independent units of government."

Around the same time, other pockets of support for tax-exempt bonds were appearing. For example, on March 8, 1941, the newspaper reported that Fiorello LaGuardia, mayor of New York and president of the U.S. Conference of Mayors, told a meeting of the mayors that a survey of members of Congress indicated there was little desire to tax municipal bond interest.

FDR JOINS THE FRAY

President Roosevelt entered the debate in his budget message to Congress in January 1942, saying it "seems right and just that no further tax-exempt bonds should be issued." He added that, "as a matter of equity, I recommend legislation to tax all future issues of this character." The paper warned that President Roosevelt "is known to be much more insistent this year than last for Congressional action for the taxing of state, municipal and authority bonds."

Later that month, on January 14, the newspaper reported that Fed Chairman Marriner S. Eccles, "supported the administration's demand that the tax exempts be eliminated" in a speech to the U.S. Conference of Mayors. The newspaper described how Mr. Eccles told the mayors "to exert all your influence to put an end to the issuance of tax-exempt securities."

Mr. Eccles's ill-conceived directive was a classic case of a speaker not knowing his audience, for the group of city officials responded by passing a resolution firmly opposing President Roosevelt's position on bonds.

The rhetoric became even more alarming a few days later, when Treasury Secretary Morgenthau called for taxation of interest on outstanding bonds and on new issues. That prompted Henry Epstein, the solicitor general of New York State, to say Morgenthau's statement was "not only shocking, but it probably will do more to destroy the confidence of the people of this country in the promise and good faith of their own government than anything that I can recall to this time."

But the paper said in an editorial the next week that Mr. Morgenthau's statement was so outlandish that all it probably did was kill "whatever chance the President's proposal to tax only future issues may have had."

The market apparently was watching events in Washington with more than a little concern. In a prescient statement, the newspaper said on March 7, 1942, that investors "are now keenly aware of the probability that the matter is going to come up again and again until it is finally settled by a Supreme Court ruling, and their appraisal of the long-term value of the tax exemption privilege has undergone an abrupt revision downwards."

In April, President Roosevelt tried to link his municipal taxation proposal to the war effort, saying that "it is indefensible that those who enjoy large incomes from state and local securities should be immune from taxation while we are at war." But the U.S. Conference of Mayors objected, saying the President was hiding behind "a false pretense of national defense."

Later in 1942, the Treasury's proposal to tax municipal bond interest was rejected by the House Ways and Means Committee. It was approved by the Senate Finance Committee but voted down in the full Senate. This appears to be the last time in the 1940s that Congress tried to tax interest on municipal bonds. Then in 1945, a major court battle came to an end that had, for a time, threatened to limit the types of governmental entities that could issue tax-exempt bonds.

On March 14, 1941, the Treasury Department had sent notes of deficiency to seven holders of debt issued by the New York Port Authority, saying the interest was considered taxable. The Treasury reasoned that the authority could not be considered a true "political subdivision" of New York and thus was not eligible to issue tax-exempt debt. The department later made a similar move against holders of bonds issued by the city's Triborough Bridge Authority.

In 1944, the U.S. Tax Court in a 10-to-5 decision ruled in favor of the authorities, saying they were indeed political subdivisions and entitled to issue tax-exempt debt. The Treasury appealed the case to the Supreme Court, but the justices in 1945 declined to hear the case. After the Supreme Court ruling, Port Authority Chairman Frank C. Ferguson said he trusted "that this decision will mark an end to efforts to interfere with the fiscal affairs of the states and cities." As the municipal market now knows, he could not have been more wrong.

NOT THE END OF THE MATTER

"Judging by the reaction of the municipal bond market to the denial of a review of the Port case, municipal bond buyers feel that the threat of taxation is now pretty completely removed," the newspaper said in an editorial on the subject. The publication itself was less sanguine, however, saying that "there is no indication" that the ruling "ends the matter."

The year 1945 also appears to be the first time abusive arbitrage deals were publicized. On July 11, the paper reported that it had discovered "a recent proposed offering of bonds by a Southern city for the purpose of buying higher yielding U.S. government bonds." The paper published an opinion by David M. Wood, of Wood, Hoffman, King & Dawson, who said municipal bonds must be issued for a public purpose and that investing in other securities is not such a purpose.

Congress took note of the issue, as Sen. George Wharton Pepper of Pennsylvania told the Municipal Bond Club around the same time that issuance of arbitrage bonds "may be perfectly valid in a technical legal sense, but it is a dangerous trend, which if carried too far, will undoubtedly result in reviving the federal Treasury's demand that Congress remove from the income tax law the exemption of all state and municipal bonds." He said it could prompt the Supreme Court to review the implied constitutional doctrine of intergovernmental tax immunity.

As the 1950s began, the Treasury was back at it again. The department sent to Capitol Hill in 1951 yet another proposal to tax municipal bond interest. Once again, Marriner Eccles—now no longer the Fed chairman but still on the Board of Governors—called for Congress to tax interest on municipal bonds. That proposal got nowhere, but in 1953 Congress began work on a sweeping revision of the tax code, and proponents of municipal bonds worried they would end up on the cutting room floor after the reforms were made.

During that same year, the junior senator from Massachusetts spoke out against the fledgling practice of issuing bonds to benefit private corporations. The newspaper reported that Sen. John F. Kennedy, D-Mass., gave a speech in Chattanooga, Tenn., in which he said he "heartily dislikes municipal bond financing in aid of private industry because it promotes 'unfair competitive practices.'"

In 1954, as the process of revising the tax code continued, it looked as if issuers' worst fears would be realized: The House Ways and Means Committee included in its tax bill that year an amendment that would have outlawed tax-exempt bonds issued to build factories or other facilities used substantially by private entities. The amendment passed the House, but was not included in the Senate bill, and was dropped during the subsequent House-Senate conference to resolve differences. It took a long time for Congress to finally achieve success in curbing IDBs: For the next 14 years, those bonds would remain free from restrictions.

INTO THE 1950s

Though the 1950s saw little else in the way of legislative efforts to hinder issuance of municipal bonds, the subject continued to be a hot topic in Congress, particularly in 1959. On March 11 of that year, *The Daily Bond Buyer* reported that the Joint Economic Committee released a report sharply criticizing the continued existence of the municipal tax exemption and challenging its constitutionality.

"The immunity of the state and municipal securities from federal taxation is not an expressed provision of the constitution," said Rep. Wright Patman, then vice chairman of the panel, in the report. "It is doubtful whether the states and municipalities save anything as a result of the tax-exempt feature," while "purchasers of the bonds whose marginal tax rates are higher than the rate of these other taxpayers get a windfall by saving more in taxes than they must pay for the tax immunity," he said.

Later that month, an editorial in the newspaper warned that "faint grumblings" in Congress and the administration against municipal bonds like Rep. Patman's statement "had better be taken seriously, for they are almost sure to increase in about the same ratio that the outstanding total of tax-exempts increases." But the editorial also noted that the doctrine of intergovernmental tax immunity "is well established, and it has withstood many assaults, including those of former President Franklin Delano Roosevelt, in the heyday of his almost complete control of Congress."

Ultimately, bonds issued to benefit private business—or, industrial development bonds, as they came to be known—were a victim of their own runaway success. As early as 1960, the newspaper foreshadowed later moves to rein in volume. It noted in an editorial that year that the amount of bonds "issued on behalf of private industry seem[s] to be getting bigger and bigger" and that "the danger is clear, but the temptation is hard to resist."

Six years later, Rep. John W. Byrnes, R-Wis., introduced legislation that would have denied tax-exempt status to bonds issued for private business or to earn arbitrage profits. Though Rep. Byrnes' legislation was not acted on that year, Sen. Abraham Ribicoff, D-Conn., introduced an identical bill the next year.

Lambasting the IDB market on November 8, 1967, Sen. Ribicoff told Congress, "these are truly corporate bonds, and the local governments' involvement is often little more than a sham." He cited as an example Port of Astoria, Ore., which at the time was planning to issue $140 million for a Japanese aluminum plant, even though the population of the town was less than 30,000.

In his speech—a text of which was printed in the paper—Sen. Ribicoff was similarly outraged by the proliferation of arbitrage bonds. "It takes but little imagination to see that the unchecked spread of arbitrage bonds would pose as great a threat to the federal revenues and the financing costs of state and local governments as IDBs," he said.

FIRST CURBS ON IDBs

It was in 1968 that Congress finally clamped down on IDBs. But at the beginning of the year, before lawmakers had a chance to act, the Treasury stepped in and created a furor when it went ahead with action of its own. On March 25, the daily reported that the IRS announced it was denying tax exemption to municipal bonds in which private corporations use or secure "a major portion" of the proceeds. Exceptions were made, however, for such facilities as stadiums and airports.

An editorial in *The Daily Bond Buyer* noted that the Treasury's action against IDBs exposed the department's true colors. "Washington's new moves against the tax-exempt financing privilege of state and local government should disabuse the most credulous of people of any notion that the Treasury has been forthright in asserting that it is not opposed to the continued use of tax exemption in the sale of state and municipal bonds."

The move ignited opposition within Congress and bogged down action in the Senate on an excise tax bill. On March 26, the daily reported that Sen. Carl Curtis, R-Neb., proposed an amendment to the excise tax bill barring the Treasury from revoking the tax exemption. Senators supporting the amendment were not in favor of IDBs; rather, they were telling the Treasury it was Congress's right, not the Treasury's, to revoke the bond exemption.

When Senate leaders dragged their heels over allowing the amendment to be included in the bill, Sen. Wayne Morse, D-Ore., threatened to filibuster. His was no idle threat: Sen. Morse was reported to hold the modern record for filibustering, having spoken in 1956 for 74 uninterrupted hours.

While the newspaper did not support the explosion in bonds issued for private corporations, neither did it applaud the federal government's efforts to rein in bond volume.

"It was only a few years ago that the can of worms of tax-exempt industrial aid financing was opened [in the mistaken belief that] the tax-exempt financing privilege of state and local governments could be extended to benefit the long-term capital needs of private corporations," a September 1968 editorial in the paper states.

On the other hand, "It's too bad Washington has seen fit to enlarge this mess into a snake pit that dismays everybody. It is not too late to call off Washington's inept and ineffectual reprisal."

But it was too late. Later that year, Congress settled the issue by superseding the Treasury's action through passage of the Revenue and

Expenditure Control Act of 1968, and placing its own version of restrictions on IDBs. The measure made the first attempt in law to define what a "public purpose" was and to restrict issuance for private corporations.

The bill instituted the private-use test, which rendered municipal bond interest taxable if more than 25% of the proceeds of an issue were used to benefit private business. Congress did, however, exempt certain private purposes from the test: sports stadiums, multifamily housing, convention centers, airports, docks, wharves, mass-commuting or parking facilities, industrial parks, and pollution control. The bill also included a small-issue exemption for issues under $10 million.

The new law had a dramatic impact on IDB volume: Just the year before, volume had hit $1.6 billion, compared with $71.7 million in 1961, when the market was just beginning to take off. The year following the 1968 bill, volume plummeted to $24 million.

While the IDB fight was going on in 1968, bond proponents battled another incursion against the municipal exemption: The so-called taxable bond option.

In March, President Lyndon Johnson's budget message to Congress offered a proposal under which issuers of bonds for pollution control and waste treatment plants would forego the tax exemption on those bonds in exchange for a new federal subsidy and a federal guarantee of their obligations.

Rep. Patman, who by now was chairman of the House Banking Committee, offered a taxable bond option of his own that was broader than that of President Johnson: It would apply to all tax-exempt bonds. Sen. William Proxmire, D-Wis., offered a similar proposal in the Senate. The taxable bond option never quite gathered steam. Sen. Proxmire tried to rally support for his plan by arguing that it would not produce "a new federal encroachment in local affairs" because it was voluntary. He even pleaded with witnesses at a July hearing to show "just a little enthusiasm" for his plan.

LITTLE SYMPATHY FOR TAXABLE MUNIS

But those witnesses included the comptroller of the currency, who was noncommittal, a Fed governor who was skeptical, and the chairman of the Federal Deposit Insurance Corp., who objected strongly. They were concerned that the increased federal tax revenues envisioned from the issuance of taxable bonds would not make up for the money the government would spend paying out subsidies. They also objected to a federal guarantee of municipal debt.

The proposals by Rep. Patman and Sen. Proxmire were never approved. Though the taxable bond option has surfaced again at various times and in different forms, it has never gotten very far in Congress.

With the IDB problem taken care of—for the moment, at least—Congress turned its attention in 1969 to arbitrage profits, passing the first-ever curbs on the amount of arbitrage an issuer could earn. The Tax Reform Act of 1969 barred the issuance of tax-exempt bonds where more than 15% of the proceeds would be invested in higher yielding taxable securities. The newspaper did not look kindly on the change, noting that "the adverse impact on public sector financing threatens to outbalance by far any benefits from well-intentioned efforts to put an end to certain abuses."

Concerned that Congress was heading down a road of even tougher restrictions on tax-exempt bonds, the paper, for the only time in its history, took out a full page advertisement in *The New York Times* to defend the municipal tax exemption. The advertisement asked, "Must Congress cripple the financing power of state and local governments?" It also suggested bond dealers and state and local officials reprint the advertisement in their local papers.

By and large, the 1970s were a quiet decade for legislative assaults on tax-exempt bonds, though tax laws enacted in 1971, 1976, and 1978 did some minor tinkering with the 1968 law covering IDBs. The 1980s more than made up for any lapses in vigilance in the 1970s.

The next major action occurred in 1980, when Congress, frightened by the rapidly increasing volume of bonds issued for both rental units and single-family mortgages, passed the Mortgage Subsidy Bond Act of 1980. Under the act, the tax exemption for mortgage bonds was scheduled to terminate at the end of 1983. In the meantime, volume was capped on a state-by-state basis, the first time Congress had moved to directly restrict volume in that way. The cap equaled $200 million, or 9%, of the state's previous three years' activity in the bonds, whichever was greater. The act also placed the first low-income requirements on multifamily housing units built with tax-exempt bonds: 20% of the units would have to be occupied by low- and moderate-income tenants.

The next few years saw Congress cutting further into the tax exemption for IDBs. The 1982 tax law eliminated the use of small-issue IDBs beginning in 1983 if more than 25% of the bonds were used for restaurants or automobile dealerships. IDBs also were eliminated for massage parlors, racetracks, hot tubs, and golf courses. But two purposes were added to the list of eligible activities for IDBs: local furnishing of gas and electric power, and ferry boats. The act also set a termination date of December 31, 1986, for all types of IDBs.

The next blow came in 1984, when Congress placed the first arbitrage rebate requirements on IDBs. Lawmakers also eliminated more IDB uses: skyboxes, airplanes, health clubs, gambling facilities, and liquor stores. The tax exemption for mortgage revenue bonds, which had died at the end of 1983, was renewed through 1987.

In addition, Congress for the first time made a distinction between IDBs for commercial uses and for manufacturing: It maintained the December 31, 1986, termination date for commercial IDBs, but granted an extension to December 31, 1988, for manufacturing IDBs. The 1984 law also included a provision prohibiting federal guarantees of tax-exempt debt. There were several exceptions written into the law, covering mortgage revenue bonds, multifamily housing bonds, and student loan bonds.

The municipal bond market had little time to recover from the 1984 act before facing a new assault. Early in 1985, Treasury Secretary Donald Regan unveiled the department's tax reform proposal. It included, among other things, a provision that would have lowered the 25% private-use test to 1%, thus virtually eliminating tax-exempt private-activity bonds.

THE TAX REFORM ACT

Though that plan never became law, Congress in 1986 imposed the most sweeping restrictions on tax-exempt bonds in history. Along the way municipal market participants were treated to a series of shocks and jolts about what Congress might or might not pass, the most frightening being the now infamous proposal offered by Sen. Bob Packwood in March of that year.

The Oregon Republican, then chairman of the Senate Finance Committee, proposed applying an alternative minimum tax on the interest of all tax-exempt bonds acquired after January 1, 1987. The plan sent shock waves through the market and shut it down on March 13, 1986, the day the proposal surfaced.

In the end, Congress imposed a minimum tax on IDB interest earned by individuals and corporations at the full rate—21% and 20%, respectively. Interest on governmental and 501(c)(3) bonds held by corporations was taxed at an effective rate of 10%. As prescribed in the 1986 law, that rate increased to 15% on January 1, 1990.

The Tax Reform Act of 1986 also extended the arbitrage rebate requirement to governmental bonds issued after September 1, 1986. When it became apparent in early 1986 that Congress was going to impose a rebate rule, a host of arbitrage-driven blind pools began coming to market. The rush to market was so huge that the top tax leaders—Sen. Packwood, Rep. Rostenkowski, and the Treasury Department—joined forces on July 18, 1986, and announced that tax-exempt blind pool issuance would be banned as of that afternoon.

The 1986 act also turned the bond world upside down by coining a new term: the "private-activity bond." More than any other tax bill, the 1986 law drove a wedge between bonds for so-called public interests and those designed to benefit private purposes. Though public purpose bonds—alternately termed "governmental" bonds—were caught under the restrictions of the minimum tax and the arbitrage rebate requirement, they escaped relatively unscathed compared to the new curbs on private-activity bonds.

First of all, Congress eliminated a host of uses that had been eligible for tax-exempt financing, including stadiums, convention centers, industrial parks, pollution control, and parking facilities. The law also dropped the 25% private-use test to 10%, and created a unified state-by-state volume cap for bonds issued to finance private activities still deemed eligible for tax-exempt financing, including mortgage revenue bonds, multifamily housing bonds, small-issue IDBs, and student loan bonds. In addition, the law eliminated small-issue commercial IDBs and set a termination date of December 31, 1989 for small-issue manufacturing IDBs. It also set a termination date of December 31, 1988 for mortgage revenue bonds.

Why did the municipal market lose so much in 1986? Some say because Congress perceived the market mainly as a group of investment bankers trying to roll back the law as it stood in 1985. H. Ben Hartley, a senior aide to the Joint Tax Committee, told the newspaper in 1989 that municipal bonds suffered in 1986 mainly because members of Congress assumed that the only real beneficiaries of the municipal tax exemption were the underwriters and bond lawyers who assist state and local governments. Moreover, the investment bankers were refusing to negotiate or suggest compromises on the municipal bond curbs proposed by tax legislators.

"They were screaming and yelling, 'the world is coming to an end,' and not really offering constructive criticism," said Mr. Hartley, who in 1988 had left Capitol Hill to become a partner in the firm of Piper and Marbury. "They really shot themselves in the foot," he said. He later returned to the joint tax panel staff. Compared to 1986, the last four years have seen relatively little in the way of new restrictions on tax exempts.

THE 1980s WIND DOWN

In 1987, Congress passed legislation that placed under the volume cap most bonds issued by states and localities to purchase existing facilities of investor-owned utilities. Lawmakers also agreed to restrict the types of tax-exempt bonds American Indian tribes are allowed to issue.

The 1987 law may be more important for what it did not include: Two provisions passed by the House Ways and Means Committee but left out of the final version of the measure that would have played havoc with demand for municipal bonds.

One, the so-called market discount provision, would have required holders of such bonds to declare as ordinary income each year a percentage of the gains they would receive if the bonds were redeemed at par value.

The other would have drastically reduced the so-called 2% de minimis rule, a safe harbor from the tax law prohibition against incurring debt to buy tax-exempt debt, which since 1972 had effectively allowed corporations to hold tax-exempt debt equal to 2% of its assets regardless of how much debt they had outstanding.

More favorable legislation followed in 1988, as Congress passed technical corrections to the tax reform law and extended the tax exemption for mortgage revenue bonds one more year, to December 31, 1989. At the same time, however, tax lawmakers also approved legislation designed to shut down blind pools.

But earlier that year the municipal market had received a big jolt from the Supreme Court. On April 21, the justices struck down a landmark 1895 decision that had given constitutional protection to the tax exemption for municipal bonds. The court decision appeared to leave the door wide open for Congress to decide in the future whether to tax the interest earned on municipal bonds, and some market participants feared that was exactly what lawmakers would do.

But Rep. Rostenkowski and Sen. Lloyd Bentsen, D-Tex., who became chairman of the Senate Finance Committee in 1987, moved quickly to calm issuers' fears, saying the high court ruling merely affirmed what Congress believed all along it had the power to do. "There is no reason to believe that today's court decision will either prompt or deter future congressional action," Rep. Rostenkowski said in a statement on the day of the ruling. So far, Rep. Rostenkowski has been right.

CHAPTER 42

The Bond Buyer
After 100 Years*

Joe Mysak

The Daily Bond Buyer, as it was called until 1982, was founded in 1891 by William Franklin Gore Shanks. Mr. Shanks was born in Shelbyville, Ky., in 1837. His professional career began with *The New York Herald* during the Civil War. Following the pattern of journalists of the day, he also served as volunteer aide de camp on the staffs of Generals Lovell H. Rousseau and George H. Thomas. He was wounded in the battle of Chickamauga, "from the effects of which he never recovered," in the words of his obituary in 1905.

After the war, Mr. Shanks enjoyed a long and illustrious career as a New York City journalist. In 1866, he produced a fat volume of reminiscences of Civil War generals. From 1867 to 1869, he edited *Harper's Weekly.* In 1869, he became city editor of *The New York Times.* In 1870, he joined Horace Greeley's *New York Tribune,* and from 1871 to 1880 he was city editor of that paper, where, among other things, he hired Jacob Riis, the future muckraking reformer, as a police beat reporter.

As *The Daily Bond Buyer* says in its obituary, "During that time he made a reputation by his exposure of the corruption in the Supreme

---

* Reprinted with permission from *The Bond Buyer,* One State Street Plaza, New York, NY 10004-1549.

Court, which led to the impeachment and removal of Judges Barnard and Cardozo. His life was frequently threatened, and 'Boss' Tweed finally warned him personally to carry a revolver and never to go to his home by the same route two nights in succession."

The paper continues, "During 1871, while fighting the then Democratic rule in Brooklyn, he was locked up on Raymond Street Jail for contempt of court for refusing to disclose the name of a reporter on the *Tribune* who had written an article about a defalcation in a local trust company, the funds stolen having been divided among the 'ring.' He was released on habeus corpus, and the district attorney, Winchester Britton, who had been the active moving party against him, was removed by Gov. Dix."

Mr. Shanks founded the National Press Intelligence Co., a press clipping service, with $50,000 in 1885. He gradually found there was great demand for "investment news," which led to the founding of *The Daily Bond Buyer* in 1891. In the words of a story on the company published in 1897, "This is simply a daily digest on investment news, being chiefly devoted to early advance news of proposed issues of city, county, state, railway, and street railway bonds . . . Every special election to authorize issues of bonds is reported, the date on which it is to be held being first given, and the result of the vote next carefully noted. Every advertisement for sealed bids for such bonds is carefully summarized; and, when the bonds are sold, the name and address of the successful bidder is given, together with the amount of the bonds purchased, their rate of interest, and term of years they are to run, and all particulars of interest to investors."

With a few alterations, this sums up *The Bond Buyer* of today. Mr. Shanks founded something of a publishing dynasty. He had three sons: Sanders Shanks, who was the attorney of the company; Lynn Hudson Shanks, who was the treasurer, and William Rousseau Shanks, who was the paper's editor from 1905 until 1914. The attorney's son, Sanders Jr., was editor of the newspaper and president of the company from 1914 until his death in 1949, marking the longest stint at the helm so far. The Shanks family was connected with the newspaper until 1977, when William S. Shanks, then president and chief executive officer, severed his connections with the company.

The Daily Bond Buyer went through at least three distinct manifestations during its 100-year history. First, there was the newspaper of William F.G. Shanks, a small financial daily filled with items culled from various daily newspapers, as well as some of the lively, typically opinionated journalism of the period, no doubt written by the founder himself.

The founder's newspaper covered all of the bond markets: municipal, corporate, Treasury, even foreign securities. In 1904, the newspaper carried a two-page spread, with a map, on "The Japanese in Manchuria" probably as much because editor Shanks had a long-standing interest in war coverage as because both belligerents "floated large loans."

Mr. Shanks gave the newspaper a distinctive voice, a decidedly conservative, Republican voice, unabashedly Imperialist and frankly partisan. Mr. Shanks believed the Democratic Party was "the greatest curse the nation has known" and used his pages to bang the drum for the Republicans, even going so far as to produce a pamphlet in 1904 containing "some wholesome truths not generally taught in schools and colleges of the present day"—that Thomas Jefferson was, in fact, the first Republican President of the United States and that Madison, Monroe, and Adams also were early members of the GOP.

Mr. Shanks was also fond of protecting his new paper from the competition, and regularly included in *The Daily Bond Buyer* what he sometimes termed "The Deadly Acrostic," an item of bond news so arranged so that, in November 1897, for example, the first letter in each item, if read down the column, spelled "FILCHED." For years, he warred in this way against the competition, in particular *The American Banker*, from whom he also won $5,500 in libel verdicts: $5,000 in 1898 when the owners of *The American Banker* said he was blackmailing municipal bond dealers; and $500 in 1897 when the same parties alleged he was "a man of bad habits."

The American Banker, in its battles with Mr. Shanks, won 6 cents, along with 6 cents for costs in a 1900 libel suit—after a jury asked whether they could bring in a verdict for the defendant. The municipal bond market of the founding Shanks's era was litigious, and the newspaper devoted a lot of space to lawsuits, especially in regard to repudiated debt and invalidly issued debt. It also carried a fair number of articles on counterfeiting and security, and even did a supplement to the weekly (then called simply *The Bond Buyer*) about safes, and how easy they were to open—with the lone exception of the Corliss safe, a globe-shaped contraption that the newspaper heartily endorsed. The Corliss is described at length on page 60 by Sean Monsarrat.

These were the years when municipal bond volume was measured in the hundreds of millions, not billions. When the newspaper was founded, volume barely totaled $50 million, and the newspaper did not begin tallying it until 1896, when 1,294 issues totaling $119.54 million were sold.

In 1905, when the founding Shanks died, long-term volume was $197.70 million. It would not break the $1 billion mark until 1921—and dipped below that line in 1932, 1937, and from 1942 to 1945.

The Daily Bond Buyer took on the issues of the day, and those issues in Mr. Shanks's time included "repudiation" of debt and the rise of "postage-stamp" and "pool" bidders. Postage stamp bidders were so called because they bragged they could bid on a deal with no capital and no office—just a postage stamp and a postcard. If the postage stamp bidder won bonds, and sold them, nobody was the wiser. But if the market turned on him, the postage stamp bidder could, and apparently did with some frequency, walk away from deals.

There were also, in the woollier days of the municipal bond market, "poolers." As *The Daily Bond Buyer* defined them: "'Poolers' are men who usually have no capital and little standing, who seek every opportunity to be 'bought off' by other bidders by threatening to run up the bidding at sales to figures which leave no margin for profit."

The newspaper said the way to combat such rascals in the market was not to demand a good-faith check in advance of a bond sale, but rather to demand such a check after the bonds were awarded. As the newspaper editorialized in 1897, "We hoped and believed that the city treasurer of Boston had furnished a solution when, not having exacted a deposit preliminary to bidding, he required a large deposit before officially announcing an award to a house whose ability he had reason to doubt."

The newspaper continues, "We shall believe that the adoption of such a rule by all municipalities"—that is, only requiring checks if the highest bidder is unknown to the issuer—"would encourage bidding while at the same time protecting sellers of bonds from imposition. The present system requires a deposit from every house bidding, though only one check can by any possibility be retained: and as a consequence, many times the deposit named has to be drawn from bank and remain idle, not drawing interest, pending this sale. It often happens that each dealer is simultaneously called upon for several guarantee deposits, so that in the aggregate the idle money represented by these checks is a very considerable sum, and the annual loss in interest an onerous and needless tax."

As the editor wrote, nearly a century ago: "It really is in the interest of municipalities that the submission of guarantee checks should be done away with; as the bids for bonds are likely, in the absence of such requirements, to be more numerous. [This, by the way, was in an era when 117 bids on an issue was not entirely unknown.] The municipal authorities have merely to stipulate that they reserve the right to reject any bid, and to demand a deposit if the highest bidder is unknown to them or known to be irresponsible."

Mr. Shanks was definitely a man of his time, complete with the prejudices of his time and of his class. He cheered a Luzerne County, Pa., sheriff, for example, for firing into the ranks of some Hungarian-born rioters, and noted with smug satisfaction, "Such ignorant races as Hungarians, Italians, Greeks, and Spaniards ought to be excluded from the country by an amendment to our immigration laws. Skin a Hun, Italian, Greek, Spaniard or Cuban and you disclose a barbarian."

Mr. Shanks died in Bermuda in 1905, and with him, with a few exceptions, went the first age of the newspaper. His successor was his son William R. Shanks, who served until 1914, when the paper was taken over by his son, Sanders Shanks, who ran it until 1949. The Shanks family sold a controlling interest in the newspaper to C. Barron Otis in 1913. Mr. Otis bought *The American Banker* in 1918, and both newspapers remained in the Otis family until its current owners, then called International Thomson, bought the company in 1983.

But during the period not long after the founder's death, the paper had relatively few sparks of journalistic glory; it devoted itself to gathering statistics and covering federal assaults on tax exemption. The founder's newspaper effectively ended publication in October 1921, foundering on the shore of journalistic heartbreak brought on by the "Travis Inquiry."

The "Travis Inquiry" was begun by *The Daily Bond Buyer* and taken up independently by *The Brooklyn Daily Times.* As editor Shanks wrote in 1920, "Prior to June 1916, many rumors reached us via the New York financial district of the existence of a 'system' which monopolized the state's investment business to the exclusion of a majority of the legitimate bond houses and incidentally profited unduly on the large amounts of securities purchased annually by the state with tax monies appropriated to sinking funds for the protection of holders of state obligations."

The Daily Bond Buyer, having gotten its "lead" in the classic journalistic way—from sources—proceeded to do some hard nuts and bolts work, and proved that the comptroller, one Eugene M. Travis, authorized purchases of bonds from only two dealers: Albert Judson, and Geo. B. Gibbons & Co., and that the purchases were done at inflated prices that turned Mr. Judson a profit of almost $825,141.65.

In 1920, Travis, his assistant James A. Wendell, and Albert Judson were charged with grand larceny, but the indictment was dismissed in October 1921 by the state Supreme Court. Mr. Wendell won election as comptroller in 1920, and he died in 1922.

The newspaper professed its own bitter disappointment, and notes, "If public officials, entrusted with the custody and management of millions of dollars of public funds raised by taxation and held in trust for the owners of the state's bonds, may conduct themselves as did Travis and Wendell with respect to the investment of some $40 million within a period of less than six years, we cannot help but view with the gravest apprehension the future security of the state sinking funds and the many large issues of state bonds which depend upon the standing of these funds for their prompt payment at maturity."

The paper continues, "To the lay mind it would appear inconceivable that the court should ask for any more complete array of evidence indicative of criminal intent upon the part of the three defendants than the ample proof showing that time and again huge blocks of bonds were purchased at prices which the three defendants, by their own admission, must have known were substantially in excess of actual market values." The episode marked the newspaper's last foray into investigative journalism for 60 years.

The Daily Bond Buyer was not always marked by journalistic excellence. The only things that transcended what would be an almost uninterrupted snooze from the founder's death to the 1960s were its numerous defenses of tax-exemption, dealt with at length in Joan Pryde's article on page 84, and the quality of its statistics.

The newspaper, as noted above in "The Deadly Acrostic," was jealous of the information it gathered in its columns of proposed issues, sealed bids, and bond sale results columns. It gathered this data into monthly tables,—and for a few decades, put bond sales and volume figures into "pink sheet" supplements. The newspaper began its famed 20- and 11-bond indexes, which measure yields on general obligation bonds, in 1917, and retroactively figured them to 1900.

For those with a taste for trivia, the record high of the 20-bond was 13.44%, which it hit on January 14, 1982. The record low was 1.29%, which it posted on February 14, 1946. The record high of the 11-bond index was 13.05%, which it hit on January 14, 1982; the record low was 1.04% on February 21, 1946. The greatest movement in the indexes took place in 1980. On February 22, the 20-bond index jumped 71 basis points, to 8.46%. On April 18, it plunged 118 basis points, to 7.89%; the 11-bond fell 129 basis points, to 7.32%.

The newspaper introduced its revenue bond index, which uses 25 assorted revenue bonds, maturing in 30 years, ranging from Baa1 to Aaa in rating, on September 20, 1979. Its record high was 14.32%, on January 14, 1982; its low was 6.92%, on March 5, 1987.

To accompany its bond yield indexes, the newspaper began a short-term tax-exempt note index in 1989, using yields from 10 issuers.

The newspaper began compiling "The Visible Supply of Municipals," which presented, "the total volume of offerings of state and municipal issues, excluding short-term notes, as listed in our 'Calendar of Sealed Bids Offerings'" on Fridays, beginning in December 1927.

Yet, for all of its precise statistics, *The Daily Bond Buyer* for almost four decades, from the 1920s to the 1950s, was little more than a municipal bond man's "shopper." The front page was devoted to dealer advertisements—and would be until the 1950s. During the 1920s and 1930s, entire weeks would go by without any actual stories in the newspaper. The stock market crash in 1929 was not even mentioned in the daily until November 27, 1929—and then only in a brief report on a Guaranty Trust Co. survey.

What little editorial copy there was during the 1920s was generally picked up from other sources—a 1921 story, "The Bond Business as an Occupation for College Men," was reprinted from *The Outlook* magazine; coverage of the Florida hurricane in October 1926, for example, was provided by a visiting bond dealer.

Even at this editorial low point, however, the newspaper managed to stay in touch with its market. For example, *The Daily Bond Buyer* in March 1928 produced its first roundup of top municipal bond underwriters. The year was a good one for bond volume—$1.48 billion, in 7,748 issues, the seventh consecutive year tax-exempt volume topped $1 billion.

The author of the story notes, "We have analyzed the activities of the dealers participating in these underwritings and find that 82 houses were identified with the original offerings of issues aggregating $20 million or more; 65 houses were named in connection with issues of $50 million or more; and 19 appeared in underwritings aggregating more than $100 million. The largest total shown for any one house is $254.43 million."

The tabulation of the top underwriters was done on the basis of a full credit to each manager—"the total for any one house is merely the aggregate of the entire amounts of all the issues with which that dealer was associated." So said, for those with a taste for the antique, Eldredge & Co. topped the 1927 underwriters, with $254 million to its credit, and was followed by Detroit Co., with $215.29 million.

First National Bank of New York was third, at $199.28 million, and was followed by Redmond & Co., at $197.99 million; National City Co., $175.53 million; Stone & Webster and Blodget, $171.35 million; Phelps, Fenn & Co., $161.66 million; Bankers Trust, $151.57 million; Old Colony Corp., $150.42 million; and Kissell, Kinnicutt & Co., $142.43 million. It was an interesting idea, ranking underwriters. But, for reasons lost now, the newspaper would not carry another list of underwriter rankings for more than 50 years.

The newspaper also noted the rise of "the Street broker," what we today call brokers' brokers, in 1928; decried "service contracts," sort of a precursor to negotiated transactions, in 1926; and condemned the "street improvement assessment bond evil," which later became known as tax increment financing, in 1927.

To address the economic situation in the 1930s, the newspaper carried a regular column of notices on "debt readjustments, refunding plans, and defaults," beginning in 1934. During the Depression, 4,770 municipal governments defaulted on $2.85 billion in debt, about 16% of the debt outstanding in 1932.

Still, there was relatively little editorial comment or analysis of the situation. Editor Shanks reprinted a speech of his own on municipal bond defaults, and how they were being remedied; and in September 1934, the newspaper noted, "One of the outstanding features of the municipal bond business these days is the activity of those bankers, bond attorneys, and others who are participating in the working out of debt adjustments . . . Due to economic recovery, plus successful negotiation between debtor and creditor, many municipalities of importance have moved or soon will move out of the default classification. A brief review of this situation may be timely."

More typical of the day's coverage, such as it was, was the report of a "special correspondent," who provided coverage of a 1933 counterfeiting scheme in Kansas which forced Gov. Alf Landon to suspend all interest payments on the state's municipal bonds for a time. Providing a true flavor of the period, one guest author asked in 1933, "what will repeal do for municipal finance?"

The author's conclusion was that it would restore local taxes. And he noted, "With repeal, the increase in internal revenue taxes and license fees will make the old 15-cent drink a think of the past. Instead, the prices will probably be 25 to 35 cents; but even these will look cheap compared to the speakeasy prices."

The 1940s brought with them perhaps the most concentrated attacks on tax-exemption. To keep its readers informed on the attacks, *The Daily Bond Buyer* carried a weekly "Washington Letter" on Saturdays. In addition, the paper began carrying a municipal market column, also on Saturdays.

There was little editorial matter printed during the week—with the result that there was no mention of the attack on Pearl Harbor until December 13, and then only in the municipal market column. "The concussion from the Japanese bombs which fell on Pearl Harbor last Sunday caused the greatest disturbance experienced by the municipal market since the beginning of World War II in September, 1939. . . . It is difficult to measure precisely the decline in prices." Besides a listing devoted to "Municipal Men in Military Service," and an occasional letter from one of them at the front, the war had little impact on *The Daily Bond Buyer*.

But it did have an impact on rates, as shown in a timeline the newspaper put together in November 1945. The timeline, "Municipal Market During World War II" represented a first for the newspaper, showing 20-bond index yields, and their response to various events, from 3.21% at the opening of the war in 1939, to 1.64% at the end.

The 1950s saw *The Daily Bond Buyer* cease Saturday publication, and undergo a redesign of its nameplate, along the way to entering its third age, the modern age. The newspaper presented its readers with a wild gallimaufry of material. There was no more Washington Letter, but the paper began coverage of the Treasury market, picking up a column from *The American Banker* called "Speaking of Government Securities." It carried, for the first time, an editor's column, "Now—And Then," by George Wanders, later to be changed to "From the Editor's Desk," which is what the same column is called today.

The newspaper, which began the decade with advertisements on its front page and ended it with editorial once again capturing the front page, carried a number of singularly odd features, all of which died quick deaths: "Women in Municipal Bonds," featuring photographs of women who worked for bond firms; "Odd Lots of Municipal News," and "Well-Known Bond Men and Municipal Officials Visiting in New York."

The newspaper entered its third age—the daily you see today—in the 1960s. In a sense, *The Bond Buyer* of today more closely resembles *The Daily Bond Buyer* of the founder's day than it does the newspaper of the 1920s through the 1950s. The newspaper returned to being a truly journalistic enterprise, rather than just a trade paper, a municipal bond man's shopper.

In the 1960s, the newspaper carried regular coverage of the municipal and Treasury bond markets. News stories always dominated page one, although the advertisements would not disappear entirely until the late 1970s. The paper began adding bureaus during this time, always an indication of a newspaper with serious journalistic intentions. It opened one in Washington in 1961 and then, in rapid succession, San Francisco in 1982, Chicago and Atlanta in 1987, and Dallas in 1990. A regular editorial page was also established.

Finally, a note on *The Bond Buyer* of today. For most of its life, *The Bond Buyer* was a trade newspaper, an industry organ that covered the market with little question or comment. Today, it is what its founder meant it to be: A newspaper covering a trade, with neither fear nor favor.

Glossary

accreted The opposition of amortize. The process by which an increment of value is theoretically added to an asset.

accrued interest Interest due on a bond from the last interest payment to the present.

ad valorem taxes (property taxes) Taxes levied on real property.

advance refunding See **defeased**.

after-tax return The investment return after taxes are paid on investment earnings.

agreement among underwriters The written agreement setting forth terms between the underwriters participating in an underwriting syndicate.

amortize Principal payment of a debt periodically, from funds received for that purpose.

assessed valuation The estimated value of property established as a basis for levying a tax.

---

[1] This chapter was derived from Robert Boyden Lamb, "Municipal Debt," Chapter 4 in Securities Essentials Program of Stanton C. Selbst's Financial Professional's Series.

automated bond system (ABS)   The New York Stock Exchange's system for processing trades in small amounts of bonds.

basis point $1/100$th of 1 percent.

basis price yield   The value of a security quoted in yield to maturity.

bearer form   A form of security in which ownership is conveyed by possession of a certificate. No registration of owners.

Blue List   A daily publication that lists municipal bonds offered for sale by dealers.

Bond Anticipation Note (BAN)   Notes issued by states and municipalities that are funded eventually through the sale of a long-term bond issue.

bond counsel   A lawyer who issues a bond option. Often a private firm of lawyers, or, in some cases, a public official.

bond opinion (legal opinion)   An opinion by a bond counsel or legal representative of the issuer as to the exemption from federal and local income taxation of the interest income of the issue.

bond purchase contract   The agreement between the underwriting syndicate and the issuer in a bond sale in which the underwriters agree to purchase the issuer's bonds according to agreed terms and conditions.

bond resolution   The official act by a bond issuer's board of directors authorizing the issue.

bond service fund   A fund that is used to make regular payments of interest to bondholders.

bond swaps   Transactions in which bonds are sold to generate a tax loss, and similar bonds are purchased to maintain the investment.

book-entry form   A form of bond ownership in which no certificates are issued. The record of ownership usually is kept by computer.

broker's broker   A bond specialist who helps brokers locate the best bid or ask prices in the market.

bullet maturity   A bond in which the entire principal matures at once.

call   The act of retiring a bond, by paying the holder principal (and perhaps a premium) before scheduled maturity. Calls benefit the issuer, not the investor, since, if interest rates drop, the bonds can be redeemed.

call premium   The amount above par that an issuer is required to pay a bondholder for the right to call a bond.

citizen bond   A small-denomination bond issued by states, authorities, or other municipal issuers, in book-entry form (without certificates) and traded on the New York Stock Exchange. Some citizen bond issues have interest reinvestment features.

citizen bond form   Book-entry form used with municipal bonds.

competitive public sale   A new issue in which underwriters or syndicates of underwriters submit bids to form a syndicate or purchase securities.

coverage   The margin of security for payment of debt service, usually on revenue bonds, reflecting the number of times by which earnings exceed debt service.

current yield   The coupon paid by a bond divided by the current market price of the bond.

dated date   The date on which the bonds are issued for purposes of computing interest due.

debt limit   The statutory or constitutional maximum debt that an issuer can legally incur.

debt service   The money needed to pay interest and principal on a bond issue.

debt service coverage ratio   Net operating revenues divided by annual debt service.

debt service reserve fund   A fund in which a sufficient reserve is maintained to pay interest on bonds, usually for a one-year period.

default   Failure to pay principal or interest on schedule.

defeased (defeasance)   A process by which debt may be eliminated for accounting purposes by purchasing government securities, the interest on which is sufficient to pay debt service on a bond.

divided account (Western account)   An underwriting in which each syndicate member is responsible only for its own underwriting allocation. Once that allocation has been sold, the underwriter's liability ceases.

doctrine of intergovernmental tax immunity   A legal doctrine developed over the past 150 years, incorporating aspects of the U.S. Constitution and a series of Supreme Court decisions. The doctrine sets forth limitations on the powers of the states and the federal government to interfere in each others' affairs. The doctrine has supported the exemption of municipal bond interest from taxation by the federal government.

double-barreled bond   A bond secured by the pledge of two or more sources for repayment (e.g., a special tax and the general obligation of an issuer).

11-Bond Index   An index of 11 high-grade bonds published by *The Daily Bond Buyer.*

excise tax bond   A bond secured by a tax on liquor or tobacco.

feasibility study   A report on a new project, without operating history, which often includes both engineering and financial data.

flat   Trading without accrued interest. Defaulted bonds that have ceased paying interest trade flat.

floating-rate bond (adjustable-rate bond)   A bond that adjusts its coupon interest rate, according to prevailing rates and preestablished formulas.

full faith and credit bond   A type of general obligation (GO) bond that pledges the full taxing power of the issuer as security.

general obligation bonds (GO)   A bond secured by the issuer's general taxing power.

gross spread   The difference between proceeds paid to the issuer of a bond and the cost to the public. The spread is the revenue generated by the underwriter or syndicate (before expenses).

indications of interest   A preliminary expression of buying interest in a new bond issue.

industrial development bond (IDBs), industrial revenue bond (IRBs)   Securities issued by governments or agencies to construct or purchase industrial facilities to be leased to a private corporation and backed by the corporation, *not* the municipality.

issuer   A political subdivision or authority that borrows money through sale of bonds.

level annual principal payments   A repayment schedule in which the same number of bonds are retired each year by the issuer.

level total debt service   A repayment schedule similar to a standard home mortgage in which payments (combined principal and interest) remain constant. The result is that a large part of the payment is interest in the early years and principal in the later years.

liabilities   The amount of a new issue that an underwriter is responsible for distributing.

limited tax bond   A bond secured by a tax limited in rate or amount, as opposed to a bond secured by the issuer's general obligation.

maintenance fund   A fund that collects surplus revenue generated by the issuer for purposes of maintenance and repairs to the facility.

mandatory sinking-fund redemption   The process of calling bonds according to requirements of the trust indenture. The issuer must make payments to a sinking fund sufficient to make the calls.

MIGs (Moody's Investment Grades) Moody's rating symbols for short-term and intermediate-term municipal notes. (Standard & Poor's does not rate notes.)

mill A unit of measurement for the levy of property taxes. One mill is equal to $1/1000$ of a dollar.

moral obligation bond A municipal security backed by the issuer's stated intention to repay the bonds, not by the issuer's full faith and credit.

municipal bond Any debt instrument issued by a nonfederal unit of government, such as a state, city, county, or public authority.

municipal bond insurance Coverage provided by an insurance company that pays the amount of interest or principal an investor otherwise would lose in the event of a default.

municipal notes Short-term municipal debt issues.

Municipal Securities Rulemaking Board (MSRB) The body established by Congress to act as the supervisory and regulatory authority of municipal securities.

net funded debt (net direct debt) Total long-term debt for which a taxpayer base (community, jurisdiction, etc.) is responsible.

net interest cost One means by which issuers and underwriters compute the interest costs of issues of municipal securities for purposes of awarding a competitive bid.

net operating revenue A figure used in calculating debt coverage ratios. It is revenues less expenses (not counting taxes and debt service).

no-call period (call protection) A period during which the issuer is not permitted to call bonds.

official statement A description from the issuer of municipal securities about the bonds and their security; the equivalent of a prospectus in the sale of new municipal issues.

original issue discount Bonds that do not pay current interest. Return is the difference between the original discounted price and par. Annualized return must be calculated over the life of the bond.

overlapping debt The part of an obligation of governmental units for which residents of several jurisdictions are responsible (such as services or facilities shared by several municipalities).

paying agent A designated bank or other institution that pays principal on a bond.

placement ratio A ratio computed by *The Daily Bond Buyer* of the amount of new bonds sold to new bonds held in inventory by dealers.

preliminary price   In a negotiated offering, a provisional scale of rates and maturities agreed upon about a week before the official offering.

pre-refunded bonds   Bonds, the interest and principal of which have been fully provided for through the sale of refunding bonds and the establishment of an escrow trust fund, the proceeds of which will be used to redeem the pre-refunded bonds on their first call date.

primary market   The market for new bond issues.

principal   The price of a bond to be paid at maturity.

private sale (negotiated sale)   A new issue in which the issuer selects the lead underwriter before the price has been determined, usually on the basis of prior experience.

project notes (public housing authority project notes)   Short-term tax-exempt securities offered by and backed by the U.S. Department of Housing and Urban Development for local housing and urban renewal projects.

put bonds   A bond that may be put back to the issuer at a stated price, usually par.

rate covenant   A covenant that requires the issuer to charge fees or rates adequate to ensure timely payment of interest and principal.

red herring (preliminary official statement)   The document that may be distributed to investors before the official statement is approved and the offering is official.

refunding bond   A bond issue the proceeds of which are used to retire a previous issue.

refunding revenue bond   A revenue issue created by the issuer to generate funds for retiring an early issue. Usually, the refunding bond is issued at terms more favorable to the issuer than the refunded bond.

registered certificate form   A bond in which ownership is conveyed by registration on the books of the issuer.

restrictive covenants   A general term for covenants that protect bond investors by providing restrictions on the issuer.

Revenue Anticipation Notes (RANs)   Short-term securities backed by the anticipation of future revenue, often in the form of federal government payments.

revenue bonds   Bonds payable from revenues to be derived from a specific project.

self-supporting debt   Debt incurred for a public project that entails no tax support other than the revenue received from the project.

selling concession The portion of the takedown paid to a firm that is not a syndicate member.

serial bonds (serial maturities) An issue that matures annually, or over some other period, in regular intervals.

single-handed A competitive bid submitted by a firm on behalf of itself only, not a syndicate.

sinking fund A fund set aside by an issuer to retire debt; sinking funds normally are built up on a yearly basis, often beginning several years before maturity.

special assessment bond A type of special tax bond secured by the taxes or fees assessed against the owners of property who benefit from the improvements being financed.

special tax bond A bond backed by a specific tax pledge, such as a sales tax.

split rating A case in which the ratings on a bond by the two major agencies, Moody's and Standard & Poor's, are different.

syndicate A group of investment bankers and/or banks that underwrite an issue and offer it for public sale.

syndicate letter A letter sent by a lead underwriter that invites participation by other firms in an upcoming syndicate.

syndicate meeting A meeting that precedes a competitive bid at which syndicate members agree on the best price and terms they can offer.

takedown The discount allowed to a member of a syndicate on any bonds sold.

take-or-pay A form of security in which customers agree to pay revenues to the bond issuer, irrespective of whether they use the intended services.

tax anticipation notes (TANs) Short-term securities backed by the anticipation of future tax receipts.

tax base Property and resources within a government or authority that it can tax.

tax conduit The tax treatment of regulated investment companies, including municipal bond funds and unit trusts.

taxable equivalent current yield The current yield on a municipal bond equal to that of a given taxable debt instrument.

taxable equivalent yield The yield on a municipal bond equal to that of a given taxable debt instrument.

tax-exempt commercial paper (TECP) Short-term tax-exempt notes, usually under 270 days in maturity, offered on a continuing basis by an issuer.

tax-exempt current yield The nominal yield of a tax-exempt bond divided by current market price.

tax-exempt security A security, the interest of which is exempt from federal tax, and often state and local taxes as well.

term bonds Bond issues that redeem a portion of outstanding bonds over a period of years through a sinking fund.

The Daily Bond Buyer A publication that reports a variety of information about municipal bonds.

30-Day Visible Supply Report All index published by *The Daily Bond Buyer* that is watched as a measure of new issues about to come to market.

total bonded debt All the debt of a municipality issued in bond form.

total direct debt The sum of bonded and other debt (typically short-term notes) of a municipality.

triple tax-exempt Municipal securities exempt from taxation by federal, state, and local governments.

true interest cost (TIC) A method used to determine the price of a new issue, for competitive bidding purposes, that includes an estimate of the cost of money over time.

trust indenture A legal document that binds the issuer to terms of the debt issue.

trustee A bank that serves as the custodian of funds and representative of bondholders in enforcing the bond contract.

20-Bond Index The broadest index of bond yields published by *The Daily Bond Buyer.*

undivided account (Eastern account) An account in which each syndicate member is responsible for a share of the *entire* syndicate's underwriting liability (not just its own share).

unlimited tax bonds Bonds not limited by rate or amount and secured by the pledge of property taxes.

when, as, and if issued The terms under which newly issued bonds are sold to the public.

writing a scale The process of determining rates and call dates for a bond issue.

zero-coupon bond A bond that pays no current interest. Return is realized as the difference between purchase price and par value.

Index